T0145375

IFIP Advances in Information and Communication Technology

632

Editor-in-Chief

Kai Rannenberg, Goethe University Frankfurt, Germany

Editorial Board Members

IFIP – The International Federation for Information Processing

IFIP was founded in 1960 under the auspices of UNESCO, following the first World Computer Congress held in Paris the previous year. A federation for societies working in information processing, IFIP's aim is two-fold: to support information processing in the countries of its members and to encourage technology transfer to developing nations. As its mission statement clearly states:

IFIP is the global non-profit federation of societies of ICT professionals that aims at achieving a worldwide professional and socially responsible development and application of information and communication technologies.

IFIP is a non-profit-making organization, run almost solely by 2500 volunteers. It operates through a number of technical committees and working groups, which organize events and publications. IFIP's events range from large international open conferences to working conferences and local seminars.

The flagship event is the IFIP World Computer Congress, at which both invited and contributed papers are presented. Contributed papers are rigorously refereed and the rejection rate is high.

As with the Congress, participation in the open conferences is open to all and papers may be invited or submitted. Again, submitted papers are stringently refereed.

The working conferences are structured differently. They are usually run by a working group and attendance is generally smaller and occasionally by invitation only. Their purpose is to create an atmosphere conducive to innovation and development. Refereeing is also rigorous and papers are subjected to extensive group discussion.

Publications arising from IFIP events vary. The papers presented at the IFIP World Computer Congress and at open conferences are published as conference proceedings, while the results of the working conferences are often published as collections of selected and edited papers.

IFIP distinguishes three types of institutional membership: Country Representative Members, Members at Large, and Associate Members. The type of organization that can apply for membership is a wide variety and includes national or international societies of individual computer scientists/ICT professionals, associations or federations of such societies, government institutions/government related organizations, national or international research institutes or consortia, universities, academies of sciences, companies, national or international associations or federations of companies.

More information about this series at http://www.springer.com/series/6102

Alexandre Dolgui · Alain Bernard ·
David Lemoine · Gregor von Cieminski ·
David Romero (Eds.)

Advances in Production Management Systems

Artificial Intelligence for Sustainable and Resilient Production Systems

IFIP WG 5.7 International Conference, APMS 2021
Nantes, France, September 5–9, 2021
Proceedings, Part III

 Springer

Editors
Alexandre Dolgui ⓘ
IMT Atlantique
Nantes, France

Alain Bernard ⓘ
Centrale Nantes
Nantes, France

David Lemoine ⓘ
IMT Atlantique
Nantes, France

Gregor von Cieminski ⓘ
ZF Friedrichshafen AG
Friedrichshafen, Germany

David Romero ⓘ
Tecnológico de Monterrey
Mexico City, Mexico

ISSN 1868-4238   ISSN 1868-422X (electronic)
IFIP Advances in Information and Communication Technology
ISBN 978-3-030-85908-4   ISBN 978-3-030-85906-0 (eBook)
https://doi.org/10.1007/978-3-030-85906-0

This Springer imprint is published by the registered company Springer Nature Switzerland AG
The registered company address is: Gewerbestrasse 11, 6330 Cham, Switzerland

Preface

The scientific and industrial relevance of the development of sustainable and resilient production systems lies in ensuring future-proof manufacturing and service systems, including their supply chains and logistics networks. "Sustainability" and "Resilience" are essential requirements for competitive manufacturing and service provisioning now and in the future. Industry 4.0 technologies, such as artificial intelligence; decision aid models; additive and hybrid manufacturing; augmented, virtual, and mixed reality; industrial, collaborative, mobile, and software robots; advanced simulations and digital twins; and smart sensors and intelligent industrial networks, are key enablers for building new digital and smart capabilities in emerging cyber-physical production systems in support of more efficient and effective operations planning and control. These allow manufacturers and service providers to explore more sustainable and resilient business and operating models. By making innovative use of the aforementioned technologies and their enabled capabilities, they can pursue the triple bottom line of economic, environmental, and social sustainability. Furthermore, industrial companies will be able to withstand and quickly recover from disruptions that pose threats to their operational continuity. This is in the face of disrupted, complex, turbulent, and uncertain business environments, like the one triggered by the COVID-19 pandemic, or environmental pressures calling for decoupling economic growth from resource use and emissions.

The International Conference on Advances in Production Management Systems 2021 (APMS 2021) in Nantes, France, brought together leading international experts on manufacturing, service, supply, and logistics systems from academia, industry, and government to discuss pressing issues and research opportunities mostly in smart manufacturing and cyber-physical production systems; service systems design, engineering, and management; digital lean operations management; and resilient supply chain management in the Industry 4.0 era, with particular focus on artificial intelligence-enabled solutions.

Under the influence of the COVID-19 pandemic, the event was organised as online conference sessions. A large international panel of experts (497 from 50 countries) reviewed all the submissions (with an average of 3.2 reviews per paper) and selected the best 377 papers (70% of the submitted contributions) to be included in these international conference proceedings. The topics of interest at APMS 2021 included artificial intelligence techniques, decision aid, and new and renewed paradigms for sustainable and resilient production systems at four-wall factory and value chain levels, comprising their associated models, frameworks, methods, tools, and technologies for smart and sustainable manufacturing and service systems, as well as resilient digital supply chains. As usual for the APMS conference, the Program Committee was particularly attentive to the cutting-edge problems in production management and the quality of the papers, especially with regard to the applicability of the contributions to industry and services.

The APMS 2021 conference proceedings are organized into five volumes covering a large spectre of research concerning the global topic of the conference: "Artificial Intelligence for Sustainable and Resilient Production Systems".

The conference was supported by the International Federation of Information Processing (IFIP), which is celebrating its 60th Anniversary, and was co-organized by the IFIP Working Group 5.7 on Advances in Production Management Systems, IMT Atlantique (Campus Nantes) as well as the Centrale Nantes, University of Nantes, Rennes Business School, and Audecia Business School. It was also supported by three leading journals in the discipline: Production Planning & Control (PPC), the International Journal of Production Research (IJPR), and the International Journal of Product Lifecycle Management (IJPLM).

Special attention has been given to the International Journal of Production Research on the occasion of its 60th Anniversary. Since its foundation in 1961, IJPR has become one of the flagship journals of our profession. It was the first international journal to bring together papers on all aspects of production research: product/process engineering, production system design and management, operations management, and logistics. Many exceptional scientific results have been published in the journal.

We would like to thank all contributing authors for their high-quality work and for their willingness to share their research findings with the APMS community. We are also grateful to the members of the IFIP Working Group 5.7, the Program Committee, and the Scientific Committee, along with the Special Sessions organizers for their support in the organization of the conference program. Concerning the number of papers, special thanks must be given to the local colleagues who managed the reviewing process as well as the preparation of the conference program and proceedings, particularly Hicham Haddou Benderbal and Maria-Isabel Estrepo-Ruiz from IMT Atlantique.

September 2021

Alexandre Dolgui
Alain Bernard
David Lemoine
Gregor von Cieminski
David Romero

Organization

Conference Chair

Alexandre Dolgui   IMT Atlantique, Nantes, France

Conference Co-chair

Gregor von Cieminski   ZF Friedrichshafen, Germany

Conference Honorary Co-chairs

Dimitris Kiritsis   EPFL, Switzerland
Kathryn E. Stecke   University of Texas at Dallas, USA

Program Chair

Alain Bernard   Centrale Nantes, France

Program Co-chair

David Romero   Tecnológico de Monterrey, Mexico

Program Committee

Alain Bernard   Centrale Nantes, France
Gregor von Cieminski   ZF Friedrichshafen, Germany
Alexandre Dolgui   IMT Atlantique, Nantes, France
Dimitris Kiritsis   EPFL, Switzerland
David Romero   Tecnológico de Monterrey, Mexico
Kathryn E. Stecke   University of Texas at Dallas, USA

International Advisory Committee

Farhad Ameri   Texas State University, USA
Ugljesa Marjanovic   University of Novi Sad, Serbia
Ilkyeong Moon   Seoul National University, South Korea
Bojan Lalic   University of Novi Sad, Serbia
Hermann Lödding   Hamburg University of Technology, Germany

Organizing Committee Chair

David Lemoine   IMT Atlantique, Nantes, France

Organizing Committee Co-chair

Hichem Haddou Benderbal   IMT Atlantique, Nantes, France

Doctoral Workshop Chairs

Abdelkrim-Ramzi   IMT Atlantique, Nantes, France
  Yelles-Chaouche
Seyyed-Ehsan   IMT Atlantique, Nantes, France
  Hashemi-Petroodi

Award Committee Chairs

Nadjib Brahimi   Rennes School of Business, France
Ramzi Hammami   Rennes School of Business, France

Organizing Committee

Romain Billot   IMT Atlantique, Brest, France
Nadjib Brahimi   Rennes School of Business, France
Olivier Cardin   University of Nantes, France
Catherine Da Cunha   Centrale Nantes, France
Alexandre Dolgui   IMT Atlantique, Nantes, France
Giannakis Mihalis   Audencia, Nantes, France
Evgeny Gurevsky   University of Nantes, France
Hichem Haddou Benderbal   IMT Atlantique, Nantes, France
Ramzi Hammami   Rennes School of Business, France
Oncu Hazir   Rennes School of Business, France
Seyyed-Ehsan   IMT Atlantique, Nantes, France
  Hashemi-Petroodi
David Lemoine   IMT Atlantique, Nantes, France
Nasser Mebarki   University of Nantes, France
Patrick Meyer   IMT Atlantique, Brest, France
Merhdad Mohammadi   IMT Atlantique, Brest, France
Dominique Morel   IMT Atlantique, Nantes, France
Maroua Nouiri   University of Nantes, France
Maria-Isabel Restrepo-Ruiz   IMT Atlantique, Nantes, France
Naly Rakoto   IMT Atlantique, Nantes, France
Ilhem Slama   IMT Atlantique, Nantes, France
Simon Thevenin   IMT Atlantique, Nantes, France
Abdelkrim-Ramzi   IMT Atlantique, Nantes, France
  Yelles-Chaouche

Scientific Committee

Erry Yulian Triblas Adesta	International Islamic University Malaysia, Malaysia
El-Houssaine Aghezzaf	Ghent University, Belgium
Erlend Alfnes	Norwegian University of Science and Technology, Norway
Hamid Allaoui	Université d'Artois, France
Thecle Alix	IUT Bordeaux Montesquieu, France
Farhad Ameri	Texas State University, USA
Bjørn Andersen	Norwegian University of Science and Technology, Norway
Eiji Arai	Osaka University, Japan
Jannicke Baalsrud Hauge	KTH Royal Institute of Technology, Sweden/BIBA, Germany
Zied Babai	Kedge Business School, France
Natalia Bakhtadze	Russian Academy of Sciences, Russia
Pierre Baptiste	Polytechnique de Montréal, Canada
Olga Battaïa	Kedge Business School, France
Farouk Belkadi	Centrale Nantes, France
Lyes Benyoucef	Aix-Marseille University, France
Bopaya Bidanda	University of Pittsburgh, USA
Frédérique Biennier	INSA Lyon, France
Jean-Charles Billaut	Université de Tours, France
Umit S. Bititci	Heriot-Watt University, UK
Magali Bosch-Mauchand	Université de Technologie de Compiègne, France
Xavier Boucher	Mines St Etienne, France
Abdelaziz Bouras	Qatar University, Qatar
Jim Browne	University College Dublin, Ireland
Luis Camarinha-Matos	Universidade Nova de Lisboa, Portugal
Olivier Cardin	University of Nantes, France
Sergio Cavalieri	University of Bergamo, Italy
Stephen Childe	Plymouth University, UK
Hyunbo Cho	Pohang University of Science and Technology, South Korea
Chengbin Chu	ESIEE Paris, France
Feng Chu	Paris-Saclay University, France
Byung Do Chung	Yonsei University, South Korea
Gregor von Cieminski	ZF Friedrichshafen, Germany
Catherine Da Cunha	Centrale Nantes, France
Yves Dallery	CentraleSupélec, France
Xavier Delorme	Mines St Etienne, France
Frédéric Demoly	Université de Technologie de Belfort-Montbéliard, France
Mélanie Despeisse	Chalmers University of Technology, Sweden
Alexandre Dolgui	IMT Atlantique, Nantes, France
Slavko Dolinšek	University of Ljubljana, Slovenia

Sang Do Noh	Sungkyunkwan University, South Korea
Heidi Carin Dreyer	Norwegian University of Science and Technology, Norway
Eero Eloranta	Aalto University, Finland
Soumaya El Kadiri	Texelia AG, Switzerland
Christos Emmanouilidis	University of Groningen, The Netherlands
Anton Eremeev	Siberian Branch of Russian Academy of Sciences, Russia
Åsa Fasth-Berglund	Chalmers University of Technology, Sweden
Rosanna Fornasiero	Consiglio Nazionale delle Ricerche, Italy
Xuehao Feng	Zhejiang University, China
Yannick Frein	INP Grenoble, France
Jan Frick	University of Stavanger, Norway
Klaas Gadeyne	Flanders Make, Belgium
Paolo Gaiardelli	University of Bergamo, Italy
Adriana Giret Boggino	Universidad Politécnica de Valencia, Spain
Samuel Gomes	Belfort-Montbéliard University of Technology, France
Bernard Grabot	INP-Toulouse, ENIT, France
Gerhard Gudergan	RWTH Aachen University, Germany
Thomas R. Gulledge Jr.	George Mason University, USA
Nikolai Guschinsky	National Academy of Sciences, Belarus
Slim Hammadi	Centrale Lille, France
Ahmedou Haouba	University of Nouakchott Al-Asriya, Mauritania
Soumaya Henchoz	Logitech AG, Switzerland
Hironori Hibino	Tokyo University of Science, Japan
Hans-Henrik Hvolby	Aalborg University, Denmark
Jan Holmström	Aalto University, Finland
Dmitry Ivanov	Berlin School of Economics and Law, Germany
Harinder Jagdev	National University of Ireland at Galway, Ireland
Jayanth Jayaram	University of South Carolina, USA
Zhibin Jiang	Shanghai Jiao Tong University, China
John Johansen	Aalborg University, Denmark
Hong-Bae Jun	Hongik University, South Korea
Toshiya Kaihara	Kobe University, Japan
Duck Young Kim	Pohang University of Science and Technology, South Korea
Dimitris Kiritsis	EPFL, Switzerland
Tomasz Koch	Wroclaw University of Science and Technology, Poland
Pisut Koomsap	Asian Institute of Technology, Thailand
Vladimir Kotov	Belarusian State University, Belarus
Mikhail Kovalyov	National Academy of Sciences, Belarus
Gül Kremer	Iowa State University, USA
Boonserm Kulvatunyou	National Institute of Standards and Technology, USA
Senthilkumaran Kumaraguru	Indian Institute of Information Technology Design and Manufacturing, India

Thomas R. Kurfess	Georgia Institute of Technology, USA
Andrew Kusiak	University of Iowa, USA
Bojan Lalić	University of Novi Sad, Serbia
Samir Lamouri	ENSAM Paris, France
Lenka Landryova	Technical University of Ostrava, Czech Republic
Alexander Lazarev	Russian Academy of Sciences, Moscow, Russia
Jan-Peter Lechner	First Global Liaison, Germany
Gyu M. Lee	Pusan National University, South Korea
Kangbok Lee	Pohang University of Science and Technology, South Korea
Genrikh Levin	National Academy of Sciences, Belarus
Jingshan Li	University of Wisconsin-Madison, USA
Ming K. Lim	Chongqing University, China
Hermann Lödding	Hamburg University of Technology, Germany
Pierre Lopez	LAAS-CNRS, France
Marco Macchi	Politecnico di Milano, Italy
Ugljesa Marjanovic	University of Novi Sad, Serbia
Muthu Mathirajan	Indian Institute of Science, India
Gökan May	University of North Florida, USA
Khaled Medini	Mines St Etienne, France
Jörn Mehnen	University of Strathclyde, UK
Vidosav D. Majstorovich	University of Belgrade, Serbia
Semyon M. Meerkov	University of Michigan, USA
Joao Gilberto Mendes dos Reis	UNIP Paulista University, Brazil
Hajime Mizuyama	Aoyama Gakuin University, Japan
Ilkyeong Moon	Seoul National University, South Korea
Eiji Morinaga	Osaka Prefecture University, Japan
Dimitris Mourtzis	University of Patras, Greece
Irenilza de Alencar Naas	UNIP Paulista University, Brazil
Masaru Nakano	Keio University, Japan
Torbjörn Netland	ETH Zürich, Switzerland
Gilles Neubert	EMLYON Business School, Saint-Etienne, France
Izabela Nielsen	Aalborg University, Denmark
Tomomi Nonaka	Ritsumeikan University, Japan
Jinwoo Park	Seoul National University, South Korea
François Pérès	INP-Toulouse, ENIT, France
Fredrik Persson	Linköping Institute of Technology, Sweden
Giuditta Pezzotta	University of Bergamo, Italy
Selwyn Piramuthu	University of Florida, USA
Alberto Portioli Staudacher	Politecnico di Milano, Italy
Daryl Powell	Norwegian University of Science and Technology, Norway
Vittaldas V. Prabhu	Pennsylvania State University, USA
Jean-Marie Proth	Inria, France
Ricardo José Rabelo	Federal University of Santa Catarina, Brazil

Rahul Rai	University at Buffalo, USA
Mario Rapaccini	Florence University, Italy
Nidhal Rezg	University of Lorraine, France
Ralph Riedel	Westsächsische Hochschule Zwickau, Germany
Irene Roda	Politecnico di Milano, Italy
Asbjörn Rolstadås	Norwegian University of Science and Technology, Norway
David Romero	Tecnológico de Monterrey, Mexico
Christoph Roser	Karlsruhe University of Applied Sciences, Germany
André Rossi	Université Paris-Dauphine, France
Martin Rudberg	Linköping University, Sweden
Thomas E. Ruppli	University of Basel, Switzerland
Krzysztof Santarek	Warsaw University of Technology, Poland
Subhash Sarin	VirginiaTech, USA
Suresh P. Sethi	The University of Texas at Dallas, USA
Fabio Sgarbossa	Norwegian University of Science and Technology, Norway
John P. Shewchuk	Virginia Polytechnic Institute and State University, USA
Dan L. Shunk	Arizona State University, USA
Ali Siadat	Arts et Métiers ParisTech, France
Riitta Smeds	Aalto University, Finland
Boris Sokolov	Russian Academy of Sciences, Russia
Vijay Srinivasan	National Institute of Standards and Technology, USA
Johan Stahre	Chalmers University of Technology, Sweden
Kathryn E. Stecke	The University of Texas at Dallas, USA
Kenn Steger-Jensen	Aalborg University, Denmark
Volker Stich	RWTH Aachen University, Germany
Richard Lee Storch	University of Washington, USA
Jan Ola Strandhagen	Norwegian University of Science and Technology, Norway
Stanislaw Strzelczak	Warsaw University of Technology, Poland
Nick Szirbik	University of Groningen, The Netherlands
Marco Taisch	Politecnico di Milano, Italy
Lixin Tang	Northeastern University, China
Kari Tanskanen	Aalto University School of Science, Finland
Ilias Tatsiopoulos	National Technical University of Athens, Greece
Sergio Terzi	Politecnico di Milano, Italy
Klaus-Dieter Thoben	Universität Bremen, Germany
Manoj Tiwari	Indian Institute of Technology, India
Matthias Thüre	Jinan University, China
Jacques H. Trienekens	Wageningen University, The Netherlands
Mario Tucci	Universitá degli Studi di Firenze, Italy
Shigeki Umeda	Musashi University, Japan
Bruno Vallespir	University of Bordeaux, France
François Vernadat	University of Lorraine, France

Agostino Villa	Politecnico di Torino, Italy
Lihui Wang	KTH Royal Institute of Technology, Sweden
Sabine Waschull	University of Groningen, The Netherlands
Hans-Hermann Wiendahl	University of Stuttgart, Germany
Frank Werner	University of Magdeburg, Germany
Shaun West	Lucerne University of Applied Sciences and Arts, Switzerland
Joakim Wikner	Jönköping University, Sweden
Hans Wortmann	University of Groningen, The Netherlands
Desheng Dash Wu	University of Chinese Academy of Sciences, China
Thorsten Wuest	West Virginia University, USA
Farouk Yalaoui	University of Technology of Troyes, France
Noureddine Zerhouni	Université Bourgogne Franche-Comte, France

List of Reviewers

Abbou Rosa	Batocchio Antonio
Abdeljaouad Mohamed Amine	Battaïa Olga
Absi Nabil	Battini Daria
Acerbi Federica	Behrens Larissa
Aghelinejad Mohsen	Ben-Ammar Oussama
Aghezzaf El-Houssaine	Benatia Mohamed Amin
Agrawal Rajecv	Bentaha M.-Lounes
Agrawal Tarun Kumar	Benyoucef Lyes
Alexopoulos Kosmas	Beraldi Santos Alexandre
Alix Thecle	Bergmann Ulf
Alkhudary Rami	Bernus Peter
Altekin F. Tevhide	Berrah Lamia-Amel
Alves Anabela	Bertnum Aili Biriita
Ameri Farhad	Bertoni Marco
Andersen Ann-Louise	Bettayeb Belgacem
Andersen Bjorn	Bevilacqua Maurizio
Anderson Marc	Biennier Frédérique
Anderson Matthew	Bititci Umit Sezer
Anholon Rosley	Bocanet Vlad
Antosz Katarzyna	Bosch-Mauchand Magali
Apostolou Dimitris	Boucher Xavier
Arica Emrah	Bourguignon Saulo Cabral
Arlinghaus Julia Christine	Bousdekis Alexandros
Aubry Alexis	Brahimi Nadjib
Baalsrud Hauge Jannicke	Bresler Maggie
Badulescu Yvonne Gabrielle	Brunoe Thomas Ditlev
Bakhtadze Natalia	Brusset Xavier
Barbosa Christiane Lima	Burow Kay
Barni Andrea	Calado Robisom Damasceno

Calarge Felipe
Camarinha-Matos Luis Manuel
Cameron David
Cannas Violetta Giada
Cao Yifan
Castro Eduardo Lorenzo
Cattaruzza Diego
Cerqueus Audrey
Chang Tai-Woo
Chaves Sandra Maria do Amaral
Chavez Zuhara
Chen Jinwei
Cheng Yongxi
Chiacchio Ferdinando
Chiari da Silva Ethel Cristina
Childe Steve
Cho Hyunbo
Choi SangSu
Chou Shuo-Yan
Christensen Flemming Max Møller
Chung Byung Do
Ciarapica Filippo Emanuele
Cimini Chiara
Clivillé Vincent
Cohen Yuval
Converso Giuseppe
Cosenza Harvey
Costa Helder Gomes
Da Cunha Catherine
Daaboul Joanna
Dahane Mohammed
Dakic Dusanka
Das Dyutimoy Nirupam
Das Jyotirmoy Nirupam
Das Sayan
Davari Morteza
De Arruda Ignacio Paulo Sergio de
De Campos Renato
De Oliveira Costa Neto Pedro Luiz
Delorme Xavier
Deroussi Laurent
Despeisse Mélanie
Di Nardo Mario
Di Pasquale Valentina
Dillinger Fabian
Djedidi Oussama

Dolgui Alexandre
Dolinsek Slavko
Dou Runliang
Drei Samuel Martins
Dreyer Heidi
Dreyfus Paul-Arthur
Dubey Rameshwar
Dümmel Johannes
Eloranta Eero
Emmanouilidis Christos
Ermolova Maria
Eslami Yasamin
Fast-Berglund Åsa
Faveto Alberto
Federico Adrodegari
Feng Xuehao
Finco Serena
Flores-García Erik
Fontaine Pirmin
Fosso Wamba Samuel
Franciosi Chiara
Frank Jana
Franke Susanne
Freitag Mike
Frick Jan
Fruggiero Fabio
Fu Wenhan
Fujii Nobutada
Gahan Padmabati
Gaiardelli Paolo
Gallo Mosè
Ganesan Viswanath Kumar
Gaponov Igor
Gayialis Sotiris P.
Gebennini Elisa
Ghadge Abhijeet
Ghrairi Zied
Gianessi Paolo
Giret Boggino Adriana
Gloeckner Robert
Gogineni Sonika
Gola Arkadiusz
Goodarzian Fariba
Gosling Jon
Gouyon David
Grabot Bernard

Grangeon Nathalie
Grassi Andrea
Grenzfurtner Wolfgang
Guerpinar Tan
Guillaume Romain
Guimarães Neto Abelino Reis
Guizzi Guido
Gupta Sumit
Gurevsky Evgeny
Habibi Muhammad Khoirul Khakim
Haddou Benderbal Hichem
Halse Lise Lillebrygfjeld
Hammami Ramzi
Hani Yasmina
Hashemi-Petroodi S. Ehsan
Havzi Sara
Hazir Oncu
Hedayatinia Pooya
Hemmati Ahmad
Henchoz El Kadiri Soumaya
Heuss Lisa
Hibino Hironori
Himmiche Sara
Hnaien Faicel
Hofer Gernot
Holst Lennard Phillip
Hovelaque Vincent
Hrnjica Bahrudin
Huber Walter
Husniah Hennie
Hvolby Hans-Henrik
Hwang Gyusun
Irohara Takashi
Islam Md Hasibul
Iung Benoit
Ivanov Dmitry
Jacomino Mireille
Jagdev Harinder
Jahn Niklas
Jain Geetika
Jain Vipul
Jasiulewicz-Kaczmarek Małgorzata
Jebali Aida
Jelisic Elena
Jeong Yongkuk
Johansen John

Jones Al
Jun Chi-Hyuck
Jun Hong-Bae
Jun Sungbum
Juned Mohd
Jünge Gabriele
Kaasinen Eija
Kaihara Toshiya
Kalaboukas Kostas
Kang Yong-Shin
Karampatzakis Dimitris
Kayikci Yasanur
Kedad-Sidhoum Safia
Keepers Makenzie
Keivanpour Samira
Keshari Anupam
Kim Byung-In
Kim Duck Young
Kim Hwa-Joong
Kim Hyun-Jung
Kinra Aseem
Kiritsis Dimitris
Kitjacharoenchai Patchara
Kjeldgaard Stefan
Kjersem Kristina
Klimchik Alexandr
Klymenko Olena
Kollberg Thomassen Maria
Kolyubin Sergey
Koomsap Pisut
Kramer Kathrin
Kulvatunyou Boonserm (Serm)
Kumar Ramesh
Kurata Takeshi
Kvadsheim Nina Pereira
Lahaye Sébastien
Lalic Danijela
Lamouri Samir
Lamy Damien
Landryova Lenka
Lechner Jan-Peter
Lee Dong-Ho
Lee Eunji
Lee Kangbok
Lee Kyungsik
Lee Minchul

Lee Seokcheon
Lee Seokgi
Lee Young Hoon
Lehuédé Fabien
Leiber Daria
Lemoine David
Li Haijiao
Li Yuanfu
Lim Dae-Eun
Lim Ming
Lima Adalberto da
Lima Nilsa
Lin Chen-ju
Linares Jean-marc
Linnartz Maria
Listl Franz Georg
Liu Ming
Liu Xin
Liu Zhongzheng
Lödding Hermann
Lodgaard Eirin
Loger Benoit
Lorenz Rafael
Lu Jinzhi
Lu Xingwei
Lu Xuefei
Lucas Flavien
Lüftenegger Egon
Luo Dan
Ma Junhai
Macchi Marco
Machado Brunno Abner
Maier Janine Tatjana
Maihami Reza
Makboul Salma
Makris Sotiris
Malaguti Roney Camargo
Mandal Jasashwi
Mandel Alexander
Manier Hervé
Manier Marie-Ange
Marangé Pascale
Marchesano Maria Grazia
Marek Svenja
Marjanovic Ugljesa
Marmolejo Jose Antonio

Marques Melissa
Marrazzini Leonardo
Masone Adriano
Massonnet Guillaume
Matsuda Michiko
Maxwell Duncan William
Mazzuto Giovanni
Medić Nenad
Medini Khaled
Mehnen Jorn
Mendes dos Reis João Gilberto
Mentzas Gregoris
Metaxa Ifigeneia
Min Li Li
Minner Stefan
Mishra Ashutosh
Mitra Rony
Mizuyama Hajime
Mogale Dnyaneshwar
Mohammadi Mehrdad
Mollo Neto Mario
Montini Elias
Montoya-Torres Jairo R.
Moon Ilkyeong
Moraes Thais De Castro
Morinaga Eiji
Moser Benedikt
Moshref-Javadi Mohammad
Mourtzis Dimitris
Mundt Christopher
Muši Denis
Nääs Irenilza De Alencar
Naim Mohamed
Nakade Koichi
Nakano Masaru
Napoleone Alessia
Nayak Ashutosh
Neroni Mattia
Netland Torbjørn
Neubert Gilles
Nguyen Du Huu
Nguyen Duc-Canh
Nguyen Thi Hien
Nielsen Izabela
Nielsen Kjeld
Nishi Tatsushi

Nogueira Sara
Noh Sang Do
Nonaka Tomomi
Noran Ovidiu
Norre Sylvie
Ortmeier Frank
Ouazene Yassine
Ouzrout Yacine
Özcan Uğur
Paes Graciele Oroski
Pagnoncelli Bernardo
Panigrahi Sibarama
Panigrahi Swayam Sampurna
Papakostas Nikolaos
Papcun Peter
Pashkevich Anatol
Pattnaik Monalisha
Pels Henk Jan
Pérès François
Persson Fredrik
Pezzotta Giuditta
Phan Dinh Anh
Piétrac Laurent
Pinto Sergio Crespo Coelho da
Pirola Fabiana
Pissardini Paulo Eduardo
Polenghi Adalberto
Popolo Valentina
Portioli Staudacher Alberto
Powell Daryl
Prabhu Vittaldas
Psarommatis Foivos
Rabelo Ricardo
Rakic Slavko
Rapaccini Mario
Reis Milena Estanislau Diniz Dos
Resanovic Daniel
Rey David
Riedel Ralph
Rikalović Aleksandar
Rinaldi Marta
Roda Irene
Rodriguez Aguilar Roman
Romagnoli Giovanni
Romeo Bandinelli
Romero David

Roser Christoph
Rossit Daniel Alejandro
Rudberg Martin
Sabitov Rustem
Sachs Anna-Lena
Sahoo Rosalin
Sala Roberto
Santarek Kszysztof
Satolo Eduardo Guilherme
Satyro Walter
Savin Sergei
Schneider Daniel
Semolić Brane
Shafiq Muhammad
Sharma Rohit
Shin Jong-Ho
Shukla Mayank
Shunk Dan
Siadat Ali
Silva Cristovao
Singgih Ivan Kristianto
Singh Sube
Slama Ilhem
Smaglichenko Alexander
Smeds Riitta Johanna
Soares Paula Metzker
Softic Selver
Sokolov Boris V.
Soleilhac Gauthier
Song Byung Duk
Song Xiaoxiao
Souier Mehdi
Sørensen Daniel Grud Hellerup
Spagnol Gabriela
Srinivasan Vijay
Stavrou Vasileios P.
Steger-Jensen Kenn
Stich Volker
Stipp Marluci Andrade Conceição
Stoll Oliver
Strandhagen Jan Ola
Suh Eun Suk
Suleykin Alexander
Suzanne Elodie
Szirbik Nick B.
Taghvaeipour Afshin

Taisch Marco
Tanimizu Yoshitaka
Tanizaki Takashi
Tasić Nemanja
Tebaldi Letizia
Telles Renato
Thevenin Simon
Thoben Klaus-Dieter
Thurer Matthias
Tiedemann Fredrik
Tisi Massimo
Torres Luis Fernando
Tortorella Guilherme Luz
Troyanovsky Vladimir
Turcin Ioan
Turki Sadok
Ulrich Marco
Unip Solimar
Valdiviezo Viera Luis Enrique
Vallespir Bruno
Vasic Stana
Vaz Paulo
Vespoli Silvestro
Vicente da Silva Ivonaldo
Villeneuve Eric
Viviani Jean-Laurent
Vještica Marko
Vo Thi Le Hoa
Voisin Alexandre
von Cieminski Gregor
Von Stietencron Moritz
Wagner Sarah
Wang Congke
Wang Hongfeng
Wang Yin

Wang Yingli
Wang Yuling
Wang Zhaojie
Wang Zhixin
Wellsandt Stefan
West Shaun
Wiendahl Hans-Hermann
Wiesner Stefan Alexander
Wikner Joakim
Wiktorsson Magnus
Wimmer Manuel
Woo Young-Bin
Wortmann Andreas
Wortmann Johan Casper
Wuest Thorsten
Xu Tiantong
Yadegari Ehsan
Yalaoui Alice
Yang Danqin
Yang Guoqing
Yang Jie
Yang Zhaorui
Yelles Chaouche Abdelkrim Ramzi
Zaeh Michael Friedrich
Zaikin Oleg
Zambetti Michela
Zeba Gordana
Zhang Guoqing
Zhang Ruiyou
Zheng Feifeng
Zheng Xiaochen
Zoitl Alois
Zolotová Iveta
Zouggar Anne

Contents – Part III

Finance-Driven Supply Chain

Gastronomic Service System Design

Modern Scheduling and Applications in Industry 4.0

Recent Advances in Sustainable Manufacturing

Green Production and Circularity Concepts

Improvement Models and Methods for Green and Innovative Systems

Supply Chain and Routing Management

Smart Supply Chain and Production in Society 5.0 Era

Supply Chain Risk Management Under Coronavirus

Autonomous Robots in Delivery Logistics

Sustainable Facility Location-Routing Problem for Blood Package Delivery by Drones with a Charging Station

Shirin Ghasemi[ID], Reza Tavakkoli-Moghaddam[✉][ID], Mahdi Hamid[ID], and Meysam Hosseinzadeh[ID]

School of Industrial Engineering, College of Engineering, University of Tehran, Tehran, Iran
{shirin.ghasemi,tavakoli,m.hamid31400,sm.hosseinzadeh}@ut.ac.ir

Abstract. This paper proposes a multi-objective integrated facility location and drone routing problem in blood package delivery by considering sustainability factors. We seek to locate the predetermined number of capacitated launching facilities and charging stations for the drones' battery. Candidate construction points are ranked by the TOPSIS method in terms of sustainability indicators. The objectives are to maximize the weight of selected points and the amount of demand coverage while minimizing the transferring and constructing facilities cost. Then, we assign drones to open launch facility and demand points to drones and launch facility. It should be noted that we consider the drone's battery consumption, and if the drone battery is not enough to continue its mission, we assign them to an opened charging station. GAMS software is employed to solve small-sized problems. The solution result indicates the performance of our model.

Keywords: Sustainable location-routing · Drone delivery system · TOPSIS method · Blood delivery

1 Introduction and Literature Review

Unmanned aerial vehicles (UAVs) or drones have attracted significant attention in differential application areas like rescue operations [1], relief distribution [2], healthcare [3], emergency applications like search and rescue [4], civilian sector [5], agriculture [6] and military [7]. However, their role in packages delivery is more common nowadays due to high traffic jams and increased competitiveness for faster service [8, 9]. Several prominent companies (e.g., Google, UPS, Flytrex, and Amazon) have resorted to using drones for package deliveries or commercial service [10]. Drone's rapid deployment ability and mobility have led to their use for transporting perishable materials or hospital packages and drugs too. Most of these materials, particularly blood products, have a short lifespan, so their delivery should be managed accurately. One of the emerging fields of using drones is their utilization as a means of delivering blood packages.

Drones, as aerial vehicles, have a much lower payload carrying capacities and range for carrying cargo than trucks; besides, as the payload increases, their maximum range

© IFIP International Federation for Information Processing 2021
Published by Springer Nature Switzerland AG 2021
A. Dolgui et al. (Eds.): APMS 2021, IFIP AICT 632, pp. 3–14, 2021.
https://doi.org/10.1007/978-3-030-85906-0_1

of coverage decreases. That is why a drone-based delivery system needs more depots or launch sites across the distribution area. Also, unpredictable weather conditions can dramatically affect energy consumption or the drone range, so it is necessary to construct some charging stations throughout the region. It should be noted that drones are beneficial to environmental sustainability due to less carbon dioxide (CO_2) emissions in comparison with trucks [11]. Nevertheless, the charging stations release some carbon dioxide and cause air pollution. Therefore, it is necessary to consider environmental sustainability indicators for locating and constructing these facilities.

Most of the previous studies on drone delivery applications are conducted on drone scheduling and routing problems [12, 13]. Recently, researchers have much concentrated on facility location problems (FLPs) in drone delivery problems. FLPs play a crucial role in designing an efficient delivery system to increase accessibility and maximize demand coverage. Several articles focused on determining the optimal location for a relief distribution center in a post-disaster supply chain network by using drones. They aim to minimize the total cost or travel times [2, 14]. Nevertheless, the crucial aim in the relief distribution or drug and blood packages delivery is the maximum coverage of demand points, which has been rarely studied. Pulver and Wei [15] attempted to maximize primary and secondary demand point coverage in medical delivery by using drones. However, they did not take into account the capacity of each drone launching site. They also did not consider the drone's battery consumption as its payload function. Kim et al. [16] proposed a two-stage pickup and delivery model for medical delivery by using drones. First, they solved a facility location problem to construct depot facilities, second, the drone's routing problem has been addressed.

Chauhan et al. [17] developed a single-stage model for capacitated launch facilities and allocating demand points to drones. They proposed a function of drone energy consumption by considering drones' payload and demand point distance. They did not include charging stations in their model and assumed that the drones would be charged the night before the flight and they are fully charged in the planning periods. Hong et al. [18] developed a coverage model for a drone's delivery system that optimizes the location of recharging stations of drones. The study conducted by Shavarani et al. [9] addressed the refuel and launching stations for the drone delivery problem and try to minimize the total cost of the system. However, they assumed that in each mission just one demand point is covered. Several authors have mentioned the collaboration of trucks and drones for package delivery, which, despite the increased service speed, causes problems for the environment due to truck's CO_2 emissions [19, 20]. Kitjacharoenchai et al. [21] developed a synchronized truck-drone routing model. In their proposed model, the drone mission started from the truck and after serving multiple demand points, they returned to the truck. Besides, UAV charging stations emit some CO_2 gas that has not been addressed in previous research, which should be considered in locating charging stations. There are also many sustainable factors influencing the construction of launching and charging stations (e.g., availability of resources, climatic conditions of the region, and access to rescue equipment) that should be considered in the model.

In response to the urgent requirement of medical centers for blood products, we provide a sustainable integrated multi-objective facility location-routing model for blood packages delivery by drones. First, we determine several sustainable indicators to rank the potential candidate point of facility location by the TOPSIS method (as one of the well-known multi-criteria decision-making methods). Then, our FLP model attempt to find the best point for drones' launching and charging station simultaneously, by maximizing the weight of each potential candidate point. Our model also aims to minimize the total delivery and construction cost of facilities while maximizing demand coverage. Then, we assign drones to open launch facilities according to their limited capacity, afterward we assign demand points to open launch facilities and drones. It should be noted that if a drones' battery is not enough to complete its mission, drones should be assigned to an open charging station.

To the best of our knowledge, no study considers sustainability in the combination of drones' launching and charging station location and drones' routing problem together by considering drones' battery consumption in its mission together, so our contribution is novel.

The remainder of this paper is organized as follows. The problem statement and the proposed mathematical formulation are illustrated in Sect. 2. The numerical results are investigated in Sect. 3. Finally, the conclusion and the relevant future studies are provided in Sect. 4.

2   Problem Definition

In this section, we present sustainable multi-objective mixed-integer linear programming (MILP) formulations for location and routing problems in blood delivery systems by drones. At the beginning of the planning period, there is a set of potential points to construct drone charging and launching facilities, which must be decided whether to open them according to sustainable indicators, which is shown in Table 1. The weight of these indicators' importance is determined according to related papers and experts' opinions. Then, each of these candidate points is ranked and weighted based on these indicators by employing the TOPSIS method that is generally proposed by Tzeng and Huang [22], which is a multi-criteria decision analysis method. This method attempts to select an alternative that has the least geometric distance from the positive ideal solution (PIS) [23] and the greatest geometric distance from the negative ideal solution (NIS) [23]. The output of the TOPSIS method is an input parameter for the mathematical model, besides our proposed model aims to maximize the total weight of the selected points.

In our model, there is a set of demand locations k with the demand of v_{kp} from blood product p; which their demand is met by the Central Blood Bank, and a set of available fully-charged drones d. It should be noted that there are two kinds of demand points, critical and non-critical points, in which all demand of critical point should be satisfied. However, for the other points, at least 70 percent of its demands should be met. Launch stations are introduced as temporary warehouses for blood packages, which are delivered to customers by drones, too. The planning period is short-term due to the nature of blood delivery and the different blood product's shelf life is about a few days to several weeks, so, they are not exposed to corruption. We aim to locate P_s launch facilities for maximizing the service rate and demand rate coverage by minimizing the total cost, including the construction cost of facilities, delivery, and drone battery consumption cost. Then, we allocate drones to opened launch facilities by considering the facility's capacity. Then, each drone makes a one-to-many routing mission to cover the demand point, by considering the drone carrying capacity and battery consumption in its mission. In our model, if the remain drone's battery capacity is not enough for traveling between nodes i to j (it is less than the consumption battery rate between nodes i to j), it should go to an open charging station; then, it can continue its mission and visit the next demand point according to its routing. It should be noted that the amount of battery consumption rate is calculated according to the weight of the drone and its battery, the weight of the blood packets carried, and the traveled distance. Figure 1 indicates the schematic representation of our proposed drone delivery system.

Table 1. Evaluation criteria for location selection of launch site and charging station

sustainability	Indicators	No.	Criterion type	Launch site's location	Charging station's location
Economy	Tax policy	A1	maximize	✓	✓
	Being in line with the economic planning of the region	A2	maximize	✓	✓
	Possibility of development	A3	maximize	✓	
	Availability of resource	A4	maximize	✓	
	Policies and rules of government	A5	maximize	✓	✓
	Annual cost (operation and maintenance)	A6	minimize	✓	✓
Environment	Effect on the ecological perspective	B1	minimize	✓	✓
	Level of environmental protection	B2	maximize	✓	✓
	Climatic conditions of the region	B4	maximize	✓	
	Amount and speed of the wind	B5	minimize	✓	
	CO2 emissions	B6	minimize		✓
	destruction level of vegetation and water	B8	minimize	✓	✓
Social	Effect on traffic agglomeration	C1	minimize		✓
	Effect on nearby inhabitant	C2	minimize	✓	✓
	Proximity to a skilled workforce	C3	maximize	✓	
	Infrastructure status of operators' workplaces	C5	maximize	✓	✓
	Operator security	C6	maximize	✓	✓

The notation and the proposed multi-objective mathematical model are given below, by considering the following assumption:

1. The amount of demand in each planning horizon is proportional to the drone's payload capacity.
2. We did not consider the effect of weather conditions on the drone's battery capacity.
3. The weight and volume of different blood packages are the same.

$$Max \sum_{i\in s} \sum_{j\in k} \sum_{d\in D} \sum_{p\in P} \alpha_j v_{jp}\mu_{ijd} + \sum_{i\in f} \sum_{j\in k} \sum_{d\in D} \sum_{p\in P} \alpha_j v_{jp}\mu_{ijd} \tag{1}$$

$$Max \sum_{i\varepsilon f} w_i \times R_i + \sum_{i\varepsilon s} w_i \times L_i \tag{2}$$

$$Min\left(\sum_{i\in s}\sum_{j\in k}\sum_{d\in D} d_{ij}c_{ijd}\mu_{ijd}\right) + \left[\left(\sum_{i\in s}\sum_{j\in f}\sum_{d\in D} d_{ij}c_{ijd}\mu_{ijd}\right) + \left(\sum_{i\in f}\sum_{j\in k}\sum_{d\in D} d_{ij}c_{ijd}\mu_{ijd}\right)\right]$$
$$+ \sum_{i\in v}\sum_{j\in i\cup k}\sum_{d\in D}\sum_{p\in P}(p_{ijdp+m_d})r_d d_{ij}\mu_{ijd}\lambda_d + \left(\sum_{i\varepsilon s} f_i L_i\right) + \left(\sum_{i\varepsilon f} f_i R_i\right) \tag{3}$$

s.t.

$$\sum_i L_i < Ps \quad \forall i \in S \tag{4}$$

$$\sum_i R_i \le Pf \quad \forall i \in F \tag{5}$$

$$U_i.L_i \le \sum_d Q_{i,d} \quad \forall i \in S \tag{6}$$

$$\sum_{i\in S} Q_{i,d} \le 1 \quad \forall d \tag{7}$$

$$\sum_{i\in S} Z_{ji} = 1 \quad \forall j \in K \tag{8}$$

$$\sum_{j\in K} \alpha_j v_{jp} Z_{ji} \le CD_{ip}L_i \quad \forall i \in S, p \tag{9}$$

$$\mu_{kjd} + Z_{ki} + \sum_{o\in S, o\ne s} Z_{jo} \le 2 \quad \forall j,k \in K, i \in S, d, k \ne j \tag{10}$$

$$\sum_{j\in I} \mu_{ijd} = 1 \quad \forall i \in K, d \tag{11}$$

$$\sum_{j\in I} \mu_{jid} = \sum_{j\in I} \mu_{ijd} \quad \forall i \in I, d \tag{12}$$

$$\sum_{j\in I} \rho_{jidp} - \sum_{j\in I} \rho_{jidp} \ge \alpha_i v_{ip} \quad \forall i \in K, d, p \tag{13}$$

$$\sum_{j\in I} \rho_{jidp} \le CV_d \mu_{ijd} \quad \forall i \in I, d, i \ne j \tag{14}$$

$$\sum_{j\in K} \rho_{ijdp} \ge \sum_{j\in K} Z_{ji}\alpha_j v_{jp} \quad \forall i \in S, d, p \tag{15}$$

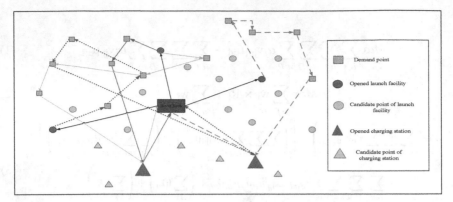

Fig. 1. Overview of the drone air delivery system

$$\rho_{ijdp} \leq \left(CV_d - \alpha_i v_{ip}\right)\mu_{ijd} \quad \forall j \in I, i \in K, p, d \tag{16}$$

$$\rho_{jidp} \geq \alpha_i v_{ip}\mu_{jid} \quad \forall j \in I, i \in K, p, d \tag{17}$$

$$BL_{jd} \leq BC_d \quad \forall j \in I, d \tag{18}$$

$$BL_{jd} \leq BL_{id} - (p_{ijdp+m_d})r_d d_{ij}\mu_{ijd} + BC_d\left(1 - \mu_{ijd}\right) \quad \forall i, j \in I, d, i \neq j \tag{19}$$

$$BL_{jd} \leq BC_d - (p_{ijdp+m_d})r_d d_{ij}\mu_{ijd} \quad \forall j \in F, i \in I, d \tag{20}$$

$$\alpha_j = 1 \quad \forall j \in k_1 \tag{21}$$

$$0.7 \leq \alpha_j \leq 1 \quad \forall j \in k_2 \tag{22}$$

$$L_i, R_i, Q_{id}, \mu_{ijd}, Z_{ij} \in \{0, 1\}, \quad \rho_{ijdp}, BL_{jd} \geq 0 \tag{23}$$

The objective (1) attempt to maximize the demand coverage according to service rate of each demand point. Objective (2) maximizes the weight of the selected points for the construction of the facility. Objective (3) tries to minimize the total cost, including the construction cost of facilities, delivery, and drone battery consumption cost. Constraints (4) and (5) ensure that the number of construction facilities (launch facility and charging station) should be less than the allowed number. Constraint (6) states drones should be assigned to launch facilities according to their limited capacity. Constraint (7) ensures each drone should be allocated to at most one open facility. Constraints (8) ensure each demand point is assigned to a launch facility exactly once. Constraint (9) is about the limited launch facility's capacity for delivering packages by considering the service rate of each demand point. Constraint (10) makes sure that two consecutive demand points on a route are assigned to the same launch facility.

Constraint (11) illustrates that each demand location should be placed on exactly one drone route. Constraint (12) is the flow constraint. Constraint (13) ensures that each customer's requirements must be met according to its service rate. Constraint (14) restricts the total package load of any arc not to exceed the drone's capacity. Constraint (15) ensures that the total demands of all customers assigned to the corresponding launch facility are more than the same facility's total load by considering the service rate of each point. Constraints (16) and (17) are bounding constraints for additional variables acourding to its service rate. Constraint (18) ensures that the battery consumption between each node is less than the drones' battery capacity. Constraints (19) and (20) guarantee that reduces battery level on entry at node j based on the distance route from node i,drone and its package weight and the drones' battery consumption rate. Constraints (21) and (22) refer to the service rate of demand points; All demand of a critical point must be met, so α_k takes the value 1 (21); for the other point, α_k will be between 0.7 and 1 (22). Constraint (23) is domain constraint.

Sets:		Parameters:	
V	Set of all node	w_i	Weight of each candidate points $(i \in M)$
F	Set of all Charging stations	f_i	Construction cost of node $i \in M$
S	Set of all potential launch facility	c_{ijd}	Cost per mile of sending packages from node i to node j by drones d
I	Set of all candidate nodes	r_d	Battery consumption rate by the drones d per weight and unit of transported
K	Set of all demand points	v_{ip}	Amount of each demand point i of blood product p $(i \in k)$
k_1	Critical demand points that all demands must be met	CV_d	Capacity of drone d
k_2	Other demand points	m_d	Weight of the drone and its battery
P	Set of all blood product $p \in P$		
Parameters:		**Variables:**	
BC_d	Drone's d battery capacity	L_i	1 if the launch facility is located at i; 0, otherwise
Ps	Maximum number of launch facility	R_i	1 if the charging station is located at i; 0, otherwise
pf	Maximum number of charging stations	Q_{id}	1 if the d-th drone d is assigned to location i; 0, otherwise
U_i	Capacity of each candidate launch facility	μ_{ijd}	1 if the arc (i, j) is traversed by drone d; 0 otherwise
d_{ij}	Travel distance between nodes i and j	Z_{ij}	1 if demand point i is assigned to launch facility j; 0, otherwise

(*continued*)

(*continued*)

Sets:		Parameters:	
CD_{ip}	Capacity of each launch facility i for blood product $p \in P$	ρ_{ijdp}	Remaining delivery demands after leaving node i if drones d travels from node i to node j (for every $i, j \in N$)
λ_d	Drone d battery consumption cost	BL_{jd}	Battery level of each drone d when arriving in vertex j
		α_k	Service rate to each demand point

3 Numerical Results

In this part, a simple numerical example with 20 candidate point for construction facilities, 8 kinds of drones, 15 demand point (in 3 groups; hospitals, clinics, and medical institutes), and 4 types of blood package include in O, A, B, and AB is presented. We aim to construct launch facilities and charging stations from the candidate point according to the weight of each location and demand point. Table 2 displays the weighted candidate point which gathers from the TOPSIS method. Some critical parameters of the problem are identified in the following tables. For instance, the total capacity of a launch facility from blood packages is in Table 3; the demand for different points from various blood packages is given in Table 4. Also, some physical characteristics of the drone (e.g., battery capacity, consumption rate, and drone capacity to carry blood packages) are prepared in Table 5. These parameters are gathered from the related articles and experts' opinions. It should be noted that the average weight of blood packages is 0.55 kg.

Since our developed model is multi-objective, we employ the ε-constraint method to achieve a Pareto-optimal solution. The validity of this model is evaluated by GAMS

Table 2. Weighted of each candidate point that gathers from the TOPSIS method.

Candidate point for the launch site	w_s	Candidate point for the charging station	w_f
1	0.12	11	0.08
2	0.13	12	0.1
3	0.14	13	0.11
4	0.11	14	0.13
5	0.15	15	0.16
6	0.04	16	0.11
7	0.05	17	0.07
8	0.1	18	0.08
9	0.11	19	0.09
10	0.05	20	0.07

Table 3. Total capacity of a launch facility from blood packages.

Launch facility	Total capacity of a launch facility for blood packages
11	105
12	80
13	70
14	90
15	100

version 25.1.3 software using the CPLEX solver in a personal computer with Intel Core i5 CPU with 2.20 GHz frequency and 8.00 GB RAM. The CPU time of this model is 10.28 s. Figure 2 illustrates Pareto solutions obtained by the ε-constraint method.

Table 4. Demand for different points from various blood packages.

Demand	p1	p2	p3	p4	Total
1	2	3	5	4	14
2	4	4	4	4	16
3	3	4	5	7	19
4	5	2	4	5	16
5	2	5	6	6	19
6	4	5	5	6	20
7	6	6	5	6	23
8	3	4	3	4	14
9	3	5	3	5	16
10	3	3	3	5	14
11	3	4	3	4	14
12	5	4	4	4	17
13	6	5	4	3	18
14	6	5	6	3	20
15	4	3	6	2	15

Table 5. Physical characteristics of each drone

Drones	Total blood packages	Drone's battery capacity (Ah)	Battery consumption rate $(^{Ah}/_{kg.Km})$	Drone and battery weight (Kg)
1	35	625	3	2.8
2	55	4425	6	6
3	30	365	2.5	2.3
4	45	2900	5	5.6
5	32	530	2.8	2.5
6	38	875	3.4	3
7	36	675	3.2	2.5
8	40	1650	4.8	4.2

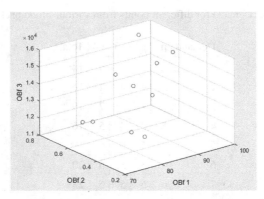

Fig. 2. Pareto solutions were obtained by the ε-constraint method

4 Conclusion

This study presented a novel location-routing problem in blood package delivery with drones by considering sustainability. The problem was supposed to locate a predetermined number of launching site and charging station of drones, considering a trade-off between three objectives, include in minimizing travel and construction cost, maximizing demand coverage, and maximizing the weight of each candidate points, which was obtained by the TOPSIS method by considering various sustainable indicators. The developed model prepares the crucial information on various aspects of the drone's location-routing problem for managers in health care seeking to construct an aerial delivery system for blood package delivery. The proposed model was solved by employing the epsilon method to validate the result. Due to the feature of the problem, developing efficient meta-heuristic or exact methods is suggested to solve large-sized problems. Moreover, the uncertainty in some parameters can be addressed in future studies.

References

1. Xiang, G., Hardy, A., Rajeh, M., Venuthurupalli, L.: Design of the life-ring drone delivery system for rip current rescue. In: Proceedings of the 2016 IEEE Systems and Information Engineering Design Symposium (SIEDS), Charlottesville, VA, USA, pp. 181–186, 26–29 April 2016, IEEE (2016)
2. Golabi, M., Shavarani, S.M., Izbirak, G.: An edge-based stochastic facility location problem in UAV-supported humanitarian relief logistics: a case study of Tehran earthquake. Nat. Hazards **87**(3), 1545–1565 (2017)
3. Scott, J., Scott, C.: Drone delivery models for healthcare. In: Proceedings of the 50th Hawaii International Conference on System Sciences, Hilton Waikoloa Village, Hawaii, USA, 4–7 January 2017 (2017)
4. Karaca, Y., et al.: The potential use of unmanned aircraft systems (drones) in mountain search and rescue operations. Am. J. Emerg. Med. **36**(4), 583–658 (2018)
5. Thiels, C.A., Aho, J.M., Zietlow, S.P., Jenkins, D.H.: Use of unmanned aerial vehicles for medical product transport. Air Med. J. **34**(2), 104–108 (2015)
6. Albornoz, C., Giraldo, L.F.: Trajectory design for efficient crop irrigation with a UAV. In: Proceedings of the 2017 IEEE 3rd Colombian Conference on Automatic Control (CCAC), Cartagena, Colombia, pp. 1–6, 18–20 October 2017, IEEE (2017)
7. Udeanu, G., Dobrescu, A., Oltean, M.: Unmanned aerial vehicle in military operations. Sci. Res. Educ. Air Force **18**(1), 199–206 (2016)
8. Hong, I., Kuby, M., Murray, A.T.: A range-restricted recharging station coverage model for drone delivery service planning. Trans. Res. Part C: Emerg. Technol. **90**, 198–212 (2018)
9. Shavarani, S.M., Nejad, M.G., Rismanchian, F., Izbirak, G.: Application of hierarchical facility location problem for optimization of a drone delivery system: a case study of Amazon prime air in the city of San Francisco. Int. J. Adv. Manuf. Technol. **95**(9–12), 3141–3153 (2017). https://doi.org/10.1007/s00170-017-1363-1
10. Mack, E.: How delivery drones can help save the world. Forbes, Forbes Magazine (2018)
11. Goodchild, A., Toy, J.: Delivery by drone: an evaluation of unmanned aerial vehicle technology in reducing CO_2 emissions in the delivery service industry. Transp. Res. Part D: Transp. Environ. **61**, 58–67 (2018)
12. Peng, K., et al.: A hybrid genetic algorithm on routing and scheduling for vehicle-assisted multi-drone parcel delivery. IEEE Access **7**, 49191–49200 (2019)
13. Hu, M., et al.: On the joint design of routing and scheduling for vehicle-assisted multi-UAV inspection. Futur. Gener. Comput. Syst. **94**, 214–223 (2019)
14. Chowdhury, S., Emelogu, A., Marufuzzaman, M., Nurre, S.G., Bian, L.: Drones for disaster response and relief operations: a continuous approximation model. Int. J. Prod. Econ. **188**, 167–184 (2017)
15. Pulver, A., Wei, R.: Optimizing the spatial location of medical drones. Appl. Geogr. **90**, 9–16 (2018)
16. Kim, S.J., Lim, G.J., Cho, J., Côté, M.J.: Drone-aided healthcare services for patients with chronic diseases in rural areas. J. Intell. Rob. Syst. **88**(1), 163–180 (2017)
17. Chauhan, D., Unnikrishnan, A., Figliozzi, M.: Maximum coverage capacitated facility location problem with range constrained drones. Transp. Res. Part C: Emerg. Technol. **99**, 1–18 (2019)
18. Hong, I., Kuby, M., Murray, A.: A deviation flow refueling location model for continuous space: a commercial drone delivery system for urban areas. In: Advances in Geocomputation, Springer, Cham. pp. 125–132 (2017). https://doi.org/10.1007/978-3-319-22786-3_12
19. Wang, D., Hu, P., Du, J., Zhou, P., Deng, T., Hu, M.: Routing and scheduling for hybrid truck-drone collaborative parcel delivery with independent and truck-carried drones. IEEE Internet Things J. **6**(6), 10483–10495 (2019)

20. Murray, C.C., Chu, A.G.: The flying sidekick traveling salesman problem: optimization of drone-assisted parcel delivery. Transp. Res. Part C: Emerg. Technol. **54**, 86–109 (2015)
21. Kitjacharoenchai, P., Min, B.C., Lee, S.: Two echelon vehicle routing problem with drones in last mile delivery. Int. J. Prod. Econ. **225**, 107598 (2020)
22. Tzeng, G.H., Huang, J.J.: Multiple Attribute Decision Making: Methods and Applications. CRC Press (2011)
23. Assari, A., Mahesh, T., Assari, E.: Role of public participation in sustainability of historical city: usage of TOPSIS method. Indian J. Sci. Technol. **5**(3), 2289–2294 (2012)

A *MILP* Formulation for an Automated Guided Vehicle Scheduling Problem with Battery Constraints

Adriano Masone[1](✉) (iD), Teresa Murino[2], Claudio Sterle[1], and Monica Strazzullo[2]

[1] Department of Electrical Engineering and Information Technology, University of Naples Federico II, Via Claudio 21, 80125 Naples, Italy
{adriano.masone,claudio.sterle}@unina.it
[2] Department of Chemical, Materials and Industrial Production Engineering, University of Naples Federico II, Piazzale Tecchio 80, 80125 Naples, Italy
teresa.murino@unina.it,mo.strazzullo@studenti.unina.it

Abstract. Nowadays, AGVs are frequently used in industries for the internal transportation of goods or pallets. The aim of an AGV-based internal transportation system is to transfer the right amount of the right material to the right place at the right time. Therefore, the determination of a good scheduling of the AGV tasks is essential to overcome delays in production and material handling processes. In this work, we study a scheduling problem arising from an internal transportation system of a company operating in the manufacturing field where AGVs subject to battery constraints are used for horizontal movement of materials. The aim of this work is to highlight the impact of the AGV battery recharge times on the completion time of the material handling process. To this aim, we propose an original mixed integer linear programming (MILP) formulation to optimally solve the addressed problem. The proposed model is validated on test instances built from real data comparing its results with those obtained disregarding the battery constraints. The results show the effectiveness of the proposed solution method and the impact of the AGV charging time on the handling process completion time.

Keywords: Parallel scheduling · AGV recharge · MILP modeling

1 Introduction

The introduction of automated guided vehicles (AGVs), due to their dexterity, efficiency and flexibility, had a great impact on logistics leading to the creation of new business models [13,16]. Currently, different kinds of AGVs are used for several logistics operations in the entire supply chain: extraction of raw materials, intermediate transport, last mile delivery to cite only a few [3,4,17,20]. In

© IFIP International Federation for Information Processing 2021
Published by Springer Nature Switzerland AG 2021
A. Dolgui et al. (Eds.): APMS 2021, IFIP AICT 632, pp. 15–23, 2021.
https://doi.org/10.1007/978-3-030-85906-0_2

particular, AGVs are frequently used in industries for the internal transportation of goods or pallets between various departments or locations within the same factory or for receiving, storage and sorting goods in shipment areas [19]. The aim of an AGV-based internal transportation system is to transfer the right amount of the right material to the right place at the right time. Therefore, the determination of a good scheduling of the AGV tasks is essential to overcome delays in production and material handling processes [10]. The research activity on AGV-based internal transportation system and, in particular, on related scheduling problems has been significant in the last twenty years. The interested reader is addressed to the survey works on the topic published by Kaoud et al. [8], Qiu et al. [18] and Xie et al. [21]. In this context, different scheduling problems were defined on the basis of the considered AGV side constraints (e.g., capacity, schedules of additional equipment and limited parking space) [7]. However, as noted in [5,12], most of the contributions on the topic paid scarce attention to the issues related to the battery usage, being it frequently omitted [6].

Nowadays, consistently with the industry 4.0 paradigm [9], several companies are adapting their processes to operate with a more intensive focus on sustainability through an increasing economic and ecological efficiency (e.g., [2,11]). In this context, an effective battery management on AGVs can have a significant impact on the overall performance of the manufacturing system, as noted in [20]. On this basis, in this work, we study a scheduling problem arising from an internal transportation system of a company operating in the manufacturing field where AGVs subject to battery constraints are used for horizontal movement of materials. In a nutshell, the AGV transportation system performs as follows: a set of AGVs must move some materials from a central warehouse to different workstations; on each trip, an AGV can be loaded with the materials of a single workstation; the AGV battery consumption depends on the travel time and the weight carried; the battery has to be recharged before it is completely depleted. The problem consists in determining the AGV scheduling that minimizes the time to supply the required materials to all the workstations. This problem will be denoted in the following as the AGV scheduling problem with battery constraints (ASP-BC). The aim of this work is to highlight the not negligible impact of the AGV battery recharge times on the completion time of the material handling process. To this aim, we proposed an original mixed-integer linear programming (MILP) formulation for the ASP-BC. The proposed model is then validated on test instances built from real data comparing its results with those obtained disregarding the battery constraints.

Similar problems have been addressed in literature through heuristic approaches [1,6]. However, to the best of our knowledge, this is the first work addressing this kind of problem through an exact solution approach. The rest of this paper is structured as follows: in Sect. 2, we provide a detailed description of the ASP-BC; the proposed MILP formulation is presented in 3; the computational results are reported in Sect. 4; conclusions and research perspectives are given in Sect. 5.

2   Problem Description

In a manufacturing facility, at the beginning of each working day, a set of work-stations must be supplied with the materials required for the production tasks. The requested materials are organized within a set of packages as follows:

- all the materials requested by a workstation are included in only one package
- a package contains the materials of only one workstation

This kind of organization creates a one-to-one workstation-package relation. The packages are arranged in a central warehouse and must be carried to the corresponding workstations by a set of AGVs. The AGVs are initially located at the central warehouse and can carry one package at a time. Moreover, the number of available AGVs is much lower than the number of packages. Therefore, an AGV should perform multiple trips since it generally has to serve more than one workstation. On this basis, in the following, We will refer the combination of an AGV loaded trip from warehouse to workstations and the empty trip back as a job. A job can be characterized by a duration given by the sum of the travel time from the warehouse to the workstation and back, and the time needed for the package load and unload operations. Moreover, each job requires a certain amount of energy to be performed by an AGV. Specifically, the required energy depends on the job duration and the package weight. Therefore, since AGVs are battery powered, the number of consecutive jobs that an AGV can perform without battery recharge is limited. The AGV battery is fully charged at the beginning of the working day and it has to be fully recharged before it is completely depleted. The charging time is fixed and does not depend on the residual energy. The manufacturer company aim is to minimize the time required to supply the materials/packages to all the workstations so avoiding delays in the production operations.

The solution of the arising optimization problem involves three kinds of decisions:

- assignment of jobs to the AGVs;
- sequencing of the jobs on each AGV;
- scheduling of AGV battery recharge.

The objective is to minimize the makespan that is given by the maximum completion time of the last job over all the AGVs.

3 Problem Formulation

To formulate the *ASP-BC*, we introduced a notation based on the the previous problem description. For the sake of readability, the notation is reported in Table 1.

Table 1. Notation used for the *ASP-BC* formulation.

Problem notation	
Sets:	
J	Set of jobs
K	Set of AGVs
$\{o\}$	Starting dummy job for each AGV
$\{d\}$	Ending dummy job for each AGV
J^+	$J \cup \{o\}$
J^-	$J \cup \{d\}$
Parameters:	
t_j^k	Processing time of the job j on the AGV k
w_j^k	Energy required for the job j on the AGV k
r	AGV battery charging time
E	AGV battery capacity
M	Sufficiently large constant
Variables:	
$C_{\max} \geq 0$	Completion time of the handling process
$C_{\max}^k \geq 0$	Completion time of the last job performed by the k-th AGV
$s_j^k \geq 0$	Starting time of job j on the AGV k
$c_j^k \geq 0$	Ending time of job j on the AGV k
$e_j^k \geq 0$	Energy spent by the AGV k from its last charge to the completion of job j
$x_j^k \in \{0,1\}$	Equal to 1 if the job j is assigned to the AGV k, 0 otherwise
$y_{ij}^k \in \{0,1\}$	Equal to 1 if job j is performed immediately after job i on the k-th AGV, 0 otherwise
$\delta_j^k \in \{0,1\}$	Equal to 1 if the AGV k is recharged before performing job j, 0 otherwise

Consistently with this notation, the *ASP-BC* can be formulated as follows:

$$\min C_{\max} \tag{1}$$

s.t.

$$C_{\max} \geq C_{\max}^k \qquad\qquad \forall k \in K \tag{2}$$

$$C_{\max}^k \geq c_j^k \qquad\qquad \forall j \in J, k \in K \tag{3}$$

$$C_{\max}^k \geq C_{\max}^{k+1} \qquad\qquad \forall k \in \{1,..,|K|-1\} \tag{4}$$

$$c_j^k \geq s_j^k + t_j^k + r\delta_j^k - M(1 - x_j^k) \qquad\qquad \forall j \in J, k \in K \tag{5}$$

$$c_o^k = 0 \qquad\qquad \forall k \in K \tag{6}$$

$$\sum_{k \in K} x_j^k = 1 \qquad\qquad \forall j \in J \tag{7}$$

$$s_j^k + c_j^k \leq Mx_j^k \qquad\qquad \forall j \in J, k \in K \tag{8}$$

$$s_i^k \geq +c_j^k - M(1 - y_{ji}^k) \qquad\qquad \forall i \in J, j \in J^+, k \in K \tag{9}$$

$$c_j^k \geq +s_i^k - M(1 - y_{ji}^k) \qquad\qquad \forall i \in J, j \in J^+, k \in K \tag{10}$$

$$\sum_{j \in J} y_{oj}^k = 1 \qquad\qquad \forall k \in K \tag{11}$$

$$\sum_{j \in J} y_{jd}^k = 1 \qquad\qquad \forall k \in K \tag{12}$$

$$\sum_{j \in J^+} y_{ji}^k = \sum_{j \in J^-} y_{ij}^k \qquad\qquad \forall i \in J, K \in K \tag{13}$$

$$\sum_{i \in J^+} y_{ij}^k = x_j^k \qquad\qquad \forall j \in J, k \in K \tag{14}$$

$$e_j^k \geq e_i^k + w_j^k - M(1 - y_{ji}^k) - M\delta_j^k \qquad\qquad \forall i, j \in J, k \in K \tag{15}$$

$$e_j^k \geq w_j^k - M(1 - x_j^k) \qquad\qquad \forall j \in J, k \in K \tag{16}$$

$$e_j^k + w_i^k \leq E + M(1 - y_{ji}^k) + M\delta_j^k \qquad\qquad \forall i \in J, j \in J^+, k \in K \tag{17}$$

$$\delta_j^k \leq x_j^k \qquad\qquad \forall j \in J, k \in K \tag{18}$$

$$\delta_j^k \leq (1 - y_{oj}^k) \qquad\qquad \forall j \in J, k \in K \tag{19}$$

The objective function (1) minimizes the makespan of the handling process. Constraints (2) set the makespan equal to the maximum completion time among the ones of the used AGVs. Constraints (3) set the makespan of an AGV equal to the completion time of its last processed job. Constraints (4) are symmetry breaking constraints. Constraints (5) ensure that if a job j is assigned to the AGV k then its completion time is equal to its starting time plus the processing time and the charging time (if a recharge is scheduled). Constraints (6) set the completion time of the initial dummy job equal to 0. Constraints (7) guarantee that each job is performed. The consistency between starting and completion time variables and job-AGV assignment variables is granted by constraints (8).

The congruence between the completion time and the starting time of jobs that are performed consecutively on the same AGV is guaranteed by constraints (9,10). Constraints (11–13) ensure that each AGV can perform one job at a time. Constraints (14) are consistency constraints among y and x variables. Constraints (15, 16) set the value of the energy consumption of each AGV after each performed job. Constraints (17) guarantee that an AGV is recharged if, performing a job, the energy consumption would exceed its battery capacity. The consistency between the recharge variables and assignment variables is granted by constraints (18). Finally, constraints (19) ensure that an AGV is not recharged without having performed at least one job.

We highlight that relaxing the battery constraints (15–19) and excluding the recharge variables, the *ASP-BC* turns out to be the well known parallel machine scheduling problem (*PSP*) [14,15]. Therefore, the optimal solution of the *PSP* is a lower bound for the *ASP-BC*.

4   Computational Results

In this section we present and discuss the computational results of the experimentation performed to validate the proposed *MILP* formulation for the *APS-BC* and to evaluate the impact of the AGV charging time on the handling process completion time. To this aim, we implemented the procedure currently used by the manufacturing company to solve the *ASP-BC*. The procedure first solves the *PSP* and then adds the recharge activities when needed (i.e., immediately before an AGV performs a job that otherwise would completely deplete its battery). The procedure, denoted in the following as *PSP+R*, has been implemented in Python 3.6 and the *ASP-BC* and *PSP* formulations have been solved with a commercial MIP solver (FICO Xpress-MP 8.2) on an Intel(R) Core (TM) i5-8250U, 1.80GHz, 8.00GB of RAM.

The experimentation has been conducted on twenty instances built from real data coming from a manufacturing company. In particular, we generated four sets of five instances each, with 6, 7, 8 and 9 jobs. The number of AGVs is equal to 2 and we considered the same charging time (r) and battery capacity (E) for all the instances. For each instance, we computed:

– the completion time of the related *PSP* solution (C_{PSP});
– the completion time of the optimal *ASP-BC* solution obtained by the proposed *MILP* formulation (C_{MILP})
– the completion time of the *ASP-BC* solution obtained using the procedure *PSP+R* (C_{PROC}).

The *PSP* and *ASP-BC* formulations were optimally solved on all the instances within a time limit of 10800 s.

The results of the experimentation are shown in Table 2. In particular, for each solution method we reported the percentage difference (%Diff) with the completion time of the *PSP* optimal solution and the number of recharge activities scheduled (Rech). The percentage differences related to the *PSP+R* and

MILP solution methods are computed as $(C_{PROC} - C_{PSP})/C_{PSP} \cdot 100$ and $(C_{MILP} - C_{PSP})/C_{PSP} \cdot 100$.

Moreover, we also compute the saving in terms of completion time obtained solving the proposed *MILP* rather than applying *PSP+R* ($\%Sav = (C_{PROC} - C_{MILP})/C_{MILP} \cdot 100$).

Table 2. Comparison of the *PSP+R* and *MILP* solutions

		PSP+R		MILP		
Id	$|J|$	%Diff	Rech	%Diff	Rech	%Sav
I_1	6	30.77	2	30.77	2	0.00
I_2		35.09	2	35.09	2	0.00
I_3		62.50	1	1.56	0	60.00
I_4		02.50	1	6.25	0	52.94
I_5		70.18	3	35.09	2	25.97
I_6	7	50.00	3	25.00	2	20.00
I_7		57.14	3	42.86	3	10.00
I_8		48.78	3	40.24	2	6.09
I_9		56.34	3	42.25	3	9.90
I_10		56.34	3	49.30	3	4.72
I_11	8	71.43	5	47.62	4	16.13
I_12		53.33	3	26.67	2	21.05
I_13		58.82	5	39.22	4	14.08
I_14		71.08	5	49.40	4	14.52
I_15		48.19	4	42.17	2	4.24
I_16	9	63.83	5	42.55	4	14.93
I_17		59.41	5	39.60	4	14.18
I_18		72.16	5	41.24	4	21.90
I_19		64.17	5	52.94	5	7.34
I_20		49.76	5	48.78	5	0.66
Average		57.09	3.55	36.93	2.85	15.93

We can observe that, on average, the completion time determined taking into account battery constraints is about 35% greater than the one obtained solving a *PSP*. This result proves the not negligible relevance of charging activities within a internal transportation system operated by AGVs. Indeed, the reported %Diff values show that charging activities represent a significant component of the handling process completion time. For example, on the instance L_20, the %Diff of the *MILP* solution is equal to 52.94%, i.e., the charging activities are around the 30% of the completion time. Moreover, we point out that if the battery issue is not effectively addressed then the charging activities can have even a greater impact on the completion time as we can observe from the average %Diff of *PSP+R* that is around the 60%. Furthermore, the average saving, equal to 15.93%, provides an idea of the completion time reduction that a company can achieve by optimally solving the *ASP-BC*.

Finally, we highlight that on average the optimal solution of the *APS-BC* determines fewer battery recharges compared to the *PSP+R* solution, even if the number of recharges is not directly considered in the objective function. This result is very important not only in terms of completion time, as previously shown, but also in terms of costs. Indeed, a company has to replace the AGV batteries when they reach their cycle life (i.e., the number of charge and discharge cycles that a battery can complete). Therefore, an effective management of the recharges can extend the battery lifespan reducing the costs for battery replacing borne by a company.

5 Conclusions

In this work, we presented a particular scheduling problem arising in the manufacturing field. It consists in the determination of the optimal scheduling of AGVs subject to battery constraints to minimize the completion time of the material handling process. An original *MILP* formulation has been proposed to tackle the problem. The performed experimentation on instances with up to 9 jobs and 2 AGVs, derived from real data, confirm the applicability and the effectiveness of the proposed approach. Preliminary results showed that the running time of the proposed approach on instances with tens of jobs and the same number of AGVs exceeds the considered time limit. Therefore, future works will be aimed at developing heuristic solution methods able to effectively address large scale instances. Moreover, it could be interesting to investigate the possibility of taking into account other operational aspects related to the battery as the performance reduction and the possibility to do partial recharges.

References

1. Abderrahim, M., Bekrar, A., Trentesaux, D., Aissani, N., Bouamrane, K.: Manufacturing 4.0 operations scheduling with AGV battery management constraints. Energies **13** (2020)
2. Boccia, M., Diglio, A., Masone, A., Sterle, C.: A location-routing based solution approach for reorganizing postal collection operations in rural areas. In: Nicosia, G., Ojha, V., La Malfa, E., Jansen, G., Sciacca, V., Pardalos, P., Giuffrida, G., Umeton, R. (eds.) LOD 2020. LNCS, vol. 12565, pp. 625–636. Springer, Cham (2020). https://doi.org/10.1007/978-3-030-64583-0_55
3. Boccia, M., Masone, A., Sforza, A., Sterle, C.: A column-and-row generation approach for the flying sidekick travelling salesman problem. Transp. Res. Part C Emerg. Technol. **124**, 102913 (2021)
4. Boccia, M., Masone, A., Sforza, A., Sterle, C.: An exact approach for a variant of the FS-TSP. Transp. Res. Procedia **52C**, 51–58 (2021)

5. De Ryck, M., Versteyhe, M., Shariatmadar, K.: Resource management in decentralized industrial Automated Guided Vehicle systems. J. Manuf. Syst. **54**, 204–214 (2020)
6. Fatnassi, E., Chaouachi, J.: Scheduling automated guided vehicle with battery constraints. In: 2015 20th International Conference on Methods and Models in Automation and Robotics (MMAR), Miedzyzdroje, Poland, pp. 1010–1015 (2015)
7. Fazlollahtabar, H., Saidi-Mehrabad, M.: Methodologies to optimize automated guided vehicle scheduling and routing problems: a review study. J. Intell. Robot. Syst. **77**, 525–545 (2015)
8. Kaoud, E., El-Sharief, M.A., El-Sebaie, M.G.: Scheduling problems of automated guided vehicles in job shop, flow shop, and container terminals. In: 2017 4th International Conference on Industrial Engineering and Applications (ICIEA), Nagoya, Japan, pp. 60–65 (2017). https://doi.org/10.1109/IEA.2017.7939179
9. Lasi, H., Fettke, P., Kemper, H.G., et al.: Industry 4.0. Bus. Inf. Syst. Eng. **6**, 239–242 (2014)
10. Luo, J., Wu, Y., Mendes, A.B.: Modelling of integrated vehicle scheduling and container storage problems in unloading process at an automated container terminal. Comput. Ind. Eng. **94**(Suppl. C), 32–44 (2016)
11. Masone, A., Sterle, C., Vasilyev, I., Ushakov, A.: A three-stage p-median based exact method for the optimal diversity management problem. Networks **74**, 174–189 (2018)
12. McHaney, R.: Modelling battery constraints in discrete event automated guided vehicle simulations. Int. J. Prod. Res. **33**(11), 3023–3040 (1995)
13. Van Meldert, B. and De Boeck, L.: Introducing autonomous vehicles in logistics: A review from a broad perspective, Facility of Economics and Business, KU Leuven, (2016). https://lirias.kuleuven.be/bitstream/123456789/543558/1/KBI_1618.pdf, Accessed Mar 2021
14. Mokotoff, E.: Parallel machine scheduling problems: a survey. Asia-Pac. J. Oper. Res. **18**, 193–242 (2001)
15. Mokotoff, E.: An exact algorithm for the identical parallel machine scheduling problem. Eur. J. Oper. Res. **152**(3), 758–769 (2004)
16. Oboth, C., Batta, R., Karwan, M.: Dynamic conflict-free routing of automated guided vehicles. Int. J. Prod. Res. **37**(9), 2003–2030 (1999)
17. Otto, A., Agatz, N., Campbell, J., Golden, B., Pesch, E.: Optimization approaches for civil applications of unmanned aerial vehicles (UAVs) or aerial drones: A survey. Networks **72**(4), 411–458 (2018)
18. Qiu, L., Hsu, W.J., Huang, S.Y., Wang, H.: Scheduling and routing algorithms for agvs: a survey. Int. J. Prod. Res. **40**(3), 745–760 (2002)
19. Ventura, J.A., Pazhani, S., Mendoza, A.: Finding optimal dwell points for automated guided vehicles in general guide-path layouts. Int. J. Prod. Econ. **170**, 850–861 (2015)
20. Vis, I.F.A.: Survey of research in the design and control of automated guided vehicle systems. Eur. J. Oper. Res. **170**(3), 677–709 (2006)
21. Xie, C., Allen, T.T.: Simulation and experimental design methods for job shop scheduling with material handling: a survey. Int. J. Adv. Manuf. Technol. **80**, 233–243 (2015). https://doi.org/10.1007/s00170-015-6981-x

Planning Autonomous Material Transportation in Hospitals

Giuseppe Fragapane[1](✉) ⓘ, Debjit Roy[2], Fabio Sgarbossa[1] ⓘ,
and Jan Ola Strandhagen[1] ⓘ

[1] Department of Mechanical and Industrial Engineering, Norwegian University of Science and
Technology, Trondheim, Norway
giuseppe.fragapane@ntnu.no
[2] Department of Production and Quantitative Methods, Indian Institute of Management
Ahmedabad, Ahmedabad, Gujarat, India

Abstract. Until recently, architects planned the layout for a new hospital based
only on design aspects, experience, and legal regulations. Today, hospital logistics
planners are included at an earlier stage in the project and support hospital layout planning with important logistics aspects. While methods supporting patient
flow are prioritized in the layout planning, methods focusing on material flow
are lacking. Therefore, this study is part of a project that aims to develop a decision support model for hospital layout planning that includes material flow. We
develop a semi-open queuing network model of a hospital with multiple floors and
compare it with agent-based simulation modeling. Simulation results show that a
semi-open queuing network is a promising approach to support hospital planners
in the decision-making process of hospital layout planning that includes planning
material flow performed by autonomous mobile robots.

Keywords: Autonomous mobile robots · Semi-open queuing network · Hospital
intralogistics · Hospital layout

1 Introduction

Until recently, architects planned the layout for a new hospital based only on design
aspects, experience, and legal regulations [1]. Today, hospital logistics planners are
included at an earlier stage in the project and support the hospital layout planning with
important logistics aspects. Layout planning for hospitals differs from that in industry.
While in industry, analyzing the material flow is the primary input to determine the layout,
in hospitals, the flows of persons, including patients, family, and staff, are prioritized [2].
Unsurprisingly, the material flow aspect has received little attention in hospital layout
planning, and methods supporting it are lacking [3].

However, material flow plays a crucial role in the daily operation of a hospital.
Activities connected to material flow consume, on average, 25–30% of a hospital's
budget [4]. One of these is material handling activities, which are still mainly performed

© IFIP International Federation for Information Processing 2021
Published by Springer Nature Switzerland AG 2021
A. Dolgui et al. (Eds.): APMS 2021, IFIP AICT 632, pp. 24–32, 2021.
https://doi.org/10.1007/978-3-030-85906-0_3

manually, especially inside the departments, which represent excellent opportunities for automation [5].

Recent advances in technology have increased flexibility in indoor mobility and human-robot collaboration, opening new opportunities to perform material handling activities, particularly in narrow, dynamic environments. Sensing devices, powerful onboard computers, artificial intelligence, and collaborative equipment allow autonomous mobile robots (AMRs) to navigate freely within a predefined area and provide material handling services [6]. AMRs can be increasingly applied in the material flow activities within departments. In contrast, automated guided vehicles cannot enter departments and deliver only in front of them. These capabilities allow deliveries to the point-of-use, the patient, and so cover a wide service area. For many years, mobile robots were a virtually unimaginable and practically unacceptable solution in healthcare support, as people did not associate hospitals with a production environment. The increased acceptance of AMRs allows their integration into departments and wards [7, 8].

The integration of AMRs as transporting, collaborating, or assisting robots can reduce humans' involvement and responsibilities in material handling activities. Including material flow and material handling activities to a stronger degree in layout planning may reduce costs. Small changes such as reducing the distance between departments with frequent material transportation or increasing elevator capacity have a strong impact on material handling performance. In a hospital layout's decision-making processes, hospital planners need to consider material flow and material handling activities.

This study is part of a project that aims to develop a decision support model for hospital layout planning, including material flow and material handling activities. Semi-open queuing network (SOQN) modeling is a promising solution for analyzing hospital layout design configurations while planning material flow performed by AMRs to achieve high performance. The present study investigates the applicability and suitability of this modeling approach and provides a basis for developing an analytical model at the next stage. To achieve this, we develop a SOQN model and compare it with agent-based simulation (ABS) modeling. Analyzing different scenarios helps identify the suitability and applicability of SOQN modeling in hospital layout planning, including material flow and material handling activities.

The rest of the paper is organized as follows. Section 2 reviews the literature on hospital layout planning, material flow and AMRs in hospitals, and SOQN modeling approaches. Section 3 provides a system description, and Sect. 4 introduces the modeling approach and assumptions. In Sect. 5, we present the results of simulations. Section 6 discusses insights related to design aspects. We conclude the study with recommendations for future research.

2 Literature Review

Hospital layout planning is conducted according to a multi-level approach in which hospital layout planning problems are often differentiated into macro- and micro-levels [1]. While the macro level focuses on the arrangement of the different departments within a hospital, the micro-level focuses on organizing the rooms and corridors within the different departments, such as the operating theater, wards, and emergency department. The approaches of quadratic assignment problems, mixed-integer programming, and discrete-event simulation have mainly been used to support the decision-making process [1]. Although quadratic assignment problems are more common in facility location planning, it has been frequently applied to support planning and optimize hospital layouts [3].

Patient flow and patient transportation are major issues in hospital planning and are often approached at the macro level. Several studies have investigated patient transportation in hospital layout planning with the objective of reducing distances to save time and resources [9–11]. However, the topic of material flow and material transportation in hospital layout planning is still lacking [3].

Material flow in hospitals focuses on providing materials to departments and medical services at the right time and quantity, facilitating patient care. Most studies have focused on procurement and inventory management, and only a few have investigated modeling and optimizing approaches for material handling activities such as material transportation in hospitals [12]. Those that have been done have mainly focused on flows of sterile instruments, food, linen, medical supplies, beds, and pharmaceuticals. Analytical models combined with mixed-integer linear programming and simulation modeling are the preferred methodologies for providing the necessary decision support to optimize work routes, workloads, and costs.

To transport materials, various manual, semi-automated, and automated material handling equipment and systems are currently used in hospitals. Many small and short deliveries of medical equipment, medicine, etc., are performed manually by nurses, physicians, porters, etc. Therefore, manual transportation is widely applied throughout the hospital, especially inside departments close to the patient [5]. The few automated material handling systems in departments, such as pneumatic tube systems, are stationary and allow low flexibility. Automated guided vehicles cannot enter departments because of their size. However, they can transport high-volume materials to many pickup and delivery locations and travel long distances within hospitals. To plan and control material handling systems, hospital planners rely mainly on discrete-event and ABS, with the main objectives of minimizing transportation time, total throughput time, and costs. These methods help to determine vehicle size, the number of vehicles, transportation schedule [13–15]. Further, simulating different scenarios such as increasing demand helps in analyzing the system's behavior and develop countermeasures to face the current challenges in hospitals [13, 16]. However, few methods are available to provide decision-making support for material transportation performed by AMRs.

Based on a recent literature review, SOQN has been identified as the most promising method to support the decision-making process for planning and controlling AMRs in hospital logistics [6]. SOQN modeling has been applied to manufacturing [17, 18], warehousing [19–22], container terminals [23, 24], and other logistics environments [24] to improve waiting and throughput time. To the best of our knowledge, the existing literature lacks modeling and proposed solutions to support hospital planners in the hospital layout planning, including material flow and material activities such as determining AMR fleet size to achieve high performance.

3   Method

To analyze the applicability and suitability of SOQN modeling for hospital layout and material flow, this study follows a three-step approach.

First, the hospital layout and AMR transportation are modeled as SOQN. SOQN modeling combines the advantages of open queuing networks (external queues to accommodate jobs whose entrances are delayed) and closed queuing networks (inner networks with a population constraint). Using a synchronization station, incoming customers waiting in an external queue can be paired with available resources in the resource queue. This modeling approach can capture external wait times and precisely estimate throughput times [25].

Second, to evaluate the SOQN model, an ABS model is developed to serve as a benchmark. ABS has recently received more interest among practitioners because it can model stochastic processes. At its core, ABS is built by autonomous resource units that follow a series of predefined rules to achieve their objectives while interacting with each other and their environment [26]. These attributes are especially salient for modeling AMRs in hospitals.

Finally, different scenarios are simulated with SOQN and ABS models to compare them and analyze the applicability and suitability of SOQN modeling for hospital layout and material flow.

4   System Description

In high-density areas, such as big cities, where area costs are high, hospital layouts can be characterized as tall and compact. The hospital layout includes few buildings with many floors and elevators. Each floor consists of several departments. At the department level, the layout is often divided into single or double corridors with treatment, operating, office, or patient rooms at each side [27].

Material flow and material handling activities are performed by AMRs, which can access the entire hospital. Communicating with the hospital infrastructure equipment, such as doors or elevators, AMRs can move to different floors and enter rooms, thereby performing the material handling activities of material transportation, which include the following steps between hospital staff and AMRs:

1. *Ordering:* A hospital staff communicates information about the job (material, pickup, and delivery points) to the AMRs.
2. *Synchronization:* The job is communicated to the AMRs, and idle AMRs receive the job after negotiating with other AMRs.
3. *Pickup:* The AMR navigates autonomously through the hospital layout to the pickup point and loads the material.
4. *Delivery:* The AMR navigates autonomously through the hospital layout to the delivery point and unloads the material. When the material arrives at its final destination, the AMR sends an arrival message to the department. A staff member receives the materials, and the AMR returns to idle.

5 Modeling Approach and Assumptions

For this study, we assume that the hospital layout is rectangular, including one building with six floors, four elevators, and 42 rooms with pickup and delivery points. The AMR can move autonomously within one floor and can enter rooms. The dwell and so the parking position of the AMR is on the first floor.

Based on the system description and assumptions, a closed queuing network (CQN) model of the hospital floor (Fig. 1) and SOQN model of a hospital with multiple floors were developed (Fig. 2).

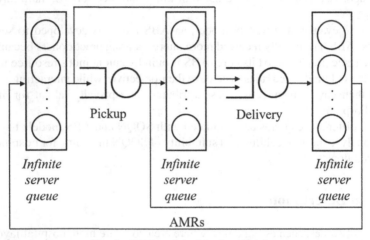

Fig. 1. CQN model of the hospital floor

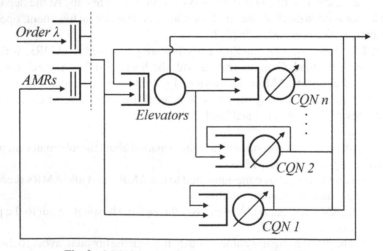

Fig. 2. SOQN model of a hospital with multiple floors

While the CQN model represents the processes within one floor, the SOQN model synchronizes the orders in the open queue with the AMRs in the closed queue. Pickup and delivery can be either on the same or at a different floor and so be grouped to several main transportation routes: a) both pickup and delivery on the first floor, b) pickup on the first floor and delivery on a different floor, c) pickup not on the first floor and delivery on the same floor, d) pickup not on the first floor and delivery on a different floor. The elevators connect the different CQN models of the hospital floor and allow to move AMRs from floor to floor to fulfill the orders. There are multiple types of orders: pickup within one CQN, delivery within one CQN, both pickup and delivery within one CQN, and pickup from one CQN and delivery in another CQN. These transaction types distinguish especially from previous studies.

To identify the mean throughput time and waiting time, we calculate the mean process times for pickup and delivery. Next, we identify the processing time for the CQN model with simulation. Varying the remaining process times in the SOQN model and conducting simulations allows identifying the transportation performance (Table 1). Seven different scenarios are developed to analyze AMR fleet size (scenarios 1, 2, and 3), the elevator response time (scenarios 1, 4, and 5), and delivery routes (scenarios 1, 6, and 7) on the transportation performance.

Table 1. Investigated scenarios

Notation	1	2	3	4	5	6	7
L $_{in\ m}$	**100**	100	100	100	100	100	100
W $_{in\ m}$	**100**	100	100	100	100	100	100
AMR	**4**	**5**	**6**	4	4	4	4
Elevator	**4**	4	4	4	4	4	4
λ $_{per\ min}$*	**1, 3.6**	1, 3.6	1, 3.6	1, 3.6	1, 3.6	1, 3.6	1, 3.6
μ $_{Pickup\ in\ min}$*	**2, 1, 3.6**	2, 1, 3.6	2, 1, 3.6	2, 1, 3.6	2, 1, 3.6	2, 1, 3.6	2, 1, 3.6
μ $_{Delivery\ in\ min}$*	**2, 1, 3.6**	2, 1, 3.6	2, 1, 3.6	2, 1, 3.6	2, 1, 3.6	2, 1, 3.6	2, 1, 3.6
μ $_{CQN\ in\ min}$*	**2, 22, 3.6**	2, 22, 3.6	2, 22, 3.6	2, 22, 3.6	2, 22, 3.6	2, 22, 3.6	2, 22, 3.6
μ $_{Elevator\ in\ sec}$*	**35, 3.6**	35, 3.6	35, 3.6	**30, 3.6**	**40, 3.6**	35, 3.6	35, 3.6
a	**0, 25**	0, 25	0, 25	0, 25	0, 25	**0, 5**	**0, 25**
b	**0, 25**	0, 25	0, 25	0, 25	0, 25	**0, 125**	**0, 125**
c	**0, 25**	0, 25	0, 25	0, 25	0, 25	**0, 125**	**0, 125**
d	**0, 25**	0, 25	0, 25	0, 25	0, 25	**0, 25**	**0, 5**

*Weilbull = α is the scale parameter, β is the shape parameter

We developed an ABS model for comparison with the SOQN model (Fig. 3). The ABS modelling approach follows the recommendations from a previous study on mobile robots in hospital intralogistics [16]. For the ABS, the AMR must be further specified. The AMR speed is 1 m/s, and it can move autonomously in 'free space,' which is framed by the walls. It chooses the shortest path to move between points and maintains a safe distance of 30 cm from all obstacles. The AMR size is 100 cm in length and 60 cm in width. The elevators can only transport one AMR at a time.

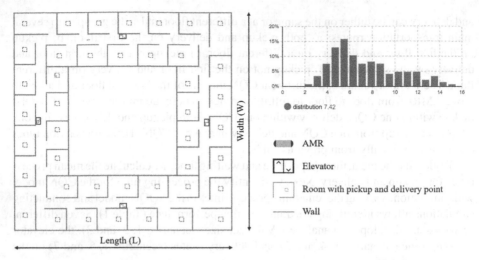

Fig. 3. Top view of ABS model for material transportation performed by AMRs in hospitals

6 Results

The simulation software Anylogic was used to simulate the SOQN and ABS models with the different scenarios (Table 2). Each scenario was conducted several times, with at least 10,000 transportation trips representing ca. 14,000 min in the simulation. On a PC with Processor Intel core i9-8950HK CPU@2.90 GHz and 32 GB installed memory RAM, the SOQN models lasted 5 s, while the ABS models took 4.75 min.

Table 2. Simulation results of the different scenarios after 10,000 transportation trips

Model	Performance	1	2	3	4	5	6	7
SOQN	Mean throughput time in min	9.88	5.73	5.19	8.68	12.17	7.5	12.43
	Mean waiting time in min	4.03	0.44	0.11	3.04	6.09	2.09	6.33
ABS	Mean throughput time in min	9.43	5.45	4.89	8.34	10.7	8.62	11.28
	Mean waiting time in min	4.95	1.09	0.57	3.97	6.11	4.17	6.75

7 Discussion and Conclusion

The SOQN and ABS models provide very close results for analyzing the AMR fleet (scenario 1, 2, and 3), while the remaining results (scenario 4, 5, 6, and 7) provide similar tendencies. Thus, either model can support hospital planners in decision-making for hospital layouts, including material flow and material handling activities. Depending on the required transportation performance, hospital planners have different alternatives to satisfy the requirements. They can either adapt the AMR fleet size (scenarios 1, 2, and

3), the elevator response time (scenarios 1, 4, and 5), or delivery routes (scenarios 1, 6, and 7). Increasing fleet size can help provide a robust transportation system but affects traffic and costs. The elevators play a crucial role in transportation between different floors. A few seconds' difference in response time has a significant effect. This can be observed in the ABS model and simulation since the elevator can only transport one AMR at a time. Waiting time can quickly increase for the next one to use it. Analyzing different transportation routes helps hospital planners to decide where to allocate departments in a hospital. Thereby, it can support finding the optimal mix of delivery routes for a hospital. Allocating departments with frequent transportation on the same floor can significantly reduce transportation time.

A significant difference can be observed between the time used to model and simulate a scenario. SOQN modeling and simulation can provide quick results, which is especially useful at an early stage of a project. It allows to investigate many different layouts in a short time and so decide which is the most appropriate for material transportation.

SOQN modeling has been demonstrated to be applicable and suitable for hospital layout and material flow, enabling hospital planners to support the decision-making process to achieve high performance. Future research should focus on extending the model to connect different buildings and investigate different hospital layouts. Further, analytical approaches to solve SOQN models should be investigated and the statistical analysis should be extended to make a solid conclusion.

References

1. Arnolds, I., Nickel, S.: Layout planning problems in health care. In: Eiselt, H.A., Marianov, V. (eds.) Applications of Location Analysis, pp. 109–152. Springer (2015)
2. Kulkarni, M., Bhatwadekar, S., Thakur, H.: A literature review of facility planning and plant layouts. Int. J. Eng. Sci. Technol. 4(3), 35–42 (2015)
3. Benitez, G.B., Da Silveira, G.J., Fogliatto, F.S.: Layout planning in healthcare facilities: a systematic review. HERD-Health Environ. Res. 12(3), 31–44 (2019)
4. Ozcan, Y.A.: Quantitative Methods in Health Care Management: Techniques and Applications, vol. 4, John Wiley & Sons (2005)
5. Fragapane, G., Hvolby, H.H., Sgarbossa, F., Strandhagen, J.O.: Autonomous mobile robots in hospital logistics. In: IFIP International Conference on Advances in Production Management System (2020)
6. Fragapane, G., de Koster, R., Sgarbossa, F., Strandhagen, J.O.: Planning and control of autonomous mobile robots for intralogistics: literature review and research agenda. Eur. J. Oper. Res. 294(2), 405–426 (2021)
7. Kriegel, J., Rissbacher, C., Reckwitz, L., Tuttle-Weidinger, L.: The requirements and applications of autonomous mobile robotics (AMR) in hospitals from the perspective of nursing officers. Int. J. Healthcare Manage. 1–7 (2021, ahead-of-print)
8. Fragapane, G., Hvolby, H.H., Sgarbossa, F., Strandhagen, J.O.: Autonomous mobile robots in sterile instrument logistics: an evaluation of the material handling system for a strategic fit framework. Prod. Planning Control 1–15 (2021, ahead-of-print)
9. Beckmann, U., Gillies, D.M., Berenholtz, S.M., Wu, A.W.: Incidents relating to the intra-hospital transfer of critically ill patients. Intensive Care Med. 30(8), 1579–1585 (2004). https://doi.org/10.1007/s00134-004-2177-9
10. Fanara, B., Manzon, C., Barbot, O., Desmettre, T., Capellier, G.: Recommendations for the intra-hospital transport of critically ill patients. Crit. Care 14(3), 1–10 (2010)

11. Segall, N., et al.: Can we make postoperative patient handovers safer? A systematic review of the literature. Anesth. Analg. **115**(1), 102 (2012)
12. Volland, J., Fügener, A., Schoenfelder, J., Brunner, J.O.: Material logistics in hospitals: a literature review. Omega **69**, 82–101 (2017)
13. Rimpiläinen, T.I., Koivo, H.: Modeling and simulation of hospital material flows. In: Tenth International Conference on Computer Modeling and Simulation (UKSim 2008), IEEE (2008)
14. Bhosekar, A., Ekşioğlu, S., Işık, T., Allen, R.: A discrete event simulation model for coordinating inventory management and material handling in hospitals. Ann. Oper. Res., 1–28 (2021, ahead-of-print)
15. Pedan, M., Gregor, M., Plinta, D.: Implementation of automated guided vehicle system in healthcare facility. Procedia Eng. **192**, 665–670 (2017)
16. Fragapane, G.I., Zhang, C., Sgarbossa, F., Strandhagen, J.O.: An agent-based simulation approach to model hospital logistics. Int. J. Simul. Model. **18**(4), 654–665 (2019)
17. Heragu, S.S., Gupta, A.: CONWIP: closed or semi-open queuing network? Int. J. Oper. Res. **24**(3), 356–367 (2015)
18. Jia, J., Heragu, S.S.: Solving semi-open queuing networks. Oper Res. **57**(2), 391–401 (2009)
19. Ekren, B.Y., Heragu, S.S., Krishnamurthy, A., Malmborg, C.J.: Matrix-geometric solution for semi-open queuing network model of autonomous vehicle storage and retrieval system. Comput. Ind. Eng. **68**, 78–86 (2014)
20. Tappia, E., Roy, D., Melacini, M., De Koster, R.: Integrated storage-order picking systems: technology, performance models, and design insights. Eur. J. Oper. Res. **274**(3), 947–965 (2019)
21. Kumawat, G.L., Roy, D.: A new solution approach for multi-stage semi-open queuing networks: an application in shuttle-based compact storage systems. Comput. Ind. Eng. **125**, 105086 (2021)
22. Roy, D., Krishnamurthy, A., Heragu, S., Malmborg, C.: Stochastic models for unit-load operations in warehouse systems with autonomous vehicles. Ann. Oper. Res. **231**(1), 129–155 (2014). https://doi.org/10.1007/s10479-014-1665-8
23. Dhingra, V., Kumawat, G.L., Roy, D., de Koster, R.: Solving semi-open queuing networks with time-varying arrivals: an application in container terminal landside operations. Eur. J. Oper Res. **267**(3), 855–876 (2018)
24. Kumawat, G.L., Roy, D.: AGV or Lift-AGV? Performance trade-offs and design insights for container terminals with robotized transport vehicle technology. IISE Trans. **53**(7), 1–19 (2020)
25. Roy, D.: Semi-open queuing networks: a review of stochastic models, solution methods and new research areas. Int. J. Prod. Res. **54**(6), 1735–1752 (2016)
26. Maidstone, R.: Discrete event simulation, system dynamics and agent-based simulation: discussion and comparison. System **1**(6), 1–6 (2012)
27. Lu, Y., Wang, Y.: Design characteristics of acute care units in China. HERD-Health Environ. Res. **8**(1), 81–93 (2014)

Collaborative Hybrid Delivery System: Drone Routing Problem Assisted by Truck

Ho Young Jeong$^{(\boxtimes)}$ (ID) and Seokcheon Lee (ID)

Purdue University, West Lafayette, IN 47907, USA
Jeong96@purdue.edu

Abstract. Unmanned Aerial vehicles (UAV) or drones have significant market potential due to their high mobility and cost savings. Simultaneously, the hybrid delivery system in which collaborative use of trucks and drones is also receiving much attention and intensively studied as traveling salesmen problem with drone (TSP-D). This delivery system has significant advantages since it can selectively exploit the strength of each vehicle. However, in many cases, drones are only used as an assistant method of supporting truck delivery. In this paper, as a reverse idea, we present a new model, named drone routing problem with truck (DRP-T), in the form of a truck assisting drones' delivery. We present a mathematical model formulated as mixed-integer linear programming (MILP) and conduct a comparative analysis with one of the existing TSP-D models with an actual map-based case study. Our experiments show that it is possible to have substantial savings with the proposed model compared to the truck-only and TSP-D model.

Keywords: Routing · Drone · Mixed integer programming

1 Introduction

Logistic companies are always looking for the most costless methods to distribute goods across their networks. Unmanned aerial vehicles (UAV), drone, is the emerging technology-driven opportunity that recently received much attention for parcel delivery [1]. Compared to a regular delivery vehicle, a drone has essential advantages such as no costly human pilot are required, high mobility avoiding the congestion of road networks, spending much lower transportation cost per kilometer. Even though drones are fast and relatively inexpensive per mile, there are inherent limitations in their practical use. Since most drones are battery-powered, their flying range and loading capacity are much more limited than fuel-based trucks.

One way to overcome this limitation is by adopting a collaborative use of trucks and drones. The problem of this collaborative system is defined as a variant of the traveling salesman problem (TSP), the TSP with drones (TSP-D) [2]. The first model of the collaboration was suggested by Murray and Chu (2015), called "Flying Sidekick Traveling Salesman Problem (FSTSP)" [3]. In the model, the delivery truck moves between different customer locations to make deliveries, and the drone simultaneously

© IFIP International Federation for Information Processing 2021
Published by Springer Nature Switzerland AG 2021
A. Dolgui et al. (Eds.): APMS 2021, IFIP AICT 632, pp. 33–42, 2021.
https://doi.org/10.1007/978-3-030-85906-0_4

serves another customer, launching from and returning to the truck each delivery. After the FSTSP, many following studies were poured out. TSP-D with minimizing operational cost including transportation cost and the cost [4], FSTSP with considering drone's energy consumption and no-fly zone as FSTSP-ECNZ [5], extended TSP-D with multiple vehicles as mTSP-D [6] and similarly extending FSTSP to multi-drone case as m-FSTSP [7].

The above TSP-D based models are using both truck and drones the same or the drone as a secondary delivery method, despite the fact that the drone is faster and cheaper than the truck. In this paper, we present the drone routing problem with truck (DRP-T) that uses only drones as the final delivery method and trucks as supportive means to help deliver drones. In DRP-T, trucks are not delivering packages to customers but carrying drones to parking locations, and drones are serving customers directly and returning to trucks. Compared to the TSP-D, the DRP-T limits the truck's use and maximizes drones' use, thoroughly enjoying the wealth of drones' mobility and costlessness. This paper proposes a new delivery model DRP-T with a new mixed-integer linear programming (MILP) formulation. The performance of the new delivery model was verified with comparative analysis with existing models, TSP, and mFSTSP.

2   Problem Description

The DRP-T can be considered an extension of the traveling salesman problem (TSP), which uses a single vehicle to serve all the customers. The FSTSP, or TSP-D, is an extension of TSP that first appeared that adds a subsidiary delivery vehicle, a drone, to help serve a part of customers in the existing route of TSP. As an extension of the FSTSP, Murray et al. recently proposed m-FSTSP, expanding the single drone availability to multi-drones that achieved further improvement in delivery time while increasing the problem's complexity [7].

The DRP-T is not an extension of the existing mFSTSP but is a model with a different approach to two delivery vehicles. In contrast to m-FSTSP, which uses drones as an auxiliary delivery method for the truck, DRP-T uses drones as the primary delivery method, and the truck does not directly serve the customers but only carrying drones to a parking location. This routing strategy constitutes an entirely different delivery network with m-FSTSP. The DRP-T can be defined as an extended model of the Two-Echelon Vehicle Routing Problem (2E-VRP) when replacing the parking location with

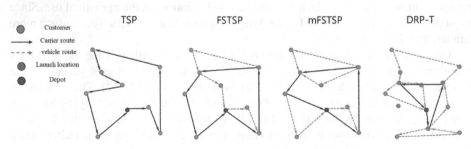

Fig. 1. Example of solutions for TSP, FSTSP, mFSTSP, and DRP-T.

a satellite that has flexible routing for delivery vehicles (drones) not restricted to the assigned satellite (parking location) and having flight endurance limit due to drone battery capacity. Figure 1 illustrates the routes of 4 different problems TSP, FSTSP, mFSTSP, and DRP-T.

2.1 Mathematical Model

The DRP-T aims to minimize the truck's arrival time at the depot after serving all the customers. The truck selectively visits parking location j ($j \in J$), close enough for drones to make delivery. After the truck arrives at a particular location, more than one drone is launched to serve the customer i ($i \in I$). While drones are delivering items to customers, the vehicle moves to another location and collects returning drones. The following represent notations and the mathematical model of DRP-T.

Notations

Variables		
I	:	Set of customer locations
J	:	Set of parking locations and depot locations
$0, |J|$	:	Starting and ending depot location ($0, |J| \in J$)
N	:	Set of all locations. ($I, J \subset N$)
K	:	Set of vehicles flights
$\tau_{ij'}$	:	Traveling time (sec) between location j and j' by truck
$\tau_{nn'}{}^d$	:	Traveling time (sec) between location n and n' by drone
E	:	Maximum flight time (sec) of drones
M	:	Positive and large number
Decision variables		
x_{jj}	:	Binary decision variable, 1 if carrier travels from location j to j'
$y_{nn'}{}^k$	:	Binary decision variable, 1 if vehicles travel from location n to n' in k-th flight
$z_{jj'}$	:	Integer decision variable, equal to available vehicles when carrier travel from location j to j'
$b_n{}^k$	:	Real number decision variable, equal to available endurance of vehicle k when vehicle visit location n
$T^t{}_j$	:	Real number decision variable, time when the truck arrives at location j
$Td_n{}^k$	:	Real number decision variable, time when the vehicle k arrives at location n

Mixed integer linear programming	

(*continued*)

(*continued*)

Minimize	$T_{|J|}$	(1)
Subject to	$\sum_{\substack{j \in J \\ j \neq 0}} x_{0j} = 1$	(2)
	$\sum_{\substack{j \in J \\ j \neq |J|}} x_{j|J|} = 1$	(3)
	$\sum_{j \in J} x_{jj'} = \sum_{j \in J} x_{j'j} \; \forall j \in J^+$	(4)
	$\sum_{n \in N} y_{jn}^k \leq M \cdot \sum_{j' \in J} x_{j'j} \; \forall k \in K, j \in J$	(5)
	$\sum_{\substack{n \in N \\ n \neq j}} y_{nj}^k \leq M \cdot \sum_{\substack{j' \in J \\ j \neq j'}} x_{j'j} \; \forall k \in K, j \in J$	(6)
	$\sum_{\substack{n \in N \\ n \neq i}} \sum_{k \in K} y_{ni}^k = 1 \; \forall i \in I$	(7)
	$\sum_{\substack{n \in N \\ n \neq i}} y_{nik} = \sum_{\substack{n' \in N \\ n' \neq i}} y_{in'k} \; \forall k \in K, i \in I$	(8)
	$T_{j'} \geq T_{j'} + \tau_{jj'} - M \cdot (1 - x_{jj'}) \forall j \in J, j' \in J$	(9)
	$Td_{j'}^k \geq T_{j'} - M \cdot (2 - \sum_{j \in J} x_{jj'}^t - \sum_{i \in I} y_{j'i}^k) \; \forall k \in K, j \in J$	(10)
	$Td_{n'}^k \geq Td_n^k + \tau_{nn'}^d - M \cdot (1 - y_{nn'}^k) \; \forall k \in K, n \in N, n' \in N$	(11)
	$T_j^k \geq Td_{j'} - M \cdot (2 - \sum_{j \in J} x_{jj'} - \sum_{i \in I} y_{ij'}^k) \; \forall k \in K, j \in J$	(12)
	$z_{0j}^t = |K| \; \forall t \in T, j \in J, j \neq 0$	(13)
	$\sum_{\substack{j'' \in J \\ j'' \neq j'}} z_{j'j''} = \sum_{\substack{j \in J \\ j \neq j}} z_{jj'} - \sum_{k \in K} \sum_{i \in I} y_{j'i}^k + \sum_{k \in K} \sum_{i \in I} y_{ij'}^k \; \forall j' \in \{J : j' \neq 0\}$	(14)
	$\sum_{k \in K} \sum_{\substack{i \in I \\ i \neq j'}} y_{j'i}^k \leq z_{jj'} \; \forall j, j' \in \{J : j \neq j\}$	(15)
	$b_i^k \geq \tau_{ij}^d - M \cdot (1 - y_{ji}^k) \; \forall k \in K, i \in I, j \in \{J : j \neq 0\}$	(16)
	$b_n^k \geq b_i^k + \tau_{in}^d - M \cdot (1 - y_{in}^k) \; \forall k \in K, i \in I, n \in N, n \neq 0$	(17)
	$0 \leq z_{jj'} \leq |K| \; \forall j, j' \in \{J : j \neq j\}$	(18)
	$0 \leq b_n^k \leq E \; \forall k \in K, n \in N$	(19)

The objective function (1) seeks to minimize the truck's returning time to the depot after completing the delivery job. Constraint (2) and (3) describe that the truck has a fixed start and end location to the depot. Constraint (4) preserves the truck routing by forcing it to depart from node j' when visiting node j'. Constraints (5) and (6) allow all drones to depart/return only to the parking location that has been visited by the truck. In constraint (7), each customer should be served precisely once by drones. Constraint (8) works the same way as a constraint (4), providing flow balance for the drones. Constraint (9) cumulatively calculates the arrival time at each parking location j that has been visited by the truck. Constraint (10) calculates the arrival time of drones at customer i that has been visited just after launched from the carrier. The constraint (11) works under the same logic as a constraint (9), which calculates the arrival time at each node n that drones have visited. Constraint (12) allows both truck and drone to wait for each other at rendezvous points.

The constraints (13) to (15) ensure that the available number of drones exceeds when the truck launch drones. First, constraint (13) states that the initial number of drones when the truck departs from the depot should be equal to the drone's index. The constraint (14) updates the number of available drones whenever the drones are launched or returned to the truck. In constraint (15), the number of drones launched from trucks should not exceed the number of drones available on the truck at that moment. The Fig. 2 illustrates the way of how the decision variable z_{jj} works as an example.

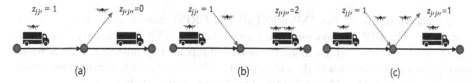

Fig. 2. Tracking the number of available drones at each location.

The available flight time is calculated through constraints (16) and (17). Constraint (16) accounts for the drone's flight time in node i where is the first visit after drone launch. From the second visit, the flight time is updated in the constraint (17). Since the drones' available flight time is limited to its endurance in constraint (19), the flight time from launch to return will not exceed the drone's endurance. The flight time limit mechanism is illustrated in detail through an example in Fig. 3.

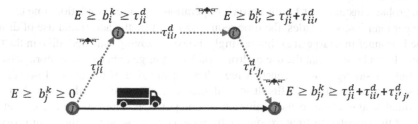

Fig. 3. Flight time monitoring formulation.

3   Computational Result

This section presents the comparative analysis result of the comparison between mFSTSP and DRP-T with a case study. The case study uses problem instances generated by GPS data of two cities Seattle and Buffalo, which is online-available at https://github.com/opt imatorlab/mFSTSP [8]. The instance set 1 (Seattle) has a broader operation area with a longer average distance than set 2 (Buffalo). The detailed specification of each instance is provided in Table 1. Each instance set has 20 problems, 10 problems with 8 customers, and 10 problems with 10 customers. Each instance has $|I|/2.5$ parking locations including the depot. The parking locations are centroid of customers found by k-mean clustering. The truck speed is set to 13 m/s. The drone of 23 m/s with a 55 min flight time is assumed according to DJI's MATRICE 300 RTK [9].

Table 1.   Case study map specification.

Set 1 (Seattle)			Set 2 (Buffalo)		
Avg Distance [m]	Width [m]	Length [m]	Avg Distance [m]	Width [m]	Length [m]
11,758.10	27,277.01	22,713.15	2,636.99	17,024.88	15,068.17

As shown in Fig. 4, the TSP, mFSTSP, and DRP-T have a distinct difference in their route. The TSP displays only truck routes because TSP is truck-only delivery. In mFSTSP, parts of the TSP route are removed and replaced by drones, and more routes are replaced as drones are added. In the case of DRP-T, compared to the other two cases, the use of trucks decreased significantly, and drones were actively used.

Table 2 shows the computational results of mFSTSP [7] and DRP-T obtained by MILP. The "% saving" captures the percentage difference of completion time compared with the TSP, truck-only delivery. The central processing unit time (CPU time) is limited to 600 s, and the best feasible solution is recorded when reached the limit. The result shows that the completion time decreases consistently with a rise in the number of drones. Specifically, when there was only one drone, the DRP-T showed a slightly shorter makespan, but the difference expanded as more drones are used. The mFSTSP and DRP-T have a maximum of 44.5% and 55.8% saving, respectively, compared to truck-only delivery.

In problem instance set 1 with a broader operation area, the completion time tends to be longer than 2 sets. Besides, the time reduction effect by the additional use of drones seemed stronger in a large area. Interestingly, however, savings showed alike in the two regions. It can be seen that the use of drone trucks in a large area can save more delivery time, but the saving ratio is constant regardless of the size of the area. However, for 10 customers cases, it was difficult to find such a trend since we often failed to find an optimal solution due to the limitation of computation time. Two more customers extended the calculation time exponentially which can be seen that the complexity of the problems is very sensitive to the number of customers. In most cases, mFSTSP takes less computation time than DRP-T, and both models consume more computation time

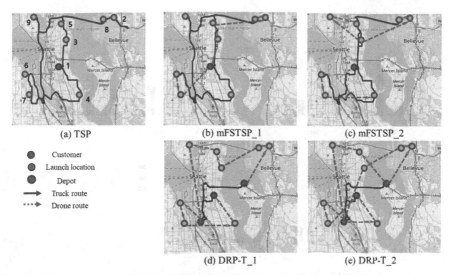

Customer
Launch location
Depot
Truck route
Drone route

(a) TSP   (b) mFSTSP_1   (c) mFSTSP_2

(d) DRP-T_1   (e) DRP-T_2

Fig. 4. Solution examples of (a) TSP, (b) mFSTSP with 1 drone, (c) mFSTSP with 2 drones, (d) DRP-T with 1 drone, (e) DRP-T with 2 drones.

Table 2. Computational result of mFSTSP and DRP-T.

Customer		Num Drones	mFSTSP			DRP-T		
			Obj value	% Savings	CPU time	Obj Value	% Savings	CPU time
8	Set 1 (Seattle)	1	2288.23	26.2317	15.8650	2211.25	29.2235	71.4610
		2	1914.69	38.0834	37.3093	1646.75	47.1858	111.8248
		3	1714.68	44.5361	49.5717	1531.63	50.8134	102.5860
	Set 2 (Buffalo)	1	587.67	26.6612	14.6771	550.49	31.3512	61.6904
		2	519.15	35.2892	33.8145	400.26	50.0400	69.0164
		3	479.58	40.2486	21.0144	353.25	55.8329	50.0477
10	Set 1 (Seattle)	1	2460.69	1.0584	495.4631	2156.96	13.4086	600.0061
		2	2168.00	12.8826	568.6874	1597.41	36.0450	600.0182
		3	2019.12	18.7561	481.1503	1446.93	41.9793	600.0315
	Set 2 (Buffalo)	1	631.81	2.7722	520.2	547.57	15.5319	600.0162
		2	537.75	17.2982	310.9816	405.13	37.8392	600.0148
		3	515.84	20.8747	385.516	359.78	44.7325	600.0337

in set1. The calculation time seems to increase as the number of drones increases, but some discrepancy has been observed. Figure 5 illustrates the computational result of two models in a bar graph.

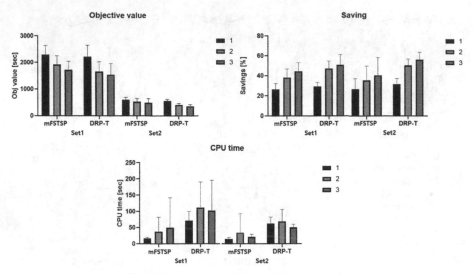

Fig. 5. Computational result of the case study.

4 Sensitivity Analysis

Drone delivery is fundamentally limited by its battery capacity. In this section, sensitivity analysis was performed to explore how these limitations work in the delivery performance in mFSTSP and DRP-T. This analysis used instance set 1 with 8 customers presented in Sect. 3. All parameters except flight time were applied the same and the flight time was set at intervals of 1000 from 2000 to 6000 s.

Table 3 provides the results of mFSTSP [7] and DRP-T with different flight time of drones. Among the 10 instances, 3 has appeared to be infeasible for the DRP-T model with 1 drone. This is because the DRP-T uses only drones, so the low flight time or the low number of drones can lead to unserviceability, unlike mFSTSP, which can serve customers by a truck when the drone's battery is not enough. Except the infeasibility, the result shows that there is not noticeably difference between flight times. With longer flight time, the DRP-T shows slightly improved performance, but there was no significant change.

Table 3. Computational result with different flight time.

		mFSTSP			DRP-T		
Flight time	Num Drones	Obj Value	% Savings	CPU time	Obj value	% Savings	CPU Time
2000	1	2169.896	1.65246	17.8794	2122.861	4.576837	64.02608
	2	1761.376	19.57147	51.35456	1483.226	32.74349	73.70463
	3	1540.837	29.41033	43.46896	1327.384	39.47884	96.59067

(continued)

Table 3. (*continued*)

| Flight time | Num Drones | mFSTSP | | | DRP-T | | |
		Obj Value	% Savings	CPU time	Obj value	% Savings	CPU Time
3000	1	2169.896	1.65246	16.96552	2091.502	5.898057	79.17365
	2	1761.376	19.57146	48.53522	1470.155	33.36129	110.835
	3	1540.837	29.41033	27.97567	1327.384	39.47884	96.57239
4000	1	2169.896	1.65246	15.08001	2058.466	7.440601	81.24646
	2	1761.376	19.57146	54.9315	1470.155	33.36129	104.1505
	3	1540.837	29.41033	59.97488	1327.384	39.47884	87.4991
5000	1	2169.896	1.65246	18.95264	2058.466	7.440601	81.0333
	2	1761.376	19.57146	45.27003	1470.155	33.36129	110.9936
	3	1540.837	29.41033	33.0208	1327.384	39.47884	94.08144
6000	1	2169.896	8.326094	126.4467	2058.466	7.440601	82.34652
	2	1761.376	19.11009	177.7154	1470.155	33.36129	120.6758
	3	1540.837	29.41033	81.27164	1327.384	39.47884	104.9229

5 Concluding Remarks

In this paper, we study a new type of collaborative delivery with drones and trucks. Empirical study shows that substantial saving is possible in the system compared to truck-only and previous truck-drone systems. Since this study proposed a new delivery system, there are many potential future research topics. One promising area is to develop a solution approach that provides a near-optimal solution with reasonable computational time. In addition, extension of the DRP-T problem with multiple trucks and consideration of drone recharging can be another interesting study. Since the model includes the battery monitoring formulation, a flexible recharging policy can be another extension.

References

1. Mack, E.: How delivery drones can help save the world. Forbes.com (2018). https://www.forbes.com/sites/ericmack/2018/02/13/delivery-drones-amazon-energy-efficient-reduce-climate-change-pollution/#77130a0a6a87. Accessed 11 Apr 2021
2. Agatz, N., Bouman, P., Schmidt, M.: Optimization approaches for the traveling salesman problem with drone. Transp. Sci. **52**(4), 965–981 (2018)
3. Murray, C.C., Chu, A.G.: The flying sidekick traveling salesman problem: optimization of drone-assisted parcel delivery. Transp. Res. Part C: Emerg. Technol. **54**, 86–109 (2015)
4. Ha, Q.M., Deville, Y., Pham, Q.D., Hà, M.H.: On the min-cost traveling salesman problem with drone. Transp. Res. Part C: Emerg. Technol. **86**, 597–621 (2018)
5. Jeong, H.Y., Song, B.D., Lee, S.: Truck-drone hybrid delivery routing: payload-energy dependency and no-fly zones. Int. J. Prod. Econ. **214**, 220–233 (2019)

6. Kitjacharoenchai, P., Ventresca, M., Moshref-Javadi, M., Lee, S., Tanchoco, J.M., Brunese, P.A.: Multiple traveling salesman problem with drones: mathematical model and heuristic approach. Comput. Ind. Eng. **129**, 14–30 (2019)
7. Murray, C.C., Raj, R.: The multiple flying sidekicks traveling salesman problem: parcel delivery with multiple drones. Transp. Res. Part C: Emerg. Technol. **110**, 368–398 (2020)
8. The Multiple Flying Sidekicks Traveling Salesman Problem (mFSTSP). https://github.com/optimatorlab/mFSTSP. Accessed 11 Apr 2021
9. DJI, Matrice-300 RTK. https://www.dji.com/matrice-300/specs. Accessed 11 Apr 2021

Drone Delivery Vehicle Routing Problem with Multi-flight Level

Yonggab Kim$^{(\boxtimes)}$ (ID), Hoyoung Jung (ID), and Seokcheon Lee (ID)

Purdue University, West Lafayette, IN 47906, USA
kim3233@purdue.edu

Abstract. The advantage of drone delivery is that it can efficiently use the vertical space in the air, allowing multiple operations at different flight levels. However, flight level and delivery efficiency come at a tradeoff, especially in a metropolitan area with many skyscrapers; placing drones higher requires more time, but the higher they are, the less detour they make due to the smaller number of buildings at higher altitudes, resulting reduced time in routing. This study integrates the problem by dividing the heights and identifying buildings that could possibly be an obstacle. We propose a novel vehicle routing problem for multi-flight level drone delivery to minimize delivery completed time.

Keywords: Drone delivery · Vehicle routing problem · Multiple flights · Logistics

1 Introduction

The desire for a faster and less expensive last-mile delivery service has always been present in the retail industry. The cutting-edge technology of unmanned aerial vehicles (UAVs), commonly known as drones, provides a new advanced option to the retail industry to fulfill its demand. Especially after the outbreak of COVID-19, drone delivery is an attractive choice to avoid human contact and help in handling the COVID-19 pandemic [1].

Many companies have already developed their drone delivery business. Amazon is the biggest player in the market; they have announced their Prime Air service. [2]. In 2020, Amazon won approval from the FAA (Federal Aviation Administration) for their prime air drone delivery fleet [3]. Alphabet is another big company testing their drone delivery service in Australia by their project Wing [4]. Other retail companies such as UPS, Walmart, and Tesco are also investing in the drone delivery business.

The contributions of this study are as follows. First, we proposed a new optimization problem with multiple flight levels in drone delivery. To the best of our knowledge, this is the first paper that takes account of the optimal flight level in the drone delivery problem. The second contribution is that we examine the advantage of operating drone service with New York City's real-world data. Lastly, we suggest a new heuristic algorithm with capacity in drone delivery.

© IFIP International Federation for Information Processing 2021
Published by Springer Nature Switzerland AG 2021
A. Dolgui et al. (Eds.): APMS 2021, IFIP AICT 632, pp. 43–51, 2021.
https://doi.org/10.1007/978-3-030-85906-0_5

The rest of this paper is organized as follows. In Sect. 2, we review the relevant literature on the drone delivery problem. Section 3 defines the problem statement and suggests the mathematical. Section 4 presents a new solution algorithm, MFLSA, which is named after multi-flight level solution algorithm. This algorithm aims to solve to solve the complex model in a timely manner. Section 5 test this algorithm to the real data-based case study on New York City. The experiment result and data analysis are presented in Sect. 6. We conclude this paper with a suggestion and potential future research.

2 Literature Review

The initial studies in the drone routing problem have been focused on the disaster situation or military applications. A group of studies has investigated the drone routing problems in information gathering and disaster control at catastrophe situations and surveillance monitoring [5–7]. As the energy efficiency and the payload capability of drone increased over several years, using the drones for the last mile delivery have gained attention in logistic field. One study introduced FSTSP, which studies the routing challenge of a drone assisting a delivery truck for last-mile delivery [8]. Researchers have used a mixed-integer linear programming (MILP) formulation and simple heuristics for a solution. Further research has been done to extend the FSTSP considering no-fly zones and using local search heuristics as a solution approach [9].

Other researchers have investigated a similar problem, the traveling salesman problem with the drone. (TSP-D) Compared to FSTSP, this study allows the drones to return to the original place where the drone has departed [10]. To solve the TSP-D, solution approaches of mixed-integer programming, heuristics, and dynamic programming were introduced [11, 12]. Furthermore, utilizing multiple drones, multiple of vehicles, and heterogeneous UAVs that have different properties were studied [13–15].

Consideration of cost, battery constraints, weights, and other important factors of drone has been by the researchers. While the drone has many advantages over conventional transportations, reduced energy capacity and lower payload weight is the major concern for drone delivery system. Battery management using efficient battery assignment and battery scheduling was studied to reduce the average waiting time and energy cost [16]. Another study considers the relationship between payload weight and energy consumption to remove the infeasible routes and construct cost-efficient route [17]. The authors use simulated annealing to find the solution in different scenarios.

3 Problem Statement and Mathematical Model Formulation

In this section, we define the capacitated drone delivery problem with multiple flight levels and propose a novel mathematical formulation to minimize the completed time while utilizing multiple flight levels and meeting the capacity constraints.

3.1 Problem Statement

- The delivery is made from a depot to one customer and then returns to the original depot.

- There are multiple flight levels drones can choose to fly to deliver.
- Customer demands are represented as weights, and all the demands need to be fulfilled.
- Depot has the capacity in weights and can have multiple drones.
- Drones have the weight capacity that they can carry in a single flight.
- Our goal is to minimize the completed time after serving all the customers.

3.2 Mathematical Formulation

Table 1. System variables

Sets		
U	:	Sets of UAVs
C	:	Sets of customers
D	:	Sets of depots
F	:	Sets of flights
W	:	Sets of weights
L	:	Sets of levels
Parameters		
Ini_u	:	Initial location of UAV u
$\tau_{i,j,l}$	:	Distance between i and j at level l
$P^w_{i,j,l}$	:	Energy consumption from i to j on level l of weight w
ϕ_l	:	Downtime for drone for level l
ψ_l	:	Uptime for drone for level l
$Capacity_d$	:	Depot capacity for depot d
$Demand_c$	:	Customer demand for customer c
E	:	Energy capacity of the drone
v	:	Drone speed
Decision variables		
$x^u_{l,c,w,f}$	:	Binary decision variable, If the UAV u is departing from i to j a level l of a weight w on flight f
T^u	:	Current time of UAV u

Table 1 is the variables that is used for constructing the mathematical model. Table 2 is the equations to solve the minimization problem suggested in this paper. Equations (1) and (2) are the objective function. The objective function minimizes the completed time after serving all the customers. Equation (3) is the constraint that ensures the drone delivery is made to the customer once or less in a single flight. Constraint (4) prevents the sum of the delivery weight fulfills the amount of weight of customer demand. Constraint

Table 2. Mathematical model

Mixed integer linear programming		
Minimize	O	(1)
Subject to	$O \geq T^u \; \forall u \in U$	(2)
	$\displaystyle\sum_{w \in W} \sum_{l \in L} \sum_{c \in C} x^u_{u,c,w,f} \leq 1 \forall f \in F$	(3)
	$Demand_c \leq \displaystyle\sum_{w \in W} \sum_{l \in L} \sum_{c \in C} \sum_{u \in U} w \cdot x^u_{l,c,w,f} \; \forall c \in C$	(4)
	$x^u_{l,u,c,w,f} \cdot \displaystyle\sum_{w \in W} \sum_{l \in L} \sum_{c \in C} \sum_{u \in U} (2 \cdot \tau_{l,Ini_u,c}/v + \psi_l + \phi_l) \leq T^u$	(5)
	$x^u_{l,u,c,w,f} \cdot (Pij^w_{l,Ini_u j} + Pij^0_{l,Ini_u j}) \leq E$	(6)
	$\displaystyle\sum_{w \in W} \sum_{l \in L} \sum_{c \in C} \sum_{u \in U} \sum_{f \in F} w \cdot x^u_{l,c,w,f} \leq Capacity_d \; \forall d \in D, Ini_u = d$	(7)

(5) calculates the completed time of each drone after serving all the customers. Constraint (6) restricts the round trip that exceeds the drone energy capacity is not being made. Lastly, constraint (7) guarantees the total delivered weight of drones from the same depot does not exceed the sum of depot capacity.

4 MFLSA

The MFLSA is a new heuristic algorithm for drone vehicle routing problem that considers the multiple flight level using local search approach.

4.1 Initial Solution Generation

The algorithm starts by generating the initial population (see Fig. 1). The first initial solution is generated by the Nearest Neighbor algorithm, and the part of the solution was generated based on the first initial solution. The other solutions were generated randomly. In this problem, when all initial solution was created randomly, too many unfeasible solutions were produced because of capacity constraints. Inserting feasible solutions created by heuristics to the randomly generated solutions led the genetic algorithm to yield a good portion of feasible solutions [18]. The optimal flight level for each flight is calculated when the destination route is given by chromosome.

4.2 Selection

The selection strategy decides which individuals are passed off from the parents to the offspring. This research adopts two selection schemes, elitist selection, and proportional roulette wheel selection. The elitist selection picks individuals with good fitness. This allows the algorithm to preserve the best solution from parents to the offspring. In a proportional roulette wheel selection scheme, individuals are chosen with a probability that corresponds to their proportion of fitness value over the sum of all fitness values. The proportional roulette wheel gives all the individuals a chance to be selected and maintained their diversity [19].

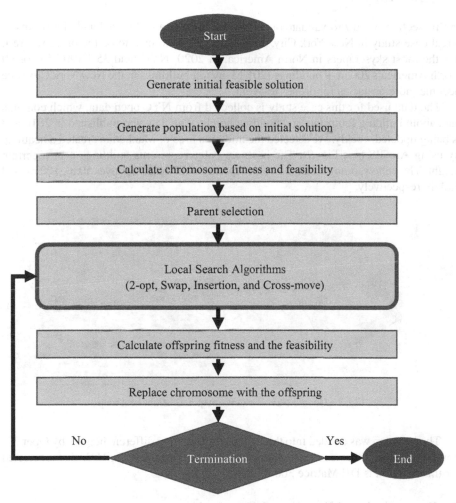

Fig. 1. Flowchart of the MFLSA

4.3 Local Search Heuristics

In a search phase, several search heuristics are used to improve the selected individuals. Two index points, I and J are randomly selected from the total length of the chromosome. The 2-opt operator selects parts from I to J and reverses the order of the index from the selected part. The swap operator exchanges the I point route and J point route. The insertion operator moves the route at the I point of the chromosome to J point. The cross-move operator interchanges the part of the chromosome between I to J and replaces the repeated route with the value outside of I and J.

5   Case Study

In this section, we try to validate our proposed mathematical model and algorithms to a real case study in New York City. New York City is known to be the place where it has the most skyscrapers in North America. In 2020, NYC held 35% (90/255) of all North America's 200 m + buildings [20]. Many tall buildings in the New York City area become more obstacles for drones to avoid.

The data used for this case study is collected from NYC open data, which contains data about building footprints and building height. The data was published in 2016 and is being updated weekly. We selected the midtown area of Manhattan created a heatmap by using ArcGIS (see Fig. 2). The heatmap color represents buildings over a certain height. The yellow, orange, and red color represents the buildings over 50 m, 100 m, and 150 m, respectively.

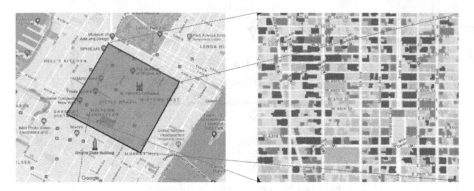

Fig. 2. Google New York city map and height heat map

The heatmap was divided into three maps representing different heights by OpenCV library. A* Algorithm was used to route from depot to customer. The UAV that is selected for this research is DJI Matrice 300 RTK.

6   Computational Result and Conclusion

In this section, we discuss the result we have obtained by running a series of numerical experiments. The number of customers was set to 20. The number of depots was set to 4, and the location was generated randomly, having 2 drones at each depot. The drones can deliver the weights between 1–2 kg to the customer. To validate the result, 20 different scenarios were generated and tested. All the algorithms are coded in Python, and experiments were run on an HP Laptop 15t-dc100 2.6 GHz processor with 16 GB of RAM.

6.1   Performance Comparison

To evaluate the performance of the MFLSA, MILP model, GA, SA, and Nearest neighbor algorithm was also tested. The objective value is the completed time after serving all the delivery, and the lower the value is the better. Table 1 is summarizing the comparison between the algorithms (Table 3).

Table 3. Performance comparison table

	MILP	MFLSA	GA	SA	Nearest neighbor
Objective value	870	966.7	1010.94	1074.83	1092.25
Computation time (seconds)	2578.97	193.69	198.83	194.21	0.06

MILP shows the optimal objective solution of 870, compared to other algorithms but shows a longer computation time, 2578.94. This makes the mathematical model hard to applicate in the real world. On the other hand, the Nearest Neighbor algorithm shows fast computation time, 0.06 but the solution is far from the optimal solution compared to other algorithms. The suggested algorithm, MFLSA shows a near-optimal solution and similar computation time compared to GA and SA. MFLSA provides the high quality of solution in a reasonable time (see Fig. 3).

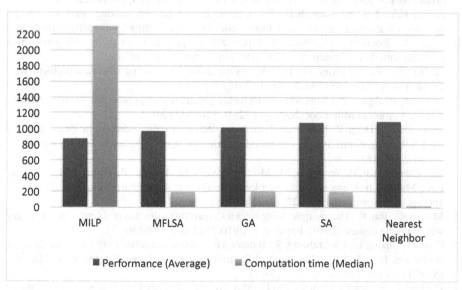

Fig. 3. Algorithm comparison bar graph

6.2 Conclusion

To take one step closer to drone delivery commercialization, some of the essential real-world life challenges should be addressed in advance. This research considered the optimal height level for drones to operate in a metropolitan area. A mathematical model and heuristic algorithm were developed to optimize the completed time after serving all the delivery. To test our model, we have done a case study in New York City and compared the result of the outcome.

Referencess

1. Kumar, A., Sharma, K., Singh, H., Naugriya, S.G., Gill, S.S., Buyya, R.: A drone-based networked system and methods for combating coronavirus disease (COVID-19) pandemic. Future Gener. Comput. Syst. **115**, 1–19 (2020). https://doi.org/10.1016/j.future
2. Amazon Prime Homepage. https://amzn.to/3t93se9. Accessed 10 Apr 2021
3. CNBC News. https://cnb.cx/2PSUWl1. 8 Apr 2021
4. Wing Homepage. https://wing.com/. Accessed 7 Apr 2021
5. Frew, E. W., Brown, T. X.: Networking issues for small unmanned aircraft systems. Unmanned Aircraft Syst. 21–37 (2009)
6. Curry, J.A., Maslanik, J., Holland, G., Pinto, J., Tyrrell, G., Inoue, J.: Applications of aerosondes in the arctic. Bull. Amer. Meteorol. Soc. **85**(12), 1855–1861 (2004)
7. Sundar, K., Rathinam, S.: Algorithms for routing an unmanned aerial vehicle in the presence of refueling depots. IEEE Trans. Autom. Sci. Eng. **11**(1), 287–294 (2014)
8. Murray, C.C., Chu, A.G.: The flying sidekick traveling salesman problem: optimization of drone-assisted parcel delivery. Transp. Res. C Emerg. Technol. **54**, 86–109 (2015)
9. Jeong, H.Y., Lee, S., Song, B.D.: Truck-drone hybrid delivery routing: payload- energy dependency and no-fly zones. Int. J. Prod. Econ. 214 (2019). https://doi.org/10.1016/j.ijpe
10. Agatz, N., Bouman, P., Schmidt, M.: Optimization approaches for the traveling salesman problem with drone. Transp. Sci. 52 (2018). https://doi.org/10.1287/trsc
11. Ha, Q., Deville, Y., Pham, Q., Ha, M.: On the min-cost traveling salesman problem with drone. Transp. Res. Part C **86**, 597–621 (2018)
12. Bouman, P., Agatz, N., Schmidt, M.: Dynamic programming approaches for the traveling salesman problem with drone. Networks **72**(4), 528–542 (2018)
13. Tu, P., Dat, N., Dung, P.: Traveling salesman problem with multiple drones. In: Proceedings of the Ninth International Symposium on Information and Communication Technology, ACM, pp. 46–53 (2018)
14. Kitjacharoenchai, P., Ventresca, M., Moshref-Javadi, M., Lee, S., Tanchoco, J.M., Brunese, P.A.: Multiple traveling salesman problem with drones: mathematical model and heuristic approach. Comput. Ind. Eng. **129**, 14–30 (2019)
15. Murray, C., Raj, R.: The multiple flying sidekicks traveling salesman problem: parcel delivery with multiple drones. (2019). https://doi.org/10.2139/ssrn.3338436
16. Park, S., Zhang, L., Chakraborty, S.: Battery assignment and scheduling for drone delivery businesses. In: IEEE/ACM International Symposium on Low Power Electronics and Design, ISLPED, Taipei, Taiwan, pp. 1–6. (2017)
17. Dorling, K., Heinrichs, J., Messier, G.G., Magierowski, S.: Vehicle routing problems for drone delivery. IEEE Trans. Systems, Man, Cybern. Syst. **47**(1), 70–85, (2017). https://doi.org/10.1109/TSMC.2016.2582745
18. Hill, R.R.: A Monte Carlo study of genetic algorithm initial population generation methods. In: Proceedings of 31st Conference on Winter Simulation–A Bridge to the Future, Phoenix, AZ, pp. 543–547 (1999)

19. Razali, N.M., Geraghty, J.: Genetic algorithm performance with different selection strategies in solving TSP. In: Proceedings of World Congress on Engineering, pp. 1–6 (2010)
20. Al-Kodmany, K.: Skyscrapers in the twenty-first century city: a global snapshot. Buildings **8**(12) (2018)

Digital Transformation Approaches in Production Management

Multi-perspective View on Sustainable Production: A Literature Review

Marko Samardzic$^{(\boxtimes)}$ and Ugljesa Marjanovic

Faculty of Technical Sciences, University of Novi Sad, Novi Sad, Serbia

Abstract. Manufactured products should be produced in a sustainable way because of their immense impact on the economy, environment and society. However, due to the many diverse parties involved and their often conflicting motivations, this is usually not the case. This paper is a literature review explaining the drivers for the transition to sustainable production from different points of view by analyzing current literature. The stakeholders are classified in the following categories: Government, Corporate, Consumer, Society. Each of the stakeholder groups has a significant impact sustainable production. Governments set the field for the corporations to operate in through rules and regulations. The effectiveness of these rules and regulations depends on government awareness and proactivity. Moreover, consumers play an important role since their demand for sustainably produced goods is an important driving factor for companies. Corporations are required to adapt to governmental regulations and consumer demand, but they can also lead the way by putting into effect sustainable methods of production. Finally, it is up to society as a whole to promote sustainable production since it profoundly benefits from it.

Keywords: Literature review · Sustainable production · Multi perspective

1 Introduction

Nowadays, manufactured products should be produced in a sustainable way due to their immense impact on the economy, environment and society [1]. This results in promotion of system innovations that aim to design out waste and increase resource-efficiency [2]. Sustainable production (SP) is defined "as production (and use) of products and services in a manner that is socially beneficial, economically viable and environmentally benign over their whole life cycle" [3]. This goes hand in hand with the triple bottom line concept that defines sustainability as the ability of a product to work continuously while ensuring lowest environmental impacts and providing economic and social benefits to stakeholders [4–6]. Thus, the fundamental pillars of sustainability are economic, environmental and social impact. According to Rosen and Kishawy [7] concerns regarding these pillars should be addressed "simultaneously and holistically", meaning that focus on all aspects is necessary to achieve sustainable development.

For production to abide by the definition and concepts of sustainability, it needs to weigh and incorporate economic, environmental and social goals, policies and practices

© IFIP International Federation for Information Processing 2021
Published by Springer Nature Switzerland AG 2021
A. Dolgui et al. (Eds.): APMS 2021, IFIP AICT 632, pp. 55–63, 2021.
https://doi.org/10.1007/978-3-030-85906-0_6

[7]. These goals are set by different stakeholders who are impacted by production. A traditional definition of stakeholders is that they are any group of individuals who are impacted by or can influence the development of organizations' objectives [8]. However, the goal of sustainable production is not just to consider the organization, but rather an increased number of stakeholders [9, 10]. These diverse stakeholders can be categorized in the following groups:

1. **Government** – an overseeing body, by whose laws the company needs to abide to operate in that domain/market,
2. **Corporate** – the company manufacturing products, including its' management and shareholders,
3. **Consumer** – the consumer purchasing the product,
4. **Society** – the third parties impacted by production.

Each group of stakeholders has unique requirements and goals. Due to their diversity these requirements and goals often do not coincide, making it challenging to satisfy each stakeholder group. Conflicting objectives can emerge in various industries and countries, even in social enterprises created with the primary goal of positive social and environmental impact rather than profit maximization [11]. This concrete example shows how, in the agricultural cooperative in Italy, the pursuance of sustainability goals creates a financial strain, leading to the abandonment of the primary sustainability objectives. When faced with the issue of waste management members of the cooperative were forced to use more chemicals or plastic packaging, negatively impacting the local society.

Trade-offs in objectives can be noticed when governmental regulation decisions favor one stakeholder rather than the other. A model created by Zhang et al. [12] deepens the effects of regulation on companies and social welfare (directly affecting the society stakeholder), finding that trade-offs between higher profitability and improved social welfare are affected by the type of legislation imposed. For example, if government advocate for the use of green technologies there are limited social welfare benefits, whereas if a carbon cap and credits strategy is implemented social welfare is increased at the expense of companies' profitability.

Collaboration [11, 13] and certain trade-offs [7] are necessary and crucial. However, this is not a disadvantage, but rather an advantage used to attain the benefits of SP as they are thoroughly and methodologically defined taking every angle and point of view into consideration and ensuring diversity and balance [14]. Unlike conventional benefit creation that concerns only a select group of stakeholders, the benefits created by sustainable production are far reaching since they impact a broad group of stakeholders. Moreover, SP focuses both on the short-term and long-term, creating immediate impact and providing lasting positive effects. It satisfies the needs of current stakeholders without putting at risk the needs of future stakeholders [10]. More specifically the benefits from SP include, but are not limited to, lower costs, improved efficiency, increased revenue, internal and external customer satisfaction, increased market shares leading to better risk management [15].

This paper seeks to explain the current literatures view on sustainable production from multiple perspectives, thus explaining the reasoning and motivation behind different drivers in a clearer way. Furthermore, each stakeholder group experiences barriers that are limiting the implementation of SP to a greater extent. Thus, this led to the following research questions: Which are the main research streams on sustainable production from the perspective of diverse stakeholders?

This paper is structured as follows. Section 2 explains the methodology used to conduct the research. Section 3 analyzes the views of different stakeholders. Section 4 concludes the discussion and suggests the potential direction for future research.

2   Research Methodology

Considering the above-mentioned research question, the present work aims at exploring scientific literature to shed the light on how research on SP has developed and evolved with a specific focus on the perspective of diverse stakeholders. To answer RQ, we focus on deriving a concept list containing a definition of the term sustainable production by performing a systematic literature review [16]. Therefore, the steps of the systematic literature review used are the following:

1. **Defining the search criteria** – only literature relevant to the research question was taken into consideration. The period analyzed considers work published from 2012 to 2021 and only English language papers were taken into consideration.
2. **Selecting a data source** – the SCOPUS and Web of Science databases were selected due to its access to global scientific publications.
3. **Collection of literature by searching for key words** in the SCOPUS and Web of Science databases

   a. The key words are: sustainable production, sustainable manufacturing, sustainable production + government, sustainable production + legislation, sustainable production + consumer, sustainable production + customer, sustainable production + third parties

4. **Analysis of the literature** by reading the title and abstract (*only the papers consistent with the research question were considered*). This filtering has led to the final set of 41 journal papers and 4 conference papers, for a total of 45 papers.
5. **Presenting the findings**

3   Research Streams on Sustainable Production from the Perspective of Diverse Stakeholders

Notwithstanding the apparent hype around sustainable production, there is still a lack of research and the implications for government, corporate, consumers, and society.

3.1   Government – Point of View

Governments set the sustainable production "playing field" for companies through the implementation of rules and regulations, promoting SP in a number of ways depending on their motivation and goals, which are described as drivers. However, not every government has incentive to promote SP. A distinction exists between SP practices in developed and developing countries. Global organizations whose concern is sustainability are compelling developing markets to adopt sustainable production because often less developed countries sacrifice the wellbeing of their citizens, either through a lack of environmental regulation or a lack of labor laws. Governments compromise to induce growth since corporations transfer production to these markets to avoid costly regulations of developed countries [17, 18]. Certainly, responsibility falls on corporations not to give in to temptation but rather employ SP.

Of course, positive examples exist in developing markets where government rules and regulations promote SP. Such is the case of Bangladesh which pushed the producers in the highly environmentally polluting leather industry to seek SP methods by implementing adequate regulations [18]. The motivation behind this regulatory push to obtain sustainable production was to allow Bangladesh to become more competitive in the global market [18]. Rigorous government regulation leads to improved production technology and therefore better global competitiveness [19].

Another reason governments create SP regulation is to reduce energy consumption, a prime pollutant of the environment [20–22]. Motivation to reduce waste and unnecessary consumption does not apply only to energy [20, 23]. A growing population leads to an increase in natural resource expenditure, in turn leading to either more governmental spending or lower quality of life. By creating rules and regulations geared towards SP governments solve these issues without compromising the quality of life for its' citizens [23]. Increased resource consumption affects international competitiveness for some countries. For example, in Malawi government legislation is crucial since the sugarcane industry on which the economy is highly dependent is being depleted due to deteriorating environmental conditions and immoderate exploitation [24].

Aside from waste reduction, global competitiveness and better life quality, a motivating factor for the push to SP from the government perspective is job creation [23].

The most effective ways governments can promote sustainable production is through legislation and incentive systems [23, 25]. Legislation by itself in some cases is not enough as proper execution is necessary for it to have an impact [19]. However, barriers exist that hinder adequate execution.

Moreover, regulation needs to be applied meticulously, with adequate research backing it. Zhu et al. [26] demonstrate how different types of policies impact firms' profit. They find that in the case of remanufacturing, specifically targeted remanufacturing subsidies promote profit, but carbon regulation can even decrease profitability. If governments seek to impose emission caps and carbon credits, corporations will adapt their production strategies accordingly. Manufacturers will either employ green technology in their production processes or seek to purchase credits [12, 27].

3.2   Corporate – Point of View

Corporations are the ones who are impacted most by sustainable production since they need to change and evolve the way they operate. There are many different motivating drivers that require this transformation that will be described in this section. Mostly drivers can be classified as the customer needs, shareholder/investor requirements, government legislation or lower cost/improved production.

SP is increasingly becoming a requirement from buyers [18, 28], in some cases companies fail to acknowledge this [29]. Moreover, to obtain it, strong commitment from top management is necessary [30]. Eventually implementing it will lead to enhanced customer communication, fidelity, and trustworthiness.

Operating within laws is a crucial driver for corporations [23]. Depending on the governmental policies imposed regarding sustainable production or carbon credits, corporations will make decisions based on profit and/or cost optimization [12, 27].

Lower energy consumption not only benefits the environment, but also significantly lowers costs for manufacturers. Thus, optimized energy consumption is essential to obtain SP [20, 22]. However, there are other elements, in addition to energy consumption, that need to be optimized. Lean and green initiatives provide a solution not just for energy consumption, bur also waste, emission, water, and chemical management [18, 20, 31]. Overall, shifting towards sustainable methods of production can lower material cost significantly [23].

The availability of big data allows for easier implementation of SP as it provides precious insight by monitoring and tracking production, leading to improved coordination and decision making [32]. Certain approaches to production can have a profound impact on sustainability without compromising the performance of producers, leading to increased competitive advantage [33], both in terms of business performance and relative quality [34]. Approaches such as zero waste manufacturing [35], smart manufacturing [36] and cloud manufacturing [37] utilize the latest technologies and best practices to optimize production, making it more efficient while taking into considerations factors of sustainability.

The black swan event of COVID-19 has exposed the traditional methods of production and their supply chains, it is the opinion of Nandi S. et al. [38], that this will lead to more "resilient, transparent, and sustainable" supply chains using the latest technologies, such as blockchain, which will involve multiple stakeholders across the value chain and serve crucially as the foundation for sustainable production.

As it often is, increased competition leads to progress, especially intertwined with customer awareness. Thus, companies are pursuing to employ SP to outperform their competition [18].

One of the main barriers limiting sustainable production is short-termism, the dominance of short-term agendas inside corporate boardrooms [39].

3.3 Customer – Point of View

One of the barriers of putting sustainable production into effect is customer perception. Consumers need to become educated and aware of the benefits of SP [29, 40–42]. If the proper education and awareness initiatives are taken up customer perception becomes a big advantage and something that drives SP [18, 23, 28].

Evidence that consumers value SP, suggests manufacturers should take on the responsibility to educate buyers [23, 28]. However, certain literature proposes governments should inform consumers in order to increase consumption of low carbon options [12].

Without doubt public awareness is one of the key factors in the enactment of SP, as customers are influential concerning environmental and social issues [18].

3.4 Society – Point of View

By definition society is impacted positively by sustainable production. Therefore, it is one of the crucial drivers for the wide utilization of SP. The most effective way society can achieve this goal is by creating pressure. Many organizations and associations are operating to promote sustainability and create the pressure for change [25, 30]. These organizations and associations educate and inform customers so they can make more responsible decisions [43], persuade corporations about the benefits of SP and influence governments to create more future oriented rules and legislations [18, 44].

Sustainable production has many and diverse positive impacts on employment, such as job creation, abiding by progressive labor laws, product health and safety, and guaranteeing a safe working environment [23, 45–48]. One such practice that has a positive impact is waste management, which creates job opportunities for local business networks and boosts economic performance [49]. Moreover, sustainable production benefits the environment through lower pollution levels and, in particular, waste management is concerned with adequate and proper disposal of hazardous materials gravely endangering the environment [49], both factors lead to healthier living conditions.

4 Conclusion

In this article, the primary aim was to explore the current state of the art of sustainable production and to provide the main implications concerning diverse stakeholders. The following conclusions can be drawn:

- Different stakeholders have different motivations for the realization of sustainable production.
- The initial phases are most effective if enacted through government awareness or customer demand, as these are the actors that can motivate production across industries and sectors within a certain market.
- Corporations are the ones that need to adapt to regulations and demand but can also lead the way by applying best practices. Therefore, it is up to corporations to put into effect sustainable methods of production.
- Society has a responsibility of promoting sustainable production since it profoundly benefits from it.

Future research can be performed by focusing on specific methods to employ sustainable production while considering multiple stakeholders.

References

1. Tarne, P., Traverso, M., Finkbeiner, M.: Review of life cycle sustainability assessment and potential for its adoption at an automotive company. Sustainability **9**(4), 670 (2017)

2. Kristensen, H.S., Mosgaard, M.A.: A review of micro level indicators for a circular economy – moving away from the three dimensions of sustainability? J. Clean. Prod. **243**, 118531 (2020)

3. Azapagic, A.: https://www.journals.elsevier.com/sustainable-production-and-consumption/. Accessed 19 Mar 2021

4. Hacking, T., Guthrie, P.: A framework for clarifying the meaning of triple bottom-line, integrated, and sustainability assessment. Environ. Impact Assess. Rev. **28**(2–3), 73–89 (2008)

5. Martens, M.L., Carvalho, M.M.: Key factors of sustainability in project management context: a survey exploring the project managers' perspective. Int. J. Project Manage. **35**(6), 1084–1102 (2017)

6. Hussain, N., Rigoni, U., Orij, R.P.: Corporate governance and sustainability performance: analysis of triple bottom line performance. J. Bus. Ethics **149**(2), 411–432 (2018). https://doi.org/10.1007/s10551-016-3099-5

7. Rosen, M.A., Kishawy, H.A.: Sustainable manufacturing and design: concepts. Pract. Needs Sustain. **4**(2), 154–174 (2012)

8. Freeman, R.E.: Strategic Management: A Stakeholder Approach. Pitman, Boston (1984)

9. Eskerod, P., Huemann, M.: Sustainable development and project stakeholder management: what standards say. Int. J. Manage. Project Bus. **6**(1), 36–50 (2013)

10. Keeys, L.A., Huemann, M.: Project benefits co-creation: shaping sustainable development benefits. Int. J. Project Manage. **35**(6), 1196–1212 (2017)

11. Pellegrini, G., Annosi, M.C., Contò, F., Fiore, M.: What are the conflicting tensions in an Italian cooperative and how do members manage them? Business goals', integrated management, and reduction of waste within a fruit and vegetables supply chain. Sustainability **12**(7), 3050 (2020)

12. Zhang, S., Wang, C., Yu, C., Ren, Y.: Governmental cap regulation and manufacturer's low carbon strategy in a supply chain with different power structures. Comput. Ind. Eng. **134**, 27–36 (2019)

13. Kemp, R., Loorbach, D., Rotmans, J.: Transition management as a model for managing processes of co-evolution towards sustainable development. Int. J. Sustain. Dev. World Ecol. **14**(1), 78–91 (2007)

14. Chih, Y.Y., Zwikael, O.: Project benefit management: a conceptual framework of target benefit formulation. Int. J. Project. Manage. **33**(2), 352–362 (2015)

15. Lintukangas, K., Kähkönen, A.-K., Ritala, P.: Supply risks as drivers of green supply management adoption. J. Clean. Prod. **112**, 1901–1909 (2016)

16. Pickering, C., Byrne, J.: The benefits of publishing systematic quantitative literature reviews for PhD candidates and other early-career researchers. High. Educ. Res. Dev. **33**(3), 534–548 (2014)

17. Rajeev, A., Pati, R.K., Padhi, S.S., Govindan, K.: Evolution of sustainability in supply chain management: a literature review. J. Clean. Prod. **162**, 299–314 (2017)

18. Moktadir, M.A., Rahman, T., Rahman, M.H., Ali, S.M., Paul, S.K.: Drivers to sustainable manufacturing practices and circular economy: a perspective of leather industries in Bangladesh. J. Clean. Prod. **174**, 1366–1380 (2018)

19. Singla, A., Ahuja, I.S., Sethi, A.P.S.: Technology push and demand pull practices for achieving sustainable development in manufacturing industries. J. Manuf. Technol. Manage. **29**(2), 240–272 (2018)

20. Tseng, M.-L., Chiu, A.S.F., Tan, R.R., Siriban-Manalang, A.B.: Sustainable consumption and production for Asia: sustainability through green design and practice. J. Clean. Prod. **40**, 1–5 (2013)

21. Su, Y., Zhang, P., Su, Y.: An overview of biofuels policies and industrialization in the major biofuel producing countries. Renew. Sustain. Energy Rev. **50**, 991–1003 (2015)

22. Zhao, G.Y., Liu, Z.Y., He, Y., Cao, H.J., Guo, Y.B.: Energy consumption in machining: classification, prediction, and reduction strategy. Energy **133**, 142–157 (2017)
23. Govindan, K., Hasanagic, M.: A systematic review on drivers, barriers, and practices towards circular economy: a supply chain perspective. Int. J. Prod. Res. **56**(1–2), 278–311 (2018)
24. Chinangwa, L., Gasparatos, A., Saito, O.: Forest conservation and the private sector: stakeholder perceptions towards payment for ecosystem service schemes in the tobacco and sugarcane sectors in Malawi. Sustain. Sci. **12**(5), 727–746 (2017)
25. Su, B., Heshmati, A., Geng, Y., Yu, X.: A review of the circular economy in China: moving from rhetoric to implementation. J. Clean. Prod. **42**, 215–227 (2013)
26. Zhu, X., Ren, M., Chu, W., Chiong, R.: Remanufacturing subsidy or carbon regulation? An alternative toward sustainable production. J. Clean. Prod. **239**, 117988 (2019)
27. Mishra, S., Singh, S.P.: An environmentally sustainable manufacturing network model under an international ecosystem. Clean Technol. Environ. Policy **21**(6), 1237–1257 (2019)
28. Jilcha, K., Kitaw, D.: Industrial occupational safety and health innovation for sustainable development. Eng. Sci. Technol. Int. J. **20**(1), 372–380 (2017)
29. van Weelden, E., Mugge, R., Bakker, C.: Paving the way towards circular consumption: exploring consumer acceptance of refurbished mobile phones in the Dutch market. J. Clean. Prod. **113**, 743–754 (2016)
30. Siemieniuch, C.E., Sinclair, M.A., Henshaw, M.J.C.: Global drivers, sustainable manufacturing and systems ergonomics. Appl. Ergon. **51**, 104–119 (2015)
31. Caldera, H.T.S., Desha, C., Dawes, L.: Exploring the role of lean thinking in sustainable business practice: a systematic literature review. J. Clean. Prod. **167**, 1546–1565 (2017)
32. Zhang, Y., Ren, S., Liu, Y., Si, S.: A big data analytics architecture for cleaner manufacturing and maintenance processes of complex products. J. Clean. Prod. **142**, 626–641 (2017)
33. Marjanovic, U., Lalic, B., Medic, N., Prester, J., Palcic, I.: Servitization in manufacturing: role of antecedents and firm characteristics. Int. J. Ind. Eng. Manage. **10**(2), 133–144 (2020)
34. Agyabeng-Mensah, Y., Ahenkorah, E., Afum, E., Owusu, D.: The influence of lean management and environmental practices on relative competitive quality advantage and performance. J. Manuf. Technol. Manage. **31**(7), 1351–1372 (2020)
35. Singh, S., Ramakrishna, S., Gupta, M.K.: Towards zero waste manufacturing: a multidisciplinary review. J. Clean. Prod. **168**, 1230–1243 (2017)
36. Kusiak, A.: Smart manufacturing. Int. J. Prod. Res. **56**(1–2), 508–517 (2017)
37. Fisher, O., Watson, N., Porcu, L., Bacon, D., Rigley, M., Gomes, R.L.: Cloud manufacturing as a sustainable process manufacturing route. J. Manuf. Syst. **47**, 53–68 (2018)
38. Nandi, S., Sarkis, J., Hervani, A.A., Helms, M.M.: Redesigning supply chains using blockchain-enabled circular economy and COVID-19 experiences. Sustain. Prod. Consum. **27**, 10–22 (2021)
39. Erhemjamts, O., Huang, K.: Institutional ownership horizon, corporate social responsibility and shareholder value. J. Bus. Res. **105**, 61–79 (2019)
40. Zhou, Y., Xiong, Y., Li, G., Xiong, Z., Beck, M.: The bright side of manufacturing–remanufacturing conflict in a decentralised closed-loop supply chain. Int. J. Prod. Res. **51**(9), 2639–2651 (2013)
41. Jiménez-Parra, B., Rubio, S., Vicente-Molina, M.-A.: Key drivers in the behavior of potential consumers of remanufactured products: a study on laptops in Spain. J. Clean. Prod. **85**, 488–496 (2014)
42. Khor, K.S., Hazen, B.T.: Remanufactured products purchase intentions and behaviour: evidence from Malaysia. Int. J. Prod. Res. **55**(8), 2149–2162 (2016)
43. Stock, T., Seliger, G.: Opportunities of sustainable manufacturing in Industry 4.0. Procedia CIRP **40**, 536–541 (2016)
44. Elmualim, A., Valle, R., Kwawu, W.: Discerning policy and drivers for sustainable facilities management practice. Int. J. Sustain. Built Environ. **1**(1), 16–25 (2012)

45. Gupta, K., Laubscher, R.F., Davim, J.P., Jain, N.K.: Recent developments in sustainable manufacturing of gears: a review. J. Clean. Prod. **112**, 3320–3330 (2016)
46. Bellantuono, N., Carbonara, N., Pontrandolfo, P.: The organization of eco-industrial parks and their sustainable practices. J. Clean. Prod. **161**, 362–375 (2017)
47. van Loon, P., Van Wassenhove, L.N.: Assessing the economic and environmental impact of remanufacturing: a decision support tool for OEM suppliers. Int. J. Prod. Res. **56**(4), 1662–1674 (2018)
48. Rakic, S., Pavlovic, M., Marjanovic, U.: A precondition of sustainability: Industry 4.0 readiness. Sustainability **13**(12), 6641 (2021)
49. Nascimento, D.L.M., et al.: Exploring Industry 4.0 technologies to enable circular economy practices in a manufacturing context: a business model proposal. J. Manuf. Technol. Manage. **30**(3), 607–627 (2019)

Determining Minimal Cost of Action for Task Allocation Within Mobile Robot Swarm in Production Environments

Elmir Babović[1], Denis Mušić[1(✉)], Bahrudin Hrnjica[2], and Adil Joldić[1]

[1] Faculty of Information Technologies, "Dzemal Bijedic" University, Mostar, Bosnia and Herzegovina
{elmir.babovic,denis,adil}@edu.fit.ba
[2] Faculty of Technical Sciences, University of Bihać, Bihać, Bosnia and Herzegovina
bahrudin.hrnjica@unbi.ba

Abstract. This paper describes the continuation of a series of research in which human behavior, in the form of models and algorithms, endeavor to be mapped into the field of mobile robotics, all with the aim of more efficient path prediction with collision detection in a dynamic obstacle environment. In our latest research [1] we proposed a new approach called Sliding Holt (SH) algorithm which is used for calculation of future spatiotemporal state of dynamic obstacle. Besides SH algorithm we also proposed method for (non)collaborative collision detection with dynamic obstacles in 2D and 3D space which ensures full de-centralization of the collision detection process. Research described in this paper focuses on the application of Computer Vision for detecting the position and movement direction of mobile robots in order to create assumptions for collision detection and path planning with within the production environment. We propose a new approach for detecting mobile robot direction based on triangular shape and use of Cost of Action in order to allocate tasks within robotic swarm.

Keywords: Mobile robots · Robot swarm · Computer vision · Collision detection · Path planning · Robot direction · Cost of action

1 Introduction

Some of the most significant discoveries of today have been made by observing natural phenomena and movements. The mechanisms that exist in nature exude harmony and precision which, even after a long and detailed observation, is not easy to model or even to understand completely. As a proof, we can mention a human who represents the most intelligent and at the same time the most complex being on Earth. The complexity of the human body is nothing special until we try to replicate in another environment or context some of the actions that a human performs with such ease and superiority. The way people make movements, path prediction, avoid static and dynamic obstacles represent particularly interesting features for the field of robotics and have been subject

© IFIP International Federation for Information Processing 2021
Published by Springer Nature Switzerland AG 2021
A. Dolgui et al. (Eds.): APMS 2021, IFIP AICT 632, pp. 64–70, 2021.
https://doi.org/10.1007/978-3-030-85906-0_7

of much research over past decades. In order to provide modest contribution to this area, our previous research [2–4, 6, 9, 10] focused on the analysis of human behavior which resulted in creation of adequate mathematical models and algorithms applicable in the field of mobile robotics.

A new industrial era called the 4th industry generation is completely dependent on the interconnectedness of all participants in the process and implies an enviable degree of intelligence and collaboration. This implies a symbiosis of human and robotic work environment that is completely safe, optimized in terms of eliminating unnecessary movement and loss of time, and making adequate decisions in real time.

The application of different types of sensors is an industry standard which brings a significant degree of autonomy and efficiency, especially when it comes to robot movement. As discussed in [5] pick and place, as one of the basic operations in most robotic applications, whether in industrial setups or in service robotics domains, are not easy to implement when it comes to manipulating parts with high variability or in less structured environments. These kind of picking systems only exist at laboratory level and have not reached the market due to factors such as lack of efficiency, robustness and flexibility of currently available manipulation and perception technologies. In fact, the manipulation of goods is still a potential bottleneck to achieve efficiency in the industry and the logistic market.

Parts of the system that oversee production management and accompanying processes to perform tasks in the shortest possible time need to consider energy consumption which usually means choosing the shortest path.

The movement of robots in a production environment brings multiple challenges, and one of the most important relates to determining the priority of performing tasks within a swarm of robots. If the robots were in charge of moving objects within the production or storage space, one of the possible solutions could be to assign the task of moving to the robot that is closest to the given object in terms of location. In the mentioned context, usage of holonomic or non-holonomic robots significantly determine the approach to problem solving. Namely, most of today's experimental or production implementations of robot applications, whether robots are intended for indoor or outdoor use, such as a Dispatch product called "Carry" or Seegrid GP8 vision-guided pallet truck, etc., involve the use of non-holonomic types of mobile robots.

In the next section of the paper, previous research in this area will be presented, after which the application of Computer Vision for detecting the position and movement direction of mobile robots and task allocation based on Cost of Action will be described.

1.1 Previous Research

Models and algorithms for collision detection in a dynamic 2D and 3D environment have been proposed in several of our previous studies [1–4, 6]. We introduced the new method of collision detection with dynamic obstacles for mobile objects space based on mathematical model of spatiotemporal de-composition of recorded motion coordinates, their respective forecast prediction using statistical methods and re-composition of future path forming metamorphous hyperspace.

Method described in [6] involves several key steps: spatiotemporal decomposition, forecast prediction using statistical methods, re-composition in metamorphous hyperspace. The inspiration for this work came from human cognitive activities executed while single unit is moving in a group of other moving units and simultaneously detecting and avoiding collision. In majority of cases, this collision detection and avoidance is done by human objects naturally without prior high level cognitive activities which lead us to the conclusion that this model is one of the most natural way of executing these activities. Path detection of object is done in non-collaborative manner as described in previous work 1. Main research hypothesis is that human behavior in collision detection can be described by statistical mathematical model and that given model can be expressed in form of algorithm and implemented in mobile robotics. In order to achieve requested results base research was divided into four segments. Since the proposed method considers two main operating modes: collaborative and non-collaborative, all model elements are analyzed from two different perspectives, as well as their similarities and differences.

Due to resolve the issue of creating metamorphous hyperspace, we proposed new approach called Sliding Holt algorithm [1] to calculate future spatiotemporal state of dynamic obstacle. Within first experimental phase, single exponential smoothing did not show satisfying results in extreme cases of dynamic obstacles with high coefficient of agility (even with high sampling frequencies of 1 kHz). Therefore, we implemented double exponential smoothing with sliding motion coordinate records in which we propose discarding of old data before motion vector alteration occurs.

2 Computer Vision Based Location and Direction Detection

As discussed in [8] robots in the industrial sector have evolved from powerful, stationary machines into sophisticated, mobile platforms to address a broader range of automation needs. Autonomous mobile robots utilize feedback from sensors to navigate their environment. State of the art mobile robots has an envious level of intelligence and are able to detect obstacles present on their path and recalculate a route around the obstacle to get it to its destination. Nevertheless, the real environment brings with it a multitude of cases that have not yet been adequately researched in terms of the existence of models and/or algorithms for solving them.

Previous research [7] described universal experimental environment for algorithm testing in the field of mobile robotics which is appropriate for tracking, collision detection and avoidance, and path planning. In order to provide precise positioning and direction detection, we proposed two-color markers which are positioned on the top of mobile robot. The initial experiment with single color marker showed low level motion path stability in the sense that it was unclear in which direction mobile object is moving. With the addition of second color marker, it became clear what is front and what is rear of the object, thus enabling straightforward definition of motion vector direction.

Although the use of two-color markers gave satisfactory results, continued research revealed some disadvantages. The main disadvantage relates to the need for fine tuning of colors and the sensitivity of the detection process to the intensity of ambient light. In order to eliminate the mentioned disadvantage, in this paper we proposed the implementation of shape detection using a triangular marker of any color. Figure 1 shows the experimental environment in which the use of triangular markers was tested. The figure illustrates a part of an application that uses the Computer Vision OpenCV library to capture a video stream that will be processed and used to detect the location and direction of the robots.

Fig. 1. Picture from video stream with indicated triangular markers

Processing an image from a video stream involves several stages that are described within the following pseudocode.

```
listOfCountours = DetectContours(stream)
foreach(contour in listOfCountours)
  if (contour == triangle)
    (shortestLine,frontPoint) = AnalizeShape(triangle)
    contour.Tail.X =(shortestLine.Begin.X+shortestLine.End.X)/2
    contour.Tail.Y =(shortestLine.Begin.Y+shortestLine.End.Y)/2
    contour.Front.X = frontPoint.X
    contour.Front.Y = frontPoint.Y
    DrawLine (shortestLine, color : green)
    DrawLine (contour.Tail, contour.Front, color : red)
    listOfTriangles.Add(contour)
```

The first phase in processing involves the detection of all shapes followed by their analysis. If the shape has a triangular form, then a more detailed analysis is performed, within which the shortest side and its corresponding points are identified. The remaining, third point is declared as the front point of the robot. Subsequently, the absolute mean between the points on the shortest line is calculated, which determines their position on the X and Y axes, and it becomes the rear point. The mentioned calculations created a precondition for plotting the location and orientation of the robots detected on the stream as indicated on Fig. 2.

By applying Computer Vision and defined processing phases, we can detect the location and direction of all members of the robot swarm which have been identified

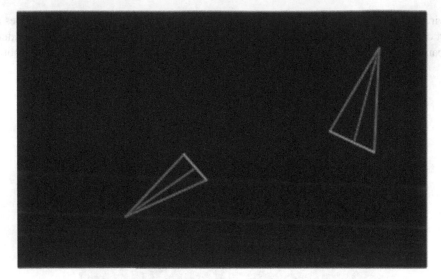

Fig. 2. Detection of robot's position and direction

in the video stream. After detecting them, it is necessary to define a model for assigning tasks (e.g., moving a certain object from one location to another) with maximum degree of efficiency, which means determining the Cost of Action (CoA) for each of the detected/available robots.

3   Cost of Action

Within this chapter, the result of initial research in the field of implementation of more efficient distribution of tasks in a swarm of robots is presented. Namely, assigning tasks to non-holonomic robots requires an analysis of several factors, not just the absolute distance from its current position to the defined location (e.g., target). The autonomous movement of non-holonomic mobile robots will very often lead to a case in which the task of moving a certain object will be assigned to a more distant robot. As shown in Fig. 3, the robot r_1 is further away from the object (e.g., target) in relation to the robot r_2 (i.e., $d_1 > d_2$) but the angle (i.e., β_1) between the shortest distance (i.e., d_1) to the destination and the movement direction (i.e., md_1) of the robot r_1 is much smaller than the angle between the shortest distance (i.e., d_2) to the destination and the movement direction (i.e., md_2) of the robot r_2.

Considering the aforementioned, it can be concluded that a higher value of the angle β will lead to a higher Cost of Action in terms of required energy (battery consumption), time to execute the action (ignoring the need to wait to avoid collisions with static or dynamic obstacles), energy caused by friction, current state of motion etc.

Analyzing the case in which the mobile robot has the possibility of free rotation (caster wheel or tracks), in order to calculate the CoA for the robot r to reach from the current to the target location, the following calculation was used:

$$CoA_r = \frac{d}{v} + \frac{\beta}{\omega} \tag{1}$$

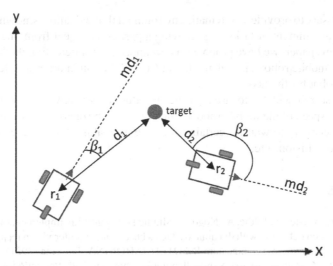

Fig. 3. Parameters used to determine cost of action in task allocation process

CoA_r – Cost of Action that robot r needs to reach the target location
d – distance to target location
v – linear velocity
β – angle between orientation and target direction
ω – angle velocity

$$\text{minCostOfAction} = \min([CoA_{r_1}, CoA_{r_2}, \ldots, CoA_{r_n}]) \qquad (2)$$

The current experimental environment is a special case of a general concept in which the CoA per unit of time for each mobile robot is identical. This implies that all robots within the production environment have identical technical characteristics meaning identical weight, battery life, vehicle frame, friction of the drive mechanism against the ground, etc. To assign a task, it is necessary to calculate CoA_r, which, in this case, represents time to reach the target, for each unallocated/idle mobile robot. The task will be assigned to the robot for which the lowest CoA value (minCostOfAction) was calculated. Taking into account the fact that the current research considered only time, in future research, a general case will be analyzed, which implies the existence of an unstructured environment with mobile robots of different technical performance.

4 Conclusion

Efficient management of production environments is a goal that is not easy to achieve. However, some of the basic prerequisites are certainly the interconnection between all participants in the production process, the application of autonomous robots that will coexist with humans within a secure work environment, maximum utilization of all resources and elimination of unnecessary actions or waiting. The movement of autonomous robots in a production facilitates the management of such environments, but it is also necessary to provide a systematic environment that will allow smooth movement and efficient assignment of tasks (e.g., moving a particular object from one location to another). In this paper, we have proposed a new approach for detecting the location and direction of a mobile robot, and calculation of Cost of Action in order to select the most appropriate robot for the task.

Future research will be focused on the introduction of new parameters such as: battery status, speed of the mobile robot (which refers to the energy needed to overcome inertia), the necessity to wait for certain actions (e.g., making turn or alter velocity) in order to avoid collisions etc.

References

1. Babovic, E., Music, D., Joldic, A., Nogo, S.: Sliding Holt algorithm implementation in mobile robots collision detection with dynamic obstacles based on computer vision technologies. In: IEEE, 20th International Symposium INFOTEH-JAHORINA, Jahorina (2021)
2. Babovic, E.: Collaborative and Non-Collaborative Dynamic Path Prediction Algorithm for Mobile Agents Collision Detection with Dynamic Obstacles in a Two-dimensional Space, IEEM 2011, Singapore (2011)
3. Babovic, E.: Collaborative and Non-Collaborative Dynamic Path Prediction Algorithm for Mobile Agents Collision Detection with Dynamic Obstacles in 3D Space, CISSE2011, Bridgeport (2011)
4. Babovic, E.: Coefficient of Agility and Sampling Frequency Issues in Mobile Agents Collision Detection with Dynamic Obstacles in 3D Space, Sarajevo, AMC 2012 (2012)
5. Iriondo, A., Lazkano, E., Susperregi, L.,Urain, J., Fernandez, A., Molina, J.: Pick and place operations in logistics using a mobile manipulator controlled with deep reinforcement learning. Appl. Sci. **9**, 348. https://doi.org/10.3390/app9020348 (2019)
6. Babovic, E.: New method and algorithm for mobile agents collision detection with dynamic obstacles in 3D space. In: 4th International Congress on Ultra Modern Telecommunications and Control Systems, ICUMT, Sankt Petersburg, pp.370–376 (2012)
7. Joldic, A., Babovic, E., Bijedic, N., Bejenaru-Vrabie, A.: Laboratory environment for algorithms testing in mobile robotics 2019 In: IEEE 17th International Symposium on Intelligent Systems And Informatics, SISY, Subotica, pp. 41–46 (2019)
8. Siegwart, R., Nourbakhsh, I.R., Scaramuzza, D.: Introduction to Autonomous Mobile Robots. MIT Press, Cambridge, USA (2011)
9. Hrnjica, B., Music, D., Softic, S.: Model-based recommender systems. In: Al-Turjman, F. (ed.) Trends in Cloud-based IoT. EICC, pp. 125–146. Springer, Cham (2020). https://doi.org/10.1007/978-3-030-40037-8_8
10. Hrnjica, B., Softic, S.: Explainable AI in manufacturing: a predictive maintenance case study. In: Lalic, B., Majstorovic, V., Marjanovic, U., von Cieminski, G., Romero, D. (eds.) APMS 2020. IAICT, vol. 592, pp. 66–73. Springer, Cham (2020). https://doi.org/10.1007/978-3-030-57997-5_8

A Hybrid Architecture for the Deployment of a Data Quality Management (DQM) System for Zero-Defect Manufacturing in Industry 4.0

Chiara Caccamo[1(✉)] ⓘ, Ragnhild Eleftheriadis[1] ⓘ, Maria Chiara Magnanini[2] ⓘ,
Daryl Powell[1] ⓘ, and Odd Myklebust[1]

[1] SINTEF Manufacturing AS, Digital Production, Raufoss, Norway
`chiara.caccamo@sintef.no`
[2] Department of Mechanical Engineering, Politecnico di Milano, Milan, Italy

Abstract. The adoption of Industry 4.0 technologies is slow and lacks homogeneity across the manufacturing landscape. Challenges arise from legacy IT systems, or a low level of digitization leading to difficult integration processes, or simply the fear of investing too much in building the necessary infrastructure versus the uncertainty of the potential benefits. The market has also become more demanding, both in terms of competition and customer requirements, so that more and more manufacturers are faced with the demand for high production flexibility, high quality, and low operating costs. This paper aims to address the implementation complexity of a cyber-physical production system for zero-defect manufacturing in dynamic, high-value, high-mix, and low-volume contexts where the level of digitalization is still low, or the IT infrastructure is rigid.

Keywords: Architecture · Cyber physical production systems · Zero defect manufacturing

1 Introduction

The introduction of new technologies in manufacturing is often painful [1]. Companies have launched costly, complicated initiatives to introduce digital tools and approaches across the enterprise, only to find that these programs fall short of their potential or stall altogether. A key factor in these shortfalls is the lack of a common, integrated operating model for digital and conventional IT teams. At least 60% of the highest value technology projects that organizations pursue require collaboration and execution across multiple technology groups in digital and IT teams. In addition, fragmented technology stacks can impact overall system stability, scalability, and resilience. Enterprises must demonstrate a willingness to test and learn, and they must design flexible, constantly evolving enterprise architectures that can support the development and delivery of new business capabilities.

A. Dolgui et al. (Eds.): APMS 2021, IFIP AICT 632, pp. 71–77, 2021.
https://doi.org/10.1007/978-3-030-85906-0_8

In the same way, the application of cyber-physical systems (CPS) in the manufacturing environment, namely cyber-physical production systems (CPPS), are still in their infancy and we see difficulties in implementation without the collaboration of manufacturing professionals with experts in cloud and ICT solutions [2]. The ICT departments of small businesses are often more focused on solving operational tasks than implementing new technologies. An important step in digital transformation is to have a clear strategy to build a suitable architecture [3]. Leveraging knowledge developed in previous projects (IFACOM [4], QU4LITY [5]) and going beyond the state-of-the-art in zero-defect manufacturing (ZDM) approaches, we have created a blueprint for a promising system architecture to address many of the challenges faced by today's manufacturing enterprises, such as integration issues, infrastructure flexibility to support production agility, and cost containment. In the following sections, we provide an overview of this concept, a description of a CPPS for a digitally enhanced quality management system (DQM) for ZDM, and the underlying hybrid architecture to support system deployment in production systems for different markets.

1.1 The Use of ZDM in Quality Management

The keys to achieving ZDM are monitoring the conditions of manufacturing equipment and processes and making decisions to implement appropriate business processes and policies to ensure zero defects in manufactured products [3]. ZDM as a quality paradigm approach goes beyond TQM, Six Sigma and other traditional quality control strategies by integrating at system level defect avoidance solutions, based on IoT and other digital or artificially intelligent systems. CPPSs play a key role in addressing the various challenges of integrating data/information (process/equipment monitoring) and knowledge (decision making and feedback controlling) to achieve the key objectives of ZDM. However, the design of CPPS is extremely challenging due to the involvement of multiple disciplines such as (i) industrial engineering, (ii) computer science, and (iii) electrical engineering [6].

1.2 The CPPS Design Concept

The term CPPS [6] refers to the application of CPS in manufacturing and production, and is characterized by the following features: (i) CPPS are systems of systems; (ii) These systems include autonomous and cooperative elements and can be connected or disconnected depending on the situation, which means that the subsystems are independent and reconfigurable; (iii) The interconnection between systems affects all levels of the production life-cycle, from manufacturing to logistics; (iv) The CPPS system learns from the knowledge generated by both human resources (human-in-the-loop) and equipment during the production process, as well as from the knowledge generated by the manufactured products during their lifecycle. Building on this concept, we propose to add in a CPPS definition that (v) it includes elements to manage data sovereignty and interoperability, to enable usage control of proprietary industry data across the whole value chain (suppliers, manufacturers, customers) in a cross-organizational, shared, virtual data space.

2   A Novel Hybrid Model for CPPS

Following a seminal work [7], an improved conceptual model of the DQM architecture is shown in Fig. 1. The improvements include the integration of cyber-security aspects for the data safety, the semantic tagging for data clustering according to data sources and functional use, as well as data integration features for advanced data fusion solutions.

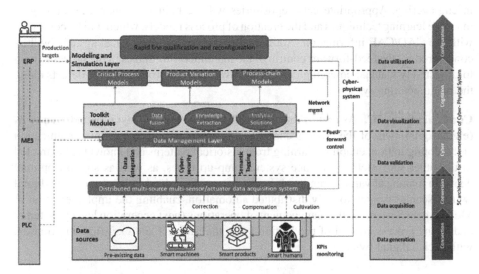

Fig. 1. Conceptual model of the DQM architecture

With this model we aim to use a multi-level approach for data processing and control strategies; we also aim to cover the whole path through the digitalization process by including pluggable SW and HW elements to overcome some of the prerequisites highlighted in [7] (i.e., (i) presence of a parts tracking system and (ii) machine state monitoring). The model is mapped to the CPS 5C architecture [8] to illustrate the logical path for design and development from initial data collection to final system control:

Smart Connection - 1C. The first layer (Data Sources) is represented by a distributed network of sensors, actuators, and other signals/data sources (e.g., HMIs, smart wearables, machines, historical company data).

Data to Information Conversion - 2C. The second layer (Distributed Data Acquisition Systems) will convert the signals into data and perform some pre-processing to support data integrity at the following processing stages.

Cyber - 3C. The Data Management Layer will take care of Data Integration, Data Integrity, Cyber Security, Semantic Tagging and Interface with Legacy Systems (i.e. Enterprise Resource Planning – ERP, Manufacturing Execution System - MES, Supervisory Control And Data Acquisition – SCADA and Programmable Logic Controllers -

PLCs), to feed the data analytics and knowledge extraction subsystem (Toolkit Modules). At this level will also be implemented a strategy for secure data sharing and traceability, using blockchain solutions and latest European standard for data sovereignty [9].

Cognition - 4C. The Toolkit Modules will support data fusion of different data sets, process mining and analytics, while the Modelling and Simulation layer will manage product and process modelling, for improved decision making at the shop floor and in engineering. Appropriate data repositories will be built to support the training of machine learning techniques and the creation of process models, which will be combined with the CAD/CAE information. Additionally, specific cyber-physical systems will be considered for the feed-forward control of the manufacturing stages in the process-chain to proactively manage emerging defects and avoiding the propagation of defects along the manufacturing system.

Configuration - 5C. As part of the Modelling and Simulation layer, data-driven tools (e.g., Digital Twin of the process chain) will be developed for rapid line qualification and reconfiguration, enabling learning from historical patterns and knowledge extracted in the other subsystems to reduce system ramp-up times, as well as support optimal decision making at value-chain level. In this perspective, the development of the digital twin is seen as the key to fully distributed automation, enabling the implementation of Multi-Agent Systems in the management of operations (next generation legacy systems) and in the process control of production lines, that interact and exchange information with such a digital twin.

2.1 A Possible Framework to Facilitate the Transition from Conventional IT Infrastructure to Industry 4.0 Digital Technology

Considering the most common design, development and deployment challenges (integration with legacy infrastructure, Real-Time Control constraints, and Company IP policy), we believe a hybrid architecture for CPPS as showed in Fig. 2, based on (i) mixed Cloud solutions (i.e. private and public) complemented by (ii) Edge Computing capabilities, combined with (iii) block chain solutions, adoption of (iv) High Security and Privacy Standards and (v) open-source technology, to be a promising one to implement the conceptual model previously introduced.

This hybrid architecture (Fig. 3) allows to transition smoothly from the traditional automation hierarchy to a fully distributed one [10]. Indeed, each functional node is decoupled from the other ones. In this way, parallel implementation of each module is possible once the interfaces and data communication protocols and standards have been fixed.

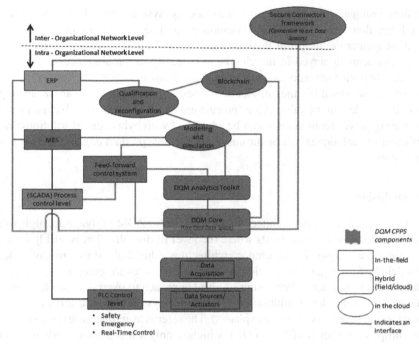

Fig. 2. Reference architecture for the DQM system

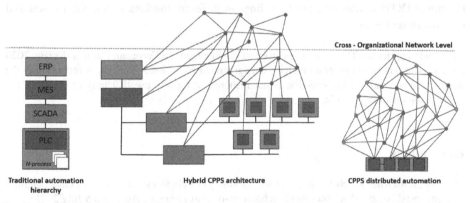

Fig. 3. Positioning of the hybrid architecture, as a bridge between the traditional automation hierarchy and a fully distributed one.

Such configuration should give the possibility to

(i) Fulfil the Real-Time Control needs as required (Edge Computing capabilities).
(ii) Manage the data processing workload (Cloud Computing).
(iii) Ensure data security along a whole value chain (block chain and secure connectors to external data spaces, mixed use of public and private cloud solutions).

(iv) Allow compatibility and synergy with legacy systems (interfaces to allow the required data flow between the DQM components and legacy systems).
(v) Exploit greater architectural flexibility and related external services offerings: the DQM components deployed in the cloud can be easily run, maintained, and replaced independently from each other, as well as accessed from anywhere; the general usage of open protocols will facilitate the introduction of new services/new hardware as developed by several providers in the value chain (no customization needed); variable data storage or computing power requirements can be addressed with hybrid cloud solutions; rapid reconfiguration techniques will be the answer to variable product demand and customer requirements.

2.2 Conclusion

This paper presents a hybrid architecture for a CPPS for ZDM in dynamic, high-value, high-mix, and low-volume contexts where the level of digitalization is still low, or the IT infrastructure is rigid. The reference architecture is highlighted in terms of conceptual modelling for design and development as well as software components and main interfaces. The advantages of choosing a hybrid approach to overcome implementation challenges due to the slow evolution of conventional systems towards advanced manufacturing technologies [11] are also explained. The reference architecture is implemented in the European project DAT4.Zero [12], which is only a first step towards the industrial implementation of CPPS for DQM in ZDM. Further results and considerations for successful implementation and adoption are expected from the future integration of the novel DQM in five selected pilot lines in different markets in the automation and healthcare segments.

Acknowledgements. This project has received funding from the European Union's Horizon 2020 research and innovation program under grant agreement No 958363. This paper reflects only the author's views, and the Commission is not responsible for any use that may be made of the information contained therein.

References

1. Digital McKinsey website: https://www.mckinsey.com/business-functions/mckinsey-digital/our-insights/toward-an-integrated-technology-operating-model. Accessed 5 July 2021
2. Acatech website: https://en.acatech.de/publication/using-the-industrie-4-0-maturity-index-in-industry-case-studies/. Accessed 15 July 2021
3. Eleftheriadis, R., Myklebust, O.: A quality pathway to digitalization in manufacturing thru zero defect manufacturing practices. In: Proceedings of the 6th International Workshop of Advanced Manufacturing and Automation, pp. 187–191. Atlantis Press, Manchester (2016)
4. Eleftheriadis, R.: Benchmark and best practice of IFaCOM industrial demonstrators. Procedia CIRP **33**, 311–314 (2015)
5. QU4LITY home page: https://qu4lity-project.eu/. Accessed 6 May 2021
6. Wu, X.: Cyber physical production systems: a review of design and implementation approaches. In: IEEE International Conference on Industrial Engineering and Engineering Management (IEEM), pp. 1588–1592. IEEE, Macao China (2019)

7. Magnanini, M.C.: Reference architecture for the industrial implementation of zero-defect manufacturing strategies. Procedia CIRP **93**, 646–651 (2020)
8. Lee, J.: A Cyber-Physical Systems architecture for Industry 4.0-based manufacturing systems. Manuf. Lett. **3**, 18–23 (2015)
9. Beuth   website: https://www.beuth.de/de/technische-regel/din-spec-27070/319111044. Accessed 16 July 2021
10. Monostori, L.: Cyber-physical systems in manufacturing. CIRP Ann. **65**(2), 621–641 (2016)
11. Cupek, R.: Agent-based manufacturing execution systems for short-series production scheduling. Comput. Ind. **82**, 245–258 (2016)
12. DAT4.Zero home page: https://dat4zero.eu/. Accessed 15 June 2021

The Survival Analysis for a Predictive Maintenance in Manufacturing

Bahrudin Hrnjica[1]($^{(\boxtimes)}$) (iD) and Selver Softic[2] (iD)

[1] University of Bihac, 77000 Bihac, Bosnia and Herzegovina
bahrudin.hrnjica@unbi.ba
[2] IT and Business Informatics, CAMPUS 02 University of Applied Sciences,
8010 Graz, Austria
selver.softic@campus02.at

Abstract. The Predictive Maintenance (PdM) as a tool for detection future failures in manufacturing has recognized as innovative and effective method. Different approaches for PdM have been developed in order to compromise availability of data and demanding needs for predictions. In this paper the Survival Analysis (SA) method was used for the probability estimation for the machine failure. The paper presents the use of the two most popular SA models Kaplan-Meier non-parametric and Cox proportional hazard models. The first model was used to estimate the probability of machine to survive certain amount of cycles time. The Cox proportional model was used to find out the most significant covariates in the observed data set. The analysis shown that use of SA in the PdM is a challenging task and can be used as additional tool for failure analysis. However, due to its foundation there are several limitations in the application of SA which in most cases are the availability of the right information in the data set.identified

Keywords: Survival analysis · Predictive maintenance · Machine learning

1 Introduction

Maintenance plays a vital role in a manufacturing and it can be defined as the set of activities in order to preserve the system in the functional state. The maintenance can be classified in different ways depending how it can be performed on the manufacturing system. Only small number of maintenance types can be performed without interrupting the manufacturing process. However, in most of cases the maintenance must be done only if the production process is shut down. When the maintenance requires production stopping it may lead for tension between the production and the maintenance departments in a way that the production needs quality and reliable maintenance without production interruption, or at least with minimum stopping time [1]. The worse case scenario may happen when the production stops due to the component failure. Such case should never happen in the production with well-planned and organized maintenance. Be able to create a perfect maintenance plan can cost more than planned by budget. It is obvious

© IFIP International Federation for Information Processing 2021
Published by Springer Nature Switzerland AG 2021
A. Dolgui et al. (Eds.): APMS 2021, IFIP AICT 632, pp. 78–85, 2021.
https://doi.org/10.1007/978-3-030-85906-0_9

that good maintenance planning can offer nearly a perfect production with minimal production interruption. How to achieve such a maintenance plan depend on adopted strategies and methods for a maintenance time calculation and prediction.

Instead of relying on planned maintenance entirely, the ability to predict possible failures in the manufacturing process has become largely popular in the last decades. By knowing the possible failure of the specific component before it occurs leads to multiple benefits in the production such as reduce maintenance costs, improve production quality and increase the productivity. Recent advancements in Artificial Intelligence (AI) and Machine Learning (ML) improved the maintenance process primarily in the ability to detect and predict errors before failure occurs. Such kind of maintenance is called Predictive Maintenance (PdM) and it requires the equipment to provide data from sensors monitoring the equipment as well as other operational data. Simply speaking, it is a technique to determine (predict) the failure of the machine component in the near future so that the component can be replaced based on the maintenance plan before it fails and stops the production process [2]. Different types of maintenance with ability to improve the production process are presented on Fig. 1.

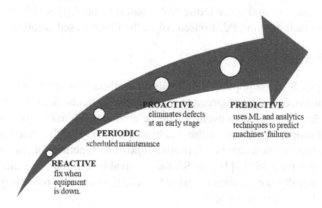

Fig. 1. Different type of maintenance

The PdM uses data collected from various sensors installed on the machines. The sensors are built into the Internet of Things (IoT) devices that send data in the cloud. Once the data are in the Cloud, different cloud solutions can use the data for processing and analysis. PdM can be implemented in the cloud solution as a part of Industry 4.0. Through the literature many different Cloud based PdM solutions have been implemented and published [3–6].

1.1 PdM and SA Literature Overview

Without doubt, the PdM plays major role in the Industry 4.0. The Industry 4.0 key components Big Data, AI, ML, Could Computing and IoT are used in the PdM to predict the machine failure and related maintenance parameters. By using IoT and Could computing PdM reaches its full potential.

Combination of Big Data ecosystem orchestrated through the IoT for various PdM approaches in industrial IoT-based smart manufacturing can be found literature. In most case the IoT provide the data in real-time while the big data eco system provides the predictive analytics algorithms in order to dynamically manage preventive maintenance and failures. Beside predictive algorithms the ecosystem include numerous technologies including big data ingestion, integration, transformation, storage, analytics, and visualization in a real-time environment using various technologies such as the Data Lake, NoSQL database, Apache Spark, Apache Drill, Apache Hive, OPC Collector, and other techniques [6–10].

PdM based on Survival Analysis (SA) can be implemented on different level. In most case PdM based SA is used for the calculation of various survival curves and then incorporated into ML models. Survival curves are used in order to calculate the probability of defects derived from the Cox proportional-hazards model. Although in most cases SA is used in medical research of various diseases such as Alzheimer's, cancer, leukemia and similar [11–13], it is possible to find examples of successful application in production and related areas [14–16].

There are few examples where PdM based SA is used in Cloud based Solutions using AI, ML, Biga Data, IoT and other Industry 4.0 based technologies [15–18]. This paper presents an approach of using PdM based SA in the cloud-based solution.

2 Survival Analysis

Survival Analysis SA is a popular data analysis method first appeared in bio science and medicine science, and later spread to other scientific fields. SA tries to estimate the time to event data. The time to event T can be anything related to maintenance such as: duration of proper operation of the machine, frequency of the machine failure, or duration of the last maintenance etc. It is always positive function. In context of science the survival means probability [19]. In SA the survival function S is defined as function of time $S(t)$. Generally, the survival function $S(t)$ is defined as the probability for survival after time t of the random variable T:

$$S(t) = \Pr(T > t) \tag{1}$$

Obviously, $S(0) = 1$, which indicate the survival function is related to the lifetime distribution function. In SA the cumulative distribution function F represents the probability that the event variable occurs earlier than t.

$$F(t) = 1 - S(t) \tag{2}$$

The first derivative of cumulative density function defines the death density function (DDF) and can be expressed as:

$$f(t) = \frac{F(x)}{dt} \tag{3}$$

Hazard density function $h(t)$ represents the probability the event to be occurred in the next instant, given survival time t:

$$h(t) = \frac{f(f)}{S(t)} = -d\frac{[\ln(S)]}{dt} \tag{4}$$

3   Case Study

The Case Study of the paper is conducted from the NASA Turbofan Engine Degradation Simulation Data Set. A number of aircraft engines were monitored throughout usage history. Each engine was employed under different flight conditions while the 21 sensors recorded various states of the engine. Depending on the recorded sensor values the amount and rate of damage accumulation for each engine can be obtained. Data generation and specific meaning of the sensors are described in the literature [20].

The data was generated in the machine learning ready data sets, consisting of four different sets. Each set was generated by different operating conditions, fault mode and train/test size. In this paper the first data set FD001 was used which consisted of 100 different engines, one operating condition and one fault mode.

The data set used in the paper consisted of the following columns (covariates) separated by space:

- Engine identification number,
- The number of cycles which can be related to time,
- Three operational settings and
- 21 sensor readings.

There are two sets of FD001: the training and testing sets. For the privacy purpose the data sets are obfuscated of the column description except the engine id and the time which is represented as the number of cycles.

3.1   Data Preparation for SA

In order to perform survival analysis on the presented data set the time to event and the indicator for censoring occurrence variables have to be defined. From the data set description file the train data set collect the information which monitored each engine till the failure time. This means that the training data set contains failure information for each engine, and it is the maximum cycle. However, the test set do not contain such information since the monitor history of engine usage is not completed. However, the third file of the data set contains such information and it is used for model test evaluation. The test set along the RUL file are used in the perdition scenario for other machine learning methods such that used in the literature [2].

As mentioned, the data set was generated so that each machine failed at certain cycle number thus the censored information is not provided. In order to provide the censored information, the data set is modified so that the maximum time cycle is defined before the engine is failed. The scenario used in the paper is defined so that the survival analysis analyzed the engines till certain number of cycles S. In such case the data set is cutoff so that the engines which have failure time greater that S are censored. The several variants of S value are used in order to get the best possible model.

3.2   Kaplan-Meier Non-parametric Model

The Kaplan – Meier survival model [1] represent a non-parametric model that estimates the survival function from the lifetime data set. The model defines the survival function

$S(t)$ which represent the probability that life is longer than time t. In our case the model estimates the probability that failure will not appear before 220 cycles:

$$\hat{S}(t) = \prod_{i, t_i \leq t = 220} \left(1 - \frac{d_i}{n_i}\right), \tag{5}$$

where,

– t_i is a time at least one event happened,
– n_i the number of engines survived up to time t_i.

The following image shows the Kaplan-Meier probability function plot for the 100 engines for the maximum of 220-time cycles (Fig. 2).

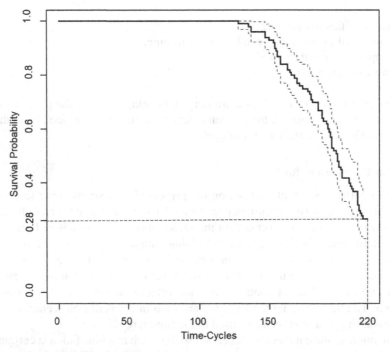

Fig. 2. Kaplan-Meier probability function plot

As can be seen all 100 engines have 100% probability of survival the first 128 cycles. Since the maximum cycle $S = 220$, one can see there is a 28% of probability that the engine will survive 220 cycles. The image also shows the confidence interval of the 95%.

3.3 Cox Proportional-Hazards Model

The Cox proportional-hazards model [1] represents the regression model used for investigating the association between the survival time of the engine and predictor variables.

In this paper the Cox proportional model was used in order to provided influence of several covariates (predictors) at rate of particular event. The model can be expressed based on the hazard function (4):

$$h(t) = h_0(t) \cdot exp(b_1 x_1 + b_2 x_2 + \ldots + b_k x_k),$$ (6)

where:

- $h(t)$ - hazard function estimated by the set of k covariates $(x_1, x_2, \ldots, x_k)$,
- $b_1, b_2, \ldots, b_k$- regressors for measuring the influence of the covariates,
- $h_0(t)$- baseline hazard which is related to the value of the hazard if all the x_i are equal to zero.

The Cox regression tests results shows several important indicators which defines the influence between the covariate and the hazard rates. The first indicator is statistical significance which defines the influence between each covariate on the hazard rate.

From the data set there are more than 20 covariates potentially be included in the Cox model. However only few have influence in the model. The following tables shows covariates which have significant influence in the model:

Table 1. Statistical significance of the regressors of the the Cox proportional regression model.

Covariates	coef	exp(coef)	se(coef)	z	Pr(>|z|)	Significance
Sensor4	8.986e−02	1.094e + 00	2.711e−02	3.314	0.000919	***
Sensor7	−8.306e−01	4.358e−01	2.631e−01	−3.157	0.001592	**
Sensor15	2.673e + 01	4.041e + 11	6.812e + 00	3.923	8.74e-05	***

Table 2. Statistical significance of the Cox proportional hazards ratios.

Cov	exp(coef)	exp(−coef)	Low.0.95	upp.0.95	Concordance = 0.773(se = 0.03)
Sensor4	1.094e + 00	9.141e−01	1.037e + 00	1.154e + 00	l.h.r.t = 91.27,3df, p = < 2e−16
Sensor7	4.358e−01	2.295e + 00	2.602e−01	7.298e−01	W.test = 44.61, 3 df, p = 1e−09
Sensor15	4.041e + 11	2.474e−12	6.430e + 05	2.540e + 17	S.test = 56.62,df, p = 3e−12

From the statistical significance (Table 2) one can see that the model is significant since all three p-values of the tests (likelihood, Wald and score) are far lower than 0.05. The tests also proved that regressors are significant.

From the Table 1 the p-value for Sensor4 is 0.000919, with hazard ration $HR = exp(coef) = 1.094$ (Table 2) indicating the strong influence between the Sensor4 values and *increased* risk of failure. The similar statement can be defined for the Sensor15. The negative value of the Sensor7 indicates that the hazard ratio has strong influence between Sensor7 and *decreased* risk of failure.

Comparison of the results with the results in the literature is hard to achieve due to the use of different data sets, tasks approaches and methods. Only qualitative analysis with limited comparison attributes can be established by several results in the literature [2, 21]. However, the comparison analysis should be our further step in the future research of this subject.

4 Conclusions, Limitations and Outlook

In this paper survival analysis method was applied for the predictive maintenance in order to estimate the probability of survival of 100 engines of the turbofan engine degradation data set. The application was carried out for the group of engines which were monitored throughout usage history. The engines were monitored by the 21 sensors and 3 different settings. During the time the amount of accumulated damage was estimated in form of number of cycles. In order to use such data set, the data transformation was performed in order to create SA compatible data set. The two most popular SA models Kaplan-Meier and Cox proportional models were created and tested. By using the first model we estimated the probability for the survival of each engine before certain amount of cycles has been reached. By using Cox proportional hazard model the influence of different sensor readings on hazard rates was estimated. General conclusion of the paper can be that the SA application in the PdM can be challenging task mostly because of leak of suitable data sets. SA for PdM can be used as additional tool for other classic PdM methods like Deep learning, Random Forest etc.

References

1. Budai, G., Dekker, R., Nicolai, R.P.: Maintenance and production: a review of planning models. In: Complex System Maintenance Handbook. Springer Series in Reliability Engineering. Springer, London (2008). https://doi.org/10.1007/978-1-84800-011-7_13
2. Hrnjica, B., Softic, S.: Explainable AI in manufacturing: a predictive maintenance case study. In: Lalic, B., Majstorovic, V., Marjanovic, U., von Cieminski, G., Romero, D. (eds.) APMS 2020. IAICT, vol. 592, pp. 66–73. Springer, Cham (2020). https://doi.org/10.1007/978-3-030-57997-5_8
3. Paolanti, M., Romeo, L., Felicetti, A., Mancini, A., Frontoni, E., Loncarski, J.: Machine learning approach for predictive maintenance in industry 4.0. In: 2018 14th IEEE/ASME International Conference on Mechatronic and Embedded Systems and Applications (MESA), Oulu, Finland, pp. 1–6 (2018). https://doi.org/10.1109/MESA.2018.8449150
4. Hrnjica, B., Mehr, A.D.: Energy demand forecasting using deep learning. In: Al-Turjman, F. (ed.) Smart Cities Performability, Cognition, & Security. EICC, pp. 71–104. Springer, Cham (2020). https://doi.org/10.1007/978-3-030-14718-1_4
5. Schmidt, B., Wang, L.: Cloud-enhanced predictive maintenance. Int. J. Adv. Manuf. Technol. **99**(1–4), 5–13 (2016). https://doi.org/10.1007/s00170-016-8983-8

6. Annamalai, S., Udendhran, R., Vimal, S.: Cloud-based predictive maintenance and machine monitoring for intelligent manufacturing for automobile industry. In: Raj, P., Koteeswaran, S. (eds.) Novel Practices and Trends in Grid and Cloud Computing, pp. 74–89. IGI Global (2019). https://doi.org/10.4018/978-1-5225-9023-1.ch006

7. Yu, W., Dillon, T., Mostafa, F., Rahayu, W., Liu, Y.: A global manufacturing big data ecosystem for fault detection in predictive maintenance. IEEE Trans. Industr. Inf. **16**(1), 183–192 (2020). https://doi.org/10.1109/TII.2019.2915846

8. Wang, J., Zhang, L., Duan, L., Gao, R.X.: A new paradigm of cloud-based predictive maintenance for intelligent manufacturing. J. Intell. Manuf. **28**(5), 1125–1137 (2015). https://doi.org/10.1007/s10845-015-1066-0

9. March, S.T., Scudder, G.D.: Predictive maintenance: strategic use of IT in manufacturing organizations. Inf. Syst. Front. **21**, 327–341 (2019). https://doi.org/10.1007/s10796-017-9749-z

10. He, Y., Han, X., Gu, C., Chen, Z.: Cost-oriented predictive maintenance based on mission reliability state for cyber man. Syst. Adv. Mech. Eng. (2018). https://doi.org/10.1177/168781 4017751467

11. Mueller, C., et al.: Associations of acetylcholinesterase inhibitor treatment with reduced mortality in Alzheimer's disease: a retrospective survival analysis. Age Ageing **47**(1), 88–94 (2018). https://doi.org/10.1093/ageing/afx098

12. Yao, H., et al.: Survival analysis of patients with invasive extramammary Paget disease: implications of anatomic sites. BMC Cancer (2018). https://doi.org/10.1186/s12885-018-4257-1

13. Gnant, M., et al.: Adjuvant denosumab in early breast cancer: disease-free survival analysis of 3,425 postmenopausal patients in the ABCSG-18 trial. J. Clin. Oncol. **36**(15) (2018). https://doi.org/10.1200/JCO.2018.36.15_suppl.500

14. de Almeida Costa, M., Braga, J.P.A.P., Andrade, A.R.: A data-driven maintenance policy for railway wheelset based on survival analysis and Markov decision process. Qual. Reliab. Eng. Int. **37**(1), 176–198 (2021). https://doi.org/10.1002/qre.2729

15. Aydin, O., Guldamlasioglu, S.: Using LSTM networks to predict engine condition on large scale data processing framework. In: 2017 4th International Conference on Electrical and Electronic Engineering (ICEEE). IEEE (2017). https://doi.org/10.1109/ICEEE2.2017.793 5834

16. Ramesh, P.G., Dutta, S.J., Neog, S.S., Baishya, P., Bezbaruah, I.: Implementation of predictive maintenance systems in remotely located process plants under industry 4.0 scenario. In: Karanki, D.R., Vinod, G., Ajit, S. (eds.) Advances in RAMS Engineering. SSRE, pp. 293–326. Springer, Cham (2020). https://doi.org/10.1007/978-3-030-36518-9_12

17. Wang, J., Li, C., Han, S., Sarkar, S., Zhou, X.: Predictive maintenance based on event-log analysis: A case study. IBM J. Res. Dev. **61**(1), 11:121–11:132, 1 Jan–Feb 2017. https://doi.org/10.1147/JRD.2017.2648298

18. Korvesis, P., Besseau, S., Vazirgiannis, M.: Predictive maintenance in aviation: failure prediction from post-flight reports. In: 2018 IEEE 34th International Conference on Data Engineering (ICDE). IEEE (2018)

19. Emmert-Streib, F., Dehmer, M.: Introduction to survival analysis in practice. Mach. Learn. Knowl. Extr. **1**(3), 1013–1038 (2019)

20. Saxena, A., Goebel, K., Simon, D., Eklund, N.: Damage propagation modeling for aircraft engine run-to-failure simulation. In: Proceedings of the Ist International Conference on Prognostics and Health Management (PHM08), Denver CO (2008)

21. Lopes, F., Sá Criticality evaluation to support maintenance management of manufacturing systems. Int. J. Ind. Eng. Manage. **11**(1), 3–18 (2020). https://doi.org/10.24867/IJIEM-2020-1-248

Detection of Fluid Level in Bores for Batch Size One Assembly Automation Using Convolutional Neural Network

Alexej Simeth[1]([⊠]) [iD], Jessica Plaßmann[2], and Peter Plapper[1] [iD]

[1] University of Luxembourg, 6, rue Richard Coudenhove-Kalergi, L-1359 Luxembourg City,
Luxembourg
alexej.simeth@uni.lu

[2] Hochschule Trier, Schneidershof, 54293 Trier, Germany

Abstract. Increased customization and shortening product life cycles pose a challenge for automation, especially in assembly. In combination with the nature of assembly tasks, which may require high level of perception, skill, and logical thinking, these tasks are often conducted manually, especially in certain industries (e.g. furniture, power tools) or small and medium-sized enterprises. One of such tasks is the liquid level monitoring in gluing processes. Existing non-manual solutions are based on conventional and less flexible algorithms to detect the current liquid level. In production environments with highly individualized products, a need for more performant models arises. With artificial intelligence (AI) it is possible to deduct decisions from unknown multidimensional correlations in sensor data, which is a key enabler for assembly automation for products with high degree of customization.

In this paper, an AI-based model is proposed to automate a gluing process in a final assembly. Images of a gluing process are taken with a camera and a convolutional neural network is used to extract images features. The features are applied to train a support vector machine classifier to identify the liquid level. The developed model is tested and validated with a Monte-Carlo-simulation and used on a demonstrator to automate a gluing process. The developed model classifies images of liquid levels with over 98% accuracy. Similar results are achieved on the demonstrator.

Keywords: Liquid detection · Artificial intelligence · Convolutional neural network · Camera · Assembly · Automation

1 Introduction

Assembly processes are still the part of manufacturing with a low overall degree of automation [1]. This is due to the nature of assembly tasks, which often require a high level of perception, skill, and logical thinking [2]. Shorter product life cycles and higher customization lead to increased variance in product portfolio with low volumes up to batch size one. Since every product is going through final assembly, complete variance

© IFIP International Federation for Information Processing 2021
Published by Springer Nature Switzerland AG 2021
A. Dolgui et al. (Eds.): APMS 2021, IFIP AICT 632, pp. 86–93, 2021.
https://doi.org/10.1007/978-3-030-85906-0_10

must be covered, which is further inhibiting automation. New trends such as industry 4.0 and the rise of artificial intelligence (AI) in manufacturing promote increased automation and are key enabler for intelligent and smart manufacturing systems [3, 4]. For a flexible automation of assembly processes of highly individual products, it is necessary to replace observations taken by humans with digital systems to start, execute, or stop (sub-) processes. For large batch sizes, tools, positions, process parameters etc. are usually adapted to fit a certain product. This procedure is not economical for small volumes with high product variability [5]. In some cases, process parameters are not known a-priori due to the characteristics of processed workpieces or the production environment. Especially in such situations manual work is still necessary. With AI it is possible to deduct decisions and actions from unknown multi-dimensional correlations in sensor data [6], which can be used for automation of highly individualized products.

The focus of the authors' research is assembly automation consisting of pick-and-place and gluing processes in batch size one assembly scenarios. Workpieces are joined by placing them into bores in a carrier workpiece and then bonded with glue. Due to the properties of the carrier workpiece, the required amount of glue is unknown and standard volumetric process control is not applicable. In this paper, a model is proposed to detect the fluid level of glue in workpieces so that the mentioned gluing process can be started, monitored, and stopped. An optical sensor is used, which is applicable for different sensing tasks in the overall assembly processes.

The next chapter gives a brief overview of related work and approaches of other authors. The methodology applied in this paper, experimental setup, results, and a conclusion are given in chapters 3–6.

2 Related Work

Detection of specific objects, features, etc. is a common issue in manufacturing and automation, and there exist many different solutions for different problems. In [7] the authors describe an image processing system directly related to glue detection, which shall be used in an LCD panel production. The authors showcase a camera-based system which monitors and measures the width of an applied glue line by identifying the edges of the glue line with standard Canny edge detection algorithm and by calculating the distance between edge pixels of two detected edges (both sides of glue line).

Several solutions for liquid/fluid detection in production environment using optical methods are proposed in the area of bottle filling. The camera is positioned so that a side view of the bottle is captured [8–12]. In [8], the authors propose to classify a bottle into under-filled, filled, and over-filled by using Canny edge detection algorithm to identify the surface of the liquid level. The detected surface is compared to a pre-defined reference line. The average vertical distance of the detected edge pixels to the reference is taken to classify the bottle. Similarly, an ISEF edge detection filter is applied in [9] to identify the surface of the liquid and the lower edge of the cap. The averaged vertical distance between edge pixels in a defined region of interest (ROI) is compared to a threshold. The proposed method in [10] uses image segmentation based on color. After changing the color space, the extracted image is smoothened, binarized, and the dark liquid is separated from the bright background. The contour of the dark area is taken to calculate the filling level. In [11], a fast and simple method is developed to automatically measure the volume of liquid and the bubble phase on top of the liquid in translucent cylindric vessels. Key of this method is the installation of an area light source and a black stripe combined with cropping and merging several image patches, which emphasize the liquid surface and bubble area. The actual detection is based on characteristic changes in histogram. In [12] the authors compare a conventional liquid detection approach via several mean filters with a neural network-based approach. Despite the very simple structure of the neural network (three layers), classification results are slightly improved compared to conventional approach. In [13] a dispensed glue drop on a workpiece is monitored to detect defects in the glue dispensing system. The authors use principal component analysis (PCA) to detect variation in the output and state whether a fault in the system exists.

Showcased methods majorly apply conventional models to detect the surface of the liquid and compare it against predefined references or thresholds. This requires a constant environment and specific settings for each product. In a continuous changing production environment (e.g., robot mounted systems) with always changing products, more flexible and robust solutions are required.

3 Methodology

In this paper, an AI-based model is developed to robustly detect a fluid on a workpiece in order to automate an industrial gluing process. The development of the model follows the workflow presented in [6], which is depicted in Fig. 1. At first, the initial data set is generated. The classification is reduced to a binary problem and single images are labelled as "empty" or "full". To achieve a sufficient size of data set, the data which is expected to be more influential, i.e., data points close to label change, are augmented following the method of importance sampling [14].

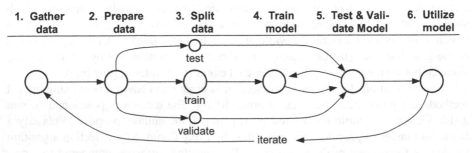

Fig. 1. Workflow for supervised and unsupervised learning [6], p. 22

The data is then randomly split into test and training set. The latter is used to train the model and to extract image features, which are used for classification. To extract the image features, a pre-trained convolutional neural network (CNN) is applied, because it is usually much faster and simpler than designing a new CNN [15]. The extracted features are used in a machine learning algorithm to classify the test set. Machine learning algorithms achieve similar performance and accuracy compared to deep learning classifiers by reducing the computational effort [16]. In the proposed model the 50 layer deep CNN ResNet50 in combination with a classifier based on a support vector machine (SVM) are applied. The learned interdependencies are highly depending on the selected training set, which depends on the random drawing of the initial data set. An additional cross-validation is conducted. Via a Monte-Carlo-Simulation (MCS) [17] the impact of the randomly selected training data on the outcome is analyzed.

In a final step, the model is used to classify new images, which are captured during a live gluing process. The gluing process is automatically stopped based on the result of the image classification.

4 Experimental Setup

4.1 Applied Detection Model

The detection of the glue is achieved with a hybrid detection model consisting of a pretrained CNN and an SVM. In a first step image features are extracted by the CNN, i.e. the activations of the output layer of the CNN. The pretrained CNN is not changed during feature extraction. Secondly, the activations of all images of the training set and their labels are used to train the SVM image classifier. The trained classifier is tested and validated with the test set. Here, image features are again extracted by the same pretrained CNN and forwarded to the SVM classifier for classification.

The introduced models of other researches in chapter 2 mostly rely on conventional filters combined with defined thresholds. The decision rules to classify an image are programmed manually and applicable only for the specific boundary conditions in each use case. In contrast, the proposed model applies a decision rule generated by the computer itself based on the training data resulting in the SVM image classifier. By changing the ground data set, the model is applicable similarly in other use cases. Additionally, the resulting SVM classifier is expected to be significantly more robust towards changes in boundary conditions than conventional methods.

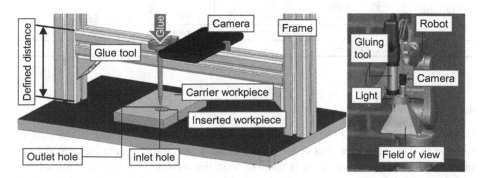

Fig. 2 . a): Designed test stand for initial data set generation. b): Demonstrator.

4.2   Generation of Data Set

In order to separate the modelling from the production line, a test stand is designed to create an initial data set. Based on this set, the CNN and the classifier are trained for later use in a real gluing process. The initial data is created by recoding manually conducted gluing trials as depicted in Fig. 2a). Glue is filled through a nozzle and an inlet hole into a workpiece. A cradle is mounted above the workpiece and a smartphone is used to record the gluing process. The region of interest (ROI), which is the outlet hole, is cropped out of each frame resulting in 41x41 resolution images. The data is transformed into 244x244x3 RGB pixel images, which are the required size for the ResNet50 input layer. The obtained images are then labelled into the categories (labels) "empty" and "full". In total 605 images were created and used for further data set optimization. In row "Label" in Table 1 examples for the images of the two labels are given.

4.3   Optimization of Data Set

For the training of the model sufficient amount of data is required. To increase the initial data set size, the data set is augmented by rotation and mirroring of selected images following the method of importance sampling. In this case, all the images which are labelled as "empty" but close to full and vice versa are augmented, since it is expected, that these images have a high impact on the decision rule to be determined. The final distribution of the data set is characterized by Table 1. Based on the initial 605 video frames, a total data set of 3,000 images is created with importance sampling method.

Table 1. Generated and optimized data set for image classification

Data	Frames from videos taken on test stand			
Label	Empty (380 images)		Full (225 images)	
	Divide into more and less influential data for "importance sampling"			
Sublabel	Clearly empty	Close to full	Sufficiently full	Overfull
		augment	_augment_	
Data Set	1830 images		1170 images	

4.4   Validation

From the label "empty" 1170 images are randomly selected so that both classes are of same size. The generated data set is randomly split into training data and test data in the ratio 70:30. The training set is used to train the model. The test set is classified, and the result is compared to the original label. In an MCS, the training of the SVM image classifier is repeated 500 times with a different random selection of label "empty", training set, and test set.

In a final validation step, the SVM trained with the identified image features extracted by CNN is used on a technology demonstrator to classify new images, which are not part of the initial data set. On the demonstrator glue is automatically pumped through a nozzle into the inlet hole and the outlet hole is monitored by an industrial fixed lens camera (see Fig. 2b). A ring light with red LED is used to illuminate the scenery and to reduce the environmental impact. The red image plane is taken for further processing. The cropped ROI has a different resolution compared to the initial data set and is grayscale but covers a similar physical area. The resulting grayscale image is transformed into the required model input size and classified by the SVM. If an image is classified as full, the gluing process is stopped. The trials are conducted in bright and dark environmental situations.

5   Results

The proposed model to detect fluid level in workpieces achieves an overall prediction accuracy of > 98%. The model is cross validated with an MCS and trained 500 times with different, randomly selected training and test set configurations. The prediction accuracy varies over the 500 simulations in the interval from 93–99.5% (see Fig. 3). All wrong classifications are on images which are directly at the boarder to the other label. I.e., the images are either of the first frames of a video, which are labelled as full or the last frames of a video which are labelled as empty (cf. categories Table 1).

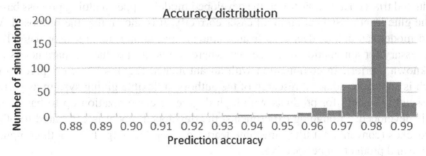

Fig. 3. Results of overall classifier performance under varying data based on MCS.

The model is then applied on a technology demonstrator. It is used to stop a gluing process based on the classification of the glue level. At 35 conducted gluing trials, the proposed method stopped the process in all cases correctly. A selection of the images classified as full during the trials is shown in Table 2 to highlight the differences between the images used for training and the images obtained during the live gluing process. As depicted, the trials are conducted in a daylight and night scenario.

Table 2. Images classified as full during demonstrator validation.

Bright environment	
Dark environment	

6 Summary

In this paper, the authors propose a new model to detect glue level in workpieces. The hybrid detection model consists of the pretrained convolutional neural network ResNet50 and a support vector machine image classifier. The used ground data set is generated on a test stand with a standard smartphone camera where images of a gluing process are taken. The obtained images are labelled into the two classes 'full' and 'empty'. Based on the generated data set, the classifier is trained with image features extracted by the neural network and used to classify new images.

The developed model classifies the test images with a very high accuracy. Based on a cross validation with 500 random distributions of training and test data of the initial data set, in average 98% of all images are classified correctly. Furthermore, the proposed model can be applied in a real gluing process with significantly different boundary conditions compared to the test stand, especially the lighting conditions. In conducted trials on a demonstrator, the developed model stopped a gluing process based on the glue level classification in all cases correctly. It is shown that the proposed AI-based model can deduct decisions from unknown multidimensional sensor data. This is necessary for automation of processes, where important production parameters are not known a-priori. In combination with an automated region-of-interest prediction, which is subject to adjacent research of the authors, a flexible gluing system as part of an assembly system for products with high degree of customization up to batch size one is developed. In ongoing experiments, the developed model is compared to other approaches (conventional filter, machine learning, deep learning) from both computer science and production perspective.

References

1. Kleindienst, M., Ramsauer, C.: Der Beitrag von Lernfabriken zu Industrie 4.0-Ein Baustein zur vierten industriellen Revolution bei kleinen und mittelständischen Unternehmen. Industrie-Manage. **3**, 41–44 (2015)
2. Scholer, M.: Wandlungsfähige und angepasste Automation in der Automobilmontage mittels durchgängigem modularem Engineering - Am Beispiel der Mensch-Roboter-Kooperation in der Unterbodenmontage. Universität des Saarlandes (2018)
3. Kolla, S.S.V.K., Sanchez, A., Minoufekr, M., Plapper, P.: Augmented reality in manual assembly processes. In: 9th International Conference on Mass Customization and Personalization – Community of Europe (MCP-CE 2020), pp. 121–128 (2020). https://www.researchgate.net/publication/344606723_Augmented_Reality_in_Manual_Assembly_Processes
4. Wang, L.: From intelligence science to intelligent manufacturing. Engineering **5**(4), 615–618 (2019). https://doi.org/10.1016/j.eng.2019.04.011

5. Burggräf, P., Wagner, J., Dannapfel, M., Fluchs, S., Müller, K., Koke, B.: Automation decisions in flow-line assembly systems based on a cost-benefit analysis. Procedia CIRP **81**, 529–534 (2019). https://doi.org/10.1016/j.procir.2019.03.150

6. Akerkar, R.: Artificial Intelligence for Business. Cham: Springer International Publishing (2019)

7. Huang, Y., Wu, C., Chang, C.-Y.: An application of image processing in flat panels. In: 2012 International Conference on Wavelet Active Media Technology and Information Processing (ICWAMTIP), pp. 8–11, December 2012. https://doi.org/10.1109/ICWAMTIP.2012.6413427

8. Felipe, M.A.A., Olegario, T.V, Bugtai, N.T., Baldovino, R.G.: Vision-based liquid level detection in amber glass bottles using OpenCV. In: 2019 7th International Conference on Robot Intelligence Technology and Applications (RiTA), pp. 148–152, November 2019. https://doi.org/10.1109/RITAPP.2019.8932807

9. Pithadiya, K.J., Modi, C.K., Chauhan, J.D.: Machine vision based liquid level inspection system using ISEF edge detection technique. In: Proceedings of the International Conference and Workshop on Emerging Trends in Technology, pp. 601–605, February 2010. https://doi.org/10.1145/1741906.1742044

10. Gonzalez Ramirez, M.M., Villamizar Rincon, J.C., Lopez Parada, J.F.: Liquid level control of Coca-Cola bottles using an automated system. In: 2014 International Conference on Electronics, Communications and Computers (CONIELECOMP), pp. 148–154, February 2014. https://doi.org/10.1109/CONIELECOMP.2014.6808582

11. Ma, H., Peng, L.: Vision based liquid level detection and bubble area segmentation in liquor distillation. In: 2019 IEEE International Conference on Imaging Systems and Techniques (IST), pp. 1–6, December 2019. https://doi.org/10.1109/IST48021.2019.9010097

12. Beck, T., Gatternig, B., Delgado, A.: Schaum-und Füllstanderkennung mittels optischer Systeme mit neuronalen Algorithmen. In: Fachtagung "Experimentelle Strömungsmechanik", pp. 17.1–17.7 (2019)

13. Huang, Z., Angadi, V.C., Danishvar, M., Mousavi, A., Li, M.: Zero defect manufacturing of microsemiconductors – an application of machine learning and artificial intelligence. In: 2018 5th International Conference on Systems and Informatics (ICSAI), pp. 449–454, November 2018. https://doi.org/10.1109/ICSAI.2018.8599292

14. Arouna, B.: Adaptative monte carlo method, a variance reduction technique. Monte Carlo Methods Appl. **10**(1), 1–24 (2004). https://doi.org/10.1515/156939604323091180

15. MathWorks: Pretrained Deep Neural Networks (2021). https://www.mathworks.com/help/deeplearning/ug/pretrained-convolutional-neural-networks.html. Accessed 08 Apr 2021

16. Kumar, T.K.A., Vinayakumar, R., Variyar, V.V.S., Sowmya, V., Soman, K.P.: Convolutional neural networks for fingerprint liveness detection system. In: 2019 International Conference on Intelligent Computing and Control Systems (ICCS), pp. 243–246, May 2019. https://doi.org/10.1109/ICCS45141.2019.9065713

17. Andrieu, C., De Freitas, N., Doucet, A., Jordan, M.I.: An introduction to MCMC for machine learning. Mach. Learn. **50**(1), 5–43 (2003). https://doi.org/10.1023/A:1020281327116

Barriers Hindering an Efficient Implementation Process of Digital Technologies; a Case Study at Norwegian Manufacturing Companies

Eirin Lodgaard[1]([✉]), Hans Torvatn[2] [ID], Johanne Sørumsbrenden[1],
and Gaute Andreas Knutstad[1]

[1] SINTEF Manufacturing, Enggata, 40-2830 Raufoss, Norway
`eirin.lodgaard@sintef.no`
[2] SINTEF Digital, SP Andersens vei 5 7031, Trondheim, Norway

Abstract. The existing wave of improvement in manufacturing industry is strongly driven by the application of digital technologies. Unfortunately, the implementation process is not straightforward. To understand the barriers which hinder a smooth implementation process is essential for successful implementation of digital technologies. Our study aims to identify the major barriers based on a case study performed at six Norwegian manufacturing companies, to know what to solve enabling a smoother implementation process. The findings shows that both technical and organizational aspects are of importance to consider, where the organizational aspects are seen as the most underestimated. The lack of digital competence alongside underestimated need for organizational development of involved people emerges as prominent barriers. Some technical problems were also pertinent, like system integration. Sharing of data was seen as a potential asset, but both legal, strategic and technical issues hampered this. The results of this study may help managers and practitioners to address the major barriers highlighted, paving the way for successful implementation and integration of digital technologies in the manufacturing industry.

Keywords: Industry 4.0 · Digitalization · Manufacturing industry · Barriers · Case study

1 Introduction

The industrial development has so far undergone three revolutions and is in the start-up phase for the fourth one, named as Industry 4.0. Each of them is related to the breakthrough of new technologies which have become the pillars of a new industrial era, where also new organizations and working methods have been developed simultaneously. The first was triggered by steam, the second by electricity, the third by computers. In the fourth revolution which is triggered by the Internet of Things (IoT), equipment, objects and users are connected to each other through advanced information and communication systems linked into the entire industrial value chains. The leaps in industrial development

Published by Springer Nature Switzerland AG 2021
A. Dolgui et al. (Eds.): APMS 2021, IFIP AICT 632, pp. 94–101, 2021.
https://doi.org/10.1007/978-3-030-85906-0_11

as each of the revolutions are representing are closely intertwined, and the technologies they opened to are still evolving.

The existing wave of improvement in manufacturing industry, is strongly driven by the application of digital technologies, affected by the concept of Industry 4.0 [1]. Digital technologies open a wealth of opportunities for the manufacturing industry, from the use of smart sensors and IoT, radio-frequency identification (RFID), big data analysis, artificial intelligence and machine learning, virtual reality, digital twins, autonomous robots, and data sharing in the entire value chain. Hence, this place new demands on the organization in terms of competence, adaptability, and innovation [2].

Upon implementation of chosen new digital technologies, efficient implementation processes are of high value. Trying to avoid pitfalls regards to the implementation process, it is a need to explore factors that determine what prevents this. Existing literature agrees upon this as a largely unexplored field and the necessity of more knowledge building [3]. Therefore, there is a need to identify the barriers inhibiting the implementation process to know what to solve, enabling a smoother implementation process of digital technologies in the era of Industry 4.0. Based on this, our research aims to answering the following research questions: *What are the most prominent barriers preventing an efficient implementation process of digital technology at shop floor level?* This gives us valuable knowledge about how to succeed with the existing digital transformation from a holistic view form a manufacturing perspective.

2 Barriers to Implementation of Digital Technologies

The implementation process of digital technologies is normally a complex process, and many organizations are facing issues due to different influencing barriers. In additional, these factors influence each other's and are intertwined and thus complicates the implementation process [3]. Several authors emphasize the complexities that will arise from the increased and intertwined human and technical interaction. This is not understood well enough and needs to be considered in the implementation process [4].

Existing literature has identified several types of barriers which will inhibiting the implementation process [3, 5, 6]. Extant findings state that barriers include both technological and organizational factors. So far, the majority of the scientific papers has dealt with technologies barriers and less on organizational barriers [7].

Regarding organizational barriers lack of knowledge and skilled workforce has been identified by several authors [3, 6, 8]. Other research studies has identified the resistance among employees' due to fear of loss of work if digital solution are able take over their work tasks [6, 7]. Resistance is also linked to the lack of skilled workforce where you react with resistance to a change due to lack of training and competencies needed for new work tasks.

Increased digitalization will change the way of working in manufacturing, and this is identified as a barrier regards to resistance to use these new technologies and the following new way of work practice [9]. One example could be use of real-time data to monitor and optimize processes, which will affect workers on several level [6]. If keeping up with traditional roles and working condition it will hampering the implementation process. It is necessary to have a process to rethink what is the new way of working and effective change management would be a key challenge for organization [3].

The lack of digital strategy alongside lack of resources are identified as the most prominent barriers by a study from Raj et al. [3]. This shows the importance of managers role of creating a roadmap and plan strategically in order to guide actions and investment in resources to manage the implementation process.

Regarding technical barriers the poor understanding of integration and systems architecture is identified as central barriers [6, 10]. Implementation of big data analytics is one concrete example, with the need of a clear understanding of the architecture of all operating IT system that potential generates the relevant data to apply. In additional, data quality is a challenge, needed to obtain quality of the decision-making process [3]. Another study shows that existing infrastructure with to old machines could be a problem in terms of the needed conversion [6]. Another key barrier is when implementing a digital technology, normally use of several different technology is needed due to dependency between each other, and this will make the implementation process more complex [6]. Here you need to understand how they function with each other.

3 Research Design

The purpose of our study is to learn from how the Norwegian manufacturing companies successfully implements digital technologies. Specifically, to identify: *What are the most prominent barriers preventing an efficient implementation process of digital technology at shop floor level?* By identifying the most pertinent barriers then we know what to solve, and simultaneously enabling a more efficient implementation process.

Given the what-type research question, an exploratory multiple case study approach was chosen [11]. Our purpose was to look for relevant evidence on what prevents an efficiency integration processes function in Norwegian manufacturing companies. Thus, the unit of analysis is the implementation processes of digital technologies at shop floor level in manufacturing industry. For the case study, six Norwegian manufacturing companies were chosen, being considered among the leading manufacturers in Norway.

Semi-structured in-depth interviews were chosen as data collection method. Well informed interviewees can provide important insight into facts of a topic in additional to their opinions [11]. Pre-developed questions were developed and formulated to cover barriers for efficiently implementation process of digital technologies. The goal was to get insight into how they approached the implementation process of digital technologies to understand theirs perceived barriers and what could be done in a better way. Least five interviews were performed at each company, including factory manager, production manager, technology manager of R&D manager, operators and a representant from the union. The interviews were conducted at case company's production site or through conference call (Teams). All the interviews were recorded enabling for more accurate representation of the conversation.

4 Case Description

The Norwegian manufacturing companies included in this study represent manufacturing industries in different markets (see Table 1), of a different size, organization, experience, and history and are in different levels in their digital development. This probably also affects their approach to digital technology. But even though the companies have different starting points, they also have some common features. They are part of a competitive industry and are global players. They have cutting-edge expertise in their specialized fields. They largely base today's productivity on efficient organization, automation and robotization of labor-intensive processes.

Table 1. Overview of the case companies.

Case	Industry	Ownership
A	Defense	Subsidiary of a Nordic corporation
B	Subsea	Subsidiary of a global corporation
C	Shipping	Subsidiary of a global corporation
D	Food	Norwegian corporation
E	Metallurgy	Subsidiary of a Norwegian group
F	Metallurgy	Subsidiary of a global corporation

To address the question about the most prominent barriers to the implementation process about digital technologies at manufacturing area, each of the case companies chosen a common project were all the respondents were involved in some way.

5 Findings and Discussion

5.1 Goals and Attitude Towards Digitalization

Before we discuss the barriers preventing implementation process, we should briefly discuss the overall goals and attitude towards digitalization in the six companies. The major overall goal for all six companies is improved efficiency in their production. Theirs is a world of intense competitiveness, where cost cutting innovation is needed to survive. This focuses their digitalization efforts most towards "Smart Production", and less towards "Smart Products", new business models and digital transformation. It might of course be argued that Smart Products, new business models and transformation would in the long run give the enterprises better long-term survival options, but this seems to be a steep step for the enterprises. Rather they focus on improved efficiency in existing processes. Within such a mindset of digitalization they are interested in understanding their own production system and optimize it, for which digital tools can be very useful. Further they want to cooperate better with suppliers and customers, exchange of various data is seen as very useful for that. Finally, and here we see the enterprises bordering on towards more transformative digitalization, they see "green" and "sustainable" as important and interesting goals to work towards. Partly because of concerns about the environment and resource expenditure, partly because they feel it is a market. Again, data collection and analytics are useful.

Regarding digital readiness and attitude towards change the whole enterprise is aware of the need, ready and willing (able being a more open question). The need for continuous improvement is accepted by all and institutionalized in the cooperation between unions and management. The Norwegian work life model and short way between management and shop floor supports broad involvement in idea generation, acquisition of knowledge and assessment of ideas. This should lead to easy implementation of digital improvement projects, but as we shall discuss more in detail there are several important barriers slowing the efforts.

When we asked about the most prominent barriers preventing an efficient implementation process of digital solution, the respondents express numerous problems they had already faced or feared, would arise.

5.2 Leadership and Human Resources

Three of the case companies highlight that the managers do not see the scope and the complexity of digitization. Thus, they are perceived as a bottleneck regarding prioritizing of technologies, hampering the implementation process and allocation of skilled resources. One reason for this emphasized from the informants is their lack of knowledge, and this is also seen as possible threat to the needed forthcoming digital transformation enabling their competitiveness.

An interesting finding in our study is the employee's acceptance of the forthcoming digital transformation, which was identified at all case companies. This is not in line with existing studies by [6, 7] which have identified resistance among employees' due to fair of loss of work. One explanation for this is the low level of hierarchical in the organization and the involvement of employees at shop floor level who are applying apply the technology at daily basis. Another explanation is the strong emphasis on the collaboration between employees, managers, and union in the Norwegian life work model [12]. This has turned into a culture based on trustful collaboration and this may be different than in the study by [6, 7]. The existing employee's acceptance of the forthcoming digital transformation in Norwegian manufacturing industry for the future is a good starting point.

5.3 Lack of Competence and Systematical Learning Process

One specific barrier was lack of competence within the field digitalization, and the explanation was about the forthcoming digital transformation requires new type of knowledge and competence. One example was within data analytics, algorithms and interaction design. This also created a longer implementation process due to more unexpected problems due to absence of competence.

As the case companies were very much aware of this problem, they had developed strategies to solving in it. Their strategies here could be divided in two: Hire external competence (consultants, technology suppliers, and researchers) or acquire in-house competence by hiring people. An experience from use of consultants is the difficultness of creating a systematical learning process in the implementation phase due to lack of continuous presence. In additional, in the end of the implementation process they lack access to the expertise. Undoubtedly, the case companies preferred in-house competence, but this was not always as easy for them to hire. For the future, they were convinced that digitalization would be one of their core competences.

5.4 Also an Organizational Issue

Another interesting finding is that the main focus in the implementation process is on technical issues and less on organizational issues. Several leaders in our study highlighted that leader of technology projects struggle to relate to the projects as organizational development projects. They believe this is an underestimated area, which is important to understand and address. They also argued that if they had focused more on the organizational issues, they may have used less resources in total. Digitization is not just about technology, but also about how people should use the technology. In practice, this means that we have to think differently about organization due to roles and distribution of functions between employees are changing. How the individual works, and who works together on the various tasks, will thus change. Therefore, it becomes important that the company analyzes the work processes and finds the best possible division of work internally and across departments.

5.5 Technical Issues

Some technical problems were also pertinent, like system integration. Systems must be integrated with other systems and here the technology suppliers have not come far enough. Another barrier was the challenges of the acquisition of data to actually obtained the needed data and with sufficient quality, enabling solution for decision support.

Sharing of data was seen as a potential asset, but both legal, strategic and technical issues hampered this. This was also a challenge within their own group due to different maturity level between the enterprises and different regulation, both due to location in different countries.

6 Concluding Remarks

The existing wave of improvement in manufacturing industry, is strongly driven by the application of digital technologies, affected by the concept of Industry 4.0. However, the implementation process for digital technologies at shop floor level is not a trivial task.

The above review indicates that both technical and organization aspects have to be taken care of in the implementation phase, where the organizational aspects are seen as the most underestimated. Undoubtedly, the need for digital competence was the most worrisome prominent barriers due to new area of knowledge the industry does not normally possess today and the lack of availability. Furthermore, this study reveals that organizational development is underestimated in the implementation process. More specifically, digitalization is not just about technology, but also about how the humans should use the technology. In additional it requires new ways of performing leadership due to the complexities that will arise from the increased and intertwined human and technical interaction. This is not understood well enough and needs to be considered in the implementation process. Some technical problems were also pertinent, like system integration. Sharing of data was seen as a potential asset, but both legal, strategic and technical issues hampered this. All the identified barriers are intertwined and interdependent and this shows the need for development of a digital strategy [3] enabling to overcome barriers as shown in Fig. 1.

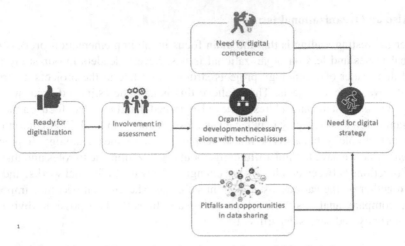

Fig. 1. The dependences of the prominent barriers and the need for a digital strategy to overcome those.

Rising awareness of these prominent barriers may help manufacturing companies to enabling a smoother implementation process of digital technologies in the era of Industry 4.0. Notwithstanding, more research is needed to enhance the results and to increase generalizability.

Acknowledgement. The authors would like to thank to all companies who took part of this study and the research project *"The lean-digitalization paradox: toward strategic digitalization"*. Latter funded by the Research Council of Norway.

References

1. Kagermann, H., Wahlster, W., Helbig, J., (eds.) Recommendations for implementing the strategic initiative Industrie 4.0 in Final report of the Industrie 4.0 Working Group. Frankfurt (2013)
2. Lall, M., Torvatn, H., Seim, E.A.: Towards industry 4.0: increased need for situational awareness on the shop floor. In: Lödding, H., Riedel, R., Thoben, K.-D., von Cieminski, G., Kiritsis, D. (eds.) APMS 2017. IAICT, vol. 513, pp. 322–329. Springer, Cham (2017). https://doi.org/10.1007/978-3-319-66923-6_38
3. Raj, A., Dwivdi, G., Sharma, A., de Sousa Jabbour, A.B., Rajak, S.: Barriers to the adoption of industry 4.0 technologies in the manufacturing sector: an inter-country comparative perspective. Int. J. Prod. Econ. **224**, 1–17 (2020)
4. Davies, R., Coole, T., Smith, A.: Review of socio-technical considerations to ensure successful implementation of industry 4.0. Procedia Manuf. **11**, 1288–1295 (2017)
5. Horvath, D., Szabo, R.Z.: Driving force and barriers of industry 4.0: do multinational and small and medium-sized companies have equal opportunities? Technol. Forecast. Soc. Change **46**, 119–132 (2019)
6. Vogelsang, K., Packmohr, S., Hoppe, U.: Barriers to digital transformation in manufacturing: development of a research agenda. In: Proceedings of the 52nd Hawaii International Conference on System Science (2019)

7. Müller, J.M.: Assessing the barriers to industry 4.0 implementation from workers' perspective. In: IFAC PapersOnLine, Elsevier, pp. 2189–2194 (2019)

8. Kiel, D., Arnold, C., Voigt, K.I.: The influence of the industrial internet of things on business models of established manufacturing companies - a business level perspective. Technovation **68**, 4–19 (2017)

9. Haddud, A., DeSouza, A., Khare, A., Lee, H.: Examining potential benefits and challenges associated with the internet of things in supply chains. J. Manuf. Technol. Manag. **28**(8), 1055–1085 (2017)

10. Dremel, C.: Barriers to the adoption of big data analytics in the automotive sector. In: Twenty-Third Americas Conference on Information Systems, Boston, pp. 1–10 (2017)

11. Yin, R.K.: Case Study Research. Design and Methods. Fourth ed. Vol. 5, Sage Publications, Beverly Hills (2009)

12. Levin, M., Nilsen, T., Ravn, J.E., Øyum, L. Demokrati i arbeidslivet. Den norske smarbeidsmodellen som konkurransefortrinn. Fagbokforlaget, Bergen (2012).

Consistent Maintenance Order Processing with Digital Assistance Systems

Robert Rost$^{(\boxtimes)}$ ⓘ and Axel Friedewald

Hamburg University of Technology, Hamburg, Germany
{robert.rost,friedewald}@tuhh.de

Abstract. Augmented reality-based digital assistance systems have proven their potential to support with instructions considering numerous application scenarios in the product life cycle. For the maintenance of machines and plants, however, their use becomes particularly efficient if the diagnosis at the operator's site can be effectively supported, so that the service provider and his experts can make accurate diagnoses for this maintenance job, plan the execution including the spare parts logistics precisely, and document as well as billing the maintenance case with low effort. For this purpose, a modular digital assistance system is presented that provides support adapted to the process phases.

Keywords: Augmented reality · Digital assistance systems · Maintenance

1 Introduction and Motivation

Performing maintenance and repair work with efficient processes and tools is a key success driver for their providers and users. For ship maintenance, for example, there are usually only short time intervals available when the ship is in port for loading and unloading. If not all the required spare parts are available in this narrow time window, a further journey by the service technician becomes necessary, as delays lead to increasing costs and decreasing customer satisfaction with the service [1]. An early assessment of the defect enables the service technician to plan the work in detail in advance and to schedule the necessary spare parts. In addition, all the relevant information must be readily available on site and subsequently documented in a structured way with minimum effort. This increases transparency for the customer and enables internal evaluations to improve service quality control loops.

Digital assistance systems represent an established means of process optimization in the described field. A special form of assistance systems are augmented reality-based systems, which are being intensively developed in research both for assembly [e.g. 2–4] and for maintenance [e.g. 5, 6]. Remote support receives a particular emphasis in numerous industrial applications, as it supports inexperienced users through contact with experts in the control center, leveraging visual cues and audio instructions during maintenance execution [e.g. 7, 8].

Published by Springer Nature Switzerland AG 2021
A. Dolgui et al. (Eds.): APMS 2021, IFIP AICT 632, pp. 102–111, 2021.
https://doi.org/10.1007/978-3-030-85906-0_12

The following section presents a more comprehensive end-to-end approach that supports the entire order processing, from diagnosis to work documentation, and is based on the assumption that it will be carried out by experienced service technicians, thus setting different priorities compared with "classic" remote support solutions. The hardware primarily used for this purpose are tablets and smartphones, as they are familiar to potential users and in this case offer greater potential than hardware found in the hands-free environment. The article firstly clarifies the individual phases of the maintenance process using a ship engine as example and presents the necessary system architecture to support them. Subsequently, the implementation for the individual phases is explained and the economic potential is demonstrated.

2   System Architecture

Different stakeholders on the customer and the service provider side are involved in processing a maintenance order and they must be supported in different ways according to their activities in the overall process. Those activities therefore give rise to requirements for the development and design of a holistic assistance environment, which should be characterized by precise issue localization and continuous information flows without media discontinuities.

2.1   Maintenance Order Processing and Its Requirements

Figure 1 shows the exemplary processing of a maintenance order. The order is triggered by the occurrence of a defect on the maintenance object, in this example a marine engine. To do this, the service provider must first be supplied with symptoms presented as extensively as possible.

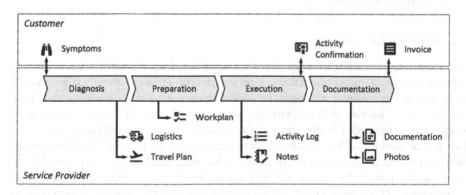

Fig. 1. Maintenance order processing

Then a diagnosis must be carried out so that corrective measures can be determined correctly. At the same time, a maintenance order is generated to reference processing and billing down the line. The service provider's technicians then organize the spare part logistics and travel arrangements. Using the customer's symptom survey and the maintenance history, the service technician carries out the case-specific work plan for the maintenance task and documents working times, work results and special features.

Based on this, an activity log is created and confirmed by the customer as an elementary part of the invoicing for the order and further case evaluation by the service specialist. Numerous process reviews with service technicians and interviews with operations managers have resulted in the following requirements with respect to the process above:

- **Symptom recording.** The less experienced onboard technician requires extensive support in symptom recording by means of a predefined symptom hierarchy, if necessary with example images or sounds. Furthermore, it must be possible to locate the symptoms for unequivocal identification.
- **Guidance.** If this support is not sufficient, support of the onboard technician in the form of remote support by experts from the service provider may be necessary. Navigation instructions and guidance are required, e.g., to perform certain measurements.
- **Expert dialog.** For the preparation of the maintenance execution, the location-specific knowledge of the symptoms is helpful. In difficult cases, the definition of remedial activities is already organized today via internal groups in relevant messengers. This expert dialog can be further optimized by a joint case review in the 3D model.
- **Connection to spare parts catalog and maintenance history.** The integration of the assistance system into the corresponding corporate IT (in particular the spare parts catalog and the maintenance history) is indispensable for end-to-end order processing.
- **Automated documentation and report generation.** Today, the effort required to log maintenance work is characterized by handwritten notes, photos and subsequent the time-consuming compilation of the report. At the same time, this leads to high expenses and a high error potential when preparing future maintenance measures on the same machine. Hence, a reduction in effort must be achieved through partial automation and structuring.

2.2 Platform Components

Augmented reality (AR) can be used for a location-based representation of work instructions, leveraging a digital assistance system that overlays real environments with virtual content while maintaining a constant positional reference between those two and allowing the user to interact with this virtual content in real-time [9]. The main reason for using augmented reality in this context is to provide an intuitive and highly productive [4] environment for on-board technicians to perform diagnostic activities. However, for holistic process support, the system needs to be integrated into the corporate IT, and needs to be optimized regarding the user interaction for the specific sub-processes of maintenance. This applies in particular a diagnosis assistant, communication via cooperation modules and extensive automation of reporting and documentation. The overall system (Fig. 2) for end-to-end maintenance assistance can be configured in three main components for this purpose [10]:

- **Creator.** A desktop-based authoring system for effortless creation of augmented reality-capable maintenance instructions. The creation of textual information is based on templates, geometrical animations can be created automatically by the system but as well individually with the help of an additional virtual reality (VR) module [11].

- **Visualizer.** An augmented reality-based diagnostic assistant for on-board technicians to easily capture symptoms. Furthermore it serves as a digital service document for service technicians to provide information during the execution as well as automatic documentation for later reporting. At the same time it performs as a communication tool for live collaboration with a remote expert.

- **Director.** The server backend for the storage, provision and processing (especially of collaborative real-time sessions) of both diagnostic and maintenance runs, that serves as a connector to the company's internal spare parts management, maintenance history and business order processing. It provides extended functions for the conversion of existing documents as well as for the preparation of 3D models for the Creator and Visualizer (especially VR / AR specific).

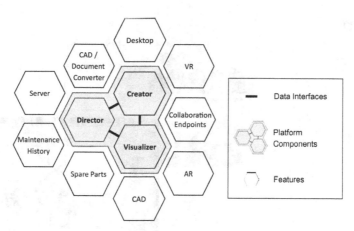

Fig. 2. DIA platform [10]

3   Diagnostic Assistant for On-Board Technicians

In order to provide the service technician with a precise view of the maintenance task as comprehensively as possible in advance, the on-board personnel must be enabled to describe the problem with the highest feasible accuracy. Therefore the diagnostic assistant (Fig. 3 right) can be supplied directly with the corresponding component. A classic aid for this purpose are fault or symptom catalogs [12], which can be linked to the underlying geometry as possible component attributes for the assistance system and can then be selected in the assistance system via selection menus, if necessary enriched with example images or typical noise samples. In addition, it is possible to create photos or sound recordings of the respective case using the assistance system, whereby the exact location of the recordings / measurements / photos are documented due to the (AR) tracking of the system. This diagnosis from the on-board personnel can be supported through predefined work instructions displayed by the assistance system in the AR display. If this form of support is not sufficient, it is possible to switch to the cooperation mode of the assistance system, in which the supervising expert sees the information recorded by the on-board personnel on his terminal and can provide further instructions. These can be navigation instructions (e.g. supported by directional arrows) for finding specific measurement points or further supplementary instructions for action that can be generated ad-hoc. Since the target group is usually familiar with smartphones (also from the private sector), an adapted smartphone interface was also created in analogy to [13], which is particularly contributory to acceptance. This can further simplify symptom recording and make diagnosis by the expert correspondingly more precise.

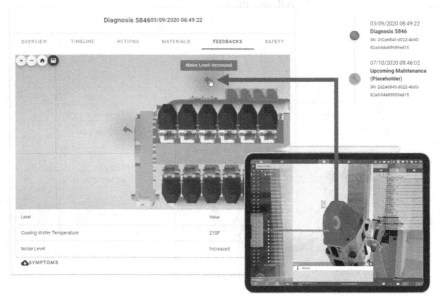

Fig. 3. Localized diagnostic measurements

4 Assistant for Service Technicians

On the service technician side, the process is divided into the three phases of preparation, execution and documentation. The following sections describe the approach for each phase.

4.1 Preparation

After the maintenance order has been placed, the symptom report generated by the customer (if necessary with the help of an export from the service provider) can be assigned to the order in the assistance system environment, thus ensuring the link to the service provider's billing systems. This is done using the corresponding functions of the Director module, which provides the interfaces to financial accounting, the spare parts catalog and the maintenance history of the defective device, where it is managed as an additional entry or case. The history includes and combines all maintenance events in a chronological order (starting from the past) as well as the detailed maintenance logs recorded by means of the digital assistance system. The maintenance tasks can then be prepared either on the PC or on the tablet, since both systems generate the same data format for later use on tablet or smartphone. The result is an instruction manual adapted to the specific case [14], which is generated from available templates. If the service expert wants to consult with his colleagues on difficult diagnoses, this is also supported by the system's collaboration mode, as the entire scope of information from the assistance system is then immediately available to the colleagues and does not have to be posted in a messenger group at great expense. Both direct communication and time-delayed annotations can be used here.

4.2 Execution

The execution of maintenance work is usually characterized by the use of the CAD view of the assistance system as well as the supplementary case-specific text information such as, for example, tightening torques of individual screws that deviate from the standard [15]. The reason lies in the service technician's basic familiarity with the subject matter, as observation of numerous cases of use has shown. The acknowledgement of individual steps (and the recording of new settings made during maintenance) (Fig. 4) also makes it easy to document how the work was carried out. Supplementary photos are captured by the assistance system (again, correctly located) and automatically assigned to the work step.

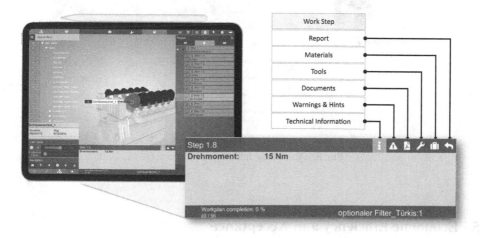

Fig. 4. Visualizer UI for service technicians [15]

4.3 Documentation

With the selection of a work step the recording of the start time takes place and with the finished message the total duration is recorded (Fig. 5). This log report helps in the subsequent calculation of the time spent on the work as well as the optimization of internal cost calculations. At the same time, the scope and type of activities are also recorded via the work step recording.

If consumables or spare parts are stored for a work step, these are also booked with the confirmation of a work step and listed in the session log for billing later on.

In the previous report generation, both the formulation of handwritten notes and the naming and assignment of photos take up a lot of time. In order to avoid this high effort of a manual report creation, the assistance system was extended by an automatic reporting feature. The entries described in 4.2 are automatically summarized in a digital maintenance log. This includes all work performed, tools used and associated photos or sound recordings. This data record can then be formatted and forwarded depending on its intended use.

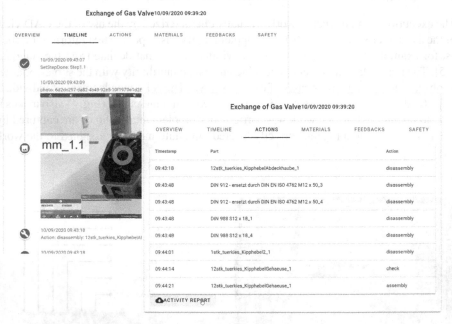

Fig. 5. Automatic maintenance report

5 Economic Efficiency and Acceptance

The benefits of the use of assistance systems were extensively investigated at several maritime component manufacturers which also provide service, with regard to their productivity increase and user acceptance. Exemplary for one engine manufacturer, savings potentials for the creation of work instructions of 51% [6] were found. The test took place in a laboratory environment where the test subjects had to create the same maintenance instructions with a conventional system and the DIA Creator solution. When it comes to the processing of the maintenance order savings the visualizer solution was used on a test basis in a two-day maintenance operation on control cabinets (see Fig. 6). In order to examine the productivity increase, the working process was recorded to find the distribution of working time across the different phases of order processing. Afterwards the key users estimated the savings per phase. Especially in the phases of condition analysis (50%), function check (20%) and action documentation (40%) a high potential for increasing productivity could be demonstrated in this way. Supplementary expert interviews in the field of engine maintenance have even shown that the documentation phase could be shortened by up to 80%.

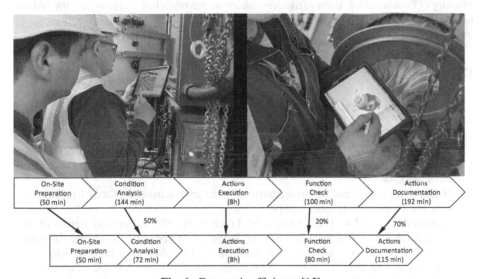

Fig. 6. Economic efficiency [15]

In addition, a second evaluation of the visualizer component was carried out together with service technicians from the engine repair division, which performed an exchange of a gas valve. Time was measured for the execution both with the help of conventional paper documents and the visualizer. It has been shown that the proportion of time spent on information-related activities could be reduced by 35% [16].

Since profitability and customer satisfaction for the system operator depend directly on accurate symptom recordings, the acceptance of a tablet or smartphone application (always at hand) is crucial for their (on-board) personnel, which was rated positively in another survey [16].

6 Outlook

It is precisely the integration into the overall process with diverse support for subtasks characterized by different challenges that demonstrates the benefits of digital AR-based assistance systems. Nevertheless, implementation in real processes is a major challenge due to the large number of interfaces to company IT systems. In particular, use across company boundaries makes operation and use of the solution more difficult. For further dissemination in other holistic process chains with several companies involved, further development into a web-based solution with reduced deployment effort can open up new potential uses.

Acknowledgements. The presented work was done in cooperation with maritime suppliers within the research project WASSER (Wartung und Service von Schiffen mit erweiterter Realität/Maintenance and Service of Ships with Augmented Reality), funded by the German Federal Ministry of Economics and Energy (Bundesministerium für Wirtschaft und Energie – BMWi) due to a decision of the German Bundestag.

References

1. Kühne, R.: Visualisierung der Prozeßqualität. In: Nedeß, Chr.; Friedewald, A. (ed.) Wissen schafft Qualität, Band III – Servicemanagement in der neuen Fabrik, FQS-DGQ-Band 96–08, Beuth, Berlin, pp. 121–131 (1997)
2. Bottani, E., Vignali, G.: Augmented reality technology in the manufacturing industry: a review of the last decade. IISE Trans. **51**(3), 284–310 (2019). https://doi.org/10.1080/24725854.2018.1493244
3. Halata, P.-S.: Augmented-Reality-gestützte Informationsbereitstellung für die Unikatproduktion, PhD-Thesis, TU Hamburg (2018)
4. Friedewald, A., Halata, P.S., Meluzov, N., Lödding, H.: The productivity impact of augmented reality in one-off manufacturing. In: Schlick, C.M. (ed.) Megatrend Digitalisierung - Potenziale der Arbeits- und Betriebsorganisation, pp. 141–162, GITO, Berlin (2016)
5. Petersen, P.: Enhancing the quality and reliability of maintenance operations using mixed reality. In: Bertram, V. (ed.) 19th International Conference on Computer and IT Applications in the Maritime Industries (COMPIT 2020), Proceedings, Pontignano, pp. 38–47 (2020)
6. Meluzov, N., Friedewald, A., Mundt, C., Lödding, H.: Produktivitätssteigerung in der Instandhaltung durch digitale Assistenzsysteme. In: Biedermann, H. (ed.) Digitalisierte Instandhaltung. Stand und Perspektiven. 33. Instandhaltungsforum (Ed. ÖVIA) Proceedimgs, TÜV-Verlag, Köln, pp. 181–197 (2019)
7. PTC Announces Vuforia Chalk App for Augmented Reality Communications. https://www.ptc.com/en/news/2017/vuforia-chalk. Accessed 07 Apr 2021
8. Features Made for a Complete New Way of Remote Collaboration. https://oculavis.de/en/product/features/. Accessed 07 Apr 2021
9. Azuma, R.T.: A survey of augmented reality. Presence: Teleoperators and Virtual Environ. **6**(4), 355–385 (1997). https://doi.org/10.1162/pres.1997.6.4.355
10. Meluzov, N., Friedewald, A., Elzalabany, A., Lödding, H.: Aufwandsarme erstellung von augmented-reality-anleitungen für die maritime instandhaltung. In: Lukas, U.v., et al. (ed.) Go-3D 2019 "Mit 3D Richtung Maritim 4.0". Proceedings, Rostock, pp. 31–44 (2019)

11. Meluzov, N., Friedewald, A.: Modular authoring of augmented reality based service instructions. In: Bertram, V. (ed.) 17th International Conference on Computer and IT Applications in the Maritime Industries (COMPIT 2018). Proceedings, Pavone, pp. 176–188 (2018)
12. Plog, J.: Expertensystemunterstützte Qualitätssicherung bei der Fertigung von Elastomerteilen, PhD-Thesis, TU Hamburg-Harburg (1989)
13. Jahn, N., Friedewald, A., Lödding, H.: Using the smartphone as an augmented reality device in ETO industry. In: Lalic, B., Majstorovic, V., Marjanovic, U., von Cieminski, G., Romero, D. (eds.) APMS 2020. IAICT, vol. 592, pp. 538–546. Springer, Cham (2020). https://doi.org/10.1007/978-3-030-57997-5_62
14. Friedewald, A., Meluzov, N., Rost, R.: Potentials of augmented reality in aircraft assembly and MRO. In: Estorff, O.v., Thielecke, F. (ed.) 6th International Workshop on Aircraft System Technologies (AST 2017). Proceedings, Shaker, Aachen, pp. 295–306 (2017)
15. Meluzov, N., Rost, R., Friedewald, A.: Holistic maintenance support with a digital as-sistance, In: Bertram, V. (ed.) 19th International Conference on Computer and IT Appli-cations in the Maritime Industries (COMPIT 2020), Proceedings, Pavone, pp. 48–62 (2020)
16. Lödding, H., Friedewald, A., Meluzov, N., Rost, R.: Wartung und Service von Schiffen mit erweiterter Realität (WASSER) – Grundlagen (GRUND). Final Report, TU Hamburg 2021

Supporting Manufacturing Processes Design Using Stakeholder Opinions and Sentiment Analysis

Egon Lüftenegger(iD) and Selver Softic(✉)(iD)

CAMPUS 02 University of Applied Sciences, Graz, Austria
{egon.lueftenegger,selver.softic}@campus02.at

Abstract. In this paper we present a novel approach of empowering the design of business processes in manufacturing and broader by using sentiment analysis on collaborative comments collected during the design phase of business processes. This method involves the implicit information of sentiment hidden behind the suggestions for the process improvements. To discover and utilize the sentiment for process redesign we trained and tested our Sentiment Analysis Module (SAM). This module classifies and scores the sentiment of comments and acts as a part of software tool for BPMN based modeling and annotation. As initial step we designed a real world use case to demonstrate the possibilities of our software. The preliminary result with evaluation test case seem to be promising regarding effective ranking and classifying the improvement proposals on BPMN design of manufacturing processes. However, there is still plenty of space for improvements in trainings data segment and in extending the tool with social BPMN functionality.

Keywords: Sentiment analysis · Business process redesign · Business process management

1 Introduction and Motivation

Traditional process design approaches often follow a top-down decomposition resulting in a long running improvement process, that requires intensive negotiations for achieving effective changes. However, unpredictable market changes require more flexibility on this matter. Changing preferences in the customer's needs require fast changes in manufacturing process models. Hence, there is a need for an agile approach for reacting to the changing business landscape.

One of the possible empowerment could be using the advanced technologies like artificial intelligence and machine learning and methods such as sentiment analysis to analyze in fast and efficient way the opinions and insights from different stakeholder in manufacturing process. In this paper we consider such case by involving a sentiment analysis module into a conventional design process scenario and using it as empowering assistant for prioritization of redesign suggestions and comments on the process.

A. Dolgui et al. (Eds.): APMS 2021, IFIP AICT 632, pp. 112–117, 2021.
https://doi.org/10.1007/978-3-030-85906-0_13

2   Related Work

2.1   Business Process Modeling

The overall goal of Business Process Modeling is to establish a common perspective and understanding for a business process within an enterprise between the relevant stakeholders involved. Hereby, the most common graphical representation such as flowchart [1] or similar serves as base to show the process steps and workflows. This approach is widely used to recognize and prevent potential weaknesses and implement improvements in companies processes as well as to offer a good base for comprehensive understanding of a processes in general.

2.2   BPMN

The BPMN 2.0 (Object Management Group, 2011) is a new standard for business process specification developed by a variety of Business Process Modeling (BPM) tool vendors. This standard is one of the most important forms of representing business process models, offering clear and simple semantics to describe the business process of a business [2,3]. This language was developed with the intention of modeling typical business modeling activities [4,5].

2.3   Business Process Redesign

Business Process Redesign (BPR) aims at improvement of vital aspects of business processes aiming at achieving some special goal e.g. reducing costs. The importance of BPR was initially outlined by the work of Davenport and Short [6] in early 90s. However, this wave of enthusiasm flattened out by the end of decade due to the concept misuse, immaturity of necessary tools and too intensive approach regarding the phase of application.

Revival of the BPR concept according to [7] happened in relation to BPM, where several studies that appeared showed that organizations which are more process oriented performed better then those which did not follow this paradigm. Studies that followed confirmed these findings. This established the new credibility to the process thinking. The BPR has been seen in this case as set of tools that can be used within BPM.

2.4   BPM Lifecycle

BPM lifecycle described in [7] represents different phases of the process beginning by analysis and ending by process monitoring and controlling and process discovery. Our usage scenario in this lifecycle is placed between the process analysis and process redesign phases. During the design phase of the BPM lifecycle, social software adequately integrates the needs of all stakeholders [8].

2.5   Sentiment Analysis and Opinion Mining in Business Processes

Data mining is being used in the field of BPM for process mining. The process mining is focused on processes at run-time, more precisely for re-creating a business process from systems logs. Opinion mining is a sub-discipline of data mining and computational linguistics for extracting, classifying, understanding and assessing opinions. Sentiment analysis is often used in opinion mining for extracting opinions expressed in text. However, current research is focused on e-business, e-commerce, social media and social networks like Twitter and Flickr rather than BPM and BPR [9].

3   Supporting the Process Design

We use our SentiPromo Tool [10] for this purpose to empower the (re)-design through integration of stakeholder's needs expressed as opinions. SentiProMo Tool[1] was developed in our department in order to provide a possibility of a role based social intervention within the business process (re)-design. The roles supported in this tool are leaned on prior research on business process knowledge management framework [11]: Activity Performer (AP), Process Owner (PO), Process Designer (PD), Superior Decision Maker (SDM) and Customer (C). According to [8] BPM tools that follow the social BPM paradigm provide a mechanism to handle priorities within a business process [8]. This also applies to SentiProMo Tool.

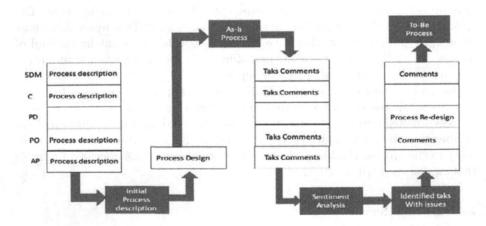

Fig. 1. Commenting workflow and the role of sentiment analysis.

Beside process modeler and business process repository module, the tool has the task commenting module which allows adding task-wise comments to process from the perspective of different roles.

---

[1] https://sites.google.com/view/sentipromo.

As empowerment of commenting process in background runs the Semantic Annotation Module (SAM) which classifies the comments and assign them to a positive or negative sentiment using a real score. Sentiment Analysis Module (SAM) was implemented using the ML .NET for classifying comments in English language [12]. The SAM module uses supervised learning as base for comment classification. The training data originates from Sentiment Labeled Sentence Data Set from UCI Machine Learning Repository[2] and from Sentiment140 data set from Stanford[3]. The training was preformed with different number of iteration on different algorithms. Averaged perceptron binary classification model turned to be the best choice in this case. This model shows best AUC (Area Under The Curve) (approx. 0,89) and other relevant measures according to [13].

4   Application Use Case

Each time we use the task commenting module to comment a single task from a stakeholders perspective as shown in Fig. 2 SAM module calculates on the fly the sentiment score for the given comment.

Figure 3, shows the processed sentiment analysis of the stakeholders' comments over all commented tasks within the SentiProMo tool. Each processed comment is presented as a row. For each row, we have the following elements presented as columns from the leftmost to the rightmost as follows: the task identifier, the task name, the stakeholders' category (from the identified stakeholders we mentioned before), the comment made by a specific stakeholders, the calculated sentiment score as positive or negative number and a timestamp that registers the time of the comment insertion by the corresponding stakeholder.

Figure 4, shows an overview score as positive or negative number performed by SentiProMo of the sentiment of the whole process as negative sentiment and positive sentiment. The software calculates the resulting number by adding all negative and positives sentiments of each task.

Additionally the same score can be seen out the perspective of single roles in process. For instance in Fig. 5 we see te sentiment score over all tasks in particular for the role of 'Activity Performer'.

5   Conclusion and Outlook

We use sentiment analysis as empowerment, in the context of process design. Sentiment analysis seems to be a perfect fit for the field of BPR because we can analyze the user's opinions with it and engage immediate changes in the process re-design. In preliminary case study we obtained also encouraging results for accuracy, sensitivity, specificity and F1-score. In the future we will provide more training data to improve the performance of sentiment analysis module and we will extend our software tool with options to comment the process remotely using the web interfaces.

---

[2] https://archive.ics.uci.edu/ml/datasets/Sentiment+Labelled+Sentence.
[3] http://help.sentiment140.com/for-students/.

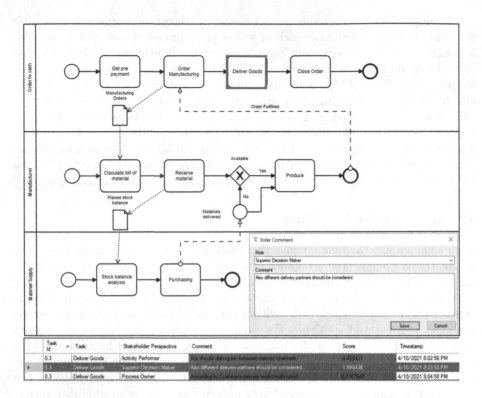

Fig. 2. Commenting Toyota supply chain management process as defined in [14].

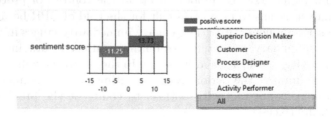

Task Id	Task	Stakeholder Perspective	Comment	Score	Timestamp
2.2	Purchasing	Activity Performer	We need to adjust the limits for purchasing to enable the flexibility regarding price changes.	-4.835219	4/10/2021 8:08:33 PM
0.3	Deliver Goods	Activity Performer	We should distinguish between delivery channels.	-4.428431	4/10/2021 8:02:56 PM
0.3	Deliver Goods	Superior Decision Maker	Also different delivery partners should be considered.	-1.990436	4/10/2021 8:03:58 PM
0.3	Deliver Goods	Process Owner	According to Customers delivery works really good.	0.274764?	4/10/2021 8:04:58 PM
2.2	Purchasing	Superior Decision Maker	Purchasing quality materials should be the main goal, even if the price is higher.	2.001694	4/10/2021 8:07:17 PM
1.3	Produce	Activity Performer	Producing speeds depends on quality of materials.	11.45397	4/10/2021 8:10:21 PM

Fig. 3. Overview over all comments and sentiment ratings.

Fig. 4. Overall sentiment score in process.

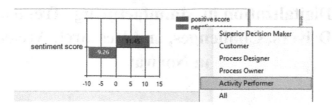

Fig. 5. Overall sentiment score of 'Activity Performer' role in process.

References

1. Wynn, D.C., Clarkson, P.J.: Process models in design and development. Res. Eng. Des. **29**(2), 161–202 (2017). https://doi.org/10.1007/s00163-017-0262-7
2. Allweyer, T.: BPMN 2.0: Introduction to the Standard for Business Process Modeling. Books on Demand (2009)
3. Zor, S., Schumm, D., Leymann, F.: A proposal of bpmn extensions for the manufacturing domain. In: Proceedings of the 44th CIRP International Conference on Manufacturing Systems (2011)
4. Recker, J., Indulska, M., Rosemann, M., Green, P.: How good is BPMN really? Insights from theory and practice. In: Proceedings of the 14th European Conference on Information Systems, ECIS 2006 (January 2006)
5. Muehlen, M., Recker, J.: How much language is enough? Theoretical and practical use of the business process modeling notation. In: Bellahsène, Z., Léonard, M. (eds.) CAiSE 2008. LNCS, vol. 5074, pp. 465–479. Springer, Heidelberg (2008). https://doi.org/10.1007/978-3-540-69534-9_35
6. Davenport, T.H., Short, J.E.: The new industrial engineering: information technology and business process redesign. Sloan Manage. Rev. **31**(4), 11–27 (1990)
7. Dumas, M., La Rosa, M., Mendling, J., Reijers, H.A.: Process-aware information systems. In: Fundamentals of Business Process Management, pp. 341–369. Springer, Heidelberg (2018). https://doi.org/10.1007/978-3-662-56509-4_9
8. Schmidt, R., Nurcan, S.: BPM and social software. In: Ardagna, D., Mecella, M., Yang, J. (eds.) BPM 2008. LNBIP, vol. 17, pp. 649–658. Springer, Heidelberg (2009). https://doi.org/10.1007/978-3-642-00328-8_65
9. Chen, H., Zimbra, D.: AI and opinion mining. IEEE Intell. Syst. **25**(3), 74–76 (2010)
10. Lüftenegger, E., Softic, S.: SentiProMo: a sentiment analysis-enabled social business process modeling tool. In: Del Río Ortega, A., Leopold, H., Santoro, F.M. (eds.) BPM 2020. LNBIP, vol. 397, pp. 83–89. Springer, Cham (2020). https://doi.org/10.1007/978-3-030-66498-5_7
11. Hrastnik, J., Cardoso, J., Kappe, F.: The business process knowledge framework, vol. 1, pp. 517–520 (2007)
12. Hrnjica, B., Music, D., Softic, S.: Model-based recommender systems. In: Al-Turjman, F. (ed.) Trends in Cloud-based IoT. EICC, pp. 125–146. Springer, Cham (2020). https://doi.org/10.1007/978-3-030-40037-8_8
13. Manning, C.D., Raghavan, P., Schütze, H.: Introduction to Information Retrieval. Cambridge University Press, USA (2008)
14. Shapiro, R., et al.: BPMN 2.0 Handbook Second Edition: Methods, Concepts, Case Studies and Standards in Business Process Management Notation. Future Strategies Inc. (2011)

Digitalization in Manufacturing: Trends, Drivers, Challenges, and Research Areas in Norway

Emrah Arica$^{(\boxtimes)}$ and Daryl Powell

SINTEF Manufacturing, Horten, Norway
emrah.arica@sintef.no

Abstract. The manufacturing industry has encountered a need for digital trans-formation during the past decade. To stay competitive, more and more manufac-turing companies are adopting digital technologies, either by internal efforts or through external help from consultants or collaborative research projects. This paper presents an overview of trends and challenges in the Norwegian industry and provides a framework of critical research areas for further efforts in the digi-talization of manufacturing. The framework is developed based on an analysis of six exemplary industrial research projects that focus on the subject of digitaliza-tion in manufacturing. The paper contributes to the literature by bringing practical insights that guide the digital transformation of manufacturing companies.

Keywords: Digitalization · Manufacturing · Industry 4.0

1 Introduction

The manufacturing industry is transforming to the Industry 4.0 era characterized by a high degree of automation and continuous data exchange in production, through the utilization of new digital solutions (e.g.. Sensorics, Augmented Reality, and industrial internet) and methodologies (e.g. Big Data Analytics) [1].

With the primary focus on knowledge-driven, complex, and technologically advanced products and services, Norwegian manufacturers' competitiveness and growth depend largely on the utilization of new digitalization technologies to achieve higher pro-ductivity as a high-cost country. Norwegian SMEs are especially challenged by investing in potentially capital-intensive systems and technologies, which makes research-driven innovation projects an essential driver of digital transformation.

This paper draws the digital transformation trends, drivers, and challenges in the Norwegian manufacturing industry, extracted from the industry-driven research projects conducted and coordinated by the SINTEF research center. Six exemplifying research project cases are analyzed and discussed. While existing frameworks point out the poten-tial applications and benefits of enabling technologies, studies on industrial application areas and implementation efforts are still scarce. The paper contributes to the literature by providing insights on the digitalization projects of manufacturing companies, as well as illustrates their requirements to guide further research activities.

© IFIP International Federation for Information Processing 2021
Published by Springer Nature Switzerland AG 2021
A. Dolgui et al. (Eds.): APMS 2021, IFIP AICT 632, pp. 118–125, 2021.
https://doi.org/10.1007/978-3-030-85906-0_14

2 Digitalization in Manufacturing

With the increasing industrial interest in Industry 4.0, researchers and policymakers have developed frameworks to define and characterize this emerging concept, and guide the industries in the digital transformation processes. The research work for guiding digital transformation in manufacturing can be categorized into three aspects: *application areas, enabling technologies, reference frameworks.*

Application areas of digitalization in manufacturing are growing with industrial interests. Some examples of the application areas are the following: (i) managing the material flows and production logistics more efficiently by for example implementing a cyber physical logistics system to increase the Kanban system with many variants of products [1]. (ii) enhancing the operator work, training, and their interaction with the systems by for example implementing Augmented Reality for work instructions and accelerating operator learning [2]. (iii) new business models and product services supported by digital technologies such as adopting a service platform that leverages the value of smart and connected resources for advanced service offerings (e.g. productivity improvement offering based on risk and reward sharing) [3]. (iv) sustainable manufacturing enhanced by new digital technologies such as developing a digital platform enabling a marketplace for sharing unused manufacturing capacities (e.g. materials, resources, technologies, and byproducts) [4].

Enabling technologies incorporate various technologies, including but not limited to sensors, robotics/automation, big data analytics, augmented reality to realize the vision of a data-driven, connected supply network, and to improve manufacturing operations at all levels (i.e. shop floor, factory, supply chain) of the supply network [1].

Reference frameworks aim to match the requirements of the companies with the application of enabling technologies and to guide them in the digital transformation process. The reference frameworks help companies at different levels, including but not limited to: (i) building a digitalization strategy aligned with the business and corporate strategies, and supporting the long-term digitalization transformation [5]. (ii) assessing the current digital maturity of a company, identifying the development requirements, and outlining the opportunities and constraints by digital maturity assessment tools [6]. This step is critical to match the requirements with implementation opportunities and constraints to avoid exceeding time and budget, and the underperformance of the implemented technologies. (iii) guiding the digital transformation steps by roadmaps [7]. (iv) evaluating the implementation of the enabling technologies in various aspects (e.g. performance, use) by evaluation methodologies [2].

3 Industry-Driven Projects on Digitalization in Manufacturing

This section presents the research projects conducted and coordinated by the SINTEF research center within the area of digitalization in manufacturing, and summarizes them in Table 1. The projects were defined by combining the research interests with industrial partner requirements.

3.1 Circulær

CIRCULÆR promises to enable the Norwegian industry to tackle economic and environmental challenges by combining lean thinking and digitalization with circular economy

(CE) principles. The European Green Deal defines the EU's environmental strategy and CE plan to halve waste by 2030. Following this notion, Norway's environmental policy brings to focus that its industries must reduce greenhouse gas emissions, minimize harmful discharges to water and increase energy efficiency. As such, the Norwegian industry must embark on the twin transition to zero- /low-emission solutions, while simultaneously advancing beyond the dominant (analog) linear economy, to remain competitive. For Norwegian companies, this transition requires new skills and capabilities throughout the organization. The underpinning idea and motivation for this project is to encourage and help organizations to discover and learn new ways of realizing opportunities for digitalization and circularity throughout their entire product portfolio.

3.2 Digitally-Enhanced Operator

The Digitally enhanced Operator (DEO) project was a Norwegian user-driven innovation project aimed to strengthen the autonomy, situation awareness, and teamwork of the production shop floor operators. An autonomous approach supported by enabling technologies was taken to enable the operators to make effective decisions. Strengthening the situation awareness of the operators aimed at increasing their responsibility in production, by providing continuously updated production status, implications of status, and precise projections of what will happen in the future. At the same time, operators depend on effective coordination in their teams to take a larger area of responsibility. The project involved two use cases to investigate, test, evaluate, and implement the digitalization methods and technologies in pilot cases. The first use case involved a producer of jet engine components that focused on testing Augmented Reality glasses for operator learning, placing dashboards on the shop floor to increase the situation awareness of the operators, and integrating sensors into the production system to obtain an overview of machine status in real-time. The second use case involved a producer of machine dampening tools and focused on developing a decision support tool for situation awareness and production control in the assembly department. The project has also characterized the need for developing a maturity assessment tool to analyze and evaluate the level of digital support given to the production operators in their daily activities and tasks and point out the needs and priorities for digitalization efforts on the production shop floor toward the Operator 4.0.

3.3 HUman MANufacturing (HUMAN)

The HUman MANufacturing (HUMAN) project was a European H2020 project coordinated by SINTEF and aimed to develop a platform that supports the human operator in performing their tasks with the desired quality, whilst ensuring their well-being. Co-creation principles with iterative study and feedback loops were used to engage with the manufacturing companies and operators, elicit the requirements, and develop, test, evaluate, and deploy the solutions.

AR was the primary enabling technology tested and implemented in the use cases with the main goal to increase productivity while ensuring the well-being of the operators. Three distinct end-users contributed to this co-creation process. The first use case involved an airplane manufacturer, targeting the operator that assembles multiple clamps in the assembly department. Due to its repetitive nature, this process may lead to mistakes that require additional time for fixing thereby reducing the production rate in the assembly department. The deployed AR solution provided step-by-step instructions to the operator on what and how to assemble, complemented by the verification of correct assembly thereby reducing the error probability. The second use case involved a designer and producer of industrial robots, targeting the assembly of a robot forearm, where due to multiple options and configuration may lead to assembly mistakes. The AR solution provided stepwise instructions where a quality checkpoint verified the correct application of the sealant before allowing the operator to proceed with the assembly. The third use case involved a furniture manufacturer where the work is seasonal and requires the recruitment of additional operators who may lack the necessary knowledge. Their training may result in a reduction of productivity as more experienced operators are required to support the new trainees. The AR solution supported the training process and reduced the need of involving experienced operators and the time to competence. An evaluation method was developed to evaluate the use cases, consisting of the following life cycle stages: data collection, technical testing, UX testing formative evaluation study, and a final study. The details of the evaluation method are provided in [2].

3.4 Lean Digital

The lean-digitalization paradox: Toward strategic digitalization (Lean Digital) aims to develop theories and managerial guidelines for digitalization of Norwegian industry based on lean principles with respect to planning, decisions systems, supplier collaboration, and work organization. The main concepts in this research project are lean management and digital manufacturing technologies. We propose that novel theoretical insights can be developed by framing the relationship between the two main concepts as a paradox. These insights will form the basis for improved managerial guidelines, leading to greater levels of workplace innovation.

3.5 Lean 4.0

The Lean European Action-learning Network utilizing Industry 4.0 (LEAN 4.0) project is a European Erasmus+ Knowledge Alliance project that seeks to integrate Industry 4.0 smart technologies with the proven Lean Manufacturing paradigm. The four partner countries (Belgium, Germany, Netherlands, and Norway) face many of the same problems with skill development and are preparing to address this significant challenge together. A readiness assessment for Industry 4.0 technologies in Northern Europe's high-value manufacturing industry has been created and deployed in the discrete manufacturing operations of four industry partners. A blended network action learning (BNAL) methodology has also been developed and is being used to guide problem-solving initiatives in the industry partners to develop digital lean solutions. LEAN 4.0 aims to develop novel education methods for the operations managers of the future.

3.6 SmartChain

The SmartChain was a Norwegian user-driven innovation project aimed at developing a lean value chain management system, by continuous real-time data exchange, monitoring, and control. The use case involved a producer of complex underwater surveillance systems, focusing on digitalizing the production value chain by designing, testing, and implementing a manufacturing execution system (MES). The project has initially focused on developing an overall digitalization strategy that considers lean implementation, establishes process stability and standardization, before automation and digitalization efforts. Once the suitable environment was established, a manufacturing execution system was designed, tested, and prototyped, involving the potential users of the system and benefitting largely from automation standards.

Table 1. Summary of the research projects on digitalization in manufacturing

Project	Application areas	Reference frameworks	Enabling technologies
Circulær	Lean manufacturing, sustainable production value chains, new business models	Enterprise-wide value stream mapping, Life cycle analysis	Dashboard, digital twin
Digitally enhanced operator	Production scheduling, monitoring and control, operator training	Digital maturity assessment tool	Sensors, dashboard, AR
HUMAN	Knowledge management operator learning and training	Co-design principles evaluation method	AR, exoskeleton
Lean digital	Digital Lean manufacturing dustainable production value chains	N/A	Sensors, dashboard, Big data
Lean 4.0	Digital Lean manufacturing	LEAN 4.0 Self assessment	Smart glasses, dashboard
Smart-chain	Production value chain monitoring and control	Digitalization strategy, automation standards (ISA95)	Manufacturing execution system

4 Critical Areas for Digitalization in Manufacturing Industry

Based on the lessons learned from the previous and current research projects recently conducted at the SINTEF research center, the following trends, drivers, challenges, research areas are identified for digitalization in the Norwegian manufacturing industry.

4.1 Trends and Drivers for Digitalization in Norwegian Manufacturing

Figure 1 illustrates the trends of digitalization in the Norwegian manufacturing industry and is explained below.

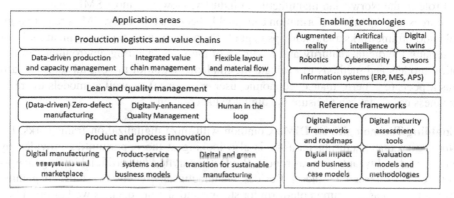

Fig. 1. Digitalization trends in the Norwegian manufacturing industry

Application Areas for DiM. The main application areas in the Norwegian companies can be classified into the following three main areas:

1) Lean and quality management: This area incorporates the topics such as data-driven zero-defect manufacturing, digitally enhanced quality management, and human-in-the-loop that incorporates human-machine interface, knowledge sharing, technology-supported learning, and augmentation and autonomy of the workers are of great interest in the Norwegian context. These trends are largely driven by the following characteristics of the Norwegian manufacturing industry: (i) flat organizational structure that aims to increase the autonomy of the employees to take more responsibilities on the production system. (ii) competitiveness goals as a high-cost country in the production and delivery of the customized, technologically advanced, and complex products and services, which require a highly competent workforce (iii) while producing customized and advanced products, minimizing the operating costs.

2) Product and process innovation: This area incorporates the topics such as digital manufacturing ecosystems and marketplaces, digital and green transition for sustainable manufacturing, and product-service systems and business models. These trends are largely driven by the following characteristics of the Norwegian manufacturing industry: (i) growing sustainability concerns and regulations in Norway (ii) clustering strategy and initiatives of the Norwegian authorities and companies that has resulted in dozens of clusters all over the country to facilitate cooperation, collaboration, and co-innovation. (iii) creating new values from digital transformation and increase the competitiveness of the manufacturing industry, which largely depends on providing advanced and customized solutions.

3) Production logistics and value chains: This area incorporates the topics such as data-driven production and capacity management, integrated value chain execution and management, and flexible layout and material flow. The main drivers of these trends are

again minimizing the operating costs and providing the operating flexibility to deliver customized products and services.

Reference Frameworks for DiM. Small and medium enterprises (SME) play a critical role in the Norwegian manufacturing industry. However, most SMEs have limited resources and digital transformation can quickly become too costly. SMEs require digitalization frameworks and roadmaps to guide the process, maturity assessment tools for assessing the digital maturity and readiness of the manufacturing environment, evaluation models and methods to evaluate the implementation of the digital tools in various aspects (e.g. performance, economic, user experience), as well as models to create business cases that can measure the digital value creation.

Enabling Technologies for DiM. Common with most digitalization frameworks, the Norwegian manufacturing industry is also looking at the opportunities provided by augmented reality, autonomous robots, Big Data analytics, and artificial intelligence, as outlined in the research projects. Besides, manufacturing execution systems are gaining strong interest as a common platform for storing and sharing data, as well as providing the integration between the enterprise levels both horizontally and vertically.

4.2 Challenges

A prominent challenge for the successful digitalization of Norwegian manufacturing environments is the lack of consideration of human aspects. Acceptance of the enabling technology may vary between the employees, depending on whether they see the value created by the enabling technology in the work practices, on their interests in utilizing new technologies, and/or convincing the employees on the role of the technology to support their work rather than replacing their tasks. Data capture and exchange also imply important challenges. Most manufacturing companies still consist of old machines and equipment, making it difficult to implement real-time data acquisition solutions. While continuous data exchange is fundamental to achieve digitally integrated value chains and creating digital marketplaces, companies are reluctant to share information given the confidentiality concerns. Implementation of new technologies (e.g. real-time data capture by sensors, AR support) also implies potential changes in the allocation of the functions between the enterprise management levels, as the abilities to make decisions at the lower levels are strengthened. For example, enhancing the decision-making abilities of the operators requires considering the allocation of production scheduling and routing functions to the shop floor systems. As such, careful consideration of the functional processes is needed along with the digitalization project.

4.3 Research Areas

Firstly, there is a need for studying efficient digitalization strategies for establishing the underlying needs of digitalization and creating a business case with clear links to value creation. Further, methodologies to guide the digitalization are needed, encompassing the requirement elicitation of the companies, ensuring the match between the requirements and technologies, application of the enabling technologies, and evaluating the implementation. Demonstration pilots in our projects have also shown that there is still a need for further development of the core enabling technologies, to make them more application-friendly in the industry. For example, users were reluctant to carry AR glasses in their work practice due to ergonomic challenges. Lastly, more field-based studies on post-implementation experiences are needed to verify the potential benefits, to better understand the critical factors for a successful digitalization process, and modify the guiding frameworks and methodologies.

5 Conclusion

The discussed trends, challenges, and research areas for digitalization in manufacturing are connected to our experiences with research projects in Norway. They are not comprehensive but provide practical insights on the digitalization of real industrial work environments towards establishing a good practice of research on digitalization in manufacturing. This study was partially funded by the SINTEF research center through strategic funding.

References

1. Thoben, K.-D., Wiesner, S., Wuest, Z.: "Industrie 4.0" and smart manufacturing-a review of research issues and application examples. Int. J. Autom. Technol. **11**(1), 4–16 (2017)
2. Dahl, T.L., Oliveira, M., Arica, E.: Evaluation of augmented reality in industry. In: Lalic, B., Majstorovic, V., Marjanovic, U., von , G., Romero, D. (eds.) APMS 2020. IAICT, vol. 591, pp. 495–502. Springer, Cham (2020). https://doi.org/10.1007/978-3-030-57993-7_56
3. Cenamor, J., Sjödin, D.R., Parida, V.: Adopting a platform approach in servitization: leveraging the value of digitalization. Int. J. Prod. Econ. **192**, 54–65 (2017)
4. Arica, E., Oliveira M.: Requirements for adopting digital B2B platforms for manufacturing capacity finding and sharing. In: 2019 24th IEEE International Conference on Emerging Technologies and Factory Automation (ETFA), pp. 703–709 (2019). https://doi.org/10.1109/ETFA.2019.8869016
5. Björkdahl, J.: Strategies for digitalization in manufacturing firms. Calif. Manage. Rev. **62**(4), 17–36 (2020)
6. Mittal, S., Khan, M.A., Romero, D., Wuest, T.: A critical review of smart manufacturing and Industry 4.0 maturity models: implications for small and medium-sized enterprises (SMEs). J. Manuf. Syst. **49**, 194–214 (2018)
7. De Carolis, A., Macchi, M., Negri, E., Terzi, S.: Guiding manufacturing companies towards digitalization a methodology for supporting manufacturing companies in defining their digitalization roadmap. In: 2017 International Conference on Engineering, Technology and Innovation (ICE/ITMC), pp. 487–495 (2017). https://doi.org/10.1109/ICE.2017.8279925

Exploring Accidental Digital Servitization in an Industrial Context

Matthew Anderson[1]([⊠]) (iD), Shaun West[2] (iD), and David Harrison[1] (iD)

[1] Glasgow Caledonian University, Glasgow G4 0BA, Scotland
mander237@caledonian.ac.uk, D.K.Harrison@gcu.ac.uk
[2] Lucerne University of Applied Sciences and Arts, 6002 Luzern, Switzerland
shaun.west@hslu.ch

Abstract. Recent advances in the Industrial Internet of Things (IIoT) and 'Smart Products' within manufacturing industries have promoted a shift to service-related offerings [1], often inadvertently and without the prerequisite foundations in place, in terms of operating models, impact upon revenue streams, and business strategy. This paper endeavors to investigate this by reviewing three distinct examples of 'smart innovations' for medium-sized industrial businesses and considers the impact upon the business when a service becomes 'smart.' We further review the impact and suggest mitigation approaches relevant to Servitization, and the key factors to enable a more effective digital transformation. Findings indicate that 'Accidental Servitization' can occur within industrial firms, irrespective of their digital experience. Also, that these firms need to ensure an underpinning organizational change is established to support new, disruptive business.

Keywords: Product service systems · Digital servitization · Smart products

1 Introduction

Evidence suggests increasing activities within industrial businesses where 'smart products' are a catalyst for digital transformation, with the potential to reshape business. Most notable is a shift to Cyber-Physical Systems (CPS) [2], where an industrial asset is augmented with monitoring or control functionality as part of a complex eco-system [3]. This leads to ongoing data generation via sensors, which industry is leveraging for data-driven insights at a lower cost. The CPS removes a gap between customer and supplier and provides new insights into product performance.

The motivation for the study is that these new smart product innovations can unexpectedly generate new services, particularly for CPS efforts that combine an IoT element with an asset. This asset may have an effective lifespan of many decades [4] and complex lifecycle management, from initial tender through to support and aftersales. To ensure repeatable quality and minimize risks, a stage-gate methodology is the norm, leading to extended quality assurance and predictable consistency [5].

This is an area that deserves more research. Failure to plan for this shift from product to service reduces the financial benefit gained from such a disruption and impedes

A. Dolgui et al. (Eds.): APMS 2021, IFIP AICT 632, pp. 126–135, 2021.
https://doi.org/10.1007/978-3-030-85906-0_15

establishing a sustainable service. To date, most studies have focused on technology transformation aspects and not the day-to-day impact on operational or business processes. Considering three use case examples, this paper aims to highlight instances of this inadvertent servitization, and answer the following question: *"what is the impact of smart product innovations upon the established business value?"*.

2 Literature Review

Porter and Heppelmann's [2, 6] articles give an overview of the nature of 'smart products' and their impact upon business transformation. Porter defined these as physical products with some degree of technological augmentation to allow connectivity, plus a 'smart component' focused on data generation/capture and analysis. Porter highlights the potential of these products to drive substantial business transformation due to the greater insights gained throughout the value chain. The articles reference the consequent change needed to business organization and skillsets; however, the focus remains on product impact, rather than the shift to service.

Numerous scholars, according to Baines et al. [7], have researched the move from products to integrated service, particularly in manufacturing. Baines et al. [7] describes a comprehensive overview of servitization within industry from the perspective of leveraging unexploited value. They observe the lack of applicable frameworks available to assist successful implementations. However, the importance of offering service as a series of options to drive value from the customer's perspective is well established. Lay [8] provides a selection of studies on the adoption of servitization in different sectors, plus barriers for adoption, and highlights the need to adapt processes. However, there is limited research regarding applying these learnings to servitization resulting from a digital catalyst. Marjanovic et al. [9], raise the importance of this research, employing a statistical analysis of industrial firms, while considering the potential impact on business strategy. Rymaszewska et al. [1], give a case-based overview of the value-driven impact of a digital servitization shift, but with a focus limited to successful projects. Of note, there is limited analysis of the barriers faced, possible mitigation steps, or what changes were required within the companies to fully leverage a new offering. Likewise, there is limited study of the need to re-engineer business processes to fully enable new opportunities. However, significant focus is afforded to potential value propositions. Freitag and Hämmerle [10] recognize the need to address how to manage the shift from product to service focus, particularly in industry, but also across firms of all sizes. They apply a novel, 'design thinking' approach to understand the problem scope which merits further study, this same approach is leveraged by Keiser [11] for a case study on Manufacturing Execution System implementation. Leminen et al. [12], reflect upon current knowledge, stating: *"existing literature lacks understanding… On what IoT business models are and how they are connected to the underlying eco-system"*, and the need for new business models is a theme across the literature.

3 Methodology

This study used qualitative techniques to analyze a cross-case analysis and reflection of three distinct case studies from industrial companies operating in the B2B sector. The case companies are at the earlier stages of digital adoption but have shifted from product to servitization models due to these innovations. Each case will be reviewed to highlight specific aspects relevant to identifying the impact of smart product innovation upon a business and the subsequent shift to servitization, according to the IMPULS model for Industrie 4.0 Readiness [13].

The key characteristics of each case are compared in a cross-case analysis, Table 1 provides the scoring rational using a five-point Likert scale for each of the characteristics. The characteristics are group based on the four major dimensions, which have been taken from the literature [14]. The lead author built up the cases and then scored the cases, these were then moderated by the second author to support the remove of bias.

Table 1. Cross case analysis review framework

Major dimension	Key characteristic	1 – low	5 – high
New service opportunity	Service evolution	Not embraced	Growth into new areas
	New service in adjacent area	Not embraced	New services
	Complementor service	Not embraced	Add-on services offered
Value proposition	New business opportunity	Not embraced	New service offerings
	Improved relationship with customer	Not embraced	New relationship dynamic/improved feedback
	Improved insights	Limited	Data feedback used
	Value co-creation for all parties	Limited	opportunities established
Impact on operating model	Process re-engineered	None	Services redefined
	Focus on product lifecycle	None	Holistic approach adopted
	Specialist roles assigned	None	Multiple assigned
Impact on business model	Shift from product to service	None	Recognized and embraced
	Cannibalization of existing business	Avoided/ ignored	Recognized and embraced
	Shift to data driven company	N/A	Strategic view clearly defined

4   Results

Three examples used for this analysis are: light industrial hand tools; digital optimization service from a product test service; and, an industrial sensor.

4.1   Case Study 1. Light Industrial Hand Tools

A handheld tool manufacturer produces various battery-operated machine tools used in light industrial work, where key business drivers are quality and safety. This firm is at the 'beginner' stage of digital transformation, and this is one of their earliest 'smart product' ventures. They are an OEM provider to resellers/redistributors, so interaction with the end-user is limited to warranty and repair issues. Feedback from resellers and warranty claims showed end-users had supply chain issues with non-OEM consumable materials, reducing output quality and damaging tools. This reduced the tool's availability and introduced 3rd party involvement into the warranty process. Another issue was that the tools are not connected to shop floor data collection systems, so their location and status is not tracked, and neither is operators' exposure to vibration in adherence to safety regulations.

The firm added a variety of sensors and remote monitoring capabilities to a range of tools to counter these gaps. The IIoT components were mounted to existing devices cost-effectively in a simple 'sleeve'. An RFID reader confirmed the provenance of consumables and read/write material-specific metadata for tool usage, while a range of sensors measured usage and ambient parameters such as vibration. Bluetooth Low Energy was used for data transfer to an end-user smartphone, and to the cloud. These technology choices drove new functionality for the resulting smart product. Using a smartphone for data transfer from the hand tool simplified the connection into IT/OT environments, and also created the opportunity to send configuration data to the device, allowing greater control and the recording of usage macros to automate operator efforts.

There was a notable change with the relationship dynamic, shifting from the sequential 'OEM, reseller, end-user' pattern to a 'three-way' relationship. The reseller gained insight into application patterns, gaining the option to shift their service to tool and material usage, and to automate replenishment There were also notable changes with the warranty service. The tool manufacturer was previously constrained by lack of access to end-user and complications in the service support model. Gaining operational data, and limiting potential causes of damage to the tool, makes the service more transparent and collaborative for the three parties. Table 2 summarizes.

Table 2.   Case 1: light industrial hand tools

Industry 4.0 attributes	IoT sensors for monitoring and control Smartphone app, cloud reporting
Target markets	Reseller ecosystem End users in light industry
Resulting product service system	Product improvement feedback Reseller service improvement from usage patterns Replenishment service model
Impact	Improved feedback from end-users, but notable reluctance from resellers to change
Comments	Suggest joint workshops with all parties to establish needs

4.2   Case Study 2. Digital Optimization Service from a Product Test Service

An industrial asset producer manufactures bespoke engineered-to-order (ETO) products for use in heavy industries. Key business drivers vary but cover performance, efficiency, and availability. The firm is established in this market and is usually approached by the customer for tenders. This customer can be a system integrator or the end-user. The firm has a strong relationship with its user-base due to the close collaboration required for ETO projects and a range of aftersales service (i.e., spare parts, repairs, and retrofit). The digital maturity of the firm would be classified as 'intermediate'. Performance tests in the firm's test facilities are typically required before shipment, simulating the customers' environment as closely as possible, although with higher instrumentation and monitoring. The firm created in-house software to perform the test calculations on real-time data and found that the in-house test tool created a demand for a similar offering for customers to use at their facilities for ongoing monitoring. The firm started to sell a cut-down version of the service via a cloud-based dashboard. This gained the firm the flexibility of a centralized environment to support and manage while safeguarding their intellectual property in a secure cloud environment.

This raised new opportunities: gaining access to anonymized data across a range of customers, assets, and failure modes allowed the firm to go beyond its initial offering. Using this centralized data source and employing more advanced analytics, new insights allowed them to provide predictive support with estimating the remaining useful lifespan of assets and guiding targeted maintenance activities. This benefited both parties, as the provider gains real-world asset application knowledge, and the customer experiences a more tailored service. Providing this information is helpful, but the customer needs guidance in applying the insights. The firm employed equipment specialists to liaise with the customers to interpret the data and guide operational improvements, using the service as 'intelligence augmentation' for decision support. The outcome was some cannibalization of existing aftermarket services, improved customer experience, and improved customer operational challenges. A short summary is given in Table 3.

4.3   Case Study 3. An Industrial Sensor

The third case study considers an industrial asset producer that manufactures and assembles configured-to-order products. These are used throughout process industries such as water treatment and food production, which focus on availability, reliability, cost efficiency and safety. With regards to their digital maturity, this case firm would be considered 'experienced' according to the IMPULS model. They have a well-established e-commerce platform, and several digital innovations underway. The firm sells a wide range of configured industrial assets, which the customer orders via a sales representative or via an online configurator. The cost of automation for asset monitoring is too high to justify its use, resulting in manual measurements that do not identify problems early enough to avoid unplanned downtime. Access to equipment can be restricted, leaving snapshot data collation to be made on an ad hoc basis, losing opportunities to see underlying patterns that would allow more reliable predictions to be made.

A low-cost IoT sensor system for automated measurement of temperature and vibration at critical areas that connects to the Internet via a smartphone app was developed

Table 3. Case 2: digital optimization service from a product test service

Industry 4.0 attributes	Data transport and ingestion to cloud machine learning, advanced analytics
Target markets	Engineer-to-order asset operators in heavy industry
Resulting product service system	Asset optimization and benchmarking Detection of anomalous behavior Targeted maintenance activities R&D feedback
Impact	Initial gaps with leveraging the data and customer communication Opportunities beyond the initial requirement identified and leveraged Better customer relationship
Comments	Gap addressed by hire of specialist resource, and customer training

to overcome these challenges. Equipment data is collected from the ERP system and recombined in an e-commerce platform, extending the offering to include monitoring. Using a web dashboard, customers can see the asset's condition, set thresholds for alerts, receive event notifications and reports, and export data for their analytics. Lastly, the firm manages the sensors and gateway's product lifecycle, scheduling updates for sensors and gateways and remote troubleshooting. The customer gained 24/7 monitoring coupled with trending, enabling them to adopt a risk-based maintenance approach.

The solution was sold as a one-off investment, priced to cover the sensor production and the R&D costs. An operating model for the sensor lifecycle was not defined, but both sensors and gateway require remote support for implementation and connectivity issues, plus firmware updates and similar factors. Customer feedback identified that the cloud-based solution was complicated, and customers needed help to get the system's value. This was overcome by a specialist team who provided customer training. Installation of sensors to the equipment as part of the standard design and later activation on customer requests has yet to be implemented and could reduce costs and complexity in the medium-term. Table 4 summarizes this.

5 Discussion

The information gathered for the three cases was combined into a cross-case analysis (see Table 5). Leading to several notable managerial implications. Firstly, it is shown that companies make greater profit from services than from products [15]. However, as the studies show, this is often not the focus of smart product innovation. A common theme across all of the cases is the focus solely on the innovation aspect, which is common in industry. Businesses with both a long industrial heritage and well-established product ranges often employ a stage-gate approach to production, and consequently to innovation [5]. This results in a slow but measured approach to what is perceived as 'sustainable

Table 4. Case 3: an industrial sensor

Industry 4.0 attributes	Data generation, transport, cloud storage Analytics and visualization Web API for data extraction
Target markets	Configured-to-order asset operators in process industry
Resulting product service system	Internet-enabled condition monitoring
Impact	Initial gaps with sales effort Lack of target operating model for ongoing support and maintenance of service Ongoing costs and support not considered Complimentary service not considered
Comments	Recruitment of IIoT sales specialists, better explanations to customers Ongoing costs and support to be factored into operating model review service offerings and synergies across the company

innovation', which is at odds with the 'fail fast, fail often, and learn' approach inherent to digital innovation. Also notable was the singular focus on a digital product. More digitally mature companies tend towards 'proof of concepts' being tried and rapidly discarded if not fit for purpose. Service innovation needs this 'start-up mentality'. Such traditional approaches also fail to capitalize on potential smart service opportunities due to business model limitations. A frequent comment was the need to review a process when limitations were met, but this resulted in a considerable reluctance to adapt. Likewise, a change in the structure is required to harness opportunities, but barriers were met with established status quo, particularly with product-centric sales efforts and a focus on immediate return on investment, rather than driving greater customer value and collaboration. However, this need for organizational transformation also includes their partner network and interaction with the customer base. One of the other barriers met was with the skillsets required.

This is an area where medium-sized industrial firms struggle and usually default to buying-in such skills and innovation mindsets. Of note, the first use case firm used the opportunity to identify key skills required and where they existed within different business units, opening those areas of the business, creating opportunities for innovation. In each of the cases a clear pattern emerges of servitization arising unexpectedly from smart products. With the immediate focus being on achieving the technical innovation without consideration of the required underpinning factors to leverage opportunity. A more holistic approach is needed. Firstly, with a systems level thinking, the realization that the smart product does not exist in isolation, but is part of an adapting eco-system that requires ongoing service such as upgrades, and leverage of the insights gained. Likewise, adaptation to existing sales process needs to be embraced. Smart products create a different relationship pattern with customers, upending the traditional dynamic. Shifting from discreet product sales to a data driven solution, results in value co-creation

Table 5. Cross case analysis

Major dimension	Key characteristic	Case 1	Case 2	Case 3
New service opportunity	Service evolution	2	4	3
	New service in adjacent area	2	4	2
	Complementor service	2	3	1
Value proposition	New business opportunity	2	3	3
	Improved relationship with customer	2	4	3
	Improved insights	3	4	3
Impact on operating model	Value co-creation for all parties	2	4	3
	Focus on product lifecycle	2	4	3
	Specialist roles assigned	1	5	3
Impact on business model	Shift from product to service	2	3	3
	Cannibalization of existing business	1	4	2
	Shift to data driven company	2	4	3

for both company and customer, in terms of upgrades and service, often resulting in cannibalization of existing products, and creating a blurred distinction between initial sales and aftersales.

Returning to the research question posed by this paper, there is an impact of Smart Product innovation upon the established business value. This occurs in three ways: first, there is an ongoing cost burden to the supplier for the digital aspects of the product; second, there is a change to the value proposition offered by the supplier as they are moving to a servitized business model predicated on product-service system; finally, the revenue model for value capture can be adapted to better reflect value in use or value in context.

This is an initial study and subject to several limitations. Due to the relatively recent trend of digital servitization, there are a limited number of case studies available for comparison. Another factor is, the firms operate in similar industrial sectors. The authors wish to build upon this and introduce case studies across a range of studies, allowing more quantitative approaches. Future research on digital-driven servitization should address a greater range of business models and impact on value once these initiatives are more commonplace. These studies should eventually lead to a common body of knowledge which can be leveraged as templates for the implementation of digital service across industry.

Of note, some seminal works, such as Porter and Heppelmann [2, 6], were commonly referenced by the firms as providing a vital catalyst for their initial digital transformation. The subsequent barriers these firms met when shifting from product to service would imply a need to revisit such papers and critically review with hindsight.

5.1 Managerial Implications

The critical lesson for management is that Smart Products are similar in many key characteristics to more traditional ones, in that much of the value can be attributed to their application. What differs is that connectivity and data analysis create ongoing costs for the supplier. In effect, the firm has unintentionally created a sophisticated product-service system where value is based upon value-in-use or -in-context, however value capture can be problematic. The challenge is to recognize the change and shift to more advanced servitization-based business models, rather than charge for the product and then provide the digital value for free. The move to Smart Products requires a change in the firm's value proposition, a new revenue model, and modifications to the underlying business model, beyond incremental product development. Without this, sales may find it difficult to attain the full value that Smart Products promise, and the business may build a growing cost base that they cannot cover adequately with their revenue streams. Therefore, when developing new Smart Products, managers should ensure that the cost model for the whole lifecycle is well defined, and the revenue model provides value capture in excess of the ongoing cash requirements. A new value proposition will be required to achieve this, and sales must adapt to sell the solution.

5.2 Theoretical Implications

The three cases illustrate that Smart Products are a 'Trojan Horse' for services and, in effect, should be considered as Service Innovation, leading to a major impact on the supplier business model. This finding is in agreement with servitization literature, Kohtamäki et al. [16] and service science literature, Grönroos and Vargo [17, 18]. The findings highlight that product development with a digital aspect fundamentally changes the underlying supplier business model and value proposition, thus changing customer relationship and experiences, and may need to shift from traditional product development process to one that integrates product and service innovation concurrently.

6   Conclusions

In each of the cases a clear pattern emerges of servitization arising unexpectedly from innovative work related to smart products that are customer oriented. It is clear that in order to establish value, smart products invariably lead to smart services, and yet the firms, irrespective of their perceived digital maturity, seem ill prepared for such an eventuality. Notably, these technology-driven innovations outpace the business transformation required to sustain them, with a delayed response in adaptation to operating models. The organizational transformation required to support these can be a complex and far-reaching endeavor. The firms referenced in the case study have invested heavily over many years into processes that support their 'heritage products' via incremental innovation. Disruptive approaches in these environments are often perceived as a risk, resulting in an understandable inertia. It is a clear necessity to accommodate both operational modes to support core business, starting with a strategic epiphany to embrace far reaching change, otherwise industrial firms' risk relinquishing such opportunities to more organizationally agile upstarts.

References

1. Rymaszewska, A., Helo, P., Gunasekaran, A.: IoT powered servitization of manufacturing – an exploratory case study. Int. J. Prod. Econ. **192**, 92–105 (2017). https://doi.org/10.1016/j.ijpe.2017.02.016
2. Porter, M., Heppelmann, J.: How smart, connected products are transforming companies. Harvard Bus. Rev. **93**(10), 96–114 (2015)
3. Monostori, L., et al.: Cyber-physical systems in manufacturing. CIRP Ann. **65**(2), 621–641 (2016). https://doi.org/10.1016/j.cirp.2016.06.005
4. Budris, A., Bloch, H.: Pump User's Handbook: Life Extension. River Publishers, New York (2021)
5. Grönlund, J., Sjödin, D.R., Frishammar, J.: Open innovation and the stage-gate process: a revised model for new product development. Calif. Manage. Rev. **52**(3), 106–131 (2010). https://doi.org/10.1525/cmr.2010.52.3.106
6. Porter, M., Heppelmann, J.: How smart, connected products are transforming competition. Harvard Bus. Rev. **92**(11), 64–88 (2014)
7. Baines, T., Lightfoot, H., Benedettini, O., Kay, J.: The servitization of manufacturing: a review of literature and reflection on future challenges. J. Manuf. Technol. Manag. **20**(5), 547–567 (2009). https://doi.org/10.1108/17410380910960984
8. Lay, G. (ed.): Servitization in Industry. Springer, Cham (2014). https://doi.org/10.1007/978-3-319-06935-7
9. Marjanovic, U., Rakic, S., Lalic, B.: Digital servitization: the next "big thing" in manufacturing industries. In: Ameri, F., Stecke, K.E., von Cieminski, G., Kiritsis, D. (eds.) APMS 2019. IAICT, vol. 566, pp. 510–517. Springer, Cham (2019). https://doi.org/10.1007/978-3-030-30000-5_63
10. Freitag, M., Hämmerle, O.: Agile guideline for development of smart services in manufacturing enterprises with support of artificial intelligence. In: Lalic, B., Majstorovic, V., Marjanovic, U., von Cieminski, G., Romero, D. (eds.) APMS 2020. IAICT, vol. 591, pp. 645–652. Springer, Cham (2020). https://doi.org/10.1007/978-3-030-57993-7_73
11. Kesier, Y.: Digital twin in manufacturing: improving the efficiency of a furniture production by means of a digital twin (Master's thesis). Lucerne University of Applied Sciences and Arts, Lucerne (2021)
12. Leminen, S., Westerlund, M., Rajahonka, M., Siuruainen, R.: Towards IOT ecosystems and business models. In: Andreev, S., Balandin, S., Koucheryavy, Y. (eds.) NEW2AN/ruSMART -2012. LNCS, vol. 7469, pp. 15–26. Springer, Heidelberg (2012). https://doi.org/10.1007/978-3-642-32686-8_2
13. C.a.R. Hilger, J.: Auto-ID integration-a bridge between worlds. German Harting Mag., 14–15 (2013)
14. Anderson, J., Narus, J.: Business market management: understanding, creating, and delivering value. J. Bus. Ind. Mark. **14**(3), 76–80 (1999). https://doi.org/10.1108/08858629910272265
15. Toivonen, M. (ed.): Service Innovation. TSS, vol. 6. Springer, Tokyo (2016). https://doi.org/10.1007/978-4-431-54922-2
16. Kohtamäki, M., Rajala, R.: Theory and practice of value co-creation in B2B systems. Ind. Mark. Manage. **56**, 4–13 (2016). https://doi.org/10.1016/j.indmarman.2016.05.027
17. Grönroos, C., Helle, P.: Adopting a service logic in manufacturing: conceptual foundation and metrics for mutual value creation. J. Serv. Manag. **21**(5), 564–590 (2010). https://doi.org/10.1108/09564231011079057
18. Vargo, S.L., Lusch, R.F.: Service-dominant logic: continuing the evolution. J. Acad. Mark. Sci. **36**(1), 1–10 (2008)

Finance-Driven Supply Chain

Financing and Cost Sharing for a Supply Chain Under CSR - Sensitive Demand

Franck Moraux, Dinh Anh Phan[(✉)], and Thi Le Hoa Vo

Université de Rennes 1, CNRS, CREM UMR6211 IGR-IAE de Rennes,
11 Rue Jean Macé, CS 70803, 35708 Rennes Cedex 7, France

Abstract. Downstream firms nowadays adopt either financing or cost sharing (CS) mechanisms to enhance the corporate social responsibility (CSR) perfor-mance of their suppliers. In this paper, we are interested in combining these two mechanisms in a supply chain. We consider a supply chain where the demand is CSR-dependent and where a large retailer shares the costs of CSR activities under-taken by a SME supplier. We investigate how the retailer's choice of two financing mechanisms, namely Bank Financing (BF) and Reverse Factoring (RF), can influ-ence the various operational decisions of both parties and the performance of the supply chain. Our findings demonstrate that no matter which financing mechanism is applied (BF or RF), CS leads to higher CSR effort and higher profits for all sup-ply chain members. Moreover, a CS contract affects the financing preferences of both the retailer and the supplier. Managerially, a CS contract combined with an appropriate financing mechanism help to improve the CSR performance and the profitability of a supply chain.

Keywords: Corporate social responsibility · Supply chain · Bank financing · Reverse factoring · Cost-sharing contract

1 Introduction

Many companies nowadays support their suppliers in adopting CSR, by sharing costs or co-financing the CSR. For example, Hewlett-Packard Company incentivizes its main suppliers by sharing CSR investment costs [1], while Wal-Mart Stores Inc. launched in 2010 a Global Social Compliance Program that co-finances CSR investment costs with suppliers. For financing, in recent years, large retailers recourse to BF and RF to support the supplier's CSR efforts. E.g., PUMA uses BF to pay its suppliers early, if they show a high sustainability performance in terms of environment, health and safety, and social welfare. PUMA also cooperates with the International Finance Corporation (IFC), a member of the World Bank Group, to offer a lower financing rate for suppliers with a high CSR score. Motivated by the aforementioned practices, our research explores whether and how the buying companies should use financing and cost-sharing together to promote the CSR performance of suppliers. The existing literature in supply chain management has mainly considered situations where only one of these two mechanisms is viable. Early

© IFIP International Federation for Information Processing 2021
Published by Springer Nature Switzerland AG 2021
A. Dolgui et al. (Eds.): APMS 2021, IFIP AICT 632, pp. 139–148, 2021.
https://doi.org/10.1007/978-3-030-85906-0_16

studies (such as [2–4]) show that CS contracts can coordinate supply chains engaged in CSR efforts and improve the supply chain performance, but none of these early investigations integrate financing issues. This contrasts a lot with the observation that most upstream suppliers are SMEs located in developing countries and need financial supports for entering such CSR practices. The literature logically introduces and explores some BF and RF solutions to mitigate the aforementioned concern. Under BF, the retailer can get some direct financing from banks to pay the suppliers early [5]. By contrast, under RF, the retailer, the supplier and a factor enter a contract that can help the supplier receive early payments from the factor [6]. Most of investigations in this stream of research focus on the influence on BF and RF on the operational and financing decisions (see respectively [5, 7] and [8–10]).

In this study we explore the joint impact of financing and cost-sharing on the CSR performance and efficiency of a supply chain. Intuitively, under BF, we can expect that a CS contract granted by the retailer, financed by cash and coupled with a bank loan to early pay the supplier, raises the financial burden of the retailer. Indeed, the cash provided by the retailer to the supplier for sharing the CSR investment directly impacts the loan amount to borrow and indirectly the loan interest rate charged by the bank. This means that, ceteris paribus, the retailer's final benefits decrease. By contrast, under RF, the level of cost-sharing has no impact on the financial burden for the retailer, because RF simply engages invoices. Given these potential interactive effects, understanding how to combine cost-sharing and financing so as to improve the profitability of the supply chain and the performance of the CSR effort is important for both the supplier and the retailer. Our research addresses specifically the three following questions. (1) Given a financing mechanism, is it beneficial for the buyer to offer a CSR CS contract to the supplier? (2) Does the financing affect the effectiveness of the CS contract in order to boost the supplier's CSR effort? (3) What is the effect of cost-sharing on the preferences of each supply chain member with regards to the financing?

The rest of the paper is organized as follows: Sect. 2 describes the model framework, assumptions and notations. Section 3 investigates the combination of CSR cost sharing with each financing mechanism BF or RF. Some numerical results and managerial observations will be presented in Sect. 4. Finally, we conclude the paper with some remarks and perspectives.

2 Model Description

Consider a supply chain with one upstream supplier "S", referred as "he" and one downstream retailer "R", referred as "she". S produces and delivers a single type of finished product to R. R then sells these products to some final consumers during a single selling season at a known (unit) retail price p. R and S have some initial levels of capital denoted by k^R and k^S respectively. The CSR-dependent random demand $\tilde{D}$ is well described by $\tilde{D}(\theta) = \tilde{D}_0 + \beta\theta$ where β is the marginal effect on the demand of any additional CSR effort θ undertaken by S, and $\tilde{D}_0$ is the random demand in absence of any CSR effort. To encourage S to undertake CSR activities, R announces her willingness to co-finance any CSR investment[1]. The CSR investment cost is variable and increases with the CSR effort nonlinearly; it is formally equal to $d\theta^2$ where θ stands for the level of S's CSR efforts and d is a positive parameter. The proportion of the CSR investment cost shared by R is denoted by λ a parameter such that $0 \leq \lambda < 1$. The setting of the parameter λ occurs after the nature of the CSR activities is revealed by S but before he announces his effort. Consequently, the parameter λ can influence θ the associated level of effort chosen by S and this latter is better denoted by $\theta(\lambda)$. Similarly, the decisions to invest in CSR and to share CSR investment costs are taken *before* the retailer placed an order from the supplier, so that both decisions should influence the following ordering of R and the R's order quantity is better denoted by $q(\lambda, \theta(\lambda))$. Three important remarks deserve to be made. First of all, we assume, without loss of generality, that all unmet demand is lost and the salvage value of products is zero. Secondly, regarding the cost sharing, we investigate two different ways to set the parameter λ. The first approach leads to a R-led CS contract, where R determines and sovereignly proclaims the level of her contribution λ alone (that is on the sole basis of her profit function π_i^R). The second approach leads to a negotiated CS contract where S and R bargain on the parameter λ. The design of this latter bargaining then follows the line exposed in [11] and the optimal sharing ratio is determined by maximizing $\pi_i^B = \pi_i^R \times \pi_i^S$, the product of individual profits of parties under strategy i, respectively denoted by π_i^R and π_i^S. Thirdly, regarding the decision-making process, one will assume that both S and R can internalize the steps ahead and that the objective function to consider in the different decision-making processes is designed backward. For instance, if R chooses her contribution alone, then she maximizes $\pi_i^R\left(\lambda, \theta_S^*(\lambda), q_R^*\left(\lambda, \theta_S^*(\lambda)\right)\right)$ where $\theta_S^*(\lambda)$ results from the optimization of the CSR effort undertaken by S and where $q_R^*\left(\lambda, \theta_S^*(\lambda)\right)$ results from the optimization

Table 1. List of notations

θ	CSR effort level	k^R	Initial capital of R
q	Ordered quantity of products	k^S	Initial capital of S
r^R	Interest rates of the loan granted by the bank to R	r^S	Interest rates of the loan granted by the bank to S
γ_R	RF Discount	d	CSR investment parameter
λ	Cost sharing ratio	$\tilde{D}_0$	Random demand without CSR
v	Proportion of invoice financed by RF	β	Marginal effect of the CSR effort on demand
p	Sale price	cs	Credit spread
w	Wholesale price	r_f	Risk-free interest rates
η	Price discount granted by S to R	Δt_p	The production delay
c	Unit cost of production	Δt_s	The lead time of sales season

---

[1] Most cost-sharing contracts mentioned in the literature take the form of a financing that is granted by the retailer and that the supplier must reimburse later. Consequently, the commonly investigated CS contract does not improve the financial situation of the supplier/that much.

of the order quantity undertaken by R. In other words, the backward sequential decision-making approach allows the parties to internalize the subsequent decisions and to choose the optimal parameters. We thus employ a standard backward induction approach to derive the equilibrium strategies for players (Table 1).

3 Financing Mechanisms and CSR Cost-Sharing

3.1 The Competitive Interest Rate

We assume that to finance the buying of products, R contracts a credit to borrow an amount L at the reference credit spread cs. Then, following Kouvelis and Zhao [12], the competitive interest rate r^R must satisfy

$$Le^{(r_f+cs)\Delta t_s} = E[\min\left(rec\left(\tilde{D}\right), Le^{r^R \Delta t_s}\right)] \qquad (1)$$

where $rec\left(\tilde{D}\right)$ is the demand-dependent recovery the lender can expect in case of default. As an example, consider a bank loan whose recovery is the retailer's revenue, the bank's competitive interest rate then is implicitly determined by Eq. (2)

$$Le^{(r_f+cs)\Delta t_s} = E[\min\left(p\tilde{D}, Le^{r^R\Delta t_s}\right)] \qquad (2)$$

3.2 CSR Cost-Sharing Under Bank Financing (CS-BF)

The sequence of events and decisions in the CS-BF is illustrated in Fig. 1.

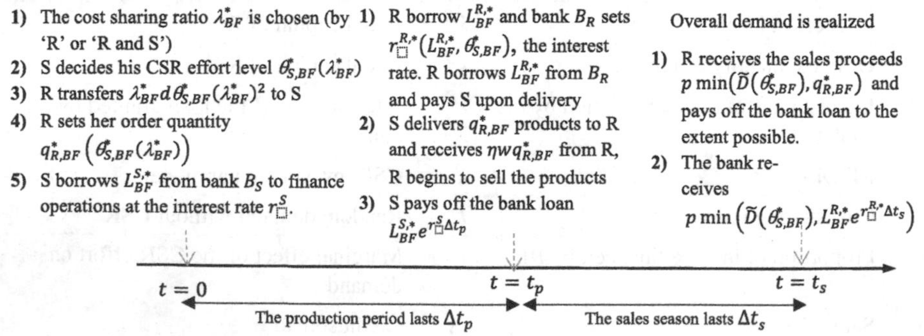

1) The cost sharing ratio λ_{BF}^* is chosen (by 'R' or 'R and S')
2) S decides his CSR effort level $\theta_{S,BF}^*(\lambda_{BF}^*)$
3) R transfers $\lambda_{BF}^* d\theta_{S,BF}^*(\lambda_{BF}^*)^2$ to S
4) R sets her order quantity $q_{R,BF}^*\left(\theta_{S,BF}(\lambda_{BF}^*)\right)$
5) S borrows $L_{BF}^{S,*}$ from bank B_S to finance operations at the interest rate $r_\square^S$.

1) R borrow $L_{BF}^{R,*}$ and bank B_R sets $r_\square^{R,*}(L_{BF}^{R,*}, \theta_{S,BF}^*)$, the interest rate. R borrows $L_{BF}^{R,*}$ from B_R and pays S upon delivery
2) S delivers $q_{R,BF}^*$ products to R and receives $\eta w q_{R,BF}^*$ from R, R begins to sell the products
3) S pays off the bank loan $L_{BF}^{S,*}e^{r_\square^S\Delta t_p}$

Overall demand is realized

1) R receives the sales proceeds $p\min(\tilde{D}(\theta_{S,BF}^*), q_{R,BF}^*)$ and pays off the bank loan to the extent possible.
2) The bank receives $p\min\left(\tilde{D}(\theta_{S,BF}^*), L_{BF}^{R,*}e^{r_\square^{R,*}\Delta t_s}\right)$

$t=0$ $t=t_p$ $t=t_s$

The production period lasts Δt_p The sales season lasts Δt_s

Fig. 1. The sequence of events and decisions in the CS-BF

The expected profit (hereafter, profit for short) of S at the end of sales season can be formulated as

$$\pi_{BF}^S = \left(\eta w q_{R,BF} - \left(cq_{R,BF} + (1-\lambda_{BF})d\theta_{S,BF}^2 - k^S\right)e^{r^S\Delta t_p}\right)e^{r_f\Delta t_s} - k^S e^{r_f t_s} \qquad (3)$$

and the profit of R at the end of sales season is

$$\pi_{BF}^{R} = E\left[\max\left(p\min\left(\tilde{D}, q_{R,BF}\right) - L_{BF}^{R} e^{r^{R}\Delta t_{s}}; 0\right)\right] - k^{R} e^{r_{f}t_{s}} \tag{4}$$

where $L_{BF}^{R} = \eta w q_{R,BF} - \left(k^{R} -_{BF} d_{S,BF}^{2}\right)e^{r_{f}\Delta t_{p}}$, and by virtue of the competitive interest rate charged by the bank, the profit of R becomes

$$\pi_{BF}^{R} = E\left[p\min\left(\tilde{D}, q_{R,BF}\right)\right] - L_{BF}^{R} e^{(r_{f}+cs)\Delta t_{s}} - k^{R} e^{r_{f}t_{s}} \tag{5}$$

3.3   CSR Cost-Sharing Under Reverse Factoring (CS-RF)

The sequence of events and decisions in the CS-RF is depicted in Fig. 2. Given a credit spread cs, the proportion v of invoice financed by RF and by virtue of the Eq. (2), the RF discount γ_{R} satisfies

$$\gamma_{R}vwqe^{(r_{f}+cs)\Delta t_{s}} = E\left[\min\left(p\tilde{D}, wq_{R,RF}\right)\right] - E\left[\min\left(p\tilde{D}, (1-v)wq_{R,RF}\right)\right] \tag{6}$$

The profit functions of S and R can be formulated as

$$\pi_{RF}^{S} = E\left[\min\left(p\tilde{D}, (1-v)wq_{R,RF}\right)\right] + \left(\gamma_{R}vwq_{R,RF} - L^{S}e^{r^{S}\ \Delta t_{p}}\right)e^{r_{f}\Delta t_{s}} - k^{S}e^{r_{f}t_{s}} \tag{7}$$

where $L^{S} = cq_{R,RF} + (1-_{RF})d\theta_{S,RF}^{2} - k^{S}$.

$$\pi_{RF}^{R} = E\left[p\min\left(\tilde{D}, q_{R,RF}\right)\right] - E[\min\left(p\tilde{D}, wq_{R,RF}\right)] - \lambda_{RF}d\theta_{S,RF}^{2}e^{r_{f}t_{s}} \tag{8}$$

From (7), both S and the factor can understand that $\partial\pi_{RF}^{S}/\partial v < 0$ and this in turn implies that (if S is free to choose v) S will choose v to be as low as possible, namely $v = v_{min} = \frac{L^{S}e^{r^{S}\Delta t_{p}}}{\gamma_{R}wq_{R,RF}}$, and the resulting profit function of S is equal to

$$\pi_{RF}^{S} = E\left[\min\left(p\tilde{D}, wq_{R,RF}\right)\right] - L^{S}e^{r^{S}\Delta t_{p}}e^{(r_{f}+cs)\Delta t_{s}} - k^{S}e^{r_{f}t_{s}} \tag{9}$$

and no longer depends on v or γ_{R}. Consequently, when S maximizes his profit the solution will not depend directly on the RF conditions.

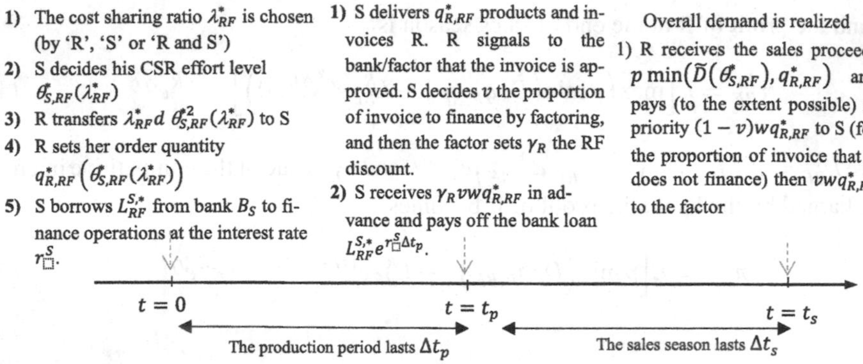

1) The cost sharing ratio λ_{RF}^* is chosen (by 'R', 'S' or 'R and S')

2) S decides his CSR effort level $\theta_{S,RF}^*(\lambda_{RF}^*)$

3) R transfers $\lambda_{RF}^* d\,\theta_{S,RF}^{*2}(\lambda_{RF}^*)$ to S

4) R sets her order quantity $q_{R,RF}^*\left(\theta_{S,RF}^*(\lambda_{RF}^*)\right)$

5) S borrows $L_{RF}^{S,*}$ from bank B_S to finance operations at the interest rate $r_\square^S$.

1) S delivers $q_{R,RF}^*$ products and invoices R. R signals to the bank/factor that the invoice is approved. S decides v the proportion of invoice to finance by factoring, and then the factor sets γ_R the RF discount.

2) S receives $\gamma_R v w q_{R,RF}^*$ in advance and pays off the bank loan $L_{RF}^{S,*} e^{r_\square^S \Delta t_p}$.

Overall demand is realized

1) R receives the sales proceeds $p\min\left(\tilde{D}(\theta_{S,RF}^*), q_{R,RF}^*\right)$ and pays (to the extent possible) in priority $(1-v)w q_{R,RF}^*$ to S (for the proportion of invoice that S does not finance) then $v w q_{R,RF}^*$ to the factor

$t = 0$ $t = t_p$ $t = t_s$

The production period lasts Δt_p The sales season lasts Δt_s

Fig. 2. The sequence of events and decisions in the CS-RF

4 Numerical Study and Managerial Observations

4.1 The Parameter Setting

We denote $_i^{k*}$ as the equilibrium profit of the entity k under strategy i. Here, $k \in \{S, R\}$ represent S and R respectively, and $i \in \{BF, RF, CS^R BF, CS^B BF, CS^R RF, CS^B RF\}$ represent for the strategies of BF, RF, BF with R-led CS contract, BF with bargaining CS contract, RF with R-led CS contract, and RF with bargaining CS contract, respectively. We explore the differences $\Delta^k = \pi_{RF}^{k*} - \pi_{BF}^{k*}$ to quantify the value of RF to the entity k when the supply chain shifts from BF to RF. Similarly, $\Delta\theta = \theta_{S,RF}^* - \theta_{S,BF}^*$ informs on the difference of CSR effort between RF and BF. We consider a normal distribution, namely $\tilde{D} \sim N(\mu, \sigma)$, for modelling the market demand uncertainty without CSR investment due to the advantage in describing separately the mean and variance. The following base case parameters are: $\mu = 100$, $\sigma = 50$, $p = 1$, $w = 0.6$, $c = 0.3$, $\eta = 0.9$, $\beta = 1$, $d = 0.01$, $k^S = 0$, $cs = 0.05$, $R_f = 2\%(r_f = 1.98\%)$, $\Delta t_p = 1$, $\Delta t_s = 1.5$, $R^S = 18\%(r^S = 16.55\%)$ and $k^R = 20$.

4.2 The Supply Chain Performance Without a CS Contract

a. Impact of Credit Spread

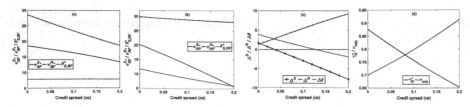

Fig. 3. Impact of the credit spread

The effects of the credit spread (cs) on the equilibrium CSR effort and the profits of S and R are shown in Fig. 3. This figure shows that there exists a certain cs threshold (around 13% in our setting) beyond which the CSR effort under RF is lower than that under BF. Panel (c) of Fig. 3 shows that R has a clear incentive to promote RF instead of BF, especially when cs increases. We can observe that both R and S agree to adopt RF for small values of cs only. There exists a cs threshold (around 4%) beyond which S would favor BF and this of course contrasts with the opinion of R. The bottom line of this numerical illustration is that when cs is below 4%, the adoption of RF is profitable for S and R, and it enhances the CSR effort. Finally, panel (d) shows that cs impacts almost linearly both v_{min} and γ_R but positively for v_{min} and negatively for γ_R. The effect highlighted in panel (d) finally suggests a sort of compensation between both parameters (even if $\gamma_R \times v_{min}$ is not exactly a constant). Consequently, we can conclude from this approximate compensation that S cannot (under RF) instrumentalize the proportion of invoice to mitigate the rise of cs that is the rise of the financing cost.

b. **Impact of demand variability**

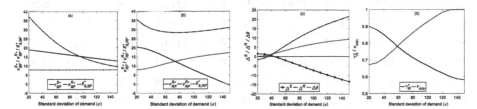

Fig. 4. Impact of the demand variability

The effects of the demand variability (measured by the variance or the standard deviation) on the equilibrium CSR effort and the profits of S and R are shown in Fig. 4. Panel (a) shows that the demand variability does not influence the CSR effort under BF. In contrast, the CSR effort under RF increases and is highly sensitive to demand variability (see Panel (b)). This suggests that RF incites S to invest more in CSR effort when the demand variability is high. Panel (c) shows different signs for Δ^S and Δ^R in many instances suggesting that the preferences of parties are irreconcilable. The adoption of RF will bring relatively more benefit for R when the variation of the market demand is high and the reverse holds for S. Panel (d) shows that the RF discount γ_R and the proportion of invoice v_{min} vary significantly and nonlinearly with the demand variability.

4.3 The SC Performance with CS Contract

4.3.1 The Feasibility of CS Contract

Table 2 shows the equilibrium under RF and BF with R-led cost sharing contract with different values of demand variance. It can be seen that the optimal cost sharing ratios under BF and RF are higher than zero, meaning that the feasibility of a cost sharing contract does not depend on the financing choice. However, we find that the optimal cost sharing under BF does not depend on the demand variance, whereas, the optimal cost sharing under RF decreases with the demand variance. Hence, a higher demand variance discourages R to grant a CS contract to S under RF.

Table 2. Equilibrium under RF and BF with R-led cost sharing contract

	BF					RF				
σ	λ^*_{BF}	$q^*_{R,BF}$	$\theta^*_{S,BF}$	π^{S*}_{BF}	π^{R*}_{BF}	λ^*_{RF}	$q^*_{R,RF}$	$\theta^*_{S,RF}$	π^{S*}_{RF}	π^{R*}_{RF}
20	0.64	116.57	21.62	20.27	39.24	0.64	116.57	22.62	20.27	39.24
30	0.64	114.05	21.62	19.78	35.38	0.63	116.49	22.21	19.99	34.47
40	0.64	111.52	21.62	19.30	31.59	0.59	117.29	21.19	19.99	32.00
50	0.64	109.00	21.62	18.81	28.07	0.52	120.38	20.25	18.28	30.38
60	0.64	106.48	21.62	18.33	24.97	0.45	125.22	19.52	16.35	29.40
70	0.64	103.95	21.62	17.85	22.33	0.38	131.28	18.99	14.34	28.88
80	0.64	101.43	21.62	17.36	20.10	0.31	138.18	18.61	12.34	28.67
90	0.64	98.91	21.62	16.88	18.23	0.26	145.66	18.32	10.36	28.69
100	0.64	96.38	21.62	16.40	16.66	0.20	153.57	18.13	8.44	28.87
110	0.64	93.86	21.62	15.91	15.32	0.16	161.79	17.98	6.56	29.18
120	0.64	91.34	21.62	15.43	14.19	0.12	170.23	17.87	4.72	29.57
130	0.64	88.81	21.62	14.95	13.22	0.08	178.85	17.78	2.91	30.04
140	0.64	86.29	21.62	14.46	12.39	0.05	187.61	17.71	1.13	30.57
150	0.64	83.77	21.62	13.98	11.67	0.03	196.48	17.66	−0.61	31.14

4.3.2   Joint Impact of Bargaining and Financing Choice on the Performance of Cost Sharing Contract

Observation 1. The equilibrium CSR effort satisfies the following order: $\theta^*_{CS^BRF} > \theta^*_{CS^RRF} \geq \theta^*_{RF}; \theta^*_{CS^BBF} > \theta^*_{CS^RBF} \geq \theta^*_{BF}$.

Observation 1 demonstrates the impact of the CS contract and the bargaining during the cost-sharing on CSR effort. It shows that under both BF and RF the CSR effort is highest in the bargaining CS contract, followed by an R-led CS contract, and lowest for the case without cost-sharing agreement. Thus, the CS contract can effectively enhance the CSR effort. In addition, the bargaining CS contract can make the CSR effort even higher than that under an R-led CS contract. Therefore, negotiations during cost-sharing are necessary for promoting CSR investment in the chain.

Observation 2. The equilibrium values of profits satisfy the following relationship.

(i) $\pi^{R*}_{CS^RRF} > \pi^{R*}_{CS^BRF} > \pi^{R*}_{RF}; \pi^{R*}_{CS^RBF} > \pi^{R*}_{CS^BBF} > \pi^{R*}_{BF}$,

(ii) $\pi^{S*}_{CS^BRF} > \pi^{S*}_{CS^RRF} > \pi^{S*}_{RF}; \pi^{S*}_{CS^BBF} > \pi^{S*}_{CS^RBF} > \pi^{S*}_{BF}$.

Observation 2 (i) reveals that under both BF and RF the R profit is highest in the bargaining CS contract, followed by the R-led CS contract, and lowest for the case without a cost-sharing agreement. In Observation 2 (ii) the S profit is highest in the bargaining CS contract, followed by the R-led CS contract, while it is the lowest in the case without a cost-sharing agreement. Overall, Observation 2 shows that no matter which financing mechanism is applied, the CS contract results in higher profits for all partners in the chain and subsequently increases the overall profitability of the supply chain. Regarding the impact of bargaining on the performance of CS contracts, Observation 2 implies that R may be unwilling to negotiate a cost-sharing parameter as it results in lower profits than the case where R determines the cost-sharing parameter. In contrast, bargaining on the CS benefits S as it leads to higher profit for S.

5 Concluding Remarks

In this study, we consider the two financing mechanisms of BF and RF, and a CSR cost-sharing contract for a capital-constrained supply chain where a downstream retailer's sales are influenced by the upstream supplier's CSR effort. Based on the equilibrium analysis, we find that no matter which financing mechanism of RF and BF is applied, a CS contract always results in higher supplier's CSR effort and higher profits for all supply chain members when compared with the case without a CS contract. This finding corroborates with the literature [2, 3]. However, our numerical results contribute to the extant literature by revealing that the effectiveness of the CS contract does not depend on the characteristics of the supply chain such as wholesale price, capital constraint, and demand variability. Our study also suggests that the performance of the CSR effort and the profitability of all members of the supply chain really depend on the financing mechanism they choose. In most situations, a RF tailored to meet the supplier's best interests appears the best way to achieve these double goals. Combining these financing mechanisms with a (sharing) coordination between members will always ensure a higher engagement, a larger gain as well as a more sustainable support of the CSR development by the supply chain. Therefore, our findings confirm the increasing propensity of using RF to support CSR goals of many big companies like PUMA, Hewlett-Packard Company, etc. with their suppliers. Finally, our work serves as an initial step for future work in designing mechanisms to improve CSR performance and efficiency of the supply chain, based on a combination of financing and sharing mechanisms. Pursuing the efforts to integrate supply chain finance and supply chain coordination should be a fertile direction for future research.

Acknowledgments. The authors would like to thank CNRS, CREMUMR 6211, University of Rennes 1 and FILEAS FOG-ANR-17-CE10–0001-01 Project for their support. All remaining errors are ours.

References

1. Rammohan, S.: Business benefits to Hewlett-Packard suppliers from socially and environmentally responsible (SE) practices in China – a case study. Working paper

2. Ghosh, D., Shah, J.: Supply chain analysis under green sensitive consumer demand and CS contract. Int. J. Prod. Econ **164**, 319–329 (2015)
3. Raj, A., Biswas, I., Srivastava, S.K.: Designing supply contracts for the sustainable SC using game theory. J. Clean. Prod **185**, 275–284 (2018)
4. Phan, D.A., Vo, T.L.H., Lai, A.N., Nguyen, T.L.A.: Coordinating contracts for VMI systems under manufacturer-CS and retailer-marketing efforts. Int. J. Prod. Econ. **211**, 98–118 (2019)
5. Kouvelis, P., Xu, F.: A supply chain theory of factoring and reverse factoring. Manage. Sci. https://doi.org/10.2139/ssrn.3241484
6. Martin, J., Hofmann, E.: Towards a framework for SC finance for the supply side. J. Purch. Supply Manag **25**(2), 157–171 (2019)
7. Kouvelis, P., Zhao, W.: The newsvendor problem and price-only contract when bankruptcy costs exist. Prod. Oper. Manag **20**(6), 921–936 (2011)
8. Klapper, L.: The role of factoring for financing small and medium enterprises. J. Bank Finan. **30**(11), 3111–3130 (2006)
9. Tanrisever, R.F., Cetinay, H., Reindrop, M., Fransoo, J.C.: Reverse factoring for SME finance. In: Working Paper (2015). https://doi.org/10.2139/ssrn.2183991
10. Gelsomino, L.M., de Boer, R., Steeman, M., Perego, A.: An optimisation strategy for concurrent supply chain finance schemes. J. Purch. Supply Manag. **25**(2), 185–196 (2019)
11. Nash, J.: The bargaining problem. Econometrica J. Econ. Soc. **18**(2), 155–162 (1950)
12. Kouvelis, P., Zhao, W.: Who should finance the SC? Impact of credit ratings on SC decisions. Manuf. Serv. Oper. Manag. **20**(1), 19–35 (2017)

Integrated Business Planning Process: Link Between Supply Chain Planning and Financial Planning

Mohamed Haythem Selmi[1]($\boxtimes$), Zied Jemai[2], Laurent Gregoire[1], and Yves Dallery[1]

[1] Industrial Engineering Laboratory, CentraleSupelec, University of Paris Saclay, Gif-sur-Yvette, Paris, France
mohamed-haythem.selmi@centralesupelec.fr
[2] LR-OASIS, National Engineering School of Tunis, University of Tunis El Manar, Tunis, Tunisia

Abstract. In this paper, we explore the interactions between supply chain planning and financial planning. To do so, we investigate the integrated business planning (IBP) process as a suitable interface between them. We focus on the French business culture. First, we provide the results and conclusions of a survey on the structure and details of the sales and operations planning (S&OP) processes of five top French multinational corporations and the extent to which finance is integrated into these processes. These companies have achieved a revenue of over 16 billion euros in 2020. Then, we conclude on the steps that the participating companies have implemented to transition from the traditional S&OP process to the complete IBP process, and thus on the steps that remain to be taken. We note that all participating companies have taken their first steps towards adopting an integrated business planning approach. They have all embraced scenario analysis. However, they are lagging behind on the other steps that require cross-functional and cross-company collaboration, such as financial integration. Finally, we define how the IBP process interacts with financial planning on four fronts, namely revenue and costs budgeting, monthly updates to budgets, capital expenditures budgeting, and working capital requirements planning.

Keywords: Sales and operations planning · Integrated business planning · Financial planning

1 Introduction

Supply chain management operates by implementing actions and decisions at three managerial levels, namely, strategic, tactical, and operational. These decisions are related to the different levels of a supply chain (upstream, internal, and downstream) as well as to the processes at each of these levels. They are varied in nature and form the basis for steering a supply chain [1]. These decisions generally influence the supply chain organization and the planning of its activities. Strategic decisions are made with a long-term horizon (generally 3 to 5 years with annual granularity). They include questions

© IFIP International Federation for Information Processing 2021
Published by Springer Nature Switzerland AG 2021
A. Dolgui et al. (Eds.): APMS 2021, IFIP AICT 632, pp. 149–158, 2021.
https://doi.org/10.1007/978-3-030-85906-0_17

of supply chain design and strategic choices of partners. Tactical planning decisions are made over a medium-term horizon (12 to 24 months with monthly granularity) and concern demand and supply balancing. Operational decisions are made over a short-term horizon (6 to 16 weeks with a weekly granularity) and concern operational planning issues (procurement plan, master production schedule, distribution resource planning, etc.). Operational execution addresses very short-term issues, such as scheduling. As supply chain management's approach began to evolve from functional to holistic and from intra-organizational to inter-organizational, links to the financial aspects of supply chains and their management become the focus of research and business. Despite this, a comprehensive map of the interactions between supply chain planning and financial planning is still lacking in the literature.

In this paper, we examine these interactions by investigating the integrated business planning (IBP) process as their potential framework. The IBP literature highlights the importance of financial integration within the process. However, it does not offer descriptive or prescriptive studies on organizational practices. To remedy this, we present a case study conducted with top French multinational companies.

The remainder of this study is structured as follows. Section 2 presents the traditional sales and operations planning (S&OP) process. Section 3 introduces the IBP process. In Sect. 4, we provide the results and conclusions of our case study. Finally, in Sect. 5, we explain our conclusions regarding the relationship between the IBP process and financial planning.

2 Traditional Sales and Operations Planning Process

The idea of the S&OP process emerged in the 1970s with the work of the business consultants Oliver Wight and Tom Wallace [2]. Conceptually, the S&OP process evolved from aggregate production planning (APP) to manufacturing resources planning (MRP II) [3, 4]. The traditional S&OP process focused on customer service and inventory. To manage them effectively, the drivers, namely demand and supply, must be aligned [5–8]. Hence, the main objective is to consolidate planned demand and to guarantee that it can be supplied by manufactured products in the medium-term to long-term planning horizon at an appropriate aggregated planning level. This helps companies create a demand and supply plan that is technically feasible using the resources of the company, cross-functionally agreed upon, and unique [9]. In practice, the traditional S&OP process represents a monthly, rolling, and multistage decision-making process with a typical planning horizon between 12 and 18 months. During the month, three meetings are held: A sales planning meeting called demand review and led by the sales manager, a supply review organized by the manufacturing, and an S&OP meeting. The output of the S&OP process is an operating plan, which is generally a consolidated view of sales, production, and inventories by month on a volume basis. Then, following the S&OP meeting, some reconciliation of volumes with financials is done to check against the budget.

After the first wave of implementation, the excitement faded. The traditional S&OP process began to be seen as a mere logistics exercise focusing on a simple demand and supply volume planning with too much detail [10]. Demand planners, often associated with the supply chain function, led the demand review with little inclusion of the sales and marketing functions. In fact, the single operating plan was the supply chain managers' objective. Finance and general management were most interested in planning and analyzing financial scenarios. Therefore, without a tangible financial link, volume forecasts became less of a priority than financial forecasts. Besides, the budget was given priority in this context, overruling any decisions made as part of the S&OP process. Moreover, many companies were increasingly driving innovation and responsiveness to customer needs. However, the traditional S&OP process was not developed to accurately forecast demand for new products and integrate it into the overall demand plan.

3 Evolution Towards the Integrated Business Planning Process

IBP is also commonly referred to as advanced S&OP. The new name reflects significant changes to the existing one. The IBP process represents the evolution of the S&OP process from its production planning origins to a fully integrated management and supply chain collaboration process [11]. The development of the S&OP process towards the IBP process started with the introduction of financial integration. The integration of product and portfolio management was the second evolutionary change. In fact, in the traditional S&OP process, product management was often seen as a separate creative process belonging to the R&D or marketing function, hence excluding an important business planning aspect. These two steps were shortly introduced after the S&OP process appeared. Equally, scenario analysis, which consists of examining the impact of potential changes on the entire company and making comparisons with strategy, represents a substantial advance over simple supply and demand planning. The latest evolution is the increased collaboration along the end-to-end supply chain to manage demand effectively and thus link suppliers and customers S&OP processes.

The goal of an effective S&OP process has always been to achieve alignment. Still, whereas the traditional S&OP process was simply aligning sales and manufacturing, the IBP process aligns sales, marketing, R&D, operations, purchasing, logistics, finance, HR, and even IT. Therefore, the IBP process is a decision-making process that realigns tactical plans for all business functions in all geographies (local, regional, and global) and in all business sectors (manufacturing, retail, and service) at an appropriate aggregated planning level (product family, brand, etc.). It has a minimum 24-month rolling planning horizon [12]. It is based on a monthly cycle of business reviews: product management, demand, supply, integrated reconciliation, and the management business review. These are not a simple sequence of meetings but an ongoing process of coordinating those accountable for reviewing, presenting, and communicating progress and change. Besides, they need to be action-oriented. Thorough preparation is required to identify the issues and scenarios to be discussed before each meeting. In this way, decisions can be made efficiently and updated plans approved before rendered available throughout the integrated process.

The Product Management Review focuses on product planning, which includes analyzing the product lifecycle, understanding where products fit into this cycle, and optimizing the product portfolio to decide to launch or discard products [13]. The objective of the demand review process is to agree upon a complete, unconstrained, and consolidated view of the expected demand situation in the medium-term to long-term planning horizon. It considers sales, marketing, and supply chain actions aimed at shaping demand to ensure that sales, profit, and service quality targets are met [14]. The supply review process's main objective is to match the updated demand plans with production, logistics, and procurement capabilities. It aims to identify potential pitfalls that hinder the development of a technically feasible supply plan and to find solutions that consider the company's financial objectives [13]. The integrated reconciliation is a continuous transversal process where gaps with financial goals and their implications are identified, understood, and addressed throughout the product, demand, and supply review processes. Scenario modeling and simulation are the basis for the integrated reconciliation process [15]. The integrated reconciliation meeting is the last opportunity to reach a cross-functional agreement. The management business review is the final decision-making meeting in the monthly IBP cycle. This meeting addresses gaps with respect to financial and strategic plans. Senior management needs to arbitrate between scenarios based on financial forecasts and make decisions concerning unresolved issues [16].

4 Survey

The conducted survey took place as a part of the activities of the supply chain Chair regrouping our research team and top five French multinational corporations from various business lines. In the following, we call them A, B, C, D, and E, where A is a retail chain, B is a luxury goods company, C is an aeronautics manufacturer, D is a pharmaceutical company, and E is a perfumes and cosmetics retailer. These companies have achieved a revenue of over 16 billion euros in 2020. In total, twelve senior managers with an operational or financial background and affiliated with the supply chain function were approached and participated in semi-structured interviews.

The objective of this survey is to investigate the structure and details of their S&OP processes and the extent to which finance is integrated into these processes. Company A, which does not have an S&OP process, was promptly dropped from the study. Company C has a process for each of its five subsidiaries. Here, we focus on two of them, namely C1 and C2.

4.1 Processes Structure

The following questions were prepared as a guide for discussions: Is your process formalized? Who is the process owner? What is the main objective of your process? What is the frequency of your process? What is the planning horizon? At what geographical level is your process conducted? At which aggregation levels does planning take place? Are there any KPIs to measure the efficiency of the process? Does the process include the product management review?

Table 1 summarizes the participating companies' answers.

A prerequisite for a well-functioning S&OP process is a complete and widely shared formalization. This is the case for most participating companies that use an ARCI matrix to define each stakeholder's responsibilities. However, another essential success factor is to define and monitor KPIs on the efficient execution of the process. This is currently

Table 1. Survey on S&OP structure

	B	C1	C2	D	E
Formalization	None	ARCI matrix	ARCI matrix	ARCI matrix	ARCI matrix
Objective	Balancing production capacity and sales objectives	Matching production load and capacity	Matching production load and capacity	Balancing demand and supply	Aligning the sales vision between finance, marketing, and supply chain
Planning horizon	12 to 18 months	5 years	24 to 36 months	12 to 18 months	3 months
Frequency	Monthly	Monthly	Monthly	Monthly	Monthly
Geographical level	World	World	World	Country and region	Country
Aggregation levels	Product activity and industrial typology	Product family and large customer	Product family	Product and distribution channel	Product category, brand, and product family
Process owner	Global distribution manager	Group supply chain methods manager	Supply chain manager of the subsidiary	Regional supply chain manager	Country supply chain manager
Process efficiency KPIs	None	S&OP stability (Adherence to time schedules)	S&OP stability (Adherence to time schedules)	No KPIs but an internal audit	None
Product management review	Yes	No	Partial	Yes	Partial

lacking in most participating companies. These KPIs may include decisions in time, people and information availability, and quality of information.

Moreover, choosing an adequate level of aggregation at which planning takes place significantly affects the efficiency and performance of the S&OP process. The participating companies plan their S&OP volumes mainly at an aggregated level corresponding to a product structure such as product families and brands. The industrial ones usually use two product structures. First, the demand plan is usually created based on a sales-oriented product structure, reflecting sales and marketing considerations. Second, the supply plan is usually created based on a production-oriented product structure, reflecting industrial resources and technologies needed. When constructing the supply plan from the updated demand plan, these two structures must be matched. However, conversion difficulties occur often.

Company D is the only company to have a process at several geographical levels. It points out the complexity of synchronizing local and regional processes, which is a recurring issue in this configuration. One of the consequences is the existence of a one-month delay between the two levels. This is an organizational and technological issue caused by the absence of an information system to integrate and coordinate both processes.

4.2 Financial Integration

To achieve full financial integration within the IBP process, the following requirements must be met:

- The finance function needs to be involved in all the process reviews (I).
- A financial assessment of all volumes is necessary (II).

  - During the product management review, changes in the product pipeline and portfolio must be translated in terms of projections of sales revenue.
  - During the demand review, sales volume forecasts need to be translated in terms of projected revenues and associated marketing costs.
  - During the supply review, produced or procured volumes need to be translated in terms of cost of goods sold (COGS), distribution costs, and overhead costs. Moreover, the evolution of the value of all inventories needs to be measured.

- During the reconciliation meeting, discussions and scenario analysis need to be based on revenue, margin, and working capital projections analysis (III).
- Financial KPIs need to be defined and monitored (IV). These may include budget vs. projected sales forecast, overhead costs as a percentage of revenue, distribution costs as percentage of revenue, EBITDA/EVA, working capital utilization, etc.

The following questions were prepared to see if the participating companies are fulfilling these requirements: In which reviews does the finance function participate? Does the process include scenario analysis? Are sales revenues and costs tracked? Are changes in inventory levels tracked? Are changes in working capital requirements (inventory value) tracked? Are investments discussed during certain reviews? Are the revenue and costs budgets updated?

Table 2 summarizes the participating companies' answers.

By crosschecking the responses of the participating companies with the requirements described above, we present, in Table 3, an assessment of the degree of financial integration in the S&OP processes of the participating companies. We provide a qualitative evaluation. A company's fulfillment of a requirement is graded into three levels: Absent when it does not meet any aspect of the requirement described above, partial when some of the requirement is met, and complete when all aspects are met.

Table 2. Survey on financial integration.

	B	C1	C2	D	E
Finance function participation	Management business review	No	No	No	S&OP meeting
Scenario analysis	Yes	Yes	Yes	Yes	Yes
Tracking sales revenues and costs	Yes	No	Yes	Yes	Yes
Tracking inventory levels	Yes	No	Yes	No	Yes
Tracking working capital requirement (inventory value)	No	No	Yes	No	Yes
Discussing investments	Yes	No	No	Yes	No
Updating revenue and costs budgets	No	No	No	No	No

The degree of financial integration is established in the same way. It is absent when all requirements are rated absent, partial when at least one requirement is rated partial and complete when all requirements are fully met.

Table 3. Degree of financial integration.

	I	II	III	IV	**Financial integration**
B	Partial	Partial	Absent	Absent	**Partial**
C1	Absent	Absent	Absent	Absent	**Absent**
C2	Absent	Partial	Partial	Absent	**Partial**
D	Absent	Partial	Partial	Absent	**Partial**
E	Partial	Partial	Partial	Absent	**Partial**

We notice a growing interest in translating volume forecasts into financial forecasts. This reflects a growing awareness among supply chain managers of the importance of reconciliation with finance. In contrast, the finance function's absence reflects a low interest and ignorance of the potential S&OP process's impact on financial aspects. This also explains the difficult accessibility to financial data by supply chain managers and the absence of financial KPIs.

4.3 Transitioning to Integrated Business Planning

As mentioned in Sect. 3, four steps must be completed for the company to fully transition from the traditional S&OP process to the IBP process. Based on the results of the two parts of the survey, we identify the steps each company has taken to adopt the IBP process.

Table 4. Transitioning to the IBP process

	Scenario analysis	New product integration	Financial integration	Supply chain collaboration	**Transitioning to the IBP process**
B	Complete	Complete	Partial	Absent	**Partial**
C1	Complete	Absent	Absent	Absent	**Partial**
C2	Complete	Partial	Partial	Absent	**Partial**
D	Complete	Complete	Partial	Absent	**Partial**
E	Complete	Partial	Partial	Absent	**Partial**

We use the same evaluation scale as in the previous analysis. Table 4 summarizes the outcome of this study.

We note that all companies have taken their first steps towards adopting an integrated business planning approach. They have all embraced scenario analysis. Companies B and D are the most advanced in their transition project, followed by companies C2 and E. Subsidiary C1 lags behind the others, but this can be explained by the nature of its products, which have a very long life cycle and R&D phase. In addition, all its orders are fixed for five years. We can also conclude that, in the context of the sample studied, the more the steps require cross-functional and cross-company collaboration, the more difficult the implementation becomes.

5 Links Between Integrated Business Planning and Financial Planning

In addition to the semi-structured interviews, focus group sessions were held to understand how integrated business planning interacts with financial planning. We concluded that the IBP process interacts with financial planning at four levels, namely revenue and costs budgeting, monthly updates to budgets, capital expenditures budgeting, and working capital requirements planning.

Revenue and costs budgeting is still an essential task, even though it is time-consuming for managers. It usually requires multiple iterations until the figures (revenues and costs) are adjusted and correspond to senior management's expectations. The IBP process cannot replace the budgeting process and the need for multiple adjustment iterations, but it can be very useful for the first set of inputs. Without the IBP process, budgeting starts with the actual year-to-date sales data, previous historical years sales data, information about future customers and trends, and an estimation of future growth. With the IBP process, the product, demand, supply, and inventory plans for the next fiscal year are used as primary inputs into the budget process. These plans being aligned reflect future reality far better than raw sales forecasts. The use of outputs from the IBP process is more persuasive to senior managers because they are involved in the decision-making process. This can help reduce the number of iterations during the annual budgeting process.

As discussed above, finance has an important role throughout the entire IBP process. It explains the financial implications of product, demand, and supply plans potential changes, starting by transforming volume assumptions into economic assumptions regarding costs and revenues. Afterward, finance gradually establishes a comprehensive assessment of the company's financial health over the planning horizon and identifies gaps in relation to financial plans (especially the budget) and strategy. This assessment should include profit and loss projections, margin projections, and cash flow analysis. After validation by senior management of the revised financial forecasts, budgets are updated.

The majority of logistic and industrial investments are needed to accommodate product volumes that are part of both current or future demand and supply plans. Linking the capital planning and justification process with the IBP process ensures that all capital investment decisions are based on the latest, most robust, and most accurate product volume plans. In this case, all needs for logistic and industrial investments are initiated by the IBP process results. Nevertheless, studying each investment's profitability and making the final decision are carried out within the capital budgeting process. The main obstacle to achieve this synchronization is that capital budgeting is usually annual and sometimes updated in the middle of the year, whereas the IBP is monthly.

Implementing the IBP process usually leads to significant inventory reductions, which results in cash flow improvement. Moreover, continuously balancing supply and demand ensures optimal inventory levels. Therefore, the IBP process can be considered as an important lever to manage working capital. It provides a simple and effective mechanism for communicating inventory targets to the entire company and ensuring they are respected.

6 Conclusion

The literature does not offer descriptive or prescriptive studies on organizational practices related to financial integration within the S&OP process. To remedy this, we present in this paper a case study conducted with multinational companies with focus on top French corporations. A survey is conducted to explore the structure and details of these companies' S&OP processes and the extent to which finance is integrated into them according to requirements we have defined. We also conclude what steps the participating companies have implemented to adopt the complete IBP process. And thus, what steps remain to be taken and need to be addressed. We note that all participating companies have taken their first steps towards adopting an integrated business planning approach. They have all embraced scenario analysis. However, they are lagging behind on the other steps that require cross-functional and cross-company collaboration, especially, financial integration, and supply chain collaboration.

After further discussions sessions with the interviewees, we conclude that implementing a complete IBP process is the bridge between supply chain planning and financial planning. Besides, complete financial integration is the first step. Finally, we explain how the IBP process interacts with financial planning on four fronts, namely revenue and costs budgeting, monthly updates to budgets, capital expenditures budgeting, and working capital requirements planning.

In most companies, the initial budget is established in a multi-month process, whether it is the revenue and cost budget or the capital expenditures budget. Besides, they are usually updated once or twice a year. Linking these updates to the IBP process presumes it will be done monthly. Certainly, it is no easy task to revise all of these data monthly and share them with all members of the organization. This requires a solid and widely shared information system. Furthermore, all these organizational challenges require more empirical research.

References

1. Berrah, L.: L'indicateur de Performance: Concepts et Applications. Cépadues-Editions, Toulouse (2002)
2. Wallace, T.F., Stahl, R.: Sales & Operations Planning: The Executive's Guide; Balancing Demand and Supply; Aligning Units and Enhancing Teamwork. TF Wallace & Company, Cincinnati (2006)
3. Singhal, J., Singhal, K.: Holt, Modigliani, Muth, and Simon's work and its role in the renaissance and evolution of operations management. J. Oper. Manag. 25(2), 300–309 (2007)
4. Olhager, J.: Evolution of operations planning and control: from production to supply chains. Int. J. Prod. Res. 51(23–24), 6836–6843 (2013)
5. Lapide, L.: An S&OP maturity model. J. Bus. Forecast. 24(3), 15 (2005)
6. Grimson, J.A., Pyke, D.F.: Sales and operations planning: an exploratory study and framework. Int. J. Logistics Manage. 18(3), 322–346 (2007)
7. Feng, Y., D'Amours, S., Beauregard, R.: The value of sales and operations planning in oriented strand board industry with make-to-order manufacturing system: cross functional integration under deterministic demand and spot market recourse. Int. J. Prod. Econ. 115(1), 189–209 (2008)
8. Ivert, L.K., Jonsson, P.: The potential benefits of advanced planning and scheduling systems in sales and operations planning. Ind. Manag. Data Syst. 110(5), 659–681 (2010)
9. Thomé, A.M.T., Scavarda, L.F., Fernandez, N.S., Scavarda, A.J.: Sales and operations planning: a research synthesis. Int. J. Prod. Econ. 138(1), 1–13 (2012)
10. Coldrick, A., Ling, D., Turner, C.: Evolution of Sales & Operations Planning-From Production Planning to Integrated Decision Making. Strata Bridge, Gloucester (2003)
11. White, O.: Transitioning from S&OP to IBP. Retrieved from Oliver White paper series (2018)
12. Palmatier, G., Crum, C.: Why companies are evolving to integrated business planning – and what they are gaining by doing so. Retrieved from Oliver White paper series (2006)
13. Tinker, E.J.: Revitalize your S&OP. J. Bus. Forecast. 29(3), 4 (2010)
14. Grüne, G., Lockemann, S., Kluy, V., Meinhardt, S.: Mapping business processes in the process industry: selected examples. In: Business Process Management within Chemical and Pharmaceutical Industries, pp. 69–162. Springer, Heidelberg (2014). https://doi.org/10.1007/978-3-642-11717-6_3
15. Moon, M., Alle, P.: From sales & operations planning to business integration. Foresight Int. J. Appl. Forecast. 37, 5–12 (2015)
16. Coldrick, A., Ling, D., Turner, C.: Integrated decision making–the choices. Retrieved from Stratabridge (2003)

An EOQ-Based Lot Sizing Model with Working Capital Requirements Financing Cost

Yuan Bian[1(✉)], David Lemoine[2,4], Thomas G. Yeung[2,4], Nathalie Bostel[3,4], Vincent Hovelaque[5,6], and Jean-Laurent Viviani[5,6]

[1] University of Chinese Academy of Sciences, Beijing, China
bianyuan@ucas.ac.cn
[2] IMT Atlantique, Nantes, France
{david.lemoine,thomas.yeung}@imt-atlantique.fr
[3] Université de Nantes, Nantes, France
nathalie.bostel@univ-nantes.fr
[4] LS2N UMR CNRS 6004, Nantes, France
[5] IGR-IAE of Rennes, University of Rennes 1, Rennes, France
{vincent.hovelaque,jean-laurent.viviani}@univ-rennes1.fr
[6] CREM UMR CNRS 6211, Rennes, France

Abstract. In time of financial crisis, bank loans are often extremely difficult to obtain for many companies. However, companies always need free cash flow to efficiently react against to any uncertainty. This work demonstrates the impact of financial consequences on operational decisions in the single-product, single-level, infinite capacity EOQ model. We propose an operation-related working capital requirement (WCR) model in a tactical planning context. The classic EOQ model is extended by integrating the WCR financing cost with a cost minimization objective and deriving its analytical solution. Compared with the optimal policy of the classic EOQ model, our approach leads to a new policy with a smaller production lot size due to the new cost trade-offs. Furthermore, an analytical analysis with a classic EOQ-based formula that considers the cost of capital demonstrates the sensitivity of approximating financial costs compared to our exact approach. Finally, sensitivity analysis and numerical examples are also provides.

Keywords: Working capital requirements · Payment delays · EOQ model · Cost of capital

1 Introduction

In the context of the recent financial crisis, many companies suffer from a lack of credit and working capital. Furthermore, they must accept longer payment

Supported by the Fundamental Research Funds for the Central Universities.

A. Dolgui et al. (Eds.): APMS 2021, IFIP AICT 632, pp. 159–166, 2021.
https://doi.org/10.1007/978-3-030-85906-0_18

terms from their customers which exacerbates their working capital level [4]. Moreover, tight or unavailable bank credit impacts the company's performance by halting their operations and starving the supply chain[1]. For this reason, in recent years working capital management (WCM), especially the working capital requirement(WCR) has drawn more attention for mainly two reasons. The first is the direct link to the cash flow level. The second reason is the potential of generating additional cash flow. As reported in the Working capital management report 2012 of Ernst, $1.1 trillion in cash have been unnecessarily tied up in working capital in the largest American and European companies. For its important role in practice, the WCR is chosen as the financial aspect to be integrated.

To do so, the WCR is remodeled for adapting the context of tactical planning following its financial signification based on cash conversion cycle [2]. However, its non-linear formulation brings additional difficulty in resolution. More essentially, due to this non-linearity, all existing theorems and properties of classic lot-sizing model must be revalidated. New ones may be necessarily proposed. For example, the Zero-Inventory Property has been proven valid in Uncapacitated Lot-Sizing (ULS) case. As mentioned in [3], to tackle more complex and realistic cases, some heuristic algorithms are established based on the Economic Order Quantity(EOQ) and the trade-off between the setup cost and inventory holding cost that minimizes the total cost. (When the EOQ model is adopted for lot-sizing problem, the EOQ represents the optimal production quantity and the fixed order cost is the fixed setup cost for one setup.) Therefore, we do not use the classic Economic Production Quantity (EPQ) model, but adopt the classical EOQ model and consider all operation costs including purchasing, setup, production and inventory holding (noted as holding for the rest of paper) costs. Furthermore, the WCR financing cost is integrated into the cost minimization objective in order to obtain a new form of the EOQ of this new problem. Such a new EOQ can thus be used for building heuristic in the future and to better understand the financial consequence of operation decision on the production program. The main contributions are summarized as follows:

- First, we propose a model of WCR adapted to the EOQ context. With this model, we are able to measure the evolution of WCR over the continuous planning horizon;
- Second, we give the closed-form, analytical formula for the optimal production quantity. Then, we prove that our result extends Wilson's formula. Furthermore, we identify the trade-offs between different costs that minimize the total cost. Sensitivity analysis is also provided in order to show the influence of parameter variations, particularly those which are finance related.

2 EOQ Based Cost Minimization Model

2.1 WCR Modeling and Differences Compared with the Trade Credit Concept

In the field of accounting and finance, the WCR is measured adopting the cash conversion cycle (CCC) methodology. It is calculated as the sum of the account payable and the inventory value minus the account receivable using the balance sheet and the profit & loss statement. However, it only represents an aggregated financial situation of the company at the moment of elaboration. Therefore, we propose a new generic WCR model based on the CCC. It is adapted for introducing the financial costs linked to operational decisions (i.e., the financing cost of WCR) in the EOQ context. Both the delay in payment to supplier and from client (i.e., downstream and upstream) are taken into account in this formulation. Moreover, only production-related WCRs are considered in this WCR model. They thus depend on the amount of investment for the related operations (e.g., purchasing, setup, production and inventory holding) and the associated financing duration before recovering by corresponding revenue. More precisely, the financing cost of the WCR is the interest (i.e., cost of capital) multiplied by the amount of WCR.

Comparing our WCR model with the concept of the trade credit in the inventory model literature, the essential difference is found on the consideration of sales revenue. In the literature, the trade credit is modeled with the assumption that the unpaid revenue from the customer is charged as a whole by the retailer for earning interest. From a financial point of view, it assumes, by default, that the cost part and the profit part of the revenue are reinvested in the same operating cycle. In practice, the profit can be allocated to any of a number of objectives for the firm including debt reduction, internal or external investment, or dividend payments. Consequently, the above-mentioned assumption does not reflect the financial management in real world situation. Since the profit reinvestment problem should be more carefully investigated. Therefore, we separate the investment problem and the WCR management and focus on the latter.

To do so, we assume that the WCR is only financed by the cost part of the revenue, not by the profit part. It is because the profit of the company has never been required, it does thus not correspond to the WCR definition and should not be considered as the WCR. In consequence, we adopt the scheme that the WCR generated by producing a product is only effectively recovered when that product is sold. Thus, we progressively and uniformly receive all production related cost from the sales revenue of products over time. Nonetheless, since we do not designate the allocation of profit (to WCR financing or others objectives), our model remains a partial model for companies.

2.2 Assumptions

In this section, we present an EOQ-based model with a cost minimization objective considering the financing cost of WCR. The WCR formulation and the corresponding proposed model are built under the following assumptions:

– Production:
  • Demand is constant and uniform during the planning horizon;
  • For each production lot, all purchasing, setup, production and inventory holding costs must be financed;
  • Production capacity is infinite;
  • No backlogging is allowed;
  • Only inventory of final product is considered;
  • Initial and final stocks are defined as zero;
  • No delivery delay of material and production is immediate.
– Financial:
  • Production, inventory and setup costs should be paid instantaneously (but may be financed);
  • WCR is only financed by the cost part of revenue;

As previously discussed, we only consider the cost portion in revenue (not the profit margin) for financing the WCR because the margin may be reinvested in another operation cycle. With this assumption, we do not need to consider the opportunity cost of using the margin to finance the WCR. Moreover, we consider that the WCR is generated due to the timing mismatch between revenue and costs to finance. Therefore, we set the last assumption in the list in order to precisely calculate the setup cost in revenue of selling each product. More specifically, all products in the same production lot share the fixed setup cost equally and it will be refunded progressively by selling the products.

2.3   Parameters Et Decision Variables

Notation is defined for the single-site, single-level, single-product with infinite capacity case in Table 1. These parameters are all assumed to be nonnegative. The decision variable is the production lot size, denoted as Q. Accordingly, Q^* represents the optimal production lot size.

Table 1. Parameters for WCR modeling

Parameter	Definition
T	Horizon length
D	Total demand in units
d	Demand rate in units per time unit $\left(d = \dfrac{D}{T} \right)$
h	Unit inventory cost in dollars per unit during a time unit
p	Unit production cost in dollars per unit
s	Unit setup cost per time in dollars per lot
a	Unit raw material cost in dollars per unit
r_c	Delay in payment from client in time units
r_f	Delay in payment to supplier in time units
α	Interest rate for financing WCR per dollar per time unit

2.4 WCR Formulation

Following the concept of the cash conversion cycle methodology, we propose a generic WCR formulation for purchasing, setup, production and holding inventory by taking into account the interest accrued by financing the WCR during the planning horizon. In the EOQ model, a uniform time division is established in which, for each cycle, a quantity Q is instantly supplied at the beginning of the cycle and uniformly consumed over the cycle. Thus, for a horizon with total duration, T and a global demand, D, each period will last $\dfrac{QT}{D}$ time units. Since the WCR represents the financing need for these operations between when we pay for them and when we collect the payment from customer, these two timings are the key elements of the WCR measurement. Explicitly, we product a lot of Q products at the beginning of the cycle (i.e., instant 0) with the following cost and revenue timing assumptions:

- The setup and production costs are paid immediately, while the purchasing cost is paid at a delay to the supplier at instant $0 + r_f$.
- A product sold (from inventory) at instant $t \in \left[0, \dfrac{QT}{D}\right]$ will be paid at a delay by the customer at the instant $t + r_c$.

The three diagrams in Fig. 1 illustrate the financing needs for purchase, production and setup operations over time. Since the WCR is the financial need to cover between the timing of paying for expenses and collecting the revenue, the surfaces in these figures represent the WCR of these operations in each production cycle. We can then easily establish the formulation of the WCR for each lot, generated by purchasing, setup and production, as follows:

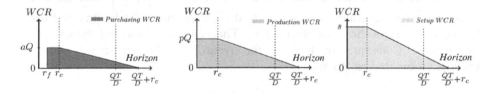

Fig. 1. Illustration of WCR of purchasing, setup and production costs in a cycle

$$WCR_{purchasing}(Q) = a\left[Q(r_c - r_f) + \frac{Q^2 T}{2D}\right]$$

$$WCR_{production}(Q) = p\left(Qr_c + \frac{Q^2 T}{2D}\right)$$

$$WCR_{setup}(Q) \quad = s\left(r_c + \frac{QT}{2D}\right)$$

Contrary to purchasing, set-up and production, which are all one-time payments, a unitary inventory holding cost must be paid regularly for each item for the entire duration of its storage. Therefore, there is a cumulative effect in financing the inventory holding costs. More precisely, for one product sold at $t \in \left[0, \frac{QT}{D}\right]$, we must pay its inventory holding costs generated in all instants over the entire duration 0 to t. Thus, all these costs must be financed from the instant when they occur (instant 0) until the arrival of client's payment at $t + r_c$, as presented in Fig. 2.

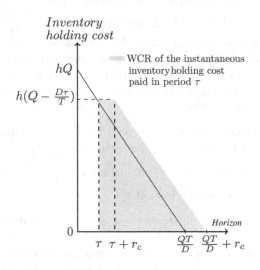

Fig. 2. Illustration of the WCR calculation for inventory holding cost

Consider an item that is sold at instant t, where $t \in \left[0, \frac{QT}{D}\right]$) and one of its inventory payment which occurs at $\tau \in [0, t]$. This cost must be financed until the customer pays the product at $t + r_c$. Therefore, the financing duration will be $t + r_c - \tau$. Consequently, the WCR for inventory holding cost in a production cycle is formulated as follows:

$$
\begin{aligned}
WCR_{inventory}(Q) &= \int_0^{\frac{QT}{D}} \int_0^t h\frac{QT}{D}(t + r_c - \tau)\ d\tau dt \\
&= h\left(\frac{Q^3 T^2}{6D^2} + \frac{r_c Q^2 T}{2D}\right)
\end{aligned}
\tag{1}
$$

Following the above formulations of WCR, the total WCR for a production cycle can be expressed as follows:

$$
\begin{aligned}
WCR(Q) &= WCR_{inventory} + WCR_{purchasing} + WCR_{production} + WCR_{setup} \\
&= \frac{hT^2}{6D^2}Q^3 + \frac{T}{2D}(hr_c + a + p)Q^2 + \left[a(r_c - r_f) + pr_c + \frac{sT}{2D}\right]Q + sr_c
\end{aligned}
$$

Accordingly, the total WCR is formulated as follows:

$$WCR_{total} = \frac{hT^2}{6D}Q^2 + \frac{T}{2}(hr_c + a + p)Q + D\left[a(r_c - r_f) + pr_c + \frac{sT}{2D}\right] + sr_c D\frac{1}{Q}$$

2.5 Objective Function

The aim of our contribution is to minimize the total cost (TC) including the production-related logistic cost and associated financial cost for satisfying constant demands. In our case, the interest is the cost of financing the WCR. The formulations of these components are

- The logistic cost (denoted as CL) is the sum of purchasing, setup, production and inventory holding costs: $CL = aD + s\dfrac{D}{Q} + pD + hT\dfrac{Q}{2}$;
- The interest to pay for financing the WCR (denoted as CF) based on an interest rate α: $CF = \alpha WCR_{total}$.

Consequently, the objective function is formulated as

$$
\begin{aligned}
TC =\;& CL + CF \\
=\;& D\left\{a + p + \alpha\left[a(r_c - r_f) + pr_c + \frac{sT}{2D}\right]\right\} \\
& + \frac{hT + \alpha(hr_c + a + p)T}{2}Q + \frac{\alpha hT^2}{6D}Q^2 + \frac{Ds(1 + \alpha r_c)}{Q}
\end{aligned}
\tag{2}
$$

We observe that the objective function is convex because all negative terms are either stationary, linearly increase or convex which means a unique minimum solution exists.

3 Optimal Solution and Structural Properties

To calculate the optimal production lot size, Q^*, we take the first-order derivative of TC.

$$\frac{dTC}{dQ} = -\frac{s(1 + \alpha r_c)D}{Q^2} + \frac{\alpha hQT^2}{3D} + \frac{[h + \alpha(hr_c + a + p)]T}{2} \tag{3}$$

The optimal solution is obtained when the Eq. (3) is set equal to zero. In order to calculate it, we adopt the Cardano method which is devoted to resolve a cubic equation in a special form.

Proposition 1. *We denote that* $\Delta = \dfrac{3\alpha^2 h^2 T^4}{s^2(1 + \alpha r_c)^2 D^4} - \dfrac{[h + \alpha(hr_c + a + p)]^3 T^3}{2s^3(1 + \alpha r_c)^3 D^3}$

$-$ *if* $\Delta > 0, Q^* = \dfrac{1}{\sqrt[3]{\dfrac{hT^2\alpha}{6D^2 s(1+\alpha r_c)}}\left\{\sqrt[3]{1 + \sqrt{1 - \dfrac{D[h(1+\alpha r_c)+\alpha(a+p)]^3}{6h^2 s(1+\alpha r_c)\alpha^2 T}}} + \sqrt[3]{1 - \sqrt{1 - \dfrac{D[h(1+\alpha r_c)+\alpha(a+p)]^3}{6h^2 s(1+\alpha r_c)\alpha^2 T}}}\right\}}$

$$- \text{ if } \Delta = 0, \ Q^* = \frac{D[h + \alpha(hr_c + a + p)]}{2\alpha hT}$$

$$- \text{ if } \Delta < 0, \ Q^* = \frac{1}{2\sqrt{\dfrac{[h(1 + \alpha r_c) + \alpha(a + p)]T}{6Ds(1 + \alpha r_c)}} \cos\left\{\dfrac{1}{3} \arccos\left[\sqrt{\dfrac{6h^2 s(1 + \alpha r_c)\alpha^2 T}{[h(1 + \alpha r_c) + \alpha(a + p)]^3 D}}\right]\right\}}$$

We can immediately remark that the optimal solution does not depend on the delay in payment to the supplier. This is not surprising as it remains constant whatever the value of Q in the WCR formulation. We can also deduce from this proposition to the fact that our result extends the Wilson formula.

Proposition 2. *For any value of* Δ,

- Q^* *is an increasing function of* s *and* r_c
- Q^* *is a decreasing function* h, a, p *and* α

Proposition 3. *For any value of* Δ, *let* Q^*_{EOQ} *be the optimal solution for the classic EOQ model, then* $Q^* \leq Q^*_{EOQ} = \sqrt{\dfrac{2Ds}{hT}}$

From a managerial point of view, this corollary has great significance as the setup and inventory holding costs are often very difficult to estimate in practice. The fact that our proposed model is less sensitive to variations in these costs yields a more robust economic order quantity.

4   Conclusions

We propose a new generic model of operations-related working capital requirements. Such a modeling allows us to measure the evolution of WCR over the entire planning horizon. Furthermore, an EOQ-based cost minimization model is developed considering the financing cost of WCR for the single-site, single-level, single-production and infinite production capacity case. We derive the analytical formula of the optimal EOQ and provide analysis to highlight some managerial insights.

References

1. Benito, A., Neiss, K.S., Price, S., Rachel, L.: The impact of the financial crisis on supply. Bank Engl. Q. Bull. Q2 (2010)
2. Bian, Y., et al.: A dynamic lot-sizing-based profit maximization discounted cash flow model considering working capital requirement financing cost with infinite production capacity. Int. J. Prod. Econ. **196**, 319–332 (2018)
3. Brahimi, N., Absi, N., Dauzère-Pérès, S., Nordli, A.: Single-item dynamic lot-sizing problems: an updated survey. Eur. J. Oper. Res. **263**, 838–863 (2017)
4. Zeballos, A.C., Seifert, R.W., Protopappa-Sieke, M.: Single product, finite horizon, periodic review inventory model with working capital requirements and short-term debt. Comput. Oper. Res. **40**(12), 2940–2949 (2013)

Put Option Contracts in Newsvendor Model with Bankruptcy Risk

Pooya Hedayatinia[1]($\boxtimes$)(iD), David Lemoine[2]($\boxtimes$)(iD), Guillaume Massonnet[2]($\boxtimes$),
and Jean-Laurent Viviani[1]($\boxtimes$)(iD)

[1] Univ Rennes, CNRS, CREM - UMR6211, 35000 Rennes, France
{pooya.hedayatinia,jean-laurent.viviani}@univ-rennes1.fr
[2] IMT Atlantique, LS2N, 4 Rue Alfred Kastler, 44300 Nantes, France
{david.lemoine,guillaume.massonnet}@imt-atlantique.fr

Abstract. This paper studies a newsvendor problem in which the retailer can mix two contracts, a wholesale price and a put option contract. We consider that the newsvendor is financially constrained and may need to contract a loan to cover her ordering costs, with a probability that she becomes bankrupted. We show that when a put option contract is available, the retailer's order quantity increases, while the bankruptcy risk and therefore the loan's interest rate decrease. We illustrate these results with numerical experiments on a simple example for different demand sizes and variability.

Keywords: Newsvendor · Finance · Bankruptcy · Put option contracts

1 Introduction

We consider a newsvendor problem in which a retailer has to decide its optimal inventory level for a future selling season. The classical objective is to find the best tradeoff between ordering too many units, inducing a holding cost for every unit of remaining product, or end up with insufficient inventory, leading to lost sales for unmet demands. This problem is rising because of the uncertainty in future demand and it becomes even more significant for the retailer when she needs to use a credit to cover her ordering costs and has to repay borrowed credit after realizing her sale. In that case, she usually refers to a bank to receive a loan to cover her expenses, possibly using a collateral to secure the loan and reduce her interest rate [17]. If the retailer cannot pay her credit obligation, she becomes bankrupted and loses all her wealth. Thus the demand's uncertainty is leading to newsvendor problem and may lead to a bankruptcy risk.

We focus on the above problem, that involves a financially constrained retailer, when she can orders her product through a mixture of wholesale price

This work was partially supported by the French National Research Agency and this is the project ANR-17-CE10-0001-01 called *FILEAS FOG*.

© IFIP International Federation for Information Processing 2021
Published by Springer Nature Switzerland AG 2021
A. Dolgui et al. (Eds.): APMS 2021, IFIP AICT 632, pp. 167–174, 2021.
https://doi.org/10.1007/978-3-030-85906-0_19

and put option contract. Units ordered with the latter are equipped with an option that allows the retailer to sell them back to the supplier at a predefined price. Traditionally, the put option contracts are a financial derivative tool used in the capital market, but it is a recent trend to use a similar concept in operations management. In essence, these contracts are similar to the well-known buyback contract, except that in this case the retailer needs to pay a premium for each unit she may sell back. In other words, the retailer can secure a part of her ordering quantity through a put option contract.

Different industries have used the put option contracts to deal with inventory risk management. Hewlett Packard (HP) are implying these kinds of contracts from 2000 to manage the inventory risk [15]. Put options have been used by the agricultural industries to hedge against unexpected weather situation in Chicago Mercantile Exchange [22]. Implying option contracts in the operation is an increasing trend to deal with supply chain management [19].

In this paper, we analyze the ordering decisions of the retailer with wholesale and put option contract, then we investigate how the bank selects a proper interest rate for a requested loan. Finally, we compare the performance, bankruptcy risk and received loan's interest rate of the retailer with and without a put option contract besides the wholesale price contract.

2   Literature Review

Decentralizing the decision making in a supply chain generally leads to a global performance reduction [16]. Since demand uncertainty directly affects the retailer, she suffers from the lack of flexibility in her ordering decision and the induced risk on her profit [18], [3]. Different mechanisms have emerged to mitigate these effects, such as buyback, emergency purchase or option contracts. It is shown that option contracts can improve the flexibility of the supply chain [10] and can be used as a risk hedging tool [11] and [2]. In the operations management literature, three main kinds of option contracts have been studied: (i) call option contracts that the retailer can use to receive the product immediately at the selling season [1] (similar to capacity reservation contracts), (ii) put option contracts that the retailer can use to sell back unsold products [7], [2] (similar to buyback contracts), or (iii) bidirectional option contracts that the retailer can choose to use it as a call or put option contract at the time of exercise [8], [21]. It is shown that under certain conditions, the supplier and retailer can both improve their performances with the existence of an option contract [4]. Other works illustrate that the option contracts can reduce the over/under inventory risk, see e.g. [23] for an application to the agricultural industry. In this study, we focus on the put option contract. In a recent article [19], the authors show that the supplier can design the put option contract in order to achieve the supply chain coordination, which means that the whole supply chain behaves like a centralized system. The put option contract is analyzed for a price setting newsvendor which can hedge her risk by using this contract [20]. [2] studied the put option contract under information asymmetry and risk-averse retailer.

The other aspect of our study focuses on the financial constraints of a retailer which can affect the performance of the global supply chain. Indeed, financial considerations on the operational decisions of the retailer can help improve the supply chain efficiency [5,6,9]. In this case that retailer has a limitation on her capital and may refer to a creditor to cover her ordering cost, inducing a bankruptcy risk in the process. This scenario is analyzed comprehensively by Kouvelis and Zhao [12,13]. In this article, we consider a financially constrained retailer who can use a put option contract to secure part of her ordering from the wholesale price contract. We first investigate the retailer and the bank decisions analytically. Then we analyze numerically the effect of a put option contract on the bankruptcy risk and performance of the retailer for different demand sizes.

3 Model Description

We consider a supply chain that consists of a financially constrained newsvendor (retailer) who faces a stochastic demand D at the beginning of the selling season (time 0). We assume that D follows an IFR (*Increasing Failure Rate*) distribution with probability density function (pdf) ϕ and cumulative distribution function (cdf) Φ and has finite mean μ. In order to satisfy her customers' demand, the retailer has the possibility to buy units of product using two types of contracts offered by her supplier. The first one is a classical wholesale price contract, in which the retailer purchases units at a given wholesale cost $w > 0$. With the second one, the retailer has the possibility to add a put option contract on some of the units purchased for an additional upfront payment $o > 0$ per unit. In return if the retailer decides to exercise her option once demand is realized, the supplier has to buy unsold units from her at a predefined per-unit exercise price e. Note that this option is only available for units to which the put option applies. At time 0, the retailer chooses a total quantity q to purchase from the supplier and an option quantity $q_p \leq q$. We note her decision vector at time 0 $\mathbf{q} = (q, q_p)$. At the end of the selling season (time 1), uncertainty is resolved and the retailer sells as much of her available inventory at a per-unit price p to satisfy the realized demand d. If she has leftover units that were purchased with a put option, she exercises her option and thus collects an additional revenue equal to $(e \min\{q - d, q_p\})^+$. The objective of the retailer is to decide how many units to purchase in total, as well as the quantity subject to the put option in order to maximize her profit at time T. Let r_f be the risk-free interest rate over the planning horizon. To avoid trivial cases, we consider in the remainder of this paper that $p > (w + o)(1 + r_f) > e > o(1 + r_f)$: The first inequality ensures that using the put option is profitable for the retailer, while the second and third one guarantee that she recovers a strictly positive part of the wholesale price when she exercises her option. We consider that the retailer is financially constrained, i.e. she has finite working capital y and collateral x. When the working capital is not enough to pay the quantity ordered by the retailer, she has the possibility to request a loan from a risk-neutral bank that offers a fairly priced loan. In that case, the interest rate offered by the bank depends on the risk incurred by the retailer and the collateral is used to secure the loan in order to reduce the bank's interest rate. In particular if the future value of the loan amount L is lower that the retailer's collateral ($x \geq L(1 + r_f)$), the loan is fully secured and the bank offers and interest rate equal to the risk-free rate r_f. On the other hand when the loan is not secured ($x < L(1 + r_f)$) there exists a probability that the retailer does not have enough capital at the end of the selling season to fully repay the loan obligation. Therefore in that case, the bank chooses an interest rate $r > r_f$ to compensate the retailer's bankruptcy risk. Note that when the retailer becomes bankrupted, the bank seizes all her sales and collateral.

3.1   The Retailer's Decision

We start by considering the case of a retailer with no financial constraint. The revenue generate by sales and buybacks at time 1 are equal to:

$$R(\mathbf{q}) = p \min\{q, \mathrm{D}\} + e \min\{q - \mathrm{D}, q_p\}$$

and we can express its expected cash flow as:

$$\Pi(\mathbf{q}) = \mathbb{E}\left[R(\mathbf{q}) + (1 + r_f)(y - wq - oq_p)^+ + x\right]^+ \tag{1}$$

The following proposition states that the retailer can always find an unique optimal decision to maximize her expected cash flow.

Proposition 1. *When the retailer is not financially constrained, her expected cash flow function is jointly concave. The corresponding optimal total quantity q and put option quantity q_p are:*

$$q^* = \Phi^{-1}(1 - \frac{(w + o)(1 + r_f) - e}{p - e})$$

$$q_p^* = q^* - \Phi^{-1}(\frac{o(1 + r_f)}{e}) \tag{2}$$

We now focus on the case where the retailer as a limited working capital y, with x the equities that can be used as collateral to secure the bank loan. If the retailer working capital is not sufficient to cover her cost at time 0, i.e. $wq + oq_p > y$, she needs to borrow a amount equal to $L = (wq + oq_p - y)^+$ from the bank. At time 1, the bank loan's repayment is then equal to $L(1 + r)$, where r is the interest rate decided by the bank. Since the bank is risk neutral, its expected repayment Π_{bk} at time 1 must equal the present value of the amount borrowed by the retailer:

$$\mathbb{E}\left[\Pi_{bk}\right] = (1 + r_f)(wq + oq_p - y)^+ \tag{3}$$

When the loan is secured by the collateral of the retailer ($L(1 + r_f) \leq x$), the bank bears no risk of default from the retailer and receives a repayment $\Pi_{bk} = (wq + oq_p)(1 + r_f)$ from the retailer with probability 1. As a consequence, it sets an interest rate equal to the risk-free rate r_f. Otherwise, the bank uses

Eq. (3) to define an interest rate $r > r_f$. The expected cash flow of the retailer then depends on the value of her collateral:

$$\Pi(\mathbf{q}) = \begin{cases} \mathbb{E}\left[R(\mathbf{q}) - L(1+r_f) + x\right]^+ & \text{if } L(1+r_f) \leq x \\ \mathbb{E}\left[R(\mathbf{q}) - L(1+r) + x\right]^+ & \text{otherwise} \end{cases} \tag{4}$$

At the end of the selling season, the retailer has to payback the loan with its interest rate. If the retailer's wealth (possibly including a portion of its collateral) is sufficient, the bank receives a full repayment of the loan. Otherwise, the retailer becomes bankrupted and the bank seizes all of her revenue and collateral. Formally, the expected repayment of the bank loan is:

$$\mathbb{E}[\Pi_{bk}] = \mathbb{E}\left[\min\left\{R(\mathbf{q}) + x, L(1+r)\right\}\right]$$
$$= \mathbb{E}\left[R(\mathbf{q}) + x\right] - \mathbb{E}\left[R(\mathbf{q}) + x - L(1+r)\right]^+ \tag{5}$$

Since the bank is risk neutral and chooses an interest rate that satisfies Eq. (3), we can substitute the right-hand side of Eq. (5) to derive the following expression of the cash flow of the retailer:

$$\Pi(\mathbf{q}) = \mathbb{E}\left[R(\mathbf{q}) + x\right] - (1+r_f)(oq_p + wq - y)^+ \tag{6}$$

Equation (6) shows that the retailer decisions are not influenced by the bank loan and thus she always behaves as an unconstrained newsvendor. This result is compatible with M&M theory [14]. It says that under perfect market assumption (including no bankruptcy cost) and competitively priced loan (fairly), the retailer choose her operational and financial decision separately.

3.2 Bank's Problem

According to our assumptions, the bank always offers a fairly priced loan and is risk neutral. Thus when the loan is fully secured by the collateral of the retailer, the bank chooses risk-free rate r_f as the interest rate of the loan. When the loan is not secured, the bank bears the risk of default loan and uses the probability of bankruptcy of the retailer to compute an interest rate $r = r(\mathbf{q})$ in order to compensate the risk of default on average. As in [12], we can use on the bankruptcy threshold $b(\mathbf{q})$ instead of $r(\mathbf{q})$ from the following relationship:

$$pb(\mathbf{q}) + e \min\left\{q - b(\mathbf{q}), q_p\right\} = \left[(oq_p + wq - y)^+(1+r) - x\right]^+ \tag{7}$$

In other words, $b(\mathbf{q})$ is the minimum realized demand such that the cash flow of the retailer is enough to repay the loan with its interest. Since the probability of bakruptcy for the retailer is equal to $\Phi(b(\mathbf{q}))$, the bank can calculate its expected loan repayment as a function of $b(\mathbf{q})$:

$$\mathbb{E}\left(\Pi_{bk}(b(\mathbf{q}))\right) = \begin{cases} p \int_0^{b(\mathbf{q})} \xi\phi(\xi)d\xi + eq_p + x + pb(\mathbf{q})\bar{\Phi}(b(\mathbf{q})) & \text{if } b \leq q - q_p \\ \\ (p - e)\int_0^{b(\mathbf{q})} \xi\phi(\xi)d\xi + e(q_p - q)\Phi(q - q_p) \\ + eq + x + (p - e)b(\mathbf{q})\bar{\Phi}(b(\mathbf{q})) & \text{otherwise} \end{cases}$$
$$\tag{8}$$

Table 1. Numerical results with different demand size.

Offered contracts	μ	σ	q	q_p	Π_r	%	r	$b(\mathbf{q})$
Put & wholesale	100	30	96.99	25.61	19.29	4.80%	2.00%	0.00
Only wholesale	100	30	83.05	–	18.04	–	2.00%	0.00
Put & wholesale	200	60	193.97	51.22	38.56	4.82%	2.01%	12.19
Only wholesale	200	60	166.09	–	36.79	–	2.01%	17.84
Put & wholesale	300	90	290.96	76.84	57.72	4.93%	2.08%	68.82
Only wholesale	300	90	249.14	–	55.01	–	2.14%	77.28
Put & wholesale	400	120	387.95	102.45	76.70	5.03%	2.18%	125.64
Only wholesale	400	120	332.19	–	73.03	–	2.30%	136.98
Put & wholesale	500	150	484.93	128.06	95.51	5.17%	2.29%	182.59
Only wholesale	500	150	415.23	–	90.81	–	2.48%	196.87

Thus we can find $b(\mathbf{q})$ by substituting Eq. (8) in the risk neutral equation:

$$(oq_p + wq - y)(1 + r_f) = \mathbb{E}\left(\Pi_{bk}(b(\mathbf{q}))\right) \tag{9}$$

Finally, $r(\mathbf{q})$ is easily found from Eq. (7). Note that $\mathbb{E}\left(\Pi_{bk}(b(\mathbf{q}))\right)$ is a increasing function in $b(\mathbf{q})$ and $b(\mathbf{q})$ is a increasing function in $r(\mathbf{q})$. Therefore, there exists a unique interest rate for the requested loan from the bank's perspective.

4   Numerical Experiments

In this section, we present the results of numerical experiments that illustrate the effect of put option on the bankruptcy risk, loan's interest rate and the performance of the retailer. First we consider that the retailer is facing two contracts, wholesale price $w = 0.7$, the put option with option price $o = 0.1$ and exercise price $e = 0.6$. The retailer has a working capital $y = 40$, a collateral $x = 60$ and sells her product to the final customers price $p = 1$. The demand is normally distributed (hence IFR). We assume that the risk-free rate is equal to $r_f = 2\%$.

We conduct these numerical experiments for different demand sizes. For the same capital structure, increasing the demand size is equivalent to consider a poorer retailer. Table 1 summarizes the results of our experiments and shows the performance of the retailer, the bankruptcy risk (indicated by $b(\mathbf{q})$) and the loan interest rate proposed by the bank. For each demand size we consider the results of two scenarios, namely the presence of absence of a put option contract. The numerical results show that the existence of a put option always increases the expected profit of the retailer and her order quantity while having financial constraint or not. When the retailer receives a loan and there exists a bankruptcy risk, the interest rate of the loan and the bankruptcy risk are reduced by using a put option contract in addition to the wholesale price contract. The effect of the put option contract on the retailer's performance is more significance when the retailer is facing financial constraints.

5   Conclusion and Further Research

We investigate the effect of complementing a wholesale price contract with a put option contract on the performance of a newsvendor with limited capital. The retailer uses her working capital to cover her costs but has the possibility to receive a loan from a bank if necessary. Our numerical results illustrate that existence of the put option contract increases her order quantity to reach a greater expected terminal cash flow while lowering both the bankruptcy risk and the loan's interest rate.

It is shown in the literature that the supplier can design such contracts to achieve the supply chain coordination [19]. An interesting question is thus whether a put option contract benefits every partner in the supply chain by reducing the probability of bankruptcy for the retailer. One may also consider the behavior of a supplier with the different contracts presented above, or even add the possibility of a trade credit instead of a bank loan. Finally as option contracts are risk hedging tools, the risk attitude of the retailer is likely to play a significant role in the performance of the whole system, hence incorporating this aspect into the model may bring valuable information for managers.

References

1. Martínez-de Albéniz, V., Simchi-Levi, D.: Competition in the supply option market. Oper. Res. **57**(5), 1082–1097 (2009)
2. Basu, P., Liu, Q., Stallaert, J.: Supply chain management using put option contracts with information asymmetry. Int. J. Prod. Res. 1–25 (2018)
3. Birge, J.R.: Option methods for incorporating risk into linear capacity planning models. Manuf. Serv. Oper. Manag. **2**(1), 19–31 (2000)
4. Burnetas, A., Ritchken, P.: Option pricing with downward-sloping demand curves: the case of supply chain options. Manag. Sci. **51**(4), 566–580 (2005)
5. Buzacott, J.A., Zhang, R.Q.: Inventory management with asset-based financing. Manag. Sci. **50**(9), 1274–1292 (2004)
6. Chao, X., Chen, J., Wang, S.: Dynamic inventory management with cash flow constraints. Nav. Res. Logist. **55**(8), 758–768 (2008)
7. Chen, F., Parlar, M.: Value of a put option to the risk-averse newsvendor. IIE Trans. **39**(5), 481–500 (2007)
8. Chen, X., Wan, N., Wang, X.: Flexibility and coordination in a supply chain with bidirectional option contracts and service requirement. Int. J. Prod. Econ. **193**, 183–192 (2017)
9. Dada, M., Hu, Q.: Financing newsvendor inventory. Oper. Res. Lett. **36**(5), 569–573 (2008)
10. Eriksson, K.: An option mechanism to coordinate a dyadic supply chain bilaterally in a multi-period setting. Omega **88**, 196–209 (2019)
11. Feng, Y., Mu, Y., Hu, B., Kumar, A.: Commodity options purchasing and credit financing under capital constraint. Int. J. Prod. Econ. **153**, 230–237 (2014)
12. Kouvelis, P., Zhao, W.: Financing the newsvendor: supplier vs. bank, and the structure of optimal trade credit contracts. Oper. Res. **60**(3), 566–580 (2012)
13. Kouvelis, P., Zhao, W.: Supply chain contract design under financial constraints and bankruptcy costs. Manag. Sci. **62**(8), 2341–2357 (2015)

14. Modigliani, F., Miller, M.H.: The cost of capital, corporation finance and the theory of investment. Am. Econ. Rev. **48**(3), 261–297 (1958)
15. Nagali, V., et al.: Procurement risk management (PRM) at Hewlett-Packard company. Interfaces **38**(1), 51–60 (2008)
16. Spengler, J.J.: Vertical integration and antitrust policy. J. Polit. Econ. **58**(4), 347–352 (1950)
17. Tirole, J.: The Theory of Corporate Finance. Princeton University Press, Princeton (2010)
18. Van Mieghem, J.A.: Investment strategies for flexible resources. Manag. Sci. **44**(8), 1071–1078 (1998)
19. Wang, C., Chen, J., Wang, L., Luo, J.: Supply chain coordination with put option contracts and customer returns. J. Oper. Res. Soc. **71**(6), 1003–1019 (2020)
20. Wang, C., Chen, X.: Joint order and pricing decisions for fresh produce with put option contracts. J. Oper. Res. Soc. **69**(3), 474–484 (2018)
21. Wang, Q., Tsao, D.b.: Supply contract with bidirectional options: the buyer's perspective. Int. J. Prod. Econ. **101**(1), 30–52 (2006)
22. Xue, W., Ma, L., Shen, H.: Optimal inventory and hedging decisions with CVaR consideration. Int. J. Prod. Econ. **162**, 70–82 (2015)
23. Yang, H., Chen, J., Chen, X., Chen, B.: The impact of customer returns in a supply chain with a common retailer. Eur. J. Oper. Res. **256**(1), 139–150 (2017)

Pricing Decisions for an Omnichannel Retailing Under Service Level Considerations

Minh Tam Tran[1,2]([envelope])[iD], Yacine Rekik[1][iD], and Khaled Hadj-Hamou[2][iD]

[1] Emlyon Business School, 23 Avenue Guy de Collongue, 69134 Ecully, Lyon, France
[2] Univ Lyon, INSA Lyon, Université Claude Bernard Lyon 1, Univ Lumière Lyon 2, DISP, EA4570, 69621 Villeurbanne, France

Abstract. An increasing number of retailers are presently moving to omnichannel configurations and embracing modern innovations to integrate the physical store and the online store to provide customers a comprehensive shopping experience. We develop a classical newsvendor model where a retailer buys items from a supplier and distributes them through two market segments, online vs. offline. We seek optimal prices for the product in the two channels under the newsvendor model with a single period, price-based stochastic demand, and cycle service level-based order quantity to maximize the retailer's profit. Motivated by market share models often used in marketing, we focus on a demand model involving multiplicative uncertainty and interaction between the two sales channels. The pricing problem arising is not to be well behaved because it is difficult to verify the joint concavity in prices of the objective function's deterministic version. However, we find that the objective function is still reasonably well behaved within the sense that there is a unique solution for our optimal problem. We observe such a situation through the visualization graphs in bounded conditions for prices and find the approximate optimal point.

Keywords: Inventory control · Newsvendor · Stochastic demand · Pricing · Omnichannel

1 Introduction

E-commerce has shown impressive growth in the past decade in all the principal markets. In 2020, the global retail e-commerce sales amounted to 4.28 trillion US dollars and were projected to grow to 5.4 trillion US dollars in 2022. Online shopping is one of the most popular online activities worldwide [1].

This paper deals with demand modeling, stock management, and pricing under omnichannel configuration. Indeed, omnichannel also opens numerous modern challenges for price optimization. Classical retail pricing models augment channels' cost upon the presumption that there's no stock sharing and

© IFIP International Federation for Information Processing 2021
Published by Springer Nature Switzerland AG 2021
A. Dolgui et al. (Eds.): APMS 2021, IFIP AICT 632, pp. 175–185, 2021.
https://doi.org/10.1007/978-3-030-85906-0_20

integration between channels. This inference does not hold in omnichannel where physical store's inventory is also utilized for matching the online client's orders. Another challenge is by cause of potential substitution of demand between the online and offline channels, which is influenced by the prices associated with them. Channel substitution is rejected in classical earnings management models, who admit that price only influences demand within the same channel. In spite of these difficulties owing to the omnichannel environment, numerous retailers apply the classical price optimization frameworks that don't take into account channel interdependencies.

In literature, the interest in studying critical subjects relating to omnichannel retailing and pricing has progressively expanded, with a rapid increase in the contributions of academic experts covering this aspect [2,3]. Moreover, omnichannel retailing seems to be a promising stream for future research [4]. Only a few literature reviews are already available that specifically analyze the distribution and optimal pricing problems faced by retailers selling items both online and through physical channels.

To formulate an omnichannel setting, a formal strategy is to extend the single channel pricing model. Concerning the optimal inventory levels and prices in a single channel, we refer them to the pricing newsvendor problem. Whitin [5], Mills [6], and Karlin [7] proposed the formulations of price-setting newsvendor problem for a single product and identified its optimal solutions. The unimodality of the objective function under certain assumptions on the statistical distribution was proved in [8], which was later extended by Petruzzi and Dada [9] on the price-dependent newsvendor problem. Aydin and Porteus [10] built on previous investigations by adding customer choice among multiple substitutable products through modeling demands for competing products by the multinomial logit demand model. Kocabiyikoglu and Popescu [11] studied the newsvendor problem with a more general demand function and derived general conditions for the unimodality of the objective function. The effect of demand uncertainty in a price-setting newsvendor model was studied in [12]. Kyparisis and Koulamas [13] investigated the price-setting newsvendor problem with nonnegative linear additive demand and showed that the problem still possesses an optimal solution and analyzed when the expected profit function is quasiconcave in price so that a unique optimal solution can be found. Given the nature of the subject, these reviews are somewhat ancient. They discuss neither multichannel systems, the correlation across channels in an omnichannel configuration, nor the impact of cycle service levels on the pricing problem. It leads to a research question on how to develop omnichannel modeling under these constraints.

Motivated by the prevailing omnichannel retailing practices and unexplored issues regarding customer service level, we utilize a newsvendor model to explore the impacts of customer service level on the retailer's pricing and ordering decisions considering each channel. Specifically, a retailer sells products to consumers via online and traditional stores, and the retailer maximizes the total profit of both channels. Our framework is inspired by the price-dependant demand model suggested by [2] in order to illustrate the integrated stock-pricing decision under an omnichannel configuration. Hence, we use attraction demand models to represent consumer choice across various channels when that the total market faces uncertainty. In contrast to [2], we consider a stochastic assumption for the attraction model where the global market facing the two channels is uncertain, and we adapt this model to the newsvendor configuration by trading-off underage and overage costs. [10] demonstrate the analytical complexity of the attraction model through a single period inventory and pricing problem. The authors show that the objective function is not necessarily jointly quasi-concave in prices, even for deterministic demand. We show in this paper that the omnichannel attraction demand model suggested by [2] can lead to poor service levels for one or both channels. Such as poor service level resulting from the integrated pricing-stock decision is conflicting with the practitioners objective to offer a better service level to customers through the omnichannel experience. Our paper revisits the attraction model for the newsvendor by integrating the service level in the optimization process. We now summarize the main contributions of this paper:

– Omnichannel demand modelling and optimization framework: We introduce an omnichannel demand modeling configuration over which a series of advanced omnichannel retail analytical solutions can be built upon.
– Omnichannel price optimization: We study optimal pricing behavior within a given model and conditions on price and order quantity.

The rest of our study is structured as follows. The next section provides the problem formulation. The third section reports and discusses the results.

2   Problem Formulation

Consider a supply chain consists of a supplier, a retailer, and clients. The retailer purchases items from the supplier and sells them to clients through two channels: online and physical stores. At the beginning of the selling season, the retailer is interested in determining the optimal order quantities and the optimal prices corresponding to two channels. Let I be the set of channels' indexes containing index 1 for online channel and 2 for physical channel. For each channel i, we let $r = [r_1, r_2]$ be the vector of the unit retail selling prices and s_i the unit salvage value ($s_i < r_i$). The demand for each channel is assumed to be stochastic characterized by a random variable $D_i(r)$ depending on the vector of prices. The order quantity Q_i for each channel is purchased by the retailer from the supplier on a fixed cost per unit, including operating expense c_i ($s_i < c_i < r_i$). The supplier is assumed to operate with no capacity restrictions, and an order placed by the buyer with the supplier is immediately filled. We denote Π_i the expected profit induced by the channel i.

2.1   Formulation of the Demand Distribution

We use the attraction demand functions to model the channel choice of consumers. We assume the demand $D_i(r)$ in each channel i has the following form

$$D_i(r) = \xi \frac{g_i(r_i)}{g_0 + \sum_i g_i(r_i)}, \tag{1}$$

where ξ is the total market size defined with the cumulative distribution function $F_\xi(x)$ and the probability density function $f_\xi(x)$, $g_i(r_i)$ is the attraction function of customers to channel i, g_0 is the attraction function of the non-purchase option usually assumed positive.

The market size represents the measure of consumers interested in the product and the market share, also generally referred to the purchase probability, shows how consumers prefer one through several channels. The attraction function depending on price is used to model the market share through channels. There are some well-known attraction models: linear attraction $g_i(r_i) = a_i - b_i r_i$ ($a_i, b_i, \min a_i - b_i r_i > 0$), multinomial logit (MNL) $g_i(r_i) = \exp(a_i - b_i r_i)$ ($a_i > 0$) and multiplicative competitive interaction (MCI) $g_i(r_i) = a_i r_i^{-b_i}$ ($a_i > 0$, $b_i > 1$). The constants a_i and b_i are assumed to satisfy the negative price elasticity of demand. This attraction demand is used by [2] to model the omnichannel setting. The authors consider the case when ξ is a positive deterministic scalar. In order to measure of market's uncertainty, we assume that ξ is a modeled by a continuous random variable. In this scheme, we see that the channel i's demand depends on both the prices r on two channels. Thus, the clients' demand in channel i is a continuous random variable $D_i(r) = \xi G_i(r)$, with

$$G_i(r) = \frac{g_i(r_i)}{g_0 + \sum_i g_i(r_i)}. \tag{2}$$

2.2   Formulation of the Objective Function

Before the sales period, the retailer favors determining order quantities Q_i, and then finding the related prices r_i corresponding to each channel i to maximize the expected total profit. Sales of the item occur at the end of selling season and: (i) if $Q_i \geq D_i(r)$, then $Q_i - D_i(r)$ units which are left over at the end of the period are salvaged by the retailer for a per unit revenue of s_i; and (ii) if $Q_i < D_i(r)$, then $D_i(r) - Q_i$ units which represent lost sales cost the buyer zero per unit. Then, the actual end of period profit for the retailer is:

$$\Pi_i\left(D_i(r), Q_i, r_i\right) = (r_i - s_i)D_i(r) - (c_i - s_i)Q_i - (r_i - s_i)[D_i(r) - Q_i]^+, \tag{3}$$

$$\Pi_i(\xi, Q_i, r_i) = (r_i - s_i)G_i(r)\xi - (c_i - s_i)Q_i - (r_i - s_i)\left[G_i(r)\xi - Q_i\right]^+. \tag{4}$$

Thus, assuming $G_i(r) > 0$, the profit within the channel i is:

$$\Pi_i(\xi, Q_i, r_i) = (r_i - s_i)G_i(r)\xi - (c_i - s_i)Q_i - (r_i - s_i)G_i(r)\left[\xi - \frac{Q_i}{G_i(r)}\right]^+. \tag{5}$$

Since the demand has not been realized at the beginning of the selling season, the retailer cannot observe the actual profit. Hence, the traditional approach to analyze the problem is based on assuming a risk-neutral retailer who makes the optimal pricing decision at the beginning of the sales season to maximize total expected profit.

The expected profit within the channel i is:

$$\Pi_i(Q_i, r_i) = (r_i - s_i)G_i(r)E[\xi] - (c_i - s_i)Q_i - (r_i - s_i)G_i(r)\int_{\frac{Q_i}{G_i(r)}}^{\infty}\left(x - \frac{Q_i}{G_i(r)}\right)f_\xi(x)dx. \quad (6)$$

The expected profit for all channels is $\Pi(Q, r) = \sum_i \Pi_i(Q_i, r_i)$.

Induced Profit Function. Π is a function of Q_i and r_i, it is separable and concave in the Q_i. Then, for any price vector r, the optimal order quantity in channel i, denoted $Q_i^*(r)$, is given by (see appendix I for the proof)

$$Q_i^*(r) = G_i(r)F_\xi^{-1}\left(\frac{r_i - c_i}{r_i - s_i}\right). \quad (7)$$

Let Q^* be the vector of all Q_i^*, the problem can be rewritten as maximizing the induced profit function below (see appendix II for the proof):

$$\Pi(Q^*, r) = \sum_i\left((r_i - s_i)G_i(r)\int_{-\infty}^{\frac{Q_i^*(r)}{G_i(r)}} xf_\xi(x)dx\right). \quad (8)$$

Let CSL_i^* be the induced cycle service level to channel $i \in I$ when the order quantity is set to Q_i^*, defined as

$$CSL_i^* = P\left(D_i(r) \leq Q_i^*(r)\right) = P\left(\xi \leq \frac{Q_i^*(r)}{G_i(r)}\right) = F_\xi\left(\frac{Q_i^*(r)}{G_i(r)}\right) = \frac{r_i - c_i}{r_i - s_i}. \quad (9)$$

Numerical Application: Let us consider the numerical setting and values considered in [10]: a pricing problem with stochastic logit demand in which the online (resp. physical) channel demand is characterised by $a_1 = 10$ and $b_1 = 1$ (resp. $a_2 = 25$ and $b_2 = 1$). We assume the non-purchased option normalised with the parameter $g_0 = 1$. With the higher parameter a_2, the physical channel has more selling potential. We set the unit purchase costs $c_1 = 6$ and $c_2 = 20$. Here, the smaller value of c_1 comparing to c_2 tells that the total purchase cost and operation cost for the online channel is lower than the physical's one. The unit salvage costs are $s_1 = 4$ and $s_2 = 15$. We consider a uniform distribution for the global market demand with two settings: highly variable demand $\xi \sim U(100, 900)$ and low variable demand $\xi \sim U(400, 600)$.

The Table 1 represents the expectation and variation coefficient of total market (μ, σ), online channel (μ_1^*, σ_1^*), and physical channel (μ_1^*, σ_1^*) given the optimal prices r_1^*, r_2^*. CV is the coefficient of variation for both of them. G_i^*, Q_i^*, CSL_i^*, PR_i, and Π_i^* are the market sharing ratio, order quantity, service level, penalty ratio (the ratio between shortage penalty ($k_i = r_i - c_i$) and the overstock penalty ($h_i = c_i - s_i$), and profit induced from channel i under the optimal pricing. Π^* is the maximum total profit.

When the shortage cost is close to the overstock cost, the optimal order quantity is close to the mean of the demand. The safety stock is close to 0. This corresponds to channel 2 with two penalty ratios 0.95 and 0.85. If $k_i > h_i$, then the order quantity is higher than the demand expectation; thus the safety stock $Q_i^* - \mu_i$ is positive. This corresponds to channel 1 with two penalty ratios equal 1.98 and 2.05. Comparing two given cases, the optimal prices are close. In the higher deviation setting, the order quantities, the market sharing ratios, and the induced profits in the two channels are also close, which is false in the other case with a dominant channel. The more the market risk there is, the lower the maximum profit. In both cases, we have not very high service levels for both two channels. Moreover, since the shortage penalty doubles the overstock penalty of channel 1, the service level tends to be higher in order to avoid shortages.

Table 1. Characteristics of optimal pricing solution for induced profit function

ξ	μ	σ	μ_1^*	σ_1^*	μ_2^*	σ_2^*	CV	r_1^*	r_2^*
$U(100, 900)$	500	230.94	155.25	71.71	195.27	90.19	0.46	9.96	24.73
$U(400, 600)$	500	57.74	112.73	13.02	261.84	30.23	0.12	10.11	24.26

ξ	G_1^*	G_2^*	Q_1^*	Q_2^*	CSL_1^*	CSL_2^*	PR_1	PR_2	Π_1^*	Π_2^*	Π^*
$U(100, 900)$	0.31	0.39	196.13	190.98	0.66	0.48	1.98	0.95	450.05	544.38	994.43
$U(400, 600)$	0.23	0.52	120.51	257.68	0.67	0.46	2.05	0.85	432.64	996.31	1428.95

Cycle Service Level Criteria for Quantity Ordering. Instead of using the quantity order as the critical fractile solution, we can initially set the order quantity by the cycle service level. Let CSL_i be the target cycle service level to channel $i \in I$ when the order quantity is set to $\hat{Q}_i$ defined as $P(D_i \leq \hat{Q}_i)$. By definition, the related order quantity $\hat{Q}_i$ satisfies

$$CSL_i = P(D_i \leq \hat{Q}_i) = P\left(\xi \leq \frac{\hat{Q}_i}{G_i(r)}\right) = F_\xi\left(\frac{\hat{Q}_i}{G_i(r)}\right), \tag{10}$$

$$\text{thus } \hat{Q}_i = G_i(r)F_\xi^{-1}(CSL_i). \tag{11}$$

The profit function is now as below (see the appendix III for the proof):

$$\Pi(\hat{Q}, r) = \sum_i \left((r_i - c_i)\hat{Q}_i - (r_i - s_i)CSL_i\hat{Q}_i + (r_i - s_i)G_i(r)\int_{-\infty}^{\frac{\hat{Q}_i}{G_i(r)}} xf_\xi(x)dx\right). \tag{12}$$

3   Characterization of Objective Function: A Case of Study

For comparison purposes, let us consider the same setting for parameters as the numerical application for the induced profit function in the previous section. The Fig. 1 shows the shape of profit function varying with prices within high and low variation market. The characteristics of optimal pricing solutions are given in Table 2. Table 3 shows the dynamic of approximate optimal prices and profit with a set of different targeted CSLs. Comparing with induced optimal profit in the first numerical application, our new formulation improves the CSLs from $(0.66, 0.48)$, $(0.67, 0.46)$ to the targeted values $(0.90, 0.90)$ on both low and high variation market. However, the profit is degraded from 994.43 to 777.73 and from 1428.95 to 1334.32, respectively. Table 3 illustrates the results for other different targeted values of the two CSLs. In Table 2, within two schemes, the optimal prices are not very much different, the same situation as Table 1.

The CSLs setting and boundary conditions on prices can cause the negativity on the total profit. The global market uncertainty also has a negative impact on this value. However, it is not necessary to balance the two channels in the high demand variability case. One channel can dominate the other in order to secure the service level and maximise profit. It can be seen that if the global market is more uncertain, then the maximum total profit is lower, but each channel' profit is not necessarily decreasing. Although the shortage penalty related to the first channel still doubles the overstock penalty, the service level is high as 0.9.

Table 2. Characteristics of optimal pricing solution under service level constraints

ξ	μ	σ	$\hat{\mu}_1^*$	$\hat{\sigma}_1^*$	$\hat{\mu}_2^*$	$\hat{\sigma}_2^*$	CV	$\hat{r}_1^*$	$\hat{r}_2^*$
$U(100, 900)$	500	230.94	220.80	101.98	84.54	39.05	0.46	9.87	25.83
$U(400, 600)$	500	57.74	136.27	15.73	227.60	26.28	0.12	10.00	24.49

ξ	$\hat{G}_1^*$	$\hat{G}_2^*$	$\hat{Q}_1^*$	$\hat{Q}_2^*$	CSL_1	CSL_2	PR_1	PR_2	$\hat{\Pi}_1^*$	$\hat{\Pi}_2^*$	$\hat{\Pi}^*$
$U(100, 900)$	0.44	0.17	362.11	138.65	0.9	0.9	1.94	1.17	562.38	215.35	777.73
$U(400, 600)$	0.27	0.46	158.07	264.02	0.9	0.9	2.00	0.90	499.69	834.63	1334.32

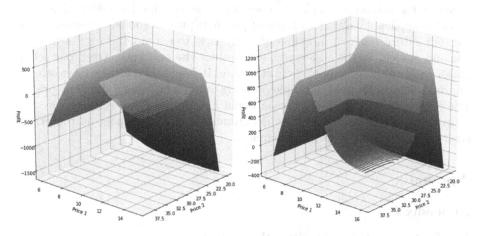

Fig. 1. The expected profit as a function of the prices, where the quantity order satisfies a constraint in service with the market's high and low variation, resp.

Table 3. Optimal prices and profit for given service levels

CSL		$\xi \sim U(100, 900)$			$\xi \sim U(400, 600)$		
CSL_1	CSL_2	$\hat{r}_1^*$	$\hat{r}_2^*$	$\Pi(\hat{Q}^*, \hat{r}^*)$	$\hat{r}_1^*$	$\hat{r}_2^*$	$\Pi(\hat{Q}^*, \hat{r}^*)$
0.7	0.5	9.98	24.73	993.22	10.11	24.27	1427.73
0.7	0.7	9.86	25.13	937.44	10.05	24.35	1401.78
0.7	0.9	9.66	25.96	841.80	9.94	24.50	1343.35
0.8	0.5	10.09	24.70	981.70	10.13	24.26	1425.63
0.8	0.7	9.96	25.10	922.19	10.08	24.35	1399.43
0.8	0.9	9.75	25.92	819.25	9.96	24.50	1340.43
0.9	0.5	10.24	24.65	959.10	10.17	24.26	1420.96
0.9	0.7	10.11	25.04	893.01	10.12	24.34	1394.30
0.9	0.9	9.87	25.83	777.73	10.00	24.49	1334.32

4   Conclusion

In this paper, we proposed and investigated a pricing problem in an omnichannel scheme using the newsvendor model with a price-dependent stochastic demand and cycle service level-based order quantity. Under a demand model coming from an attractive interpretation of clients' preference over the sales channels, our model adapts well within the nature of management. Within a set of boundary conditions, there exists a unique optimal price vector, which can be calculated numerically (by gradient descent algorithm). Being aware of the high level of customer expectations in omnichannel settings, we firstly showed the limitation of only considering profit maximization, and we then proposed a new formulation of the attraction model by considering service level considerations. Our model is applicable in various types of product: private goods, consumer goods, etc. For future research, one line of analysis is to extend the results to other demand models. In the case study, we consider the uniform market, one selling season, and one stage supply chain structure. It would therefore be interesting to improve our model under multiple ordering opportunities and dynamic pricing. The decentralized supply chain case would be an interesting research direction to investigate the supply chain (un)coordination and its impact on the pricing strategies for the different sales channels.

Appendix

Appendix I

Proof. The expected profit within the channel i is:

$$\Pi_i(Q_i, r_i) = (r_i - s_i)G_i(r)E[\xi] - (c_i - s_i)Q_i - (r_i - s_i)G_i(r) \int_{\frac{Q_i}{G_i(r)}}^{\infty} \left(x - \frac{Q_i}{G_i(r)} \right) f_\xi(x)dx.$$

To find the order quantity Q_i^* that maximizes the expected profit associated to the channel i within a given prices r_i, we compute the derivative of $\Pi_i(Q_i, r_i)$:

$$\frac{\partial \Pi_i(Q_i, r_i)}{\partial Q_i} = -(c_i - s_i) + (r_i - s_i)G_i(r)\frac{1}{G_i(r)}\int_{\frac{Q_i}{G_i(r)}}^{\infty} f_\xi(x)dx$$

$$= -(c_i - s_i) + (r_i - s_i)\left(1 - F_\xi\left(\frac{Q_i}{G_i(r)}\right)\right)$$

$$= (r_i - c_i) - (r_i - s_i)F_\xi\left(\frac{Q_i}{G_i(r)}\right).$$

In addition, the second derivative is negative:

$$\frac{\partial^2 \Pi_i(Q_i, r_i)}{\partial Q_i^2} = -(r_i - s_i)\frac{\partial F_\xi\left(\frac{Q_i}{G_i(r)}\right)}{\partial Q_i}$$

$$= -(r_i - s_i)\frac{1}{G_i(r)}f_\xi\left(\frac{Q_i}{G_i(r)}\right) < 0.$$

The function $\Pi_i(Q_i, r_i)$ is therefore concave and is minimal if and only if:

$$\frac{\partial \Pi_i(Q_i, r_i)}{\partial Q_i} = 0 \Leftrightarrow (r_i - c_i) - (r_i - s_i)F_\xi\left(\frac{Q_i}{G_i(r)}\right) = 0 \Leftrightarrow F_\xi\left(\frac{Q_i^*(r)}{G_i(r)}\right) = \frac{r_i - c_i}{r_i - s_i}.$$

This proves the Eq. 7.

Appendix II

Proof. The induced profit function for the channel i:

$$\Pi_i(Q_i^*, r) = (r_i - s_i)G_i(r)E[\xi] - (c_i - s_i)Q_i^*(r) - (r_i - s_i)G_i(r)\int_{\frac{Q_i^*(r)}{G_i(r)}}^{\infty}\left(x - \frac{Q_i^*(r)}{G_i(r)}\right)f_\xi(x)dx$$

$$= (r_i - s_i)G_i(r)E[\xi] - (c_i - s_i)Q_i^*(r)$$

$$\quad -(r_i - s_i)G_i(r)\left(E[\xi] - \int_{-\infty}^{\frac{Q_i^*(r)}{G_i(r)}} xf_\xi(x)dx - \frac{Q_i^*(r)}{G_i(r)}\left(1 - F_\xi\left(\frac{Q_i^*(r)}{G_i(r)}\right)\right)\right)$$

$$= -(c_i - s_i)Q_i^*(r) + (r_i - s_i)G_i(r)\int_{-\infty}^{\frac{Q_i^*(r)}{G_i(r)}} xf_\xi(x)dx + (r_i - s_i)Q_i^*(r)$$

$$\quad -(r_i - s_i)Q_i^*(r)F_\xi\left(\frac{Q_i^*(r)}{G_i(r)}\right)$$

$$= (r_i - c_i)Q_i^*(r) + (r_i - s_i)G_i(r)\int_{-\infty}^{\frac{Q_i^*(r)}{G_i(r)}} xf_\xi(x)dx - (r_i - s_i)Q_i^*(r)\frac{r_i - c_i}{r_i - s_i}$$

$$= (r_i - s_i)G_i(r)\int_{-\infty}^{\frac{Q_i^*(r)}{G_i(r)}} xf_\xi(x)dx.$$

Since $\Pi(Q^*, r) = \sum_i \Pi_i(Q_i^*, r)$, the Eq. 8 holds.

Appendix III

Proof. For each index i, we have

$$\int_{\frac{\hat{Q}_i}{G_i(r)}}^{\infty} \left(x - \frac{\hat{Q}_i}{G_i(r)} \right) f_\xi(x)dx = \int_{\frac{\hat{Q}_i}{G_i(r)}}^{\infty} x f_\xi(x)dx - \frac{\hat{Q}_i}{G_i(r)} \int_{\frac{\hat{Q}_i}{G_i(r)}}^{\infty} f_\xi(x)dx$$

$$= E[\xi] - \int_{-\infty}^{\frac{\hat{Q}_i}{G_i(r)}} x f_\xi(x)dx - \frac{\hat{Q}_i}{G_i(r)} \left(1 - \int_{-\infty}^{\frac{\hat{Q}_i}{G_i(r)}} f_\xi(x)dx \right)$$

$$= E[\xi] - \int_{-\infty}^{\frac{\hat{Q}_i}{G_i(r)}} x f_\xi(x)dx - \frac{\hat{Q}_i}{G_i(r)} \left(1 - F_\xi \left(\frac{\hat{Q}_i}{G_i(r)} \right) \right).$$

Thus

$$\Pi_i(\hat{Q}_i, r) = (r_i - s_i)G_i(r)E[\xi] - (c_i - s_i)\hat{Q}_i - (r_i - s_i)G_i(r)\int_{\frac{\hat{Q}_i}{G_i(r)}}^{\infty} \left(x - \frac{\hat{Q}_i}{G_i(r)} \right) f_\xi(x)dx$$

$$= (r_i - s_i)G_i(r)E[\xi] - (c_i - s_i)\hat{Q}_i$$

$$-(r_i - s_i)G_i(r)\left(E[\xi] - \int_{-\infty}^{\frac{\hat{Q}_i}{G_i(r)}} x f_\xi(x)dx - \frac{\hat{Q}_i}{G_i(r)} \left(1 - F_\xi \left(\frac{\hat{Q}_i}{G_i(r)} \right) \right) \right)$$

$$= -(c_i - s_i)\hat{Q}_i + (r_i - s_i)G_i(r)\int_{-\infty}^{\frac{\hat{Q}_i}{G_i(r)}} x f_\xi(x)dx + (r_i - s_i)\hat{Q}_i - (r_i - s_i)\hat{Q}_i F_\xi \left(\frac{\hat{Q}_i}{G_i(r)} \right)$$

$$= (r_i - c_i)\hat{Q}_i - (r_i - s_i)CSL_i\hat{Q}_i + (r_i - s_i)G_i(r)\int_{-\infty}^{\frac{\hat{Q}_i}{G_i(r)}} x f_\xi(x)dx.$$

Since $\Pi(\hat{Q}, r) = \sum_i \Pi_i(\hat{Q}_i, r)$, the Eq. 12 is proved.

References

1. Retail e-commerce sales worldwide from 2014 to 2024 (in billion U.S. dollars). https://www.statista.com/statistics/379046/worldwide-retail-e-commerce-sales/. Accessed 6 Apr 2021
2. Pavithra, H., Subramanian, S., Ettl, M.: A practical price optimization approach for omnichannel retailing. INFORMS J. Optim. **13** (2019)
3. Yuqing, J., Liu, L., Lim, A.: Optimal pricing decisions for an omni-channel supply chain with retail service. Int. Trans. Oper. Res. **27**(6), 2927–2948 (2020)
4. Yang, C., Cheung, C., Tan, C.: Omnichannel business research: opportunities and challenges. Decis. Support Syst. **109**, 1–4 (2018)
5. Whitin, T.M.: Inventory control and price theory. Manag. Sci. **2**(1), 61–68 (1955)
6. Mills, E.S.: Uncertainty and price theory. Q. J. Econ. **73**(1), 116–130 (1959)
7. Karlin, S., Carr, C.R.: Prices and optimal inventory policy. Stud. Appl. Probab. Manag. Sci. **4**, 159–172 (1962)
8. Young, L.: Price, inventory and the structure of uncertain demand. New Zealand Oper. Res. **6**(2), 157–177 (1978)
9. Petruzzi, N.C., Dada, M.: Pricing and the newsvendor problem: a review with extensions. Oper. Res. **47**(2), 183–194 (1999)
10. Aydin, G., Porteus, E.L.: Joint inventory and pricing decisions for an assortment. Oper. Res. **56**(5), 1247–1255 (2008)

11. Kocabiyikoglu, A., Popescu, I.: An elasticity approach to the newsvendor with price-sensitive demand. Oper. Res. **59**(2), 301–312 (2011)
12. Xu, M., Chen, Y., Xu, X.: The effect of demand uncertainty in a price-setting newsvendor model. Eur. J. Oper. Res. **207**(2), 946–957 (2010)
13. Kyparisis, G.J., Koulamas, C.: The price-setting newsvendor problem with non-negative linear additive demand. Eur. J. Oper. Res. **269**(2), 695–698 (2018)

Gastronomic Service System Design

Forecasting the Number of Customers Visiting Restaurants Using Machine Learning and Statistical Method

Takashi Tanizaki[1]([✉]), Shunsuke Kozuma[1], and Takeshi Shimmura[2]

[1] Graduate School of Systems Engineering, Kindai University, 1 Takaya-Umenobe, Higashi-Hiroshima 739-2116, Japan
tanizaki@hiro.kindai.ac.jp
[2] Ritsumeikan University, 1-1-1 Nogi-Higashi, Kusatsu 525-8577, Japan

Abstract. In this paper, it is proposed the forecasting of the number of customers visiting restaurants using machine learning and statistical method. There are some researches on forecasting the number of customers visiting restaurants. Since the beginning of last year, the number of customers visiting restaurants has plummeted due to COVID-19. A machine learning-based approach can be applied to forecast something including stable trends. Therefore, in this paper, machine learning that incorporates the moving average method is proposed to reflect the latest fluctuation trend. Furthermore, a forecasting method using deep learning is proposed to improve forecasting accuracy. In the method using deep learning, the analysis results on the normalization of training data and the contribution of meteorological data to the forecasting accuracy are described. It was found that the introduction of the moving average into the explanatory variables is effective when the trend of the number of customers visiting fluctuates rapidly. It was also found that normalization for each year of training data is effective when the annual average number of customers visiting restaurants increases or decreases monotonically.

Keywords: Forecasting customers visiting · Machine learning · Deep learning

1 Introduction

The GDP of the service industry accounts for more than 70% of that of Japan. The productivity of the service industry is lower than that of the manufacturing industry. In order to improve the productivity of the service industry, it is important to improve "efficiency" and "customer satisfaction and service quality" at the same time by using engineering methods. The goal of our research is to improve a store management method by optimizing employee job arrangements and cooking material orders based on accurate forecasts of the number of customers visiting restaurants. In our research up to last year, we made forecasts using machine learning and statistical method [1, 2]. Since the beginning of last year, the number of customers visiting restaurants has plummeted due to COVID-19. A machine learning-based approach can be applied to forecast something including

© IFIP International Federation for Information Processing 2021
Published by Springer Nature Switzerland AG 2021
A. Dolgui et al. (Eds.): APMS 2021, IFIP AICT 632, pp. 189–197, 2021.
https://doi.org/10.1007/978-3-030-85906-0_21

stable trends. In this paper, machine learning that incorporates the moving average (MA) method is proposed in order to reflect the latest fluctuation trend in the forecast for 2020, when the number of customers visiting the restaurant has dropped sharply affected by the COVID-19. Furthermore, a forecasting method using deep learning is proposed to improve forecasting accuracy. In deep learning, we also analyzed the normalization method of training data and the effect of the presence or absence of meteorological data.

2   Forecasting Method

In this paper, "Gradient Boosting Regression (GBR) [3]", "Bayesian Linear Regression (Bayesian) [4]", "Boosted Decision Tree Regression (Boosted) [5]", "Decision Forest Regression (Decision) [6]", "Random Forest Regression (RFR) [7]", and "Stepwise Method [8]" are used as machine learning and statistical method. In addition, "Simple Recurrent Neural Network (RNN)" and "long short-term memory (LSTM)" are used as deep learning methods [9].

3   Forecasting the Number of Customers Visiting Restaurants

3.1   Target Data

Using the customers visiting data of four stores from restaurant chain A of the joint research, the number of customers visiting was forecasted. Table 1 shows the period of training data set and test data set. The number of customers visiting restaurants was forecasted by machine learning incorporating the MA method using the training data set for the past four years. In order to compare the forecasting accuracy with and without the influence of COVID-19, we compared the forecasting results using the training dataset from 2018/5/1 to 2019/4/30 and 2019/5/1 to 2020/4/30. In deep learning, two-year, three-year, and four-year training data were used to compare the forecasting accuracy depending on the amount of training data.

Table 2 shows the explanatory variables used for the forecasting. The meteorological data used was the data from the Japan Meteorological Agency's observation station closest to the location of each store. From our last year's research [10], we obtained

Table 1. Training data set and test data set.

Method	Data set	Period	From	To
Machine learning	Training data set	Four years	2014/5/1	2018/4/30
		Four years	2015/5/1	2019/4/30
	Test data set	Year 2018	2018/5/1	2019/4/30
		Year 2019	2019/5/1	2020/4/30
Deep learning	Training data set	Four years	2014/5/1	2018/4/30
		Three years	2015/5/1	2018/4/30
		Two years	2016/5/1	2018/4/30
	Test data set	Year 2018	2018/5/1	2019/4/30

the result that meteorological data do not affect the forecasting accuracy in machine learning, thus those data were excluded from explanatory variables. On the other hand, in deep learning, the effect on the forecasting accuracy of the presence or absence of meteorological data was analyzed.

Table 2. Explanatory variable.

Category	Explanatory variable	Definition
Month	January	Jan/1-Jan/31
	February	Feb/1-Feb/28
	March	Mar/1-Mar/31
	April	Apr/1-Apr/30
	May	May/1-May/31
	June	Jun/1-Jun/30
	July	Jul/1-Jul/31
	August	Aug/1-Aug/31
	Septemner	Sep/1-Sep/30
	October	Oct/1-Oct/31
	Novenber	Nov/1-Nov/30
	December	Dec/1-Dec/31
The day of the week	Monday	Weekday and the next day is weekday
	Tuesday	Weekday and the next day is weekday
	Wednesday	Weekday and the next day is weekday
	Thuesday	Weekday and the next day is weekday
	Fryday	Weekday and the next day is weekday
	Saturday	Even if the target day is a holiday it is Saturday.
	Sunday	Sunday and the next day is weekday
		Even if the target day is a holiday it is Sunday.
	Sunday during holidays	Sunday and the next day is holiday
		Even if the target day is a holiday it is Sunday.
	Holiday	Holiday and the nextday is weekday
	Holiday during holidays	Holiday and the nextday is holiday
	Before holiday	Weekday and the next day is holiday
	Lastday during holidays	The last day of three or more consecutive holidays
5 day pitch week	First week	1st day - 5th day
	Second week	6th day - 10th dat
	Third week	11th day - 15th day
	Fourth feek	16th day - 20th day
	Fifth week	21th day - 25th day
	Sixth week	26th day - Last of the month
Event	January 1st	January 1st
	January 2nd	January 2nd
	January 3rd	January 3rd
	Year-end	Dec/29-Dec/31
	End of year party	Weekday of December
	Christmas eve	December 24th
	Coming-of-age day	Second Monday in January
	Setsubun	February 2nd
	Obon	Aug/13-Aug/15
	New year's party	Weekday till the coming-of-age day except Jan/1-Jan/3
	Farewell party	Weekday in March
	Welcome party	Weekday in April
Meteorology	Average wind speed	Average wind speed per day (m/s)
	Maximum wind speed	Maximum wind speed per day (m/s)
	Highest temperature	Highest temperature in a day （°C）
	Lowest temperature	Lowest temperature in a day （°C）
	Amount of precipitation	Amount of precipitation in a day (mm)
	Maximum precipitation	Maximum amount of precipitation in ten minutes (mm)
	Maximum instantaneous wind speed	Maximum instantaneous wind speed in a day (m/s)
Moving average	Simple moving average	Simple moving average value

The forecasting accuracy α, that is a ratio of the number of forecasted customers to that of actual customers, is calculated using the Eqs. (1) and (2). The reasons for excluding reserved customers in Eq. (1) are as follows. Since many of the reserved customers of restaurant chain A are for business use such as social gatherings associated with business trips, factors related to reserved customers are not included in the explanatory variables.

p_i: Actual number of customers visiting without reservation on i-th day.
e_i: Forecasted number of customers visiting without reservation on i-th day.
α_i: Forecasting accuracy without reservation on i-th day.
N: Forecasting period

$$\alpha_i = \frac{p_i - |p_i - e_i|}{p_i} \tag{1}$$

$$\alpha = \frac{\sum_{i=1}^{N} \alpha_i}{N} \tag{2}$$

3.2 Order of MA

The relationship between the order of MA and the forecasting accuracy value was investigated to find the best order of MA. Using visitor data from 2014/5/1 to 2018/4/30, we forecasted the number of visitors visiting the four stores using only MA. In doing so, the order of MA was varied from 2 to 31. Figure 1 shows the forecasting accuracy. There was no significant change in forecasting accuracy for all four stores for 7 or higher of the order of MA. Figures 2 and 3 show the actual number of customers visiting over the four years and the forecasting results when the order of MA is set to 7, 14, 21, and 28 at store A. As the order of MA increased, the forecasting results tended to become smoother. Based on the above, and from the perspective of reflecting the weekly trend the next day, the order of MA was set to 7 in the following research.

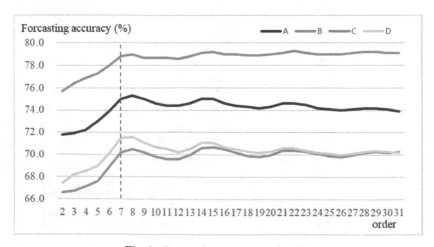

Fig. 1. Forecasting accuracy using MA

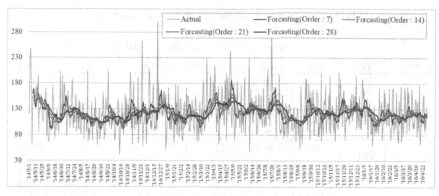

Fig. 2. Forecasting results and actual result (2014/5–2016/4)

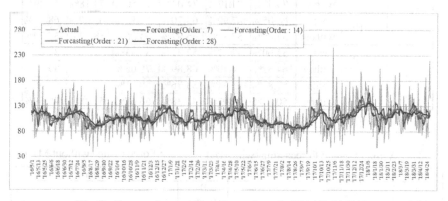

Fig. 3. Forecasting results and actual result (2016/5–2018/4)

3.3 Forecasting Results of Machine Learning

Table 3 shows the forecasting accuracy using machine learning. With the MA method, the method with the highest forecasting accuracy in 2018 was different for each store. In 2019, the stepwise method was the highest except for store B. Without the MA method, the forecasting accuracy of the Decision method was the highest in 2018 except for store A. In 2019, the Boosted method was the highest except for store D. Comparing with and without the MA method, the forecasting accuracy was higher with the MA method. This tendency was remarkable in 2019, which was affected by COVID-2019.

Figure 4 shows the transition in the actual customers visiting values and the forecasting values for the most accurate method in Table 3 for each store. Since January 2020, which was affected by the COVID-2019, the forecasting method with MA was able to follow the sharp decrease in the actual visiting. This is probably because the latest trend information could be reflected in the forecast by MA. However, since the forecast period is short (4 months), consideration will be given based on the forecast results for a longer period.

Table 3. Forecasting accuracy using machine learning.

:better result between 'with MA' and 'without MA'

Store	Year	MA	GBR	Bayesian	Boosted	Decision	RFR	Stepwise
A	2018	with	79.10%	78.27%	66.08%	77.12%	78.39%	78.89%
		without	77.86%	75.67%	72.16%	74.57%	75.67%	75.83%
	2019	with	65.17%	68.50%	66.60%	66.56%	66.02%	68.95%
		without	63.92%	63.39%	68.44%	65.21%	61.86%	63.66%
B	2018	with	76.03%	76.72%	74.62%	76.57%	74.03%	76.88%
		without	74.33%	73.15%	74.58%	76.15%	71.97%	72.92%
	2019	with	65.78%	73.76%	57.06%	66.47%	64.40%	72.96%
		without	65.28%	64.86%	67.11%	66.46%	65.47%	65.20%
C	2018	with	79.02%	79.59%	76.71%	78.27%	78.57%	79.56%
		without	74.57%	74.17%	74.03%	76.50%	74.18%	74.29%
	2019	with	66.05%	67.99%	63.70%	64.19%	65.00%	68.24%
		without	57.48%	57.84%	65.92%	64.26%	58.12%	57.79%
D	2018	with	53.00%	37.27%	52.77%	55.03%	55.21%	34.04%
		without	64.62%	44.40%	68.89%	70.05%	50.10%	39.22%
	2019	with	57.81%	58.34%	53.76%	58.51%	57.89%	58.65%
		without	50.23%	49.97%	41.38%	56.67%	51.38%	49.59%

──── : Actual   ──── : Forecasting (with MA)   ──── : Forecasting (without MA)

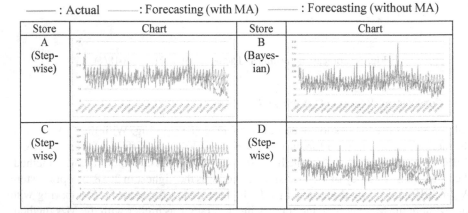

Store	Chart	Store	Chart
A (Step-wise)		B (Bayes-ian)	
C (Step-wise)		D (Step-wise)	

Fig. 4. Forecasting results using machine learning

3.4 Forecasting Results of Deep Learning

Table 4 compares the accuracy of the forecast using the training data normalized for all years (all years) and the training data normalized for each year (each year). At stores, C and D, the forecasting accuracy of both RNN and LSTM using the training data normalized for each year was higher. On the other hand, at store A, there were many cases where the forecasting accuracy using normalized data for all years was high.

At store B, there was no significant tendency. Table 5 shows the average number of customers visiting per day compared to 2014. At stores, C and D, the average number of customers visiting per day has decreased almost monotonically, and 2018, which is the forecast target, has decreased by more than 20% compared to 2014. Furthermore, this is also considered to be the reason why the forecasting accuracy is higher when the training data of the last 2 years is used than the 4 years that the number of training data is more.

Table 4. Forecasting accuracy using deep learning comparing normalization.

Store	Traing data	With meteorological data				Without meteorological data			
		RNN		LSTM		RNN		LSTM	
		All year	Each year	All year	Each year	All year	Each year	All year	Each year
A	four	76.90%	65.77%	75.20%	75.18%	81.05%	72.58%	73.90%	73.84%
	three	80.67%	67.52%	73.00%	68.31%	75.40%	67.65%	73.90%	66.26%
	two	68.96%	69.41%	70.95%	70.55%	69.10%	76.14%	70.11%	70.96%
B	four	65.99%	58.28%	63.73%	57.48%	64.10%	63.75%	63.52%	57.73%
	three	75.16%	74.44%	71.81%	74.44%	71.50%	72.48%	71.68%	71.76%
	two	72.04%	63.27%	69.86%	72.25%	69.22%	70.63%	69.03%	71.36%
C	four	29.95%	70.24%	41.81%	71.39%	63.44%	74.27%	40.34%	70.20%
	three	64.77%	74.43%	65.69%	72.95%	68.21%	76.47%	64.44%	72.36%
	two	69.86%	74.65%	70.57%	72.33%	75.04%	67.77%	70.40%	72.53%
D	four	36.17%	69.25%	25.52%	71.54%	15.89%	62.73%	18.89%	70.71%
	three	53.57%	75.94%	54.53%	73.33%	34.50%	74.66%	55.05%	73.06%
	two	65.24%	66.21%	73.02%	73.87%	63.89%	64.99%	72.98%	74.28%

Table 5. The average number of customers visiting per day.

Year	Store			
	A	B	C	D
2014	100.0%	100.0%	100.0%	100.0%
2015	100.7%	104.9%	84.9%	101.5%
2016	87.8%	87.6%	78.8%	94.7%
2017	89.4%	84.8%	76.5%	86.6%
2018	86.5%	85.8%	71.6%	79.5%

Table 6 compares the accuracy of the forecast using the training data including meteorological data (with data) and not (without data). In the forecasting using RNN, the accuracy of the forecasting using the training data with the meteorological data was higher at store D and was lower at stores A and C. At store B, there was no significant tendency. In forecasting using LSTM, the accuracy of the forecasting using the training data with the meteorological data was higher. Since the tendency is different between RNN and LSTM, more detailed analysis and tuning will be performed in the future.

Table 6. Forecasting accuracy using deep learning comparing meteorological data.

Store	Traing data	All year				Each year			
		RNN		LSTM		RNN		LSTM	
		With data	Wiout data	With data	Wiout data	With data	Wiout data	With data	Wiout data
A	four	76.90%	81.05%	75.20%	73.90%	65.77%	72.58%	75.18%	73.84%
	three	80.67%	75.40%	73.00%	73.90%	67.52%	67.65%	68.31%	66.26%
	two	68.96%	69.10%	70.95%	70.11%	69.41%	76.14%	70.55%	70.96%
B	four	65.99%	64.10%	63.73%	63.52%	58.28%	63.75%	57.48%	57.73%
	three	75.16%	71.50%	71.81%	71.68%	74.44%	72.48%	74.44%	71.76%
	two	72.04%	69.22%	69.86%	69.03%	63.27%	70.63%	72.25%	71.36%
C	four	29.95%	63.44%	41.81%	40.34%	70.24%	74.27%	71.39%	70.20%
	three	64.77%	68.21%	65.69%	64.44%	74.43%	76.47%	72.95%	72.36%
	two	69.86%	75.04%	70.57%	70.40%	74.65%	67.77%	72.33%	72.53%
D	four	36.17%	15.89%	25.52%	18.89%	69.25%	62.73%	71.54%	70.71%
	three	53.57%	34.50%	54.53%	55.05%	75.94%	74.66%	73.33%	73.06%
	two	65.24%	63.89%	73.02%	72.98%	66.21%	64.99%	73.87%	74.28%

3.5 Comparison of Machine Learning and Deep Learning

Table 7 shows the comparison of machine learning and deep learning. In order to compare the difference in forecasting accuracy between machine learning and deep learning, it is necessary to make the conditions other than the method the same. Therefore, among the forecasts for 2018 with training data of 4 years, without meteorological data as explanatory variables, and with MA data as explanatory variables, we compared the forecasting results of the most accurate methods for both machine learning and deep learning. The forecasting accuracy of deep learning was high in stores A and D, and that of machine learning was high in stores B and C. From this, it is unclear which machine learning and deep learning are better for forecasting the number of customers visiting. However, deep learning is at the beginning of the research, and we plan to adjust the parameters in the future.

Table 7. Comparison of machine learning and deep learning.

Store	Machine learning	Deep learning	
		RNN	LSTM
A	79.10%	81.05%	73.90%
B	76.88%	64.10%	63.52%
C	79.59%	74.27%	70.20%
D	55.21%	62.73%	70.71%

4   Conclusion

In this paper, it is proposed the forecasting of the number of customers visiting restaurants using machine learning and statistical method. The following results were obtained.

(1) The MA is effective when the trend of the number of customers visiting fluctuates rapidly. However, since the forecast period is short (4 months), consideration will be given based on the forecast results for a longer period.
(2) Normalization for each year of training data is effective when the annual average number of customers visiting increases or decreases monotonically.
(3) Depending on the location of the store, the meteorological data may affect the forecasting accuracy.

We will proceed with research on deep learning in forecasting the number of customers visiting, aiming to improve the forecasting accuracy.

References

1. Takashi, T., Tomohiro, H., Takeshi, S., Takeshi, T.: Demand forecasting in restaurants using machine learning and statistical analysis. Procedia CIRP **79**, 679–683 (2019)
2. Takashi, T., Tomohiro, H., Takeshi, S., Takeshi, T.: Restaurants store management based on demand forecasting. Procedia CIRP **88**, 580–583 (2020)
3. Jerome, H.M.: Greedy function approximation: a gradient boosting machine. Ann. Stat. **29**(5), 1189–1232 (2001)
4. Yoichi M., Takeshi K., Yoshinobu Y.: Community-Based Participatory Service Engineering, Case Studies and Technologies, Global Perspectives on Service Science, pp. 63–78. Springer, New York (2016)
5. Bernard, S., Fabio, R., Flavio, R., Fabricio, F., Jonice, O.: Scholar performance prediction using boosted regression trees techniques. In: European Symposium on Artificial Neural Networks 2017 Proceedings, pp. 329–334 (2017)
6. Antonio, C., Jamie, A., Ender, K.: Decision forests: a unified framework for classification, regression, density estimation, manifold learning and semi-supervised learning. Found. Trends Comput. Graph. Vis. **7**(2–3), 81–227 (2012)
7. Sebastian, R.: Python Machine Learning (Japanese Edition), pp. 86–87. Impress Corp, Taipei (2016)
8. Boich, B.W., Huang, C.J.: Applied Statistics Analysis (Japanese Edition), pp. 27–28, pp. 167–172. Morikita Publishing Co. Ltd., Tokyo (1968)
9. Kouki, A.: Deep Learning from Scratch 2, pp. 175–187, pp. 223–244. O'reilly Japan, Chiba (2018)
10. Takashi, T., Yuta, H., Takeshi, S.: Forecasting customers visiting using machine learning and characteristics analysis with low forecasting accuracy days. In: Lalic, B., Majstorovic, V., Marjanovic, U., von Cieminski, G., Romero, D. (eds.) Advances in Production Management Systems. Towards Smart and Digital Manufacturing, pp. 670–678. Springer, Cham (2020). https://doi.org/10.1007/978-3-030-57997-5_77

Digital Ordering Improves Labor Productivity in Multiproduct Restaurants

Takeshi Shimmura[1,2]($\boxtimes$) and Syuichi Oura[2]

[1] Ritsumeikan University, 1-1-1 Noji-Higashi, Kusatsu, Shiga, Japan
t-shinmura@gankofood.co.jp
[2] Ganko Food Service Co. Ltd., 1-2-13 Shin-kitano, Yodogawa-ku, Osaka, Japan

Abstract. This study assessed a digital ordering system (DOS) for use in a multi-product Japanese cuisine restaurant to enhance labor productivity. Labor productivity of restaurants is lowest among Japanese service industries. After DOS is introduced, restaurant operation processes were changed: order receiving duties are allocated to the DOS, not staff members; also, the number of dishes for preparation is decided based on the DOS promotion contents. Thereafter, restaurant managers can change the work schedule to reduce the total labor hours necessary for operations. Work hours and sales per labor hour measured before/after DOS introduction are recorded as a KIP showing productivity improvement. Results show that DOS introduction reduces labor hours, but increases sales per labor hour. However, the system should be improved to provide greater utility for customers. Moreover, DOS has no character size expansion function. Therefore, elderly customers have difficulties caused by poor vision. Also, DOS does not show all menus together. Therefore, customer selection of dishes to order can take some time and effort.

Keywords: Labor productivity · Restaurant · Service engineering

1 Introduction

In recent years, service industries have come to account for 75% of Japanese GDP. The trend is not only prevalent in Japan. Economies of industrialized nations are shifting to service industries. Nevertheless, labor productivity of service industries is lower than that of manufacturing industries. Especially, labor-intensive industries such as transportation, retail, and hotel industries have lower labor productivity than other service industries such as information services and web services. The restaurant industry can be regarded as a typical labor-intensive service.

The restaurant industry has strived to improve labor productivity since the mid-20th century. In the 1950s, some innovative American restaurant companies introduced chain store management systems. In the 1970s, the Japanese restaurant industry adopted such systems [1], introducing a central kitchen to reduce the number of chefs in restaurant kitchens. The system also introduces multi-store operations to realize economies of scale. The strategy rapidly expanded Japanese restaurant markets.

© IFIP International Federation for Information Processing 2021
Published by Springer Nature Switzerland AG 2021
A. Dolgui et al. (Eds.): APMS 2021, IFIP AICT 632, pp. 198–205, 2021.
https://doi.org/10.1007/978-3-030-85906-0_22

In the 1980s, the industry introduced information systems to improve store operations and supply chains. For instance, point of sales (POS) systems were developed and introduced in restaurants [2]. Before POS introduction, when a service staff member received order information, the staff member wrote it on a sheet of paper and brought it from the floor to the kitchen. By contrast, POS systems communicate order information electronically from a service staff member to a kitchen. The POS printer issues an order sheet. Restaurants reduce order information distribution operations, which reduces workloads of the service staff members.

In the 1990s, cooking machines and production systems were enhanced for more efficient kitchen operations. For instance, sushi production systems were developed for Japanese sushi restaurants [3]. Such systems include sushi preparation machines. The machines require no special sushi preparation skills. Restaurants need not hire sushi chefs. Restaurants can therefore reduce staff wages. Similarly, bulk cooking machines were developed to improve production capacity. For instance, convection ovens were used for simmered and baked dishes. The ovens require no special preparation skills. Restaurants were thus able to reduce the total number of chefs [4].

In the 2000s, the industry improved information systems for better store operations. For instance, process management systems (PMS) were developed. A POS manages order information by paper, but a PMS manages order information by display; PMS updates it regularly (kinds of dishes, total numbers, and lead times). Chefs can raise cooking speeds by referring to the information. In addition, the industry developed simulation systems for facility design and shift scheduling [5]. For instance, kitchen operation simulators were developed for facility layout design and cooking capacity control. Simulators calculate the lead times of dishes and cooking machine workloads. Kitchen designers can refer to simulation results for new kitchen design and cooking machine volume [6]. Furthermore, digital signage was introduced to enhance sales revenue and customer satisfaction. Digital signage shows information for dishes and ingredients: they promote customer orders [7]. Customers can gain knowledge related to ingredients and dishes, and can feel that the waiting time is short. Waiting time is an important factor affecting customer satisfaction [8].

Although many machines, systems and methods have been developed, restaurant labor productivity is lowest among service industries. Conventional studies mainly address kitchen (production) processes because they can be easily augmented by production management methods developed for manufacturing industries. Improving floor (service) process productivity is difficult because the process is a typical service product. Low productivity for service products arises from service characteristics. Services are intangible (intangibility). Therefore, products must be produced at the moment a customer orders them (simultaneity). In restaurant service, a POS system obviates order information transmission processes, but service staff members must wait at the restaurant floor to receive customer orders (thus service staff members are called waiters). To reduce the total number of service staff (labor hour input), the order receiving process must be eliminated, not only the order transmission process. Also, the total order (production output) should be increased to improve labor productivity because productivity is calculated by division (output/input).

To resolve difficulties, a digital ordering system (DOS) was developed and applied for an actual restaurant. In addition, service operations and working shifts are changed to reduce work hours. Kitchen operations are changed to adopt the system. Work hours and the total of orders before/after the system introduction are measured to confirm the system efficacy for productivity improvement. In addition, interviews are conducted to confirm the qualitative efficacy of the system.

2 Digital Ordering System Introduction

2.1 Usage and Structure of Digital Ordering System

Conventionally, order information is recorded in the staff member's memory or order sheet. When a customer orders, the customer calls a service staff member and conveys an order. The service staff member memorizes it or writes it on paper before delivering it to the restaurant kitchen. If a restaurant is busy, then many customers call staff members to convey orders in succession. Therefore, the restaurant manager should assign service staff members to avoid customer complaints.

A POS system automatically transmits order information from the service staff members to the restaurant kitchen using the order input device and transmission system, but the customer order information is received by service staff members. Input devices are operated by service staff member.

By contrast, the DOS can omit staff members' order receiving and delivery processes. Moreover, DOS has sales promotion functions to increase sales revenue. Figure 1 portrays the system structure: it consists of a control server, order input devices, kitchen printers, communication devices, and cashiers. The ordering program, dish information database (food category, name, price and picture), and promotion movie data are stored in a control server. When a customer inputs the order information, the communication device transmits it from the device to a kitchen printer and to a cashier via the control server. The printer issues an order sheet. The cashier calculates the account. If the customer uses no device, then the controller displays recommended information for sales promotion.

The DOS reduces the total number of service staff members because customers input order information by themselves. If a customer decides on an item to order, the customer inputs the information using the order tablet placed on a table. Menu categories are indicated on the main screen. When the customer taps a menu category, the category dishes and drinks are shown on the display. When the customer taps a dish or drink that the customer wants to eat or drink, the order quantity input command pops up; then the customer inputs the order quantity and taps the call button. Therefore, service staff members need not receive and deliver order information except if the customer is unable to do so. They need only to serve the ordered dishes, clear dishes, and clean and prepare the table. Restaurant managers can reduce the total number of service staff members because several operations of staff are allocated to the system.

In addition, the tablet can show product and promotion information. A restaurant manager determines a recommended dish, creates a recommendation movie or still image, and uploads it to the system. The system displays the information when a customer is not operating the device. The information provokes customer buying interest [7].

Therefore, kitchen staff can forecast the increase in the volume of recommended dishes and make arrangements to prepare it quickly. Reduction of lead times is important for productivity enhancement [9].

Decreasing the total number of staff and lead times is important for labor input reduction, and for increasing total of order is factor for output growth. They enhance labor productivity because it is defined by deduction (output volume/labor input).

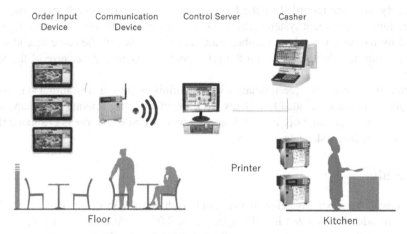

Fig. 1. Digital ordering system structure.

2.2 System Introduction

The system was introduced to a multiproduct Japanese cuisine restaurants located in Kyoto (2 floors, 1 kitchen, 123 sheets, and 1,234 m^2). Before system introduction, operation training was conducted for restaurant A staff members. The menu category, menu database, and promotion movie are created by a menu planning division staff. The system line, equipment configuration (1 control server, 2 cashiers, 30 order input device, 15 kitchen printer, and 1 communication device), and transmission setting (which kitchen printer receive and issue for dish a, b, c) are prepared by an information system division staff member.

At the time of system introduction, the restaurant manager changes restaurant staff operations. As explained above, customers input order information directly to an order input device. Therefore service staff members can stop visiting customer tables for order receipt, except in cases where customers ask for device operation support. Kitchen staff members can change preparation operations. They increase preparation volumes of system recommended dishes. Based on operation change, the restaurant manager changes the work schedule (service staff member number is reduced).

To confirm the system efficacy for labor productivity enhancement, work hours of the restaurant were measured for 9 weeks as a KPI for labor input reduction. Work hour reduction is a KPI for labor productivity, because Labor productivity is calculated by division; divide total of production by work hour. Work hours of the respective staff members are recorded by an attendant management system. They are calculated daily. Work hours of the same calendar day of the system introduced year and in the previous year are compared because restaurant operations fluctuate seasonally.

Sales per labor hour are measured for the same term as a KIP for output volume. As explained above, numerator of labor productivity formula is total of production, and sales is a index for production number. Therefore hourly sales per labor hour indicates productivity output volume.

Hourly sales are recorded by the DOS cashier. Hourly staff numbers are recorded by attendant management systems. Sales per labor hour are calculated from hourly sales divided by the hourly working number. Sales per labor hour of the same calendar day of the system introduction year and the prior year are compared because of the same reason.

After the experiment, questionnaires were administered to the restaurant staff members. Questionnaires included four items (DOS is effective for operation efficacy, sales promotion, customer support, and work hour reduction). Staff members evaluated them using an ascending risk scale of 1 to 5.

3   Results

Average work hour per day before the system introduction is 356.4 hr (SD = 32.2). That of after introduction is 339.4 hr (SD = 38.1, P = 0.0942). Assuming unequal variance with one-sample t tests, we found a significant difference in the means ($t(63) = 2.686$, $p < 0.05$) Average sales per labor hour is 4,003 yen (Sd = 575). That of after system introduction is 4,454 yen (SD = 730, P = 0.0167). Assuming equal variance with one-sample t tests, we found a significant difference in the means ($t(63) = 3.847, p < 0.05$). Figure 2 (left) presents work hours and sales point diagrams for the prior year. Figure 2 (right) shows those of the present year.

Results of questionnaires include the following: The average score of question 1 (DOS is effective for operation efficacy) was 4.1. That of question 2 (DOS is effective

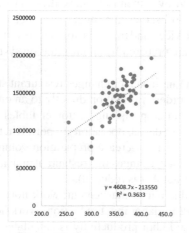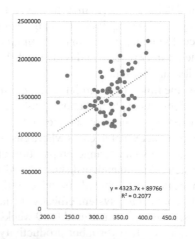

Fig. 2. Digital ordering system structure (y axis, sales in yen; x axis, work hour).

for sales promotion) was 4.0). That of question 3 (DOS is effective for customer support) was 3.4. That of question 4 (DOS is effective for work hour reduction) was 4.4. Table 1 presents the questionnaires results).

Table 1. Responses to questionnaires

Questionnaire item	1	2	3	4	5	Avg.
DOS is effective for operation efficacy	0	0	1	7	2	4.1
DOS is effective for sales promotion	0	0	2	6	2	4.0
DOS is effective for customer support	0	0	7	2	1	3.4
DOS is effective for work hour reduction	0	0	1	4	5	4.4

4 Discussion

First, DOS introduction effects on work hour reduction are discussed. As results show, average work hours were reduced from 356.4 hr to 339.4 hr. The purpose of DOS was to obviate order receiving operations by service staff. Because the restaurant manager reduced the total of service staff after adoption by the system, work hours of the restaurant decreased. In addition, as Table 1 shows, staff members evaluated the most effective DOS function is to reduce work hours (average score is 4.4). The restaurant manager remarked that DOS is effective especially during idle times. On two floors, there are two large rooms in each floor in the restaurant. If DOS is not introduced, then at least four service staff members must be assigned because staff members must wait at each room to receive customer orders. If DOS is introduced, then staff members need only to wait at each floor, and need only serve dishes when they are finished cooking.

Secondly, DOS introduction effects for output volume are discussed. Average sales per labor hour increased from 4,003 yen to 4,454 yen (+11.3%). Work hours decreased by 4.8%. Therefore, the sales increase effect for sales per labor hour was 6.5%. As explained, promotion and product information elicit customer orders [7]. In addition, the ordering system itself increases the total number of orders. If DOS were not introduced, then customers would call a service staff member for ordering. If a restaurant is busy, staff members can not receive all customer orders conveniently. Therefore some customers hesitate or stop orders because they become too busy. By contrast, DOS resolves the difficulty; customers can order dishes timely using an ordering device, even if the restaurant is busy. Employees evaluated DOS as useful for sales promotion.

Thirdly, the DOS qualitative evaluation is discussed. As Table 1 shows, the highest score of the questionnaire is "work hour reduction". The second score is "operation efficacy". The purpose of DOS is to enhance labor productivity. Naturally, restaurants reduce work hours by changing service operations and work scheduling. In addition, increased output volume is important for enhancing labor productivity Employees evaluate that the system supports increased sales. However, employees evaluated the "customer support" function as low, although service quality is a primal factor for the restaurant industry.

Several reasons can explain this finding. First, older customers are not accustomed to IT device operations. In addition, senior customers have bad eyesight, but the display system does not have a character size transformation function. Order input function should be improved for easier ordering. Secondly, looking at all menus is not easy compared to a paper menu. If a customer decides to order an item, then they need only to tap the "menu category" "menu item" and "number". However, if a customer does not decide to order something, the customer should search all kinds of menu categories to ascertain which menu items are available.

5 Conclusions

For this study, a digital ordering system was developed and introduced in a multiproduct Japanese cuisine restaurant to enhance labor productivity. Before the system introduction, operation training was conducted for staff members. Then the menu of the restaurant was set up. Thereafter, the system was actually introduced. Store managers changed staff operations; order receiving processes were allocated to the system. Numbers of dish preparation were decided based on the system promotion contents. Subsequently, the manager changed the work scheduling to reduce total work hours. Results show that reducing work hours of restaurant staff members can be achieved by introducing the system. A restaurant can improve sales per labor hour using the system. Results demonstrate that the system enhances labor productivity of restaurants by reducing input (work hour) and by increasing output volume (sales per labor hour). However, the system should be improved: it is less useful for elderly customers because the system can not show large characters. Also, the system does not show the entire menu at once. Therefore a customer can not view all items easily.

References

1. Chase, R.B., Apte, U.M.: A history of research in service operations: what's the big idea? J. Oper. Manage. **25**(2), 375–386 (2007)
2. Stein, K.: Point-of-sales systems for foodservice. J. Am. Diet. Assoc. **105**(12), 1861–1863 (2005)
3. Ngai, E.W.T., Suk, F.F.C., Lo, S.Y.Y.: Development of an RFID-based Sushi management system: the case of a conveyer belt sushi restaurant. Int. J. Prod. Econ. **112**(2), 630–645 (2008)
4. Danowsca-Oziewicz, M., Karpinsca-Tymoszczyk, M., Borowski, J.: The effect of cooking in a steam-convection oven on the quality of selected dishes. J. Food Serv. **18**(5), 187–197 (2007)
5. Takeshi, S., Takeshi, T., Motoyuki, A.: Improvement of restaurant operation by sharing order and customer information. Int. J. Organ. Collecting Intell. **1**(3), 54–70 (2010)
6. Nobutada, F., Toshiya, K., Minami, U., Tomomi, N., Takeshi, S.: Facility layout planning of central kitchen in food service industry – application to the real-scale problem. In: Proceedings of International Conference Advances in Production Management Systems, pp. 33–40 (2013)
7. Takeshi, S., Toshiya, K., Nobutada, F., Takeshi, T.: Improving customer's subjective waiting time introducing digital signage. In: Proceedings of International Conference Advances in Production Management Systems, p. 165 (2012)

8. Hwang, J., Lambert, C.U.: The interaction of major resources and their influence on waiting times in a multi-stage restaurant. Int. J. Hospitality Manage. **274**, 541–551 (2007)
9. Takeshi, S., et al.: Using a cooking operation simulator to improve cooking speed in a multi-product Japanese cuisine restaurant. In: Proceedings of International Conference Advances in Production Management Systems, pp. 33–40 (2014)

Geospatial Intelligence for Health and Productivity Management in Japanese Restaurants and Other Industries

Takeshi Kurata[1,2]([⊠])

[1] Human Augmentation Research Center AIST, Chiba, Japan
t.kurata@aist.go.jp
[2] University of Tsukuba, Tsukuba, Japan

Abstract. Health and Productivity Management (HPM) requires simultaneous improvement of labor productivity and Quality of Working (QoW), which consists of health, workability, and rewarding. In order to deal with a wide range of issues for HPM, engineering approaches are much more effective rather than just relying on experience and intuition. First, this paper outlines Geospatial Intelligence (GSI) as a tool for such engineering approaches, which supports problem solving by linking geospatial data with other data. Next, we summarize use cases of GSI in service and manufacturing sites, including Japanese restaurants, which have addressed labor productivity and QoW. Finally, we extract the metrics regarding labor productivity and QoW used in those use cases.

Keywords: Health and productivity management (HPM) · Geospatial intelligence (GSI) · Quality of working (QoW) · Indoor positioning

1 Introduction

In 2015, SDGs were adopted by the United Nations, and in the same year, the Ministry of Economy, Trade and Industry (METI) and the Tokyo Stock Exchange (TSE) started to select HPM stocks in Japan. HPM requires the simultaneous improvement of labor productivity and QoW [1]. As shown in Fig. 1, QoW consists of health, workability, and rewarding, which is closely related to occupational safety and health, QWL, and decent work, as well as social capital. To improve both labor productivity and QoW in a well-balanced manner, it is necessary to deal with a wide range of issues. Therefore, there is limitation in taking action by experience and intuition, and engineering approaches are essential.

2 Geospatial Intelligence

It is natural to incorporate ideas such as digital twin and DX as engineering approaches that contribute to HPM. An effective tool for this purpose is GSI, which supports problem

A. Dolgui et al. (Eds.): APMS 2021, IFIP AICT 632, pp. 206–214, 2021.
https://doi.org/10.1007/978-3-030-85906-0_23

solving by linking geospatial data, including positioning data, with other sources of data. This is often described as GEOINT, but it has a strong national security nuance, so here we call it GSI. The conceptual diagram of GSI is shown in Fig. 2 [2].

GSI makes organic use of both (1) digital twin/IoT/IoH technologies and methodologies and (2) social technologies and methodologies cultivated in service engineering, IE, etc. to provide a comprehensive picture of the current situation in service and manufacturing sites while acquiring 6M data there. Furthermore, GSI can support process modelling, improvement activities, and preliminary evaluation (simulation). It has been reported that about 60–80% of data is related to location [3], and that humans spend about 90% of their time indoors [4]. In light of these facts, we believe that GSI, especially Indoor GSI is an effective way to promote DX (Fig. 1).

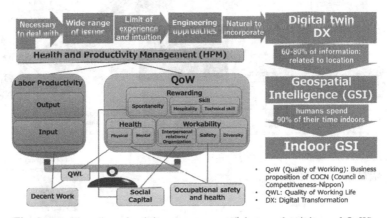

Fig. 1. Health and productivity management (labor productivity and QoW).

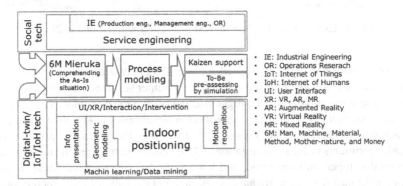

Fig. 2. Conceptual diagram of GSI.

3   Use Cases of GSI

Tables 1 and 2 aggregate the use cases of GSI in service and manufacturing sites, including Japanese restaurants, that AIST has been involved in or investigated. As shown in the tables, both of productivity and QoW have been addressed in most of the cases. Although we have started applied GSI with a clear awareness of QoW and HPM only since 2015, it is confirmed that both productivity and QoW have been targeted since 2010 when we started applying GSI for 'Kaizen (improvement)'. Table 1 lists the objectives, methods, effects and results, positioning technologies used, joint research partners, investigation sites, and references for each case study, and each row of Table 2 presents the evaluation items, indicators, and contents related to labor productivity and QoW used for each case in the same row of Table 1.

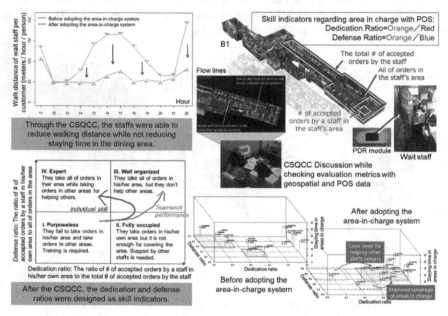

Fig. 3. Example of CQSCC with GSI in a Japanese restaurant in 2012.

The sites and job categories covered include helpers and nurses at nursing homes [6], guest room attendants at Japanese inns [7], customer service assistants and catering staff at Japanese restaurants [8–11], flight attendants on passenger planes [12], building maintenance workers [13], pickers at distribution warehouses [14], office workers, and manufacturing workers at cable factories [2, 15]. Over the years, especially through practical experiments in Japanese restaurants, GSI-related techniques and methodologies have been developed and improved, and knowledge has been accumulated [8–11]. In addition, in the past few years, we have confirmed that the technologies, methodologies, and knowledge can be transferred from the service sites to the manufacturing sites [2, 15].

As an example of GSI utilization, we briefly present a case study of a Japanese restaurant in 2012 [9] along with each item in Tables 1 and 2 (Fig. 3). The purpose of using GSI in this case was to reduce the physical workload of the employees while maintaining hospitality, which had been improved in the previous year [8]. In order to achieve this goal, a CSQCC (Computer Supported Quality Control Circle) activity [8]

Table 1. Use cases using GSI: Purposes, objectives, methods, effects and results, positioning techs, joint research partners, and references. (PDR: Pedestrian Dead Reckoning, RFID: Radio Frequency Identification, BLE: Bluetooth Low Energy, MAP: Map matching, QC: Quality Control, OJT: On-the-Job Training).

Site [Job category]	Year	Purpose	Method	Effect and result	Positioning technologies	Joint research partners/ investigation sites	References
Nursing home [helpers, nurses]	2010	As-Is comprehension of care work flow	Flow-line measurement, descriptive statistics, interview	Process modeling, visualization of issues		SUPER COURT	[6]
Japanese inn [guest room attendants]	2011	Skill analysis	Flow-line measurement, descriptive statistics, retrospective interview	As-Is comprehension of skill		Kinosaki hot springs	[7]
Japanese restaurant 1 [Customer service assistants and catering staff]	2011	Hospitality improvement		Increase in duration of stay in guest areas and additional orders	PDR+ Active RFID +MAP		[8]
	2013	Physical load reduction while hospitality improvement		(In addition to the above) reduction of walking distance, skill modeling			[9]
Japanese restaurant 2 [Customer service assistants and catering staff]	2014	Support of new restaurant launch	Flow-line measurement, descriptive statistics, QC activity	visualization of issues. Kaizen effect check, rapid launch		GANKO FOOD SERVICE Co,Ltd.	[10]
Japanese restaurant 3 [Customer service assistants and catering staff]	2018 -19	Effectiveness verification of robot installation		Increase in sales per man hour and dedication in charge			[11]
Passenger plane [Flight attendant]	2015	Constructing training support environments to facilitate awareness learning	Flow-line measurement, descriptive statistics, process modeling, retrospective interview	Skill modeling in serving drink, training support	PDR+BLE +MAP	University of Tokyo, ANA Strategic Research Institute Co., Ltd.	[12]
Office [office worker]	2016	Improving office environmens (Communication/exercie space installation)	Flow-line measurement, descriptive statistics	Increase in usage rate of communication and exercie spage	RGB-D camera	Fujikura Ltd.	—
Building [Building maintenance worker]	2017	Investigating effects and impacts of work restructuring	Flow-line measurement, descriptive statistics, Questionnaire, Interview	Clarification of effects and issues before and after the restructuring	PDR+BLE +MAP	KAJIMA TATEMONO SOGO KANRI CO.,LTD.	[13]
Distribution warehouse 1 [Picker]	2014	As-Is comprehension of picking work flow, Kaizen simulation	Flow-line measurement, descriptive and inferential statistics, process modeling, interview	Process modeling, To-Be simulation to compare Kaizen plans	Visible Light Communication	Frameworx, Inc., TRUSCO NAKAYAMA Corporation	[14]
Distribution warehouse 2 [low-vision/blind subject]	2018 -19	Effectiveness check of work support of low-vision and blind workers	Picking operation Instructions based on positioning	Feasibility confirmed	Passive RFID	GOV Co.,Ltd., TRUSCO NAKAYAMA Corporation	—
Cable factory 1 [Manufacturing worker]	2018 -19	Workload leveling	Flow-line measurement, descriptive statistics, Information sharing, OJT, retrospective interview	Workload leveling, Clarification of issues	BLE		—
Cable factory 2 [Manufacturing worker]	2018 -	Simultaneous support for productivity improvement, safety management, and health management	Flow-line measurement, descriptive statistics, Information sharing, POC	—	PDR+BLE +MAP	Sumitomo Electric Industries, Ltd.	[2][15]

Table 2. Use cases using GSI: Evaluation items on labor productivity and QoW (outside { }: evaluation items, inside { }: evaluation indicators and contents used, bold: indirectly related to geospatial data, bold underlined: directly related to geospatial data).

Site [Job category]	Labor productivity		QoW							
			Health		Rewarding				Workability	
					Skill					
	Output	Input	Physical	Mental	Hospitality		Spontaneity	Interpersonal relations/ Organization	Safety	Diversity
Nursing home [helpers, nurses]		**Wasted movement {Flow lines}**				Individual and team skills **{Flow lines, duration of stay}**				
Japanese inn [guest room attendants]					Subjective skill description **{Pseudo FPV video}**					
Japanese restaurant 1 [Customer service assistants and catering staff]	Number of additional orders {POS}	**Wasted movement {Flow lines}**	Physical load **{Walking distance}**		Customer service time **{Heat maps, Duration of stay in guest areas}**	Individual and team skills {POS, **Dedication/defense rate in charge**}	Kaizen proposal			
Japanese restaurant 2 [Customer service assistants and catering staff]	Labor productivity {Sales per man hour}				Dedication **{Heat maps}**			Information sharing, transparency of work conditions **{Geospatial data}**		
Japanese restaurant 3 [Customer service assistants and catering staff]						Individual and team skills **{Dedication rate in charge}**				
Passenger plane [Flight attendant]					Interpersonal defference in serving drink **{Flow lines}**		Look-back			
Office [office worker]	Amount of added value {Operating profit (rate)}		**Exercise space usage rate {Duration of stay}**					descriptive statistics of communication **{Flow lines, duration of stay}**		
Building [Building maintenance worker]	Service quality {Customer complaints}	Workload in office, **Wasted movement {Flow lines}**	Physical load **{Walking distance}**					ES {Questionnaire}		
Distribution warehouse 1 [Picker]		**Traffic congestion {Heat maps}**, Workload per man hour, working hours per team		Mental load **{Relaxation/contingency allowance}**		Objective skill **{movement speed, working hours}**		Fairness **{Unevenness of workload among workers}**		
Distribution warehouse 2 [low-vision/blind subject]		Comparison between sighted and low-vision/blind subjects {working hours}								Feasibility of work support of low-vision and blind people {Working hours}
Cable factory 1 [Manufacturing worker]		Deviation from code of operation **{Duration of stay}**				Interpersonal difference **{Duration of stay}**		Information sharing, transparency of work conditions **{Geospatial data}**		
Cable factory 2 [Manufacturing worker]		**Wasted movement {Flow lines}**	Physical load/Exercise intensity **{Walking distance}**					Information sharing, transparency of work conditions, 6M visualization **{Geospatial data}**	Working alone/Intersection situation between workers and vehicles **{Flow lines, heat maps}**	

was conducted by measuring flow lines, analyzing descriptive statistics of each indicator, and visualizing them. For measuring flow lines, the CSQCC installed an integrated indoor positioning system based on PDR, active RFID, and map matching. It was proposed spontaneously by the CSQCC participants to adopt an area-in-charge system, and it resulted in a shorter walking distance while maintaining hospitality.

In addition, as a spinoff effect of adopting the area-in-charge system, skill indicators for individuals and teams were designed as in the dedication and defense ratios (precision and recall in [9]) regarding the area in charge. These indicators were derived from POS (Point of Sales) data, and it allowed us to visualize the distribution of the skills of each wait staff. Thus, it can be seen that productivity (waste), health (physical load), rewarding (hospitality skills, spontaneity), and workability (information sharing, transparency of work conditions) were efficiently and simultaneously handled by GSI in this case study.

4 Summary of Use Cases

The purposes of each case have progressed from understanding the current (As-Is) situation alone to supporting improvement and pre-assessing (To-Be) hypotheses by simulations. In addition, the specific objectives have become broader such as skill analysis, training support, simultaneous support for productivity improvement, safety management, and health management, effect verification of introducing robots, and feasibility verification of employment support for the visually impaired (Fig. 4).

In some cases, existing indicators can be applied, while in other cases, the process starts with designing indicators. The evaluation items {indicators} for labor productivity include those that can be obtained directly from geospatial data, such as wasted movement {flow lines}, traffic congestion {heat maps indicating duration of stay}, and deviation from code of operation {duration of stay in each area}; those that can be applied indirectly from geospatial data, such as workload and working hours; and other items (number of additional orders {POS}, service quality {customer complaints}, added value {operating profit (rate)}, and labor productivity {sales per hour}) are used (Fig. 5).

As described above, QoW consists of health, workability, and rewarding. Regarding health, the walking distance is used for both the negative aspect of physical load and the health-promoting aspect of exercise intensity, and geospatial data is also applied to the evaluation of exercise space usage rate {duration of stay in the area} and mental load {relaxation/contingency allowance}. As for rewarding, individual and team skills are evaluated based on the flow lines, movement speed, duration of stay, working hours, or the dedication/defense ratio in charge. For qualitative evaluation of skills by retrospective interviews, pseudo FPV (First-Person View) videos generated with 3D models of work sites and flow lines [5] are sometimes used as visual geospatial contents.

And with respect to interpersonal relations and organization out of workability, it is confirmed whether information sharing, transparency of work conditions, and visualization of the 6M data have been carried out, and geospatial data such as flow lines and heat maps are used as contents for this purpose. Other evaluation items for interpersonal relations and organization include fairness {unevenness of workload among workers}, descriptive statistics of communication {flow lines and duration of stay}, and Employee Satisfaction (ES) {questionnaire}. Flow lines and heat maps are also utilized to validate the safety when working alone and the intersection situation between workers and vehicles. There is also a diversity-related case in which the feasibility of work support of low-vision and blind people is evaluated with working hours.

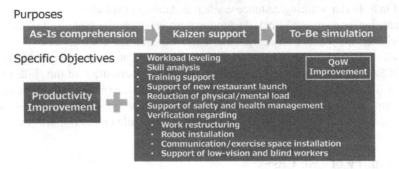

Fig. 4. Purposes and specific objectives extracted and summarized from Table 1.

5   Conclusion

In this paper, a wide range of actual cases are summarized to contribute to the study of how to utilize GSI to promote DX for the purpose of HPM. By dealing with multiple items related to labor productivity and QoW at the same time, the organizations will be able to maintain a high balance between them. We summarized the indicators used in each of the cases listed in Table 2 as shown in Fig. 5. It demonstrates that there are diverse but common indicators obtained directly or indirectly from geospatial data, and that they can be easily applicable by GSI. In fact, in the specific case of the Japanese restaurant introduced in Sect. 3, the combination of geospatial data such as flow lines and POS data was able to simultaneously handle multiple indicators associated with productivity, health, rewarding, and workability for HPM. In addition, the organizations also receive the advantage of being able to disperse the initial/running costs of GSI over several purposes rather than just for a single purpose [15].

DX means digitizing 6M information, including geospatial information, and transforming products, services, business processes, and ultimately the organization. However, it takes a long time to see results after digitization, and not a few organizations find it difficult to gain understanding of GSI implementation from both the executive labor sides. The only way to achieve this drastically is to spread the concept of DX throughout society, but making it easier to introduce, operate, and maintain the GSI infrastructure and improving interoperability in groups such as supply chains using 6M data will also contribute to promoting the application of GSI at the practical level. In addition, geospatial artificial intelligence (GeoAI) technologies [16] based on machine learning are likely to attract more and more attention from service and manufacturing industries from now on. We will continue our research and development on how GeoAI can combine the evaluation indicators summarized in Fig. 5 and utilize them for the purpose summarized in Fig. 4, or whether new metrics can be acquired by GeoAI.

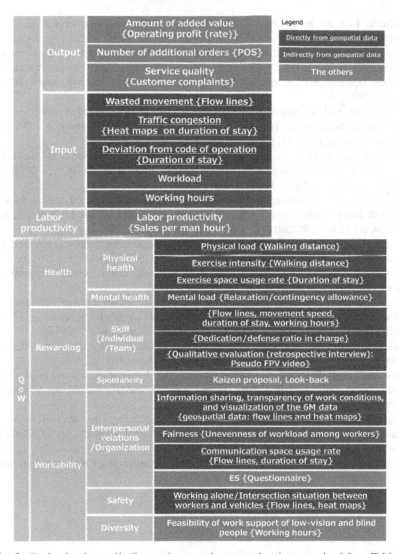

Fig. 5. Evaluation items {indicators/contents} extracted and summarized from Table 2.

References

1. QoW: http://www.cocn.jp/report/thema91-L.pdf. Accessed 21 Mar 2021
2. Kurata, T., et al.: Towards realization of 6M visualization in manufacturing sites. In: The First IEEE VR Workshop on Smart Work Technologies, 4 p. (2019)
3. Hahmann, S., Burghardt, D.: How much information is geospatially referenced? Networks and cognition. Int. J. Geograph. Inf. Sci. **27**(6), 1171–1189 (2013)
4. Klepeis, N.E., et al., The National Human Activity Pattern Survey (NHAPS): A Resource for Assessing Exposure to Environmental Pollutants, Lawrence Berkeley National Laboratory (2001)

5. Ishikawa, T., et al.: Interactive 3-D indoor modeler for virtualizing service fields. Virtual Reality **17**(2), 89–109 (2013)
6. Motomura, Y., et al.: Community-based participatory service engineering: case studies and technologies. In: Kwan, S.K., Spohrer, J.C., Sawatani, Y. (eds.) Global Perspectives on Service Science: Japan, pp. 63–78. Springer-Verlag, New York (2016). https://doi.org/10.1007/978-1-4939-3594-9_5
7. Nakajima, M., et al., Cognitive chrono-ethnography lite, work: a journal of prevention, assessment and rehabilitation. In: (IEA 2012: 18th World Congress on Ergonomics - Designing a Sustainable Future), vol. 41, pp. 617–622 (2012)
8. Fukuhara, T., et al.: Improving service processes based on visualization of hu-man-behavior and POS data: a case study in a Japanese restaurant. In: Proceedings ICServ 2013, pp.1–8 (2013). https://doi.org/10.1007/978-4-431-54816-4_1
9. Fukuhara, T., et al., Estimating skills of waiting staff of a restaurant based on behavior sensing and POS data analysis: a case study in a Japanese cuisine restaurant. In: Proceedings AH-FE2014, pp. 4287–4299 (2014)
10. Okuma, T., et al.: Role of servicing activity visualization in quality control circle. In: Proceedings ICServ 2015, 6 p. (2015)
11. Shinmura, T., et al.: Service robot introduction to a restaurant enhances both labor productivity and service quality. In: CIRP ICME 2019 (2019)
12. Tachioka, K., et al.: Behavioral measurements of cabin attendants together with observations and an analysis of their tasks by using service process model. In: Proceedings of the 4th International Conference on Serviceology (ICServ2016), pp. 271–277 (2016)
13. Ichikari, R., et al.: A case study of building maintenance service based on stakeholders' perspectives in the service triangle. In: Proceedings ICServ 2018, pp. 87–94 (2018)
14. Myokan, T., et al.: Pre-evaluation of Kaizen plan considering efficiency and employee satisfaction by simulation using data assimilation - toward constructing Kaizen support framework. In: Proceedings ICServ 2016, 7 p. (2016)
15. Kurata, T., et al.: IoH technologies into indoor manufacturing sites. In: IFIP International Conference on Advances in Production Management Systems (APMS), pp. 372–380 (2019). https://doi.org/10.1007/978-3-030-29996-5_43
16. Openshaw, S., Openshaw, C.: Artificial Intelligence in Geography, Chichester. John Wiley & Sons, Hoboken (1997)

Engineering Large Event Catering Services

Kai-Wen Tien[✉] and Vittaldas V. Prabhu

The Pennsylvania State University, University Park, PA 16802, USA
kut147@psu.edu

Abstract. In the United States, catering services constitute about $8.6 billion annually. The main objective in managing large catered events is centered around ensuring good customer satisfaction while minimizing food wastage. Achieving this management objective is challenging because of some of the key characteristics of such service systems such as long setup time, time varying demand, and complex customer food preferences. Industry practice heavily relies on the experience of individuals with little use of model-driven decision-making for planning such events. This paper takes a service system engineering approach for event catering by developing an analytical framework for decision-making by event planners to determine kitchen capacity, temporary storage capacity for warmers, and staffing level for buffet service. The proposed model is distribution-free and provides intuitive visualization for decision-making. As a practical case study, the model is applied to a large catered event with an attendance of about 10,000 over three hours.

Keywords: Event catering · Food services · Gastronomic services · Buffet-style catering

1 Introduction

Event catering plays a vital role in creating memorable events. Researches have shown that the quality of food, the quality of services, and the fit for the event's atmosphere are essential for increasing satisfaction and creating a holistic experience for guests [1]. Good food experiences also attract attendees to participate in the events and increase customers' return intention in the future [2]. Therefore it is important to plan event catering as well as possible.

Food wastage is one of the main issues of event catering. Reports by FAO indicate that one-third of all food produced for human consumption is wasted [3, 4]. In particular, in developed countries, food services cause 14% of food wastage [4]. In the United States, catering services constitute about $8.6 billion annually. Thus, event catering is a significant source of food wastage. Monteiro et al. studied the food wastage in event catering in higher education institutions in the UK and investigated the possible causes for food wastage [5]. They suggested that there is a need for planning tools to help inexperienced planners reduce wastage.

© IFIP International Federation for Information Processing 2021
Published by Springer Nature Switzerland AG 2021
A. Dolgui et al. (Eds.): APMS 2021, IFIP AICT 632, pp. 215–223, 2021.
https://doi.org/10.1007/978-3-030-85906-0_24

Recent efforts in modeling for catering services focus on linking food production with its transportation to the location where the event is held, with the main emphasis on the freshness of the food when served. Farahani et al. introduced a heuristic method based on vehicle routing problems to help catering companies integrate the decision on both their short-term production and distribution plan [6]. Yağmur and Kesen developed a fast algorithm for joint production and distribution scheduling with perishable products [7]. Wu et al. studied the catering services for high-speed rail in China [8]. They developed a lot-sizing network optimization model to determine the location for producing foods and control the on-train inventories with capacity limits and time-varying demand.

To our best knowledge, there is no published work focusing on analytical models for decision-making for planning event catering. Such a model can help reduce reliance on the experience of individual planners and help improve customer service along with reductions in food wastage. This paper takes a service engineering approach for event catering by developing an analytical framework for decision-making by event planners to determine kitchen capacity, temporary storage capacity for warmers, and staffing level for buffet service. In Sect. 2, the characteristics of large catering events are discussed. Section 3 presents the "distribution-free" analytical framework in detail. Also, a case study is used to demonstrate the framework. We conclude and discuss possible future work in Sect. 4.

2   Characteristics of Large Event Catering

There are many types of event catering services. Its design depends on the event scale, venue types, or the types of food provided [5]. This research studies large buffet-type catering services which coordinate with kitchen operation in close proximity to the venue and provide hot food. There are three critical characteristics in these events: long setup, time-varying demand, and high food wastage.

2.1   Long Setup

A catering event is often less than three hours, but the planning time and preparation time are much longer than the event duration. During the event, the demand can be large range from a few hundred to several thousand and kitchen operations need to prepare enough food before the demand surge occurs. Therefore kitchen needs to have surge capacity planned for such operation, e.g., setup more grills or fryers along with corresponding staff members. This installed capacity can be reduced to some extent by preparing food ahead of time and storing it appropriately. For food items whose quality depends on their temperature, insulated boxes (bags) or food warmers would be needed for this temporary storage.

Therefore, determine the setup time, i.e., when kitchen operations commence, is crucial for event catering. For example, if the setup time is advanced to an earlier time, then kitchen operations can be slowed down with corresponding reductions in installed capacity but more storage capacity would be needed. Installed kitchen capacity may be constrained by venue-specific parameters such as space and utilities (e.g., maximum power that can be drawn).

2.2 Time-Varying Demand

An event catering demand profile can exhibit significant dynamics and swings depending on the timing of other activities in the event. For example, a huge surge of guests would join a lunch buffet if several sessions at a conference end simultaneously just before the lunch break resulting in a demand profile that is shown in Fig. 1 (a). If event catering is before an important activity then the demand profile could have a profile as shown in Fig. 1 (b) or (c). If the event catering is planned between two important activities, then the resulting profile could be as shown in Fig. 1 (d).

It should be emphasized that the demand profile has a significant impact on decision-making for event planning. For example, the kitchen might need to start earlier and stop earlier if the demand profile is as Fig. 1 (a). On the other hand, demand profiles like Fig. 1 (b), (c), (d) do not impact the setup time significantly.

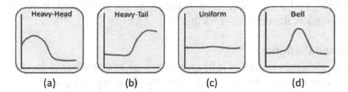

Fig. 1. Different demand profile

2.3 Customer Food Preference

Customer food preference is one of the essential factors for planning a good event catering. It determines how much food should be prepared. It should be considered when creating the menu, especially for hot food items, since most of these may be disposed of after the event if guests do not consume them. Good design of menu considering customer preference reduces the plate waste during event. However, customer food preference in event catering is largely unknown compared to restaurants that have recurring guests over several years of operation. Moreover, the food preference in event catering is influenced by many factors including weather, time, type of event, type of guests, and menu design [9]. One way to consider customer preference in planning is to estimate guest preference probabilities for each food item from some historical data.

In order to assist event planners in dealing with the challenges of long setup times, dynamic demand, and unknown food preferences, we propose an analytical model for decision-making through the context of a case study in the next section.

3 Analytical Model for Planning Event Catering: A Case Study

In this section, through a case study we propose a three-phase decision framework to plan event catering for a buffet-style catering with hot food. The framework shown in Fig. 2 includes three phases: system analysis and design, kitchen and service capacity synchronization, and detailed planning. The main objective of this planning is to synchronize kitchen capacity (e.g., number of grills), service capacity (e.g., number of buffet lines and employees). Consequently, the space of food capacity (e.g., number of warmer) and the kitchen operation time can be determined.

Phase I: System Analysis and Design
In the first phase, some primary operational data should be collected: arrival profile of guests (see Fig. 1), kitchen cooking times, service times for each food item, and food preference. It should be noted that some food items such as bottled water, which does not seize the kitchen capacity, need not be considered in the plan.

Phase II: Kitchen and Service Synchronization
In the second phase, the planner uses rough capacity planning to determine the overall kitchen capacity and overall service capacity with the demand profile predicted in Phase-I. With different kitchen capacity and service capacity decisions, kitchen operation time, max storage level, and max queue level of the event are computed. It could provide an intuitive visualization for decision-making.

Phase III: Detail Planning
The last phase calculates pieces of kitchen equipment, the number of food lines, and the number of warmer required by the rough capacity planning in Phase-II.

3.1 Case Study Description

Penn State University serves the military and veteran community every year by giving special recognition to our service members, veterans, and their families by offering free admission to sporting events, including an annual tailgate party and tickets to football games. The tailgate party, attended by over 8,000 people, consisted of military appreciation, entertainment shows, and food catering. The layout is as shown in Fig. 2.

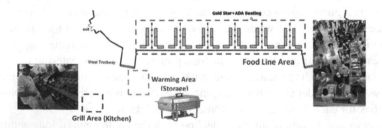

Fig. 2. Event catering layout

The tailgate is organized at a sports arena. Volunteers are stationed to direct the flow of people and to staff the food lines. The venue consists of two seating areas and L-shaped food lines containing nine servers each and two counters for dessert and drinks. All the food lines and dessert counters serve guests simultaneously. The kitchen is located outside of the main venue, where the food is prepared and brought to the food lines by volunteers. The cooked hot food is stored between the kitchen and the venue if food items in the food lines are sufficient.

3.2 Operation Analysis and Design

In the following case study, the data collected in the 2016 tailgate party is used. The event started from 2:00 pm to 6:00 pm, four hours in total.

Demand Analysis

In record, there were 8160 guests at the event. The event was right after the sports event, so a demand surge occurred in the first 20 min (Fig. 3). After the demand surge, the demand became smooth. Thus, we model the demand profile with two sections: rush hours and non-rush hours. In rush hours, the average demand rate was 120 guests/minute. On the other hand, during the non-rush hours, the average rate was 36 guests/minute. The average demand rate (D) during the event is 45.33 guests/minute.

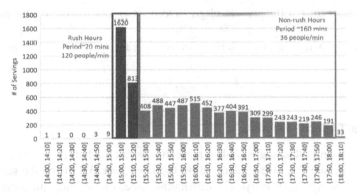

Fig. 3. Demand profile

Kitchen Operation Analysis

All the hot foods produced by the kitchen were cooked by grills. The cook batch size, cook time for each batch are shown in Table 1. The unit cook rate of a grill (p), calculated by Eq. (1), is 2.50 servings/minute/grill. Also, the number of serving can be stored in a warmer for each item was also measured.

$$p = \left(\sum_i \frac{f(i) \cdot T_c(i)}{B(i)} \right)^{-1} \tag{1}$$

Food Service Analysis

There were nine servers in each food line and the service times are in Table 2. Since the food line service is like an assembly line, the bottleneck server dominates the service rate. The bottleneck in this case is the Chicken station with a service time of 14.04 s/serving.

Table 1. Kitchen operation time analysis

Item	Burger	Hotdogs (S)	Hotdogs (L)	Chicken
Cook Batch Size [$B(i)$] (servings/batch)	40	40	40	40
Cook Time [$T_C(i)$] (minutes/batch)	12	8	10	10
Storage Vol. (servings/warmer)	12	12	12	12
Food preference [$f(i)$] (%)	90%	70%	50%	85%

Table 2. Foodservice time analysis & food preference probabilities (***bottleneck**)

Server	Plates	Bread	Burgers	Hotdog (S)	Hotdog (L)	**Chicken***	Mac & Cheese	Beans	Salad
Proc. Time (secs)	6.61	9.01	8.49	9.19	7.35	**14.04**	7.73	8.39	7.18

3.3 Rough Capacity Planning

The rough capacity planning is to determine the overall kitchen cook rate (P) and the overall service rate (S), given a demand profile from Sect. 3.2, using the sample path analysis [10]. Sample path analysis is "distribution-free" for studying queueing systems. Thus, the planning can be evaluated even only a few historical data exists. It considers the interaction between cumulative demand, cumulative service and provides a visualization tool for decision-making like Fig. 4. The analysis considered three steps. The first step is to decide the cumulative demand curve $D(t)$. In Sect. 3.2, we construct the demand curve into two sections: rush and non-rush, thus the cumulative demand curve is a piece-wise increasing function shown in Fig. 4 (a).

The second step, the cumulative production curve $P(t)$ is determined with three assumptions: (1) the kitchen should be closed before the end of the event, (2) the first guest should get served right after he arrives, and (3) the kitchen production rate keeps constant during the event. To avoid overproduction, which may cause food wastage, the cook start time (t_s) is,

$$t_s = \begin{cases} \left(\frac{D}{P} - 1\right)T, & \text{if } P < D \\ 0, & \text{if } P \geq D \end{cases}. \tag{2}$$

where D is the average demand rate calculated in Sect. 3.2; P is the overall kitchen production rate, the slope of $P(t)$; T is the length of event duration. In this step, the maximum storage level can be computed, which determines the number of warmer needed. For the scenario in Fig. 4, T is 3 h (3 pm to 6 pm). If the designed production rate is 37 servings/minute, the cook start time is at least 40 min before the start of the event.

The final step is shown in Fig. 4 (c). The service rate s is assumed to be constant during the event as well. However, the service rate is always dominated by production rate and demand rate. If the food cooked was not enough or no demand came, the server would not work. Thus, the cumulative service curve $S(t)$ cannot surpass the cumulative demand curve $D(t)$ and cumulative production curve $P(t)$.

$$S(t) = \min\{sl, P(t), D(t)\} \tag{3}$$

where l is the number of food lines designed. In this case, the number of food lines is 12, so the maximum service rate is 50.40 customers/minute. However, $S(t) = 36$ after 4:56 p.m since the service rate is dominated by the demand rate.

In this step, the maximum number of guests waiting in the queue is computed. This information can help design the waiting spaces. Here, the max storage level is 1774 servings during the event, and the max queue in length is 1329 customers.

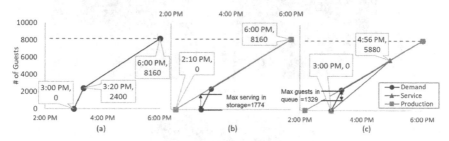

Fig. 4. Rough capacity planning

3.4 Detail Planning

The rough capacity plan shows that P is 37 servings/minutes; the maximum storage level is 1774 servings; the maximum customer waiting is 1329 customers. These figures are as input to the detailed planning stage to compute the number of equipment needed. Using information from Table 1, the number of grills and warmers can be calculated as Fig. 5. "Adjustment" columns are for fine-tuning the number of grills and heaters; "Batch in Food Line" shows the average amount of food already placed on the food lines.

| Prod Rate | 37.00 | servings/min |

	Item	Adjustment	Batch	Cook Time	Preference	# Grills
1	Burger	44%	40	12	0.9	4.44
2	Hotdog(S)	57%	40	8	0.7	2.96
3	Hotdog(L)	80%	40	10	0.5	3.70
4	Chicken	47%	40	10	0.85	3.70
#Grills = (Prod Rate x Cook Time x Preference / Batch) x Adjustment					Total Grills	15.00

| Max Inv | 1774 | servings |

	Item	Adjustment	Batch	Preference	Batch in Foodline	# Heater
1	Burger	44%	40	90%	6	11.74
2	Hotdog(S)	57%	40	70%	6	11.74
3	Hotdog(L)	80%	40	50%	6	11.74
4	Chicken	47%	30	85%	6	17.65
#Heaters = (Max Inv x Preference / Batch) x Adjustment - Batch in Food Line					Heaters needed	53.00

Fig. 5. Illustration of detail planning calculations

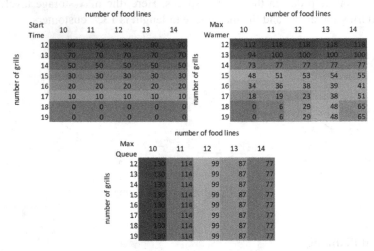

Fig. 6. Detail planning

The planners can use a table such as Fig. 6 from the analysis done in Sects. 3.2 and 3.3 to decide the system: the number of grills, the number of food lines, and the number of warmer. Different kitchen capacity (grills) and service capacity (food lines), different cook start times, the numbers of warmers, and the sizes of waiting buffer are needed. The result shows that, given the demand profile (2016), the latest cook start time (Fig. 6(a)) is determined by the kitchen capacity planned. On the other hand, the waiting buffered required (Fig. 6(c)) at each food line depends on the number of food lines designed.

4 Conclusion

Event catering plays a vital role in creating memorable events. Due to some distinct characteristics such as long setup time, time-varying demand, and complex customer food preferences, it is hard to keep high customer satisfaction with low food wastage. However, planning event catering still highly relies on planners' experience nowadays, there is a lack of decision models developed for planning aid.

This paper uses a service engineering approach to develop a framework for planning event catering to guide planners to determine kitchen capacity, temporary storage level (warmers), and staffing level in buffet service. The framework consists of three phases: System Analysis and Design, Kitchen and Service Synchronization, and Detail Planning. The tool provides planners a systematic way to plan event catering and intuitive visualization for decision making. Another benefit of the framework is that the queueing analysis in the framework is distribution-free, so only a few parameters are needed to run the analysis. A case study – military day tailgate party held by Penn State University is studied. In the future, we will extend this model with other critical features in event catering, such as food wastage and cook lead time. Also, the model will be validated with different types of case studies.

References

1. Doppler, S., Steffen, A., Wurzer, L.-M.: Event catering: enhancing customer satisfaction by creating memorable holistic food experiences. In: Case Studies on Food Experiences in Marketing, Retail, and Events, pp. 133–145. Elsevier (2020)
2. Kim, Y.S., Lee, Y.Y., Love, C.: A case study examining the influence of conference food function on attendee satisfaction and return intention at a corporate conference. J. Conv. Event. Tour **10**, 211–230 (2009). https://doi.org/10.1080/15470140903178567
3. Food Wastage Footprint model: Food Wastage Footprint Impacts on natural resources. Technical Report (2013)
4. Birisci, E., McGarvey, R.G.: Optimal production planning utilizing leftovers for an all-you-care-to-eat food service operation. J Clean Prod. **171**, 984–994 (2018). https://doi.org/10.1016/j.jclepro.2017.10.052
5. Monteiro, D.M.S., Brockbank, C., Heron, G.: Food waste in event catering: a case study in higher education. J Food Prod. Mark. **26**, 262–278 (2020). https://doi.org/10.1080/10454446.2020.1765935
6. Farahani, P., Grunow, M., Günther, H.O.: A heuristic approach for short-term operations planning in a catering company. In: IEEM 2009 - IEEE International Conference on Industrial Engineering and Engineering Management, pp. 1131–1135 (2009)
7. Yağmur, E., Kesen, S.E.: A memetic algorithm for joint production and distribution scheduling with due dates. Comput. Ind. Eng. **142**, 106342 (2020). https://doi.org/10.1016/j.cie.2020.106342
8. Wu, X., Nie, L., Xu, M., Zhao, L.: Distribution planning problem for a high-speed rail catering service considering time-varying demands and pedestrian congestion: a IoT-sizing-based model and decomposition algorithm (2019)https://doi.org/10.1016/j.tre.2019.01.003
9. Takenaka, T.: Analysis and prediction of customer behaviors for restaurant management. In: Shimmura, T., Nonaka, T., Kunieda, S. (eds.) Service Engineering for Gastronomic Sciences, pp. 29–41. Springer, Singapore (2020). https://doi.org/10.1007/978-981-15-5321-9_2
10. Gross, D., Shortie, J.F., Thompson, J.M., Harris, C.M.: Fundamentals of Queueing Theory, 4th edn. Wiley, New York (2013)

A Study on Menu Planning Method Considering the Variation in Menu Orders - Application to Daily Foods in a Company Cafeteria

Ruriko Watanabe[1]($\boxtimes$), Nobutada Fujii[1], Daisuke Kokuryo[1], Toshiya Kaihara[1], Kyohei Irie[1], Kenji Yanagita[2], and Kenichi Harada[2]

[1] Kobe University, 1-1 Rokkodai-cho, Nada, Kobe, Hyogo 657-8501, Japan
`r.watanabe@crystal.kobe-u.ac.jp, nfujii@phoenix.kobe-u.ac.jp,`
`kokuryo@port.kobe-u.ac.jp, kaihara@kobe-u.ac.jp`
[2] TMES Corporation, Tokyo, Japan
`{kenji_yanagita,kenichi_harada}@tte-net.com`

Abstract. It is a problem that dietitians have a shortage of labor and a large amount of work per person. The work of a dietitian includes menu planning, ordering meals, nutritional guidance, etc. Among them, menu planning is an important work. Menu planning is an advanced work that considers dietitians adjustment, safety and economic efficiency based on basic knowledge such as cooking combination, food combination, appropriate amount for one-person, seasoning ratio, cooking method, etc. It is thought that reducing the burden on menu planning will lead to more efficient work for dietitians. The subjects for which a dietitian makes a menu plan are classified into managed meals such as those provided at hospitals and daily meals provided to healthy people in a company cafeteria. This paper proposes a menu planning method that meets the requirements for menu plans for regular meals in the company cafeteria, which has more constraints than managed meals and is a complicated problem. The menu planning is optimized by a DGA (Distributed Genetic Algorithm) using an evaluation function that expresses the variations in menu orders.

Keywords: Genetic algorithm · Menu planning · Information entropy

1 Introduction

It is a problem that dietitians have a shortage of labor and a large amount of work per person. The work of a dietitian includes menu planning, ordering meals, nutritional guidance, etc. Among them, menu planning is an important work. Menu planning is an advanced work that considers dietitians adjustment, safety and economic efficiency based on basic knowledge such as cooking combination, food combination, appropriate amount for one-person, seasoning ratio, cooking method, etc. It is regarded as a problem that dietitians have a large amount of work per person due to labor shortage [1]. It is

© IFIP International Federation for Information Processing 2021
Published by Springer Nature Switzerland AG 2021
A. Dolgui et al. (Eds.): APMS 2021, IFIP AICT 632, pp. 224–231, 2021.
https://doi.org/10.1007/978-3-030-85906-0_25

thought that reducing the burden on menu planning will lead to more efficient work for dietitians.

The subjects for which a dietitian makes a menu plan are classified into managed meals [2] such as those provided at hospitals and daily meals [3] provided to healthy people in a company cafeteria. Table 1 shows the requirements for preparing menus for managed meals and daily meals.

Table 1. Menu planning requirements for managed meals and daily meals

	Managed meals	Daily meals
Diversity of dishes	Considering the variety of dishes and the order of serving so that the eaters will not get bored	
Nutrition	Adjusted based on dietary intake standards	Adjusted based on the standards set for each business establishment
Ingredient cost	Considering of keeping within a limited budget	Considering by cost rate
Menu style	Considering the combination of one meal	Considering many kinds of dishes for one meal

This study focuses on menu planning for daily meals in a company cafeteria. As shown in Table 1, menu planning for daily meals is a more complex problem structure with more constraints than managed meals.

Four decades ago, the need for computer-based methods for menu planning was recognized. In 1964, Balintfy [4] applied linear programming techniques to build the first computer-based menu planner, which optimized menus for nutritional adequacy and budgeted food cost. Subsequently, menu planning methods using random sampling techniques [5], interactive [6] and evolutionary computation [7] were proposed. In this research, which has a complex problem structure with many constraints, a menu planning method using GA (Genetic Algorithm) has been proposed [8], which is an algorithm that only requires information to determine the degree of adaptation to a given environment and requires little information about the nature of the problem to be solved, such as a mathematical model. By expanding the method of the previous study [8], the developed menu planning method is suggested that takes into account the variation in the characteristics of dishes in consecutive days, the variation in the characteristics of dishes in the same category provided on the same day, the event menu for each day of the week, and the cost rate.

2 Menu Planning Using Genetic Algorithm

In this study, menus are planed from a cooking database using a genetic algorithm.

2.1 Target Problem

The menu is for a company cafeteria where meals are served in a cafeteria style, and the menu is planned for 20 days (4 weeks) only for lunch on weekdays. In addition, the categories of dishes offered per day are main dish A, main dish B, main dish C, bowl, curry, Japanese noodles, Chinese noodles, pasta, small bowl A, small bowl B, small bowl C, salad and dessert.

The total number of dishes registered in the cooking database is 1770. The information that each dish data has is "cooking number", "cooking name", "cost", "characteristic 1", "characteristic 2", and "characteristic 3". Regarding the characteristics of cooking, characteristic 1: main ingredients, characteristic 2: cooking method, and characteristic 3: classification, are held as numerical values of each item. The number of items for each characteristic differs depending on the cooking category.

2.2 Distributed Genetic Algorithm

Since the daily meals have more constraints than the case of the managed meals and the search ability is not sufficient in the single-population Genetic Algorithm, Distributed Genetic Algorithm (DGA) [9] having a higher search ability is used.The flow of DGA is shown below.

Step 1.   Generation of early individuals
          Individuals are randomly generated until the default number of individuals is reached.
Step 2.   Fitness calculation
          The fitness of the individual is calculated.
Step 3.   Confirmation of the number of generations
          If generations have not reached the default number, go to step 4. If they reach, the calculation ends.
Step 4.   Selection
          Next-generation individuals are selected according to the evaluation value of each individual. The best individuals of that generation remain in the next generation.
Step 5.   Migration judgement
          If generations have reached the default number, proceed to step 6. If they have not been reached, go to step 7.
Step 6.   Migration
          The number of individuals determined by the migration rate from each sub-population is transferred to another population.
Step 7.   Crossover
          Two individuals are randomly selected and uniformly crossed with a certain probability.
Step 8.   Mutation
          Each individual is mutated with a certain probability, return to step 2.

2.3 Gene Coding

The genetic coding is shown in Fig. 1. 20 pieces for each of the 13 cooking categories (main dish A, B, C, bowl, curry, Japanese noodles, Chinese noodles, pasta, small bowls A, B, C, salad and dessert) They are arranged one by one (5 days on weekdays x

4 weeks), and each is arranged according to the menu orders. Each individual holds the dish number of the corresponding category. The information contained dish data, which is not included in the gene, is linked to the dish number.

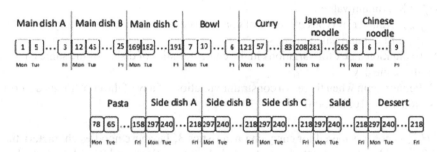

Fig. 1. Cording of individuals

2.4 Fitness Function

The fitness function F consists of the evaluation value H of the variability of the order of appearance of the features of a dish, the evaluation value S of the variability of the features of the same category of dishes on the same day, and a penalty term p. With reference to the calculation method of the evaluation function in the previous study [10], the entropy $H_{m,i}$ for measuring the variation in the appearance order of the characteristics for each dish of each category is calculated as the average of the all intervals, shifting the intervals with the number of items $J|_{m,i}$ as one interval. The expressions and the meanings of the characters in the expressions are shown below.

$$F = \sum_{m=1}^{M} \sum_{i=1}^{I} \frac{H_{m,i}}{H_{m,i}^*} + S + p$$

$$H_{m,i} = -\frac{1}{T - J|m, i + 1} \sum_{t=1}^{T-J|m,i+1} \sum_{j|m,i=1}^{J|m,i} P_{j|m,i=1}(t) \log P_{j|m,i}(t)$$

$$P_{j|m,i}(t) = \frac{1}{J|m,i} \sum_{k=0}^{J|m,i-1} \alpha_{J|m,i}(t+k)$$

$$S = \frac{1}{MTI} \sum_{m=1}^{M} \sum_{t=1}^{T} \sum_{i=1}^{I} \frac{\beta_{t,j_{m,i}}}{\beta_{t,j_{m,i}}^*}$$

- $m = 1, 2, \ldots, M$: Cooking category
- $i = 1, 2, \ldots, I$: Characteristics of cooking
- $j_{m,i} = 1, 2, \ldots, J_{m,i}$: Characteristic i item of dish type m
- $t = 1, 2, \ldots, T$: Menu ordinal number (for T days)

- $P_{i|m,i}$: Serving frequency ratio in one section from t of dishes with $j_{m,i}$
- $\alpha_{j|m,i}$: 1/0 binary variable representing the serving/non-serving of dishes with the feature $j_{m,i}$ in t
- $H_{m,i}$: Average of entropy of characteristic i of all sections of dish type m
- $H^*_{m,i}$: Maximum value of $H_{m,i}$
- $\beta_{t,j,m,i}$: Number of types of item i of characteristics of dishes in category m on day t
- $\beta^*_{t,j,m,i}$: Maximum value of $\beta_{t,j,m,i}$
- S: Evaluation index for variations in the characteristics of dishes of the same category on the same day
- P: Penalty term when there is a constraint violation (if any of the constraints described is violated: -10, if not: 0)

$H_{m,i}$ is not considered for curry characteristics 3, Japanese noodles characteristics 1 and 2, small bowl A characteristics 2, salad characteristics 1 and 2, and desserts due to data bias.

2.5 Constraints

The restriction that the event menu specified for each day of the week is included in the target day of the week, the menu categorized as "high profit" is included once a week, and the menu categorized as "popular TOP20" is included twice a week. The cost rate is restricted so that the average cost rate falls within a certain range. Since there is a target value for the usage ratio of the main ingredients (characteristic 1) for the main dish and rice bowl dishes, the usage ratio of the main ingredients is set so that the error from the target value is within ±5%.

3 Computer Experiments

These experiments are conducted to create a menu using the proposed method and verify its effectiveness by comparing it with the comparison method (single-population Genetic Algorithm) and the menu prepared by a dietitian.

3.1 Experimental Conditions

Use the cooking database in which the 1770 kinds of dishes described in Sect. 2.1 are registered. The number of trials was 10.

The parameters of GA and DGA are shown in Table 2.

3.2 Experimental Results

Comparative Experiment Between DGA and Single-Population GA
Table 3 shows the maximum, minimum, average, standard deviation of the evaluation value F of the solution obtained in 10 trials and value F of menu prepared by a dietitian used in the actual cafeteria.

Table 2. Experimental conditions

	GA	DGA
Population	1000	1000
Number of islands	–	5
Number of genetically manipulated generations	100,000	100,000
Migration interval	–	1000
Migration rate	–	0.01
Target individuals for migration	–	Descending order of fitness
Selection method	Tournament selection (Tournament size: 2)	Roulette tournament selection (Tournament size: 2)
Crossing method	Uniform crossing (crossing rate: 0.9)	Uniform crossing (crossing rate: 0.9)
Mutation rate	0.1	0.1

Table 3. Comparison of the degree of fitness

	F			
	Max.	Min.	Ave.	Std.
Proposed method (DGA)	26.36	25.69	26.10	0.21
Comparison method (single-population GA)	25.10	17.00	24.12	2.51

From Table 3, it was confirmed that a solution with higher fitness was obtained using DGA than single-population GA. The minimum value of fitness by single-population GA is extremely low, and it can be confirmed that the search performance of the algorithm is insufficient without getting out of the solution with the constraint violation. On the other hand, the minimum value of fitness by DGA is 25.69, and it can be confirmed that the search performance is improved.

Figure 2 shows comparison of the diversity of solutions in the population. The horizontal axis represents the number of generations, and the vertical axis represents the type of solution in the population. For the single-population GA, it is confirmed that the diversity of solutions within the population is lost and converges at an early stage. For the DGA, the diversity of solutions is maintained, so the search performance is improved and a solution with better fitness is obtained.

Comparison with the Menu Prepared by Dietitians
Table 4 shows the fitness of the menu obtained by the proposed method and the menu actually prepared by the dietitian.

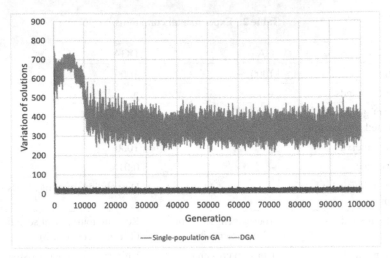

Fig. 2. Comparison of the diversity of solutions in the population

Table 4. Comparison of the degree of fitness

	Proposed method	Menu prepared by the dietitian
F	26.36	14.29
Main dish A	2.32	1.84
Main dish B	2.32	1.82
Main dish C	2.40	1.98
Bowl	2.58	1.77
Curry	1.69	1.08
Noodle J	0.97	0.54
Noodle C	2.32	1.70
Pasta	2.44	1.32
Side dish A	1.90	0.00
Side dish B	2.63	0.51
Side dish C	2.76	1.09
Salad	0.97	0.00
Duplication	0.82	0.64

The proposed method has a higher fitness. Even when the objective function value is divided into the degree of variation in each cooking category, the proposed method gives a higher value in all cases. It can be confirmed that the fitness is increasing in the proposed method even in the cooking category such as Side dish A, where diversity was not taken into consideration when the dietitian made the menu.

From the discussion with the dietitian, it was suggested that the proposed method would be useful in the real world, as it would be able to create menus with a variety of cooking category that cannot be fully considered by humans.

4 Conclusion

This study proposed a menu planning method that considers the menu order so that eaters will not get tired of dishes, targeting the daily meals in the company cafeteria where food is served in a cafeteria format.

As a result of computer experiments, it was confirmed that proposed method could search for the solution while maintaining the diversity of solutions within the population and obtain the solution with a high fitness, compared with the single-population GA. By comparing the menus obtained by the proposed method with the menus prepared by the dietitians, the menus obtained by the proposed method had a more varied order of appearance of the characteristics of the dishes. Although omitted in this paper, it is confirmed that the proposed method can meet the restrictions that the registered dietitian cannot meet.

Future prospects include consideration of the expiration date and inventory of ingredients, and consideration of nutrients by establishing categories such as healthy menus.

References

1. Kamata, H., Hasumi, M., Aikawa, R.: A study of menu planning ability on a dietitian course: an analysis of factors related to menu planning. J. Jpn. Soc. Food Educ. **7**(4) (2013). (in Japanese)
2. Okamura, Y., Yuka, N., Atsuko, H., Naoko, H., Mayumi, Y., Toyoko, O.: Nutritional management for the dietary reference intake in the hospital diet: about nutrients whitch is apt tp be short. Senri Kinran Univ. Bull. 1–13 (2007). (in Japanese)
3. Yoshioka, Y., Kobayashi, Y., Ogawa, A., Murasawa, H.: An approach to nutrition education of company cafeteria lunches by industry, government and a college. J. Nagano Prefectural Coll. (69), 21–29 (2014). (in Japanese)
4. Balintify, J.L.: Menu planning by computer. Commun. ACM **7**(4), 255–259 (1964)
5. Brown, R.M.: Automated menu planning. M.S. thesis, Kansas State University (1966)
6. Hinrichs, T.: Problem Solving in Open Worlds: A Case Study in Design. Lawrence Erlbaum Associates, Hillsdale (1992)
7. Seljak, B.K.: Computer-based dietary menu planning. J. Food Compos. Anal. **22**(5), 414–420 (2009)
8. Irie, K., Fujii, N., Kokuryo, D., Kaihara, T.: A study on planning method for managed meal – consideration of the cost of ordering ingredients. In: APMS 2020 International Conference Advances in Production Management Systems, pp. 679–685 (2020)
9. Kajima, T., Orito, Y., Someya, H.: Consecutive meals planning on meals support system: verification of solutions obtained by permutation GA. The papers of Technical Meeting on Intelligent Transport Systems, IEE Japan, pp. 1–6 (2017). (in Japanese)
10. Tanese, R.: Distributed genetic algorithms. In: Proceedings of the 3rd ICGA, pp. 434–439 (1989)

Systems Engineering Analysis for Cooking Recipes from the Perspective of Work Instructions

Tomomi Nonaka[1]([⊠]), Kaoru Kamatani[1], and Nobutada Fujii[2]

[1] College of Gastronomy Management, Ritsumeikan University, 1-1-1 Noji-higashi,
Kusatsu, Shiga 525-8577, Japan
nonaka@fc.ritsumei.ac.jp
[2] Graduate School of System Informatics, Kobe University, Kobe, Japan

Abstract. In this paper, we focus on the labour-intensive human cooking process and analyze cooking recipes using systems engineering techniques. The purpose of this is paper to help analyze the impact of specifying cooking recipes from the perspective of work instructions on the reproducibility and development of food. Specifically, we use as an example the recipe for "Fuhafuha Tofu," which appears in number 21 of the cookbook "Tofu Hyakuchin" published in the Edo period between 1603 and 1868 in Japan. We focus on the ambiguity of the description method in this cooking recipe. First, we extract expressions that are described as explicit textual information in the cooking recipe. Next, we analyze the information containing the ambiguity described in the cooking recipe and the information that is not directly described. These are assumed to be information containing ambiguities that can be inferred from the context even without being instructed when the operator performs the cooking task. We will take the specifications of modern cooking recipes and compare and analyze how they are written from the perspective of work instructions.

Keywords: Cooking recipe · Systems engineering · Work instruction · Gastronomic sciences · Food

1 Introduction

A recipe is defined as a method of preparing a dish. A recipe describes the necessary information on ingredients and the cooking process, and the cook attempts to reproduce the described dish based on the information obtained from the recipe. In addition to paper, recipes can be passed on orally through hearsay in the community or region or memorized implicitly in the mind without being directly written on a medium. In recent years, research has been conducted on recommending dishes based on lifestyle and preferences [1–3], recognizing food images and using deep learning to estimate cooking recipes and information such as nutrients contained in them [4], and businesses utilizing recipe data.

A. Dolgui et al. (Eds.): APMS 2021, IFIP AICT 632, pp. 232–237, 2021.
https://doi.org/10.1007/978-3-030-85906-0_26

Salvador et al. have proposed an Inverse cooking system that generates cooking recipes from food images [5]. The information generated is the name of the dish, the ingredients, and a description of the cooking method (Instruction). The system comprehensively determines the ingredients that make up the dish from the image and generates a cooking recipe by estimating the transformation processes such as slicing, stirring, and mixing with other ingredients as interactions between the image and the ingredients. Here, we focus on the process of estimating the cooking method in the reverse direction, using the cooking image as the final form. The given cooking image shows the finished state of the dish. In other words, the process is oriented toward reproduction.

However, in general, when a person cooks based on the information in a cooking recipe, the degree of fidelity to the recipe is left to the discretion of the cook. It is not uncommon for the cook to change the seasoning or heat level, or substitute ingredients within the range of available ingredients, depending on the preferences of the family or the cook. When cooking recipes are considered as work instructions, they can be used in a variety of ways according to the cook's purpose of cooking, unlike the conventional work instructions that standardize and describe the work to improve productivity and quality. Therefore, in this paper, we focus on the labour-intensive manual cooking process and analyze the influence of the cooking recipe on the reproducibility and development of the dish. In this paper, we focus on the labour-intensive manual cooking process, and analyze the effect of the cooking recipe on the reproducibility and development of the dish. We also analyze the cooking recipe using the system engineering method, in order to examine how the method of information presentation and work instructions in the cooking recipe stimulates the creativity and ideas of the cook or worker, and which tasks should be left as human tasks, and which should be automated or robotized in the future. In this paper, we analyze cooking recipes using the system engineering method. Specifically, the ambiguity of the description method will be analyzed using "Tofu Hyakuchin" (Tofu Hyakuchin), a cookbook published in the Edo period (1782), as a case study. The characteristics of the recipes will also be discussed by comparing them with modern cooking recipes.

2 Systems Engineering Analysis of Cooking Recipes

In this section, we analyze "Tofu Hyakuchin", a cookbook published in the Edo period. The ambiguity of the description in the recipe is analyzed using "Fuhafuha Tofu," which is described in number 21 of the book, as a case study. We extract the expressions that are explicitly described as textual information in the recipe and sort out the content of the explicit description and the ambiguous information when executing the cooking process.

First, the textual information described in "Fuhafuha Tofu" shown in Fig. 1 is translated into modern Japanese. In this analysis, we focus on the textual information. The following steps are used to analyze the text information translated into modern Japanese.

- **STEP1:** Extraction of information explicitly described in cooking recipes
  Extract character strings that are explicitly described in the cooking recipe and divide them into morphemes. These include noun phrases for ingredients and verb phrases for processes.

- **STEP2:** Process description
  Describe the process diagram using the extracted morphemes (Fig. 2). Noun phrases are written as squares, verb phrases as circles, and other words as text.
- **STEP3:** Identifying non-unique information for cooking reproduction
  Organize the information that is not uniquely determined when attempting to reproduce the cooking based on the described process diagram. These include the specific amount of food, the amount of heat and mixing, and adverbial expressions such as frequency and degree for verb phrases.
- **STEP4:** Estimation from ambiguous information

Fig. 1. Left: "Tofu Hyakuchin" (National Diet Library website (Japan)), Right: reprint result

In Step 3, information that is not uniquely determined in the cooking reproduction is defined as ambiguous information in this paper. This can be interpreted as inducing a state in which the cook cannot specify the specific cooking process when he or she sees the cooking recipe as a work instruction. The cook is required to proceed with the cooking by inferring the ambiguous information from the information before and after the explicit description in the cooking recipe and the context of the dish or supplement the information with the cook's own ideas and devices.

The following is an example of applying the steps described above to Fuhafuha Tofu. The explanation follows the steps from the left of the process diagram (Fig. 2). The original recipe, translated into English, is described as follows.

1. Mix equal amounts of chicken egg and tofu and scrape well.
2. Boil it fluffy
3. Sprinkle with pepper

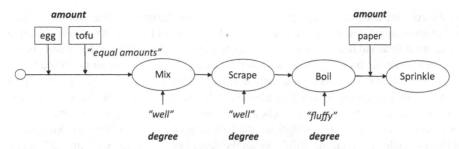

Fig. 2. Process description diagram for "Fuhafuha Tofu".

Note: The egg fluffy and flavor will not change. Therefore, thrifty one uses tofu instead of eggs.

Ingredient: Tofu, egg, pepper.

The first step is to mix equal amounts of egg and tofu. However, no specific amount is given here. In the section on mixing well and boiling to a fluffy consistency, the expressions "well" and "fluffy" are ambiguous as to the specific level of detail. The cook cannot uniquely identify the cooking process because there is no detailed description as in modern cooking recipes, such as mixing with a whisk until the mixture becomes angular or until the egg is no longer sticky, and no image information is given to confirm the process. The final step is to sprinkle pepper. The cook is required to imagine the cooking process based on the context associated with the name of the dish and the information before and after the cooking process, because the process of adding liquid such as broth or water to the boiling process is not described.

3 Estimation of Ambiguous Information

When cooking a cooking recipe that contains ambiguous information, the cook needs to estimate the task from the context and the context before and after as shown in the previous section. In this section, as one of the estimation approaches, we consider the cooking recipe as an optimal design problem.

First, the objective variable is set based on the information described explicitly in Step 1. The objective variable is set by assuming the goal that the recipe is intended to achieve from the explicitly described recipe information. It is possible to estimate multiple optimal design problems from a single recipe, and objective variable settings can be defined for each problem. For example, in the case of "Fuhafuha Tofu," for the description of "Fuhafuha" in the name of the dish, the objective is how to make the finished dish into a Fuhafuha state, which is assumed to be a maximization problem of the Fuhafuha state. In Japanese, "fluffy" means very soft and fluffy. In other words, it can be regarded as a problem of maximizing softness and fluffiness. Next, in STEP 3, ambiguous information that is not uniquely determined is set as explanatory variables. In the estimation of explanatory variables, we focus on the following two perspectives. One is the existence of a quantitative expression for the foodstuff. Quantitative amount for a foodstuff can be set as an explanatory variable, if the required input of the foodstuff is not specifically specified. The second is the presence or absence of degree expressions for the cooking and processing operations. We focus on the time required for the cooking and processing operations, and the amount and intensity of the operations. For example, the heating time and heat level in the heating process, and the degree of force and stirring time in the stirring process. Here, we add that even if the specific amount and degree of manipulation are not described as quantitative expressions, the state of change of the food after the cooking and processing operation can be described specifically. For example, whipping cream until it becomes cubed, or continuing heating until the surface of the food becomes white, such descriptions can be interpreted as unambiguous expressions. In this example of "Fuhafuha Tofu", we set the degree of mixing in "well-mixed" and the degree of heat and heating time in "simmering". In this example, the degree of mixing in "well-mixed" and the degree of heat and heating time in "simmering" were set as explanatory variables.

Fig. 3. Cooking results of "Fuhafuha Tofu".

The information that is not explicitly described in the cooking recipe, such as the process and the amount of ingredients, was regarded as incomplete information and was considered as design variables. As a result of cooking with multiple combinations of these design variables as different conditions, the finished products varied depending on the combination of conditions. The different features of appearance in finished products and nutritional components differed depending on the combination of different conditions were observed, i.e., cooking process and ingredients. For example, the different appearances observed in the cooking results of "Fuhafuha Tofu" were like scrambled eggs and pancakes (Fig. 3). Near-infrared spectroscopy NIRS analysis showed that the nutritional components also differed due to the effects of cooking wear and tear caused by the different cooking processes.

In recent years, many recipes have been published using videos and photographs. The information given to cooks by video recipe representation is discussed in order to compare it with the recipe containing ambiguous information analyzed in this study. In a video recipe, the cook can check the condition of the ingredients and the degree of processing from the images at each time in a series of snapshots. It is possible to determine from the image information how much heat should be added and when the condition of the food should be changed to the next step. Therefore, video recipes can be said that a suitable way for faithfully reproducing recipes. On the other hand, the recipe analyzed in this paper contains ambiguous information. It is possible that recipe descriptions containing ambiguous information were created due to the fact that the measurement technology for describing quantitative expressions was not yet developed at that time. Therefore, the cook has the discretion to reflect environmental constraints and/or regional and personal preferences within the range of information that is not uniquely defined in the cooking process. Cooks can add various interpretations and imaginations for targeted ambiguous information. The accumulation of such actions may have led to the development and diversity of home tastes and local cuisine.

4 Conclusions

In this paper, we considered cooking recipes as work instructions and conducted systems engineering analysis focusing on ambiguity. It is future work to analyze the effect of ambiguity on the cook's ingenuity and the development and variability of the dish.

References

1. Mino, Y., Kobayashi, I.: Recipe recommendation for a diet considering a user's schedule and the balance of nourishment. In: Proceedings of IEEE International Conference on Intelligent Computing and Intelligent Systems 2009, pp. 383–387 (2009)
2. Karikome, S., Fujii, A.: A system for supporting dietary habits: planning menus and visualizing nutritional intake balance. In: Proceedings of the 4th International Conference on Ubiquitous Information Management and Communication, pp. 386–391 (2009)
3. Freye, J., Berkovsky, S.: Intelligent food planning: personalized recipe recommendation. In: Proceedings of the 2010 International Conference on Intelligent User Interfaces, pp. 321–324 (2010)
4. Jingjing, C., Chong-wah, N.: Deep-based ingredient recognition for cooking recipe retrieval. In: Proceedings of the 24th ACM International Conference on Multimedia, pp. 32–41 (2016)
5. Salvador, A., Drozdzal, M., Giro-i-Nieto, X., Romero, A.: Inverse cooking: recipe generation from food images. In: Proceedings of the IEEE Conference on Computer Vision and Pattern Recognition (CVPR), pp. 10453–10462 (2019)

Modern Scheduling and Applications in Industry 4.0

Electric Bus Charging Scheduling Strategy with Stochastic Arrival Time and State of Charge

Ming Liu[1], Yueyu Ding[2], Feng Chu[3(✉)], Feifeng Zheng[4], and Chengbin Chu[5]

[1] School of Economics and Management, Tongji University, Shanghai
, People's Republic of China
[2] Urban Mobility Institute, Tongji University, Shanghai, People's Republic of China
[3] IBISC, Univ Évry, University of Paris-Saclay, Évry, France
feng.chu@univ-evry.fr
[4] Glorious Sun School of Business and Management, Donghua University, Shanghai,
People's Republic of China
[5] Laboratoire d'Informatique Gaspard-Monge (LIGM), UMR 8049,
Univ Gustave Eiffel, ESIEE Paris, 93162 Noisy-le-Grand Cedex, France

Abstract. To alleviate the range anxiety of drivers and time-consuming charging for electric buses (eBuses), opportunity fast-charging has gradually been utilized. Considering that eBuses have operational tasks, identifying an optimal charging scheduling will be needed. However, in the real world, arrival time and state of charge (SOC) of eBuses are uncertain. Therefore, it is challenging for the charging station to efficiently schedule charging tasks. To solve the problem, this paper develops a two-stage stochastic eBus charging scheduling model. In the first stage, eBuses are assigned to designated chargers. After the arrival time and SOC are realized, the second stage determines the charging sequence of eBuses on each charger. The objective is to minimize the penalty cost of tardiness by determining the charging start time and the corresponding charging duration time. Then, a sample average approximation (SAA) algorithm is applied. Additional numerical experiments are performed to verify the efficiency of the stochastic programming model and algorithm.

Keywords: eBus charging scheduling problem · Uncertain arrival time and SOC · Stochastic two-stage programming · Sample average approximation

1 Introduction

The reduction of fossil and the increase of carbon emissions force people to turn their attention to renewable energy. Electric buses are widely welcomed for their

Supported by the National Natural Science Foundation of China (NSFC) under Grants 72021002, 71771048, 71432007, 71832001, 71972146, and 72071144.

A. Dolgui et al. (Eds.): APMS 2021, IFIP AICT 632, pp. 241–249, 2021.
https://doi.org/10.1007/978-3-030-85906-0_27

smooth driving process, low noise, and zero emission [8,13]. However, the limited range is a key challenge in operating eBuses. The range of an eBus is about 265 mi, while diesel buses can run for nearly 2.5 times more than eBuses, which may cause severe range anxiety among drivers [12]. Another challenge is charging. Though there is a relatively wide-scale adoption of eBuses, the charging supply is in shortage for the limited space of charging stations. Therefore, efficient charging scheduling to meet the charging needs is necessary.

Overnight charging is the most popular charging strategy, which needs sufficient capacity of the battery. However, increased battery size may reduce the passenger capacity. Thereby opportunity charging is gradually received more and more attention, which not only makes smaller, lighter batteries possible, but also keeps eBuses stay in service without driving range restrictions. With charging stations at the end point of each route, eBuses are charged at higher power – a level of around 300 to 450 kW – during their layover time of 15 to 25 min. Then the bus can run the route again several times. Taking Fig. 1 as an example, the eBus departs according to the timetable at the bus terminal, and the initial SOC should meet the energy required for at least one run of the driving route. After finishing a driving route, it returns to the original departure station, and makes an appointment for charging during layovers. Then the charging station schedules charging tasks when the eBus arrives at the station. Finally, the eBus will drive back to the bus terminal after completing the charging task and wait for the next departure. Since eBuses are susceptible to weather, road conditions, and human flow factors, they may arrive at the charging station before or after the reservation time point, and the SOC is also unknown before the actual arrival.

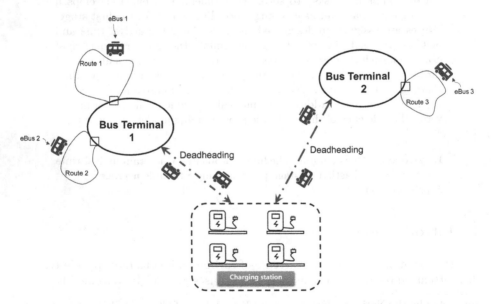

Fig. 1. Charging structure of two bus terminals and single charging station

Considering that charging times should be less than layovers, this can be challenging to schedule charging tasks during peak periods, which may require either partial charging or risk a tardiness. Previous studies have analyzed the impact of different charging scheduling on the power grid and operational costs with deterministic settings [3,6,7,11,13]. However, it is hard for the charging station to receive full information about eBuses for the complexity of road conditions. Therefore, our work investigates how to allocate chargers to the eBuses during their layovers with uncertain arrival times and SOC in order to minimize the total cost.

To the best of our knowledge, we are the first to introduce a two-stage stochastic programming model in this domain. The main contributions of this work include (1) a two-stage stochastic charging scheduling problem is studied for the first time, (2) SAA algorithm is proposed to deal with the considered problem.

The rest of this paper is organized as follows. Section 2 describes the problem and a two-stage stochastic programming model is developed. In Sect. 3, the SAA method is applied to solve the problem. Computational experiments are presented in Sect. 4 and conclusion is given in Sect. 5.

2 Problem Description and Formulation

In this section, the problem is described in detail and a two-stage stochastic programming formulation is proposed.

2.1 Problem Description

In this work, we focus on investigating a stochastic eBus charging scheduling problem, where the eBus arrives at a random time with a random arrival SOC, to minimize the penalty cost of eBuses' tardiness. For the addressed problem, given a set of chargers K, the set of eBuses to be charged is denoted by $B = \{1, 2, ..., n\}$. The eBuses run from two different bus terminals to the same charging station for charging. Therefore, the transportation time of eBus $j \in B$ to the charging station is related to the distance Dis_j between them and calculated as Dis_j/v_j, where v_j denotes the average speed of eBuses. We allow for tardiness of the operation plan if the eBus does not have enough energy before the charging deadline for the next trip [4]. To reduce battery consumption, the eBus must stop charging when the charge level reaches the upper SOC limit. The remaining work is based on the following assumptions:

(1) Adopt intermittent charging mode. Reference proved that when the battery always in the "half-and-half-discharge" state has a long cycle life [13];
(2) Each eBus $j \in B$ can only be allocated to one charger $k \in K$;
(3) One charger $k \in K$ can only charge one eBus $j \in B$ at the same time;
(4) The chargers are of the same type, using constant current charging, and the relationship of charging capacity and charging time is linear, i.e., the charging time is calculated by dividing the expected charging capacity by the charging power p;

(5) The charging capability of the charging station is sufficient;
(6) Once an eBus starts charging, it must be continuously charged until the charging task is completed;
(7) To protect the batteries and ensure the service life of eBuses, each residual capacity of the battery should be greater than SOC_{min} (i.e., 30%) of its full capacity for the departure of next trip, and less than SOC_{max} (i.e., 70%).

2.2 Two-Stage Stochastic Mathematical Model

In this section, input parameters and decision variables are presented, then the problem is formulated into a two-stage stochastic mathematical model [**P1**].

Input Parameters

Ω: Set of scenarios, indexed by ω;
B: Set of eBuses, $B = \{1, 2, ..., n\}$, indexed by i, j;
K: Set of chargers, indexed by k;
$a_j(\omega)$: Uncertain arrival time of eBus $j \in B$ under scenario $\omega \in \Omega$;
$\theta_j(\omega)$: Uncertain SOC of bus $j \in B$ under scenario $\omega \in \Omega$
$\xi(\omega)$: Vector of uncertain arrival time and SOC under scenario $\omega \in \Omega$, and $\xi(\omega) = [a_1(\omega), a_2(\omega), ..., a_n(\omega), \theta_1(\omega), \theta_2(\omega), ..., \theta_n(\omega)]^{\mathsf{T}}$;
$P(\omega)$: Probability of scenario $\omega \in \Omega$;
Dis_j: The distance of eBus $j \in B$ from each bus terminal to the charging station;
v_j: Average driving speed of eBus $j \in B$;
d_j: Charging deadline of eBus $j \in B$;
SOC_{max}: Upper limit SOC of each eBus;
SOC_{min}: Lowest allowed SOC of each eBus;
Q_j: Energy consumed for performing a trip by eBus $j \in B$;
p: Charging power of each charger;
Cap_j: Battery energy capacity of eBus $j \in B$;
e_j: Energy consumption per kilometer of eBus $j \in B$;
$L_j^{\max}$: The maximum charging time allowed for eBus $j \in B$;
$L_j^{\min}$: The minimum charging time that eBus $j \in B$ must meet;
c_j: eBus $j's$ per-unit-time tardiness penalty cost;
$\mathcal{M}$: A large enough number.

Decision Variables

x_{jk}: Binary variable, equal to 1 if eBus $j \in B$ is assigned to charger $k \in K$, and 0 otherwise;
$y_{ij}^k(\omega)$: Binary variable, equal to 1 if eBus $i \in B$ is charged immediately before eBus $j \in B$ on charger $k \in K$ under scenario $\omega \in \Omega$, and 0 otherwise;
$S_j(\omega)$: Start charging time of eBus $j \in B$ under event $\omega \in \Omega$;
$E_j(\omega)$: Charging end time of eBus $j \in B$, i.e., the time when eBus $j \in B$ is completed charging under scenario $\omega \in \Omega$;

$C_j(\omega)$: Completion time of eBus $j \in B$, i.e., the time when eBus $j \in B$ is completed charging and back to the bus terminal under scenario $\omega \in \Omega$;

$T_j(\omega)$: Tardiness of eBus $j \in B$ under scenario $\omega \in \Omega$.

The two-stage stochastic programming model [**P1**] can be constructed as follows:

[**P1**]:

$$\min \quad f = \sum_{\omega \in \Omega} \sum_{j \in B} c_j \cdot T_j(\omega) \cdot P(\omega) \tag{1}$$

$$s.t. \quad \sum_{k \in K} x_{jk} = 1, \quad \forall j \in B \tag{2}$$

$$y_{ij}^k(\omega) + y_{ji}^k(\omega) \geq 1 - \mathcal{M} \cdot (2 - x_{ik} - x_{jk}), \quad \{i \neq j\} \in B, k \in K, \omega \subset \Omega \tag{3}$$

$$y_{ij}^k(\omega) + y_{ji}^k(\omega) \leq 1 + \mathcal{M} \cdot (2 - x_{ik} - x_{jk}), \quad \{i \neq j\} \in B, k \in K, \omega \in \Omega \tag{4}$$

$$S_j(\omega) \geq a_j(\omega) + \sum_{k \in K} \frac{Dis_j}{v_j} \cdot x_{jk}, \quad \forall j \in B, \omega \in \Omega \tag{5}$$

$$S_j(\omega) \geq E_i(\omega) - \mathcal{M} \cdot \left(1 - y_{ij}^k(\omega)\right), \quad \{i \neq j\} \in B, k \in K, \omega \in \Omega \tag{6}$$

$$E_j(\omega) \leq S_j(\omega) + L_j^{\max}, \quad \forall j \in B, \omega \in \Omega \tag{7}$$

$$E_j(\omega) \geq S_j(\omega) + L_j^{\min}, \quad \forall j \in B, \omega \in \Omega \tag{8}$$

$$C_j(\omega) = E_j(\omega) + \sum_{k \in K} \frac{Dis_j}{v_j} \cdot x_{jk}, \quad \forall j \in B, \omega \in \Omega \tag{9}$$

$$T_j(\omega) \geq C_j(\omega) - d_j, \quad \forall j \in B, \omega \in \Omega \tag{10}$$

$$x_{jk} \in \{0,1\}, \quad \forall j \in B, k \in K, \omega \in \Omega \tag{11}$$

$$y_{ij}^k(\omega) \in \{0,1\}, \quad \forall i, j \in B, i \neq j, k \in K, \omega \in \Omega \tag{12}$$

$$S_j(\omega), C_j(\omega), T_j(\omega) \in \mathbb{R}, \quad \forall j \in B, k \in K, \omega \in \Omega \tag{13}$$

The objective function (1) is to minimize the penalty cost of eBuses' tardiness. Constraint (2) implies that each eBus $j \in B$ can only be allocated to one charger. Constraints (3)–(4) mean if both eBuses i and j are charged on the same charger k (i.e., $x_{ik} = 1$ and $x_{jk} = 1$), there must exist a precedence relation, i.e., $y_{ij}^k(\omega) + y_{ji}^k(\omega) = 1$. Constraint (5) implies that each eBus $j \in B$ should be charged after the arrival time at the bus terminal plus the travel time to the charging station under scenario $\omega \in \Omega$. Constraint (6) restricts that no eBus can be charged before the charging end time of its predecessor under each scenario $\omega \in \Omega$, which is linearised by the big-M method. Constraint (7) represents the maximum time when eBus j is completed charging under scenario $\omega \in \Omega$, where $L_j^{max} = 60 \cdot (SOC_{\max} - \theta_j(\omega)) \cdot Cap_j/p$. Constraint (8) represents the minimum time when eBus j is completed charging under scenario $\omega \in \Omega$, where $L_j^{\min} = 60 \cdot [e_j \cdot Dis_j + Q_j + Cap_j \cdot (SOC_{min} - \theta_j(\omega))]/p$. Constraint (9) defines the completion time of eBus $j \in B$ under scenario $\omega \in \Omega$. Constraint (10) defines tardiness of eBus $j \in B$ under scenario $\omega \in \Omega$. Constraints (11)–(13) give the domains of decision variables.

3   Solution Approach

SAA is a well known approach for solving stochastic programs with a set of smaller and tractable scenarios [1,5,9,10]. When the number of given scenarios $|\Omega|$ is sufficiently large and $|\Omega| \to +\infty$, the optimal objective value of **P2** almost certainly converges to the true optimal target value [2]. For our problem, a set Ω of scenarios is randomly generated by Monte Carlo simulation, corresponding to Ω realisations of uncertain vector ξ, denoted by $\xi(1), \xi(2), ..., \xi(\Omega)$. The SAA approach approximates problem **P1** by the following problem **P2**:

[**P2**]:

$$\min \quad \hat{f} = \frac{1}{\Omega} \sum_{\omega \in \Omega} \sum_{j \in B} c_j \cdot T_j(\omega) \tag{14}$$

$$s.t. \quad (2) - (13) \quad \omega = 1, 2, \ldots, \Omega \tag{15}$$

4   Numerical Experiments

In this section, numerical experiments are conducted to evaluate the performance and efficiency of the solution approach we propose. The stochastic model is implemented by the off-the-shelf commercial optimisation solver CPLEX 12.8. And all the numerical experiments are run on a PC with Core I7 3.4 GHz processor and 8 GB RAM under Windows 10 Operating System. The computation time of the SAA is limited to 3600 s.

4.1   Scenario Generation and Data Description

The input data involve $B = 5$ eBuses from two different bus terminals and $k = 2$ chargers in a charging station. In Table 1, it is noted that (1) the first column denotes eBus indexes; (2) column 2 denotes the average speed of each eBus; (3) column 3 reports the charging deadline of each eBus; (4) column 4 provides the energy consumption per kilometer of each eBus; (5) column 5 provides the distance between the bus terminals and charging station; (6) the 6th column provides the penalty costs; (7) column 7 provides battery energy capacity of each eBus.

Table 1. Input parameter data about eBuses

j	v_j	d_j	e_j	Dis_j	c_j	Cap_j
1	25	20	1.2	2	2	250
2	22	25	1.5	3	1	300
3	28	20	1.5	3	3	300
4	23	30	1.2	2	3	250
5	27	30	1.5	3	2	300

4.2   The Performance of SAA Algorithm

In the computational experiments, the arrival time and SOC are randomly generated. And two probability distribution, i.e., uniform and normal distributions are tested. We assume the mean values of arrival time and SOC are $\mathbb{E}[a_j] = 3$ and $\mathbb{E}[\theta_j] = 0.3$, respectively. The corresponding standard deviations are set to 1 and 0.1. Let sample size $\Omega = 10$, and each instance is tested $M = 10$ times to obtain its average results. Additionally, mean values, coefficient of variation (CV), 85th percentiles and 99th percentiles of the total costs over all the scenarios are employed to evaluate the proposed SAA algorithm. Computational results are reported in Table 2. We can observe that (1) the objective value under uniform distribution is 21.34, which is 8.25% lower than that under normal distribution; (2) the coefficient of variation under uniform distribution is 47.04%, about 31.93% lower than under normal distribution; (3) the 85th percentile under uniform distribution is about 5.49% larger than under normal distribution. This may be because the random numbers generated by normal distribution are closer to the mean values. However, the 99th percentile obtained under uniform distribution is 39.09, about 28.06% smaller than that under normal distribution. This may be explained that the extreme case under normal distribution may be worse; (4) the average computation time under uniform distribution is 14.01, about 63.1% larger than that under normal distribution.

Table 2. Computational results under uniform and normal distributions

$M = 5$	Uniform distribution	Normal distribution
Objective	21.34	23.26
CV (%)	47.04	69.11
85th percentile	31.51	29.87
99th percentile	39.09	54.34
Time(s)	14.01	8.59

Considering that SAA has unstable objective values in small sample experiments. Therefore, we conduct the experiment to illustrate the role of sample size Ω in the SAA algorithm. The arrival time and SOC are randomly generated under normal distribution. The results are detailed in Table 3. With the increase of the sample size Ω, the optimal value decreases continuously, but at the cost of increasing calculation time greatly.

Table 3. Quality of solutions with various sample size Ω (M=10)

Ω	Objective	85th percentile	99th percentile	Time(s)
5	121.67	142.95	153.54	1.72
10	23.40	29.45	34.29	8.97
15	22.33	39.46	44.78	64.47
20	18.8	25.76	32.16	417.56
25	–	–	–	>3600

4.3   Sensitivity Analysis

In this section, sensitivity analysis results are presented based on the illustrative example. We examine the impact of standard deviation for arrival time. The standard deviations of a_j for any $j \in B$ is among $0.1\ldots1$ (fixed $M = 10, \Omega = 10$). The results are shown in Table 4. We can find that large standard deviations of arrival time under normal distribution lead to smaller objective values.

Table 4. The impact of standard deviation of arrival time

Standard deviation	Objective	85th percentile	99th percentile	Time (s)
0.1	21.21	30.24	40.13	17.06
0.2	23.09	38.56	58.35	21.83
0.3	24.27	32.04	36.09	18.39
0.4	24.19	30.64	37.78	17.86
0.5	21.77	33.66	44.10	19.58
0.6	22.30	38.99	41.22	16.91
0.7	22.85	35.34	40.03	17.24
0.8	19.56	32.41	33.56	12.98
0.9	18.72	31.96	39.43	14.22
1.0	21.02	37.34	39.91	15.38

5   Conclusion

In this work, we investigate a two-stage stochastic eBus charging scheduling model, in which arrival time and SOC are assumed to be uncertain. The objective is to minimize the penalty cost of tardiness by determining the charging start time and the corresponding charging duration time. Then, SAA algorithm is applied to solve the problem. Additional numerical experiments are carried out to illustrate the effectiveness of SAA algorithm. For further research, one of the directions is to develop more efficient heuristic algorithms to shorten the computation time.

References

1. Ahmed, S., Shapiro, A., Shapiro, E.: The sample average approximation method for stochastic programs with integer recourse. Submitted for publication, pp. 479–502 (2002)
2. Bertsimas, D., Gupta, V., Kallus, N.: Robust sample average approximation. Math. Program. **171**(1–2), 217–282 (2018)
3. Chen, H., et al.: Coordinated charging strategies for electric bus fast charging stations. In: 2016 IEEE PES Asia-Pacific Power and Energy Engineering Conference (APPEEC), pp. 1174–1179. IEEE (2016)
4. De Filippo, G., Marano, V., Sioshansi, R.: Simulation of an electric transportation system at the Ohio state university. Appl. Energy **113**, 1686–1691 (2014)
5. Habibi, M.K.K., Battaïa, O., Cung, V.D., Dolgui, A., Tiwari, M.K.: Sample average approximation for multi-vehicle collection-disassembly problem under uncertainty. Int. J. Prod. Res. **57**(8), 2409–2428 (2019)
6. He, Y., Liu, Z., Song, Z.: Optimal charging scheduling and management for a fast-charging battery electric bus system. Transp. Res. Part E Logist. Transp. Rev. **142**, 102056 (2020)
7. Jahic, A., Eskander, M., Schulz, D.: Charging schedule for load peak minimization on large-scale electric bus depots. Appl. Sci. **9**(9), 1748 (2019)
8. Kebriaei, M., Niasar, A.H., Asaei, B.: Hybrid electric vehicles: an overview. In: 2015 International Conference on Connected Vehicles and Expo (ICCVE), pp. 299–305. IEEE (2015)
9. Long, Y., Lee, L.H., Chew, E.P.: The sample average approximation method for empty container repositioning with uncertainties. Eur. J. Oper. Res. **222**(1), 65–75 (2012)
10. Pagnoncelli, B.K., Ahmed, S., Shapiro, A.: Sample average approximation method for chance constrained programming: theory and applications. J. Optim. Theor. Appl. **142**(2), 399–416 (2009)
11. Qin, N., Gusrialdi, A., Brooker, R.P., Ali, T., et al.: Numerical analysis of electric bus fast charging strategies for demand charge reduction. Transp. Res. Part A Policy Pract. **94**, 386–396 (2016)
12. Shell, C.: Electric buses and cities: can innovation lead the way? https://www.cleantech.com/electric-buses-and-cities-can-innovation-lead-the-way/. Accessed 30 June 2020
13. Zhou, D., Ren, Z., Sun, K., Dai, H.: Optimization method of fast charging buses charging strategy for complex operating environment. In: 2018 2nd IEEE Conference on Energy Internet and Energy System Integration (EI2), pp. 1–6. IEEE (2018)

Group Scheduling and Due Date Assignment Without Restriction on a Single Machine

Ying Chen[1] and Yongxi Cheng[1,2]([✉]) [iD]

[1] School of Management, Xi'an Jiaotong University, Xi'an 710049, China
`guolichenying@stu.xjtu.edu.cn`, `chengyx@mail.xjtu.edu.cn`
[2] State Key Lab for Manufacturing Systems Engineering, Xi'an 710049, China

Abstract. We consider a single machine scheduling problem in which the scheduler decides optimal due dates for different jobs under a group technology environment, in which the jobs are classified into groups in advance due to their production similarities, and jobs in the same group are required to be processed consecutively to achieve efficiency of high-volume production. The goal is to determine an optimal job schedule together with a due date assignment strategy to minimize an objective function that includes earliness, tardiness, due date assignment and flow time costs. The due date assignment is without restriction, that is, it is allowed to assign different due dates to jobs within one group. We present structural results that fully characterize the optimal schedule, and give an optimal $O(n \log n)$ time algorithm for this problem.

Keywords: Single machine scheduling · Due date assignment · Group technology

1 Introduction

Consider a multinational company exports products to overseas destinations. The products are often adapted to local regulations, require labeling in different languages, or are even modified to meet different electricity and other infrastructure standards. In order to meet different demands, improve the efficiency and reduce costs, the company join orders coming from the same area of the world to be processed together. These orders can be considered as a group of jobs where each job can be assigned a different due date, which is often determined during sales negotiations with the customers. Each job completed ahead of its due date has to be stored and thus an inventory (earliness) cost is incurred, and each job that is not completed by its due date incurs a tardiness cost.

Supported by the National Natural Science Foundation of China under Grant No. 11771346.

The above scenario forms the due date assignment problem in a group technology (GT) scheduling environment, which has attracted much attention in the past few decades due to the increasing interest in Just-In-Time systems, together with the current changing of manufacturing industries from mass production to customized production with the coming of Industry 4.0 [1,2]. GT is an approach to manufacturing and engineering management that seeks to achieve efficiency in high-volume production, by exploring similarities of different products in their production. After classified into groups, products (jobs) within a group are consecutively sequenced. Many advantages have been claimed through the wide applications of group technology, e.g., by Lv et al. [3] and Keshavarz et al. [4]. When analyzing a group technology scheduling problem, it is commonly assumed that a job is completed when its processing is finished, irrespective of when the other jobs in the group may be finished.

Meeting due dates has always been one of the most important objectives in scheduling and supply chain management. Products which complete processing prior to their due date often incur earliness costs, which include storage costs, insurance fees and so on. On the other hand, products completed past their due date often incur tardiness penalties, e.g., in the form of compensation of customers. An increasing number of studies have viewed due date assignment as part of the scheduling process, motivated by the fact that the due date is often determined during sales negotiations with the customer. Earlier due dates are more attractive to customers but may incur higher tardiness cost, while setting further due dates may result in lost sales. Hence, there is also a cost associated with the due date assignment. Due to limited production capacity, it is often unlikely to complete all jobs exactly on their respective due dates. Thus, it is crucial for manufacturing systems to take into account all associated costs and develop policies which focus on the aggregate cost.

Research in scheduling with due date assignments was initiated by Seidmann et al. [5] and Panwalkar et al. [6]. Seidmann et al. [5] analyzed a single machine non-preemptive scheduling problem where all jobs are available for processing at time zero. They used a due date assignment method where each job can be assigned a due date without any restriction, and presented an $O(n \log n)$ time optimization algorithm to determine the set of due dates. Panwalkar et al. [6] studied a problem where the scheduler has to assign a common due date to all jobs, to minimize an objective function which is a combination of earliness, tardiness, and due date costs. They provided an $O(n \log n)$ optimization algorithm to solve the problem. Li et al. [7] considered a single machine scheduling problem involving both the due date assignment and job scheduling under a group technology environment, with three different due date assignment methods. The objective is to find an optimal combination of the due date assignment strategy and job schedule, to minimize an objective function that includes earliness, tardiness, due date assignment and flow time costs. Shabtay et al. [8] investigated a due date assignment problem under a group technology environment in which jobs within a family (group) are restricted to be assigned the same due date, while the due dates for different families are allowed to be different. The objective is to find the job schedule and the due date for each group that minimizes an objective function which includes earliness, tardiness and due date assignment costs. They also extended the analysis to the case in which the job processing times are resource dependent. Shabtay [9] considered a due date assignment problem where each job may be assigned a different due date whose value cannot exceed a predefined threshold. Bajwa et al. [10] investigated a single machine problem of minimizing the total number of tardy jobs in a GT environment with individual due dates. They proposed a hybrid heuristic approach to solve the problem. Li et al. [11] and Ji et al. [12] considered group scheduling problem on a single machine with multiple due windows assignment.

For the third due date assignment method in [7], the unit due date, earliness, tardiness and flow time costs are the same for jobs within one group. Though classified into groups according to similarities in their production, jobs within one group could be different from each other, and so these unit costs could be different as well. Based on the research gap found, in this paper we consider the group scheduling problem with due date assignment, in which jobs within one group may have different unit due date, earliness, tardiness and flow time costs. Similar to the third due date assignment method in [7], in the problem studied it is allowed to assign different due dates to jobs within one group.

The rest of this paper is organized as follows. In Sect. 2, we formally describe the group scheduling problem with due date assignment studied in this paper and present some preliminary analysis. In Sect. 3, structural results of the optimal schedule are presented and an $O(n \log n)$ time optimization algorithm for the problem is given. The paper is concluded in Sect. 4.

2   Problem Formulation

There are n independent and non-preemptive jobs that are classified into m groups $G_1, G_2, \cdots, G_m$. Each group G_i, for $i = 1, 2, \cdots, m$, consists of a set $\{J_{i1}, J_{i2}, \cdots, J_{in_i}\}$ of n_i jobs, where $\sum_{i=1}^{m} n_i = n$. All the groups are given, and jobs within the same group are required to be processed contiguously. A sequence-independent machine setup time s_i precedes the processing of the first job in group G_i. All jobs are simultaneously available for processing at time zero. Each job J_{ij} has a normal processing time p_{ij}, and jobs within one group are allowed to be assigned different due dates. Let C_{ij} denote the completion time of job J_{ij}. The earliness and tardiness of job J_{ij} is given by $E_{ij} = \max\{d_{ij} - C_{ij}, 0\}$ and $T_{ij} = \max\{C_{ij} - d_{ij}, 0\}$. Clearly, E_{ij} and T_{ij} cannot both be positive. Let $\alpha_{ij}, \beta_{ij}, \gamma_{ij}$ and θ_{ij} be unit due date, earliness, tardiness and flow time costs of job J_{ij}, respectively. All $n_i, s_i, p_{ij}, \alpha_{ij}, \beta_{ij}, \gamma_{ij}$ and θ_{ij} are given parameters.

The objective is to determine a schedule π for the group sequence and job sequence within each group G_i for $i = 1, 2, \cdots, m$, and a due date assignment vector $d(\pi) = (d_{11}(\pi), d_{12}(\pi), \cdots, d_{1n_1}(\pi), \cdots, d_{m1}(\pi), \cdots, d_{mn_m}(\pi))$ specifying the due date for each job J_{ij}, to minimize a cost function that includes earliness, tardiness, due date assignment and flow time costs, given by the following equation:

$$Z(\pi, d(\pi)) = \sum_{i=1}^{m} \sum_{j=1}^{n_i} (\alpha_{ij} d_{ij} + \beta_{ij} E_{ij} + \gamma_{ij} T_{ij} + \theta_{ij} C_{ij}).$$

Table 1. Notations.

Symbol	Definition
$G_{[i]}$	The group scheduled in the ith position of a sequence
$J_{[i][j]}$	The job scheduled in the jth position in group $G_{[i]}$
$p_{[i][j]}$	The processing time of job $J_{[i][j]}$
$s_{[i]}$	The setup time for group $G_{[i]}$
$d_{[i][j]}$	The due date assigned to job $J_{[i][j]}$
$\psi_{[i][j]}$	$\min(\alpha_{[i][j]}, \gamma_{[i][j]})$
$P_{[i]} = \sum_{j=1}^{n_{[i]}} p_{[i][j]}$	The total processing time of all jobs within group $G_{[i]}$
$\Theta_{[i]} = \sum_{j=1}^{n_{[i]}} \theta_{[i][j]}$	The sum of $\theta_{[i][j]}$ for all jobs within group $G_{[i]}$
$\Psi_{[i]} = \sum_{j=1}^{n_{[i]}} \psi_{[i][j]}$	The sum of $\psi_{[i][j]}$ for all jobs within group $G_{[i]}$

Following Graham's et al. [13] three-field notation and the notations used in [7], we denote this problem by $1|GT, DIF| \sum_{i=1}^{m} \sum_{j=1}^{n_i} (\alpha_{ij} d_{ij} + \beta_{ij} E_{ij} + \gamma_{ij} T_{ij} + \theta_{ij} C_{ij})$. Please refer to Table 1 for notations that will be used in this paper.

2.1 Preliminary Analysis

The following two lemmas will be used in later analysis. They are easy to verify, we state them without giving proofs.

Lemma 1. *Fix a schedule π for the group sequence and job sequence within every group, the optimal due date assignment vector, $d^*(\pi)$, for problem*

$$1|GT, DIF| \sum_{i=1}^{m} \sum_{j=1}^{n_i} (\alpha_{ij} d_{ij} + \beta_{ij} E_{ij} + \gamma_{ij} T_{ij} + \theta_{ij} C_{ij})$$

can be determined as follows:

$$d_{[i][j]}^*(\pi) = \begin{cases} C_{[i][j]}(\pi) & if \ \alpha_{[i][j]} < \gamma_{[i][j]} \\ 0 & if \ \alpha_{[i][j]} > \gamma_{[i][j]} \\ any \ value \ in \ [0, C_{[i][j]}(\pi)] & if \ \alpha_{[i][j]} = \gamma_{[i][j]} \end{cases}$$

for $i = 1, 2, \cdots, m$, and $j = 1, 2, \cdots, n_i$.

Lemma 2. *An optimal schedule does not have idle times.*

Given a schedule π, let $d^*(\pi)$ be an optimal due date assignment as given in Lemma 1, and let $Z_{[i][j]}(\pi, d^*(\pi))$ be the contribution to the objective function from job $J_{[i][j]}$. According to Lemma 1, we can analyze $Z_{[i][j]}(\pi, d^*(\pi))$ according to the following three cases.

Case 1. $\alpha_{[i][j]} > \gamma_{[i][j]}$. According to Lemma 1, in this case we have $d^*(\pi)_{[i][j]} = E_{[i][j]} = 0$ and $T_{[i][j]} = C_{[i][j]}$, for $i = 1, 2, \cdots, m$ and $j = 1, 2, \cdots, n_i$. Hence,

$$Z_{[i][j]}(\pi, d^*(\pi)) = (\gamma_{[i][j]} + \theta_{[i][j]})C_{[i][j]}.$$

Case 2. $\alpha_{[i][j]} < \gamma_{[i][j]}$. In this case, we have $d^*(\pi)_{[i][j]} = C_{[i][j]}$ and $E_{[i][j]} = T_{[i][j]} = 0$, for $i = 1, 2, \cdots, m$ and $j = 1, 2, \cdots, n_i$. Hence,

$$Z_{[i][j]}(\pi, d^*(\pi)) = (\alpha_{[i][j]} + \theta_{[i][j]})C_{[i][j]}.$$

Case 3. $\alpha_{[i][j]} = \gamma_{[i][j]}$. Similarly, according to Lemma 1 in this case we have

$$Z_{[i][j]}(\pi, d^*(\pi)) = \alpha_{[i][j]}d_{[i][j]} + \gamma_{[i][j]}(C_{[i][j]} - d_{[i][j]}) + \theta_{[i][j]}C_{[i][j]}$$
$$= (\alpha_{[i][j]} + \theta_{[i][j]})C_{[i][j]}.$$

Recall that $\psi_{[i][j]} = \min(\alpha_{[i][j]}, \gamma_{[i][j]})$, for $i = 1, 2, \cdots, m$, and $j = 1, 2, \cdots, n_i$. Hence, for all the above three cases $Z_{[i][j]}(\pi, d^*(\pi))$ can be written in a unified way as follows:

$$Z_{[i][j]}(\pi, d^*(\pi)) = (\psi_{[i][j]} + \theta_{[i][j]})C_{[i][j]}.$$

It follows that $Z(\pi, d^*(\pi))$, the objective value of the problem, can be written as

$$Z(\pi, d^*(\pi)) = \sum_{i=1}^{m} \sum_{j=1}^{n_{[i]}} \left(\psi_{[i][j]} + \theta_{[i][j]} \right) C_{[i][j]}. \tag{1}$$

3   The Optimal Schedule

In this section, we analyze the structure of an optimal schedule for problem $1|GT, DIF| \sum_{i=1}^{m} \sum_{j=1}^{n_i}(\alpha_{ij}d_{ij} + \beta_{ij}E_{ij} + \gamma_{ij}T_{ij} + \theta_{ij}C_{ij})$, and present an $O(n \log n)$ time optimal algorithm for the problem. By Lemma 2, we can restrict our attention to schedules without idle times. Hence, for any given schedule π, the completion time for job $J_{[i][j]}$ can be calculated by the following equation:

$$C_{[i][j]} = \sum_{k=1}^{i-1} P_{[k]} + \sum_{k=1}^{i} s_{[k]} + \sum_{l=1}^{j} p_{[i][l]}.$$

Thus, by Eq. (1), the objective value can be written as

$$Z(\pi, d^*(\pi))$$
$$= \sum_{i=1}^{m} \sum_{j=1}^{n_{[i]}} \left(\psi_{[i][j]} + \theta_{[i][j]} \right) C_{[i][j]}$$

$$= \sum_{i=1}^{m} \sum_{j=1}^{n_{[i]}} \left(\psi_{[i][j]} + \theta_{[i][j]} \right) \left(\sum_{k=1}^{i-1} P_{[k]} + \sum_{k=1}^{i} s_{[k]} + \sum_{l=1}^{j} p_{[i][l]} \right)$$

$$= \sum_{i=1}^{m} \left(\Psi_{[i]} + \Theta_{[i]} \right) \left(\sum_{k=1}^{i-1} P_{[k]} + \sum_{k=1}^{i} s_{[k]} \right) + \sum_{i=1}^{m} \sum_{j=1}^{n_{[i]}} \sum_{l=1}^{j} \left(\psi_{[i][j]} + \theta_{[i][j]} \right) p_{[i][l]}. \quad (2)$$

From Eq. (2), under an optimal due date assignment, the total cost is the sum of $m + 1$ terms. The first term $\sum_{i=1}^{m} (\Psi_{[i]} + \Theta_{[i]})(\sum_{k=1}^{i-1} P_{[k]} + \sum_{k=1}^{i} s_{[k]})$ is independent of the internal job sequence with each group, and each of the remaining m terms, $\sum_{j=1}^{n_{[i]}} \sum_{l=1}^{j} (\psi_{[i][j]} + \theta_{[i][j]}) p_{[i][l]}$, only depends on the internal job sequence within group $G_{[i]}$. As a result of this separable property of the objective function, the problem reduces to $m + 1$ subproblems. We can get the optimal group sequence and job sequence in each group from the following two lemmas.

Lemma 3. *There exists an optimal group sequence such that the groups are scheduled in non-decreasing order of $\frac{P_i + s_i}{\Psi_i + \Theta_i}$.*

Proof. Assume that π is an optimal schedule which does not satisfy the property of the lemma. Then, π must contain two consecutive groups, G_u (we assume that G_u is processed as the rth group in π) followed by G_v, such that $\frac{P_u + s_u}{\Psi_u + \Theta_u} > \frac{P_v + s_v}{\Psi_v + \Theta_v}$. We exchange the positions of G_u and G_v (i.e., G_v is now at the rth position), and leave all other groups at their original positions in π. Let π' be the resulting schedule. From the above analysis, to compare the objective values between schedules π and π', we only need to consider the first term in Eq. (2). Hence,

$$Z(\pi, d^*(\pi)) - Z(\pi', d^*(\pi'))$$

$$= (\Psi_u + \Theta_u) \left(\sum_{k=1}^{r-1} P_{[k]} + \sum_{k=1}^{r-1} s_{[k]} + s_u \right) + (\Psi_v + \Theta_v) \left(\sum_{k=1}^{r-1} P_{[k]} + P_u + \sum_{k=1}^{r-1} s_{[k]} + s_u + s_v \right)$$

$$- (\Psi_v + \Theta_v) \left(\sum_{k=1}^{r-1} P_{[k]} + \sum_{k=1}^{r-1} s_{[k]} + s_v \right) - (\Psi_u + \Theta_u) \left(\sum_{k=1}^{r-1} P_{[k]} + P_v + \sum_{k=1}^{r-1} s_{[k]} + s_v + s_u \right)$$

$$= (\Psi_v + \Theta_v)(P_u + s_u) - (\Psi_u + \Theta_u)(P_v + s_v)$$

$$= (\Psi_v + \Theta_v)(\Psi_u + \Theta_u) \left(\frac{P_u + s_u}{\Psi_u + \Theta_u} - \frac{P_v + s_v}{\Psi_v + \Theta_v} \right)$$

$$> 0.$$

This contradicts the optimality of π. The lemma is established. $\square$

Lemma 4. *In an optimal schedule, the jobs within group G_i $(i = 1, 2, \cdots, m)$ are ordered in non-decreasing order of $\frac{p_{ij}}{\psi_{ij} + \theta_{ij}}$.*

Proof. Once the processing order of the groups is fixed, the first term of Eq. (2) is a constant, and the second term of Eq. (2) can be decomposed into m terms, such that each of these m terms only depends on the internal job processing order within each group, that is, does not depend on the processing order of the groups. Hence, the proof of this lemma follows directly from a standard exchange argument similar to the proof of Lemma 3. $\square$

3.1   An $O(n \log n)$ Time Optimal Algorithm

Now we are ready to present an $O(n \log n)$ time optimal algorithm for problem
$1|GT, DIF| \sum_{i=1}^{m} \sum_{j=1}^{n_i} (\alpha_{ij} d_{ij} + \beta_{ij} E_{ij} + \gamma_{ij} T_{ij} + \theta_{ij} C_{ij})$.

Algorithm 1

1. Order the groups in non-decreasing order of $\frac{P_i + s_i}{\Psi_i + \Theta_i}$.
2. Order the jobs within group G_i $(i = 1, 2, \cdots, m)$ in non-decreasing order of
   $\frac{p_{ij}}{\psi_{ij} + \theta_{ij}}$. Let π be the schedule obtained.
3. Assign the due dates for jobs according to Lemma 1.

Theorem 1. *Algorithm 1 optimally solves* $1|GT, DIF| \sum_{i=1}^{m} \sum_{j=1}^{n_i} (\alpha_{ij} d_{ij} + \beta_{ij} E_{ij} + \gamma_{ij} T_{ij} + \theta_{ij} C_{ij})$ *in* $O(n \log n)$ *time.*

Proof. The correctness of Algorithm 1 follows from Lemmas 1–4. Determining
the group sequence in Step 1 requires $O(max(n, m \log m))$ time. Calculating the
job sequence in Step 2 requires $O(\sum_{i=1}^{m} n_i \log n_i)$ time, and Step 3 requires $O(n)$
time. Since $m = O(n)$ and $\sum_{i=1}^{m} n_i = n$, the overall time complexity of the
algorithm is $O(n \log n)$.   □

4   Conclusion

In this paper, we study a single machine scheduling problem in which the scheduler decides optimal due dates for different jobs under a group technology environment. Jobs in the same group are required to be processed consecutively. The
goal is to determine an optimal job schedule and a due date assignment strategy
to minimize an aggregate cost function, which includes earliness, tardiness, due
date assignment and flow time costs. Though classified into groups according to
similarities in their production, jobs within one group could be different from
each other, and so their unit due date, earliness, tardiness and flow time costs
could be different as well. In this paper, we consider the group scheduling problem with due date assignment, in which the above mentioned unit costs of jobs
within the same group could be different. The due date assignment is without
restriction, that is, it is allowed to assign different due dates to jobs within one
group.

We present structural results that fully characterize the optimal schedule,
and give an optimal $O(n \log n)$ time algorithm for this problem. As the assumption that the processing times of jobs are constant may not be appropriate for the
modeling of many real world industrial processes, one possible future research
direction is to take into account time-dependent learning effect for job processing times, in which the actual processing time of a job is affected by the total
processing time of jobs preceding it.

References

1. Vaidya, S., Ambad, P., Bhosle, S.: Industry 4.0 - a glimpse. Procedia Manuf. **20**, 233–238 (2018)
2. Dalenogare, L.S., Benitez, G.B., Ayala, N.F., Frank, A.G.: The expected contribution of Industry 4.0 technologies for industrial performance. Int. J. Prod. Econ. **204**, 383–394 (2018)
3. Lv, D., Luo, S., Xue, J., Xu, J., Wang, J.: A note on single machine common flow allowance group scheduling with learning effect and resource allocation. Comput. Ind. Eng. **151**, 106941 (2021). https://doi.org/10.1016/j.cie.2020.106941
4. Keshavarz, T., Savelsbergh, M., Salmasi, N.: A branch-and-bound algorithm for the single machine sequence-dependent group scheduling problem with earliness and tardiness penalties. Appl. Math. Modell. **39**(20), 6410–6424 (2015)
5. Seidmann, A., Panwalkar, S.S., Smith, M.L.: Optimal assignment of due-dates for a single processor scheduling problem. Int. J. Prod. Res. **19**(4), 393–399 (1981)
6. Panwalkar, S.S., Smith, M.L., Seidmann, A.: Common due date assignment to minimize total penalty for the one machine scheduling problem. Oper. Res. **30**(2), 391–399 (1982)
7. Li, S., Ng, C.T., Yuan, J.: Group scheduling and due date assignment on a single machine. Int. J. Prod. Econ. **130**(2), 230–235 (2011)
8. Shabtay, D., Itskovich, Y., Yedidsion, L., Oron, D.: Optimal due date assignment and resource allocation in a group technology scheduling environment. Comput. Oper. Res. **37**(12), 2218–2228 (2010)
9. Shabtay, D.: Optimal restricted due date assignment in scheduling. Eur. J. Oper. Res. **252**(1), 79–89 (2016)
10. Bajwa, N., Melouk, S., Bryant, P.: A hybrid heuristic approach to minimize number of tardy jobs in group technology systems. Int. Trans. Oper. Res. **26**(5), 1847–1867 (2019)
11. Li, W., Zhao, C.: Single machine scheduling problem with multiple due windows assignment in a group technology. J. Appl. Math. Comput. **44**, 477–494 (2015)
12. Ji, M., Zhang, X., Tang, X., Cheng, T.C.E., Wei, G., Tan, Y.: Group scheduling with group-dependent multiple due windows assignment. Int. J. Prod. Res. **54**(4), 1244–1256 (2016)
13. Graham, R.L., Lawler, E.L., Lenstra, J.K., Kan, A.H.G.R.: Optimization and approximation in deterministic sequencing and scheduling: a survey. Ann. Discrete Math. **5**, 287–326 (1979)

Parallel Machine Scheduling with Stochastic Workforce Skill Requirements

Xin Liu[1($\boxtimes$)] and Ming Liu[2($\boxtimes$)]

[1] Glorious Sun School of Business and Management, Donghua University, Shanghai, China
[2] School of Economics and Management, Tongji University, Shanghai 200092, China
mingliu@tongji.edu.cn

Abstract. In the context of Industry 4.0, both of the ability to handle unexpected events and personalization customization are emphasized. This work investigates a parallel machine scheduling problem with uncertain skill requirements. The problem involves a two-stage decision-making process: (i) determining the workers' skill training plan and the number of opened machines on the first stage before the realization of uncertain skill requirements, and (ii) scheduling jobs and assigning workers to jobs on the second stage, under known skill requirements. The objective is to minimize the expected total cost, including the workers' skill training cost, machine opening cost and the expected penalty cost of jobs' tardiness. A two-stage stochastic programming formulation is proposed, and an illustrative example shows the applicability of the model.

Keywords: Parallel machine scheduling · Stochastic optimization · Skill requirements · Skill training plan

1 Introduction

Industry 4.0, also known as the fourth industrial revolution or smart manufacturing, has received widely industrial and academic attention [9,10,24]. Such a concept gains sustainable and competitive advantages, aiming at improving the cooperation and communication of Cyber-Physical Systems and Human Resources [14]. One of the goals of Industry 4.0 is to find flexible and efficient production schedules, to cope with unpredictable issues [15,18,19].

Production Scheduling is an essential role in manufacturing, and it greatly impacts the production efficiency [6,17,25]. As unexpected events often occur in practice, such as changing workers' physical conditions and dynamic manufacturing environments, stochastic production scheduling is more realistic and becoming a popular research issue in recent years [1,13,22]. Most existing works assume that the job processing times are uncertain. Industry 4.0 is also a way

A. Dolgui et al. (Eds.): APMS 2021, IFIP AICT 632, pp. 258–265, 2021.
https://doi.org/10.1007/978-3-030-85906-0_29

to customization and personalization production, which emphasizes different requirements of orders [21]. In practical manufacturing systems, requirements for workers' skills to handle different jobs are different. Due to the changeable market situations and the upgrade of technology and products, the skills required by jobs may unexpectedly vary as well, and the uncertain skill requirements largely impact the scheduling and cannot be ignored.

On the other hand, from the mid- and long-term perspectives, managers should offer specialized skill training for workers, in order to cope with the uncertain skill requirements. In the following, we describe the impacts of skills possessed by workers on the job processing times, via borrowing the concept of "skill coefficient" [12]. That is, if the standard processing time of job j is p_j, and a worker with skill l handles job j, the practical processing time of job j is $\delta_{jl}p_j$, where δ_{jl} is the skill coefficient.

Parallel machine manufacturing situations are common in practice, and the parallel machine scheduling problem have been widely investigated [7, 11, 23]. Motivated by the above observations, this work considers a stochastic parallel machine scheduling problem with skill requirements. The problem involves a two-stage decision making process: (i) in the first stage, jobs' skill requirements are unknown, workers' skill training plan and the number of opened machines are determined; and (ii) when jobs' skill requirements are known, the detailed schedule of jobs on each machine and the worker-to-job assignment are determined. The objective is to minimize the expected total cost, including the workers' skill training cost, machine opening cost and the expected penalty cost for jobs' tardiness. The contribution of this paper mainly include:

(1) A novel parallel machine scheduling problem, where jobs' skill requirements are uncertain, is studied.
(2) Skill requirements are described via a limited set of samples. A two-stage stochastic programming formulation is proposed.
(3) An illustrative example is conducted to show the applicability of the problem model.

In the following, a brief literature review is provided in Sect. 2. Section 3 describes the problem in detail and propose a two-stage stochastic programming formulation. An illustrative example is shown in Sect. 4. Section 5 summarizes this work and suggests future research directions.

2 Literature Review

Parallel machine scheduling problems under deterministic environments have been widely investigated [7, 8, 11, 20]. This work focuses on a parallel machine scheduling problem with skill training, skill coefficient, and stochastic skill requirements. Thus only the most related literature considering scheduling with workforce is reviewed in the following.

An unrealated parallel machine scheduling problem with limited human resources is investigated in [2], where workers handle the setup activities between two consecutive jobs. The authors study the effect of reducing the human resource capacity on scheduling of parts in cells. [16] consider a parallel machine scheduling problem in precision engineering industry, where multi-skill workers are considered. The problem is to determine the worker-to-workshift and worker-to-machine assignments, to minimize the total salary payment and the overtime payment. They propose a mixed-integer programming formulation and design a two-stage heuristic algorithm. [4] investigate an identical parallel machine scheduling problem to assign workers to machines, where job processing times depend on the number of workers assigned to a machine. They propose a genetic algorithm to minimize the total tardiness. Based on that, [3] study the minimization of the total flow time and design a genetic algorithm. [5] investigate an unrelated parallel machine scheduling problem with sequence-dependent setup times, in which workers handle the setup activities and worker number is limited, to minimize the makspan. The specific skill level possessed by each worker affects setup times. They design a permutation encoding-based genetic algorithm for the problem.

In sum, to our best knowledge, there is no literature investigating the parallel machine problem with stochastic skill requirements, in which the worker skill training plan should be determined.

3   Problem Description and Formulation

In this section, the considered problem is first described in detail, and then basic notations and a two-stage stochastic programming formulation are proposed.

3.1   Problem Description

This paper investigates a parallel machine problem with stochastic skill requirements. The considered problem consists of a set N of jobs to be processed by a set M of machines and handled by a set R of workers, and the skills required by jobs are collected in set L. The problem follows the basic assumptions:

(1) Each job $j \in N$ should be assigned to exactly one machine $k \in M$ for processing.
(2) One machine can process at most one job at a time unit.
(3) The set of skills capable to handle job $j \in N$ is denoted by Q_j, which is stochastic. We use a set Ω of scenarios (i.e., samples) to describe the stochastic skill requirements, and we have $Q_j(\omega)$ under scenario $\omega \in \Omega$. That is, a worker with any one skill $l \in Q_j$ can be assigned to handle job j.
(4) If a worker with skill $l \in Q_j$ handles job j, the actual processing time of job j is $\delta_{jl}p_j$, where δ_{jl} is the skill coefficient and p_j is the standard processing time of job j.
(5) The cost for training worker $r \in R$ to possesses skill $l \in L$ is denoted by c_{rl}. The due date d_j of job $j \in N$ is predetermined by the customer, and the unit-time penalty cost of jobs' tardiness is denoted by c_j^P.

The problem consists of a two-stage decision-making process: (i) the first stage determines the workers' skill training plan and the number of opened machines, before the realization of skill requirements, and (ii) for a given scenario $\omega \in \Omega$, the second stage schedules jobs on each machine and assigns workers to jobs, under realized $Q_j(\omega)$. The objective is to minimize the total cost, including the workers' skill training cost and the expected penalty cost for jobs' tardiness.

3.2 Two-Stage Stochastic Programming Formulation

In this subsection, input parameters and decision variables are presented, and a two-stage stochastic programming formulation is proposed.

Input Parameters

- N: Set of jobs indexed by i, j, there is a dummy job 0 serving as the predecessor of the first job and the successor of the last job processed on a machine;
- M: Set of machines indexed by k;
- R: Set of workers indexed by r;
- L: Set of skills indexed by l;
- Ω: Set of scenarios indexed by $\omega \in \Omega$;
- p_j: Processing time of job j;
- δ_{jl}: Skill coefficient if job j is handled by a worker with skill $l \in L$;
- $Q_j(\omega)$: Set of skills capable to process job j under scenario $\omega \in \Omega$;
- c_{rl}^T: Cost for training worker $r \in R$ to process skill $l \in L$;
- c_k^M: Cost for opening machine $k \in M$;
- c_j^P: Penalty cost for jobs' tardiness;
- $\mathcal{M}$: A large enough number.

Decision Variables

- η_{rl}: Binary variable, equal to 1 if worker $r \in R$ is trained to process skill $l \in L$, and 0 otherwise;
- $x_{ij}^k(\omega)$: Binary variable, equal to 1 if job i is processed immediately before job j on machine k under scenario $\omega \in \Omega$, and 0 otherwise;
- y_k: Binary variable, equal to 1 if machine k is opened, and 0 otherwise;
- $z_{rj}(\omega)$: Binary variable, equal to 1 if worker $r \in R$ is assigned to process job $j \in N$ under scenario $\omega \in \Omega$, and 0 otherwise;
- $S_j(\omega)$: Nonnegative variable, denoting the starting time of job $j \in N$ under scenario $\omega \in \Omega$;
- $t_j(\omega)$: Nonnegative variable, denoting the tardiness of job $j \in N$ under scenario $\omega \in \Omega$.
- $\nu_{rjl}(\omega)$: Binary variable, used to linearize $\eta_{rl}z_{rj}(\omega)$, and equal to 1 if worker $r \in R$ is trained to process skill $l \in L$ and handle job $j \in N$, and 0 otherwise.

$$\min f = \sum_{r \in R}\sum_{l \in L} c_{rl}\eta_{rl} + \sum_{k \in M} y_k c_k^M + \frac{1}{|\Omega|}\sum_{\omega \in \Omega}\sum_{j \in N} c_j^P t_j(\omega) \tag{1}$$

$$\text{s.t.} \sum_{l \in L} \eta_{rl} = 1, \quad \forall r \in R \tag{2}$$

$$\sum_{j \in N} x_{0j}^k(\omega) \leq y_k, \quad \forall k \in M, \omega \in \Omega \tag{3}$$

$$\sum_{k \in M} \sum_{i \in N \cup \{0\}} x_{ij}^k(\omega) = 1, \quad \forall j \in N \tag{4}$$

$$\sum_{i \in N \cup \{0\}, i \neq j} x_{ij}^k(\omega) - \sum_{i \in N \cup \{0\}, i \neq j} x_{ij}^k(\omega) = 0, \quad \forall j \in N, k \in M, \omega \in \Omega \tag{5}$$

$$z_{rj}(\omega) \leq \sum_{l \in Q_j(\omega)} \eta_{rl}, \quad \forall r \in R, j \in N, \omega \in \Omega \tag{6}$$

$$\sum_{r \in R} z_{rj}(\omega) = 1, \quad \forall j \in N, \omega \in \Omega \tag{7}$$

$$\sum_{j \in N} z_{rj}(\omega) \leq 1, \quad \forall r \in R, \omega \in \Omega \tag{8}$$

$$\nu_{rjl}(\omega) \leq z_{rj}(\omega), \quad \forall r \in R, j \in N, l \in L, \omega \in \Omega \tag{9}$$

$$\nu_{rjl}(\omega) \leq \eta_{rl}, \quad \forall r \in R, j \in N, l \in L, \omega \in \Omega \tag{10}$$

$$\nu_{rjl}(\omega) \geq 1 - \mathcal{M}(2 - \eta_{rl} - z_{rj}(\omega)), \quad \forall r \in R, j \in N, l \in L, \omega \in \Omega \tag{11}$$

$$S_j(\omega) \geq S_i(\omega) + \sum_{r \in R} \sum_{l \in L} p_i \delta_{il} \nu_{ril}(\omega) - \mathcal{M}(1 - \sum_{k \in M} x_{ij}^k(\omega)),$$
$$\forall i, j \in N, i \neq j, \omega \in \Omega \tag{12}$$

$$S_j(\omega) + \sum_{r \in R} \sum_{l \in L} p_j \delta_{jl} \nu_{rjl}(\omega) - t_j(\omega) \leq d_j, \quad \forall j \in N, \omega \in \Omega \tag{13}$$

$$\eta_{rl}, x_{ij}^k(\omega), z_{rj}(\omega) \in \{0, 1\}, \quad \forall i, j \in N, i \neq j, r \in R, l \in L, \omega \in \Omega \tag{14}$$

$$S_j(\omega), t_j(\omega) \geq 0, \quad \forall j \in N, \omega \in \Omega \tag{15}$$

The objective function is to minimize the expectation of the system cost, including the first-stage skill training cost (i.e., $sum_{r \in R} \sum_{l \in L} c_{rl} \eta_{rl}$) and the machine opening cost (i.e., $\sum_{k \in M} y_k c_k^M$), and the expected second-stage penalty cost of jobs' tardiness, i.e., $\sum_{\omega \in \Omega} \sum_{j \in N} c_j^P t_j(\omega)$.

Constraints (2) ensure that each worker should be trained to possess exactly one skill. Constraints (3) restrict that jobs can only be assigned to opened machines under scenario $\omega \in \Omega$. Constraints (4) ensure that each job is assigned to one machine for processing under scenario $\omega \in \Omega$. Constraints (5) serve as the flow conservations, i.e., the numbers of a job's predecessor and successor on a machine should be the same under scenario $\omega \in \Omega$. Constraints (6) ensure that only workers with the required skills can be assigned to handle job j under scenario $\omega \in \Omega$. Constraints (7) imply that a job should be handled by exactly one worker under scenario $\omega \in \Omega$. Constraints (8) restrict that a worker can handle at most one job under scenario $\omega \in \Omega$. Constraints (9)–(11) are to linearize $\eta_{rl} z_{rj}(\omega)$. Constraints (12) calculate the starting time of each job $j \in N$

under scenario $\omega \in \Omega$. Constraints (13) estimate the tardiness of each job $j \in N$ under scenario $\omega \in \Omega$. Constraints (14) and (15) provide the domains of decision variables.

4   An Illustrative Example

In this section, an illustrative example is investigated, to test the applicability of the proposed model. The input data is reported in Table 1 and Table 2, where (1) 6 jobs, 3 machines, 10 workers and 10 skills in total are involved; (2) 20 scenarios (i.e., $|\Omega|$) is tested; (3) Table 1 provides the input skill coefficient δ_{jl} and the standard processing time p_j and the due date d_j; and (4) Table 2 reports the input cost for training each worker r to possess skill l. Without loss of generality, penalty cost c_j^P for jobs' tardiness is set to be 1. Skill requirement Q_j of each job $j \subset N$ is a randomly selected subset of L. Via calling the CPLEX solver, the obtained objective value is 107.32 within 98 s. The 10 workers are trained to possess skills [6, 7, 4, 8, 6, 8, 5, 10, 2, 8], and all of the 3 machines are opened.

Table 1. Input data of the illustrative example

$j \backslash l$	δ_{jl}										p_j	d_j
	1	2	3	4	5	6	7	8	9	10		
1	1.46	1.30	1.18	1.21	1.20	1.27	1.21	0.62	1.25	1.05	9	10
2	0.99	1.46	1.26	0.53	0.82	1.30	1.26	1.00	0.75	0.64	10	11
3	1.30	1.16	1.25	0.77	1.45	0.68	0.77	1.46	1.01	0.65	2	13
4	0.64	0.53	0.89	0.54	0.53	0.99	1.18	0.84	1.20	0.76	10	13
5	0.92	1.35	1.16	0.59	0.94	0.95	1.16	1.09	1.39	1.34	7	9
6	1.42	2.44	0.67	1.33	0.88	1.15	0.66	0.72	1.46	0.75	1	13

Table 2. Input cost c_{rl} for training workers of the illustrative example

Worker $(r) \backslash$ skill (l)	1	2	3	4	5	6	7	8	9	10
1	18	16	15	13	12	10	12	13	19	12
2	12	16	18	15	20	18	12	15	20	14
3	20	20	20	11	11	18	11	14	15	11
4	13	13	11	16	19	19	11	10	15	11
5	12	18	16	12	15	10	19	12	13	20
6	12	18	15	17	20	14	16	11	19	20
7	16	14	10	17	10	12	16	12	14	16
8	15	16	13	18	14	18	11	12	11	20
9	13	10	11	14	11	14	19	14	18	12
10	19	10	18	10	20	20	16	10	14	13

5   Conclusion

This paper investigates a two-stage stochastic parallel machine scheduling problem: (1) the first stage determines the worker skill training plan and the opened machines, under unknown skill requirements, and (2) the second stage schedules the jobs on each machine and assigns workers to jobs. A two-stage stochastic programming formulation is proposed for the problem, and an illustrated example is investigated to show the applicability of the formulation.

Further research is still needed: (i) developing algorithms that can solve the problem more efficiently; (ii) investigating robust optimization of the problem, from the risk-averse perspective; (iii) considering situations where the probability of not meeting the skill requirements is restricted.

Acknowledgements. This work is supported by the National Natural Science Foundation of China (NSFC) under Grants 72021002, 71771048, 71432007, 71832001 and 72071144.

References

1. Al-Khamis, T., M'Hallah, R.: A two-stage stochastic programming model for the parallel machine scheduling problem with machine capacity. Comput. Oper. Res. **38**(12), 1747–1759 (2011)
2. Celano, G., Costa, A., Fichera, S.: Scheduling of unrelated parallel manufacturing cells with limited human resources. Int. J. Prod. Res. **46**(2), 405–427 (2008)
3. Chaudhry, I.A.: Minimizing flow time for the worker assignment problem in identical parallel machine models using GA. Int. J. Adv. Manuf. Technol. **48**(5–8), 747–760 (2010)
4. Chaudhry, I.A., Drake, P.R.: Minimizing total tardiness for the machine scheduling and worker assignment problems in identical parallel machines using genetic algorithms. Int. J. Adv. Manuf. Technol. **42**(5), 581–594 (2009)
5. Costa, A., Cappadonna, F.A., Fichera, S.: A hybrid genetic algorithm for job sequencing and worker allocation in parallel unrelated machines with sequence-dependent setup times. Int. J. Adv. Manuf. Technol. **69**(9), 2799–2817 (2013). https://doi.org/10.1007/s00170-013-5221-5
6. Dolgui, A., Ivanov, D., Sethi, S.P., Sokolov, B.: Scheduling in production, supply chain and industry 4.0 systems by optimal control: fundamentals, state-of-the-art and applications. Int. J. Prod. Res. **57**(2), 411–432 (2019)
7. Dong, C., Chen, M., Wan, G.: Parallel machine selection and job scheduling to minimize machine cost and job tardiness. Comput. Oper. Res. **32**(8), 1995–2012 (2005)
8. Edis, E.B., Oguz, C., Ozkarahan, I.: Parallel machine scheduling with additional resources: notation, classification, models and solution methods. Eur. J. Oper. Res. **230**(3), 449–463 (2013)
9. Gorecky, D., Schmitt, M., Loskyll, M., Zühlke, D.: Human-machine-interaction in the industry 4.0 era. Manage. Sci. **23**(6), 595–605 (2014)
10. Hofmann, E., Rüsch, M.: Industry 4.0 and the current status as well as future prospects on logistics. Comput. Ind. **89**, 23–34 (2017)

11. Ji, M., Cheng, T.C.E.: Parallel-machine scheduling with simple linear deterioration to minimize total completion time. Eur. J. Oper. Res. **188**(2), 342–347 (2008)
12. Liu, M., Liu, X., Chu, F., Zhang, E., Chu, C.: Service-oriented robust worker scheduling with motivation effects. Int. J. Prod. Res. (2020). https://doi.org/10.1080/00207543.2020.1730998
13. Liu, M., Liu, X., Chu, F., Zheng, F., Chu, C.: Service-oriented robust parallel machine scheduling. Int. J. Prod. Res. **57**(12), 3814–3830 (2019)
14. Longo, F., Nicoletti, L., Padovano, A.: Smart operators in industry 4.0: a human-centered approach to enhance operators' capabilities and competencies within the new smart factory context. Comput. Ind. Eng. **113**, 144–159 (2017)
15. Machado, C.G., Winroth, M.P., Ribeiro da silva, E.H.D.: Sustainable manufacturing in industry 4.0: an emerging research agenda. Int. J. Prod. Res. **58**(5), 1462–1484 (2020)
16. Pan, Q.K., Suganthan, P.N., Chua, T.J., Cai, T.X.: Solving manpower scheduling problem in manufacturing using mixed-integer programming with a two-stage heuristic algorithm. Int. J. Adv. Manuf. Technol. **46**(9–12), 1229–1237 (2010)
17. Pinedo, M., Hadavi, K.: Scheduling: Theory. Algorithms and Systems. Springer, Berlin (1992). https://doi.org/10.1007/978-1-4614-2361-4
18. Rosin, F., Forget, P., Lamouri, S., Pellerin, R.: Impacts of industry 4.0 technologies on lean principles. Int. J. Prod. Res. **58**(6), 1644–1661 (2020)
19. Rossit, D.A., Tohmé, F., Frutos, M.: Industry 4.0: smart scheduling. Int. J. Prod. Res. **57**(12), 3802–3913 (2018)
20. Vallada, E., Ruiz, R.: A genetic algorithm for the unrelated parallel machine scheduling problem with sequence dependent setup times. Eur. J. Oper. Res. **211**(3), 612–622 (2011)
21. Wang, Y., Ma, H.-S., Yang, J.-H., Wang, K.-S.: Industry 4.0: a way from mass customization to mass personalization production. Adv. Manuf. **5**(4), 311–320 (2017). https://doi.org/10.1007/s40436-017-0204-7
22. Xu, X., Cui, W., Lin, J., Qian, Y.: Robust makespan minimisation in identical parallel machine scheduling problem with interval data. Int. J. Prod. Res. **51**(12), 3532–3548 (2013)
23. Yang, D.L., Cheng, T.C.E., Yang, S.J.: Parallel-machine scheduling with controllable processing times and rate-modifying activities to minimise total cost involving total completion time and job compressions. Int. J. Prod. Res. **52**(4), 1133–1141 (2014)
24. Yin, Y., Stecke, Kathryn, E., Li, D.: The evolution of production systems from industry 2.0 through industry 4.0. Int. J. Prod. Res. **56**(1–2), 848–861 (2018)
25. Zhang, J., Ding, G., Zou, Y., Qin, S., Fu, J.: Review of job shop scheduling research and its new perspectives under industry 4.0. J. Intell. Manuf. **30**, 1809–1830 (2017)

Multitasking Scheduling Problem with Uncertain Credit Risk

Feifeng Zheng[1], Zhaojie Wang[1], Yinfeng Xu[1], and Ming Liu[2(✉)]

[1] Glorious Sun School of Business and Management, Donghua University,
Shanghai 200051, China
[2] School of Economics and Management, Tongji University, Shanghai 200092, China
mingliu@tongji.edu.cn

Abstract. Parallel machine scheduling problem in multitasking environment plays an important role in modern manufacturing industry. Multitasking is a special scheduling method, in which each waiting job interrupts the primary job, causing an interruption time and a switching time. The existing literatures discuss the problem of multitasking scheduling, however, few studies consider credit risk into such a realm of scheduling models. In this work, we combine customer credit risk into a multitasking scheduling problem. Besides, due to the existence of credit risk and the constraint of deadline of each accepted job, we also consider the job rejection into this problem. To hedge against the worst-case performance (total profit in the worst-case), we then propose a robust stochastic mathematical model with the objective of minimising the maximum difference between total job rejection cost and total revenue. As commercial solvers cannot directly solve this robust stochastic programming model, a sample average approximation model is proposed to further solve this problem. Numerical experiments are conducted to demonstrate the effectiveness of the proposed sample average approximation approach.

Keywords: Multitasking · Scheduling · Stochastic · Credit risk · Robust

1 Introduction

In the industry 4.0 environment, scheduling should deal with an intelligent manufacturing system supported by new and emerging manufacturing technologies, such as mass customization (Zhang et al. 2019). Hence, customer credit risk (or payment probability) is becoming a main challenge faced by modern manufacturing industry (Liu et al. 2020).

This work was supported by the National Natural Science Foundation of China (Grant No. 71771048, 71832001, 72021002, 72071144 and 71972146) and the Fundamental Research Funds for the Central Universities (Grant No. 2232018H-07).

Parallel machine scheduling is a classical subject of study and common problem in practice (Wu and Che 2019). As a special parallel scheduling mode, multitasking allows the machine to perform multiple tasks (Liu et al. 2017). In multitasking settings, each waiting job interrupts the primary job, causing an interruption time and a switching time. In fact, parallel machine scheduling in multitasking environment is a very common phenomenon such as chemical manufacturing, food processing, and oil refining (Gaglioppa et al. 2008). Despite this, few studies investigate the impact of customer credit risk on parallel machine scheduling under multitasking environment.

Motivated by scheduling practices, we investigate a multitasking scheduling problem considering customer credit risk. Due to the existence of credit risk and the limitation of deadline of each accepted job, the option of job rejection is a very practical and realistic feature (Mor et al. 2020). Hence, we make a reasonable assumption in this work that any job can be rejected. For solving this problem, we first establish a robust stochastic mathematical model to hedge against the worst-case performance (i.e., total profit in the worst-case), and then propose a sample average approximation (SAA) approach to solve this problem.

1.1   Literature Review

As parallel machine scheduling in multitasking environment is a very common phenomenon in manufacturing industry, the research on multitasking scheduling problem has attracted wide attention of scholars.

Gaglioppa et al. (2008) consider the planning and scheduling of production in a multitask batch manufacturing process which is typical industries. In their problem, they allow instances in which multiple sequences of tasks may be used to produce end products. For solving this problem, they first establish a mixed-integer linear program, and then propose a new family of efficient inequalities to reduce the solution time. Liu et al. (2019) investigate a multitasking scheduling problem on parallel machines with uncertain processing times. The objective of their problem is to minimize the weighted sum of the earliness and tardiness. They then propose a two-stage stochastic programming formulation based on scenarios to solving this problem. Zhu et al. (2016) study multitasking scheduling problems with a rate-modifying activity. In the problems, the processing of a selected task suffers from interruptions by other tasks that are available but unfinished, and the human operators regularly engage rest breaks during work shifts allowing them to recover or mitigate some of the negative effects of fatigue. Hall et al. (2015) develop optimal algorithms for some fundamental and practical single machine scheduling problems with multitasking. Ji et al. (2018) consider the problem of parallel-machine scheduling with machine-dependent slack (SLK) due-window assignment in the multitasking environment. The objectives of their studied problem is to minimise the total cost that comprises the earliness, tardiness, and due-window-related costs. Xiong et al. (2019) consider the multitasking scheduling problem on unrelated parallel machines to minimize the total weighted completion time. For solving this problem, they propose an exact branch and price algorithm. Li et al. (2020) present four fuzzy optimization models for scheduling multiple heterogeneous complex tasks with distributed resources/services in consideration of multiple criteria with fuzzy uncertainty in service-oriented manufacturing environment. For solving those models, they then develop corresponding heuristic algorithms in their study.

In sum, we know that few studies consider external factors, such as the impact of credit risk on multitasking scheduling problem. Liu et al. (2020) study a stochastic flowshop scheduling problem with the objective of maximizing the profit level. They show that credit risk has an important impact on the scheduling decision of enterprises. Inspired by Liu et al. (2020), we consider credit risk into parallel machine scheduling under multitasking environment. The main contributions of this work include: (1) Credit risk is considered in the multitasking scheduling problem, which makes this research more in line with the practical production; (2) A robust stochastic optimization model is established to study this problem; (3) A SAA method is proposed to further solve this problem.

The remainder of this paper is organized as follows. Section 2 describes the considered problem and establishes a robust mathematical model for the this problem. Section 3 proposes a SAA model for ease of adopting commercial solvers to solve this problem. Finally, Sect. 4 conducts numerical experiments to evaluate the performance of the proposed model.

2   Problem Statement

Suppose that there are $|\mathcal{J}|$ jobs to be processed on $|\mathcal{M}|$ parallel machines, and the release time of all jobs are 0. Due to the constraint of the deadline of each job, we make a reasonable assumption, that is, any job can be rejected.

For describing the details of multitasking scheduling process, we assume that only one machine is available. We use $\mathcal{J}_i$ to represent the job set that will be processed on the machine i. In $\mathcal{J}_i$, any job scheduled for processing at any time is called a primary job, while all the other unsatisfied (or unfinished) jobs at that time are referred to as waiting jobs (Hall et al. 2015). Beside, in $\mathcal{J}_i$, any primary job must be interrupted by all the waiting jobs during its processing. Figure 1 describes a multitasking environment in which two accepted jobs are processed on a machine. Since any accepted job have to be completed, each job is selected as a primary job exactly once, and a primary job is always completed before other waiting jobs.

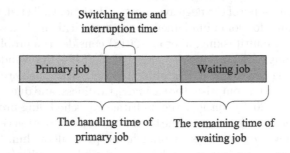

Fig. 1. Illustration of multitasking processing

Due to the uncertainty of credit risk, the total profit usually cannot be evaluated deterministicly by decision makers. To address this problem, we investigate a robust multitasking scheduling problem considering uncertain customer credit risk. The objective is to minimise the maximum difference between total penalty cost, i.e., job rejection cost and total revenue.

2.1   Mathematical Model

Below we first present basic parameters and decision variables, and then establish a robust stochastic programming model.

Input Parameters

$\mathcal{M}$: set of machines, indexed by i, and $\mathcal{M} = \{1, 2, \dots, |\mathcal{M}|\}$;

$\mathcal{J}$: set of jobs, indexed by j, and $\mathcal{J} = \{1, 2, \dots, |\mathcal{J}|\}$;

$\mathcal{W}$: set of positions, indexed by w, and $\mathcal{W} = \{1, 2, \dots, |\mathcal{W}|\}$;

Ω : set of all random events indexed by ω.

$\xi_j(\omega)$: stochastic payment probability of job j under event $\omega \in \Omega$;

p_j : the processing time of job j;

π_j : revenue for processing job j;

e_j : penalty cost for rejecting job j;

η : the parameter given in the switching time function $f(|S_j|) = \eta * |S_j|$, where $|S_j|$ denotes the number of waiting jobs processed on the same machine as the job j when processing job j;

ν_j : the parameter given in the interruption time function $g_j(p_j') = \nu_j * p_j'$, where p_j' is the remaining time of job j, $g_j(p_j')$ is the interruption time;

d_j : deadline of job j;

M : a sufficiently large positive integer.

Decision Variables

$x_{ij}^w(\omega)$: a binary variable equal to 1 if job j is processed by machine i at position w under event $\omega \in \Omega$, 0 otherwise;

$\lambda_i(\omega)$: the number of jobs that are processed on machine i under event $\omega \in \Omega$;

$\tilde{p}_j(\omega)$: the handling time of job j under event $\omega \in \Omega$;

$y_j(\omega)$: a binary variable equal to 1 if job j is accepted under event $\omega \in \Omega$, 0 otherwise;

$l_{jj'}(\omega)$: a binary variable equal to 1 if the position assigned to job j ahead of that assigned to job j' on the same machine under event $\omega \in \Omega$, 0 otherwise;

$h_{ij}^w(\omega)$: the remaining time of job j on machine i at position w under event $\omega \in \Omega$, where $h_{ij}^w(\omega) = (1 - \nu_j)^{w-1} * p_j$;

$\theta_j(\omega)$: the interruption time of all the waiting jobs for processing job j under event $\omega \in \Omega$;

$s_j(\omega)$: the start processing time of job j under event $\omega \in \Omega$;

$c_j(\omega)$: the completion time of job j under event $\omega \in \Omega$.

Robust Stochastic Programming Formulation [P1]

$$\min \max \left\{ \sum_{j\in\mathcal{J}} (1 - y_j(\omega)) * e_j - \sum_{j\in\mathcal{J}} y_j(\omega) * \xi_j(\omega) * \pi_j \right\} \tag{1}$$

subject to

$$\sum_{i\in\mathcal{M}} \sum_{w\in\mathcal{W}} x_{ij}^w(\omega) = y_j(\omega), \quad j \in \mathcal{J}, \omega \in \Omega \tag{2}$$

$$\sum_{j\in\mathcal{J}} x_{ij}^w(\omega) \leq 1, \quad i \in \mathcal{M}, w \in \mathcal{W}, \omega \in \Omega \tag{3}$$

$$\sum_{j\in\mathcal{J}} x_{ij}^w(\omega) \geq \sum_{j\in\mathcal{J}} x_{ij}^{w'}(\omega), \quad i \in \mathcal{M}, w, w' \in \mathcal{W}, w < w', \omega \in \Omega \tag{4}$$

$$h_{ij}^w(\omega) \geq (1 - \nu_j)^{w-1} * p_j - M * (1 - x_{ij}^w(\omega)), \quad i \in \mathcal{M}, j \in \mathcal{J}, w \in \mathcal{W}, \omega \in \Omega \tag{5}$$

$$\lambda_i(\omega) = \sum_{j\in\mathcal{J}} \sum_{w\in\mathcal{W}} x_{ij}^w(\omega), \quad i \in \mathcal{M}, \omega \in \Omega \tag{6}$$

$$\theta_j(\omega) \geq \sum_{j'\in\mathcal{J}} \sum_{w'=w+1}^{|\mathcal{W}|} \nu_j * (1 - \nu_j)^{w-1} * p_j * x_{ij}^{w'} - M * (1 - x_{ij}^w(\omega)),$$

$$i \in \mathcal{M}, j \in \mathcal{J}, w \in \{\mathcal{W}\} \backslash |\mathcal{W}|, \omega \in \Omega \tag{7}$$

$$\tilde{p}_j(\omega) = h_{ij}^w(\omega) + \eta * (\lambda_i(\omega) - w) + \theta_j(\omega), \quad i \in \mathcal{M}, j \in \mathcal{J}, w \in \mathcal{W}, \omega \in \Omega \tag{8}$$

$$l_{jj'}(\omega) \geq 1 - M * (2 - x_{ij}^{w'}(\omega) - x_{ij'}^w(\omega)),$$

$$i \in \mathcal{M}, j, j' \in \mathcal{J}, w, w' \in \mathcal{W}, w > w', \omega \in \Omega \tag{9}$$

$$s_j'(\omega) \geq c_j(\omega) - M * (1 - l_{jj'}(\omega)), \quad j, j' \in \mathcal{J}, j \neq j', \omega \in \Omega \tag{10}$$

$$c_j(\omega) = s_j(\omega) + \tilde{p}_j, \quad i \in \mathcal{M}, j \in \mathcal{J}, \omega \in \Omega \tag{11}$$

$$c_j(\omega) \leq d_j, \quad j \in \mathcal{J}, \omega \in \Omega \tag{12}$$

$$x_{ij}^w(\omega), y_j(\omega), l_{jj'}(\omega) \in \{0, 1\}, \quad i \in \mathcal{M}, j \in \mathcal{J}, w \in \mathcal{W}, \omega \in \Omega \tag{13}$$

$$s_j(\omega), c_j(\omega), \lambda_i(\omega), \theta_j(\omega), \tilde{p}_j(\omega), h_{ij}^w(\omega) \geq 0, \quad i \in \mathcal{M}, j \in \mathcal{J}, w \in \mathcal{W}, \omega \in \Omega \tag{14}$$

Formula (1) is the objective function, which is used to minimise the maximum difference between total penalty cost and total revenue. Constraint (2) denotes that the accepted job must be processed under event $\omega \in \Omega$. Constraint (3) implies that no more than one job can be processed at a certain position of a machine under event $\omega \in \Omega$. Constraint (4) guarantees that the position of machine $i \in \mathcal{M}$ is continuous when processing the jobs under event $\omega \in \Omega$. Constraint (5) calculates the remaining processing time of job $j \in \mathcal{J}$ on machine $i \in \mathcal{M}$ under event $\omega \in \Omega$, where $(1 - \nu_j)^{w-1}$ represents the $w - 1$ power of ν_j. Constraint (6) calculates the number of jobs assigned to machine $i \in \mathcal{M}$ under event $\omega \in \Omega$. Constraint (7) calculates the interruption time of all the waiting jobs for processing job $j \in \mathcal{J}$ under event $\omega \in \Omega$. Constraint (8) calculates the handling time of job $j \in \mathcal{J}$ on machine $i \in \mathcal{M}$ under event $\omega \in \Omega$, which includes three parts: its remaining processing time, the switching and the interruption time of all the waiting jobs. Constraints (9)–(11) calculate the start processing time and completion time of job $j \in \mathcal{J}$ under event $\omega \in \Omega$, respectively. Constraint (12) guarantees that the completion time of job $j \in \mathcal{J}$ is less than its deadline under event $\omega \in \Omega$. Constrains (13)–(14) limit the ranges of the variables.

3   SAA Approach

Sample average approximation (SAA) has widely used to deal with stochastic optimization problem (e.g., Li and Zhang 2018). The main idea of this approach is to adopt deterministic optimization techniques with Monte Carlo simulation (Zheng et al. 2018).

In this section, we assume that the random vector $\xi_j (j \in \mathcal{J})$ has finite support, i.e. Ω contains a finite number of random events, and $\omega - 1, 2, \cdots, |\Omega|$ index its possible realisations. [**P1**] can be approximately transformed into [**P2**].

$$[\mathbf{P2}] : \mathbf{min}\ \theta \tag{15}$$

subject to

$$(2) - (14)$$

$$\sum_{j \in \mathcal{J}} (1 - y_j(\omega)) * e_j - \sum_{j \in \mathcal{J}} y_j(\omega) * \xi_j(\omega) * \pi_j \leq \theta, \quad \omega \in \Omega \tag{16}$$

Constraint (16) implies that the maximum difference between total job rejection cost and total revenue under event $\omega \in \Omega$ cannot be larger than θ.

4   Numerical Experiments

For demonstrating the effectivess of the proposed SAA approach, we carry out numerical experiments via Matlab R2017a. All numerical experiments are conducted on a PC with AMD Ryzen 7 4800U with Radeon Graphics 1.80 GHz.

4.1   Experiment Setup

In this work, we test two probability distribution of ξ_j ($j \in \mathcal{J}$), i.e., uniform and normal distributions. For normal distributions, according to Ng (2015), the variance (σ^2) of ξ_j is set as $\sigma^2 = 0.005 * \mu^2$, where μ is the estimates of mean of ξ_j. In order to compare the results of the two distributions, we set the mean value of the normal distribution to 0.5, which is the same as that of the uniform distribution. For each probability distribution, the instances to be tested and the values or ranges of generated other parameters are shown in Table 1.

Table 1. Parameter settings

Instance	p_j	d_j	e_j	η	ν_j	π_j
$(|\mathcal{M}| = 2; |\mathcal{J}| = 5; |\Omega| = 3)$	[5,10]	[20, 30]	[1, 3]	0.5	[0.1, 0.3]	[5,10]
$(|\mathcal{M}| = 2; |\mathcal{J}| = 7; |\Omega| = 3)$	[5,10]	[30, 50]	[3, 5]	1	[0.3, 0.5]	[8,10]
$(|\mathcal{M}| = 3; |\mathcal{J}| = 5; |\Omega| = 3)$	[5,10]	[20, 30]	[1, 3]	0.5	[0.1, 0.3]	[5,10]
$(|\mathcal{M}| = 3; |\mathcal{J}| = 7; |\Omega| = 3)$	[5,10]	[30, 50]	[3, 5]	1	[0.3, 0.5]	[8,10]
$(|\mathcal{M}| = 2; |\mathcal{J}| = 5; |\Omega| = 5)$	[5,10]	[20, 30]	[1, 3]	0.5	[0.1, 0.3]	[5,10]
$(|\mathcal{M}| = 2; |\mathcal{J}| = 7; |\Omega| = 5)$	[5,10]	[30, 50]	[3, 5]	1	[0.3, 0.5]	[8,10]
$(|\mathcal{M}| = 3; |\mathcal{J}| = 5; |\Omega| = 5)$	[5,10]	[20, 30]	[1, 3]	0.5	[0.1, 0.3]	[5,10]
$(|\mathcal{M}| = 3; |\mathcal{J}| = 7; |\Omega| = 5)$	[5,10]	[30, 50]	[3, 5]	1	[0.3, 0.5]	[8,10]
$(|\mathcal{M}| = 2; |\mathcal{J}| = 5; |\Omega| = 8)$	[5,10]	[20, 30]	[1, 3]	0.5	[0.1, 0.3]	[5,10]
$(|\mathcal{M}| = 2; |\mathcal{J}| = 7; |\Omega| = 8)$	[5,10]	[30, 50]	[3, 5]	1	[0.3, 0.5]	[8,10]
$(|\mathcal{M}| = 3; |\mathcal{J}| = 5; |\Omega| = 8)$	[5,10]	[20, 30]	[1, 3]	0.5	[0.1, 0.3]	[5,10]
$(|\mathcal{M}| = 3; |\mathcal{J}| = 7; |\Omega| = 8)$	[5,10]	[30, 50]	[3, 5]	1	[0.3, 0.5]	[8,10]

4.2   Experimental Results

Experimental results of SAA approach under the two distributions are shown in Table 2.

Table 2 summarizes that the average objective value of SAA under uniform distribution is −16.5, which about 29.8% larger than that under normal distribution (−23.5). It can also be observed that the increase of the number of scenarios

Table 2. Experimental results of SAA approach with uniform and normal distributions

Instance	Uniform distribution		Normal distribution	
	Obj	Time (s)	*Obj*	Time(s)
1	−14.8	5	−16.6	4
2	−16.4	5	−31.6	5
3	−14.8	8	−16.6	8
4	−16.4	9	−31.6	9
5	−12.0	6	−15.9	6
6	−22.7	14	−30.7	14
7	−12.0	5	−15.9	5
8	−22.7	12	−30.7	12
9	−8.0	9	−15.4	9
10	−25.1	21	−30.7	21
11	−8.0	7	−15.4	7
12	−25.1	18	−30.7	18
Average	−16.5	10	−23.5	10

and instance size may lead to the increase of computation time. Decision makers can first determine the distribution of stochastic payment probability of each job according to historical data, and then use the proposed robust stochastic programming model and SAA approach to make a scheduling plan to hedge against the worst-case performance.

In the future research, we will explore several rule-based heuristics, and then compare them with existing algorithms through numerical experiments. Besides, multitasking environment with unrelated machines can also be considered to further study the considered problem.

References

Gaglioppa, F., Miller, L.A., Benjaafar, S.: Multitask and multistage production planning and scheduling for process industries. Oper. Res. **56**(4), 1010–1025 (2008)

Hall, N.G., Leung, J., Li, C.: The effects of multitasking on operations scheduling. Prod. Oper. Manage. **24**(8), 1248–1265 (2015)

Ji, M., Zhang, W., Liao, L., Cheng, T.C.E., Tan, Y.: Multitasking parallel-machine scheduling with machine-dependent slack due-window assignment. Int. J. Prod. Res. **57**(6), 1667–1684 (2018)

Li, F., Liao, T.W., Cai, W.T., Zhang, L.: Multitask scheduling in consideration of fuzzy uncertainty of multiple criteria in service-oriented manufacturing. IEEE Trans. Fuzzy Syst. **126**(11), 2759–2771 (2020)

Li, X., Zhang, K.: A sample average approximation approach for supply chain network design with facility disruptions. Comput. Ind. Eng. **126**, 243–251 (2018)

Liu, M., Liu, X., Chu, F., Chu, C.B.: Profit-oriented distributionally robust chance constrained flowshop scheduling considering credit risk. Int. J. Prod. Res. **58**(8), 2527–2549 (2020)

Liu, M., Wang, S., Zheng, F., Chu, C.: Algorithms for the joint multitasking scheduling and common due date assignment problem. Int. J. Prod. Res. **55**(20), 6052–6066 (2017)

Liu, M., Liu, R., Liu, X.: Two-stage stochastic programming for parallel machine multitasking to minimize the weighted sum of tardiness and earliness. In: 16th International Conference on Service Systems and Service Management (ICSSSM) (2019)

Mor, B., Mosheiov, G., Shapira, D.: Flowshop scheduling with learning effect and job rejection. J. Sched. **23**(6), 631–641 (2020)

Ng, M.W.: Container vessel fleet deployment for liner shipping with stochastic dependencies in shipping demand. Transp. Res. Part B **74**, 79–87 (2015)

Wu, X., Che, A.: A memetic differential evolution algorithm for energy-efficient parallel machine scheduling. Omega **82**, 155–165 (2019)

Xiong, X., Zhou, P., Yin, Y., Cheng, T.C.E., Li, D.: An exact branch and price algorithm for multitasking scheduling on unrelated parallel machines. Naval Res. Logist. **66**(6), 502–516 (2019)

Zhang, J., Ding, G., Zou, Y., Qin, S., Fu, J.: Review of job shop scheduling research and its new perspectives under Industry 4.0. J. Intell. Manuf. **30**(4), 1809–1830 (2019)

Zheng, F., Man, X., Chu, F., Liu, M., Chu, C.: A two-stage stochastic programming for single yard crane scheduling with uncertain release times of retrieval tasks. J. Prod. Res. **57**(13), 4132–4147 (2018)

Zhu, Z., Zheng, F., Chu, C.: Multitasking scheduling problems with a rate-modifying activity. Int. J. Prod. Res. **55**(1), 296–312 (2016)

A Mathematical Model for Bus Scheduling with Conditional Signal Priority

Ming Liu[1], Yecheng Zhao[1], Feng Chu[2(✉)], Feifeng Zheng[3], and Chengbin Chu[4]

[1] School of Economics and Management, Tongji University,
Shanghai, People's Republic of China
[2] IBISC, Univ Évry, University of Paris-Saclay, Évry, France
`feng.chu@univ-evry.fr`
[3] Glorious Sun School of Business and Management, Donghua University, Shanghai,
People's Republic of China
[4] Laboratoire d'Informatique Gaspard-Monge (LIGM), UMR 8049,
Univ Gustave Eiffel, ESIEE Paris, 93162 Noisy-le-Grand Cedex, France

Abstract. Inaccuracy of buses is a common situation. A common practice is that a certain amount of slack is usually added to the schedule of bus operation, so that the bus can execute the schedule in most cases. On the other hand, slack means that buses sometimes have to wait for a while at the station or slow down while driving. Since the bus cannot accelerate the driving process by itself, this method cannot make the bus fully implement the schedule. Researchers invented the Transit signal priority (TSP) and conditional signal priority (CSP), the purpose of which is to give the bus signal priority to speed up when it is delayed to a certain extent. Some previous work has studied the driving process of buses with CSP. However, there is still room for further improvement in the mathematical description of the bus driving process based on CSP. In this article, we analyze the driving state of the bus under different CSP states, that is, positive and negative. Then a series of representative and operational assumptions are given. These assumptions can be used as the basis for future research on such topics. With the assumptions, we give a mathematical model of the bus driving process using CSP. According to some performance indicators of the bus driving process obtained in the modeling process, an optimization goal is established to comprehensively improve the driving effect of the bus. Mathematical analysis and numerical solution verify the applicability of the model.

Keywords: Bus scheduling · Signal priority · Bus driving process · Mathematical model

1 Introduction

As a kind of public transportation, buses are expected to have high schedule reliability. But due to many reasons, bus delays are common occurrences. In order

© IFIP International Federation for Information Processing 2021
Published by Springer Nature Switzerland AG 2021
A. Dolgui et al. (Eds.): APMS 2021, IFIP AICT 632, pp. 274–281, 2021.
https://doi.org/10.1007/978-3-030-85906-0_31

to solve this problem, decision makers often leave a certain slack when designing the bus schedule to ease it. This has caused a waste of traffic resources. In today's era where efficiency and resource conservation are increasingly concerned, the optimization of the bus driving process has become a valuable topic.

Setting a certain amount of slack for bus driving is a common way to adjust the pace of the bus to meet the schedule. In this way, the bus will face a situation where slack is useless. Many methods are used to control the driving process of buses. The classic approach involves setting a station as control point so that the bus can stay at the station for a period of time [7]. It is true that this intentional deceleration will slow down the entire driving process. But this approach does allow most buses to reach control point according to schedule.

The pursuit of efficiency makes it impossible to set slack too much. And this kind of setting cannot deal with unexpected events during driving, such as traffic accidents on the route or sudden natural disasters. Some studies take these conditions into consideration and introduce different modes of driving with failure of schedule. Given the concept of forward headway, which is the distance between current bus and the bus in front, some research study how long the bus is held based on the forward headway [3]. Another research concerns the backward headway between current bus and the behind one [5]. There are also some related papers that combine the two headway to consider, such as [4,8].

Transit signal priority (TSP) is a means used to speed up the process of public transport. Since it is difficult for a bus to recover from a late arrival by itself, TSP is an effective method to assist the bus to recover to the schedule. When the bus calls for TSP, the traffic lights will help it continue driving without stopping and waiting for the red light to end. While TSP is effective for buses, it will inevitably have a certain impact on traffic. Therefore, reducing the impact of TSP on the transportation system has also received attention. One idea is to use TSP only when the bus is late to a certain extent, in order to reduce the negative impact of TSP on the transportation system [6]. And the conception is called conditional signal priority (CSP). Other studies, such as [2], not only consider the application of CSP to request traffic signal priority to speed up the bus, but also use CSP to slow down the early bus by adding additional red lights. But the latter behavior can also be replaced by letting the bus stay at the station for a period of time, which seems to have a smaller impact on the transportation system. Anderson et al. [1] study the impact of CSP on bus reliability. Their research considered three situations, namely no holding, holding by schedule and holding by headways without schedule. Their results show that CSP can not only improve the speed of buses, but also improve the reliability of buses.

2 Problem Description and Assumptions

In this section, we analyze the driving mode of the bus according to the traffic signal priority request or without traffic signal priority request, and describe the process of the bus driving according to the CSP as an abstract process through a series of clear assumptions.

2.1 Problem Description

Suppose there is a bus driving on an infinitely long route. For example, the route of a bus is a loop, and there is enough power to drive more loops. In theory, the bus has two driving modes, one is driving at a relatively low speed V_u, and the other is driving at a relatively high speed V_c realized by requesting signal priority. The unit of speed here is km/s. In this study, we do not consider setting up any holding at stations, which means that high speed and low speed can be achieved by relying solely on the request signal light or not. Correspondingly, there are two kinds of average paces for buses, τ_u and τ_c (s/km). It can be known that $V_u = \frac{1}{\tau_u}$ and $V_c = \frac{1}{\tau_c}$. Obviously $\tau_u > \tau_c$. There is also a schedule-based pace called τ_s. In order for the schedule to be useful to the bus,

$$\tau_u > \tau_s > \tau_c,$$

otherwise the bus will not be able to achieve τ_s regardless of whether the bus is driving at a high speed or a low speed.

In order to prevent from requesting signal priority when the bus is slightly late, we artificially set a gap, namely δ. At the station x, if and only if the lateness caused by low speed is larger than δ, signal priority is requested and the bus switches to high speed. The requesting continues until lateness reached $-\delta$.

We ignore the influence between buses, including the trend of aggregation, so that we regard each bus as independent. When a bus wants to switch CSP, it can switch immediately, regardless of whether other buses need CSP. Suppose that distance between all adjacent stations is equal and each station is equipped with a traffic light. Furthermore, we assume that the entire driving process passes through an infinite number of stations, and the distance between each station is infinitely small. The entire bus driving process is therefore considered a continuous control process and distance x is assumed as continuous. Also, we ignore the time that the bus stops at the traffic lights and stations. Switching of CSP only affects the bus by switching the average pace of driving, that is, τ_u and τ_c.

The difference between actual arrival time and schedule is called lateness, written as $\varepsilon(x)$. The expectation of lateness per unit time is called drift, written as m. It is conceivable that if m is not 0, then as x increases, the absolute value of lateness drifts larger. If the traffic signal priority is not requested during the whole journey (NSP), the drift is m_u. If a traffic signal priority is requested (TSP), the drift is m_c. So the drift under NTP is

$$m_u = \tau_u - \tau_s > 0,$$

and the drift under TSP is

$$m_c = \tau_c - \tau_s < 0.$$

As mentioned earlier, the bus has only two driving modes, namely low speed $V_u = \frac{1}{\tau_u}$ and high speed $V_c = \frac{1}{\tau_c}$. When the bus departs from the departure station, if it is not the scenario that lateness is positive and greater than δ

which means $\varepsilon > 0$ and $\varepsilon = \delta$, the signal priority is not requested, that is, the CSP is negative. The bus is therefore running at a low speed V_u. With the assumption that x is continuous, the bus can immediately change its driving mode by switching CSP when it finds that the lateness is large enough. When the first occurrence of $\varepsilon > 0$ and ε is equal to the upper limit of lateness gap δ, a signal priority is requested, that is, CSP turns positive. CSP remains positive until the lateness of the bus is negative due to high-speed driving and its absolute value is greater than $-\delta$. That is, when $\varepsilon < 0$ and ε touches the lower limit of lateness gap $-\delta$, CSP turns negative. We call this duration between two CPS shifts a period. Until the next time $\varepsilon > 0$ and $\varepsilon = \delta$, repeat to request signal priority and the two periods occur alternately. If the scenario when the bus departs from the departure station is $\varepsilon > 0$ and $\varepsilon = \delta$, the bus starts with CSP positive and then acts the same as the former scenario. In both scenarios, the two periods occur the same number of times during a long journey.

2.2   Detail of Assumptions and Analysis

Based on the above analysis, the following assumptions are given.

Assumption 1: No holding at stations.
Assumption 2: The route that the bus travels is infinitely long with infinite number of stations.
Assumption 3: No influence between buses, which means that the bus is independent.
Assumption 4: Switching of CSP only affect the bus by switching the average pace of driving, that is, τ_u and τ_c.

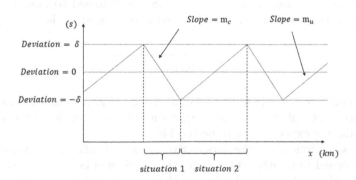

Fig. 1. Basic driving process of the bus with CSP

Although these assumptions represent a certain abstraction of reality, they also have practical significance. For example, Assumption 2 is derived from the fact that some buses return after reaching the destination without additional rest, and some buses travel in loop routes. Without Assumption 2, the analysis and modeling of buses under CSP will be difficult. Assumption 2 is also reflected in previous research [1]. With the assumptions, the basic driving process of the bus is shown in the figure. In the actual bus driving process, there will always be behaviors such as acceleration, deceleration and stopping. Here, straight lines are used to represent the average driving of the bus under two situations.

The distance of situation 1 that CSP is positive is

$$S_c = \frac{2\delta}{-m_c},$$

and duration time of situation 1 is

$$T_c = \frac{S_c}{V_c} = \frac{S_c}{1/\tau_c} = -\frac{2\delta\tau_c}{m_c}.$$

The distance of situation 2 that CSP is negative is

$$S_u = \frac{2\delta}{m_u},$$

and duration time of situation 2 is

$$T_u = \frac{S_u}{V_u} = \frac{S_u}{1/\tau_u} = \frac{2\delta\tau_u}{m_u}.$$

The duration time of a cycle of two situations is

$$T = T_c + T_u = -\frac{2\delta\tau_c}{m_c} + \frac{2\delta\tau_u}{m_u} = 2\delta\left(\frac{\tau_u}{m_u} - \frac{\tau_c}{m_c}\right).$$

Therefore, the number of times that CSP is switched to positive per unit time, that is, the frequency that CSP is switched to positive is

$$\omega = \frac{1}{T} = \frac{1}{2\delta\left(\frac{\tau_u}{m_u} - \frac{\tau_c}{m_c}\right)}.$$

In practice, from the customer's point of view, the customer hopes that the bus can arrive at stations on time so that the bus can provide better service. In other words, δ is expected not to be too big.

At the same time, from the perspective of entire traffic, if the frequency that CSP is switched to positive is too high, the traffic will be frequently disturbed, which is an abuse of signal priority. In other words, we hope ω is not too big.

The traffic managers also do not want the distance with CSP positive too long, which is also an abuse of traffic signal priority. On the other hand, too short distance with CSP positive is a waste of CSP resource. It is a parameter specified according to people's needs that the fraction of distance where CSP is positive on the route. Here we specify that the ideal fraction is $\frac{1}{2}$. The degree of deviation of the fraction from $\frac{1}{2}$ can be expressed by the following formula.

$$\rho = \left(\frac{S_c}{S_c + S_u} - \frac{1}{2} \right)^2 = \left(\frac{\frac{2\delta}{-m_c}}{\frac{2\delta}{-m_c} + \frac{2\delta}{m_u}} - \frac{1}{2} \right)^2$$

$$= \left(\frac{m_u}{m_u - m_c} - \frac{1}{2} \right)^2 = \left(\frac{m_u + m_c}{2(m_u - m_c)} \right)^2$$

The form of the quadratic function makes that the distance of CSP positive deviate more from $\frac{1}{2}$, the more obvious the penalty is.

Based on the above analysis, the goal we need to optimize is the combination of lateness gap δ, the frequency of CSP is switched to positive ω, and the fraction of distance where CSP is positive. Here, we set the objective function as the weighted sum of the three as below.

$$F = \alpha\delta + \beta\omega + \gamma\rho$$

$$= \alpha\delta + \frac{\beta}{2\left(\frac{\tau_u}{m_u} - \frac{\tau_c}{m_c} \right)} \frac{1}{\delta} + \gamma\left(\frac{m_u + m_c}{2(m_u - m_c)} \right)^2$$

$$= \alpha\delta + \frac{\beta}{2\left(\frac{\tau_u}{\tau_u - \tau_s} - \frac{\tau_c}{\tau_c - \tau_s} \right)} \frac{1}{\delta} + \gamma\left(\frac{\tau_u + \tau_c - 2\tau_s}{2(\tau_u - \tau_c)} \right)^2$$

The whole problem can be described as

$$\min_{\delta,\tau_s} \quad F = \alpha\delta + \frac{\beta}{2\left(\frac{\tau_u}{\tau_u - \tau_s} - \frac{\tau_c}{\tau_c - \tau_s} \right)} \frac{1}{\delta} + \gamma\left(\frac{\tau_u + \tau_c - 2\tau_s}{2(\tau_u - \tau_c)} \right)^2$$

$$\text{s.t.} \quad \delta > 0,$$
$$\tau_c < \tau_s < \tau_u. \tag{1}$$

Here we use three parameters α, β and γ to control the weights of θ, ω and ρ, and all three parameters are positive. It is worth mentioning that since θ, ω and ρ have different units respectively, the three parameters α, β and γ may have different orders of magnitude. The specific value of each parameter needs to be determined according to the specific situation.

3   Analysis and Solution of the Optimization Problem

We can find the first partial derivative of F with respect to δ as follows.

$$\frac{\partial F}{\partial \delta} = \theta - \frac{1 - \theta}{2\left(\frac{\tau_u}{\tau_u - \tau_s} - \frac{\tau_c}{\tau_c - \tau_s} \right)} \frac{1}{\delta^2}$$

The second partial derivative of F with respect to δ is

$$\frac{\partial^2 F}{\partial \delta^2} = \frac{\partial}{\partial \delta}\left(\frac{\partial F}{\partial \delta} \right) = \frac{1 - \theta}{\frac{\tau_u}{\tau_u - \tau_s} - \frac{\tau_c}{\tau_c - \tau_s}} \frac{2}{\delta^3}.$$

According to these two preconditions that $0 < \theta < 1$, $\delta > 0$ and $\frac{\tau_u}{\tau_u - \tau_s} - \frac{\tau_c}{\tau_c - \tau_s} > 0$, it always exists that $\frac{\partial^2 F}{\partial \delta^2} > 0$. That is to say, $\delta = \sqrt{\dfrac{1-\theta}{2\theta\left(\frac{\tau_u}{\tau_u - \tau_s} - \frac{\tau_c}{\tau_c - \tau_s}\right)}}$ is the only minimum for F.

$\frac{\partial F}{\partial \tau_s}$ can be calculated as

$$
\begin{aligned}
\frac{\partial F}{\partial \tau_s} &= -\frac{\beta}{2\left(\frac{\tau_u}{\tau_u - \tau_s} - \frac{\tau_c}{\tau_c - \tau_s}\right)^2} \frac{1}{\delta} \frac{\partial}{\partial \tau_s}\left(\frac{\tau_u}{\tau_u - \tau_s} - \frac{\tau_c}{\tau_c - \tau_s}\right) + \gamma \frac{2\tau_s - \tau_u - \tau_c}{(\tau_u - \tau_c)^2} \\
&= -\frac{\beta}{2\delta} \frac{1}{\left(\frac{\tau_s(\tau_c - \tau_u)}{(\tau_u - \tau_s)(\tau_c - \tau_s)}\right)^2}\left(\frac{\tau_u}{(\tau_u - \tau_s)^2} - \frac{\tau_c}{(\tau_c - \tau_s)^2}\right) + \gamma \frac{2\tau_s - \tau_u - \tau_c}{(\tau_u - \tau_c)^2} \\
&= -\frac{\beta}{2\delta} \frac{\tau_u(\tau_c - \tau_s)^2 - \tau_c(\tau_u - \tau_s)^2}{\tau_s^2(\tau_c - \tau_u)^2} + \gamma \frac{2\tau_s - \tau_u - \tau_c}{(\tau_u - \tau_c)^2}.
\end{aligned}
$$

Since the partial derivative of F with respect to τ_u has a complicated form, we use the YALMIP solver to find its numerical solution.

Here we set the values of the parameters as $\alpha = 1$, $\beta = 10000$ and $\gamma = 200$. And we set $\tau_c = 90\,\text{s/km}$ and $\tau_u = 144\,\text{s/km}$ that correspond to the speed of $40\,\text{km/h}$ and $25\,\text{km/h}$. The best delta is $23.6182\,\text{s}$ and the best τ_s is $119.7508\,\text{s/km}$. F is 47.7554 according to them. In order to speed up the solving process, we change the constraints in Eq. (1) to the following three constraints.

$$
\begin{cases}
1 \le \delta \le 1000 \\
\tau_s \ge \tau_c + 1 \\
\tau_s \le \tau_u - 1
\end{cases}
$$

These three constraints are used to replace the original strict inequality constraints to make the solver easier to run. At the same time, although we have restricted δ, given that the two limit values, namely $1\,\text{s}$ and $1000\,\text{s}$, are too small or too large to appear in practical applications. The restriction on τ_s is also in line with our expectation that the journey with CSP positive will not be too close to τ_u or τ_c.

Our analysis and constraints processing are enlightening, and the results obtained can also reflect certain physical meaning and application value. The lateness gap from tens to hundreds of seconds is reasonable for buses. That is, it will not deviate too much from the schedule to affect the satisfaction of passengers, and it can also make the bus not need to request signal priority too frequently. The reasonable value of τ_u also effectively controls the proportion of the distance of the request signal priority within a reasonable range.

This result can be further improved by more information about real bus conditions and more adjustments to the above parameters.

4   Conclusion

The non-punctuality of buses has always been a phenomenon that the industry and academia are trying to change. In order to allow buses to execute schedules more stably, schedule designers usually add some slack to schedules. This results in buses sometimes having to wait at the station or slow down while driving. But this approach does not make the bus fully implement the schedule. Transit signal priority (TSP) and its conditional form CSP are invented to accelerate the bus in its driving process.

There is still room for further improvement in the mathematical description of the process of bus driving in accordance with the CSP. In this article, we describe this process in detail. We describe the process of bus driving according to CSP as a continuous control process through a series of assumptions, and establish our bus driving process model. These assumptions can be useful to the basis for future researchers. We analyze the process of bus acceleration due to CSP positive and the process of deceleration due to CSP negative, and describe the process of bus driving as alternating acceleration and deceleration. Through analysis, we have obtained the period and frequency of the bus switching driving state. Then an objective function that takes into account gap of lateness, frequency of switching and the fraction of distance where CSP is positive is established. Through mathematical analysis and numerical solution, we verified the feasibility of the model.

Future work includes improving the expression of different parts of the objective function to better serve practical applications, and introducing other bus driving indicators that people pay attention to in the objective function.

Acknowledgement. This work was supported by the National Natural Science Foundation of China (NSFC) under Grants 72021002, 71972146, 71771048, 71432007, 71832001 and 72071144.

References

1. Anderson, P., Daganzo, C.F., Mannering, F.: Effect of transit signal priority on bus service reliability. Transp. Res. Part B Method. **132**, 2–14 (2020)
2. Chow, A.H.F., Li, S., Zhong, R.: Multi-objective optimal control formulations for bus service reliability with traffic signals. Transp. Res. Part B Method. **103**, 248–268 (2017)
3. Daganzo, C.: A headway-based approach to eliminate bus bunching. Transp. Res. Part B Method. **43**(10), 913–921 (2009)
4. Daganzo, C.F., Pilachowski, J.: Reducing bunching with bus-to-bus cooperation. Transp. Res. Part B Method. **45**(1), 267–277 (2011)
5. Iii, J., Eisenstein, D.D.: A self-cordinating bus route to resist bus bunching. Transp. Res. Part B **46**(4), 481–491 (2012)
6. Janos, M., Furth, P.: Bus priority with highly interruptible traffic signal control: simulation of san juans avenida ponce de leon. Transp. Res. Rec. J. Transp. Res. Board **1811**, 157–165 (2002)
7. Newell, G.F.: Unstable Brownian motion of a bus trip. In: Landman, U. (eds.) Statistical Mechanics and Statistical Methods in Theory and Application. Springer, Boston (1977). https://doi.org/10.1007/978-1-4613-4166-6_28
8. Xuan, Y., Argote, J., Daganzo, C.: Dynamic bus holding strategies for schedule reliability: optimal linear control and performance analysis. Transp. Res. Part B Method. **45**(10), 1831–1845 (2011)

Charging Scheduling Optimization of Battery Electric Bus with Controllable Task Completion

Feifeng Zheng[1], Zhixin Wang[1], Yinfeng Xu[1], and Ming Liu[2(✉)]

[1] Glorious Sun School of Business and Management, Donghua University, Shanghai 200051, China
[2] School of Economics and Management, Tongji University, Shanghai 200092, China
mingliu@tongji.edu.cn

Abstract. In order to reduce carbon emissions, various government organizations have taken measures to promote the development of the electric vehicle industry. Motivated by scheduling practices, this work proposes a battery electric bus (BEB) charging scheduling problem. Different from the existing research on scheduling, the completion level of each task in this problem is controllable, because the charging level of BEB can be controlled. Besides, for saving charging cost, bus companies usually charge their battery electric buses (BEBs) at night. Because of the concentration of charging time, the decision-maker must make charging scheduling decision under a departure schedule to ensure charging with no delay. For solving this problem, we first establish a mixed integer linear programming model with the aim of minimising the total electricity cost and battery loss cost. Numerical experiments demonstrate the electiveness of the proposed model.

Keywords: Scheduling · Optimization · Bus charging · State of charge · Battery loss cost

1 Introduce

With the rapid development of the world economy and the excessive development of natural resources, the energy crisis and the deterioration of the ecological environment have become a focal topic (Ibarra-Rojas et al. 2015; Mahmoud et al. 2016). As the dominant position of petroleum energy consumption and greenhouse gas emissions, traditional fuel vehicles are facing revolutionary changes. In the long run, new energy vehicles will become the main direction of the future development of the automobile industry (Lajunen 2014; Nurhadi et al. 2014; Liu

---

This work was supported by the National Natural Science Foundation of China (Grant No. 71771048, 71832001, 72021002, 71972146 and 72071144) and the Fundamental Research Funds for the Central Universities (Grant No. 2232018H-07).

A. Dolgui et al. (Eds.): APMS 2021, IFIP AICT 632, pp. 282–289, 2021.
https://doi.org/10.1007/978-3-030-85906-0_32

and Song 2017; Grande Yahyaoui and Gómez 2018). In recent years, many countries and regions have issued policies to promote the development of new energy vehicles. Especially battery electric buses (BEBs) are the main way to improve environmental quality and promote people's green travel (Wesseling 2016; Hao et al. 2014).

Due to many advantages of BEBs, their number has increased rapidly. However, the construction speed of charging piles is slow, and the problem of insufficient charging resources is prominent. Under the premise of the limited resources available, a reasonable BEB charging scheduling can effectively solve this problem (Rogge et al. 2018; He et al. 2020; Abdelwahed et al. 2020). In this work, we describe the process of BEB charging as a parallel machine problem that controllable task completion level. As an important means to optimize industrial resource allocation and promote industrial structure upgrading, parallel machine scheduling theory can improve the competitiveness of enterprises (Liu et al. 2012; Zheng et al. 2013; Karhi and Shabtay 2017; Aschauer et al. 2020). We combined the parallel machine scheduling theory to establish a BEB charging scheduling model with a controllable task completion level. In our mathematical model, the task completion level is regarded as a variable to be decided. The current research on BEBs mainly concentrates on the fields of charging site selection, charging resource optimization and allocation, and there are relatively few studies on bus charging scheduling (Kang et al. 2016; He et al. 2020). And our research is mainly devoted to the formulation of a charging scheduling plan, the purpose is to save the cost of charging and battery loss. In addition, the model incorporates the cost of battery loss into the minimization goal, and explores the charging scheduling plan for BEBs.

The remainder of this paper is organized as follows. In Sect. 2, we describe the problem. In Sect. 3, we establish a mixed integer linear programming model. In Sect. 4, we have verified the applicability of the model through a case study. In Sect. 5, gives the conclusion.

2   Problem Description

In this part, we introduce the concept of BEB charging with a controllable task completion level. The controllable task completion level means the BEBs charging level can be controlled, and the BEB departure time and residual state of charge (SOC) will affect its charging level decision. When the BEB starts to charge, the residual SOC of the battery is known. There are $|\mathcal{M}|$ ($\mathcal{M}$ is charging pile set) can be used to serve $|\mathcal{J}|$ ($\mathcal{J}$ is BEB set) BEBs. For the convenience of calculation, we use a charging level set $\mathcal{B} = \{1, 2, \cdots, |\mathcal{B}|\}$ to replace the charging power quantity set $Q = \{1\%, 2\%, \cdots, |Q|\%\}$. In details, charging level 1 denotes 1% of the battery capacity is charged. Once a BEB arrives at the charging depot, its remaining SOC a_j is known. We define H_j as the actual SOC of BEB j after charging activity. The controllable task completion degree in this work means that the charging level of each BEB is controllable. Figure 1 describes the controllable task completion degree. Notice that the red bracket part in Fig. 1 denotes the controllable charging interval, while the green part means the actual charging level.

In practice, a safe remaining SOC is usually set to ensure battery health of each BEB. If the remaining SOC of a BEB less than its safe remaining SOC, it is unavailable. In the actual operation process, such a safe remaining SOC usually set as 20% of the battery capacity. Under the given the fixed bus schedules, we make a reasonable assumption that the departure time, arrival time and driving route of each BEB are fixed and known before charging activity. Hence, the lower SOC limits l_j of BEB $j \in \mathcal{J}$ to meet a day's operation is known. Besides, for reducing the damage to the battery caused by overcharging and over-discharging, BEB $j \in \mathcal{J}$ is set with an optimal SOC, i.e., $\bar{H}_j$. If $H_j > \bar{H}_j$, there is a overcharging risk. While $H_j < \bar{H}_j$, it may cause the battery's discharge depth to be too deep the next day, thus, there is a over-discharge risk. Therefore, the closer the SOC after charging activity is to $\bar{H}_j$, the lower the loss of the battery.

In addition, this research is also based on the following assumptions:

1. Only one charging depot is available to satisfy the charging demand of BEBs.
2. Each BEB has a fixed departure time.
3. The type of charging pile are the same, that is to say, the charging powers are the same and known before charging activity.
4. All BEBs are homogeneous and have the same cruising range.
5. The charging rate of all charging piles is the same, and the charging process is continuous.

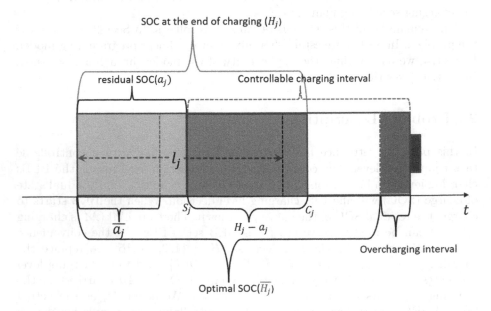

Fig. 1. Charging process of BEB with controllable task completion (Color figure online)

3 Model Formulation

In this work, we assume that only one charging depot is available to satisfy the charging demand of BEBs. Under the given the fixed bus schedules, we make a reasonable assumption that the departure time, arrival time and driving route of each BEB are fixed and known before charging.

Below we first present other basic parameters and decision variables, and then establish a mixed integer linear programming model.

Parameters	
$\mathcal{M}$:	Set of charging piles indexed by i, i.e., $i \in M = \{1, 2, \ldots, \|\mathcal{M}\|\}$
$\mathcal{J}$:	Set of BEBs index j, i.e., $j \in J = \{1, 2, \ldots, |\mathcal{J}|\}$
$\mathcal{B}$:	Set of charging level indexed b, $b \subset B = \{1, 2, \ldots, |\mathcal{B}|\}$
a_j :	Initial sate of charge (SOC) of BEB $j \subset \mathcal{J}$
l_j :	The lower limit of the SOC of the BEB $j \in \mathcal{J}$ after charging
r_j :	Arrival time of BEB $j \in \mathcal{J}$
d_j :	Departure time of BEB $j \in \mathcal{J}$
c :	Unit electricity price
$\bar{a}_j$:	The lower limit of SOC before charging activity
$\bar{H}_j$:	The optimal SOC $j \in \mathcal{J}$
λ :	The penalty coefficient for overcharging and over-discharging
τ_b :	The charging time spent when charged to level b
L :	A sufficiently large positive real number
Variables	
S_j :	Charging start time of BEB $j \in \mathcal{J}$
C_j :	Charging end time of BEB $j \in \mathcal{J}$
p_j :	The charging time of BEB $j \in \mathcal{J}$
H_j :	The actual SOC at the end of charging activity
z_{jb} :	A binary variable equal to 1 if the BEB $j \in \mathcal{J}$ is charged to level $b \in \mathcal{B}$, 0 otherwise
x_{ij} :	A binary variable equal to 1 if BEB $j \in \mathcal{J}$ is assigned to charging pile $i \in \mathcal{M}$, 0 otherwise
$y_{jj'}^i$:	A binary variable equal to 1 if both BEBs $j \in \mathcal{J}$ and $j' \in \mathcal{J}\{j\}$ are charged on the charging pile i and j is charged before j', and, 0 otherwise

The complete model is provided in (1)–(15):

$$min \sum_{j \in \mathcal{J}} \sum_{b \in \mathcal{B}} c \cdot \tau_b \cdot z_{jb} + \sum_{j \in \mathcal{J}} \lambda \cdot |H_j - \bar{H}_j| \qquad (1)$$

Subject to:

$$\sum_{i \in \mathcal{M}} x_{i,j} \leq 1 \quad \forall j \in \mathcal{J} \qquad (2)$$

$$H_j \geq l_j \quad \forall j \in \mathcal{J} \tag{3}$$

$$H_j = a_j + \sum_{b \in \mathcal{B}} b \cdot z_{jb} \quad \forall j \in \mathcal{J} \tag{4}$$

$$x_{ij} + x_{ij'} \geq 2 - L(1 - y_{jj'}^i) \quad \forall i \in \mathcal{M}, \quad \forall j, j' \in \mathcal{J}, \quad j \neq j' \tag{5}$$

$$\sum_{i \in \mathcal{M}} (y_{jj'}^i + y_{j'j}^i) \leq 1 \quad \forall j, j' \in \mathcal{J}, \quad j \neq j' \tag{6}$$

$$S_j \geq C_{j'} - L(1 - \sum_{i \in \mathcal{M}} y_{jj'}^i) \quad \forall j, j' \in \mathcal{J}, \quad j \neq j' \tag{7}$$

$$C_j = p_j + S_j \quad \forall j \in \mathcal{J} \tag{8}$$

$$p_j = \sum_{b \in \mathcal{B}} \tau_b \cdot z_{jb} \quad \forall j \in \mathcal{J} \tag{9}$$

$$\sum_{b \in \mathcal{B}} z_{jb} = \sum_{i \in \mathcal{M}} x_{i,j} \quad \forall j \in \mathcal{J} \tag{10}$$

$$\sum_{b \in \mathcal{B}} z_{jb} \leq 1 \quad \forall j \in \mathcal{J} \tag{11}$$

$$C_j \leq d_j \quad \forall j \in \mathcal{J} \tag{12}$$

$$S_j > r_j \quad \forall j \in \mathcal{J} \tag{13}$$

$$z_{jb}, x_{ij}, y_{jj'}^i \in \{0, 1\} \quad \forall i \in \mathcal{M} \quad \forall j, j' \in \mathcal{J} \quad \forall b \in \mathcal{B} \quad j \neq j' \tag{14}$$

$$s_j, c_j, p_j \in \mathbb{Z}^+ \quad \forall j \in \mathcal{J} \tag{15}$$

Formula (1) is to minimize the total charging cost. Constraint (2) denotes that each BEB can only be assigned to a certain charging pile. Constraint (3) ensures that the SOC of BEB $j \in \mathcal{J}$ after charging activity is not less than the power required for BEB $j \in \mathcal{J}$ to complete a day's operation. Constraint (4) calculates the SOC of the battery after charging activity. Constraints (5) and (6) define $y_{jj'}^i$, which means that if both buses $j \in \mathcal{J}$ and $j' \in \mathcal{J}$ are charged on the same charging pile $i \in \mathcal{M}$, bus j is charged before j'. Constraints (7)–(9) calculate the charging start time S_j, charging completion time C_j, as well as charging time p_j of each BEB $j \in \mathcal{J}$. Constraints (10) and (11) guarantee that each BEB can only be charged to a certain level. Constraint (12) and (13) express the constraints of charging start time and completion time. Constraints (14) and (15) give the value range of decision variables.

4   Case Study

For demonstrating the effectiveness of the proposed mixed integer linear programming, we apply it to solve a case study, i.e., the transit sub-network in the city of Shanghai, China.

4.1 Sub-network Description and Data Preparation

We select a certain bus sub-network in the Shanghai area for analysis. This bus sub-network includes one charging depot and 6 bus lines. For ease of expression, bus lines are defined Line1 to Line6, and all bus lines are loop lines. The bus departs from a terminal station and returns to the starting point after a round detour. The bus sub-network is equip with BYD K9 BEBs. This type of BEB has a cruising range of up to 350 km, and the battery can be reused more than 4000 times.

In this bus sub-network, the bus company arranges the number of buses according to the length of each line. In the same bus route, the time interval between adjacent flights is 5 min. the travel time between two bus stops is 5 min. In the same bus, the interval between the arrival time of the previous flight and the start time of the next flight is 20 min. The real data is shown in Table 1:

Table 1. Basic information of each bus line

Bus line	Bus stops	Temiral	Mileage	Number of BEBs	Number of tasks per BEB
Line 1	11	2	16.9 km	17	11
Line 2	14	3	22.1 km	21	9
Line 3	12	2	18.2 km	18	10
Line 4	11	1	15.6 km	16	12
Line 5	9	2	14,3 km	15	13
Line 6	9	2	14.3 km	15	13

Table 1 shows the basic operation information of buses on different lines. For example, on bus line 1, there are 11 bus stops and two terminal stations, the total length is 16.9 km. There are 17 buses operating together on this bus Line, each bus needs to perform 11 flights of transportation tasks, and the daily mileage is 185.9 km.

4.2 Parameter Setting and Numerical Experiment

Assigning values to the involved parameters according to the actual operating conditions of the BEB. In order to protect the battery of the BEB, the bus will set a minimum SOC requirement when it leaves the factory, the general setting value is 20%, so we set $\bar{a}_j = 20$; We set the minimum SOC based on the average daily mileage of the BEB. Through calculation, after the charging activity, the minimum SOC of the BEBs of line 1 to line 6 are set to 75%, 78%, 77%, 78%, 78%, and 76%, respectively. According to the physical properties of the battery, when the SOC reaches 90%, the battery loss is minimal, so it is the optimal SOC. The rated power of all charging piles in this charging depot is $60kw$, and the battery capacity of the BEB is $600Ah$.

The charging depot serves 102 BEBs, and there are 30 charging piles in common. BEB earliest start time is 5:30, the latest end time is 22:35. For ease of description, we let 5:30 as the starting point discretize one day into 288 time intervals, with every five minutes as an interval. The proposed model was programmed in Matlab R2018a and solved by using the commercial solver CPLEX 12.4. All numerical experiments were run on a Surface book with 8 GB of RAM and 4.0 GHz of CPU under a Windows 10 environment.

Table 2. Numerical experiment results

Line	$a_j(\%)$	$p_j(h)$	$H_j(\%)$	$\tau_b \cdot z_{jb}$	$\lambda \cdot |H_j - \bar{H}_j|$	obj
Line 1	25%	2.190	86%	131.40	136	2369.80
Line 2	27%	2.088	85%	125.28	210	2840.88
Line 3	30%	2.052	87%	123.12	108	2324.16
Line 4	25%	2.124	84%	127.44	192	2231.04
Line 5	36%	2.160	86%	129.60	120	2064.00
Line 6	27%	2,160	87%	129.60	90	2034.00
Total	-	-	-	-	-	13863.88

The problem is solved in 13 min. The results are shown in Table 2. Since the BEBs on the same route have the same transportation tasks and mileage, the charging quantity and charging time after the decision is the same. The total cost of charging for the bus sub-network is 13,863.88 RMB, which is 4.35% lower than the average daily charging cost before the decision. At present, bus companies do not take into account the battery loss cost when calculating the charging cost. Therefore, the true ratio is higher than 4.35%.

5   Conclusion

In this work, we study a BEB charging scheduling model with a controllable task completion degree. This model combines the physical properties of the power battery, taking into account the impact of overcharge and over-discharge on battery loss, and incorporates the cost of battery loss into the model's minimization goal. In addition, the applicability of the model is verified by numerical experiments. However, the current solution method consumes a long calculation time, and it is even more unsolvable for large-scale multi-network problems. Therefore, our next step is to develop efficient algorithms for this problem to solve large-scale problems.

References

Ibarra-Rojas, O.J., Delgado, F., Giesen, R., Muñoz, J.C.: Planning, operation, and control of bus transport systems: a literature review. Transp. Res. Part B **77**, 38–75 (2015)

Mahmoud, M., Garnett, R., Ferguson, M., Kanaroglou, P.: Electric buses: a review of alternative powertrains. Renew. Sustain. Energy Rev. **62**, 673–684 (2016)

Lajunen, A.: Energy consumption and cost-benefit analysis of hybrid and electric city buses. Transp. Res. Part C Emerg. Technol. **38**, 1–15 (2014)

Nurhadi, L., Borén, S., Ny, H.: A sensitivity analysis of total cost of ownership for electric public bus transport systems in Swedish medium sized cities. Transp. Res. Procedia **3**, 818–827 (2014)

Liu, Z., Song, Z.: Robust planning of dynamic wireless charging infrastructure for BEBs. Transp. Res. Part C Emerg. Technol. **83**, 77–103 (2017)

Grande, L.S.A., Yahyaoui, I., Gómez, S.A.: Energetic, economic and environmental viability of off-grid PV-BESS for charging electric vehicles: case study of Spain. Sustain. Cities Soc. **37**, 519–529 (2018)

Wesseling, J.H.: Explaining variance in national electric vehicle policies. Environ. Innov. Soc. Transitions **21**, 28–38 (2016)

Hao, H., Ou, X., Du, J., Wang, H., Ouyang, M.: China's electric vehicle subsidy scheme: rationale and impacts. Energy Policy **73**, 722–732 (2014)

Rogge, M., van der Hurk, E., Larsen, A., Sauer, D.U.: Electric bus fleet size and mix problem with optimization of charging infrastructure. Appl. Energy **211**, 282–295 (2018)

Abdelwahed, A., van den Berg, P.L., Brandt, T., Collins, J., Ketter, W.: Evaluating and optimizing opportunity fast-charging schedules in transit battery electric bus networks. Transp. Sci. **54**(6), 1439–1731 (2020). https://doi.org/10.1287/trsc.2020.0982

Liu, M., Zheng, F., Chu, C., Xu, Y.: Single-machine scheduling with past-sequence-dependent delivery times and release times. Inf. Process. Lett. **112**(21), 835–838 (2012)

Zheng, F., Cheng, Y., Liu, M., Xu, Y.: Online interval scheduling on a single machine with finite lookahead. Comput. Oper. Res. **40**(1), 180–191 (2013)

Karhi, S., Shabtay, D.: Single machine scheduling to minimise resource consumption cost with a bound on scheduling plus due date assignment penalties. Int. J. Prod. Res. **56**(9), 3080–3096 (2017)

Aschauer, A., Roetzer, F., Steinboeck, A., Kugi, A.: Efficient scheduling of a stochastic no-wait job shop with controllable processing times. Expert Syst. Appl. **162**, 113879 (2020). https://doi.org/10.1016/j.eswa.2020.113879

Kang, Q., Wang, J., Zhou, M., Ammari, A.C.: Centralized charging strategy and scheduling algorithm for electric vehicles under a battery swapping scenario. IEEE Trans. Intell. Transp. Syst. **17**(3), 659–669 (2016)

He, Y., Liu, Z., Song, Z.: Optimal charging scheduling and management for a fast-charging BEB system. Transp. Res. Part E Logistics Transp. Rev. (2020). https://doi.org/10.1016/j.tre.2020.102056

Research on the O2O Takeout Orders Merger and Routing Optimization

Wenjie Wang$^{(\boxtimes)}$, Xue Xia, Lei Xie, Li Jiang, and Yangyun Song

Glorious Sun School of Business and Management, Donghua University,
Shanghai 200051, China
wenjiew@dhu.edu.cn

Abstract. Delivery service of O2O takeout platforms requests the high timeliness, which frequently results in explosive orders during peak period. Because the order must be completed delivery during committed service time, the orders merger and delivery routing optimization are essential to O2O takeout delivery service. Taking into consideration the amount of the different order locations, this paper studies the order delivery with the closest pickup distance principle in O2O takeout platform. Firstly, we use the K-means algorithm to cluster and merge the orders. Secondly, due to the strictly time constraints of real-time order, we propose the delivery routing optimization model of order cluster with soft time window, and which can be solved with simulated annealing algorithm. Finally, using the actual delivery data of O2O takeout platform, we further demonstrate the orders merger and delivery routing optimization mode we proposed with Python.

Keywords: O2O takeout real time delivery · Cluster analysis · Soft time window · Delivery routing optimization · Simulated annealing algorithm

1 Introduction

Motivated by Internet and e-commerce, O2O (Online To Offline) takeout delivery platform has shaped a new service mode of takeout ordering and delivery, which influences consumers' eating habits. By the end of 2018, there are 358 million users choosing O2O takeout platform of China, after that, the development of takeout delivery has entered a stable growth period [1]. Meanwhile, the timeliness becomes a large challenge with the accelerating social pace. Furthermore, O2O takeout platform usually faces the huge orders issue in peak period. For example, during peak period of Eleme takeout delivery platform, the quantity of real-time orders per second can reach 20000. Also, different from the traditional commodity logistics

Supported by the key project of the National Natural Science Foundation of China (Grant No. 71832001) and project of the National Natural Science Foundation of China (Grant No. 71872038).

delivery network, there not exists the fixed delivery center in O2O takeout delivery platform, it means that the pickup and delivery location of each takeout order are generally non-fixing [2]. Because of the huge orders quantity in peak period and the non-fixed location of the pickup and delivery in O2O takeout platform, they bring great challenge to the delivery service optimization. Thus, this paper studies the delivery routing optimization problem (VRP) in O2O platform, based on the orders merger in peak and the non-fixed pickup and delivery location, aiming at reducing the order delivery time. The study has vital theoretical significance and practical value for the service management optimization of O2O takeout delivery platform.

The traditional logistics delivery vehicle routing problem (VRP) mainly studies the fixed delivery center location, which is not suitable for the real-time routing optimization problem of the O2O takeout delivery platform, due to its different delivery locations. For example, Clarke et al. [3] develop an iterative procedure that enables the rapid selection of an optimum or near-optimum route to find the optimum routing of a fleet of trucks of varying capacities from a central depot to a number of delivery points. Thus, on the basis of the related research, this paper adopts cluster analysis to merge orders of O2O takeout delivery platform, purposes to reduce the time cost of pickup orders under large orders quantity and different delivery locations in real-time delivery.

Delivery problem is noteworthy in the study, and many scholars have done a lot of research on this issue. Reference to reducing the time cost, Liu et al. [4] first propose a Crowdsourcing Dynamic Congestion Model, using the congestion model, he develop efficient algorithms for non-myopic adaptive routing to minimize the collective travel time of all vehicles in the entire transportation system. Dantzig et al. [5] find a way to assign stations to trucks in such a manner that station demands are satisfied and total mileage covered by the fleet is a minimum. Taking into account the multi-pickup and delivery problem with time windows, Naccache et al. [6] solve the problem exactly via branch-and-bound and heuristically developing a hybrid adaptive large neighborhood search with improvement operations. Muñoz-Carpintero et al. [7] present a methodology based on generic evolutionary algorithms to solve a dynamic pickup and delivery problem formulated under a hybrid predictive control approach, which consider different configurations of particle swarm optimization and genetic algorithms. Considering a family of time-dependent pickup and delivery problems with time windows, Sun et al. [8] propose an exact solution approach for solving problems from this family that is based upon branch and price. To achieve the global optimal order fulfillment performance, Zhang et al. [9] study the online integrated order picking and delivery problem for an O2O community supermarket, and the online algorithm A is established. Cherkesly et al. [10] propose models and algorithms for the pickup and delivery vehicle routing problem with time windows and multiple stacks, that is, two different branch-price-and-cut algorithms.

Taking into account the high timeliness of O2O takeout delivery platform, we establish the delivery routing optimization model of orders cluster and merger orders with soft time window, aiming at reduce the time cost of O2O takeout

orders. Furthermore, considering the complexity of NP-hard vehicle routing optimization model and the high timeliness requirement of O2O takeout delivery platform, we solve the model via simulated annealing algorithm. Finally, using the
actual delivery data of O2O takeout platform, we simulate the delivery routing
optimization model with clustering and merging orders.

2   Modelling

2.1   Problem Description

O2O takeout platform based on the Internet accepts the customer's takeout order
at any time, and distributes the order to deliverer in time. The distribution area of
deliverer is generally within a few kilometers. Different from the traditional commodity logistics distribution network, O2O takeout distribution problems generally have the following characteristics: 1) takeout order distribution is mostly takeout food, beverage and other fresh and perishable goods, which timeliness is very
strong, the delivery time is very high, takeout delivery must be delivered immediately within the prescribed time window. 2) O2O takeout orders have obvious
peak period, peak order burst, takeout platform needs to merge orders reasonably,
with limited capacity to meet the timely delivery of a large population of orders.
3) O2O takeout delivery often does not have a fixed distribution center, each O2O
takeout order delivery location is generally different, O2O takeout deliverer needs
to pickup goods in different delivery locations, and then give them to customers in
different delivery locations. After completing an order delivery task, the deliverer
goes directly to the next order cluster.

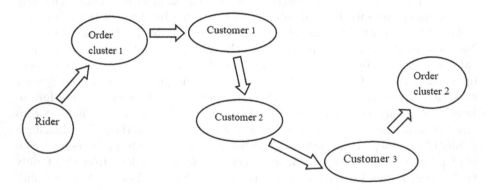

Fig. 1. A schematic diagram of the delivery O2O takeout order clustering and distribution process.

Aimed at the characteristics of high timeliness of O2O takeout order and
different location of distribution, based on clustering analysis and vehicle route
optimization theory, this paper studies the cluster merging of O2O takeout peak
explosive orders and the optimization of O2O takeout distribution route with soft
time window. O2O takeout order clustering and distribution process is shown in

Fig. 1. During the O2O takeout peak burst period, the takeout order is clustered and distributed. Then the combined order cluster is assigned to deliverer who is currently idle and close to the takeout order cluster. After receiving the order, according to the optimized route provided by the O2O takeout platform, multiple takeout orders in the order cluster are delivered to each customer on time. The specific delivery time window requirement for each O2O delivery order is $[E_i, F_i]$, E_i of which, express the earliest delivery time and F_i express the latest delivery time required for orders, delivery orders in advance or overtime will cause O2O takeout platform to produce a certain time penalty cost. As shown in Fig. 1, after picking up the goods at the order cluster 1, the delivery order is delivered to the customer 1 on time according to the optimized distribution route provided by the platform, then the customer 2, finally the customer 3. After completing the delivery of all customer orders in order cluster 1 on time, according to the assignment of the platform, the deliverer directly starts the new distribution task in order cluster 2.

2.2   Order Cluster Distribution Routing Optimization Model

O2O takeout instant delivery service has strict delivery time requirements, takeout orders must be delivered in accordance with the promised delivery time. Therefore, considering that O2O delivery order is not delivered on time will have a certain penalty cost, for the takeout customer time window constraints $[E_i, F_i]$, the distribution routing optimization model of takeout order merging cluster with soft time window is established. When establishing the model, we also consider the constraints of delivery point location of each takeout order and deliverer ability, optimize the distribution order of multiple orders in the order cluster after the takeout order is merged, and generate the optimal delivery route of the order cluster.

The number of orders contained in each order cluster after O2O takeout order clustering is m, regardless of the mileage limit of the takeout deliverer, assuming that the maximum delivery capacity Q^r by the takeout deliverer is r, the average delivery speed is v. The important time node of the instant delivery process of O2O takeout is shown in Fig. 2. After receiving the delivery task assigned by the platform, the deliverer starts with timing from its location, the time requires to arrive at the designated order cluster is recorded as t_w, the pickup time for each delivery order is t_q. t_{ij}^r represents the delivery time required from the delivery location of the order i in the order cluster to the delivery location of the order j by deliverer r. In particular, t_{01}^r represents the time required from the center of the order cluster to the delivery location of the first order. The production time of takeout goods is short, and the merchants can use the time that deliverers drive to the order cluster to prepare the meal. In this study, the time that deliverer waiting for the merchant to prepare the meal is ignored. After the takeout deliverer arrives at the customer's location and needs to wait for the customer to confirm the goods, then the order delivery process will finally end. The time t_s for the customer service is set up by the deliverer. Take an order as an example, The delivery completion time T_{0i}^r is equal to the sum of the time

t_w taken by the takeout deliverer to the pickup location, order cluster pickup time mt_q, delivery time t^r_{ij}, customer service time t_s. The unit time cost factor of the distribution process is u_{ij}. The soft time window indicates that if the requirement of time window $[E_i, F_i]$ is not satisfied by the delivery completion time of the order i, it will incur a penalty cost. Earlier than the earliest delivery time E_i, the corresponding waiting cost coefficient is λ_1, later than the latest delivery time F_i, the corresponding penalty cost coefficient is λ_2. At the same time, the decision variable x^r_{ij} is introduced to indicate that when the takeout deliverer r from the delivery location i to the delivery location j, the value is 1, otherwise the value is 0. The decision variable z^r_m indicates that when the takeout order i assigned to the deliverer r, value is 1, otherwise the value is 0.

Since there is no fixed distribution center for O2O takeout distribution, the constraint of returning the distribution vehicle to the distribution center is not considered when establishing the order cluster distribution routing optimization model with O2O takeout order clustering with soft time window. Taking minimizing the total delivery time cost of O2O takeout platform as the objective function f, the mathematical model of order cluster distribution routing optimization combined with O2O takeout order clustering with soft time window is shown below.

Objective function:

$$f = \min \left\{ \sum_{i,j=1}^{n} u_{ij} T^r_{0i} x^r_{ij} + \lambda_1 \sum_{i,j=1}^{n} \sum_{r=1}^{R} x^r_{ij} \max \left(E_i - T^r_{0i}, 0 \right) \right. \\ \left. + \lambda_2 \sum_{i,j=1}^{n} \sum_{r=1}^{R} x^r_{ij} \max \left(T^r_{0i} - F_i, 0 \right) \right\} \tag{1}$$

Constraints:

$$m \leq Q^r, \forall r \in R, m = 1, 2, 3... \tag{2}$$

$$T^r_{0i} = t_w + mt_q + t^r_{0(i-1)} + t^r_{(i-1)i} + t_s, m = 1, 2, 3..., i = 1, 2, 3... \tag{3}$$

$$\sum_{r=1}^{R} z^r_m = 1, \forall r \in R, m = 1, 2, 3... \tag{4}$$

$$\sum_{i=1}^{m} x^r_{ij} = \sum_{i=1}^{m} x^r_{ji}, \forall r \in R, j = 1, 2, 3... \tag{5}$$

$$\sum_{i=1}^{m} x^r_{ij} = 1, \forall r \in R, j = 1, 2, 3... \tag{6}$$

$$\sum_{j=1}^{m} x^r_{ij} = 1, \forall r \in R, i = 1, 2, 3... \tag{7}$$

$$x^r_{ij} = \{0, 1\}, \forall r \in R, i = 1, 2, 3..., j = 1, 2, 3... \tag{8}$$

$$z^r_m = \{0, 1\}, \forall r \in R, m = 1, 2, 3... \tag{9}$$

The objective function f in the model is the total delivery time cost of the O2O delivery platform (the first item is the delivery process time cost, the second is the waiting cost when earlier than the earliest delivery time, the third is the penalty cost when later than the latest delivery time) minimize, Constraint (2) indicates that the number of orders in the order cluster after the merger of the takeout order does not exceed the ability constraint of the takeout deliverer, Constraint (3) indicates the delivery arrival time of the delivery order i, that is, the time taken by the deliverer to pick up the goods, the time of delivery and customer service, Constraint (4) ensures that each order is assigned to only one deliverer, to avoid duplicate assignments, Constraint (5) requires the O2O takeout deliverer to leave for the next delivery location after arriving at one delivery location, Constraints (6), (7) indicate that the deliverer must visit each delivery location once during delivery, and only once to the delivery location, Constraints (8), (9) are the range of values of the introduced decision variables.

2.3   Orders Merger Based on K-Means Algorithm

In addition, as a result of O2O takeout platform in the urgent time window, on time, efficient, low-cost to complete a large population of orders instant delivery, is not easy. High order quantity and different delivery positions of different orders bring great complexity to O2O delivery problem. The deliverer needs to go to different pickup locations of different orders to pick up goods. If the different pickup locations of different orders assigned to the deliverer are far apart, it will obviously bring inconvenience to the deliverer, make takeout delivery instant difficult to meet, and increase delivery time cost. Therefore, this paper uses clustering analysis algorithm to combine a large population of orders to be delivered according to the principle of similar location of O2O takeout orders, so as to save the time cost of O2O takeout platform. The parameter a_i expresses the pickup location of takeout order i, such as a_1, a_2, a_3, as the locations of order 1, order 2, order 3, are close, these three orders can be grouped into a class of combined distribution. The pickup location a_4, a_5 of delivery order 4, order 5 are close, these two orders also can be grouped into a class of combined distribution. The pickup locations a_6, a_7, a_8, a_9, of delivery order 6, order 7, order 8, order 9 have close distance, the four orders are clustered into a class of combined distribution.

Taking into account the characteristics of the real-time delivery process of O2O takeout orders and the different order locations, the K-means algorithm is used to cluster and merge O2O takeout orders. K-means algorithm is a dynamic fast clustering method, which can combine order clustering into K clustering centers according to the minimum distance criterion. The objective function of merging O2O takeout order cluster is D, which means the minimum sum of the distance from the order cluster c_k to the center of the order cluster p_k, that is

$$\min D = \left\{ \sum_{k=1}^{K} \sum_{i \in c_k} d\left(a_i, p_k\right) \right\} \qquad (10)$$

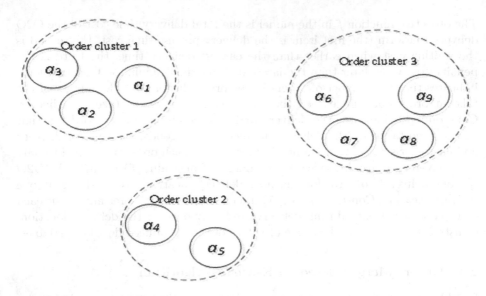

Fig. 2. Clustering and merging delivery orders according to the principle of close location.

After processing the merger and allocation of orders based on the K-means algorithm, then we got order clusters R, and deliverer r who is in charge of a designated order cluster. Based on these order clusters, algorithm is applied to the next order routing planning.

3   SA Algorithm and Simulation

Immediacy of O2O takeout distribution requires that the optimal route solving process must be fast and efficient. In this paper, aiming at the NP-hard characteristics of routing optimization problems, simulated annealing algorithm (Simulated Annealing, SA) is used to solve the mathematical model of O2O takeout clustering and order cluster distribution route optimization. Analog annealing algorithm is a random optimization algorithm based on Monte-Carlo iterative solution strategy, it has the characteristics of small influence of initial solution and strong global optimization ability.

Using python language programming to simulate the order cluster distribution optimization model of O2O takeout order clustering and merging, and we select 30 orders to be delivered at a certain time in a certain takeout platform. Takeout delivery time-consuming t_w from current location of the deliverer r to the designated order cluster, the average pickup time of each order in the order cluster is $t_q = 2$ min, average customer service time $t_s = 2$ min, average delivery speed $v = 10$ km/h, unit time delivery cost for delivery $u_{ij} = 1$, the penalty coefficient that does not meet the distribution time window $\lambda_1 = 2$, $\lambda_2 = 3$. Test data including pickup location for 30 orders a_i, corresponding delivery location b_i, 2D coordinates are used to the location $a_i(x_i, y_i)$, $b_i(x_i, y_i)$. Earliest delivery time

(E_i) of orders, latest delivery time (F_i), the distance between any two points is calculated by Euclidean distance.

Combined with the requirement of high timeliness and the scale of example of O2O delivery, the initial temperature of the simulated annealing algorithm is set to $T_0 = 1000$, termination temperature $T_{end} = 0.01$, the temperature attenuation rate $q = 0.9$, and the maximum number of iterations at the current temperature, that is, metropolis chain length $L = 100$. The simulated annealing algorithm is used to obtain the optimal solution of the five order cluster distribution routes of O2O takeout orders clustering and merging as shown in Table 1.

Table 1. Cluster route solution for delivery order.

Order clusters	Delivery orders in order clusters	Optimized delivery route
c_1	1, 10, 21, 22, 23, 24, 28, 29	10-24-22-1-23-21-29-28
c_2	4, 6, 7, 14, 15, 27	15-4-6-7-27-14
c_3	2, 3, 5, 12, 13, 20, 25, 30	5-13-12-25-20-3-2-30
c_4	9, 11, 17, 19	9-19-17-11
c_5	8, 16, 18, 26	8-16-18-26

According to the actual delivery time of each order in the order cluster, each order can be delivered in the specified time window, minimizing the total delivery time cost while ensuring the delivery order delivered on time, verified the feasibility and effectiveness of the order cluster distribution route optimization scheme based on O2O takeout order pickup location clustering and merging.

On the whole, the reasonable cluster and distribution of orders in the process of O2O takeout delivery can ensure that O2O takeout platform can meet the demand of a large population of orders and the demand of customer's delivery limitation with lower total delivery cost. Significantly, it improves the delivery efficiency of O2O delivery platform peak delivery order.

4   Conclusion

The time requirement of O2O takeout delivery service is strict, especially in the peak period of takeout order exploding, the order distribution can be completed quickly and on time, which can improve the customer satisfaction of takeout delivery service and improve the income of O2O takeout platform. To meet the immediate requirements of O2O takeout delivery and the situation of peak order explosion, the K-means clustering analysis method is used to cluster and merge the O2O takeout delivery orders according to the principle of similar location, in order to reduce the time cost of takeout delivery. The order cluster distribution routing optimization model of O2O takeout clustering with soft time window is further established, and the simulated annealing algorithm is used to solve the model to optimize the O2O delivery time cost. Numerical simulation results show that under the condition of meeting the constraints of delivery time window, the optimization effect of order cluster distribution route is ideal, which can ensure the immediate delivery of each order in the order cluster.

In the cluster analysis of O2O takeout orders, this paper mainly clusters and single according to the principle of similar location of delivery orders. Since the delivery locations of O2O takeout delivery orders are different, in the future research, we can consider the clustering and merging of orders and delivery locations at the same time to further improve the immediacy and punctuality of O2O takeout delivery, and reduce the total delivery time cost of the takeout platform. Moreover, for the real-time requirement of delivery scheduling of O2O takeout platform, designing fast heuristic algorithm will also be the research direction of operation optimization of O2O takeout platform.

References

1. Chinese online takeout industry development report 2018–2019. https://www.iimedia.cn/c400/64223.html. Accessed 4 Mar 2021
2. He, Z., Han, G., Cheng, T.C.E., Fan, B., Dong, J.: Evolutionary food quality and location strategies for restaurants in competitive online-to-offline food ordering and delivery markets: an agent-based approach. Int. J. Prod. Econ. **215**, 67–72 (2019)
3. Clarke, G., Wright, J.W.: Scheduling of vehicles from a central depot to a number of delivery points. Oper. Res. **12**(4), 568–581 (1964)
4. Liu, S., Qu, Q.: Dynamic collective routing using crowdsourcing data. Transp. Res. Part B: Methodol. **93**, 450–469 (2016)
5. Dantzig, G.B., Ramser, J.H.: The truck dispatching problem. Manage. Sci. **5**(1), 80–91 (1959)
6. Naccache, S., Côté, J., Coelho, L.C.: The multi-pickup and delivery problem with time windows. Eur. J. Oper. Res. **269**(1), 353–362 (2018)
7. Muñoz-Carpintero, D., Sáez, D., Cortés, C.E., Núñez, A.: A methodology based on evolutionary algorithms to solve a dynamic pickup and delivery problem under a hybrid predictive control approach. Transp. Sci. **49**(2), 239–253 (2015)
8. Sun, P., Veelenturf, L.P., Hewitt, M., Van Woensel, T.: The time-dependent pickup and delivery problem with time windows. Transp. Res. Part B: Methodol. **116**, 1–24 (2018)
9. Zhang, J., Liu, F., Tang, J., Li, Y.: The online integrated order picking and delivery considering pickers' learning effects for an O2O community supermarket. Transp. Res. Part E: Logistics Transp. Rev. **123**, 180–199 (2019)
10. Cherkesly, M., Desaulniers, G., Irnich, S., Laporte, G.: Branch-price-and-cut algorithms for the pickup and delivery problem with time windows and multiple stacks. Eur. J. Oper. Res. **250**(3), 782–793 (2015)

A MILP Model for the Scheduling of a Multiproduct Tree-Structure Pipeline Network in Mining Industry

M. Bamoumen[1] , S. Elfirdoussi[1] , L. Ren[2] , and N. Tchernev[3]([✉])

[1] EMINES School of Industrial Management, Université Mohammed VI Polytechnique, Ben Guerir, Morocco
{Meryem.Bamoumen,Selwa.Elfirdoussi}@emines.um6p.ma
[2] CRCGM EA3849, Université Clermont Auvergne, Clermont-Ferrand, France
libo.ren@uca.fr
[3] LIMOS, UMR CNRS 6158, Université Clermont Auvergne, Aubière, France
nikolay.tchernev@uca.fr

Abstract. The scheduling of multiple products through pipelines, to meet a demand over a considered time horizon, is a challenging problem that many researchers have been interested in. Although pipelines are considered mainly in the petroleum industry, they can also be used in other industries. This paper deals with the multiproduct pipeline network scheduling problem in the context of mining industry. The objective is to schedule a sequence of batches, to be transported through the pipeline network, to ensure all product demand, while respecting the different technical constraints. The proposed approach is a MILP model with a continuous representation of time and batch volume. It provides maximizes the volume of batches to satisfy all product demands. The model was tested using different instances over a short-term horizon.

Keywords: Pipeline network · Phosphate products · Scheduling · MILP

1 Introduction

1.1 Research Context

The use of pipelines to transport petroleum products has increased significantly during the last few years, as they are considered to be the most reliable and safe way to move these products [6]. Although pipelines are mainly related to petroleum industries, this paper presents a system composed of multiple pipelines used in the mining industry. The considered pipeline network transports phosphate products, which are produced by the Moroccan firm "OCP Group". In fact, phosphate is transferred through the pipelines by mixing phosphate grains with water to obtain "phosphate slurry", which is considered a homogenous liquid product. Phosphate slurry is characterized by its Bone Phosphate of Lime (BPL) composition, storage capacity and demand during a fixed time horizon.

A. Dolgui et al. (Eds.): APMS 2021, IFIP AICT 632, pp. 299–306, 2021.
https://doi.org/10.1007/978-3-030-85906-0_34

Therefore, the system considered is destined to transport multiple products. This transportation is achieved by pumping a sequence of batches from the source point to the different destinations. Each batch is composed of one product and has a volume which is comprised between an upper and a lower bound. In order to identify each batch during the unloading phase at the destination points, each two successive batches are separated by injecting a volume of water.

In this paper, we tackle the multi-product pipeline network scheduling problem in mining industry. The objective is to determine the schedule of batches to be pumped and transported through the pipelines to satisfy the demand on a predefined time-horizon, by taking into consideration different technical constraints, while maximizing the amount of product to be delivered. We propose a Mixed Integer Linear Program (MILP) model with a continuous time and volume formulation to study this problem.

1.2 Problem Definition

The system under study is the pipeline network of "OCP Group" (see Fig. 1) a tree-structure type network, and consists of a multi-product main pipeline that connects a source "Head Station" to several destinations using secondary pipelines. The first destination is for local customers, and the second destination is referred to as "Downstream" unit, which delivers phosphate products to international customers.

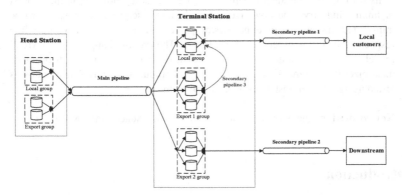

Fig. 1. Pipeline network of "OCP Group"

There exist eight different products: one local product delivered to the local customers and seven export products, which are delivered to international clients via the Dowstream unit. These products are unloaded in different tanks organized in groups at the "Terminal Station": the local product is unloaded in the "local group" and the "export 1 group", due to its high demand; the "export 2 group" is shared by the export products, where each tank can contain only one product at a time. If the export product to be unloaded has a higher BPL composition than the previous one contained in a tank, then a flushing operation occurs: a volume of the product with the high BPL is added to the previous product to avoid any contamination. Based on the demands from local customers and those received by Downstream from international customers over a predefined planning horizon, the objective is to provide the scheduling of batches to meet these demands, while maximizing the volume of the planned batches. For this, the following input settings are assumed to be known: 1) the length of the time horizon (in hours); 2) the number of products; 3) the flowrate of all pipelines; 4) the storage capacity of each tank/group; 5) the initial inventory of each tank/group; 6) the upper and lower volume of batches, depending on the products; 7) the demand of local customers and the Downstream; 8) the matrix of product compatibility; and 9) the matrix of flushing.

The following assumptions are considered: A) the phosphate slurry is considered to be a homogenous material; B) the flowrate of each pipeline is considered to be uniform; C) all tank groups have an initial inventory; D) the filling level of each tank is bounded by an upper value (90%) and a lower value (13%); E) the tanks of a group can be filled simultaneously; F) the tanks can be filled and flushed at the same time; G) the "export 1 group" at the "Terminal Station" is destined to contain the local product, which can be transferred to the "local group" via a secondary pipeline; and H) the demand is uniformly distributed over the planning horizon. The resulted schedule should contain the following elements: a) the batches to be transported through the pipelines over the planning horizon, and the product contained in each batch; b) the volume of each batch; c) the start and completion time of unloading each batch; d) the duration of unloading each bloc of a batch, and the storage group destined for each bloc; and e) the inventory level of storage groups before unloading each bloc of a batch.

The rest of the paper is arranged as follows: Sect. 2 presents a literature review on the multi-products straight pipeline network scheduling problems; Sect. 3 details the proposed approach; Sect. 4 gives computational experiments; finally, Sect. 5 provides the conclusion and perspectives of future work.

2 Literature Review

The numbers of researchers interested in the multiproduct pipeline scheduling problem has considerably increased over the last few years. Many published works tackle this problem in the context of petroleum industry. To the best of our knowledge, no article related to the scheduling of phosphate slurries in a pipeline network has been published in the literature.

According to [7], the multiproduct pipeline scheduling problems could be classified conforming to the pipeline structure: straight (linear), network, etc. In this paper, our focus is on the works which deal with multiproduct pipeline network scheduling problems. These problems could also be divided into two categories, depending on the structure of the pipeline network: tree-structure, where the pipelines link between one source and multiple destinations; and mesh-structure, in which the pipelines connect multiple sources to multiple destinations.

In order to study these two categories of problems, many approaches were proposed, such as discrete event simulation tools [3], mixed integer linear and non-linear programming formulations (MILP and MINLP) [9] and [10], and hybrid approaches that combine between multiple methods [4] and [7].

[1] were among the first works which focused on the multiproduct pipeline network scheduling problems. The authors consider a mesh-structure system and propose a

genetic algorithm that uses multi-objective optimization. Later, [2] presented an extensive version of [1], where they propose a hybrid method that combines between a MILP model and the genetic algorithm. The performance of the hybrid method is compared to that of the model and the algorithm. The results show that the hybrid method provides a solution with the lowest number of product changes, compared to the model and algorithm. However, no information in relation to the calculation time is presented.

Recently, [10] developed MILP model to deal with tree-structure pipeline network scheduling problem. The linear model is based on continuous time and volume representation: the time horizon is divided into several periods, the duration of which is to be determined by the model. Moreover, the model allows the loading and unloading of several batches in parallel during each period of time. The objective function is to minimize the time horizon. The model is tested by considering different instances presented in [5] and [8]. The results obtained show that the proposed model provides solutions which satisfy the demand in a shorter time horizon than the models of [5] and [8] for certain scenarios.

It is interesting to note that the cited works use different optimization criteria, so the comparison between these studies is difficult. In addition, the some of the studied articles consider the product compatibility constraint in their approach to avoid contamination between products. Other works consider inserting a plug which is a small volume that separates between two successive batches to avoid contamination. However, no information is provided on how these plugs are unloaded at the destination points.

3   Proposed Approach

In this paper, we propose a MILP model to tackle the multiproduct tree-structure pipeline network scheduling problem. The MILP model uses continuous variables to represent time and the volume of batches. In addition, it provides the optimal schedule of batches based on only determining the unloading time of these batches. The loading time of each batch is deduced from its unloading time and transport duration. Other technical constraints regarding inventory management at the destination points are detailed in this section.

3.1   Objective Function and Decision Variables

The objective function is composed of two optimization criteria: the maximization of the total volume of products, noted vp_total, transported through the pipeline network over the time horizon; and the minimization of the number of blocks of batches, denoted nb_bloc, by using a penalty ρ:

$$(max)vp\_total - \rho * nb\_bloc \tag{1}$$

Two decision variables are considered in the model: the first one is the binary variable $y_{i,p}$ which indicates the products allocated to batches in order to create the batch sequence. It is equal to 1 if batch i ($i = 1, \ldots, N$) contains product p ($p = 0, \ldots, P$); 0 otherwise. The second decision variable is the binary variable $sz_{k,i,j}$ which represents the allocation of products to the tanks at the "Terminal Station". It is equal to 1 if block j ($j = 1, \ldots, NB$) of batch i is allocated to tank/group k ($k = 1, \ldots, 5$) during the unloading operation of batch i; 0 otherwise.

3.2 MILP Constraints

Constraints for Product Selection. The allocation of products to batches is achieved by considering the binary variable $y_{i,p}$. In addition, the number of scheduled batches, denoted by the variable nb, is determined by using the binary variable $y_{i,p}$ and the maximum number of products, noted by the parameter N. Therefore, no products are all the batches i numbered from nb to N (i.e., $y_{i,p} = 0 \; \forall i = nb, \ldots, N$).

Product Compatibility Constraints. The separation of consecutive batches by using a volume of water can be modeled by a matrix of product compatibility m, where water is considered a product numbered $p = 0$. Each element $m_{p,q}$ is equal to 1 if the sequence of products (p, q) is allowed. In this case, only water is compatible with each product p ($p = 1, \ldots, P$) (i.e., $m_{0,p} = m_{p,0} = 1 \; \forall p = 1, \ldots, P$). The product compatibility constraint also consider the use of the binary variable $y_{i,p}$ to determine the possible sequences between two successive batches $(i - 1)$ et i, containing products p and q respectively.

Lot Sizing Constraints. The variable Q_i. Represents the volume of batch i. It must be comprised between an upper bound $Vmax_p$ and a lower bound $Vmin_p$, depending on product p contained in the batch i, and determined by the binary variable $y_{i,p}$. In addition, the variable BQ_{ij} amount to the volume of block j of batch i. This volume is comprised between an upper bound, which is the batch volume Q_i, and a lower bound, which is equivalent to an hour of product pumping in the main pipeline. In addition, the sum of all block volumes BQ_{ij} must be equal to the batch volume Q_i.

Constraints for Block Unloading Control. The allocation of blocks to tanks/groups at the "Terminal Station" is represented by the binary variable $sz_{k,i,j}$. Another binary variable $z_{i,j}$ is introduced, which indicates that block j exists for batch i. If batch i contains water ($p = 0$), then only one block is considered for this batch. The block unloading constraints are summed as follow: 1) only one tank/group k is allocated to each existing block j of batch i; 2) two successive blocks j and $(j + 1)$ cannot be unloaded in the same tank/group k; 3) the variable $sz_{0,i,j}$ indicates that water is allocated to a fictive tank where it is unloaded ($sz_{k,i,j} \; \forall k = 1, \ldots, 5$); 4) if batch i contains the local product ($p = 1$), then $sz_{k,i,j} = 0$ for each tank $k = 3, \ldots, 5$ of the "export 2 group"; 5) if batch i contains an export product ($p = 2, \ldots, P$), then $sz_{k,i,j} = 0$ for the "local group" ($k = 1$) and the "export 1 group" ($k = 2$). Moreover, the sum of all binary variables $z_{i,j}$ is equal to the total number of blocks nb_bloc, which is minimized in the objective function.

Constraints Related to the Unloading Time and Duration. The variables T_i. and D_i amount respectively to the time and the duration of unloading batch i. The unloading time T_i is determined by adding to the previous one T_{i-1} the duration D_{i-1} of the previous batch, starting with $T_1 = 0$, since no pipeline stoppages are considered. The sum of all unloading durations D_i must be equal to the time horizon h_max. In addition, the variable $BD_{i,j}$ represents the unloading duration of block j of batch i. It is equal to the block volume BQ_{ij} divided by the flowrate of the main pipeline db_pp. Moreover, the sum of all the block unloading durations $BD_{i,j}$ must be equal to the batch unloading duration D_i.

Constraints Related to Inventory Management. Two variables are introduced for inventory management: $S_{k,i}$. Represents the inventory level of tank/group k before unloading batch i; $BS_{k,i,j}$ defines the inventory level of tank/group k before unloading block j of batch i. These inventory levels are updated by using the variable $vs_{k,i,j}$, which indicates the stock variation of tank/group k while unloading block j of batch i. The stock variation $vs_{k,i,j}$ is determined for each tank/group k by considering different scenarios: 1) unloading a batch containing water ($p = 0$); 2) unloading a batch which comprises the local product ($p = 1$); 3) unloading a batch which contains an export product ($p = 2, \ldots, P$); 4) if the operations of filling and flushing of a tank/group are done simultaneously or separately. The inventory level $BS_{k,i,j}$ is determined by considering the previous level $BS_{k,i,j-1}$, to which is added the stock variation $vs_{k,i,j}$. In addition, the inventory level $S_{k,i+1}$ is calculated by considering the inventory level $BS_{k,i,NB}$ before unloading the last block NB of the previous batch i, and by adding the stock variation $vs_{k,i,NB}$. Moreover, the inventory levels $S_{k,i}$ and $BS_{k,i,j}$ must be positive and lower than the maximum allowed level.

Constraints Related to the Total Demand of Export Products. The variable $vpE_{i,p}$. Amounts to the total volume of export product p ($p = 2, \ldots, P$) contained in batch i. The total demand of a product p, denoted dem_p, must be higher or at least equal the of batches containing product p, to which is added two volumes: the variable $SvrB_p$ (where $SvrB_p \geq 0$) represents the total volume received by product p if the latter has a low bpl; and the variable $SvrH_p$ (where $SvrH_p \leq 0$) amounts to the total volume lost by product p if the latter has a high BPL. These volumes are determined by using a flushing matrix mr. Each element of the matrix $mr_{p,q}$ is equal to 1 if a flushing operation must occur in "export 2 group" to change from product p with low BPL to product q with higher BPL.

Constraints for Total Product Volume. The variable vp_i. refers to the volume of product contained in batch i (i.e. $p = 1, \ldots, P$). This variable is equal to the batch volume Q_i if batch i is not composed of water (i.e. $y_{i,0} = 0$); and is equal to 0 if $y_{i,0} = 1$. In addition, the sum of all volumes vp_i containing the local product and export products is equal to the total product volume vp_total, which is maximized in the objective function.

4   Case Study

In order to evaluate the performance of the proposed model, we consider the tree-structure pipeline network in Fig. 1. The main pipeline has a length of 187 km and an average flowrate of 4000 m^3/h. The average flowrate of the secondary pipelines 1, 2 and 3 are respectively: the total demand the local product divided by the time horizon, 600 m^3/h and 1000 m^3/h. We use different instances generated arbitrary from a typical instance with a short term time horizon (2 days): a set of 10 instances with 3 products and two scenarios of instance 3 with respectively 4 and 5 products. For the 10 instances with 3 products, the tanks of "export group 2" are aggregated, since only one export is considered. However, these tanks are separated in the two scenarios with 4 and 5 products.

Table 1. Results provided for the instances with 3 products and 2 days

Instances	Objective function	Total product volume (m^3)	Total number of blocks	CPU time (s)	GAP
1	180615.52	182715.52	21	13.6	0.00%
2	182800.00	185000.00	22	5.4	0.00%
3	184100.00	186000.00	19	4.8	0.00%
4	172611.54	174811.54	22	12.3	0.00%
5	181227.80	183327.80	21	25.5	0.00%
6	182700.00	185000.00	23	10.8	0.00%
7	184100.00	186000.00	19	5.6	0.00%
8	171014.20	173214.20	22	17.0	0.00%
9	183100.00	185000.00	19	11.1	0.00%
10	184000.00	186000.00	20	6.1	0.00%

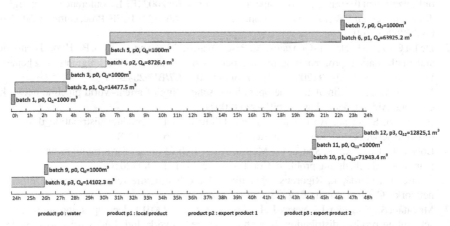

Fig. 2. Batch schedule obtained for scenario 1 of instance 3 (with 4 products)

Table 1 gives information about the results of the 10 instances with 3 products: the objective function; the two optimization criteria (the total product volume and the total number of blocks of batches); the CPU time and the GAP. We can note that the model provides the optimal solution of all considered instances within a CPU time of few seconds with Gurobi 9.1.1. In addition, the two scenarios of instance 3 with 4 and 5 products were also tested by the proposed model using the same solver, with a time limitation of one hour. The results showed that the solutions provided by the model at the end of the time limit is 0.16% for both scenarios. Figure 2 represents the schedule of batches over 2 days provided by the model for the first scenario of instance 3 with 4 products.

5 Conclusion

In this paper, a MILP model is proposed to deal with the multiproduct tree-structure pipeline network in the context of mining industry. The model aims to maximize the volume of batches which contain phosphate products to satisfy all demands over a fixed planning horizon. It also divides each batch into several blocks in order facilitate inventory management at the destination points. Different constraints were considered in the model, such as flushing operation of tanks and the use of water as batch separator to avoid contamination. The performance of the model was evaluated using different instances over a short-term horizon. It proved to be efficient by providing optimal and near-optimal solutions of these instances.

For future work, it would be interesting to adapt some constraints of the model in order to test other instances with longer planning horizon.

References

1. de la Cruz, J.M., de Andres-Toro, B., Herrán, A., Porta, E.B., Blanco, P.F.: Multiobjective optimization of the transport in oil pipelines networks. In: 2003 IEEE Conference on Emerging Technologies and Factory Automation, vol. 1, pp. 566–573. IEEE Proceedings (Cat. No. 03TH8696) (2003)
2. De La Cruz, J.M., Herrán-González, A., Risco-Martín, J.L., Andrés-Toro, B.: Hybrid heuristic and mathematical programming in oil pipelines networks: use of immigrants. J. Zhejiang Univ.-SCI. A 6(1), 9–19 (2005). https://doi.org/10.1007/BF02842471
3. Mori, F.M., et al.: Simulating the operational scheduling of a real-world pipeline network. Comput. Aided Chem. Eng. 24, 691–696 (2007)
4. Boschetto, S., et al.: An operational scheduling model to product distribution through a pipeline network. Ind. Eng. Chem. Res. 49(12), 5661–5682 (2010)
5. Lopes, T., Ciré, A., de Souza, C., Moura, A.: A hybrid model for a multiproduct pipeline planning and scheduling problem. Constraints 15(2), 151–189 (2010)
6. Cafaro, D., Cerdá, J.: Rigorous scheduling of mesh-structure refined petroleum pipeline networks. Comput. Chem. Eng. 38, 185–203 (2012)
7. Magatão, S., Magatão, L., Neves-Jr, F., Arruda, L.: Novel MILP decomposition approach for scheduling product distribution through a pipeline network. Ind. Eng. Chem. Res. 54(18), 5077–5095 (2015)
8. Castro, P.M., Mostafaei, H.: Batch-centric scheduling formulation for treelike pipeline systems with forbidden product sequences. Comput. Chem. Eng. 122, 2–18 (2018)
9. Liao, Q., Zhang, H., Wang, Y., Zhang, W., Liang, Y.: Heuristic method for detailed scheduling of branched multiproduct pipeline networks. Chem. Eng. Res. Des. 140, 82–101 (2018)
10. Liao, Q., Castro, P.M., Liang, Y., Zhang, H.: Computationally efficient MILP model for scheduling a branched multiproduct pipeline system. Ind. Eng. Chem. Res. 58(13), 5236–5251 (2019)

Exploiting the Full Potential of I4.0 Technologies for Products EOL Recovery Process

Valentina Popolo[✉], Mose Gallo, Andrea Grassi,
and Maria Grazia Marchesano

University of Naples Federico II, 80125 Napoli, NA, Italy
{valentina.popolo,mose.gallo,andrea.grassi,
mariagrazia.marchesano}@unina.it

Abstract. The recent advancements of technology have been radically transforming the industrial world and our societies as well. The application of the new technologies is ubiquitous involving various domains from industrial production to everyday life. This paper investigates whether and how it is possible to better support product life-cycle management by exploiting product's enhanced capabilities stemming from an I4.0 ecosystem. To this aim, this paper proposes the new concept of Product 4.0 that is a product archetype combining the functionalities of an intelligent product with those permitted by I4.0 technologies. As Product 4.0 has the potential to benefit the various phases of the product life cycle, this paper also provides further details on the end-of-life recovery options for this new product archetype, by means of an explanatory case dealing with a laser-jet printer.

Keywords: Smart product · Product 4.0 · End-of-Life · Recovery options · Industry 4.0

1 Introduction

The technological advance of the Fourth Industrial Revolution (I4.0) is bringing strong changes in manufacturing and service industries as well. The potential of I4.0 technologies is apparent in various aspects of industrial operations, such as sustainability, smart products, End of Life (EoL) and remanufacturing.

[7] propose a sustainable I4.0 framework that includes three main components: I4.0 technologies, process integration and sustainable outcomes. The authors also suggest future research developments investigating the implementation of I4.0 technologies for better man-machine and machine-to-equipment integration through the use of sensors. Another important impact of these technologies is on the design of efficient supply chains, which through information gathered from products themselves, logistics and production operations and a seamless integration between the physical and digital worlds could further

© IFIP International Federation for Information Processing 2021
Published by Springer Nature Switzerland AG 2021
A. Dolgui et al. (Eds.): APMS 2021, IFIP AICT 632, pp. 307–316, 2021.
https://doi.org/10.1007/978-3-030-85906-0_35

improve product's lifecycle permitting also a more effective and efficient product recovery at its End of Use (EoU) and/or End of Life (EoL).

Nowadays products are not exclusively composed of mechanical and electrical parts, they have become complex systems that combine hardware, sensors, data storage, microprocessors, software and connectivity capabilities [15]. Classifying smart products allows a clearer their definition and application. The [16] archetypes are an example of the classification of smart products according to their features.

[8] identify Remanufacturing as a key strategy for the full achievement of Circular Economy, which, in turn, represents an important research area for many companies worldwide and for our societies as a whole. This "smart remanufacturing" review focuses on the remanufacturing industry and the sustainable application of I4.0 enablers. The results are used to create a framework that links to the research agenda needed to fully achieve smart remanufacturing. Other authors have tried to define the types of intelligent recovery options. [1] detailed the characteristics that intelligent reuse, intelligent remanufacturing and intelligent recycling must have in relation to smart products.

In light of the above, there are a lack of articles dealing with these topics in the current literature. Few authors deal with smart products as aggregation systems of innovative technologies. Recovery options exploiting I4.0 tools are little studied in the literature.

According to these premises and within the outlined context, the first aim of this work is to propose the novel concept of "Product 4.0" (P4.0). This concept builds upon product archetypes and explores the augmented capabilities of an intelligent product in a I4.0 environment. In fact, we highlighted the aspect of the smart product with the use of I4.0 tools. Furthermore, this paper has the aim of investigating the possibilities that arise when recovering an intelligent product, at its EoU or EoL, in a I4.0 environment.

The remaining part of this paper is as follows. Section 2 presents the literature review of the I4.0 tools and the recovery options. After defining Product 4.0, Sect. 3 deals with the recovery options with respect to Product 4.0. Finally, Sect. 4 draws conclusions and future development.

2   Literature Review

In this section, the relevant literature is presented in two parts. The first part describes the I4.0 tools that can be used in smart products, and the second part will analyse aspects of the different recovery options.

A notable starting point when dealing with so called *Smart Products* and their possible classification is represented by the work carried out by [16]. The authors classify smart products according to 4 archetypes based on 16 criteria/characteristics of the products themselves. The proposed archetypes are classified as follows: *Digital Product, Connected Product, Responsive Product, Intelligent Product.*

The so called smart products are the most used technological products today. The capabilities of these products can be expanded by the integration of more advanced I4.0 tools and with the aspects of the different end-of-life recovery options.

2.1 Suitable Industry 4.0 Technologies

From a literature review, we identified those advanced technologies that could be included as additional features to the archetypes proposed by [16] and briefly described above. In particular, we found out that the main tools are: Internet of Thing (IoT), Cloud Computing (CC), Big Data (BD), Digital Twin (DT), Machine Learning (ML) and Human-Machine Cooperation (HMC). The previous innovative tools and technologies were chosen because they are the most representative for an innovative product. Although the IoT technology was swiftly mentioned by [16], any other of the above cited technologies was explicitly considered in the proposed archetypes.

In order to proper ascribe to the various archetypes the different I4.0 tools, we will start this discussion from their very definition. For the IoT, we adopt the same definition as [22] who argues that virtual 'things' have virtual identities, physical attributes and virtual personalities.

The BD technology has been largely investigated in scientific literature and, among its different definitions, we consider that provided by [5] who argues that Big Data is a set of techniques and technologies that require new forms of integration to discover great hidden values from large datasets.

According to [12], CC can be defined as "a model for enabling ubiquitous, affordable, on-demand network access to a range of configured computing resources".

[2] define the DT as a simulation technology available for use in the real system, allowing the equipment's self-adaptive behaviour. The machine can simulate the different environment, establishing the best decision to make in a particular situation.

ML is a subject that studies how to use computers to simulate human learning activities and to study methods of self-improvement of computers to obtain new knowledge and new skills, identify existing knowledge and continuously improve performance and results [21]. From a practical point of view, machine learning allows automatic data processing and can be considered an advanced analysis tool for intelligent production.

We decided to include also HMC as another important advanced technology that features an I4.0 environment. According to [14], HMC is a technology that allows to incorporate more and more decision-making capabilities in both material (e.g. machines, products) and immaterial (e.g. production orders) elements, transforming them into efficient assistance systems to help human beings improve their performance.

Finally, Cyber Physical System (CPS) can be seen as systems of systems, which emerge through complex networking, integration of embedded systems, application systems and infrastructures, made possible by human-machine interaction [19].

2.2 EoL Recovery Options

Literature reports on several different EoL recovery options for a generic product. [13] grouped these options into ten recovery strategies, including Recovery, Recycle, Repurpose, Remanufacture, Refurbish, Repair, Reuse, Rethink, Reduce. [10] considered only seven recovery options, while distinguishing for recycling between a primary and a secondary type. [18] in their review of key regeneration activities grouped the recovery options into Reconditioning, Dismantling/Disassembly, Refurbishment, Repair, Salvage, Incineration, Resale, Cannibalisation. In addition, the authors interestingly classified extant research papers, according to the level of decision, i.e., whether the recovery option is applied to the entire product or components. [3], while tackling the disassembly problem, identified five options for product recovery, in particular they assigned to each level of disassembly also which elements could be recovered from the product itself, i.e. product, module, part and material level.

For the purpose of this research, we decided to focus only on the main EoL options, i.e. reuse, remanufacturing, recycling, cannibalization and disposal. In accordance with the relevant literature, we adopted the following definitions for the recovery options mentioned above. Reuse is considered to be an operation whereby a few non-destructive improvements are made in order to bring the product back to its initial state. Remanufacturing, on the other hand, is a more complex operation where the product is disassembled and worn or broken components are replaced. Recycling is the operation where raw materials are recovered and a complete conversion is carried out. Disposal is the last possible operation, where nothing can be recovered from the product and it is therefore thrown away. Finally, cannibalisation is the operation that allows us to recover from a product only the components that are still functional and then reuse them on another product as replacement components.

3 Conceptualization of Product 4.0

In a I4.0 environment, we argue that the product, as a whole, along with its parts and components can "interact" with the various resources it encounters during its lifecycle. These interactions turn out to be greatly enhanced or augmented by the implementation of I4.0 technologies. Needless to say, that this enhancement strongly depends upon the embedded capabilities of the product and its parts and components.

As a consequence of the previous considerations and according to the tools of I4.0, we can extend the archetypes of product of [16] in a I4.0 perspective (see Fig. 1). Based on the definitions previously given, we decided to suitably attribute the I4.0 tools among the different archetypes. In fact, the possibility to make different decisions in different situations makes DT a suitable element for the fourth archetype, i.e. Intelligent product. Depending on the definition of IoT and taking into account that most of current products are equipped with Radio Frequency Identification (RFID), sensors and communication technologies [6], the archetype that could exploit at most this advanced technology is the second one, i.e., Connected product. By taking into account the considerations made about BD, we expect that Responsive product is the archetype that could have more advantages stemming from BD technology. It is worth noting here that, although the first archetype, i.e. the Digital product, already has data archiving capability, the BD technology has not been linked to it as the data involved in this case are not complex or various. Still according to the definitions given above, we can attribute the tools of CC in the third archetype and ML and HMC in the fourth archetype. Once defined, categorized and imputed to the appropriate archetype the various I4.0 tools in a separated way, it can be argued that all these technologies epitomize what literature defines as CPS. This object turns out to be the union of different technological systems, for this reason we decided to group all the I4.0 tools within the umbrella term of CPS.

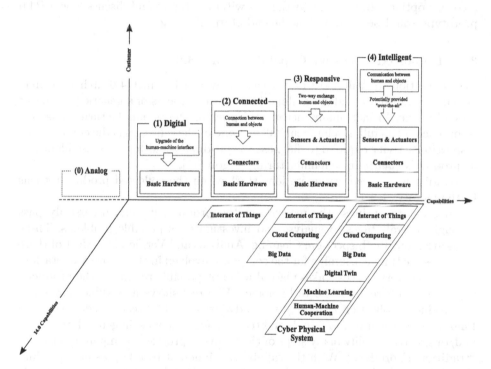

Fig. 1. Extension of [16] archetypes with I4.0 technologies

Figure 1, turns out to be an extension of the image originally proposed by [16] to pictorially represent the various archetypes of products. We give a three-dimensional representation of the various archetypes by adding an axis, labelled as I4.0 Technologies, along which the innovative tools and technologies of I4.0 are shown in relation to the various archetypes. By jointly considering the capabilities of the fourth archetype proposed by [16], i.e. the Intelligent product, along with the new ones available in the so called CPS while interacting in an I4.0 environment, we could introduce the new concept of *Products 4.0.*

As a consequence of the previous definition, we can argue that the Product 4.0 concept involves not only the product itself but also the ecosystem where the product life cycle takes place. In fact, it includes *a smart product that can communicate with humans and objects as well, having basic hardware and intrinsic characteristics (sensors, actuators and connections) and implementing I4.0 technologies (IoT, CC, BD, DT, ML and HMC)*.

The enhanced capabilities of Product 4.0 have the potential to deliver several benefits during the product lifecycle. It can also effectively support logistic and production activities and, in general, all the activities involved from product's conception to its EoU or EoL.

In this perspective, P4.0 may represent the hinge upon which circular economy models could rest. In fact, it would lead to a better investigation of product recovery options. In the next section we will investigate and discuss how a P4.0 prototype could be recovered at the end of its life cycle.

3.1   Enhanced Recovery Capabilities of P4.0

In this section we will show and discuss how the Product 4.0 archetype may heavily revolutionize and streamline the recovery process of a generic product at its end of life. In fact, many factors still prevent the remanufacturing business from reaching its full development [20] and one of these factors is the cumbersome inspection activity required to diagnose the product's health status also identified as product's *quality* in remanufacturing jargon [17].

Traditionally, recovery operations start when the collected product returns to the factory [4, 9, 11].

In order to optimise the recovery of the product, it must necessarily pass through several stages to analyse and investigate its possible problems. These steps are typically: Inspection, Cleaning, Analysis and Verification. Most of these activities are time-consuming for the company involved in the recovery operation.

This recovery process takes place if it is not possible to exploit the product's capabilities inherent to I4.0 technologies. Figure 2 shows a possible flow chart for product's collection that fully take advantage of I4.0 technologies. Under a P4.0 scenario the use of I4.0 tools and technologies allow us, in general, to reduce and/or greatly simplify many steps of the recovery process if compared to that of "traditional" products. With the capabilities inherent to P4.0, a smart product that interact with a smart environment, we can take advantage of available technologies to collect detailed information about product's health even before it returns to the factory for recovery purposes.

In general, it is possible to gather and exploit two types of data. A first set of information is that pertaining the various products belonging to the installed base and sent by products themselves to a cloud platform. This data usually refer to the average behaviour of the products of the installed base. A second set of information is the product-specific data collected once the product enters the factory and, therefore, it is able to communicate with the Industry 4.0 system.

Thanks to the combined use of these data sets, the diagnostic phase of the recovery process is noticeably simplified and sped up, in fact there is no need to carry out the various levels of inspection and problem analysis as we already know in advance the health and usage status of the product, which can then go straight to the cleaning stage.

As a consequence, Inspection and Analysis phases may not appear in the flowchart of the recovery process. In order to identify the more appropriate recovery option for the specific product, it is possible to make use of product's status and use data. Depending on product's "health state" and "use" parameters, the different recovery options can be properly chosen. Once defined the product category, it is crucial to identify the "use" parameters and "health state" to better address recovery operations. Specifically, in the case of intensive use of the product and a good health state, it would be viable to first cannibalize the still valuable components, then materials recovery from parts and components, and, finally, the disposal of remaining parts. If the "use" parameters and "health state" are appropriate, product could undergo the reuse option provided that minor repairs and replacements are carried out. If, despite the low values of "use" parameters, the "health state" is not adequate, the product could conveniently

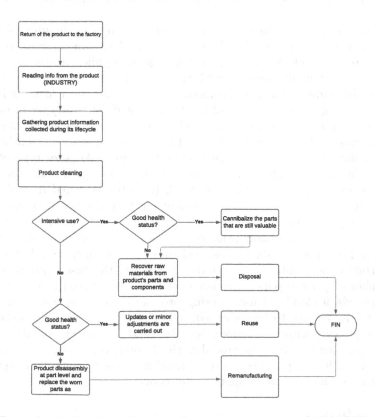

Fig. 2. Example of a flowchart diagram of a recovery process exploiting I4.0 technologies.

undergo the remanufacturing process where it is disassembled at component level, and relevant parts of the product are replaced.

It is worth noting that, because of the augmented capabilities of P4.0, it could perform by itself the verification phase that conclude the remanufacturing process.

In order to show the potential of P4.0 in terms of its recovery process, we provide the readers with a simple but effective example. We considered here the case of a consumer electronics product, that is, a multi-function laser jet printer. This kind of products are usually capable of and actually share many information on product use and product performance with Original Equipment Manufacturer (OEM) on the basis of sharing agreements. These agreements are usually framed within a win-win Product Service System logic and are mainly intended to gather information on the installed base in order to deliver more customer value during the product use and, at the same time, to allow the OEM to sell secondary products and ancillary services. In our use case, both the aggregated information about the installed base and the product-specific data may be used to support a more efficient and environmental friendly recovery process.

In fact, some data related to product's operation (e.g., number of printed pages, number of scans on the glass) as well as data coming from product's event log (e.g., document feeder jam, paper jam, supplies status, double feed error) could be put into relation with the general health state of the product and its main modules, parts and components in a cause-effect logic. It is worth noting that, in general, this type of products is made of two types of modules, parts and components: the first type, such as toner cartridges, drums and fuser, are to be classified as "consumables" as they are purchased recurrently during product's lifecycle as part of its regular maintenance. Another type of parts, such as scan unit, transfer module, sheet feeder, edge guides, electric motors and gears, imaging unit are those more likely to be recovered from discarded products provided that a reliable assessment on their status can be performed.

For example, a malfunctioning of the printer's transfer module may be signalled by an abnormal consumption of electrical power of its motors, that can be obtained by minor product's design changes as well as cheap additional sensors to collect those data. While the data related to the "use" parameters (i.e., the number of printed pages, number of scans on the glass) could be already exchanged via a cloud platform during product's life-cycle, when the printer returns to the factory to be recovered, it is also able to exchange stored data of its components with its environment. By jointly exploiting the data related to "use" parameters and those stored in the printer, it is possible to assess the health state of its components in a more reliable manner, thus better supporting the identification of the more appropriate recovery options.

4   Conclusion

The first goal of this paper was to combine advanced industrial technologies with the product archetypes identified by [16] in order to propose the new concept of

Product 4.0. To this aim, the tools with the highest potential for implementation in smart products have been analysed. This analysis identified as the main tools IoT, CC, BD, DT, ML and HMC. The concept of Product 4.0 stems from the combination of the I4.0 technologies with the fourth archetype proposed by [16].

A second goal of this paper was to conduct an exploratory analysis of product recovery scenarios in presence of a Product 4.0 prototype. In particular, the most common product recovery options were presented. We highlighted the potential advantages of recovering P4.0s in comparison with those products not exploiting I4.0 technologies. An explanatory case dealing with laser jet printer allow us to exemplify these benefits.

Future development of this research could focus on the other phases of Product Lifecycle Management, such as Beginning of Life (BoL) and Middle of Life (MoL). With reference to the BoL, the main aspects of product design, creation and verification could be analyzed. In fact, Product 4.0, in order to deliver specified functionalities and to suitably interact with its environment, has to be designed with proper hardware and software features. A further aspect to investigate would be that of properly addressing the design process in order to widen as much as possible the recovery options to which Product 4.0 could undergo at its end of life.

References

1. Alcayaga, A., Wiener, M., Hansen, E.G.: Towards a framework of smart-circular systems: an integrative literature review. J. Cleaner Prod. **221**, 622–634 (2019)
2. Bottani, E., Cammardella, A., Murino, T., Vespoli, S.: From the cyber-physical system to the digital twin: The process development for behaviour modelling of a cyber guided vehicle in M2M logic. In: Proceedings of the Summer School Francesco Turco, September 2017, pp. 96–102 (2017)
3. Desai, A., Mital, A.: Evaluation of disassemblability to enable design for disassembly in mass production. Int. J. Ind. Ergonomics **32**(4), 265–281 (2003)
4. Gaspari, L., Colucci, L., Butzer, S., Colledani, M., Steinhilper, R.: Modularization in material flow simulation for managing production releases in remanufacturing. J. Remanufacturing, 139–157 (2017). https://doi.org/10.1007/s13243-017-0037-3
5. Hashem, I.A.T., Yaqoob, I., Anuar, N.B., Mokhtar, S., Gani, A., Ullah Khan, S.: The rise of "big data" on cloud computing: review and open research issues. Inf. Syst. 47, 98–115 (2015)
6. Ivanov, D., Dolgui, A., Sokolov, B.: Multi-disciplinary analysis of interfaces "supply Chain Event Management - RFID - control theory". Int. J. Integr. Supply Manage. **8**(1-3), 52–66 (2013)
7. Kamble, S.S., Gunasekaran, A., Gawankar, S.A.: Sustainable industry 4.0 framework: a systematic literature review identifying the current trends and future perspectives. Process Saf. Environ. Protect. **117**, 408–425 (2018)
8. Kerin, M., Pham, D.T.: Smart remanufacturing: a review and research framework (2020)
9. King, A., Barker, S., Cosgrove, A.: Remanufacturing at xerox: evaluating the process to establish principles for better design. In: Proceedings of ICED 2007, the 16th International Conference on Engineering Design DS 42(August), pp. 1–11 (2007)

10. Lee, S.G., Lye, S.W., Khoo, M.K.: A multi-objective methodology for evaluating product end-of-life options and disassembly. Int. J. Adv. Manuf. Technol. **18**(2), 148–156 (2001)
11. Ma, Y.S., Jun, H.B., Kim, H.W., Lee, D.H.: Disassembly process planning algorithms for end-of-life product recovery and environmentally conscious disposal. Int. J. Prod. Res. **49**(23), 7007–7027 (2011)
12. Mell, P., Grance, T.: The NIST-National Institute of Standards and Technology - Definition of Cloud Computing. NIST Special Publication 800-145, p. 7 (2011)
13. Morseletto, P.: Targets for a circular economy. Resour. Conserv. Recycl. **153**, 104553 (2020)
14. Pacaux-Lemoine, M.P., Trentesaux, D., Zambrano Rey, G., Millot, P.: Designing intelligent manufacturing systems through human-machine cooperation principles: a human-centered approach. Comput. Ind. Eng. **111**, 581–595 (2017)
15. Porter, M.E., Heppelmann, J.E.: How smart, connected products are transforming competition. Harvard Bus. Rev. **92**(11), 64–88 (2014)
16. Raff, S., Wentzel, D., Obwegeser, N.: Smart products: conceptual review, synthesis, and research directions. J. Prod. Innov. Manage. **37**(5), 379–404 (2020)
17. Ridley, S.J., Ijomah, W.L., Corney, J.R.: Improving the efficiency of remanufacture through enhanced pre-processing inspection-a comprehensive study of over 2000 engines at Caterpillar remanufacturing, U.K. Prod. Planning Control **30**(4), 259–270 (2019)
18. Sitcharangsie, S., Ijomah, W., Wong, T.C.: Decision makings in key remanufacturing activities to optimise remanufacturing outcomes: a review. J. Cleaner Prod. **232**, 1465–1481 (2019)
19. Thoben, K.D., Wiesner, S., Wuest, T.: "Industrie 4.0" and smart manufacturing-a review of research issues and application examples. Int. J. Autom. Technol. **11**(1), 4–16 (2017)
20. Vogt Duberg, J., Johansson, G., Sundin, E., Kurilova-Palisaitiene, J.: Prerequisite factors for original equipment manufacturer remanufacturing. J. Cleaner Prod. **270**, 122309 (2020)
21. Wang, H., Ma, C., Zhou, L.: A brief review of machine learning and its application. In: Proceedings - 2009 International Conference on Information Engineering and Computer Science, ICIECS 2009, pp. 2–5 (2009)
22. Xu, L.D., He, W., Li, S.: Internet of things in industries: a survey. IEEE Trans. Ind. Inform. **10**(4), 2233–2243 (2014)

An Approximation Algorithm for the k-Connected Location Set Cover Problem with Color-Spanning Constraint

Yin Wang[1,2] and Yinfeng Xu[1,2(✉)]

[1] School of Management, Xi'an Jiaotong University, Xi'an, Shaanxi 710049, China
yinaywang@stu.xjtu.edu.cn, yfxu@mail.xjtu.edu.cn
[2] The State Key Lab for Manufacturing Systems Engineering,
Xi'an, Shaanxi 710049, China

Abstract. Motivated by the need for a more sensitive server assignment strategy in supply-chain network management, our total cost comprises coverage area (i.e., disk) sizes and "moving" service modes that facilitate multiple and flexible demand fulfillment. Selection of k color-spanning centers to achieve cost minimization is the aim of our k-Connected Location Set Cover Problem with Color-spanning Constraint (k-CLSCPCC). The cost reflects the sum of the radii of the color-spanning disks plus the cost of connecting to disk regions. The farthest-color Voronoi diagram(FCVD) helps to assign an individual radius to each selected color-spanning center with aims to minimal cost. The main idea behind our greedy algorithm, which integrates the ideas of the classical minimum-power coverage problem and k-maximum coverage problem, is to minimize the measurable gap between the cost of connecting all nodes and the reduced cost of coverage with k disks. Our proposed algorithm can approximate a 3.368-factor solution within $O(n^2 m \log m)$ running time, equal to time cost of generating FCVD, where n is the number of input nodes and m is the number of demand types.

Keywords: Color-spanning set · Approximation algorithm · Maximum coverage problems · Farthest-Color Voronoi Diagram(FCVD) · Minimum spanning tree

1 Introduction

Demand fulfillment, one of the most important components of complex supply-chain network management, is the basic aim for both location and routing problems. Demand in a cluster with requirement of a multi-type facility, represents same type or the possible locations of an object. This multiple-choice problem as "color-spanning set" should cover each given subset but not all given elements [1–3].

© IFIP International Federation for Information Processing 2021
Published by Springer Nature Switzerland AG 2021
A. Dolgui et al. (Eds.): APMS 2021, IFIP AICT 632, pp. 317–325, 2021.
https://doi.org/10.1007/978-3-030-85906-0_36

Facility location always involve long-term decisions and large investments in supply-chain management, and is difficult to correlate them with organizational changes, particularly those involving diversification of products and varying demand. To fulfil multiple and varying demands in a wide variety of domains, location plans must account for both stable and dynamic demands that arise in a wide variety of domains.

A center with multiple service types is always appropriate to a long-term location plan for stable and multi-type demands. However, once the organization commits to a location, resource and location-related costs are often difficult to reduce. Dynamic dispatching can facilitate rapid response times and accurately adapt to variability in customer requirements. A location decision process with appropriate parameter settings should reduce operating costs. We are interested in establishing covered zones using fixed multi-type server and allocate regions via routing to make server assignments more sensitive to diversification of products and varying demand.

The problem discussed in this paper can be traced back to the location set covering problem (LSCP) [4]. The goal of LSCP is to meet the customer demand using the minimum number of facilities. The classical k-center location model aims to find optimal locations for k facilities while minimizing the coverage radii. In most cases, the classical LSCP is required to satisfy demands within a certain distance or standardized arrival time. The fixed coverage radius was relaxed by employing variable radii as the influence of facilities [5]. Some special constraints on facilities help to generate coverage regions. Considering demands with different types or uncertainty, the minimum diameter color-spanning set problem focused on finding the smallest color-spanning regions [1]. As its NP-hardness [6], designing an approxiamtion is a natural choice.

The Farthest Color Voronoi Diagram (FCVD) is a color weighted version of the furthest point Voronoi diagram to find the furthest colored elements [7]. The minimum or maximum color-spanning objects can be find via the FCVD graph [2,8,9]. Especially, the approximated smallest disk is no more twice size than its optimal one in $\mathbb{R}^2$ within time complexity of $O(n \log n)$ based on generated FCVD graph [3]. The time cost of FCVD construction was reduce from $\Omega(mn)$ [7] to $O(n^2 \alpha(m) \log m)$, where m is the number of given color sets [10]. Under the condition of $m \leq \frac{n}{2}$, its performance was improved to $O(n^2 \log n)$ [11,12].

The color-spanning problems focus on finding k objects whose union could cover a fixed number of points for each given color [6]. The connectivity between objects is approximated to be bounded by the minimum color-spanning set (MCSS) [13].

For node set without colors, a constraint specifying an equal maximum coverage distance is a classical setting for the connected set cover location problem. The coverage tour problem (MCTP) always defines this influence as coverage based on the lengths of paths and trees [14]. MCTP aims to generate a tour with exactly k elements selected from a ground set. An algorithm for a generalized version of MCLP improved the performance based on a tree allowing individual radii [15]. Focusing on minimization of total radius cost, the minimum sensor coverage problem and the minimum-power coverage (MPC) problem define a "sensing area" as a disk centered at one of sensors , and finds the minimum radius that covers the required area of targets.

In our variations, the connective costs arise from locating the facilities, as well as transportation costs for distributing the remaining nodes. Differing from previous studies, this paper introduces the k-Connected Location Set Covering Problem with Color-spanning Constraint(k-CLSCPCC), which seeks to find a selection set of exact k color-spanning disks such that the total cost is as less as possible. The total cost considered in our study is motivated by the need for a more sensitive server assignment strategy and arises from coverage area sizes and "moving" service modes that allow stable and flexible demand fulfillment.

The objecitve value of the MPC problem were within 2 times the length of a generated MST [16]. A minimum spanning tree (MST) is a natural choice for ensuring that facilities and uncovered nodes can connect with each other. We first recall how the MST plays an important role in assigning the node connective weights by ranges from the MPC problem. The main idea behind our strategy is to minimize the measurable gap between the cost of connecting all nodes and the reduced cost of coverage with a specified number of disks (center/radius combinations).

This is the background and related works of our study. Our problem description and approximation design were then emphasized. The remainder of this paper is organized as follows. Our problem description and approximation design were then emphasized in Sect. 2 and Sect. 3. Section 4 presents our main results relating to the approximation ratio and overall complexity. At last, Sect. 5 contains our concluding thoughts and scope for future work.

2 Problem Definition

Consider a finite set of potential facility locations that are available; however, without loss of generality, we assume that the demand points and the potential locations are a set of nodes $V(|V| = n)$ of an all-connected network G with shortest Euclidean distances $dist_{xy}, \forall v_x, v_y \in V$. Any pair of nodes (i, j) and (i', j') cannot have the same weights to ensure the uniqueness of a generated MST [17].

Given integer $1 \leq k \leq n$ as number of selected centers. The selection $D = \{o_1, o_2, \cdots, o_k\}$ with k cites is our decision variable, and generate the assigned radii as $R(D) = \{r(o_1), r(o_2), \cdots, r(o_k)\}$ under the "color-spanning" constraint.

Color-Spanning Constraint. A finite family $\mathcal{P} = \{P_1, P_2, \cdots, P_j, \cdots, P_m\}$ is m distinct colored sets for all given nodes V in $\mathbb{R}^2$. Each node only belongs to one of m colored set and all nodes in each set $P_j \in \mathcal{P}$ have the same color. Our selected regions with center o_i and range r_i should cover all types in P with minimum distance to each set $P_j \in P$, i.e. $dist(o_i, P_j) = \min_{x \in P_j} dist(o_i, x) \leq r_i$. Conceptually, we define any range of each selected region $R_i \in R(D)$ as $r_i = \max_{P_j \subset \mathcal{P}}^m \min_{x \in P_j} dist(o_i, x)$, and generated a set of subsets $S(D) = \{s_i\} = \{s(o_1), \cdots, s(o_k)\}$.

Each selected color-spanning region $s_i \in S(D)$ contains all types of colors by the smallest enclosing disk of radius r_i. Given integer k as size of selection, let $Cov(D) = \bigcup_i^k s(o_i)$ be the nodes covered by color-spanning sets and rest node set $B = D \cup Cov(D)$.

This paper focus on achieving "accessibility". All demand points should be covered by color-spanning disks regions or through reallocation with minimum total covering cost $F(D)$. This study addresses the total cost arising from two defined service types: centers providing coverage with cost as the color-spanning radius $r \in R(D)$, and remaining uncovered nodes whose connective cost is the "moving" length from paths or subtrees to covered elements. Thus, our objective function $F(D)$ is the cost obtained by summation of coverage radius $r \in R(D)$ and the cost $Cost(B)$ of connecting centers or uncovered parts to covered regions. We have $F(D) = \sum^k r(i) + Cost(B)$, where $r(i)$ is assigned color-spanning radius of selected cite $o_i \in D$, and $Cost(B)$ is allocation cost depending on the connective cost or accessibility cost between uncovered node set B and covered elements $Cov(D)$.

3 Proposed Algorithm

3.1 Algorithm Design Notations

After generating the given n nodes with all edge weights for an all-connected undirected graph $G = (V, E)$, our approximation algorithm performs three main procedures: The color-spanning set generation, the MPC procedure and a deducting procedure based on the greedy strategy of the Max-k-cover problem.

The Voronoi diagram of high order is a common method to solving color-spanning set [3,8]. The farthest color Voronoi diagram (FCVD) is a $max - min$ diagram generating the bounds on maximal distance to each type [12]. Our approximation algorithm decides the color-spanning radius sequence $CSR(V) = \{r(v_1), r(v_2), \cdots, r(v_n)\}$ for all points by FCVD at first.

The result of the MCP problem can provide a measurable approximation processing to assign all nodes weights. The MST generation helps to solve the MCP problem [15,16]. With ranges $W(V) = \{w(v_1), w(v_2), \cdots, w(v_n)\}$ of the MCP problem, all nodes can be connected, where w_i is range of cite v_i.

After these two steps, each set s_i captures the nodes in disk $\odot_i(v_i, r_i)$ centered on v_i with radius r_i, but $v_i \notin s_i$. Once two element $v_x, v_y \in V$ was selected to center set D, $dist(v_x, v_y) = w_y$ or $dist(v_x, v_y) = w_y$, these two elements set need w_x or w_y ranges to connected with each other. Then weight of each s_i is $H(i) = \sum_{x \in s_i} w_x$. The final Max-k-cover subproblem is seeking the "best" collection to "peel off" the weights of nodes covered by k disks as much as possible. When computing the intersection of two or more sets, our only concern is determining whether these sets have any common union values arising from the elements such as $\Delta_t = f(\bigcup_i^{t-1} s_{t-1} \cup s_t) - f(\bigcup_i^{t-1} s_{t-1})$. The first one of center sequence sorted by $f(s_i)$ in nondecreasing order is the initial solution D_1.

The rest $k - 1$ ones should ensure that each addition Δ_t at step t is maximal. Let $Cov_{t-1} = \bigcup_i^{t-1} s(t-1)$ with initial solution $Cov_0 = \varnothing$.

3.2 Approximation Algorithm Design

We provide a step-by-step description of our algorithm, followed by details on constraint identification.

Algorithm 1. Approximation Algorithm

1: Generate the FCVD for given $G = (V, E)$ with m colors
2: **for** each $v_i \in V$ **do**
3:   $r(v_i) \leftarrow \max_{P_j \subset \mathcal{P}}^m \min_{x \in P_j} dist(v_i, x)$;
4: **end for**
5: Save $CSR(V) = \{r(v_1), r(v_2), \cdots, r(v_n)\}$
0: Compute the minimum spanning tree (MST) $G_{MST} = (V, E^{MST})$
7: $\forall w(u) \leftarrow 0$
8: $S_0 = \varnothing$
9: **for** each $v_i \in V$ **do**
10:   $w(v_i) \leftarrow \max_{e(i,x) \in E^{MST}} w(v_i, v_x)$;
11: **end for**
12: $Solution(MPC) \leftarrow \sum_{v_i \in V}^n w(v_i)$
13: **for** each $v_i \in V$ **do**
14:   **if** $dist(v_i, v_x) \leq r(v_i)$ **then**
15:     $s(v_i) \leftarrow v_x$;
16:   **end if**
17:   Save $s(v_i)$, short as $s(i)$, and count $|s(v_i)|$;
18: **end for**
19: **for** $v_i \in V$ **do**
20:   $f(v_i) \leftarrow \sum_{v_x \in s(i)}^{|s(i)|} w(v_x) - w(v_i)$;
21: **end for**
22: Save sorted sequence $V^I = \{v_1, v_2, \cdots, v_i, \cdots, v_n\}$ in nonincreasing order by value $f(v_i)$ as the covering set;
23: Save subsets to $S = \{s(v_1), s(v_2), ..., s(v_i), ..., s(v_n)\}$;
24: $D_0 \leftarrow \varnothing, Cov(D_0) \leftarrow \varnothing$;
25: Select the first item with maximal $f(v)$ in $L = (V^I, S)$
26: $r_1 \leftarrow r(v_1)$, and $D \leftarrow v_1$
27: $S(D_1) \leftarrow s_1$, and $Cov(D_1) \leftarrow s_1$
28: **for** $t = 2$ to k **do**
29:   choose $v_t \in V$ to maximize $\Delta_t f(\bigcup_i^{t-1} Cov_{t-1} \cup s_t)$
30:   $D_t \leftarrow D_{t-1} \cup \{v_t\}, Cov(t) \leftarrow Cov(t-1) \cup \{s_t\}$
31: **end for**
32: **return** Selected center set D^A with color-spanning radii $R^A(D) = \{r_1, \cdots, r_k\}$;
33: **return** covered node subset $S(D^A) = \{s_1, ..., s_k\}, Cov(D^A) = \bigcup_i^k s(D_i)$, and the uncovered node set $B = U \setminus (Cov(D) \cup D)$;
34: **return** $F^A = Solution(MPC) - \max_{D \subseteq V} f(D) + \sum^k r(i)$

---

4   The Performance of Our Algorithm

4.1   The Approximation Ratio

The classical and k-maximal cover problem are NP-hard. When objective function is under submodular and monotone condition, Feige et al. [18,19] proved a best-possible factor approximation ratio of $1-e^{-1}$ by the greedy algorithm unless $NP = P$. Submodular is a very natural property of various functions. In set function $f : 2^V \mapsto \mathbb{R}$, f is submodular iff. $f(X \cup Y) + f(X \cap Y) \leq f(X) + f(Y)$ for any $X, Y \subseteq V$. The corollary below helps us to estimate the gap between our approximation value f^A and the optimal solution f^* of the Max-k-cover step.

Lemma 1. *The function in our Max-k-cover subproblem is submodular and monotone.*

Proof. Let D_t be the selected center by greedy strategy up to t iterations and $Cov(D_t)$ be the corresponding sets.

The $Cov(D_1)$ is the maximum coverage one in all $s_i \subseteq S$. Then the rest $k-1$ selection is added by maximum added coverage value at each iteration. It is obvious that the improvement from $f(t)$ to $f(t+1)$ is always positive and monotone decreasing or nonincreasing for any integer $t \in [1, k)$. This step shows serious monotonicity firstly.

Let $w(i) = \sum_{v_x \in s_i}^{|s_i|} p(v_x) - p(i)$ be the value covered by disk $\odot(o_i, r_i)$ centered on node o_i with radius r_i, and $Cov(D_k) = \{s_1 \cup ... \cup s_k\} - D_k$ be union of each covered nodes by selected centers except centers themselves. Next proof of submodularity is based the definition above. As we know, our Max-k-cover subproblem aims to find k sets with maximal coverage value $f(D_k) = \sum_{v_x \in Cov(k)}^{|Cov(k)|} p(v_x) - \sum_{v_i \in D_k} p(i)$, where $r(i)$ is the radius of color-spanning disk, and $p(i)$ is assigned weight to node $v_i \in V$ for connectivity based on of MCP subproblem.

It has an influence on the total coverage $f(D_t)$ that whether the new added set s_t in t-th iteration contains previous selected centers D_{t-1}. Based on this property, we divide two cases by whether $s_t \cap D_{t-1} \neq \varnothing$.

One case is $s_t \cap D_{t-1} = \varnothing$, $\forall t \in [2, k]$, when no selected centers is contained by new added coverage sets. The total coverage value would be summation. We have $f(A \cup B) = f(A) + f(B)$ for any $A, B \subseteq V$, as $f(A \cap B) = 0$. Another case exists $s_t \cap D_{t-1} \neq \varnothing$. We assume it appeared at the t-th iteration. Let $v_x \in D_{t-1}$ be the covered element by s_t. When element v_t added, function $f(t)$ would move out value $p(x)$ counted in $w(t)$. As $\forall p(x) \geq 1$, we have $f(D_{t-1} \cap X) < f(D_{t-1}) + f(X) - f(D_{t-1} \cup X)$, where X is any other set contained $v_x \in D_{t-1}$.

Combined these two cases, we can conclude that $f(A \cup X) + f(A \cap X) \leq f(A) + f(X)$ with $A, X \subset V$. Submodularity is proved based on its definition.

Theorem 1. *Our approximation algorithm can solve the k-CCSLPCC within a ratio of $3 + \frac{1}{e}$.*

Proof. There are three main parts for our algorithm.

The first FCVD graph for color-spanning constraints can find an approximation solution r_i^A no more twice than optimal one for $v_i \in V$. Note the case with ratio 2 as instance I_1. Let $R^A(I)$ be the solution of our approximation algorithm for any instance I, and R^* be optimal solution. We have $\frac{R^A(I)}{R^*} \le \frac{R^A(I_1)}{R^*(I_1)} \le 2$.

Let $P(I_2) = Length(MST)$ is the solution under instance I_2 with gap 2 to our MCP solutions [16]. Thus, we have $\frac{Solution(MCP)}{OPT(MCP)} \le \frac{Solution(MCP)}{P(I_2)} \le 2$.

The Max-k-cover part is the last step of our approximation algorithm. Let $F(D)$ be our objective function and $f(D_i)$ be value function of the Max-k-cover value. Let $f(I_3)$ be the results in instance I_3 with the maximal gap between our greedy strategy and the optimal one f^*. As Corollary 1 proved, we claim that $\frac{f^A(I)}{f^*} \ge \frac{f^A(I_2)}{f^*(I_2)} \ge 1 - \frac{1}{e}$ [19].

We denote an instance I_{worst} arising the upper bound of gap between our approximation solution $A(I)$ and the optimal result OPT(I) for our k-CLSCPCC. With the help of case I_{worst}, the approximation ratio $ratio(A)$ of our algorithm can be estimated as follow:

$$ratio(A) = \max \frac{A(I)}{OPT(I)} = \frac{Solution(MCP) - f^A(I) + R^A(I)}{OPT(I)} \tag{1}$$

$$\le \frac{2P(I_2)}{OPT(I_{worst})} - \frac{f^A(I_3)}{OPT(I_{worst})} + \frac{R^A(I_1)}{OPT(I_{worst})} \tag{2}$$

$$\le \frac{2P(I_2)}{OPT(I_2)} - \frac{f^A(I_3)}{f*(I_3)} + \frac{R^A(I_1)}{R*(I_1)} \le 2 - (1 - \frac{1}{e}) + 2 = 3 + \frac{1}{e} < 3.368 \tag{3}$$

4.2   The Complexity

Theorem 2. *The computing time of our approximation algorithm costs no more than $O(n^2 m \log m)$, where n is the input size of ground set, m is the number of colors.*

Proof. Our total running time is the longest time of our three main steps.

Firstly, the disk coverage region must satisfy the color-spanning constraint. Generation of FCVD costs $O(n^2 m \log m)$ for given n nodes with m colors [10]. Based on FCVD graph, n nodes need at most n times $n \log n$ to get their diameter of color-spanning circle.

Secondly, Primal Algorithm helps generate the minimum spanning tree T_n on dense graph with timing of $O(n^2 \log n)$. The selection of the maximum weighted runs n times for all nodes on tree. Then, the total cost of second main step is $O(n^2 \log n) + O(n^2 \log n) = O(n^2 \log n)$.

The set operations help compute covered value $u_i = \sum_{v_j \in Cov(v_i, r_i)} p_j$ and n elements cost $n \times O(n)$ time. It costs $O(n^2)$ time to sort elements by value u_i. At most k times loops to finish the selection of rest D_i. Even based on the basic List and Array List data structure, all selections cost $O(kn^3)$ time at most.

All in all, as parameter m is much less than n and k is given integer, the total computing time is $T(n^2 m \log m + n^2 \log n + kn^3 + n) = O(n^2 m \log m)$, where n and m is the number of nodes and colors of in a given node set V.

5   Conclusions

Our k-CLSCPCC assigns an individual radius to each selected color-spanning center such that the total cost is minimized. A more sensitive server assignment is achieved using the nearest-first rule in disk coverage for stable performance in high-density and multi-class scenarios. A moving service mode to fulfill the remaining demand arises rest part of cost except all k individual radius. In this study, we propose a $3+\frac{1}{e}$ ratio algorithm for a variant connected location problem within $O(n^2 m \log m)$ running time.

Applying our method or adjusting our method on a wider range of networks can be considered in the future.

References

1. Ju, W., Fan, C., Luo, J., et al.: On some geometric problems of color-spanning sets. J. Comb. Optim. **26**(2), 266–283 (2013)
2. Graf, T., Hinrichs, K.: Algorithms for proximity problems on colored point sets. In: Proceedings of 5th Canada Conference Computer Geometric, Universität Münster. Angewandte Mathematik und Informatik, pp. 420–425 (1993)
3. Abellanas, M., et al.: Smallest color-spanning objects. In: auf der Heide, F.M. (ed.) ESA 2001. LNCS, vol. 2161, pp. 278–289. Springer, Heidelberg (2001). https://doi.org/10.1007/3-540-44676-1_23
4. Toregas, C., Swain, R., ReVelle, C., et al.: The location of emergency service facilities. Oper. Res. **19**(6), 1363–1373 (1971)
5. Berman, O., Ingco, D.I., Odoni, A.: Improving the location of minimax facilities through network modification. Networks **24**(1), 31–41 (1994)
6. Banerjee, S., Misra, N., Nandy, S.C.: Color spanning objects: algorithms and hardness results. In: Govindarajan, S., Maheshwari, A. (eds.) CALDAM 2016. LNCS, vol. 9602, pp. 37–48. Springer, Cham (2016). https://doi.org/10.1007/978-3-319-29221-2_4
7. Huttenlocher, D.P., Kedem, K., Sharir, M.: The upper envelope of Voronoi surfaces and its applications. Discrete Comput. Geom. **9**(3), 267–291 (1993)
8. Fleischer, R., Xu, X.: Computing minimum diameter color-spanning sets. In: International Workshop on Frontiers in Algorithmics, FAW 2010, LNCS, vol. 6213, pp. 285–292. Springer, Berlin, Heidelberg (2010). https://doi.org/10.1007/2F978-3-642-14553-7_27
9. Fleischer, R., Xu, X.: Computing minimum diameter color-spanning sets is hard. Inf. Proc. Lett. **111**(21–22), 1054–1056 (2011)
10. Abellanas, M., Hurtado, F., Icking, C., et al.: The farthest color voronoi diagram and related problems. In: Abstracts 17th European Workshop Computing. Geometry, CG 2001, pp. 113–116. Freie, Universität Berlin (2001)
11. Eppstein, D., Overmars, M., Rote, G., et al.: (1992). Finding minimum area k-gons. Discrete Comput. Geom. **7**(1), 45–58 (1992)
12. Mantas, I., Papadopoulou, E., Sacristán, V., Silveira, R.I.: Farthest color voronoi diagrams: complexity and algorithms. In: Kohayakawa, Y., Miyazawa, F.K. (eds.) LATIN 2021. LNCS, vol. 12118, pp. 283–295. Springer, Cham (2020). https://doi.org/10.1007/978-3-030-61792-9_23

13. Fan, C., Luo, J., Zhu, B.: Tight approximation bounds for connectivity with a color-spanning set. ISAAC **2013**, 590–600 (2013). https://doi.org/10.1007/978-3-642-45030-3_55
14. Current, J.R., Schilling, D.A.: The median tour and maximal covering tour problems: formulations and heuristics. Eur. J. Oper. Res. **73**(1), 114–126 (1994)
15. Spoerhase, J., Wirth, H.C.: An $O(n(\log n)^2/log\log n)$ algorithm for the single maximum coverage location or the (1, Xp)-medianoid problem on trees. Inf. Proc. Lett. **109**(8), 391–394 (2009)
16. Chen, W.T., Huang, N.F.: The strongly connecting problem on multihop packet radio networks. IEEE Trans. Commun. **37**(3), 293–295 (1989)
17. Sedgewick, R., Wayne F. K.: Algorithms. 4th edn. Addison-Wesley, Boston (2011)
18. Nemhauser, G.L., Wolsey, L.A.: Best algorithms for approximating the maximum of a submodular set function. Math. Oper. Res. **3**(3), 177–188 (1978)
19. Feige, U.: A threshold of $\ln n$ for approximating set cover. J. ACM (JACM) **45**(4), 634–652 (1998)

Recent Advances in Sustainable Manufacturing

Sustainable Process Plan Generation in RMS: A Comparative Study of Two Multi-objective Evolutionary Approaches

Imen Khettabi[1], Lyes Benyoucef[2(✉)], and Mohamed Amine Boutiche[1]

[1] DGRSDT, LaROMaD Laboratory, USTHB University, Algiers, Algeria
khettabi.imen@usthb.dz, mboutiche@usthb.dz
[2] Aix Marseille University, University of Touloun, CNRS, LIS, Marseille, France
lyes.benyoucef@lis-lab.fr

Abstract. In today's manufacturing industry, staying competitive requires being both cost and time effective, as well as being environmentally benign. In this paper, two versions of the well-known non-dominated sorting genetic algorithm (NSGA) namely Dynamic-NSGA-II and NSGA-III are proposed and compared to solve an environmental oriented multi-objective single unit process plan generation problem in a reconfigurable manufacturing environment. In addition to the traditional total production cost and total production time, two other criteria namely, total amount of hazardous liquid waste and total amount of greenhouse gases (GHG) emitted are minimized. Firstly, a non-linear multi-objective integer program (NL-MOIP) is proposed. Secondly, to illustrate the efficiency of the two approaches, several instances of the problem are experimented and the obtained results are analyzed using three metrics respectively spacing metric, inverted generational distance and cardinality of the mixed Pareto fronts.

Keywords: Sustainability · RMS · Process plan generation · Multi-objective optimization · Dynamic-NSGA-II · NGSA-III

1 Introduction

Reconfigurable manufacturing system (RMS) is one of the latest manufacturing paradigms. In this paradigm, machine components, machines softwares or material handling units can be added, removed, modified or interchanged as needed and when imposed by the necessity to react and respond rapidly and cost-effectively to changing requirements. RMS is regarded as a convenient manufacturing paradigm for variety productions as well as a flexible enabler for this variety. Hence, it is a logical evolution of the two manufacturing systems already used in the industries respectively dedicated manufacturing lines (DML) and flexible manufacturing systems (FMS). According to Koren [1], father of RMS, DMLs are inexpensive but their capacities are not fully utilized in several situations especially under the pressure of global competition, thus they engender

© IFIP International Federation for Information Processing 2021
Published by Springer Nature Switzerland AG 2021
A. Dolgui et al. (Eds.): APMS 2021, IFIP AICT 632, pp. 329–339, 2021.
https://doi.org/10.1007/978-3-030-85906-0_37

losses. On the other hand, FMSs respond to product changes, but they are not designed for structural changes. Hence, in both systems, a sudden market variation cannot be countered, like demand fluctuation or regulatory requirements. RMS combines the high flexibility of FMS with the high production rate of DML. It comprises the positive features of both systems, thanks to its adjustable structure and design focus.

Nowadays, RMS is a very active research field where multiple state of the arts have been dedicated covering many areas, such as design, layout optimization, reconfigurable control, process planning and production scheduling, etc. In a multi-objective context, [2] used an adapted version of NSGA-II to integrate process plan generation to the design problem. In [3], the authors introduced the concept of reconfigurable and energy efficient manufacturing system (REMS) and proposed a discrete event simulation model to evaluate its energy efficiency. Moreover, [4] presented a quantitative framework for sustainable manufacturing explaining how it can be applied to the automotive industry and how material alternatives can help to achieve sustainability objectives. Toward sustainable RMSs and system design through process plan generation, the authors in [5] proposed a comparative study of an iterative multi-objective integer linear programming (I-MOILP) approach with adapted versions of AMOSA and NSGA-II algorithms. Recently, [6] showed how the RMSs concepts can lead to the design of sustainable and energy efficient manufacturing systems and how to decrease the emissions and energy consumption during the life cycle.

In this paper, we adapt two evolutionary approaches, respectively Dynamic-NSGA-II and NSGA-III, to solve an environmental oriented multi-objective single unit process plan generation problem in a reconfigurable environment. Some experimental results are presented and analyzed using three metrics namely spacing metric, inverted generational distance and cardinality of the mixed Pareto fronts. The rest of the paper is organized as follows. Section 2 presents the problem under consideration and its mathematical formulation. Section 3 describes the proposed two approaches. Section 4 discusses the experimental results and analyzes. Section 5 concludes the paper with some future work directions.

2   Problem Description and Mathematical Formulation

2.1   Problem Description

Let us consider a single unit of a product to be manufactured in a reconfigurable environment. The product is composed of a set of operations linked by precedence constraints (see Fig. 1). Moreover, three key data define an operation: the precedence constraints, the set of candidate tools and the tool approach directions (TADs) (i.e. x±,y±,z±). Once the operations requirements are identified, a machine is able to perform a certain number of operations. Given that, for each machine, the sets of available configurations and compatible tools are identified. Thus, each operation OP_i requires an association of machine-configuration-tool

(M, C, T) called triplet TO_i. The generation of process plan consists of sequencing the operations to be performed on the used machines under the configurations and tools, through the precedence graph as well as the triplets to perform each operation in the sequence. Table 1 presents a simple example of a generated process plan in our case.

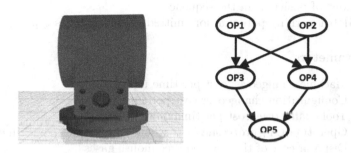

Fig. 1. An illustrative product schema and operations precedence graph

Table 1. Illustrative structure of a process plan

Operation	OP_1	OP_2	OP_3	OP_4	OP_5
Machine	M_2	M_1	M_3	M_3	M_1
Configuration	C_2	C_3	C_1	C_1	C_2
Tool	T_2	T_1	T_3	T_1	T_1

2.2 Mathematical Formulation

The following notations are used:

Parameters

n Number of operations
OP Set of operations
i, i' Index of operations
PR_i Set of predecessors of operation OP_i
m Number of machines
M Set of machines
j, j' Index of machine
G Set of greenhouse gases
g Index of greenhouse gases
$l_{i,t}$ Required liquid for operation OP_i when using triplet t per time unit
$EP_{i,t}$ Estimated hazardous liquid waste for operation OP_i when using triplet t
f_{ef} Emission factor for electricity consumption
$f_{i,g}$ Operation OP_i emitting greenhouse gas type g per time unit

t, t' Index of triplet
TO_i Set of available triplets for operation OP_i
TM_j Set of available triplets using machine M_j
T Set of triplets, where $T = TO_i \cup TM_j$
c, c' Index of configurations
tl, tl' Index of tools
p, p' Index of positions in the sequence
GWP_g Global warning potential for emitted greenhouse gas type g

Cost Parameters

$CCM_{j,j'}$ Machine changeover cost per time unit
$CCC_{c,c'}$ Configuration changeover cost per time unit
$CCT_{tl,tl'}$ Tool changeover cost per time unit
$Pc_{i,t}$ Operation OP_i processing cost when using triplet t per time unit
DC_{GHG} Disposal cost of the emitted greenhouse gases
DC_{LHW} Disposal cost of the hazardous liquid waste

Time Parameters

$TCM_{j,j'}$ Machine changeover time
$TCC_{c,c'}$ Configuration changeover time
$TCT_{tl,tl'}$ Tool changeover time
$Pt_{i,t}$ Operation OP_i processing time when using triplet t

Energy Parameters

$ECM_{j,j'}$ Machine changeover energy per time unit
$ECC_{c,c'}$ Configuration changeover energy per time unit
$ECT_{tl,tl'}$ Tool changeover energy
$Pe_{i,t}$ Operation OP_i processing energy when using triplet t per time unit
IEC_j Initial energy consumption of machine M_j

Decision Variables

$x^t_{i,p} = 1$ if operation OP_i is using triplet t at the pth position, 0 otherwise.
$y^m_{p,t} = 1$ if machine M_j is using triplet t at the pth position, 0 otherwise.
$MC^{p-1}_p(j, j') = 1$ if there has been a change from machine M_j to machine M'_j between positions $p - 1$ and p, 0 otherwise.
$TC^{j,p-1}_p(t, t') = 1$ if there has been a change from triplet t to triplet t' of machine M_j between positions $p - 1$ and p, 0 otherwise.

Objective Functions

Our problem can be formulated as a non-linear multi-objective integer program (NL-MOIP), where four objectives are minimized:

1. The total production cost f_c: Eq. (1) shows the total production cost to be minimized. It includes the following costs: machine changeover cost, configuration changeover cost, tool changeover cost, processing cost, emitted greenhouse gases cost and disposal cost of the emitted hazardous waste during the production.

$$
\begin{aligned}
f_c = &\sum_{p=1}^{n}\sum_{i=1}^{n}\sum_{t\in TO_i} x_{i,p}^t \times Pc_{i,t} \times Pt_{i,t} \\
&+ \sum_{p=2}^{n}\sum_{j=1}^{m}\sum_{j'=1}^{m} MC_p^{p-1}(j,j') \times CCM_{j,j'} \times TCMj,j' \\
&+ \sum_{p=2}^{n}\sum_{j=1}^{m}\sum_{t\in M_j}\sum_{t'\in M_j} TC_p^{j,p-1}(t,t') \times (CCT_{tl,tl'} \times TCT_{tl,tl'} \\
&+ CCC_{c,c'} \times TCC_{c,c'}) + (DC_{GHG} \times f_{GHG} + DC_{LWH} \times f_{LHW})
\end{aligned}
\tag{1}
$$

2. The total production time f_t: Eq. (2) defines the total production time to be minimized. It includes: machine changeover time, configuration changeover time, tool changeover time and processing time.

$$
\begin{aligned}
f_t = &\sum_{p=1}^{n}\sum_{i=1}^{n}\sum_{t\in TO_i} x_{i,p}^t \times Pt_{i,t} \\
&+ \sum_{p=2}^{n}\sum_{j=1}^{m}\sum_{j'=1}^{m} MC_p^{p-1}(j,j') \times TCM_{j,j'} \\
&+ \sum_{p=2}^{n}\sum_{j=1}^{m}\sum_{t\in M_j}\sum_{t'\in M_j} TC_p^{j,p-1}(t,t') \times (TCC_{c,c'} + TCT_{tl,tl'})
\end{aligned}
\tag{2}
$$

3. The amount of hazardous liquid waste f_{LHW}: Eq. (3) defines the amount of hazardous liquid waste to be minimized. It comprises the hazardous liquid waste during processing of the operations, including: wastes oils/water, hydrocarbons/water mixtures, emulsions; wastes from the production, formulation and use of resins, latex, plasticizers, glues/adhesives; wastes resulting from surface treatment of metals and plastics; residues arising from industrial waste disposal operations.

$$
f_{LHW} = \sum_{p=1}^{n}\sum_{i=1}^{n}\sum_{t\in TO_i} x_{i,p}^t \times l_{i,t} \times Pt_{i,t} \times EP_{i,t}
\tag{3}
$$

4. The amount of greenhouse gases emitted f_{GHG}: Eq. (4) defines the amount of greenhouse gases emitted during the manufacturing process to be minimized. It is composed of two parts. The first considers the energy consumption taking into account the emission factor for consumed electricity. The second considers the emitted gases taking into account the factor of global warning potential (GWP). In this research work, GWP factor is used to convert emissions of the other greenhouse gases into CO_2 equivalents.

$$f_{GHG} = f_{ef} \times f_{EC} + \sum_{p=1}^{n} \sum_{i=1}^{n} \sum_{t\in TO_i} \sum_{g\in G} x_{i,p}^t \times Pt_{i,t} \times f_{i,g} \times GWP_g \qquad (4)$$

Equation (5) describes how to compute the total energy consumption f_{EC} during the production process.

$$
\begin{aligned}
f_{EC} = & \sum_{p=1}^{n} \sum_{i=1}^{n} \sum_{j=1}^{m} \sum_{t\in TO_i} y_{p,t}^j \times x_{i,p}^t \times IEC_j \\
& + \sum_{p=1}^{n} \sum_{i=1}^{n} \sum_{t\in TO_i} x_{i,p}^t \times Pe_{i,t} \times Pt_{i,t} \\
& + \sum_{p=2}^{n} \sum_{j=1}^{m} \sum_{j'=1}^{m} MC_p^{p-1}(j,j') \times ECM_{j,j'} \times TCM_{j,j'} \\
& + \sum_{p=2}^{n} \sum_{j=1}^{m} \sum_{t\in TM_j} \sum_{t'\in TM_j} TC_p^{j,p-1}(t,t') \times \\
& (TTC_{tl,tl'} \times ETC_{tl,tl'} + TCC_{c,c'} + ECC_{c,c'})
\end{aligned}
\qquad (5)
$$

f_{EC} is a non-linear function. To linearize it, we can use the following equations:
$y_{p,t}^j \times x_{i,p}^t = z \ S.t : z \le x_{i,p}^t, z \le y_{p,t}^j, z \ge y_{p,t}^j + x_{i,p}^t - 1, z \in \{0,1\}$

A complete description of the nine constraints associated to our problem are depicted in [7].

3   Proposed Approaches

In this section, we describe the adapted two evolutionary approaches, namely Dynamic-NSGA-II and NSGA-III. Two genetic operators, respectively crossover and mutation, are used as illustrated in Fig. 2 and Fig. 3. For clear descriptions of the considered coded process plan as well as the crossover and the mutation operators, refer to [8].

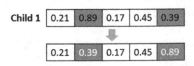

Fig. 2. Illustrative crossover operator

Fig. 3. Illustrative mutation operator

3.1   Dynamic Non Dominated Sorting Genetic Algorithm II (Dynamic-NSGA-II)

NSGA-II is an updated version of the non-dominated sorting genetic algorithm (NSGA) [9], well-known for solving multi-objective problems. The NSGA-II mechanism begins by ranking the solutions according to their non-domination score to get a set of Pareto front solutions. Then, the crowding distance technique, which guarantees diversity along the obtained Pareto front solutions, is applied on the last front to complete the next generation parent population size. Nevertheless, the lateral diversity is not maintained. For better convergence, we proposed an adapted version of NSGA-II called Dynamic-NSGA-II. It uses a new diversity preservation technique called dynamic crowding distance, which can maintain lateral diversity and a uniform distribution of the Pareto front solutions. Algorithm 1 presents the main steps of the Dynamic-NSGA-II.

1: input data
2: initialize $populationSize$, $iteration$, $p_{mutation}$, $mutationRatio$, $p_{crossover}$
3: randomize $parentPopulation$
4: **for** $iter = 1 : iteration$ **do**
5:     generate $childPopulation$ from $parentPopulation$
6:     $population = parentPopulation \cup childPopulation$
7:     $F = $ fastNonDominatedSorting($population$)
8:     **for** $l = 1 : size(F)$ **do**
9:         **if** size($newPopulation$)+size(F_l) $< populationSize$ **then**
10:             $newPopulation+ = F_l$
11:         **else**
12:             DynamicCrowdingDistanceSorting(F_l)
13:             **for** $k = 1 : size(F_l)$ **do**
14:                 **if** size($newPopulation$) $< populationSize$ **then**
15:                     $newPopulation+ = F_l^k$
16:                 **else**
17:                     break;
18:                 **end if**
19:             **end for**
20:         **end if**
21:     **end for**
22:     $parentPopulation = newPopulation$
23: **end for**
24: **return** $parentPopulation$

3.2   Non Dominated Sorting Genetic Algorithm III (NSGA-III)

The NSGA-III's [10] framework is based on the NSGA-II. The major difference between the two algorithms is the selection mechanism. NSGA-III replaces the crowding distance with a reference point based niche mechanism, which can help spread out Pareto optimal fronts and improve population diversity. Note that, the same procedures (i.e., initial population, crossover and mutation operators) used for Dynamic-NSGA-II are being considered for NSGA-III. Algorithm 2 presents the main steps of NSGA-III.

1: Compute the number of reference points (H) to place on the hyper-plan
2: Generate the initial population randomly taking into account the resources assignment constraints (POP chromosomes)
3: Realize the non-dominated population sorting
4: **for** $i = 1$ Stopping criteria **do**
5:     Select two parents $P1$ and $P2$ using the tournament method
6:     Apply the crossover between $P1$ and $P2$ with a probability P_c
7:     Compute the non-dominated population sorting
8:     Normalize the population members
9:     Associate the population member with the reference points
10:     Apply the niche preservation (counter)
11:     Keep the niche obtained solutions for the next generation
12: **end for**

4   Experimental Results and Analyses

The following experiments were implemented with a 4.0 GHZ Intel Core i7 processor and 16 GB RAM. The two approaches were implemented with a Java-Cplex. An instance is defined by the number of operations and the number of available reconfigurable machines and represented by nbOperations-nbMachines. To analyze the Pareto solutions, two metrics, respectively Spacing metric [11] and inverted generational distance (IGD) [12], are used. Due to the space limitation, we replace Dynamic-NSGA-II by D-NSGA-II in the following tables.

For both Dynamic-NSGA-II and NSGA-III, the used parameters are as follows: Population-size = 40, number of iterations = 1000, probability of mutation = 90%, probability of crossover = 10% and mutation ratio = 0.3. Furthermore, to show the impact of the number of iterations on the quality of the Pareto fronts, instance 100-20bis refers to the situation where the number of iterations = 2000.

Table 2 presents the obtained numerical results, where two performance indicators are used, the CPU calculation time (in seconds) and the cardinality of the Pareto front (number of Pareto optimal process plans) of each instance.

Table 2. CPU time and cardinality of the pareto fronts: D-NSGA-II vs NSGA-III

Instance	CPU (seconds)		Cardinality of the Pareto fronts	
	D-NSGA-II	NSGA-III	D-NSGA-II	NSGA-III
10-5	417.87	**212.35**	3	**7**
13-6	484.41	**309.86**	8	**9**
15-10	495.17	**337.73**	3	**5**
25-10	673.23	**536.46**	19	19
35-15	937.36	**808.39**	13	**21**
40-15	1057.23	**950.05**	16	**26**
50-20	1541.40	**1485.96**	20	13
100-20	3894.79	**3740.28**	16	13
100-20bis	15005.70	**14281.22**	44	37

Table 3 presents a comparison of the Pareto fronts obtained by Dynamic-NSGA-II and NSGA-III, where # Pareto front corresponds to the number of Pareto optimal process plans maintained in the new Pareto front (i.e., contributions of Dynamic-NSGA-II and NSGA-III Pareto fronts in the new mixed Pareto front). The idea is to construct a new Pareto front based on the two Pareto fronts of respectively Dynamic-NSGA-II and NSGA-III. Moreover, Table 4 shows the obtained metric values.

Table 3. Performances comparisons: D-NSGA-II vs NSGA-III

Instance	Combination of the pareto fronts of D-NSGA-II, NSGA-III			
	Total of cardinality	# Pareto front of D-NSGA-II	# Pareto front of NSGA-III	# Pareto front in common between D-NSGAII & NSGA-III
10-5	4	1	1	2
13-6	11	2	**3**	6
15-10	5	0	**5**	0
25-10	32	16	**16**	0
35-15	28	8	**20**	0
40-15	37	11	**26**	0
50-20	23	10	**13**	0
100-20	24	11	**13**	0
100-20bis	60	23	**37**	0

Table 4. Spacing metric and IGD values: D-NSGA-II vs NSGA-III

Instance	Spacing metric		IGD	
	D-NSGA-II	NSGA-III	D-NSGA-II	NSGA-III
10-5	695.13	**128.72**	64.28	**48.36**
13-6	**40.26**	108.74	36.05	36.05
15-10	2.89	**2.24**	17.03	**10.44**
25-10	**328.76**	613.40	524.31	**426.61**
35-15	302.38	**264.62**	**357.54**	761
40-15	340.74	**179.48**	**192.93**	310.27
50-20	**265.18**	321.57	**229.98**	230.36
100-20	**805.53**	5941.80	**379.44**	594.32
100-20bis	**126.56**	185.24	**329.95**	549.28

From the above three tables, we can distinguish three observations:

- Observations 1: From Table 2, we can see that, NSGA-III has better computational time, where Dynamic-NSGA-II has acquired more Pareto solutions for large instances.
- Observations 2: From Table 3, we observe that, NSGA-III completely dominates Dynamic-NSGA-II.
- Observations 3: From Table 4, we can conclude that Dynamic-NSGA-II algorithm has a great advantage in promoting diversity. Moreover, it indicates a major progression of the region covered by the Pareto front.

5 Conclusion and Perspectives

In this paper, we considered an environmental oriented multi-objective process plan generation problem in a reconfigurable manufacturing environment. We adapted two evolutionary approaches, respectively, Dynamic-NSGA-II and NSGA-III. To show the efficiencies of both approaches, some experimental results were realized and the obtained results were analyzed using three metrics respectively, spacing metric, inverted generational distance and cardinality of the mixed Pareto fronts.

For future works, shortly, in addition to reducing the traditional total production cost and completion time, minimizing the maximum machines exploitation time can be considered as a novel optimization criterion for high quality products. Moreover, other evolutionary-based approaches such as AMOSA, MOPSO, etc., can be adapted and compared.

References

1. Koren, Y.: The Global Manufacturing Revolution: Product-Process-Business Integration and Reconfigurable Systems, vol. 80. Wiley, Hoboken (2010)

2. Bensmaine, A., Dahane, M., Benyoucef, L.: A non-dominated sorting genetic algorithm based approach for optimal machines selection in reconfigurable manufacturing environment. Comput. Indus. Eng. **66**(3), 519–524 (2013)
3. Zhang, H., Zhao, F., Sutherland, J.W.: Energy-efficient scheduling of multiple manufacturing factories under real-time electricity pricing. CIRP Ann. **64**(1), 41–44 (2015)
4. Stoycheva, S., Marchese, D., Paul, C., Padoan, S., Juhmani, A.S., Linkov, I.: Multi-criteria decision analysis framework for sustainable manufacturing in automotive industry. J. Cleaner Prod. **187**, 257–272 (2018)
5. Touzout, F.A., Benyoucef, L.: Multi-objective sustainable process plan generation in a reconfigurable manufacturing environment: exact and adapted evolutionary approaches. Int. J. Prod. Res. **57**(8), 2531–2547 (2019)
6. Battaïa, O., Benyoucef, L., Delorme, X., Dolgui, A., Thevenin, S.: Sustainable and energy efficient reconfigurable manufacturing systems. In: Benyoucef, L. (ed.) Reconfigurable Manufacturing Systems: From Design to Implementation. SSAM, pp. 179–191. Springer, Cham (2020). https://doi.org/10.1007/978-3-030-28782-5_9
7. Khezri, A., Haddou Benderbal, H., Benyoucef, L.: Towards a sustainable reconfigurable manufacturing system (SRMS): multi-objective based approaches for process plan generation problem. Int. J. Prod. Res. **59**(15), 4533–4558 (2021)
8. Touzout, F.A., Benyoucef, L.: Sustainable multi-unit process plan generation in a reconfigurable manufacturing environment: A comparative study of three hybrid-meta-heuristics. In: Proceedings of IEEE 23rd International Conference on Emerging Technologies and Factory Automation (ETFA), vol. 1, pp. 661–668. IEEE (2018)
9. Deb, K., Pratap, A., Agarwal, S., Meyarivan, T.: A fast and elitist multiobjective genetic algorithm: NSGA-II. IEEE Trans. Evol. Comput. **6**(2), 182–197 (2002)
10. Deb, K., Jain, H.: An evolutionary many-objective optimization algorithm using reference-point-based nondominated sorting approach, part I: solving problems with box constraints. IEEE Trans. Evol. Comput. **18**(4), 577–601 (2014)
11. Deb, K., Agrawal, S., Pratap, A., Meyarivan, T.: A fast elitist non-dominated sorting genetic algorithm for multi-objective optimization: NSGA-II. In: Schoenauer, M., Deb, K., Rudolph, G., Yao, X., Lutton, E., Merelo, J.J., Schwefel, H.-P. (eds.) PPSN 2000. LNCS, vol. 1917, pp. 849–858. Springer, Heidelberg (2000). https://doi.org/10.1007/3-540-45356-3_83
12. Sierra, M.R., Coello Coello, C.A.: Improving PSO-based multi-objective optimization using crowding, mutation and ε-dominance. In: Coello Coello, C.A., Hernández Aguirre, A., Zitzler, E. (eds.) EMO 2005. LNCS, vol. 3410, pp. 505–519. Springer, Heidelberg (2005). https://doi.org/10.1007/978-3-540-31880-4_35

How Is Value Created in the Circular Economy? Evidence from Remanufacturing and Repair Businesses

Melissa Correa Marques$^{(\boxtimes)}$, Umit Sezer Bititci, and Amos Peter Haniff

Heriot-Watt University, Edinburgh EH14 4AS, UK
M.Correa_Marques@hw.ac.uk

Abstract. The circular economy refers to a cluster of strategies which are necessary in the pursuit of more sustainable production-consumption systems. In despite of the importance of repair and remanufacturing in the context of circular economy and sustainability, research in value creation within this sector is limited. There is little empirical evidence pertaining to the different ways that repair and remanufacturing activities can contribute to value creation across firms. This study therefore aimed to investigate value creation in the circular economy, particularly in context of fifteen repair and remanufacturing firms. Through a multi-method approach, data pertaining to value creation strategies were collected in both original equipment manufacturers (OEMs) and non-OEMs, and inductively analyzed with the aid of mapping tools. As a result, four generic patterns of value creation were identified, expanding upon previous literature by highlighting that 'OEM status' and 'servitization' are important variables of value generation.

Keywords: Remanufacturing · Value creation · Business model · Circular economy

1 Introduction

The circular economy is frequently interpreted as a set of strategies to implement the concept of sustainable development, including reducing, reusing, repairing, remanufacturing, and recycling materials. Although these strategies have the potential to transform business models, the literature pertaining to the various forms that repair and remanufacturing firms create value remains limited. One of the most significant studies was conducted by Lüdeke-Freund and colleagues [1] who identified a generic pattern of value creation asserting that repairing, remanufacturing, and upgrading allow companies to offer greener products at lower prices. The authors highlighted that value is generally captured through reduced material costs and additional revenues from price-sensitive customers seeking functionality. Nevertheless, it was acknowledged that additional costs are required to establish the required reverse logistics and labor skills [1]. Whilst it can be useful to generalize remanufacturing and repair organizations through a broad pattern of value creation, the authors themselves noted that not all firms capture

© IFIP International Federation for Information Processing 2021
Published by Springer Nature Switzerland AG 2021
A. Dolgui et al. (Eds.): APMS 2021, IFIP AICT 632, pp. 340–350, 2021.
https://doi.org/10.1007/978-3-030-85906-0_38

value in the same way [1]. Their framework, created from a literature review rather than own empirical data, was more applicable to an original equipment manufacturer (OEM) rather than an independent remanufacturer (or non-OEM).

Indeed, a bias towards the OEM perspective in the limited body of literature pertaining to repair and remanufacturing business models has been previously identified [2]. Additionally, there is a dearth of empirical evidence regarding the relationship between the circular economy and value creation. This includes a lack of comparisons across several repair and remanufacturing firms, with most articles adopting theoretical lenses or conducting one to four case studies. We therefore sought to address these knowledge, contextual, and methodological gaps within the literature. Specifically, this study aimed to answer '*how is value created across repair and remanufacturing business models?*' through a comprehensive empirical approach including fifteen case studies.

The remainder of this paper is structured as follows. Section 2 provides a literature review on value creation in repair and remanufacturing business models. Section 3 describes the method employed in this study, followed by analysis in Sect. 4 and discussion in Sect. 5. Finally, Sect. 6 provides a conclusion.

2 Literature Review

The literature pertaining to repair and remanufacturing businesses models is skewed towards the perspective of OEMs. Their primary concern when adopting such models is the risk of cannibalizing the sales of new products, although this is assessed against the profit potential of repair and remanufacturing and the risk of third parties conducting such activities [3]. Consequently, several studies have attempted to identify factors that OEMs should consider when deciding whether to engage with repair and remanufacturing. Matsumoto et al. [4] asserted that product characteristics are an important factor arguing that suitable products contain subparts with a physical lifetime significantly longer than the product usage time and have stable product and process technologies. Repair and remanufacturing are challenging from the operations management standpoint due to uncertainties related to the volume, timing, and conditions of returned products. Therefore, it was suggested that OEMs consider the product lifecycle and branding strategies to determine the most appropriate moment to introduce remanufacturing [5]. In addition to the right timing, decisions such as the ratio of new and remanufactured products and pricing of rebates might vary across the product lifecycle [6].

OEMs must guarantee that the costs for reverse logistics and re-processing are lower than the cost to produce new goods to make repair and remanufacturing viable [7]. Underpinning this idea is the assumption that consumers will misperceive remanufactured products as being of lower quality thus requesting a lower price. Consequently, if costs were not lower, the OEM would lose profitability. As revenues from the sales of reprocessed products are typically lower, OEMs seek to maintain the demand for new products stable whilst using reprocessed products to expand sales to new price-sensitive markets [8]. Such approach promotes growth at the firm level; however, the overall environmental impact might increase as the total of products created is higher [9].

Despite findings involving increased costs and reduced revenues, the literature also suggested advantages for OEMs conducting repair and remanufacturing such as the possibility of extending contact with consumers, facilitating returns, and reducing uncertainties through leasing models [10]. This could be enabled by sensors that track the state of components in real-time increasing the efficiency of planning, sorting, and remanufacturing processes, and that provide information for the design of new products [11]. Nevertheless, a challenge associated with leasing is that the product's lifetime costs depend on how the material is used by the customer, which is difficult to predict [12]. Additionally, leasing models shift the manufacturer's focus from production and distribution to asset management, requiring changes in customer relationships [13].

The bias towards the OEMs perspective within the literature is clear with little discussion focusing on third parties [2]. Non-OEM firms are typically treated as a threat as they can compete with OEMs. Even though third parties do not hold the prestige of the brand, they can offer long warranties, quick processing times, and proximity to clients [14]. To combat such threat, some OEMs prevent independent remanufacturing trough design and intellectual property rights [15]. Nevertheless, the rise in competition can benefit OEMs, for example increasing the perceived value of new products by up to 7% [16]. Furthermore, OEMs and non-OEMs do not necessarily need to compete, as OEMs can license their remanufacturing. Liu et al. [17] argued that such strategy is optimal for the OEM when the consumers' preference on refurbished product is not high - which would make the contracted company a strong competitor once authorized. However, it is not always profitable for non-OEMs to accept OEM licensing [18].

In summary, the literature review indicated the existence of limited empirical evidence pertaining to value creation in the circular economy, particularly in remanufacturing and repair business models and across both OEM and non-OEM firms.

3 Research Design

A multiple case study design was adopted in this qualitative study. Qualitative case studies are useful for exploring an understudied topic and allow theory building through inductive reasoning [19]. In this study, fifteen firms that conduct repair and remanufacturing were selected based upon theory-based variation, as the literature review indicated that including both the OEM and non-OEM perspectives were essential. Therefore, care was taken in selecting a comparable number of OEMs or OEM-associated firms (7) and non-OEMs (8). Although all businesses conducted repair and/or remanufacturing, a range of types of companies was obtained, whereby firms varied in terms of the level of product complexity and demand uncertainty for their products [20].

The companies' profiles are as follows. Companies A, B, C, D, E, F, and G were OEMs or OEM-associated. Company A was associated to OEMs both in the marine sector and in the industrial sectors. Firm B was a subsidiary conducting engine remanufacturing in the aviation industry. OEM C manufactured high-end audio equipment, offering modular upgrades throughout the product's lifetime. Company D designed and assembled new pumps for mining and industrial applications; nevertheless, repair and remanufacturing services were responsible for most of the revenues, with their share having increased over recent years. Likewise, OEM E assembled pumping equipment, with the firm also offering remanufacturing services and spare parts for other brands. Firm F focused on remanufacturing and servicing high-voltage generators for the power and oil sectors worldwide. Company G was an OEM of gearboxes for wind power and repaired and upgraded their own gearboxes or ones from other brands.

Differently than the previous companies, H, I, J, K, L, M, N, and O were non-OEMs. H and I were smaller independent remanufacturers in the automobile industry. Company H remanufactured gearboxes and transmissions, whilst firm I focused on turbocharges. Firm J was an independent remanufacturer of toners and cartridges. Firms K and L were providers of aftermarket services including repairs for the oil and marine sectors respectively, although K was a larger firm. Furthermore, companies M, N and O were also independent but focused on IT equipment, with N and O providing services for businesses wishing to dispose of equipment, whilst M offered repairs and exchanges on behalf of the OEM.

Table 1. Case studies and data collection approach

Company	Industry	OEM status	Approach
A	Generators and turbines for Industrial, Power and Marine	OEM-associated	Site visits and in-company workshops
B	Engines for Aviation	OEM	Site visit
C	Hi-fi sound equipment	OEM	Several site visits
D	Mining and Industrial pumps	OEM	Phone interview with CEO
E	Oil and Industrial pumps	OEM	Primary data in Bititci [20]
F	Generators for Power and Oil	OEM	Phone interview with CEO
G	Drivetrain and services for Wind power	OEM	In-person interview with shareholder
H	Automobile gearboxes and automatic transmissions	Non-OEM	In-person interview with CEO; site visit
I	Turbochargers for Automobile, Marine and Public sectors	Non-OEM	Two site visits and interview with CEO
J	Toners and cartridges	Non-OEM	Primary data in Bititci [20]
K	Asset management services for Oil and Renewable Energy	Non-OEM	Phone interview with the company's previous CEO
L	Engineering and repair services for Industrial and Marine	Non-OEM	Site visit; phone interview with CEO
M	Electronic monitors	Non-OEM	Primary data in Bititci [20]
N	Asset management for IT equipment	Non-OEM	Primary data in Cheng et al. [22]
O	IT equipment repair, recycling, and data destruction services	Non-OEM	Primary data in Cheng et al. [22]

Data were collected through the multi-method approach detailed in Table 1. The inductive data analysis process focused in understanding in-depth each of the companies' business models and value creation mechanisms, making use of the business model canvas [21] and value proposition tools [20].

4 Findings

After analyzing and comparing fifteen companies, two variables emerged as drivers of value creation in repair and remanufacturing. They were 'OEM status', i.e., how much companies were able to exploit the reputation of their established brand in the remanufacturing side of the business, and 'level of servitization', or how companies increased the level of services offered to enhance their appeal to customers. Therefore, a set of generic business models was proposed (Fig. 1). In Fig. 1, higher levels of servitization in the horizontal axis result in value creation through additional revenues, whilst higher OEM status in the vertical axis results in higher profit margins.

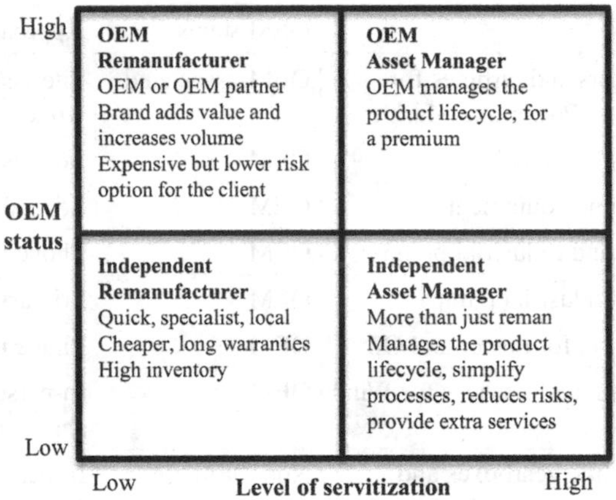

High

	OEM **Remanufacturer** OEM or OEM partner Brand adds value and increases volume Expensive but lower risk option for the client	**OEM** **Asset Manager** OEM manages the product lifecycle, for a premium
OEM **status**	**Independent** **Remanufacturer** Quick, specialist, local Cheaper, long warranties High inventory	**Independent** **Asset Manager** More than just reman Manages the product lifecycle, simplify processes, reduces risks, provide extra services

Low

Low   **Level of servitization**   High

Fig. 1. Generic patterns of value creation in repair and remanufacturing

The proposed matrix identifies four patterns of value creation:

- **OEM remanufacturers:** firms that add value through OEM brand reputation and focus on clients who desire a low-risk option albeit at a higher price.
- **OEM asset managers:** firms that add value through real-time asset management of their OEM product. Customers accept paying a premium for the OEM service.
- **Independent remanufacturers:** this group creates value through operational excellence. They are generally SMEs, and offer quicker, specialist, and cheaper solutions for their customers. Interestingly, some OEMs can behave as independent remanufacturers by performing repair and remanufacturing irrespective of the product brand.
- **Independent asset managers:** this group creates value by increasing the services offered to the customer. They collaborate with other firms and simplify client processes.

The following sub-sections explain each pattern in detail.

4.1 OEM Remanufacturers: High OEM Status, Low Servitization

Firms A and C utilized their OEM status or association to position their repair and remanufacturing unit as the brand or technology leader. Firm A targeted segments of risk-averse customers willing to pay a higher price in return for OEM warranties and for a higher residual value at the product end-of-life. Concurrently, firm C provided consumers who desired the best audio experience with high quality products, albeit for a higher price. Firm C's unique selling proposition was the durability of the product due to its modular design which allowed the product to be upgraded when a new technology became available. Due to their OEM status and premium prices, A and C achieved high profit margins in remanufacturing and upgrading. They relied on the OEM partnership and the technical capability of employees as key resources, respectively.

4.2 OEM Asset Managers: High OEM Status, High Servitization

As with firm A, firm B also utilized their strategic partnership with the OEM to their advantage which allowed the creation of high profit margins. However, value creation for firm B went beyond repair and remanufacturing, as the company also provided services that simplified customer processes by tracking the engine's performance in real time, which was aligned with the OEM pay-per-hour-flying service offering. Interestingly, B was the only OEM to use asset management services as a value creation strategy. As B was in the aviation sector where security is a crucial factor, they maintained dedicated resources for their real-time tracking services for their clients.

4.3 Independent Remanufacturers: Low OEM Status, Low Servitization

Non-OEMs I and J competed through operational excellence by minimizing prices, offering quick turnarounds, and possessing knowledge across different brands. Their target segments were mainly other businesses – such as dealerships and organizations with large car fleets for I, and firms with several printers for J. Their customers prioritized low prices and speed, placing less importance on brand reputation.

It is commonly assumed that independent remanufacturers are a threat for OEMs. This appeared to be the case for firm J as they faced the fiercest competition with OEMs. Price was a crucial value driver for J, which offered a low cost per-printed-page by upgrading cartridges with bigger sponges. Due to such competition, several OEMs of printers are now introducing subscription models to acquire back used parts. Additionally, OEMs keep reinventing their technology to avoid aftermarket competition. Consequently, keeping up with OEMs' innovations was a key activity for company J and balancing revenues from cheaper sales with the costs of reverse engineering and acquiring cores was challenging for the firm. Nevertheless, the situation was slightly different for I, which maintained good relationships with OEMs as they focused on a low-price product. Therefore, it appeared more interesting for automobile OEMs to cooperate rather than to compete with I. In addition to cheaper turbochargers, firm I was known for being a specialist in sourcing rare components, and occasionally even competitors placed orders. However, to deliver short turnarounds, the company maintained large stocks, including of rare products with low probability of being sold.

4.4 OEMs Under 'Brand Dilution' Behaving as Independent Remanufacturers

Whereas the cases of I and J supported the literature, it was surprising to observe firms D, E, F and G not exploiting their established OEM brand in their remanufacturing business unit and competing as independent firms. Company E had a history of expansion through acquisitions that helped constantly reducing operational costs and appeared to pursue a price minimization strategy in remanufacturing. In parallel, firms D and F were innovative in their new products business unit, both engineering specialist equipment for their clients. However, the remanufacturing side of those firms competed mostly through price minimization. This dynamic was the result of an interesting phenomenon over time. Specifically, D and F were initially OEMs producing new products exclusively. With time, seeking to fully exploit their capabilities, D and F started offering remanufacturing services to their own-brand products. As more time passed and market challenges made difficult to grow organically, they identified an opportunity to generate revenues by also servicing third-party equipment. Even though repairing other brands increased revenues, D and F observed their manufacturing of new products shrink in proportion to aftermarket services. Over time, their aftermarket services transitioned from competing through brand leadership to competing through lower prices and closer proximity to the customer, similarly to how independent remanufacturers compete. Therefore, a 'brand dilution' process and loss of focus were observed in these firms. Whilst revenues have grown as a result, their business model had changed significantly. As margins were narrower in the aftermarket services due to higher labor costs, these businesses have experienced a reduction in profitability over time, combined with a reduction in cash to invest in the development of new technology.

The challenges related to managing an OEM business whilst also remanufacturing, repairing, and upgrading products from other brands were also observed in firm G. In their case, they also started manufacturing new products, but such strategy depends on intensive research and development, which is an expensive process. As their technology aged, they too started repairing and remanufacturing; however, the OEM (centralized in Europe) and repair business (worldwide) were separate business units. In one instance, the repair unit in North America required cheaper spare parts, but the OEM in Europe refused, forcing the repair business to reverse engineer and engage with local manufacturers to produce them cheaply and quickly. This illustrated how conflicting the OEM and remanufacturing business units can be within the same organization.

4.5 Independent Asset Managers: Low OEM Status, High Servitization

Similarly to company I, H was an independent firm in the automobile market, although it repaired and remanufactured higher value items (transmissions and gearboxes). Company H also offered cheaper and quicker solutions and used high stocks to cope with uncertainties and to deliver short lead times. However, the difference between H and I was that firm H demonstrated a higher level of servitization to OEM clients. The relationship between H and OEMs was cooperative. For OEMs, the benefit was the provision of a 'risk reduction' service, as company H would repair or remanufacture any returned product without additional costs during extended warranty periods. For H, repetitive orders from OEMs created economies of scale increasing productivity. In parallel, firm M was a contracted party under an agreement involving the repair of any returned computer monitor on behalf of the OEM during the warranty period. Like H, a close relationship with OEMs provided economies of scale for M, whilst M offered fixed-price contracts to OEMs in return thus eliminating uncertainties and making the warranty process less risky for the OEM, although not necessarily cheaper as the total costs depended on how many products were actually repaired at the end of the period.

Firms K, N and O also added value through servitization. By managing several assets for their clients, they offered a broader scope of services than OEMs could, providing simplification. Specifically, N and O helped businesses disposing of electronic goods by performing data security services, assuring clients that any confidential data were destroyed. Their margin was complemented by repairing and re-selling items whenever possible. In the oil industry, K managed client's assets, keeping customers within their expensive 'day rate'. They were process simplifiers and innovators, for instance they used licensed smart glasses to provide real-time specialist advice for less-skilled repair workers on the field, helping the client reducing the costs of bringing a specialist to an offshore platform. Firm K offered remanufactured parts and services to the oil industry with very distinct gross profit margins (35–50% for parts and 20–30% for services).

Each company analysed in this study was categorized within the proposed framework (Fig. 2).

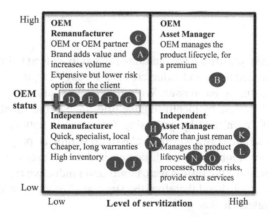

Fig. 2. Categorization of the studied firms

5   Discussion

The findings of this study contribute to addressing a knowledge gap within the literature pertaining to value creation in the circular economy, particularly in repair and remanufacturing business models. Previous studies had fragmentally identified value-adding elements in repair and remanufacturing [3, 6, 10, 13, 17, 18], and proposed a general pattern of value creation [1]; however, such pattern was not fully applicable to all companies analysed in this study. Additionally, this study contributed to addressing a methodological gap within the literature, through empirical evidence from fifteen case studies, whilst previous literature either adopted a theoretical standpoint [1, 3, 4, 6, 10, 15, 17, 18] or provided up to four cases [2, 7, 8, 11–13]. Furthermore, a contextual gap was addressed by including the perspectives of both OEMs and non-OEMs.

The framework provided in Fig. 1 differentiates how companies add value based on their OEM status and level of servitization. The identification of the first variable – OEM status – was a result of the design of this research including both OEMs and non-OEMs. It was interesting to observe that remanufacturing products of any brand destroyed value over time for four OEMs. This phenomenon was not predicted through the literature review as longitudinal case studies in repair and remanufacturing companies are rare. One of the few longitudinal studies was provided by Hopkinson et al. [8] which also contained negative findings describing why a company decided to move away from remanufacturing after years of conducting such activity. Such findings indicate the need for future research to investigate value creation in the circular economy through longitudinal case studies. Furthermore, the identification of the second variable – servitization – was not surprising as product service-systems are a commonly discussed topic. Nevertheless, servitization is typically argued as a strategy favoured by leasing models [11], although only one firm (B) conducted leasing in this study. All other companies were able to repair, remanufacture and offer upgrades through traditional sales models – a finding that contributes to the empirical literature [12, 23].

6 Conclusion

This study addressed a gap within the literature related to understanding the relationship between the circular economy and value creation through empirical data from several repair and remanufacturing businesses. With fifteen cases, our comprehensive findings complemented the literature by identifying the relevance of the variables 'OEM status' and 'level of servitization' and by proposing four generic patterns of value creation (Fig. 1). Each of the studied firms were also classified within the proposed matrix (Fig. 2) and had their value creation strategies discussed in detail. Nevertheless, a limitation of this project was that, since the results were based upon inductive reasoning, the validity applies to the cases studied and therefore the suggested framework should continue to be tested in future research.

Acknowledgements. We thank the Scottish Institute for Remanufacturing for funding this research.

References

1. Lüdeke-Freund, F., Gold, S., Bocken, N.M.P.: A review and typology of circular economy business model pattern. J. Ind. Ecol. **23**(1), 36–61 (2018). https://doi.org/10.1111/jiec.12763

2. Kalverkamp, M., Young, S.B.: In support of open-loop supply chains: expanding the scope of environmental sustainability in reverse supply chains. J. Clean. Prod. **214**, 573–582 (2019). https://doi.org/10.1016/j.jclepro.2019.01.006

3. Kwak, M., Kim, H.: Green profit maximization through integrated pricing and production planning for a line of new and remanufactured products. J. Clean. Prod. **142**, 3454–3470 (2017). https://doi.org/10.1016/j.jclepro.2016.10.121

4. Matsumoto, M., Yang, S., Martinsen, K., Kainuma, Y.: Trends and research challenges in remanufacturing. Int. J. Precis. Eng. Manuf.-Green Technol. **3**(1), 129–142 (2016). https://doi.org/10.1007/s40684-016-0016-4

5. Atasu, A., Guide, V.D.R., Jr., van Wassenhove, L.N.: So what if remanufacturing cannibalizes my new product sales? Calif. Manag. Rev. **52**(2), 57–76 (2010). https://doi.org/10.1525/cmr.2010.52.2.56

6. Ferrer, G., Swaminathan, J.M.: Managing new and differentiated remanufactured products. Eur. J. Oper. Res. **203**(2), 370–379 (2010). https://doi.org/10.1016/j.ejor.2009.08.007

7. Ranta, V., Aarikka-Stenroos, L., Makinen, S.J.: Creating value in the circular economy: a structured multiple-case analysis of business models. J. Clean. Prod. **201**, 988–1000 (2018). https://doi.org/10.1016/j.jclepro.2018.08.072

8. Hopkinson, P., Zils, M., Hawkins, P., Roper, S.: Managing a complex global circular economy business model: opportunities and challenges. Calif. Manag. Rev. **60**(3), 71–94 (2018). https://doi.org/10.1177/0008125618764692

9. Zink, T., Geyer, R.: Circular economy rebound. J. Ind. Ecol. **21**(3), 593–602 (2017). https://doi.org/10.1111/jiec.12545

10. Aboulamer, A.: Adopting a circular business model improves market equity value. Thunderbird Int. Bus. Rev. **60**(5), 765–769 (2018). https://doi.org/10.1002/tie.21922

11. Bressanelli, G., Adrodegari, F., Perona, M., Saccani, N.: Exploring how usage-focused business models enable circular economy through digital technologies. Sustainability **10**(3), 639 (2018). https://doi.org/10.3390/su10030639

12. Linder, M., Williander, M.: Circular business model innovation: inherent uncertainties. Bus. Strategy Environ. **26**(2), 182–196 (2017). https://doi.org/10.1002/bse.1906

13. Lieder, M., Asif, F.M.A., Rashid, A., Nihelic, A., Kotnik, S.: A conjoint analysis of circular economy value propositions for consumers: using "washing machines in Stockholm" as a case study. J. Clean. Prod. **172**, 264–273 (2018). https://doi.org/10.1016/j.jclepro.2017.10.147

14. Berssaneti, F.T., Berger, S., Saut, A.M., Vanalle, R.M., Santana, J.C.C.: Value generation of remanufactured products: multi-case study of third-party companies. Sustainability **11**(3), 584 (2019). https://doi.org/10.3390/su11030584

15. Krystofik, M., Wagner, J., Gaustad, G.: Leveraging intellectual property rights to encourage green product design and remanufacturing for sustainable waste management. Resour. Conserv. Recycl. **97**, 44–54 (2015). https://doi.org/10.1016/j.resconrec.2015.02.005

16. Agrawal, V.V., Atasu, A., van Ittersum, K.: Remanufacturing, third-party competition, and consumers' perceived value of new products. Manag. Sci. **61**(1), 60–72 (2015). https://doi.org/10.1287/mnsc.2014.2099

17. Liu, H., Lei, M., Huang, T., Leong, G.K.: Refurbishing authorization strategy in the secondary market for electrical and electronic products. Int. J. Prod. Econ. **195**, 198–209 (2018). https://doi.org/10.1016/j.ijpe.2017.10.012

18. Ma, Z., Zhou, Q., Dai, Y., Guan, G.: To license or not to license remanufacturing business? Sustainability **10**(2), 347 (2018). https://doi.org/10.3390/su10020347

19. Barratt, M., Choi, T.Y., Li, M.: Qualitative case studies in operations management: trends, research outcomes and future research implications. J. Oper. Manag. **29**(4), 329–342 (2011). https://doi.org/10.1016/j.jom.2010.06.002

20. Bititci, U.S.: Managing Business Performance: The Science and the Art. Wiley, Chichester (2015). ISBN: 978-1-119-02567-2

21. Osterwalder, A., Pigneur, Y.: Business Model Generation: A Handbook for Visionaries, Game Changers, and Challenger. Wiley , Hoboken (2010). ISBN: 978-0470876411
22. Cheng, S.Y., Bititci, U.S., Greening, P., Rutherford, C., Karamperidis, S.: WEEE flows: a case study of a reverse supply chain for mixed small electrical waste. In: 23rd International Symposium on Logistics Proceedings, pp. 469–477 (2018). ISBN: 9780853583240
23. Copani, G., Behanm, S.: Remanufacturing with upgrade PSS for new sustainable business models. CIRP J. Manuf. Sci. Technol. **29**, 245–256 (2020). https://doi.org/10.1016/j.procir.2016.03.055

Modeling the Parallel Machine Scheduling Problem with Worker- and Position-Dependent Processing Times

Jairo R. Montoya-Torres[1]($\boxtimes$) (iD), Valérie Botta-Genoulaz[2] (iD), Nick Materzok[2],
Þorgeir Páll Gíslason[2], and Sélène Mendiela[2]

[1] School of Engineering, Universidad de La Sabana, Chia, Colombia
jairo.montoya@unisabana.edu.co
[2] Univ Lyon, INSA Lyon, Université Claude Bernard Lyon 1, Univ Lumière Lyon 2, DISP,
E4570, 69621 Villeurbanne, France
valerie.botta@insa-lyon.fr

Abstract. Traditional deterministic scheduling problems consider that processing times of jobs are fixed and constant over time. However, this assumption is not realistic in practice in hand-intensive manufacturing contexts. To deal with this, the current paper studies the deterioration effect of processing times on a parallel machine scheduling problem. In such a case, job processing times depend on the position of jobs in the execution sequence. The objective function is the minimization of the maximum delay of the set of jobs, that is the makespan. A mixed-integer linear programming model is provided for the basic case in which the processing time of jobs deteriorate only as a function of their position in the schedule. Then, two original extensions are proposed. The first one considers that both the position and the worker do impact the processing time, while in the second situation workers can have a break after a given period of time. Preliminary experiments are carried out to illustrate the impact of such situations on the objective function. Results are promising.

Keywords: Scheduling · Workers · Deterioration effect · Position-dependent processing times · Mathematical modeling

1 Introduction

Personnel scheduling in productive or service systems (e.g., hospitals, universities, call centers, banks, postal services, airlines and hand-intensive manufacturing industries) does require to make decisions in regard to the assignment of workers for the execution of a number of tasks during a time horizon. As pointed out in [1], this problem impacts on both the cost of operations and the service level to customers. In addition, some other physical or psychological issues can impact the actual performance of the schedule as well as moral, mental health and social welfare of workers [16, 17].

© IFIP International Federation for Information Processing 2021
Published by Springer Nature Switzerland AG 2021
A. Dolgui et al. (Eds.): APMS 2021, IFIP AICT 632, pp. 351–359, 2021.
https://doi.org/10.1007/978-3-030-85906-0_39

In traditional scheduling models, human conditions of workers are ignored, and assumptions consider that he/she is a predictable agent in the system with perfect availability, deterministic processing times, and that fatigue or learning has no effects on productivity [2]. These assumption does reduce the complexity and computational tractability of the problem. However, important characteristics of workers are neglected as a factor of variability in the productive system [2, 11, 16, 18]. Under this context, this paper is motivated by the inclusion of particular work conditions, as the "deterioration effect". Hence it deals with the problem of scheduling a set of jobs on a group of workers with homogeneous skills, where the productivity of workers deteriorates over time, and so the actual execution times of jobs are increased. According to the literature [8], this deterioration can be model either as a function of the position of jobs in the schedule or as a cumulative function of the time the execution of jobs started. Each approach has advantages and drawbacks. In any case, mathematical and computational complexity of the problem is increased. The introduction of a decrease in the productivity rate of workers during the scheduling horizon results in a more realistic representation of the system, especially in hand-intensive production, and support the construction of better decision-making models [8]. In the scheduling literature, the deterioration effect has been studied from two main approaches, either the processing times of a job increase depending on the waiting time until the start of its execution (starting time deterioration, or time-dependent processing times), or the processing times increase depending on the number of jobs previously scheduled until the beginning of the execution of a given job (position deterioration or sequence-dependent processing times) [13]. This paper considers the second approach since it has been less studied, even though this is the case of the decrease in the workers productivity due to physical exhaustion by repetitive work [10].

For the case of multiple parallel resources, Mosheiov [14] proposed to convert the position-dependent scheduling problem with linear deterioration of processing times to an assignment problem. The option of job rejection was considered in the works of [4]. Mosheiov [15] studied the minimization of the maximum workload. Huang & Wang [5] evaluated the minimization of the absolute deviation of both the completion time and the waiting time of jobs. Chen et al. [3] considered a deterioration function by parts to minimize the sum of completion times. Finally, Moreno-Camacho et al. [12], evaluated the performance of various mathematical models for makespan and tardiness minimization. All these works considered the same deterioration factor for all workers.

The problem under studied is an extension of the job scheduling problem in parallel resources with minimization of the makespan. This latter is known to be strongly NP-hard, even for the 2-machines case [7]. The case with simple linear deteriorating jobs is also proven to be NP-hard in strongly sense [6, 9]. Although some works have studied scheduling with the deteriorating effect in processing times with identical parallel resources (i.e., workers), majority of those studies focus on the analysis of mathematical properties of the deteriorating effect. Scarcity of works propose solution procedures, except the work in [12], where the complexity (in terms of efficiency and capacity) of mixed-integer linear programming (MILP) models for makespan and tardiness minimization is deeply explored. The objective of this paper is to formally model, through an MILP approach, the parallel resources scheduling problem with position-dependent deteriorating processing times under two new original conditions: (i) considering worker-dependent deterioration rates, and (ii) breaks during the scheduling. The impact of these situations is analyzed using an illustrative example.

To this end, Sect. 2 formally describe the basic problem under study, as well as the variants considered. Section 3 presents the results of the computational experiment. Finally, the conclusions of the work and perspectives of future research are outlined in Sect. 4.

2 Problem Description and Mathematical Modeling

We have a set of n independent jobs $i = 1, \ldots, n$ and m identical workers $j = 1, \ldots, m$ who can perform any of the n jobs, under the same conditions. Each worker can only perform one job at a time and pre-emption is not allowed. For each job i, a baseline deterministic processing time p_i is known in advance, representing the expected duration to execute the job without any deterioration and independent of the allocated worker. The special characteristic of the problem studied here is that the actual execution time of a job depends on the position in the sequence: processing times increase as a function of their positions in the schedule. That is, the actual processing time of job i in the k-th position of the schedule is computed as $p_{ik} = p_i k^{\alpha}$, where α is the deterioration rate. This exponential deterioration rate follows the original proposition given in [11], where the factor α models the decrease in worker productivity.

A MILP model is first proposed for makespan minimization with a single position-dependent deterioration rate. Then, a first realistic extension of the model is presented to allow both position- and worker-dependent deterioration. The second extension consists in another realistic condition in which workers are allowed to have breaks during the production period.

2.1 Makespan Minimization with Position-Dependent Deterioration

The set of jobs is denoted as N, the set of identical workers is denoted as M, and the set of positions in the sequence is denoted as R, where $|R| = |N| - |M| + 1$. The parameters are the number $n = |N|$ of jobs, the number $m = |M|$ of available workers, the deterioration rate α, with $0 \leq \alpha \leq 1$, and the processing time p_{ik} of job $i \in N$ scheduled on position $k \in R$. The set of decision variables: $x_{jik} = 1$ if job $i \in N$ is executed by worker $j \in M$ at position $k \in R$ in the schedule, 0 otherwise; C_{jk} is the completion time of the job executed by worker $j \in M$ at position $k \in R$; and C_{max} is the makespan. The model reads as follows:

$$\text{Min } C_{max} \tag{1}$$

Subject to:

$$\sum_{j \in M} \sum_{k \in R} x_{jik} = 1 \quad \forall i \in N \tag{2}$$

$$\sum_{i \in N} x_{jik} \leq 1 \quad \forall j \in M, k \in R \tag{3}$$

$$C_{j1} = \sum_{i \in N} p_{i1} x_{ji1} \quad \forall j \in M \tag{4}$$

$$C_{jk} = C_{j,k-1} + \sum_{i \in N} p_{ik} x_{jik} \quad \forall j \in M, k \in R \setminus \{1\} \tag{5}$$

$$C_{max} \geq C_{j,(n-m+1)} \quad \forall j \in M, k \in R \tag{6}$$

$$x_{jik} \in \{0, 1\} \quad \forall j \in M, i \in N, k \in R \tag{7}$$

In the above formulation, the objective function (1) minimizes the maximum completion time of all jobs (makespan). Constraints (2) and (3) ensure that one and only one job i is assigned to only one worker j in only one position k. Constraints (4) compute the completion time for the job scheduled in the first position to be executed by the worker j. Constraints (5) compute the completion time of the job in the k-th position of the worker j. Constraints (6) compute the value of decision variable C_{max}. Finally, the description of binary decision variables is given by Constraints (7).

2.2 Position- and Worker-Dependent Deterioration

The previous basic model assumes that the processing time of jobs deteriorates equally for all workers at an identical rate; therefore all workers share the same deterioration factor α. In real-life, however, the decrease of productivity can differ from one worker to another depending on their physical or psychological conditions. In consideration of this aspect, an extension can now be formulated where the parameter of the processing time changes from p_{ik} to p_{jik}. Consequently, the processing time no longer dependents only on the position k in the schedule but on both the position k and the worker j that executes the respective job i. That is, the deteriorating factor becomes α_j for worker j. By integrating the worker-dependency in the deterioration factor and thus in the parameter of the processing time, the model can still be classified as a parallel machine scheduling problem with identical resources.

To formulate the problem as a MILP model, the new parameter for the actual processing time is defined as $p_{jik} = p_{ik} k^{\alpha_j}$ for job $i \in N$ scheduled on position $k \in R$ while executed by worker $j \in M$. Constraints (4) and (5) are now rewritten as follows:

$$C_{j1} = \sum_{i \in N} p_{ji1} x_{ji1} \quad \forall j \in M \tag{4a}$$

$$C_{jk} = C_{j,k-1} + \sum_{i \in N} p_{jik} x_{jik} \quad \forall j \in M, k \in R \setminus \{1\} \tag{5b}$$

2.3 Position- and Worker-Dependent Deterioration and Breaks

Another extension that improves the practical applicability of the model is the implementation of breaks in the schedule. Breaks allow workers to rest and recharge to continue working. The underlying assumption of our model is that breaks lead to a decrease of the deterioration factor depending on the duration of the break, i.e. a recovery for the worker. Formally speaking, a break of duration d_{break} takes place after a given position k_{break} for every worker j. In a given schedule, the duration of breaks is fixed and identical for all workers. As a result, the deterioration factor decreases by the following function: $a(k_{break}+1) = a(k_{break}) - 0,1 * d_{break}$. In Sects. 2.1 and 2.2, the deterioration rate α has been considered to be constant which means that it is identical at any position k in the schedule. By including breaks and assuming that the deterioration decreases but remains constant after the decrease, the following definition can be used, where α_0 represents the deterioration rate at position $k = 0$. Figure 1a depicts an exemplary function for $\alpha_0 = 0,5$ and a break of $d_{break} = 2$ at position $k = 5$ which leads to a decreased deterioration factor of $a = 0,3$ after the break, computed as follows:

$$\alpha(k) = \alpha_0 \quad \forall k < k_{break} \tag{8}$$

$$\alpha(k) = \alpha_0 - 0,1 * d_{break} \quad \forall k > k_{break} \tag{9}$$

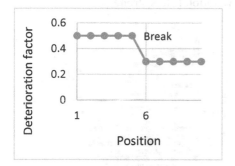
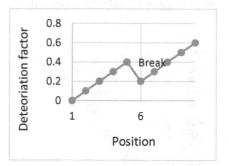

a) Constant deterioration factor with break.   b) Increasing deterioration factor with break

Fig. 1. Constant and increasing deterioration factor with break.

A second and more realistic way of modelling the deterioration rate is to include a general increase over the positions in the schedule. By that, it is considered that workers become less and less productive throughout the day. Assuming that the increase is also linear and breaks are still in place, the following definition can be used. Figure 1b shows an example of an increasing deterioration factor with a break, computed as follows:

$$a(k) = 0,1 * (k-1) + a_0 \quad \forall k \leq k_{break} \tag{10}$$

$$a(k) = 0,1 * (k-1) + a_0 + a(k_{break}) - 0,1 * d_{break} \quad \forall k > k_{break} \tag{11}$$

3   Comparison Between Models

The basic MILP model and its extensions have been implemented to carry out an illustrative computational experiment. Models were coded on GAMS (General Algebraic

Modeling System) and run on a PC with Windows 10, processor Intel® Core™ i5-8250U at 1.6 GHz, and 8 GB of RAM. A set of 10 jobs and two workers are considered in this experiment, with baseline processing times being 8, 7, 5, 6, 7, 3, 2, 9, 10, and 2. Running times were about 16 min.

In a first instance, the behavior of the basic model is analyzed by looking into how different deterioration factors affect the scheduling. It is human nature to fatigue, but people usually do at different rates. This is represented by the different values of the deterioration factor, that was set from 0 to 1. Figure 2a depicts the solution obtained by the MILP model. For every deterioration factor, there are two bars, one for each worker, that show the assignment of jobs and their duration. The longest bar represents the makespan. As observed, when the deterioration factor is set to zero (i.e., workers never get fatigued), the makespan is the lowest; the makespan generally increases as the deterioration factor increases. Note that the solution schedules jobs in such a way that jobs with higher processing times are allocated at the beginning, while jobs with low processing time are at the end. That happens because the equation for deteriorated processing times leads to a higher absolute increase for jobs with high processing times. Since this increase would have a greater impact on the makespan, they get assigned to the beginning of the schedule where the deterioration is less strong.

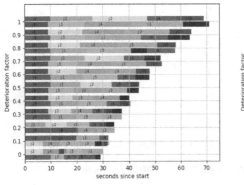

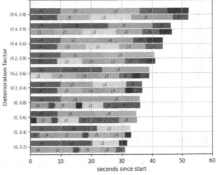

a) Schedule for two workers and different deterioration factors from 0 to 1.

b) Schedule for two workers with different deterioration factors from 0 to 0.8

Fig. 2. Two-workers schedule for (a) the basic scenario, and (b) worker-dependent deterioration.

The second analysis was carried out on how the scheduling is performed if the workers would have different deterioration factors. Recall that this approach models the situation in which workers do not necessarily fatigue at the same rate. For this instance, the deterioration factors were set between 0 and 0.8 but never as the same number. Figure 2b shows the obtained assignment and makespan (the ordinate axis indicates the deterioration factors of the two workers). As per the results, in most cases the worker with the lower deterioration factor executes more jobs. In some cases, however, both workers perform an equal number of jobs but the worker with the lower deterioration factor gets assigned the jobs that have a higher baseline processing time. This is due to the same reason that jobs with high processing time are assigned earlier in the schedule, that is, the solver tries to minimize the absolute increase of processing times by deterioration as it would have an impact on the makespan. For example, looking at Figs. 2a and 2b, in most of cases, having the same deterioration rate for both workers drives to a worst performance than modeling independent deterioration. As a matter of fact, the makespan is 42 time-units with both workers having $\alpha = 0.4$, while it decreases to 36 time-units with $\alpha_1 = 0$ and $\alpha_2 = 0.8$. This represents a decrease of 14.3% on the makespan value.

The second extension includes the assumption of breaks that decrease the deterioration factor. In order to see the benefits, the model was run for different break durations from 0 to 4 units of time. To compare the results, the respective break duration was added to the total makespan. It is assumed that the deterioration factor is constant before and after the break and that it begins with $\alpha_0 = 0.5$. The input data is the same as before. Figure 3 shows the makespan for each break duration and visualizes the time of the break by a white space between two consecutive jobs. Comparing the makespans for the different break durations, it is observed that there is a trade-off which has to be balanced. On the one hand, breaks decrease the deterioration factor which keeps the processing times and thus the makespan lower. On the other hand, breaks increase the makespan as they lead to idle-time in the schedule. Looking at the makespan, it shows that the first effect of decreasing the deterioration factor becomes dominant with a longer break duration. Until a break duration of 2, the makespan increases whereas it decreases again for durations of 3 and 4. This consideration is quite relevant for the planning of breaks in real life applications.

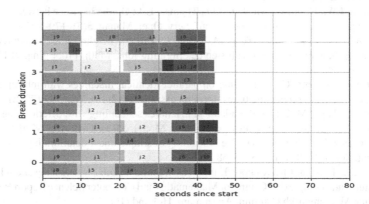

Fig. 3. Exemplary schedule of two workers with breaks.

4   Conclusions and Perspectives

This paper studied the problem of job scheduling in hand-intensive production systems. Workers are considered with homogeneous skills, but their productivity decrease over time according to a deterioration rate. A mixed-integer linear programming approach was employed to model three situations. The former "all workers deteriorate at the same rate", already studied in the literature is the basic situation that serves as a reference to analyze two new original situations: (i) "each worker has his/her own deterioration rate", and (ii) the latter coupled with "the impact of breaks for worker recovery". The first experiments allow us to see the interest of individualizing the deterioration rate per worker (by comparison with a global average rate), and also to identify the duration of breaks as a lever for optimization.

Since this is one of the few works in the literature addressing these problems, several lines for future research are open. For instance, behavior of workers is also impacted (not necessarily in the same ratio) by learning effects. One line for further research can focus on the simultaneous evaluation of deterioration rates and recovery curves, in addition to include breaks during the scheduling horizon. Also, non-linear deterioration or recovery functions can be considered, as well as stochastic modeling. Heterogenous labor or worker preferences are also characteristics to be included. Other lines for future research include the possibility to extend the study to other non-classical optimization criteria such as maximization of machines exploitation time, workload balance among workers, tardiness, etc. Finally, because of its computational complexity, the use of heuristics and/or meta-heuristics can be a promising line for future research in order to solve large-scale versions of the problem.

References

1. Alfares, H.K.: Survey, categorization, and comparison of recent tour scheduling literature. Ann. Oper. Res. **127**(1–4), 145–175 (2004)
2. Boudreau, J.W., Hopp, W., Mcclain, J.O., Thomas, L.J.: On the interface between operations and human resources management. Manuf. Serv. Oper. Manag. **5**(3), 179–202 (2003)
3. Chen, W., Guo, P., Zhang, Z., Zeng, M., Liang, J.: Variable neighborhood search for parallel machines scheduling problem with step deteriorating jobs. Math. Probl. Eng. **2012** (2012). Article no. 928312
4. Gerstl, E., Mosheiov, G.: Scheduling on parallel identical machines with job-rejection and position-dependent processing times. Inf. Process. Lett. **112**(19), 743–747 (2012)
5. Huang, X., Wang, M.-Z.: Parallel identical machines scheduling with deteriorating jobs and total absolute differences penalties. Appl. Math. Model. **35**(3), 1349–1353 (2011)
6. Ji, M., Cheng, T.C.: Parallel-machine scheduling of simple linear deteriorating jobs. Theoret. Comput. Sci. **410**(38–40), 3761–3768 (2009)
7. Lawer, E.L., Lenstra, J.K., Rinnooy Kan, A.H.G., Shmoys, D.B.: Sequencing and scheduling: algorithms and complexity. Centre for Mathematics and Computer Science Report BS-R8909, Stichting Mathematisch Centrum, Amsterdam, Holland (1989)
8. Lodree, E.J., Geiger, C.D., Jiang, X.: Taxonomy for integrating scheduling theory and human factors: review and research opportunities. Int. J. Ind. Ergon. **39**(1), 39–51 (2009)
9. Miao, C., Zou, J.: Parallel-machine scheduling with time-dependent and machine availability constraints. Math. Probl. Eng. **2015** (2015). Article no. 956158
10. Montoya-Torres, J.R., Sánchez, S., Moreno-Camacho, C.: A literature-based assessment of human factors in shop scheduling problems. IFAC-PapersOnLine **52**(10), 49–54 (2019)
11. Moreno-Camacho, C.A., Montoya-Torres, J.R.: Workforce scheduling with social responsibility considerations. In: Proceedings of the 4th IEEE International Conference on Advanced Logistics and Transport (ICALT), pp. 24–29. IEEE Publishing (2015)
12. Moreno-Camacho, C.A., Montoya-Torres, J.R., Vélez-Gallego, M.C.: A comparison of mixed-integer linear programming models for workforce scheduling with position-dependent processing times. Eng. Optim. **50**(6), 917–932 (2018)

13. Mosheiov, G.: A note on scheduling deteriorating jobs. Math. Comput. Model. **41**(8–9), 883–886 (2005)
14. Mosheiov, G.: Minimizing total absolute deviation of job completion times: extensions to position-dependent processing times and parallel identical machines. J. Oper. Res. Soc. **59**, 1422–1424 (2008)
15. Mosheiov, G.: A note: multi-machine scheduling with general position-based deterioration to minimize total load. Int. J. Prod. Econ. **135**(1), 523–525 (2012)
16. Petrovic, S., Vanden Berghe, G.: A comparison of two approaches to nurse rostering problems. Ann. Oper. Res. **194**(1), 365–384 (2012)
17. Puente, J., Gómez, A., Fernández, I., Priore, P.: Medical doctor rostering problem in a hospital emergency department by means of genetic algorithms. Comput. Ind. Eng. **56**(4), 1232–1242 (2009)
18. Thompson, G.M., Goodale, J.C.: Variable employee productivity in workforce scheduling. Eur. J. Oper. Res. **170**(2), 376–390 (2006)

The Most Critical Decisions in Manufacturing: Implications for a Circular Economy

Nina Pereira Kvadsheim[1]([⊠]), Bella B. Nujen[2], and Deodat Mwesiumo[3]

[1] Møreforsking AS, Britvegen 4, Molde, Norway
nina.p.kvadsheim@moreforsking.no
[2] Department of International Business, Norwegian University of Science and Technology, Trondheim, Norway
bella.nujen@ntnu.no
[3] Molde University College, Specialized University in Logistics, Molde, Norway
Deodat.E.Mwesiumo@himolde.no

Abstract. Through product development and design, manufacturers wield great influence on the entire product's life cycle resulting in creating value to customers and thus, have great potential to decouple this value provision from linear resource consumption to a Circular Economy (CE). However, since CE is a systemic concept rooted in the principle of conservation of resources, its implementation cannot only be done in one of the firm's functions or facilities, as it requires collaboration and commitment enterprise wide and conscious management of stakeholders. In view of this, the current research focuses on the identification and evaluation of the most critical decisions across functional areas in manufacturing and how they may impact the implementation of CE. In so doing, this study contributes with building a solid base of empirical research on CE in the manufacturing sector, hence contributing to literature on CE and manufacturing.

Keywords: Critical decisions · Manufacturing · Circular Economy

1 Introduction

The progress of manufacturing sector is tantamount to the economic sustainability of a country, which requires continuous upgradation to achieve excellence. Indeed, manufacturing firms are bestowed with resources and capabilities [1] and thus, have a great potential to drive the change towards a more Circular Economy (CE). As a reaction to the prevailing economic system of 'take, make, and dispose', the concept of CE aims to create a closed-loop system where resources are conserved and brought back into the life-cycle after being used [2]. Accordingly, manufacturing firms are influential and claimed to be among the most dominant coordinating organization in the world [3] and so any strategy aiming at increasing circularity cannot be pursued without their engagement.

Despite the important role of manufacturers in achieving CE, our theoretical and managerial understanding of how their critical decisions can have implications on a CE,

© IFIP International Federation for Information Processing 2021
Published by Springer Nature Switzerland AG 2021
A. Dolgui et al. (Eds.): APMS 2021, IFIP AICT 632, pp. 360–368, 2021.
https://doi.org/10.1007/978-3-030-85906-0_40

is still limited. This study contributes to the scientific knowledge in this area. We pose that decisions concerning manufacturing can have profound impacts on the entire product's lifecycle stages, which includes but are not limited to 1) designing products for reusability, recyclability, and remanufacturing; 2) improving the product design with less material use for same service and for durability and longevity and 3) selecting 'cleaner' materials from more environmentally conscious suppliers [4]. Extending the extant body of knowledge, the study identifies and evaluates the most critical decisions across functional areas in manufacturing and their impact on the implementation of CE. Thus, while previous studies tend to focus on the products and/or industries characteristics, the approach used in this study draws on the building blocks of the [Porter's] value chain. Our results show that the overall performance of CE depends on a well-functioning collaboration across the entire firm and conscious management of stakeholders, and hence, only by including the entire lifecycle can manufacturers wholly succeed with implementing CE strategies. Besides, by focusing on manufacturing, this study responds to the call for further research on building a solid base of empirical research on CE in the manufacturing sector [5], hence contributing to literature on CE and manufacturing.

The paper proceeds as follows. Section 2 introduces the '3R principles' main actions of the CE. Section 3 highlights the methodology used in the research, followed by analysis and discussion in Sect. 4. Finally, Sect. 5 presents the closure and limitation of the study.

2 Circular Economy – The 3R Principles

Firm's implementation of CE is mainly perceived through three actions referred to as '3R principles': reduce, reuse, and recycle [6]. The goal of the reduce principle is to minimize the input of primary energy, raw materials, and waste through eco-efficiency. Eco-efficiency refers to the improvement of efficiency in production and the consumption process, by keeping or increasing the value of products while also reducing environmental impacts. This can be achieved by using fewer resources per unit of value produced and by replacing harmful substances in favor of less harmful ones per unit of value produced. The reuse principle mainly covers operations that aim to use again products or components that are not waste for the same purpose for which they are conceived. Lastly, the recycle principle refers to any recovery operation by which waste materials are reprocessed into products, materials, or substances whether for the original or other purposes. It includes the reprocessing of organic material but does not include energy recovery and the reprocessing into materials that are to be used as fuels or for backfilling operations.

3 Methodology

Our study explores an emerging phenomenon – CE, hence an embedded single-case design was deemed appropriate since it is suitable for revelatory purposes [7]. The case company (hereafter MediX) provides training, educational and therapy products for lifesaving and emergency medical care, with its headquarters located in Scandinavia. MediX was chosen due to their interest in exploring business opportunities under the circularity logic, where the business model(s) is aligned with either closing, slowing, intensifying, narrowing and/or dematerializing loops. It is, thus, worth mentioning that MediX has not implemented any of the CE strategies yet, rather they are in the process of doing it. Hence, this study aims to identify and evaluate MediX's most critical decisions in manufacturing and how they may impact their implementation of CE in the near future.

To be able to do that, data were collected through semi-structured interviews as well as informal conversational interviews with individual team managers of key functional areas (i.e., product development (PD), software development, strategic sourcing, manufacturing, distribution). The interviews were important as they helped us to detect and hence understand the most critical decisions made within and across all functions. To achieve optimum use of interview time, an interview guide was developed and was organized around a set of predetermined open-ended questions, with additional questions emerging from the dialogue with the involved managers. In so doing, the interviews resembled a dialogical action research approach [8], which helped the researchers to bypass short-term intervention and thus facilitate iterations catalyzing reflective discussions and learning [9]. More so, to gain additional viewpoints on the critical decisions, supplementary sources were collected, and a workshop was conducted, where all teams were present. This served as triangulation and reinforced additional cycles of feed-back and learning.

4   Analysis and Discussion

Based on the knowledge obtained through the above learning actions, the data material went through an individual analysis and coding process, which were later presented to all participants to increase accuracy and enhance the validity. This created an additional feedback-loop, which was beneficial for the conclusions drawn. This section discusses the most critical decisions, which are classified into the following: 1) PD decisions, 2) strategic sourcing decisions; 3) manufacturing decisions; 4) customer/user decisions and 5) distribution decisions. Taken together, such decisions provide a mixed picture when it comes to the prospects for circularity. Some of them have aspects that can either enhance or hamper implementation of CE for MediX.

Product Development Decisions

Inefficient information sharing was identified as a challenge among all the functions, and a critical decision connected to this issue is *when exactly to share information with others*. This was stressed by sourcing, manufacturing, and the distribution functions, and in particular for the PD function, as it is where the production starts. Designers greatly influence the amount of time the sourcing team has to handle a sourcing assignment, since designers usually have the initial responsibility for preparing the technical specifications for firms' products and the materials that go into them. However, designers at MediX, especially in the early phase of designing, are mostly unaware of what exactly they are building, and the materials/parts that may be needed, as such it does not make sense to have the sourcing team on board at that stage. Accordingly, the designers understand that sharing information with other functions provides adequate visibility, enabling them to make good decisions that can improve the total chain profitability.

However, the challenge is when exactly is the right time to share it with the sourcing function, resulting in untimely exchange of information between them.

Consequently, designers play vital role in designing CE-oriented products., as they control what raw materials to use, how to manufacture the products, how the product will be used and how it will perform. Hence, more than three out of four decisions directly influencing materials selection and manufacturing processes are determined in the design phase and over 80% of the environmental costs are determined before the product is even created [10]. As such, decisions made by the PD function play a major role in the shift towards a CE. Thus, if information sharing with other functions is delayed, untimely waste is generated at MediX (e.g., disposal of obsolete parts, rework, and disposal of built prototypes). This can be due to sourcing of parts starting too early, ending up not being used by the designers when done with the prototyping. To support a transition to a CE, it is essential that designers involve sourcing and manufacturing functions in the PD process as early as possible, as that will help firms to better use material and energy efficiency, and hence manage losses. Broadly, lack of collaboration and delay in information sharing can be one of the impediments to MediX's effort to build circular supply networks, as the sourcing may not be able to communicate CE requirements to their own suppliers, much less enforce them. Moreover, since a CE intrinsically requires a systems approach and the involvement of all value chain actors [6], it is crucial that MediX strengthens their internal integration before attempting to integrate themselves with other value chain actors. This supports the contention that information sharing within a firm should precede the information sharing between firms [11]. At the end of the day, it is all about mutual understanding and willingness to give and take (required from all teams), if satisfactory CE solutions are to be reached.

Strategic Sourcing Decisions

Currently, sourcing decisions are perceived as strategic and have moved up in the hierarchy resulting in decisions being made by managers at prominent positions within firms. MediX is one such firms that have embraced the concept of strategic sourcing, thus, making acquisition decisions with the intent of creating distinctive value and achieving a competitive advantage [12]. Sourcing is helping MediX create value not only by managing costs and availability, but also by collaborating with other supply chain members to improve customer responsiveness, reduce risk, develop innovative products and processes, and market innovations more effectively. Together with the decision regarding where to source from, one of the most critical strategic sourcing decisions for MediX is whether all corporate requirements for a particular part of a product should be fulfilled by one selected supplier or not. Given that more than 50% of the cost of goods sold worldwide is derived from purchased materials, supplier selection is seen as a critical strategic sourcing decision for MediX. This is consistent with [13], who assert that suppliers' capabilities heavily influence a firm's ability to produce a quality product at a reasonable cost and in a timely manner, and that supplier performance is considered one of the crucial determining factors for the firm's success.

These critical decisions imply the nature of the relationship MediX has with their suppliers, which has a significant impact on realizing a CE. In fact, supplier selection is becoming a crucial routine for implementing successful circularity. For instance, the innovative selection criteria go beyond standard features like price, quality, and lead time [14] and include eco-friendly practices, programs, and attitudes [15] Firms are now looking for suppliers that are concerned with environmental issues and are able to provide technically restorative and regenerative materials [16]. Thus, the strategic sourcing function has a role to play in relation to CE 3R principles [17]. For MediX, the reduction principle can be reflected in the function's ability to avoid unnecessary waste, through systematic evaluations of what they need pertaining to the developed specs for their products and the materials that go into them. The function does not directly affect the improvement of efficiency in production and the consumption process, i.e., eco-efficiency, but can ensure that the right parts are available. This would avoid waste in the form of the wrong materials/parts, which usually end up discarded, and can result in fewer parts used per unit of value produced, which is one way of achieving eco-efficiency [6]. Further, the reuse and recycling principles are also relevant to the strategic sourcing function, as it can contribute with evaluation of materials and parts used and provide alternatives that enable a higher degree of reuse and recycling at MediX. The ability to support 3R efforts indicates that the sourcing function can enhance CE implementation; as the function can consider multiple cycles of value creation as well as disposal when the end of life is irreversibly reached, which is especially necessary for MediX in their quest to capitalize on circular practices.

Manufacturing Decisions

When deciding whether a manufacturing process is to be executed in-house or externally, the firm's strategy, and the coordination of procurement with other functional strategies, such as logistics and production, should be considered [18]. This explains why the critical decision to *make-or-buy products* at MediX is made by both manufacturing and sourcing functions. In fact, such a decision is the starting point and a vital element in the sourcing process as it determines the number of value-adding activities that potentially can be sourced from suppliers. Although the most common make-or-buy triggers are cost and quality problems [19], for MediX it is mostly due to lack of capacity.

Product quality versus on-time delivery is another critical decision particularly in in-house production. It becomes a critical issue when there are delays, which then pose decisions about whether to compromise on quality and get the new product out on the market on-time. An intriguing question though is whether one have to choose one of them or if these factors can go hand in hand? The latter is what MediX practices. In their case the most important thing is not to compromise on quality when delivering projects on-time, but in case that happens, the decision must be done on a firm level and not restricted to individual decision makers. Indeed, in today's highly competitive market where technological innovation and its growth are significant, both quality and time are essential for the success of their products, and not least for the shift towards a CE. Hence, if quality of products is compromised right from the designing stage, it can result in a product that breaks down before its end of life, which in most cases, is either financially not viable to repair, or simply not reparable. Consequently, they are discarded and landfilled, creating detrimental environmental consequences with enormous loss of materials, energy, water, and labour embedded in them. Thus, as noted earlier, key lies in how a product is designed.

Customer/User Decisions

Customer/user team supports the PD function through understanding customer and user needs at a detailed level by meeting and interacting with them. One of the critical decisions they make is *which user information to forward to the product development function.* As MediX has a large customer base worldwide, there is just too much user information collected. This makes it hard for the customer/user team to decide which of the collected information will be useful in informing the PD decisions. Having said that, both explicit feedbacks provided from users and insight gained by interpreting user behavioral data can provide guidance on how to improve MediX's products, and thus this becomes a critical decision. Indeed, by being thoughtful about the type of user information that would be most valuable for PD or improvements can assist MediX with better decisions and thus serve their users better.

Closely related is the actual *purpose of collecting user data.* This type of decision covers aspect about e.g., data that can assist with discovering designs that provide the best outcomes, and which one would help them determine what work would have the largest impact on users. This might even be essential as explicit feedback can help surface user requirements that firms (in this case MediX) might not have thought of and opportunities to expand their offerings to address specific concerns. Undeniably, knowing the purpose of collecting user data is vital, as that enables gathering of relevant information, and if used wisely, it can give an edge over competitors and increase the impact of limited resources.

Having a deeper knowledge and understanding of customer/user needs enhances customer-focused design thinking, which can help firms to reap more value from the energy and resources they use. Simply put, the transformation to a CE will require fundamental changes in how MediX sells their products as well as how their customers/users buy them. Accordingly, an emphasis on understanding user expectations and levels of acceptability will be key to the success of many CE propositions. For example, offering services rather than products, producing more durable products by using better materials, or designing products for maintainability allowing critical components to be replaced when they wear out. Just as MediX is fully aware about taking a user-centered approach to innovation can create radical change, they know that if they do not understand their users, how then could they expect to design circular products that they aspire to?

Distribution Decisions

How to plan distribution properly is a critical decision made by the distribution function. This affects the volume of shipment, as knowing how much to ship depends on the history of how many products have previously been sold, to whom and what versions they were. It takes about six to eight weeks to transport products on a boat from Scandinavia to US, and the number of products that are sold per week is what is on a boat shipment per week. Thus, the correct shipment with regard to both volume and product type(s) becomes crucial. For instance, if the distribution personnel have missed out and shipped the wrong products, the stock in the US might fail to sell them as they are not purchased/ordered. In such a case, MediX is obliged to ship the right products by airplane. Failure to do so increases the risks additionally, as it would imply another six weeks of waiting, or in worst case scenario missing out on sales. Consequently, when shipping the products to distribution centers, the distribution function must always have a double guess; in terms of what is needed in stock (how much stock) and what exact products are to be sold. Otherwise, any minor error made in the forecasts by MediX will not only affect themselves (in terms of costs) but also their distribution centers, located in Europe, US, and Asia (e.g., stockouts and excess inventory, resulting in less efficient use of storage space, excessive use of transportation and resource waste).

In view of this, it is obvious that MediX still operates the linear model of production, as they produce their products mostly from virgin materials (i.e., except for the metal as it is recycled), and the end products are shipped to their distribution centers all over the world, where they are used, discarded, and eventually replaced by newer versions. This is an untapped potential value, which could be realized through CE implementation. Precisely, MediX could retain the utmost value embedded in products by paying close attention to the production and distribution systems that will enable them to collect and recover used products and/or components besides manufacturing new ones. By doing this, not only is the amount of waste sent to landfills minimized through repair, remanufacturing/reuse and recycling but also leads to considerable energy and economic value savings added to the products in the production phase.

Further, it can also be deduced that MediX struggles with inventory accuracy especially in their distribution centers. To be circular, it is therefore essential to have a complete visibility of what the distribution centers have in stock because inventory accuracy and CE are complementary: without one there cannot be the other [20].

5 Closure

The findings of this study suggest that of all the most critical decisions made by many functions, timely exchange of information is the most critical and yet it often fails to happen. Thus, the emphasis is on the role of time, which is more often than not, an underappreciated dimension in the study of affect at work [21]). Even though the delay in information exchange, for instance, between PD and the strategic sourcing functions at MediX is well substantiated and unintended, such a delay does not only impede work by blocking access to a needed resource, but it can also have substantial negative consequences for CE implementation. This is especially a risk, when overdue information is needed by the strategic sourcing before any further action can be taken (e.g., sourcing parts for the spec).

Additionally, based on our findings, we argue that the 3R principles are not something any function can achieve in isolation, instead it requires collaboration with various internal functions (holistic approach). Further, the involvement of the sourcing in the design and development stage and collaboration with the manufacturing is of utmost importance. Thus, such an involvement is crucial in ensuring that design changes are communicated effectively to all parties involved as well as a common understanding of what material and components are needed.

While the present study provides valuable insights, it is important to outline some limitations as they provide opportunities for further research. Firstly, the study has identified and evaluated the most critical decisions in manufacturing based on a single case study, hence future studies may further explore the subject based on multiple cases. Secondly, given the increasing recognition to embrace circular economy across different industries, future studies may consider investigating in detail the various managerial issues from different sectors that need to be addressed to assure a successful implementation. Specifically, how managers and stakeholders from different sectors in general and manufacturing in particular can benefit from analyzing the most critical decisions made in their systems.

References

1. Shrivastava, P., Ivanaj, S., Persson, S.: Transdisciplinary study of sustainable enterprise. Bus. Strategy Environ. **22**(4), 230–244 (2013)
2. Gaustad, G., Krystofik, M., Bustamante, M., Badami, K.: Circular economy strategies for mitigating critical material supply issues. Resour. Conserv. Recycl. **135**, 24–33 (2018)
3. De Angelis, R.: Business Models in the Circular Economy: Concepts, Examples and Theory. Springer, Cham (2019)
4. Wang, P., Kara, S., Hauschild, M.Z.: Role of manufacturing towards achieving circular economy: the steel case. CIRP Ann. **67**(1), 21–24 (2018)
5. Bjørnbet, M.M., Skaar, C., Fet, A.M., Schulte, K.Ø.: Circular economy in manufacturing companies: a review of case study literature. J. Clean. Prod. **294**, 126268 (2021)
6. Ghisellini, P., Cialani, C., Ulgiati, S.: A review on circular economy: the expected transition to a balanced interplay of environmental and economic systems. J. Clean. Prod. **114**, 11–32 (2016)
7. Yin, R.K.: Case Study Research and Applications: Design and Methods, 6th edn. SAGE Publications, Inc., Thousand Oaks (2018)
8. Mårtensson, P., Lee, A.S.: Dialogical action research at omega corporation. MIS Q. **28**(3), 507–36 (2004)
9. Argyris, C.: Action science and intervention. J. Appl. Behav. Sci. **19**(2), 115–140 (1983)
10. BEDA: A Design Policy for Europe. http://www.policyconnect.org.uk/apdig/sites/site_a pdig/files/report/290/fieldreportdownload/apdigtermpaperfeb2013-adesignpolicyforeurope. pdf. Accessed 05 Mar 2021
11. Carr, A.S., Kaynak, H.: Communication methods, information sharing, supplier development and performance: an empirical study of their relationships. Int. J. Oper. Prod. Manag. **27**(4), 346–370 (2007)
12. Ketchen, D.J., Russell Crook, T., Craighead, C.W.: From supply chains to supply ecosystems: implications for strategic sourcing research and practice. J. Bus. Logistics **35**(3), 165–71 (2014)
13. Krause, D.R., Scannell, T.V., Calantone, R.J.: A structural analysis of the effectiveness of buying firms' strategies to improve supplier performance. Decis. Sci. **31**(1), 33–55 (2000)
14. Hartmann, J., Moeller, S.: Chain liability in multitier supply chains? Responsibility attributions for unsustainable supplier behavior. J. Oper. Manag. **32**(5), 281–294 (2014)
15. Konys, A.: Green supplier selection criteria: from a literature review to a comprehensive knowledge base. Sustainability (Switzerland) **11**(15), 4208 (2019)
16. Dhakal, M., Smith, M.H., Newbery, R.: Secondary market: a significant aspect in reverse logistics and sustainability. Int. J. Soc. Sustain. Econ. Soc. Cult. Con. **12**, 24–35 (2016)
17. Mwesiumo, D., Kvadsheim, N., Nujen, B.: The potential for purchasing function to enhance circular economy business models for ETO Production. In: Lalic, B., Majstorovic, V., Marjanovic, U., von Cieminski, G., Romero, D. (eds.) APMS 2020. IAICT, vol. 592, pp. 557–564. Springer, Cham (2020). https://doi.org/10.1007/978-3-030-57997-5_64
18. Meyer, M.M., Glas, A.H., Eßig, M.: Systematic review of sourcing and 3D printing: make-or-buy decisions in industrial buyer-supplier relationships. Manag. Rev. Q. (2020). https://doi.org/10.1007/s11301-020-00198-2

19. Moschuris, S.J.: Triggering mechanisms in make-or-buy decisions: an empirical analysis. J. Supply Chain Manag. **43**, 40–49 (2007)
20. Schwarz, M.: Circular Economy and Inventory Accuracy: The Yin and Yang of a Sustainable Supply Chain. https://www.nordicid.com/resources/blog/circular-economy-and-inventory-accuracy/. Accessed 05 Mar 2021
21. Guenter, H., van Emmerik, I.J.H., Schreurs, B.: The negative effects of delays in information exchange: looking at workplace relationships from an affective events perspective. Hum. Resour. Manag. Rev. **24**(4), 238–298 (2014)

Challenges in Setting up a Production Line During Pandemic

Kiwook Jung[1], Scott Nieman[2], and Boonserm Kulvatunyou[3]([✉])

[1] POSTECH, Pohang, South Korea
kiwook@posetch.ac.kr
[2] Land O'Lakes, Shoreview, MN, USA
stnieman@landolakes.com
[3] National Institute of Standards and Technology, Gaithersburg, MD, USA
serm@nist.gov

Abstract. The pandemic caused by COVID-19 brought on many challenges. Sustaining manufacturing production is one of them. Some market segments may experience reductions in demands, while other market segments may experience explosions in demand. Companies have to manage these changing needs and supply uncertainties while keeping employees safe and remaining profitable. This paper characterizes the problems encountered in setting up new production lines in two different industries and describes solutions adopted and envisioned.

Keywords: New factory · Production line set up · Pandemic · Production management

1 Introduction

During the pandemic, demands for certain products changed dramatically driven by medical and economic necessities as well as consumer behavior changes such as stock-up buying, more reliance on online and direct-ship. Some product category sales skyrocketed while others plummeted, and some products that plummeted may never rebound. For example, for a diverse agrifood business, demands of grocery items such as milk, butter, and cereal went up because consumers were eating more at home [1–3]. Demands for electronics continued to grow as stayed-at-home consumers needed more electronics to do their jobs and kept them entertained [4]. The demand for printed-circuit-board (PCB) for medical devices, in particular, increased [5]; and auto-part manufacturing plants had to be adapted to producing medical devices [6].

The pressure on the supply chain for raw materials to produce in-demand finished goods shifted common ingredients away from some commodities to meet the demand of others. Animal feed for backyard chickens increased dramatically and shifted ingredients away from other more traditional animals. The closure of some ethanol plants reduced the feedstuff ingredients of by-products such as dried distillers' grains, meaning some traditional animal feed could not be produced even though the demand was there. Dairy

A. Dolgui et al. (Eds.): APMS 2021, IFIP AICT 632, pp. 369–374, 2021.
https://doi.org/10.1007/978-3-030-85906-0_41

and other livestock farmers also 'stocked up' on feed supplemental blends and additives [1–3]. Increase in plant production capacities were needed to meet this shift in demand.

Similarly, the demand for batteries continued to grow, not only due to the growing demands of electronic devices, but also due to electric cars and alternative energy. New production lines need to be added to address shifts in demands and the continued growing demands. While some companies were able to squeeze out additional productivity to deal with the demand surge [5], some of them have to set up new production lines.

This paper documents the difficulties associated with setting up a new production line during the pandemic. The intention of documenting these is that it may spur developments of new production technologies and better the preparations for similar, emergency situations in the future.

The rest of the paper is organized as follows. Section 2 gives high-level activities associated with setting up a new factory and/or production line. Section 3 documents challenges associated with some of those activities and finally Sect. 4 discusses ideas that could address those challenges.

2 Background

Setting up a production line or factory (from designing to commissioning) is a subset of a larger set of activities of the new product introduction [NPI] process. Jung et al. [7] outlined a set of activities involved in setting up or updating a factory using an IDEF0 activity model [8]. Table 1 lists these activities. While many activities can be done virtually with today's technologies, some of them require physical presence and face challenges, especially those related to the physical deployment of production equipment, network installation such as fiber optics and Wi-Fi access points, bar-code scanners and printers, conveyance equipment, and the various Test activities. Some of these activities are also challenged by supply shortages. The next section discusses more detail about these challenges.

Table 1. Activities involved in setting up a new factory as outlined in [6].

A1- Develop factory requirement	A2 - Develop basic design	A3 - Develop and deploy detail design	A4 - Test
A1.1 - Analyze Market	A2.1- Set Production Target	A3.1 - Manage Capital Procurement (order/receive)	A4.1 Verify Production & Inspection Equipment
A1.2 - Analyze Infrastructure	A2.2 - Determine Equipment & Manpower Capacity	A3.2 - Determine Manufacturing Method & Technology	Verify Process

(continued)

Table 1. (*continued*)

A1- Develop factory requirement	A2 - Develop basic design	A3 - Develop and deploy detail design	A4 - Test
A13 - Analyze Sales & Production Plan	A23 - Verify Process Throughput	A33 - Design and Deploy Production Equipment	A43 - Verify Material Handling System
A14 - Assemble Factory Requirement	A24 - Set Lot Size	A34 - Design and Deploy Inspection Equipment	A44 - Verify Factory Layout & Material Flow
	A25- Design Auxiliary Facility	A35 - Design and Setup Material Flow	A45 - Test Factory
	A26 - Design & Verify Manufacturing Line	A36 - Design and Deploy Material Handling System	A46 - Standardize Factory
	A27 - Assemble Basic Factory Layout	A37 - Design and Factory Layout	
	A28 - Develop Production Management System	A38 - Develop Material Management Plan	
	A29 - Assemble Basic Factory Specification	A39 - Assemble Detailed Factory Specification	

3   Challenges

One of the main decisions that is made when addressing increased demand (which even existed prior to COVID-19) is whether the existing plants can increase their production throughput, whether a new plant needs to be created, an existing plant can be expanded, or whether a co-manufacturing or contract-manufacturing partner can be used to handle the increased demand (expensed). For the agrifood business, a decision matrix was created to determine whether to 1) build a new plant, 2) retrofit existing, but unused, manufacturing plant the business owned through prior merger/acquisition, or 3) whether re-purpose and expand existing plant. Prior to COVID, to address the need for increased demand for feed additives and pre-mixed ingredients operated under a subsidiary, the original plan was to bring back to life an idle plant that was part of a merger and acquisition of a competitor. After COVID hit, it was determined that it was better to repurpose and expand an existing plant and convert that plant from the parent operation company to the subsidiary while STILL producing the parent company's feed supplements for livestock (dairy, beef, pig, turkey) as if it was a co-manufacturer. This decision reduced the amount of technical resources required to be on-site, as bringing back to life the old plant only needed resources to ensure the equipment was still operational, determine whether they required upgrade, etc. - less than resources that would be required for breaking a new ground for an expansion. The business decision did not take into account all the system integrations, and that required additional scoping.

Once the decision above was made, the company still faced challenges from the pandemic on three fronts. First, there was a supply chain disruption of devices and equipment needed to set up the factory. The shortages extended also to control equipment such as Programmable Logic Control (PLC) and computer systems.

The second issue was the supply chain disruption of personnel. Even if the social distance and other preventative measures such as mask wearing and air scrubbing can be employed to allow physical presence of local workers, getting experts and engineers particularly from abroad to the set-up site was next to impossible because of the travel restriction.

The third challenge stems from the first two challenges causing difficulties related to factory design and overall commissioning.

4 Discussion

This section discussed ideas that may be developed to address the challenges that have been described in Sect. 3. For the agrifood business, from a business applications perspective, it was determined that the subsidiary's Enterprise Resource Planning (ERP), Manufacturing Execution System (MES)/Inventory Management System would be used. This indicated a significant process change for existing personnel who used to use the parent companies ERP and no MES system. This meant re-training of personnel on new systems and processes that added significant lot traceability - a step in the positive direction. To support the new co-manufacturing processes, additional integration between the respective ERPs to communicate purchase orders, ship notices and invoices would need to be created. The formula bill of materials would come out of the parent company's formulation system and sent to the subsidiary's MES. The MES would now have an additional integration to the process control system that the parent company was already using at that parent location. It was decided to leverage the Open Application Group Inc. (OAGi) SME Express Pack the API definitions for all these integrations [9].

The use of web conference solutions facilitated all the workshops between the parent company, the subsidiary headquarter's personnel and the plant operations personnel. BPMN models were created as visual approaches to describe the business and manufacturing processes as it was understood. It was necessary for manufacturing engineers to travel to existing subsidiary plants to capture videos of the existing processes leveraging these systems, such as material gathering and flow, and record keeping. It was too hard to elicit this from the system documentation, emails, and screen sharing over web conferences. This put both engineering and plant personnel at risk.

To alleviate that, and as vaccines became more readily available, the agrifood company worked with the various government agencies and local health care providers in the region of the plant to conduct a one-day vaccination clinic where all personnel of the plant would be vaccinated as they were on the production line. This assisted future travel concerns to that plant by engineering and IT resources needing to do that work.

4.1 Shortage of Industrial Parts

Specific industrial equipment and devices were particularly vulnerable to instability stemming from restrained labor conditions in countries like Japan and Germany. Essential components for automated production such as PLCs were not easy to replace with alternative vendors in a short amount of time.

Short term resolutions to industrial part shortages includes subcontracting of credit. It's particularly more effective to apply subcontracting for standard parts such as PLCs. For example, each equipment vendor has a little buying power on PLC providers, but the manufacturer can exercise much bigger buying power with all demands combined. To put this into action, it is required to negotiate a separate term with a PLC vendor directly about discounted unit price and sourcing mechanisms to each equipment vendor.

Mid-to-long term resolution involves a more technical approach. Control systems in factories are slowly moving towards more PC-based controls. This opens up a new paradigm where more general programming skills become applicable in industrial applications. Therefore, manufacturers need to start considering more aggressive adoption of PC-based controls.

4.2 Immobility of Setup Engineers (Potential Delays in Commissioning)

Immobility of setup engineers to be dispatched, oftentimes to foreign soils, greatly delay debugging of equipment thus not being able to meet target dates for production ramp-ups. With travel restrictions across countries and quarantine regulations ranging 2–4 weeks, scheduling became more difficult than before. Expenses (travel cost) are also higher for commissioning jobs.

Digital technologies can be leveraged to deal with this problem. Augmented reality (AR) can enable users to interact with both virtual and real worlds simultaneously by overlaying information on real world objects. Recently, AR solutions including hardware devices, software, and contents became much more accessible. There are remote assistance tools powered by such augmented reality technologies. This allows an expert on one node and a novice on the other node. Thus, companies can leverage less skilled workers on one end to be guided by experts located elsewhere to execute the commissioning jobs. For example, PTC Vuforia provides a comprehensive AR solution that is tailored to needs of industrial applications.

4.3 Factory Design and Commissioning Difficulties

Pandemic puts more stress particularly on actual sourcing (FOB/acceptance test) and commissioning stages. Any changes in the factory design would cause significant disruptions downstream because of the challenges in the supply chain and logistics. Adhering to the concurrent engineering strategy is ever more important to minimize design changes. Then, in the downstream sourcing activity, applying the divide-and-conquer (category management) approach to supply chain management is very important. In this approach, procurement strategies for standard parts vs. customized parts need to be clearly distinguished. For standard parts, procurement strategy is driven by the procurement organization to lower the cost while keeping the supply stable. For customized parts, a collaborative approach among engineering, quality and procurement organizations is required to freeze equipment specification as early as possible. Thus, procurement practice itself needs to be engineered and highly aligned with development activities (also known as procurement engineering).

5   Conclusion

Pandemic causes hardship on virtually everyone on the planet. Manufacturing enterprises have to continue to operate while subject to contraction, expansion, or adaptation to respond to changing industry demands. This paper discussed challenges and resolves manufacturers faced and used for the case of manufacturing expansion. It also offered visions about technological development that could help faced other challenges and disruptions better in the future. While the discussions were specifically in the context of a pandemic, some resolutions and technological vision discussed could be applied during the normal time that could provide positive impact on the process flexibility and cost reductions, e.g., related to travels and supply costs. In the future, more in-depth research could be performed on the expansion case and extended to contraction and adaptation cases (e.g., adapting an auto-part plant to make ventilators by Ford Motor).

Disclaimer.   Any mention of commercial products is for information only; it does not imply recommendation or endorsement by NIST.

References

1. Silverstein, S.: Grocery sales soar as pandemic crushes overall consumer spending (2020). https://www.grocerydive.com/news/grocery-sales-soar-as-pandemic-crushes-overall-consumer-spending/576147/. Accessed 6 Apr 2021
2. Choudhury, N.R.: Covid-19: The impact on the animal feed industry (2020). https://www.allaboutfeed.net/animal-feed/raw-materials/covid-19-the-impact-on-the-animal-feed-industry/. Accessed 6 Apr 2021
3. Raia, P.: COVID-19 Economics Challenge the Horse Industry (2020). https://thehorse.com/186680/covid-19-economics-challenge-the-horse-industry/. Accessed 6 Apr 2021
4. TechXplore. Consumers boosted electronics spending in pandemic year: survey (2021). https://techxplore.com/news/2021-02-consumers-boosted-electronics-pandemic-year.html. Accessed 6 Apr 2021
5. Lloyd, E.H.: Small-Town Calumet Electronics Has Big Impact (2020). https://www.countrylines.com/cover-story/small-town-calumet-electronics-has-big-impact/. Accessed 6 Apr 2021
6. Ford to produce 50,000 ventilators in Michigan in next 100 days; partnering with GE healthcare will help coronavirus patients. https://media.ford.com/content/fordmedia/fna/us/en/news/2020/03/30/ford-to-produce-50-000-ventilators-in-michigan-in-next-100-days.html
7. Jung, K., Choi, S., Kulvatunyou, B., Cho, H., Morris, K.C.: A reference activity model for smart factory design and improvement. Prod. Plann. Control **28**(2), 108–122 (2017)
8. Cheng-Leong, A., Li Pheng, K., Keng Leng, G.R.: IDEF*: a comprehensive modelling methodology for the development of manufacturing enterprise systems. Int. J. Prod. Res. **37**(17), 3839–3858 (1999)
9. Nieman, S.T., Ivezic, N., Kulvatunyou, B.: Enabling small and medium sized enterprises to participate in a digital supply chain using the OAGi express pack. In: Proceedings of Advances in Production Management Systems, Nantes, France (2021)

Green Production and Circularity Concepts

Developing a Qualitative Maturity Scale for Circularity in Manufacturing

Federica Acerbi[1]([⊠]) [iD], Vafa Järnefelt[2], Jorge Tiago Martins[2] [iD], Leila Saari[3] [iD], Katri Valkokari[4] [iD], and Marco Taisch[1] [iD]

[1] Department of Management, Economics and Industrial Engineering, Politecnico Di Milano, Piazza Leonardo da Vinci 32, 20133 Milan, Italy
{federica.acerbi,marco.taisch}@polimi.it
[2] VTT Technical Research Centre of Finland, Tekniikantie 21, 02150 Espoo, Finland
{vafa.jarnefelt,jorge.martins}@vtt.fi
[3] VTT Technical Research Centre of Finland, Kaitoväylä 1, 90570 Oulu, Finland
leila.saari@vtt.fi
[4] VTT Technical Research Centre of Finland, Visiokatu 4, 33720 Tampere, Finland
katri.valkokari@vtt.fi

Abstract. Circular Economy (CE) is gaining momentum and its diffusion in manufacturing companies remains a key element to be addressed. Indeed, the principles and practice of circularity can enhance sustainability in the manufacturing sector, but changes are required in organizations in order to fully embrace this paradigm. Therefore, several assessment models have been proposed to quantitatively measure CE performance, yet covering niche aspects, whereas a holistic perspective is usually neglected. In addition, there is significant scope to improve the elements composing the big picture through delineating where possible improvements might occur and this can be provided through an evaluation of the current status of a manufacturing company in respect to the optimum or reference model. Therefore, the goal of this contribution is to create the building blocks for a maturity model assessment proposing a complete and exhaustive maturity scale supporting companies in clarifying strategic objectives towards circularity in manufacturing. This goal has been achieved through a review of the scientific literature and a validation exercise performed through two workshops in which practitioners and researchers have been involved. This mixed-methodology allowed to strengthen the results obtained.

Keywords: Circular economy · Maturity scale · Manufacturing

1 Introduction

Nowadays more than ever, manufacturing companies are required to update and rethink traditional activities and operations, especially through the perspective of sustainability [1], and with a focus on limiting resource consumption and extending resource lifecycles. In this regard, calls for adopting circular economy (CE) principles have proliferated based

© IFIP International Federation for Information Processing 2021
Published by Springer Nature Switzerland AG 2021
A. Dolgui et al. (Eds.): APMS 2021, IFIP AICT 632, pp. 377–385, 2021.
https://doi.org/10.1007/978-3-030-85906-0_42

on values and principles that are intended to increase sustainability in the manufacturing sector [2]. Indeed, the extant literature presents a plethora of research dealing with CE in terms of definition of the paradigm [3], description of the main principles [4], and possible circular business models adoptable by companies [5].

A common need identified across these calls is that of a reference model to enable companies to embrace CE through embarking on a structured transition, based on clear objectives. Different assessment models have been proposed, such as those to assess resource consumption and greenhouse gasses emissions [6]. Although these models often generate quantitative measures, their scope is limited usually to a specific process or a specific resource. They all tend to have either a firm-level or a network-level perspective, without providing a holistic picture. They also neglect the possibility to benchmark the current status assessed with better achievable levels. Indeed, each company requires varying time and efforts to undertake this path. Developing a qualitative maturity scale for circularity in manufacturing firms is therefore needed. The existing maturity models for circularity appear to focus on assessing structural and technical factors of manufacturing systems and tend to neglect organizational factors and the managerial practices, which indicates a limitation in the current approaches to circularity. The contribution put forward in this paper places organizational and managerial practices center-stage in order to underline the way in which things are done, i.e. the granularity in practices, which is fundamental to understand and explain performance differentials [7]. Therefore, the goal of this paper is to develop a qualitative maturity scale allowing to position manufacturing companies in the path towards circularity. The scale is essential to support companies in defining clear objectives to improve self-performance towards circularity and to understand what is needed for effective collaboration with other actors to participate in a CE.

The paper is structured as follows. Section 2 reports the methodology adopted. Section 3 reviews the literature on assessment models for CE. Section 4 presents the qualitative maturity scale developed based on the review. Section 5 reports on the workshops held to validate the scope and applicability of the scale, and finally Sect. 6 concludes the contribution with implications, limitations and future research directions.

2 Methodology

The present contribution aims to establish the basis and the building blocks to clarify the distinctive maturity levels in which a manufacturing company can be positioned concerning CE implementation. To achieve this goal, the extant literature was reviewed by querying Scopus with the following string: "circular economy" AND ("assessment" OR "maturity") AND "model*" AND "manufacturing"). This led to an initial output of 79 to which 9 were added relying on suggestions from experts in the field. Then non-English written documents were excluded and the remaining sample was spanned to select eligible papers. Therefore, non-manufacturing specific papers, and papers not focused on models to assess circularity or circular aspects were discarded. The final sample of 44 papers (only partly reported in this paper) was reviewed in Sect. 3.

This review enabled to define the maturity scale, establishing a theoretically informed basis for a comprehensive circularity maturity model, that then has been validated (see

Sect. 5) through two complementary workshops held in Italy and in Finland, involving a total of 20 European participants (10 in each workshop) from industry. Methodologically, this is consistent with the exploratory and cocreation-focused approaches employed in maturity scale development, which engage a broad range of domain experts in order to ensure that the maturity scale addresses the needs of the target audience [8]. The workshops took place online using *Mural* and *Miro* tools to actively engage participants in the collaborative validation of the scale and the discussion of its value and applicability.

3 Literature Review: Assessment Models for CE

The extant literature on models assessing CE performances is quite vast [9], since each model developed tends to be focused on a specific aspect of CE [6]. This allows companies to immediately retrieve information about a distinctive aspect without instead having the overview on the company as a complex entity operating in an even more complex network. This limits the potential of CE in coping with the linear inefficiencies like unsustainable materials, and unexploited customer engagement [10].

These assessment methods may evaluate the greenhouse gasses emissions of productive activities [11], the resources consumption starting by considering the product design [12]. These measurements are sometimes grouped in the Life Cycle Assessment (LCA) to support for instance the decision-making process towards the design of new circular products or services [13]. Moreover, in addition to the environmental performance, these models are also extended to the evaluation of the economic benefits taking the name of Life Cycle Costing (LCC) to meet the companies' economic needs [14]. These models allow to monitor the undertaking of an initial path towards circularity focusing first on the consumption of limited resources but offer only a partial view without fully capturing the range of the opportunities enabled by circularity. As a consequence, considering the network perspective characterizing CE, other models were developed such as those focused on the supplier selection process [15] or those supporting the engagement with the right partners in a reverse logistics network [16]. Following the same circular lifecycle perspective, maturity assessment models were developed to evaluate functional product requirements to ensure product circularity at the end of their lifecycle [17]. In line with these models, the LCA and the LCC were adopted also to monitor the environmental performances of an industrial symbiosis network [18] stressing the importance to engage with external stakeholders.

Although these existing models provide great tools to assess manufacturing companies' current circular performances on specific issues, they do not help them in understanding concretely where they are, to be able to put in place new actions to improve their conditions. This issue can be covered by an internal awareness generated through a thorough initial qualitative analysis concerning their general current achievements in terms of circularity, as proposed for SMEs [19]. This awareness is necessary also for larger companies requiring significant changes supported by clear plans, defined by managers, to be aligned with the external ecosystem [20]. Indeed, the strategic and the managerial indicators cover the most relevant roles in embracing CE [21].

In summary, the current approaches to measure circularity in isolation are insufficient to capture the multiple dimensions of practice that manufacturing companies need to embrace in their transitions towards improved levels of circularity. The existing measurements need to be grouped and analyzed together to provide companies with a holistic understanding of what different levels of circularity mean and require.

The evaluation of the status of a company in respect to the optimum is commonly designated as "maturity". Maturity models typically consist of a sequence of maturity levels, usually five, representing a desired evolutionary path, in which the initial stages represent a limited set of capabilities in a domain, which progressively moves towards enhanced capabilities [8] and a stage of maturity. Maturity seen as a measure to evaluate the capabilities of an entity become popular since the Capability Maturity Model (CMM) was proposed and was proven in practice on Software Engineering domain [22, 23]. This was adopted in different areas especially when dealing with an innovative paradigm requiring drastic internal change for companies such as the challenges of digital transformation [24] that require a new set of skills [25]. Indeed, it has been considered a useful tool for the CE context too [26] even though still at an emergent stage regarding the building blocks characterizing CE. This is the gap this paper addresses.

Determining the capability levels of processes, thus a maturity scale, in organizations requires the definition of best practices in a reference model [27] that outlines a process lifecycle, objectives, outputs and relationships between them. These reference models are refined into activities and base practices which exemplify attributes and characteristics of firms' practices enabling to assess performances. The proposed qualitative maturity scale for circularity in manufacturing is intended to operate as a reference, where the dimensions and categories of the activities and base practices operate as the key building blocks for a fully-fledged circularity maturity model. This contribution opens up the black box of maturity scale development, through reporting on the process of incorporating the needs of the intended users. It strengthens the transparency of the process through demonstrating how varying stakeholders were actively involved in collaboratively examining the applicability and what can be achieved using the scale.

4   Qualitative Maturity Scale for Circular Economy

Further to the review of assessment models for CE reported in Sect. 2, a clustering and systematization of circularity components into five distinct qualitative maturity levels is below proposed and illustrated in Fig. 1.

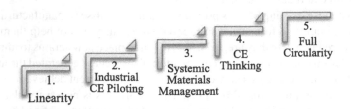

Fig. 1. Circular economy qualitative maturity scale.

A manufacturing company classified in the *Linearity* level is still stuck into the traditional concept of make-take-dispose. The only sustainable/circular-oriented activities consist in legal responsibilities mainly related to waste management and limited usage of toxic substances. Therefore, the company performance is monitored only to mitigate additional costs rather than to find new opportunities in a circular scenario.

The second level of maturity, named *Industrial Circular Economy Piloting,* corresponds to a more advanced level, within which the company is interested in changing, at least partially, the current linear pattern. Indeed, some pilot experimentation takes place, pushing performance closer to resources sufficiency. Detailed analyses are performed to diagnose resource bottlenecks and to evaluate different processes parameters in terms of material and energy consumption. In addition, led by the strategic level, the experimentation goals and results are shared within the company boundaries across different hierarchical levels, from the top management to the more operative levels, to engage employees in this transition and create internal awareness.

The third achievable level, named *Systemic Material Management,* corresponds to the adoption of CE in a more extended perspective, i.e. to the whole company. Here the "R-cycles" characterizing CE have become a standard practice adopted by the company to systematically identify possibilities to reuse, refurbish, recycle, and remanufacture materials [28]. To make this possible, the entire company is involved and the operative level is required to take an active role in this initiative. Every resource used by the company is internally analyzed to think about possible future reintroduction into (new) R-cycles. The LCA is implemented to keep the most critical processes under control. This is backed also by the monitoring of the circular performance, conducted by the local unit leaders, with an initial attempt to share the results with value chain partners and other stakeholders such as customers. Therefore, to do that, an initial adoption of information and communication technologies (ICT) to optimize material management and to make operations more sustainable is seen.

The fourth level of the scale is named *Circular Economy Thinking* since at this level the company is not only internally able to recirculate resources, but it has also understood the potential in defining stronger partnerships with external stakeholders to re-purpose industrial materials. Therefore, industrial symbiosis networks, and an attempt to establish a closed-loop supply chain is observed at this level. To support these initiatives, ICT are used in a more integrated manner. Moreover, the LCA is performed as common practice on all the production processes and products developed internally.

The highest maturity level, from which continuous improvement follows, is named *Full Circularity.* At this level, the firm is fully immersed into the circularity paradigm and committed to achieving social, economic and environmental positive performances in all the products, processes and operations. This is achieved thanks to the exploitation of synergies among forward and reverse logistics, and among local value chains by sharing a mutual vision for sustaining full circularity leading to the co-creation of new value circles within manufacturing networks. ICT are highly integrated into operations to support these interactions. Strategic, tactical and operational levels of the company are aligned with a systematic and proactive follow-up of the circular transition.

5 Maturity Scale Validation

The maturity scale developed for circularity in manufacturing has been validated through two complementary workshops evaluating its applicability and value.

In the first workshop, the importance of clearly determining the positioning of a company in respect to the improved levels achievable in CE was highly emphasized. This would enable to facilitate the clarification of internal objectives extending the traditional ones of manufacturing operations. There was wide agreement with the need to first think about internal adaptation of traditional processes by starting with piloting experimentation focused mainly on material management. This creates the awareness to also look externally into other possible stakeholders that should be involved in alignment with the maturity scale proposed. Indeed, the higher levels of maturity require the involvement of external actors to make the recirculation of resource possible.

In the second workshop, participants acknowledged the usefulness of a maturity scale to address, on the one hand, capability gaps concerning CE know-how within companies and, on the other hand, the possibility to pace the transition, since the required changes for CE would be too massive to tackle at once. The workshop has also highlighted how participating companies understood the importance of an early identification of circularity potential across supply chain individual components, which requires a common reference architecture and the adoption of an ecosystem type of thinking for the effective sharing of material information and logistics optimization. This is reflected particularly in the Systemic Material Management level of the maturity scale.

Across both workshops, participants converged on their consideration of product as a key element to be updated and innovated to address circularity, underlining also the need to ensure consumer satisfaction in modifying products, and the engagement of the labor force through strengthening their competencies for undertaking this transition. Another crucial aspect raised by participants concerned the need to be aligned with other industrial actors, especially those operating in the same supply chain, which can be achieved through better data sharing capabilities. This indeed requires the introduction of integrated platforms allowing an easy exchange of relevant information and the establishment of type of data required to be shared and exchanged.

6   Conclusions

The present contribution aimed at developing a qualitative maturity scale for circularity in manufacturing. The maturity scale represents an extensive description of a possible stage within which a manufacturing company can be found during the transition from linear to circular manufacturing. It supports a diagnosis-oriented introspective qualitative analysis, by covering the distinctive actions that should be put in place to achieve higher levels of circularity starting from an initial update of internal practices.

Our contribution of a qualitative maturity scale is a fundamental step in the formulation of a circularity maturity model for manufacturing firms. The qualitative stages of the scale correspond to a set of practices and processes to be established, and a first attempt at systematizing the sophistication and embeddedness of the proposed practices and processes, with a view to developing a validated maturity scale that enables manufacturing firms to position themselves against the maturity scale and optimize CE performance. The process presented here contributes to opening up the black-box of maturity models development, as it demonstrates how the needs of industry practitioners are reflected, how and why industry practitioners will seek to apply them, and who needs to be involved. Indeed, the present research contributes to both theory and practice through on the one hand developing a maturity scale that is a foundational building block of a fully-developed assessment model devoted to circularity performance evaluation, and on the other hand providing practitioners with a usable scale enabling the positioning of their current status against circularity.

Further developments should be focused on extending the maturity scale beyond a descriptive scope and outline a detailed range of prescriptive actions, giving manufacturing companies access to the more practical instruments and indicators they need to fully embrace circularity. This can be done by extending the validation of the scale towards its application in different industrial case studies. In addition, considering the value of data sharing expressed during the workshops, further analysis in this direction will be performed.

References

1. United Nations, Sustainable Development Goals (2015) https://sustainabledevelopment.un.org/?menu=1300
2. Geissdoerfer, M., Savaget, P., Bocken, N.M.P., Hultink, E.J.: The circular economy – a new sustainability paradigm? J. Clean. Prod. **143**, 757–768 (2017). https://doi.org/10.1016/J.JCLEPRO.2016.12.048
3. Kirchherr, J., Reike, D., Hekkert, M.: Conceptualizing the circular economy: an analysis of 114 definitions. Resour. Conserv. Recycl. **127**, 221–232 (2017). https://doi.org/10.1016/J.RESCONREC.2017.09.005
4. Ellen MacArthur Foundation, Growth within: a circular economy vision for a competitive Europe, Ellen MacArthur Found., p. 100 (2015)
5. Garza-Reyes, J.A., Kumar, V., Batista, L., Cherrafi, A., Rocha-Lona, L.: From linear to circular manufacturing business models. J. Manuf. Technol. Manag. **30**(3), 554–560 (2019). https://doi.org/10.1108/JMTM-04-2019-356
6. Kravchenko, M., McAloone, T.C., Pigosso, D.C.A.: To what extent do circular economy indicators capture sustainability? Procedia CIRP **90**, 31–36 (2020). https://doi.org/10.1016/j.procir.2020.02.118
7. Bititci, U.S., Garengo, P., Ates, A., Nudurupati, S.S.: Value of maturity models in performance measurement. Int. J. Prod. Res. **53**(10), 3062–3085 (2015). https://doi.org/10.1080/00207543.2014.970709
8. De Bruin, T., Freeze, R., Kulkarni, U., Rosemann, M.: Understanding the main phases of developing a maturity assessment model. ACIS 2005 Proceedings of (December 2005). Accessed 04 Dec 2020. https://aisel.aisnet.org/acis2005/109
9. Sassanelli, C., Rosa, P., Rocca, R., Terzi, S.: Circular economy performance assessment methods: a systematic literature review. J. Clean. Prod. **229**, 440–453 (2019). https://doi.org/10.1016/j.jclepro.2019.05.019
10. Sitra; Technology Industries of Finland; Accenture, Circular economy business models for the manufacturing industry. Circular Economy Playbook for Finnish SMEs (2020)
11. Zhang, H., et al.: Closed-circulating CO_2 sequestration process evaluation utilizing wastes in steelmaking plant. Sci. Total Environ. **738**, 139747 (2020). https://doi.org/10.1016/j.scitotenv.2020.139747

12. Desing, H., Braun, G., Hischier, R.: Resource pressure – a circular design method. Resour. Conserv. Recycl. **164**, 105179 (2021). https://doi.org/10.1016/j.resconrec.2020.105179

13. van Loon, P., Diener, D., Harris, S.: Circular products and business models and environmental impact reductions: current knowledge and knowledge gaps. J. Clean. Prod. **288**, 125627 (2021). https://doi.org/10.1016/j.jclepro.2020.125627

14. Wohner, B., Gabriel, V.H., Krenn, B., Krauter, V., Tacker, M.: Environmental and economic assessment of food-packaging systems with a focus on food waste. Case study on tomato ketchup. Sci. Total Environ. **738**, 139846 (2020). https://doi.org/10.1016/j.scitotenv.2020.139846

15. Feng, J., Gong, Z.: Integrated linguistic entropy weight method and multi-objective programming model for supplier selection and order allocation in a circular economy: a case study. J. Clean. Prod. **277**, 122597 (2020). https://doi.org/10.1016/j.jclepro.2020.122597

16. Chen, Z.S., Zhang, X., Govindan, K., Wang, X.J., Chin, K.S.: Third-party reverse logistics provider selection: a computational semantic analysis-based multi-perspective multi-attribute decision-making approach. Expert Syst. Appl. **166**, 114051 (2021). https://doi.org/10.1016/j.eswa.2020.114051

17. Martinsen, K., Assuad, C.S.A., Kito, T., Matsumoto, M., Reddy, V., Guldbrandsen-Dahl, S.: Closed loop tolerance engineering modelling and maturity assessment in a circular economy perspective. In: Kishita, Y., Matsumoto, M., Inoue, M., Fukushige, S. (eds.) EcoDesign and Sustainability I. SPLCEM, pp. 297–308. Springer, Singapore (2021). https://doi.org/10.1007/978-981-15-6779-7_21

18. Kerdlap, P., Low, J.S.C., Ramakrishna, S.: Life cycle environmental and economic assessment of industrial symbiosis networks: a review of the past decade of models and computational methods through a multi-level analysis lens. Int. J. Life Cycle Assess. **25**(9), 1660–1679 (2020). https://doi.org/10.1007/s11367-020-01792-y

19. Garza-Reyes, J.A., Valls, A.S., Nadeem, S.P., Anosike, A., Kumar, V.: A circularity measurement toolkit for manufacturing SMEs. Int. J. Prod. Res. **57**(23), 7319–7343 (2019). https://doi.org/10.1080/00207543.2018.1559961

20. Parida, V., Burström, T., Visnjic, I., Wincent, J.: Orchestrating industrial ecosystem in circular economy: a two-stage transformation model for large manufacturing companies. J. Bus. Res. **101**, 715–725 (2019). https://doi.org/10.1016/j.jbusres.2019.01.006

21. Yadav, G., Mangla, S.K., Bhattacharya, A., Luthra, S.: Exploring indicators of circular economy adoption framework through a hybrid decision support approach. J. Clean. Prod. **277**, 124186 (2020). https://doi.org/10.1016/j.jclepro.2020.124186

22. Paulk, M.C., Curtis, B., Chrissis, M.B., Weber, C.V.: Capability maturity model, version 1.1. IEEE Softw. **10**(4), 18–27 (1993). https://doi.org/10.1109/52.219617

23. Wendler, R.: The maturity of maturity model research: a systematic mapping study. Inf. Softw. Technol. **54**(12), 1317–1339 (2012). https://doi.org/10.1016/j.infsof.2012.07.007

24. Teichert, R.: Digital transformation maturity: a systematic review of literature. Acta Univ. Agric. Silvic. Mendelianae Brun. **67**(6), 1673–1687 (2019). https://doi.org/10.11118/actaun201967061673

25. Acerbi, F., Assiani, S., Taisch, M.: A methodology to assess the skills for an industry 4. 0 factory. In: Ameri, F., Stecke, K., von Cieminski, G., Kiritsis, D. (eds.) Advances in Production Management Systems. Towards Smart Production Management Systems. APMS 2019. IFIP Advances in Information and Communication Technology, vol. 567, pp. 520–527 Springer, Cham https://doi.org/10.1007/978-3-030-29996-5_60

26. Kristoffersen, E., Blomsma, F., Mikalef, P., Li, J.: The smart circular economy: A digital-enabled circular strategies framework for manufacturing companies. J. Bus. Res. **120**, 241–261 (2020). https://doi.org/10.1016/j.jbusres.2020.07.044

27. Lacerda, T.C., von Wangenheim, C.G.: Systematic literature review of usability capability/maturity models. Comput. Stand. Interfaces, **55**, 339–1351 (2018) https://doi.org/10.1016/j.csi.2017.06.001
28. Morseletto, P.: Targets for a circular economy. Resour. Conserv. Recycl. **153**, 104553 (2020) https://doi.org/10.1016/j.resconrec.2019.104553

Business Models in Circular Economy: A Systematic Literature Review

Beatrice Colombo[1,2](✉), Paolo Gaiardelli[1], Stefano Dotti[1], and Albachiara Boffelli[1]

[1] Department of Management, Information and Production Engineering,
University of Bergamo, Dalmine, Italy
{beatrice.colombo,paolo.gaiardelli,stefano.dotti,
albachiara.boffelli}@unibg.it
[2] ENEA - Italian National Agency for New Technologies, Energy and Sustainable Economic
Development, Division for Sustainable Materials, Brindisi Research Centre, Brindisi, Italy

Abstract. Scientific literature lacks a comprehensive and extensive overview of business models built upon circular economy principles. Based on this premise, this paper performs a systematic literature review, through which it aims at identifying and then categorizing circular business models processed in the literature to date. Fifteen circular business models are identified and analysed. The results show that circular business models can be associated with different circular strategies, but that some are more studied than others. The research also indicates that each circular business model can be associated with one particular life cycle stage of a product-service, thus making it more suitable for a specific circular strategy.

Keywords: Systematic literature review · Circular business model · Circular economy

1 Introduction

A Business Model (BM) is considered a fundamental driver for innovation [1]. Currently, the interest of academics and practitioners is moving towards sustainable BMs, as they are seen as a new source of competitive advantage [2]. In particular, with the recent emergence of Circular Economy (CE), the development of Circular Business Models (CBMs) has taken on a predominant role, for many reasons. Indeed, the introduction of a CBM leads to a number of positive effects in the environmental, financial, and social sphere, such as reduction of environmental impact, GDP growth, and creation of new jobs [3]. Moreover, at the micro-level, companies adopting CBMs reduce their costs, encounter new profit opportunities, improve their competitive advantage and foster their resilience in the long term [4]. Despite the significant benefits of adopting CBMs, the transition to sustainable BMs is often difficult to implement [5]. As shown by Kirchherr et al. [6] in their journey towards CBM, companies may encounter several barriers, which can be grouped into four main categories: cultural, regulatory, market, and technological. Better awareness of possible strategies of CE and associated CBMs, with their distinctive features, would allow for more effective targeting of CBM adoption. Nonetheless, existing

A. Dolgui et al. (Eds.): APMS 2021, IFIP AICT 632, pp. 386–393, 2021.
https://doi.org/10.1007/978-3-030-85906-0_43

studies do not focus on analysing this relationship. Specifically, scientific literature lacks a comprehensive and extensive overview of all the BMs which can be implemented in order to capture CE principles into business practices. For instance, [7] found that only a few articles explore two or more CBMs concurrently. Based on these premises, this paper tries to bridge the existing gap by performing a systematic literature review. The goal is to create a comprehensive map of the main CBMs and their distinctive features. In addition, through the analysis of the state of the art, this paper aims to understand the relationship between each type of CBM and the main CE strategies, to help scholars to (re)direct their efforts within this research field and organizations to identify the proper actions to take in accordance with their circular strategy.

The paper is organized as follows: Sect. 2 outlines the methodology adopted to perform the systematic literature review, while Sect. 3 and 4 propose the main results of the final sample and the categorization of the papers based upon their content. Lastly, Sect. 5 discusses the results and concludes the work by also highlighting some limitations for future improvements.

2 Methodology

This paper performs a systematic review of the literature on the topic of CBMs. This methodology was identified as the best option to pursue the research objective, as it is widely used to explore emerging topics, investigate the development of specific research stream, and propose suggestions for future works [8]. In particular, the review process was structured by following the guidelines proposed by Tranfield et al. [9]. The material collection was carried out through Web of Science (WoS) and Scopus, as they are recognised as the most complete and exhaustive scientific databases. To capture all the studies concerning CBMs across the scientific community, the generic keyword "Circular Economy" combined with "Business model" was used as a research criterion in both databases. Moreover, the research record was "Topic" in WoS and "Title, Author keywords, Abstract" in Scopus. The first round returned 1161 results and was performed in August 2020. Then, in the second round, two selection criteria were applied. Specifically, only articles written in English and published after 2015 were considered, as the study aims at assessing the most innovative and recent publications in international academic research. Subsequently, duplicates of the two databases were removed, resulting in 754 unique records. In the fourth round, abstracts of all articles were carefully read to assess their relevance and alignment to the topic under investigation. In doing so, 678 articles were rejected. The remaining 76 sources were read in their entirety. Three cited articles were found to be of interest and therefore added to the search. Thus, the total amount of papers analysed was 79. Figure 1 shows all steps of the systematic literature review process.

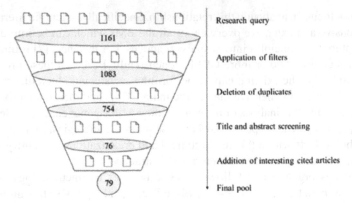

Fig. 1. Steps and number of papers along the systematic literature review

3 Papers Descriptive Analysis

In this section, the analysis of the documents selected through the systematic litera-ture review is presented. In detail, the study reveals the growth of publications over the selected period, reaching a peak in 2019 with 27 articles. This result proves the increas-ing scientific interest in this research field. The analysis also indicates that articles are mainly concentrated in Journals focused on the environmental field. The same evidence is provided by the analysis on the application field, which shows that "Environmental Sciences" occupies a core placement. Nevertheless, data depict that other sectoral areas, such as Energy, Business and Management, Engineering and Social Sciences are at the forefront of the debate. Finally, the study reveals that most of the documents involve several areas, emphasising the interdisciplinary nature of research. This feature is partly in line with the definitions of CBM proposed in the literature, which, although different, agree that a CBM has an impact not only on the company and its stakeholders but also on society as a whole [10], addressing economic, environmental and social aspects through a systemic and transdisciplinary perspective, i.e. involving science and society in the development of integrated knowledge [11].

4 Paper Categorization

As shown in Table 1 and briefly described in the following, the review of the scientific literature identified fifteen types of CBM, each with its distinctive features, and groupable into homogenous groups according to the circular strategies proposed by Bocken et al. [12] and, subsequently revised by Geissdoerfer et al. [13]. These are: closing, narrowing, slowing, intensifying, and dematerializing.

4.1 Closing Loop Strategy and Relevant CBMs

A closing loop strategy involves all BMs which seek to maintain the value of the product by exploiting the materials of which it is made of [14]. Recycling, organic feedstock, and industrial symbiosis are the three main CBMs belonging to this group. The former focuses on activities that transform waste into raw materials for manufacturing new products, which can be either the same as or different from those recycled [15]. The second proposes biomass as an input for production processes, thus closing the resource loop [14]. In fact, the organic feedstock can be converted into energy sources. Industrial symbiosis, instead, is to use the production waste of one company as an input for the processes of another company. In doing so, resources remain longer in the cycle, leading to a reduction in the demand for virgin raw materials [16], and, also, decreasing the amount of waste disposed of in landfills [17].

4.2 Narrowing Loop Strategy and Relevant CBMs

This strategy focuses on reducing resources that enter production processes [12]. It encompasses three types of CBM: resource efficiency, produce on demand, and renewable sources. Resource efficiency aims to optimize the use of virgin material and the consumption of other resources, such as water and energy, during the production phase [18]. In the produce on demand, the supplier produces only if there is demand and the products have already been ordered [19]. A company that uses renewable sources can reduce its greenhouse gas emissions [20] and the impact on natural capital [21].

4.3 Slowing Loop Strategy and Relevant CBMs

Slowing loop concerns all BMs which seek to extend the life of the product by exploiting its value for as long as possible [12]. These are long-life products, repair and maintenance, remanufacturing and reuse. The first focuses on prolonging the intrinsic life of the products through functional and aesthetic improvements that make them more resistant to damage and wear over time, encouraging users to keep them in use [22]. The second is based on the direct sale of products with associated maintenance services that make the goods last longer [23]. The third, instead, consists of rebuilding a used or unwanted product by replacing non-functional parts with new ones [24]. Finally, the fourth concerns the offer of used products that can be sold without any changes or in a slightly improved form, by cleaning and repairing small defects [21].

4.4 Intensifying Loops Strategy and Relevant CBMs

An intensifying loop strategy stresses the importance of a more intensive use phase [13]. In particular, it involves four CBMs such as sharing economy, access model, performance model, and sufficiency economy. Sharing economy encourages manufacturers to operate as service providers and to consider customers no longer as product owners or buyers, but as users [25]. The supplier continues to own the good throughout its life cycle and is responsible for end-of-life strategies [26]. Instead, the access model provides a product-oriented offer in which the value is given by temporary access to products. Specifically, companies have a continuous flow of revenues coming from subscriptions or rental payments [25]. Similarly, in the performance model, the customer buys the product performance or specifically defined results rather than the product itself [23]. Lastly, the sufficiency economy aims at moderating the consumption of end customers, thus, it represents a radical change in the concept of traditional value acquisition [27].

4.5 Dematerializing Strategy and Relevant CBMs

A dematerializing strategy is related to the formulation of a digitalization CBM which concerns the virtualization of tangible assets [24]. In this case, firms acquire the value through revenues from subscription contracts for services offered [11].

Table 1. Classification of CBMs and related percentages of papers (% per Circular strategy may be greater than 100% as one article can be associated with several CBMs).

Circular strategy	CBM	% of papers	% per Circular strategy
Closing	Recycling	30.6%	55.6%
	Organic feedstock	8.3%	
	Industrial symbiosis	16.7%	
Narrowing	Resource efficiency	13.9%	33.3%
	Produce on demand	8.3%	
	Renewable sources	11.1%	
Slowing	Long-life products	16.7%	64.0%
	Repair and maintenance	5.6%	
	Remanufacturing	25.0%	
	Reuse	16.7%	
Intensifying	Sharing economy	30.6%	114.0%
	Access model	38.9%	
	Performance model	38.9%	
	Sufficiency economy	5.6%	
Dematerializing	Digitalization	11.1%	11.1%

5 Discussion, Conclusion and Further Research

Although each CBM could be studied in more detail in the future, this initial analysis allows some insights to be extracted. First of all, it is possible to state that the topic has gained momentum over time, but that attention of academia and industry has not been paid to the different CBMs with the same intensity. Indeed, the study shows that research has mainly been focused on CBMs belonging to intensifying, slowing and closing strategies, such as sharing economy, access model, performance model, remanufacturing and recycling. Therefore, it can be stated that academics have been interested both in the issue of waste management and valorisation and in exploring new approaches to changing the way products and services are offered to customers. The attitude is perhaps still too much oriented towards a traditional view, where circular actions are mainly carried out to eliminate problems by reducing or decelerating their effects but not by acting on their causes, thus leaving the tendency to the immoderate consumption of resources unchanged. Narrowing and dematerializing circular strategies, instead, are significantly less studied than the others. This might be due to be fact that the CBMs belonging to a narrowing strategy require substantial changes to the way a company does business, e.g. by reducing the amount of resource input or producing on demand, while the dematerializing strategy concerns a relatively new subject and not yet closely related to the concept of CE. However, applying CBMs related to these two circular strategies could provide significant results for the environment, society and economy, as they are directly linked to the principle of reduction, which is considered the most important factor of CE as its implementation allows the problem to be solved at source [27]. The analysis also has revealed the key role of *servitisation* in supporting circular strategies, as highlighted by many CBMs based upon the idea of loss of ownership in favour of service provision. In particular, performance and access model have been increasingly studied over the last few years. Contrariwise, the sufficiency economy received less attention. This may be due to the different origin of the change in perspective and habits of the end customer. While *servitisation*, in fact, derives from a market need and is, therefore, more natural (pull), whereas the latter derives from the will of the company and is more difficult to implement (push).

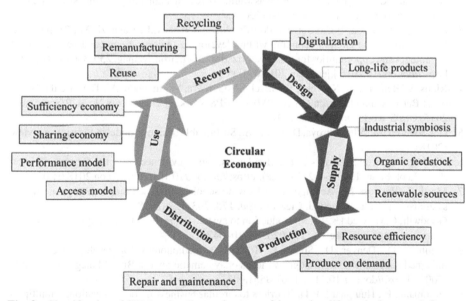

Fig. 2. Classification of CBMs according to the stage of the product life-cycle that most influences

As shown in Fig. 2, the study also made it possible to understand that each CBM is able to influence each phase of the life cycle of a product-service with different intensity. In other words, some CBMs belonging to the same circular strategy are not placed in the same stage of the life cycle. This is due to the fact that, despite aiming to pursue the same goal, they try to achieve it in different ways. Therefore, this study could help companies understand which is the most suitable CBM to adopt once they have established the circular objective to be leveraged or rather identify the best set of CBMs to be adopted at the same time to involve all stages of the life-cycle.

Finally, this study presents some limitations. First of all, the categorization of the information is necessarily affected by researcher bias. This was reduced by describing the research process as transparently as possible and by relying on well-established categories. Furthermore, only the scientific literature has been included in this study. The inclusion of grey literature could result in an important contribution to the topic, especially concerning practical examples of CBM implementation. The latter represents a promising future research avenue. Lastly, given the level of generality of the approach used in this discussion, it might be interesting in future studies to focus more attention on the most suitable CBMs with reference to the production characteristics and/or the different levels of the supply chain.

References

1. Chesbrough, H.: Business model innovation: opportunities and barriers. Long Range Plann. **43**, 354–363 (2010). https://doi.org/10.1016/j.lrp.2009.07.010
2. Nidumolu, R., Prahalad, C.K., Rangaswami, M.R.: Sustainability is the key driver of innovation. Harv. Bus. Rev. **87**, 56–64 (2009)
3. Ferronato, N., Rada, E.C., Gorritty Portillo, M.A., Cioca, L.I., Ragazzi, M., Torretta, V.: Introduction of the circular economy within developing regions: a comparative analysis of advantages and opportunities for waste valorization. J. Environ. Manag. **230**, 366–378 (2019). https://doi.org/10.1016/j.jenvman.2018.09.095
4. Rizos, V., Behrens, A., Kafyeke, T., Hirschnitz-Garbera, M., Ioannou, A.: The Circular Economy: Barriers and Opportunities for SMEs. CEPS Working Documents No. 412/September 2015. CEPS Work. Docucemnts (2015)
5. Geissdoerfer, M., Vladimirova, D., Evans, S.: Sustainable business model innovation: a review (2018)
6. Kirchherr, J., et al.: Barriers to the circular economy: evidence from the European Union (EU). Ecol. Econ. **150**, 264–272 (2018). https://doi.org/10.1016/j.ecolecon.2018.04.028
7. Merli, R., Preziosi, M., Acampora, A.: How do scholars approach the circular economy? A systematic literature review. J. Cleaner Prod. **178**, 703–722 (2018)
8. Goodwill, G.M., Geddes, J.R.: Introduction to systematic reviews (2004). http://journals.sag epub.com, https://doi.org/10.1177/0269881104042629
9. Tranfield, D., Denyer, D., Smart, P.: Towards a methodology for developing evidence-informed management knowledge by means of systematic review. Br. J. Manag. **14**, 207–222 (2003). https://doi.org/10.1111/1467-8551.00375
10. Guldmann, E., Huulgaard, R.D.: Barriers to circular business model innovation: a multiple-case study. J. Clean. Prod. **243** (2020). https://doi.org/10.1016/j.jclepro.2019.118160
11. Pieroni, M.P.P., McAloone, T.C., Pigosso, D.C.A.: From theory to practice: systematising and testing business model archetypes for circular economy. Resour. Conserv. Recycl. **162** (2020). https://doi.org/10.1016/j.resconrec.2020.105029
12. Bocken, N.M.P., de Pauw, I., Bakker, C., van der Grinten, B.: Product design and business model strategies for a circular economy. J. Ind. Prod. Eng. **33**, 308–320 (2016). https://doi.org/10.1080/21681015.2016.1172124
13. Geissdoerfer, M., Morioka, S.N., de Carvalho, M.M., Evans, S.: Business models and supply chains for the circular economy. J. Clean. Prod. **190**, 712–721 (2018). https://doi.org/10.1016/j.jclepro.2018.04.159

14. Lüdeke-Freund, F., Gold, S., Bocken, N.M.P.: A review and typology of circular economy business model patterns. J. Ind. Ecol. **23**, 36–61 (2019). https://doi.org/10.1111/jiec.12763

15. Ünal, E., Urbinati, A., Chiaroni, D.: Managerial practices for designing circular economy business models: the case of an Italian SME in the office supply industry. J. Manuf. Technol. Manag. **30**, 561–589 (2019). https://doi.org/10.1108/JMTM-02-2018-0061

16. Rosa, P., Sassanelli, C., Terzi, S.: Circular economy in action: Uncovering the relation between circular business models and their expected benefits. In: Proceedings of the Summer School Francesco Turco. pp. 228–235 (2018)

17. Fraccascia, L., Magno, M., Albino, V.: Business models for industrial symbiosis: a guide for firms. Procedia Environ. Sci. Eng. Manag. **3**, 83–93 (2016)

18. Salvador, R., Barros, M.V., da Luz, L.M., Piekarski, C.M., de Francisco, A.C.: Circular business models: current aspects that influence implementation and unaddressed subjects (2020)

19. Marke, A., Chan, C., Taskin, G., Hacking, T.: Reducing e-waste in China's mobile electronics industry: the application of the innovative circular business models. Asian Educ. Dev. Stud. **9**, 591–610 (2020). https://doi.org/10.1108/AEDS-03-2019-0052

20. Ghisellini, P., Cialani, C., Ulgiati, S.: A review on circular economy: the expected transition to a balanced interplay of environmental and economic systems. J. Clean. Prod. **114**, 11–32 (2016). https://doi.org/10.1016/j.jclepro.2015.09.007

21. Henry, M., Bauwens, T., Hekkert, M., Kirchherr, J.: A typology of circular start-ups: analysis of 128 circular business models. J. Clean. Prod. **245**, 118528 (2020). https://doi.org/10.1016/j.jclepro.2019.118528

22. Singh, J., Cooper, T., Cole, C., Gnanapragasam, A., Shapley, M.: Evaluating approaches to resource management in consumer product sectors - an overview of global practices. J. Clean. Prod. **224**, 218–237 (2019). https://doi.org/10.1016/j.jclepro.2019.03.203

23. Planing, P.: Towards a circular economy – how business model innovation will help to make the shift. Int. J. Bus. Glob. **20**, 71–83 (2018). https://doi.org/10.1504/IJBG.2018.10009522

24. Lewandowski, M.: Designing the business models for circular economy-towards the conceptual framework. Sustain. **8**, 1–28 (2016). https://doi.org/10.3390/su8010043

25. Urbinati, A., Chiaroni, D., Chiesa, V.: Towards a new taxonomy of circular economy business models. J. Clean. Prod. **168**, 487–498 (2017). https://doi.org/10.1016/j.jclepro.2017.09.047

26. Widmer, T., Tjahjono, B., Bourlakis, M.: Defining value creation in the context of circular PSS. Procedia CIRP **73**, 142–147 (2018). https://doi.org/10.1016/j.procir.2018.03.329

27. Bocken, N.M.P., Short, S.W.: Towards a sufficiency-driven business model: experiences and opportunities. Environ. Innov. Soc. Transitions **18**, 41–61 (2016). https://doi.org/10.1016/j.eist.2015.07.010

Industry 4.0 Driven Quantitative Methods for Circular Supply Chains: A Bibliometric Analysis

Biman Darshana Hettiarachchi[1]([⊠]) (iD), Stefan Seuring[1] (iD),
and Marcus Brandenburg[1,2] (iD)

[1] Chair of Supply Chain Management, University of Kassel, Kleine Rosenstraße 1–3, 34109
Kassel, Germany
{Biman.Hettiarachchi,seuring}@uni-kassel.de
[2] School of Business, Flensburg University of Applied Sciences, Kanzleistr. 91-93, 24943
Flensburg, Germany
marcus.brandenburg@hs-flensburg.de

Abstract. The Industry 4.0 (I4.0) concept comprises advanced digital technologies that facilitate the digitally enabled sustainability approach leading to a Circular Economy (CE). I4.0 driven CE initiative leads to a paradigm shift in supply chain management (SCM), where quantitative methods provide practical solutions to issues that arise when adopting circular practices. Therefore, the intersection of I4.0, CE, SCM and quantitative methods has been identified as an upcoming area worthwhile investigation. Hence, we conduct a bibliometric analysis on extant literature to visualise and unravel the current scholarly discussion while providing insights to the scholars and practitioners who pursue the current dynamics, trends, prospects pertaining to the intersection mentioned above.

Keywords: Industry 4.0 · Circular economy · Supply chain management

1 Introduction

The role of digital technologies has been identified as crucial in the transition towards the Circular Economy (CE) [1]. This digitally enabled CE approach is facilitated by the Industry 4.0 (I4.0) technologies influencing its performance with a positive impact on the life cycle management of products. Hence, several elements of I4.0 were identified as digital enablers for CE [2]. Especially, I4.0 elements such as simulation along with quantitative methods have been recognised as practical techniques to address issues related to supply chain management (SCM) when adopting circular practices [2]. However, studies disseminating such methods are dispersed in the SCM discourse, focusing on the reverse and closed-loop supply chains in the CE context. Hence, this study accumulates such scholarly work and answers which facets, factors, and limitations are to be considered when applying quantitative methods and techniques for I4.0 enabled operations and supply chains in the CE context. Moreover, this review aims to pinpoint possible research directions while highlighting the boundaries of knowledge.

© IFIP International Federation for Information Processing 2021
Published by Springer Nature Switzerland AG 2021
A. Dolgui et al. (Eds.): APMS 2021, IFIP AICT 632, pp. 394–401, 2021.
https://doi.org/10.1007/978-3-030-85906-0_44

2 Background

CE aims to achieve sustainable development along with improved social equity and environmental and economic prosperity [3]. Integrated with I4.0, a technology-driven CE centric supply chain would be more sustainable, adaptable, secured, and interactive [4], ultimately paving the path to achieve the aims of CE.

Introduced in 2011, I4.0 exemplifies a set of automation technologies such as the Internet of Things (IoT), Cyber-Physical Systems (CPS), and cloud computing in the manufacturing industry [5]. It comprises nine pillars, namely, additive manufacturing (AM), simulation, augmented and virtual reality, big data and analytics (BDA), the Internet of Things (IoT), autonomous robots and vehicles, horizontal/vertical system integration, cloud, fog, and edge technologies, and blockchain and cyber-security [6, 7]. I4.0 represents a fundamental paradigm shift in SCM [8] which presents an immense possibilities to improve the SCM processes in areas such as responsiveness, efficiency, and sustainable performance [9]. Moreover, I4.0 technologies positively influence the lifecycle management of a product where technologies such as AM, BDA and IoT were identified as digital enablers of CE [2].

3 Methodology

Bibliometric analysis is adopted to analyse the relationships among articles efficiently and reliably and visualise the results to identify future research directions while providing comprehensive insights on the analysed research field [10]. Rowley and Slack [11] proposed a systematic methodology to scan resources, design the mind map to build the bibliography and structure a literature review. Literature review underlines the boundaries of the existing literature while identifying potential research gaps through a comprehensive evaluation of the body of literature [12]. In this study, we adopted the methodology followed by Fahimnia et al. [13] to conduct the bibliometric analysis.

To identify the relevant papers related to the focus of this study, keywords related to four areas, namely, I4.0, CE, SCM and quantitative methods, were selected. I4.0 related keywords covered all nine technological pillars and related areas proposed by Rosa et al. [2]. CE related keywords captured the different approaches for CE such as "circular economy", "closed loop*", "open loop*", and 10 CE implementation strategies identified by Reike et al. [14]. SCM and quantitative method aspects were comprehended by including keywords such as "supply chain*", "simulation", "optimisation" and "quantitative methods". The literature search only focused on papers published in English in peer-reviewed scientific journals, where the search was carried on title, abstracts and keywords in the Web of Science database. The initial search resulted in 526 papers. After removing duplicate papers among the search strings, the final dataset included 414 papers with a focus on technical and management perspectives. They were published from 2003 to December 2020.

The distribution of papers over the considered time horizon, as depicted in Fig. 1, shows a compound annual growth rate (CAGR) of 35%. Within the last five years, the CAGR accounted for 58%. This highlights the interest of scholars and practitioners in the intersection of I4.0, CE, SCM and quantitative methods.

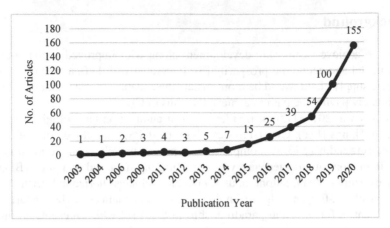

Fig. 1. Publishing trend

4   Bibliometric Analysis

We performed the bibliometric analysis using Biblioshiny software, which uses bibliometrix package of R to generate results. Moreover, data cleaning and data visualisation were completed using MS Excel. The key findings of the bibliometric analysis are discussed in this section.

Figure 2 presents the top 10 journals. These journals accounted for approximately 45% of the total number of articles selected for the study. Journal of Cleaner Production tops the list with 58 articles, closely followed by Sustainability with 53 papers. International Journal of Production Research and International Journal of Production Economics published 17 and 16 studies, respectively. This journal distribution depicts that journals from operations management and sustainability dominate the investigated research domain while journals representing the technology domain are emerging.

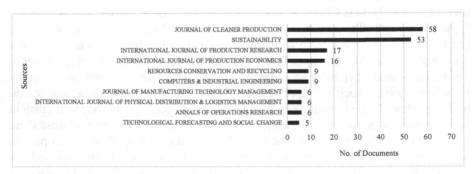

Fig. 2. Most relevant sources

Figure 3 depicts the most local cited documents, which illustrates the number of citations an article received from the articles included in the analysed collection (414 papers). The top four local cited documents are research agendas and road maps discussing the intersection of I4.0 technologies and CE/sustainability. This shows the sources where the literature has started evolving in our analysed collection, and these articles provide insights on future research directions.

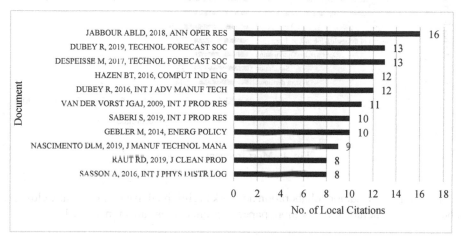

Fig. 3. Most local cited documents

A thorough scan of the content of these articles listed in Fig. 3 revealed that I4.0 technologies facilitate and enable CE implementation. For instance, Jabbour et al. [15] highlighted that I4.0 technologies may amplify the profit and efficiency by improved productivity whilst facilitating the CE. Despeisse et al. [16] also underlined that 3D printing stimulates more improved sustainable production and consumption while paving the path to enable CE. Moreover, Nascimento et al. [1] emphasised that 3D printing and I4.0 promote the CE and its related practices such as reuse, which extend the lifecycle of a product and recycle, which optimises the consumption of natural resources. It is interesting to see that blockchain also facilitates CE by improving the recycling process through enhanced data tracking and introducing various incentives such as cryptographic tokens in exchange for recyclable bottles and cans [17].

Analysis of the top 10 keywords shown in Fig. 4 reveals that sustainability and supply chains top the table, followed by the CE. AM and BDA were the most frequently discussed I4.0 related technologies. This finding is further aligned with the results of Fig. 3 where articles published by Despeisse et al. [16] and Hazen et al. [18] discuss research agendas related to AM and BDA intersecting CE and sustainable supply chains. I4.0 becoming the fourth in the most used keyword list along with AM and BDA also supports the findings depicted in Fig. 3 as the most local cited article by Jabbour et al. [15] provides a roadmap and research agenda for sustainable operations incorporating I4.0 and CE. Further, after a close investigation of all keywords listed in 414 papers, it is noteworthy that I4.0 technologies such as CPS, cloud computing, autonomous robots, augmented reality, and horizontal and vertical integration are the least explored areas intersecting CE, SCM and quantitative methods related research fields.

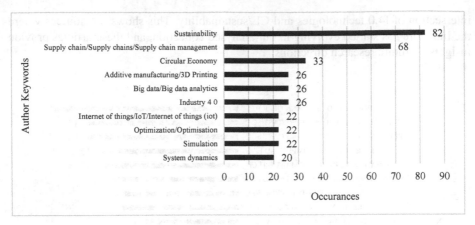

Fig. 4. Most frequent keywords

Examining the author collaboration network highlighted five main thematic clusters. These clusters include three or more papers per cluster, as shown in Table 1.

Table 1. Thematic clusters

Cluster no.	Theme of the cluster	Main methods and techniques	No. papers	Key references
1	Impact of BDA towards sustainable consumption and operation	Big data and predictive analytics (BDPA)	5	[19–21]
2	Role of I4.0 technologies in CE and sustainable SCM (SSCM)	Structural equation modelling (SEM)	5	[22–24]
3	Barriers/challenges for CE implementation in I4.0 environment	Multiple methods	5	[25–27]
4	Quantitative methods for I4.0 technologies in CE and SSCM	Multiple methods	4	[28–30]
5	Impact of digital technologies on sustainability performance	Multi-criteria decision making (MCDM) techniques	3	[31, 32]

Cluster 1 investigates the impacts of BDPA on sustainability performance measures. The effects of I4.0 technologies (specially BDA) on logistics, SSCM, CE performance and CE implementation strategies such as remanufacturing has been studied using SEM in cluster 2. Articles in cluster 3 and 4 employ multiple quantitative methods/techniques such as system dynamics, MCDM methods (e.g., DEMATEL) and mixed integer non-linear programming. Cluster 3 investigates the barriers, challenges and benefits of I4.0 technologies on sustainability performance, where cluster 4 explores how different quantitative methods can be operationalised to achieve highly efficient logistics services under the I4.0 enabled CE and SSCM environment. Cluster 5 underlines the impacts of digital technologies on sustainability performance while understanding the implications of I4.0 technologies. The comparably low number of studies per cluster suggests that the research potential of these topics is not yet fully exploited.

5 Conclusion and Future Directions

This paper presented a structured review on the intersection of I4.0, CE, SCM and quantitative methods. A comprehensive bibliometric analysis was conducted on this upcoming research arena that paves the path for new research avenues. The results identified the most influential authors, articles and pointed out the evolving research clusters in this intersection of four research fields. The study also identified research agendas and road maps discussing the juncture of I4.0 and CE/SSCM, which were identified as the most cited articles of the investigated scope of our study. Further investigation of these studies highlighted that I4.0 is becoming a digital enabler of CE. I4.0 driven sustainable supply chains and manufacturing supply chains are emerging for future research directions where AM, IoT and BDA are the most prominent technologies discussed in those research fields. Careful investigation of the author collaboration network provided several suggestions for future research opportunities connecting I4.0 with sustainable business models, sustainable operations and sustainability performance focusing CE. Moreover, it is noteworthy to mention that quantitative methods gained a new approach with the introduction of BDA.

Acknowledgements. This research has received funding from the European Union's Horizon 2020 research and innovation programme under the Marie Skłodowska-Curie Innovative Training Networks (H2020-MSCA-ITN-2018) scheme, grant agreement number 814247 (ReTraCE project).

References

1. Nascimento, D.L.M., et al.: Exploring Industry 4.0 technologies to enable circular economy practices in a manufacturing context: a business model proposal. J. Manuf. Technol. Manag. **30**, 607–627 (2019)
2. Rosa, P., Sassanelli, C., Urbinati, A., Chiaroni, D., Terzi, S.: Assessing relations between circular economy and industry 4.0: a systematic literature review. Int. J. Prod. Res. **7543**, 0–26 (2019)
3. Kirchherr, J., Reike, D., Hekkert, M.: Conceptualizing the circular economy: an analysis of 114 definitions. Resour. Conserv. Recycl. **127**, 221–232 (2017)
4. Rajput, S., Singh, S.P.: Connecting circular economy and industry 4.0. Int. J. Inf. Manage. **49**, 98–113 (2019)
5. Xu, L.D., Xu, E.L., Li, L.: Industry 4.0: state of the art and future trends. Int. J. Prod. Res. **56**, 2941–2962 (2018)

6. Rüßmann, M., et al.: Industry 4.0: the future of productivity and growth in manufacturing industries. The Boston Consulting Group (2015)
7. Machado, C.G., Winroth, M.P., Ribeiro da Silva, E.H.D.: Sustainable manufacturing in Industry 4.0: an emerging research agenda. Int. J. Prod. Res. **58**, 1462–1484 (2020).
8. Fatorachian, H., Kazemi, H.: Impact of Industry 4.0 on supply chain performance. Prod. Plan. Control. **32**, 63–81 (2020)
9. Chauhan, C., Singh, A.: A review of Industry 4.0 in supply chain management studies. J. Manuf. Technol. Manag. **31**, 863–886 (2019)
10. Feng, Y., Zhu, Q., Lai, K.H.: Corporate social responsibility for supply chain management: a literature review and bibliometric analysis. J. Clean. Prod. **158**, 296–307 (2017)
11. Rowley, J., Slack, F.: Conducting a literature review. Manag. Res. News. **27**, 31–39 (2004)
12. Tranfield, D., Denyer, D., Smart, P.: Towards a methodology for developing evidence-informed management knowledge by means of systematic review. Br. J. Manag. **14**, 207–222 (2003)
13. Fahimnia, B., Sarkis, J., Davarzani, H.: Green supply chain management: a review and bibliometric analysis. Int. J. Prod. Econ. **162**, 101–114 (2015)
14. Reike, D., Vermeulen, W.J.V., Witjes, S.: The circular economy : new or refurbished as CE 3.0 ?—exploring controversies in the conceptualization of the circular economy through a focus on history and resource value retention options. Resour. Conserv. Recycl. **135**, 246–264 (2018)
15. Lopes de Sousa Jabbour, A.B., Jabbour, C.J.C., Godinho Filho, M., Roubaud, D.: Industry 4.0 and the circular economy: a proposed research agenda and original roadmap for sustainable operations. Ann. Oper. Res. **270**, 273–286 (2018)
16. Despeisse, M., et al.: Unlocking value for a circular economy through 3D printing: a research agenda. Technol. Forecast. Soc. Change. **115**, 75–84 (2017)
17. Saberi, S., Kouhizadeh, M., Sarkis, J., Shen, L.: Blockchain technology and its relationships to sustainable supply chain management. Int. J. Prod. Res. **57**, 2117–2135 (2019)
18. Hazen, B.T., Skipper, J.B., Ezell, J.D., Boone, C.A.: Big data and predictive analytics for supply chain sustainability: a theory-driven research agenda. Comput. Ind. Eng. **101**, 592–598 (2016)
19. Dubey, R., et al.: Can big data and predictive analytics improve social and environmental sustainability? Technol. Forecast. Soc. Change. **144**, 534–545 (2019)
20. Dubey, R., et al.: Examining the role of big data and predictive analytics on collaborative performance in context to sustainable consumption and production behaviour. J. Clean. Prod. **196**, 1508–1521 (2018)
21. Jeble, S., Dubey, R., Childe, S.J., Papadopoulos, T., Roubaud, D., Prakash, A.: Impact of big data and predictive analytics capability on supply chain sustainability. Int. J. Logist. Manag. **29**, 513–538 (2018)
22. Bag, S., Yadav, G., Wood, L.C., Dhamija, P., Joshi, S.: Industry 4.0 and the circular economy: resource melioration in logistics. Resour. Policy **68**, 101776 (2020)
23. Bag, S., Dhamija, P., Gupta, S., Sivarajah, U.: Examining the role of procurement 4.0 towards remanufacturing operations and circular economy. Prod. Plan. Control. **0**, 1–16 (2020).
24. Bag, S., Gupta, S., Luo, Z.: Examining the role of logistics 4.0 enabled dynamic capabilities on firm performance. Int. J. Logist. Manag. **31**, 607–628 (2020)
25. Ozkan-Ozen, Y.D., Kazancoglu, Y., Mangla, S.K.: Synchronized barriers for circular supply chains in industry 3.5/industry 4.0 transition for sustainable resource management. Resour. Conserv. Recycl. **161** (2020).
26. Janssen, M., Luthra, S., Mangla, S., Rana, N.P., Dwivedi, Y.K.: Challenges for adopting and implementing IoT in smart cities: an integrated MICMAC-ISM approach. Internet Res. **29**, 1589–1616 (2019)

27. Luthra, S., Kumar, A., Zavadskas, E.K., Mangla, S.K., Garza-Reyes, J.A.: Industry 4.0 as an enabler of sustainability diffusion in supply chain: an analysis of influential strength of drivers in an emerging economy. Int. J. Prod. Res. **58**, 1505–1521 (2020)
28. Liu, S., Zhang, Y., Liu, Y., Wang, L., Wang, X.V.: An 'Internet of Things' enabled dynamic optimization method for smart vehicles and logistics tasks. J. Clean. Prod. **215**, 806–820 (2019)
29. Cao, C., Li, C., Yang, Q., Liu, Y., Qu, T.: A novel multi-objective programming model of relief distribution for sustainable disaster supply chain in large-scale natural disasters. J. Clean. Prod. **174**, 1422–1435 (2018)
30. Zhang, Y., Ren, S., Liu, Y., Sakao, T., Huisingh, D.: A framework for big data driven product lifecycle management. J. Clean. Prod. **159**, 229–240 (2017)
31. Li, Y., Dai, J., Cui, L.: The impact of digital technologies on economic and environmental performance in the context of industry 4.0: a moderated mediation model. Int. J. Prod. Econ. **229**, 1077 (2020)
32. Cui, L., Zhai, M., Dai, J,, Liu, Y., Zhang, P.: Assessing sustainability performance of high-tech firms through a hybrid approach. Ind. Manag. Data Syst. **119**, 1581–1607 (2019)

Rethinking Circular Business Models: The Role of the Learning Factory

Maria Flavia Mogos[1]([✉]) [ID], Sigurd Sagen Vildåsen[1,2], Johanne Sørumsbrenden[1], and Daryl Powell[1,2] [ID]

[1] SINTEF Manufacturing, Raufoss, Norway
maria.flavia.mogos@sintef.no
[2] Norwegian University of Science and Technology (NTNU), Trondheim, Norway

Abstract. There is a need for both increased knowledge and for effective solutions in the transition from linear to circular business models. Circular hubs are increasingly regarded by academia and policy makers as facilitators of circularity in industry. This paper investigates how a circular hub can better integrate circular economy principles into existing business models, through conducting case study research where we analyse 16 months of data about a circular hub, which appeared to effectively aid the participants both in the transition towards the circular utilization of resources and the pursuit of Sustainable Development Goals. The case is a circular hub for the reuse, repair, remanufacture and repurpose of furnishing in Norway. The findings of this paper include a framework for the assessment of the impact of circular hubs on existing business models, as well as the following facilitators: (i) organizing the circular hub as a learning factory for pupils and other stakeholders in collaboration with local schools, (ii) the municipality coordinating the learning factory, (iii) researchers ensuring that high-level concepts of circularity are explored by the stakeholders, and (iv) public financial support. Proposed avenues of future research include investigating the role of network action learning principles and methods in achieving higher circularity and hub maturity levels.

Keywords: Circular economy · Sustainability · Circular business model

1 Introduction

There is a call for research and innovation on the transition from linear to circular business models (CBMs). Thus, academics and practitioners are increasingly engaging in co-creative processes to develop economic value in a manner that eases the pressure on collective resources such as energy and virgin raw materials. This is the core of what we refer to as at the circular economy (CE) challenge. Central to solving the CE challenge is to develop CBMs. A CBM refers to how "[…] a company creates, captures, and delivers value with the value creation logic designed to improve resource efficiency

© IFIP International Federation for Information Processing 2021
Published by Springer Nature Switzerland AG 2021
A. Dolgui et al. (Eds.): APMS 2021, IFIP AICT 632, pp. 402–410, 2021.
https://doi.org/10.1007/978-3-030-85906-0_45

through contributing to extending useful life of products and parts (e.g., through long-life design, repair and remanufacturing) and closing material loops" [1]. Illustrative examples of CBMs in practice include circular loops where companies take back components from the market and recycle materials with sufficient quality to make new products [2], and product designs that enable repair and upgrades while the products are still in use [3]. The state-of-the-art reflects that CBMs do not emerge in a vacuum because closed material loops and extended product loops imply inter-organizational collaboration and co-creative development processes [4]. Moreover, disruptive innovation theory suggests that start-ups might yield more effective solutions with more CE impact, yet without the risks of radically transforming existing BMs [5]. Thus, it is interesting to investigate the role played by industrial hubs with different actors in developing functioning CBMs [6]. This paper explores a CBM development process, and the following question guides the research: *How can a circular hub better integrate CE principles into existing BMs?*

2 Research Design

Given the practical nature of the investigation and the how-type research question, we select case study research as our primary research method [7]. We draw on insights from a longitudinal study in which, together with practitioners from the participating organizations, researchers studied, guided, and engaged in learning over a 16-month period. The major stakeholders in the project were the manufacturer and the users (the municipality, local secondary schools, and a non-governmental organization (NGO)).

During the research process, data was both collected and generated (created) in action. Section 4 describes various learning interventions in more detail, and presents the results in the form of emergent, actionable knowledge.

3 Analytical Framework

The framework used to analyse the role of the industrial hub in the in-depth CMB innovation study is based on literature about *industrial symbiosis* (IS), circular hubs, network action learning, and on Geissdoerfer et al.'s CBM framework [5]. IS is the use by one company or sector of underutilised resources (including waste, by-products, residues, energy, water, logistics, capacity, expertise, equipment and materials) from another, with the result of keeping resources in productive use longer [8]. IS can arise through: i) direct interaction among companies (*self-organised*), ii) the facilitation of public investment networks and/or commercial brokers (*facilitated*), iii) the initiative of the users of an ICT system that manages data on resource availability and potential synergies (*ICT-supported*), and (iv) the initiative of the public sector (*strategic/planned*) [8]. Generally, the *steps* involved in establishing IS are: i) an exchange of resources (e.g. one company's waste is another company's raw material), ii) an awareness that a long-term CE strategy through IS is advantageous, and iii) a joint business model (BM) that is mutually beneficial [6]. *Barriers* to IS include a lack of a culture of trust and cooperation between independent actors, the investments needed, rules and regulations, and the unavailability of data on waste streams as attractive raw materials. Potential *facilitators* include: (i) the local proximity of the actors for increased trust, lower transportation cost and efficient infrastructure (e.g. shorter pipelines), (ii) appropriate agreements and blockchain technology for confidential data management, (iii) digital twins for process visualisation and control (e.g. to cope with fluctuations in the supply of renewable energy), (iv) proactively evaluating financing options, (v) investors focusing on sustainable finance, (vi) public financial support, (vii) the standardisation and publication of data on municipal waste streams, (viii) digital platforms for confident resource sharing, and (ix) IS included in education to ensure a sufficient skill base [6, 9]. Other facilitators include 'living labs' for experiments in real-life context together with users, and 'open innovation testbeds' with facilities and services for the upscaling of IS technology [6].

Moreover, the coordination and advancement of IS by a *circular hub*, and/or neutral actors such as the municipality, the chamber of commerce and/or an association of a cluster of companies are among the most important IS facilitators [6]. A circular hub can be defined as a cluster of interconnected industrial companies and/or public facilities within a given region, which collectively achieve a demonstrable level of circularity (including greenhouse gas (GGE) neutrality) in their use of materials/energy/water whilst boosting the global competitiveness of the industry and achieving sustainable growth [6].

A series of scholars and practitioners emphasize that the transition from linear BM (or lower levels of circularity) to CBMs (or higher levels of circularity) should be based on close stakeholder collaboration, co-creation through experimentation and iterative learning [e.g. 10]. At circular hubs, this process can be supported by the *network action learning* principles and methods, highlighting that learning (L) is an incremental process starting with the programmed knowledge (P), combined with the questioning process as individuals (Q), and with learning in action, first at organizational level (O) and then at inter-organizational level (IO). Thus, $L = P + Q + O + IO$ [11].

In a recent article, [5] developed a *CBM framework* based on a systematic review of the existing literature. Table 1 applies this lens to IS by help of circular hubs, showing that this approach can be particularly relevant for circular *value propositions* and *value creation & delivery* methods that are based on the *recycling* strategy. However, arguably *extending*, *intensifying*, and *dematerializing* strategies (see [5]) can be implemented by individual actors, e.g. through network learning. Finally, IS by help of a circular hub can contribute to *value capture*, leading to: i) economic and environmental benefits due to the reduction of waste and GGE and the reduction of energy, water and materials used, and ii) economic and social benefits due to new sales, investments, jobs, start-ups, talent to the region, revenues from export of innovative solutions, and indirect jobs that are triggered by regional growth [6].

Table 1. CBM innovation through IS & circular hubs (based on [5])

Strategy	Recycling
Value proposition:	
Goods/services	Used/repaired/remanufactured/repurposed/recycled goods
Customer needs	Affordable & eco-friendly goods; circular end-of-life/ waste management solutions for their goods
Industrial symbiosis through circular hubs: The Recycling strategy is directly relevant, yet the other strategies can be implemented by individual actors (e.g., through network learning)	
Value creation & delivery:	
Key value chain activities	Design for sustainability; modular design; repair/remanufacturing/recycling/reprocessing operations
Core competencies/Collaboration	Collaboration with suppliers/collectors/retailers/recommercers/reprocessors
Resources/capabilities	End-of-life goods; reverse supply chain
Industrial symbiosis through circular hubs: The Reycling strategy is directly relevant, yet the other strategies can be implemented by individual actors (e.g., through network learning)	
Value capture:	
Revenue stream	From residual values of goods
Cost drivers	Cheaper resource input (e.g., recycled materials)
Revenue model	Direct sales; trade of resources
Industrial symbiosis through circular hubs: Economic and environmental benefits due to reduction of waste/greenhouse gas emissions and reduction of energy/water/materials used; economic and social benefits due to new sales/investments/jobs/talent to the region/start-ups/revenues from export of innovative solutions, and indirect jobs triggered by regional growth	

4   The Case of a Circular Learning Factory in Norway

This section presents the case of a circular hub that a furniture manufacturer (with 26 employees) established in 2020, in an empty factory hall (4000 m^2) in Norway. The manufacturer developed the hub as a learning factory for pupils and other stakeholders, in collaboration with the local municipality (18115 inhabitants), five secondary schools in the municipality (around 600 pupils), and a non-profit organization (NGO) promoting entrepreneurship as an education form and the SDGs among youngsters (12 employees). The hub currently hosts 10 *pupil companies* (with around 100 pupils), which (learn to) sell, repair, refurbish, remanufacture, and repurpose used furniture and décor from the manufacturer and from other public and private actors. For example, a tabletop can be repurposed as a flower container or shelves. The companies must create their own business plan, design their own products, take orders, and conduct marketing and sales. The municipal school manager informed that they were planning to offer the sustainability and entrepreneurship subject to all the pupils in the last but one secondary school grade (the 9th). The manufacturer's CEO has also begun to establish an apprentice factory at the hub, in collaboration with the municipality, and an open innovation technology and digitalization centre for the local business community.

Since 2019, the manufacturer has been involved in a 3-year innovation project in collaboration with a private research institute (around 2000 employees). 40% of the project is financed by the Research Council of Norway and one of the work packages is dedicated to CBM innovation. The IS and the hub initiative arose through the investigation conducted by researchers in this project along with the manufacturer's interest in a long-term symbiotic agreement with an energy company (approx. 20000 employees). The agreement was signed in March 2020 and included both the sale of the manufacturer's own products to the company and circular end-of-life and waste management solutions for the company's used furnishing from offices and worker bedrooms. Thus, the *manufacturer's CBM value proposition* (see Table 1) included used goods (30% in 2021), repaired goods (20% in 2021) and remanufactured and repurposed goods (47% in 2021) to customers looking for affordable and eco-friendly furnishing. The *schools' strategy and motivation* included offering a learning-by-doing education about sustainability and entrepreneurship to the pupils in the hub, and the manufacturer together with a few sponsors provided not only the space but also the machines and tools that the pupils needed for handling the used furnishing. "We want more motivated students. We want to make the school more relevant, and we know that practice is a great way to do this. In addition, sustainability is an important part of the new curriculum, so this fits very well. There is no better way to learn about sustainability than to be a part of it, instead of sitting in a classroom and hearing about it", informed the municipal school manager.

The development of the hub started in October 2019 and during the first 6 months, it was mainly *facilitated* by the researchers. While the school representatives focused on practicalities, such as what subjects to teach and apply in the hub, and transportation costs, the researchers presented (at workshops with the hub actors) and promoted high-level concepts of sustainable development, such as design strategies to minimize recycling, and the product-as-a-service strategy including furniture rental, maintenance, and repair. However, the municipality (school management) took gradually over the coordination of the learning factory at the hub, with support from the NGO. The facilitation appeared to have increased the energy company and the schools' trust in the hub initiative. Later, the manufacturer and the schools also dedicated one employee each to the administration of the hub and the supervision of the pupils.

Apart from repair, remanufacturing and repurposing operations, the *value creation & delivery* (see Table 1) of the manufacturer's CBM included the collaboration with a furniture collector and distributor and with suppliers of used furnishing. Apart from the energy company, the manufacturer's CEO established sale and end-of-life return agreements with the local university and several schools and kindergartens. Moreover, through the innovation project and the researcher's facilitation the manufacturer was investigating and implementing principles and methods within 'design for sustainability' (e.g., modularity and the use of regenerative materials) both in their own production and at the hub.

In terms of *value capture* and *economic benefits* (see Table 1), due to the circular hub initiative, the manufacturer gained new sales contracts and attracted a series of new national and international customers, which were looking for furniture producers that could handle product return and had a substantial commitment to environmentally sound products and processes. Provided that the hub was self-financed over time and the manufacturer continued to be active in innovation projects, the CEO estimated a fourfold turnover increase due to the hub. The revenue model of the hub consisted of weekly direct sales at the hub combined with online sale of used or repaired furnishing, and other repurposed and remanufactured goods. The hub was financed with around half of the sales revenue, while the pupil-companies benefited of the rest. The materials that were used were cheaper, as the pupils and the manufacturer were benefiting of practically free wood-based materials from the used furnishing. Moreover, the wood rests from the hub (3% of the returned goods in 2021) and from the manufacture's factory were converted into heat in the manufacturer's plant, which was sufficient to heat both facilities.

Potential *environmental benefits* (see Table 1) of the hub include the prevention of waste and pollution from discarded furnishing, and the reduction of GGE and the amount of wood, metal, energy, and water used when producing new products, due to the extension of the goods' useful life. Thus, the hub can contribute to less pollution in the air, water and on land (SDGs 6 and 13–15) and to SDG 12, 'Responsible consumption and production'.

Potential *social benefits* (see Table 1) of the hub include professionals with relevant skills for sustainable development, and new jobs. At the hub, the secondary school pupils from the municipality are provided a tuition-free, learning-by-doing training on how to develop and run sustainable companies, create value adding jobs, and live and promote sustainable lifestyles. "We are happy to be up and running and see that this is where there is a potential to tear down some of the separation that you get in a regular classroom. Here, everyone can join and contribute with their own skills", said the school manager who regarded the practical education at the hub in close collaboration with the businesses as having a significant potential for reducing the school dropout and absenteeism. One of the manufacturer's employees, with over 30 years of experience as a prison employee highlighted that even if they only prevented one individual from a criminal life or long-term unemployment yearly, this would spare the society sums in the order of tens of thousands (e.g. around 120000 EUR/detention year at a juvenile centre). Thus, the hub can contribute to SDG 4 ('Good education') and SDG 3 ('Good health and wellbeing', e.g., by promoting sustainable lifestyles and striving to prevent school dropout). Moreover, the hub can also facilitate *socio-economic benefits*, by contributing to SDG 8 ('Decent work and economic growth', e.g., by supporting job creation, growing enterprises, and youth employment), SDG 9 ('Industry, Innovation, and Infrastructure', by opening the hub to other companies and contributing to upgrading the industrial community for sustainability), and SDG 17 ('Partnership for the goals', e.g. through the multi-stakeholder partnership including both public and private actors).

Nonetheless, the development of the circular hub was not exempt from salient *barriers* and challenges. These included different motivations among stakeholders, and different degrees of trust among the school representatives during the first meetings, with teachers having experience with similar teaching in collaboration with companies being more supportive. Salient examples also include the complexity of sustainability assessments, and of establishing a system for monitoring and reporting results, as well as a truly integrated joint CBM for the manufacturer and schools.

5 Discussion and Concluding Remarks

The previous section presented the case of a circular hub that appeared to be effective at integrating CE principles into the participants' BMs and strategies. It facilitated the integration of circular end-of-life and waste management services for furnishing owners, as well as the sale of affordable and eco-friendly goods. For the secondary schools, the hub eased the integration of learning-by-doing education about sustainability and entrepreneurship into their strategy. The CBM value capture and economic benefits for the manufacturer included new sales, long-term agreements with national and international customers looking for producers that can handle product return and are actively committed to sustainability, as well as a considerable projected turnover increase. For the schools, projected benefits included increased motivation among pupils, fewer school dropouts and less absenteeism. Moreover, the hub is expected to contribute to environmental benefits such as the reduction of waste, pollution and GGE from discarded furniture, and the reduction of materials and energy used for producing new furnishing (SDG 6, 12 and 13–15). The hub is also expected to have a series of socio-economic benefits – such as professionals with relevant skills for sustainable development and new jobs and start-ups – and to contribute to SDG 3, 4, 8, 9 and 17. The impact of the hub on the manufacturer's BM was assessed by help of the *CBM framework* in Table 1, based on [5]. The framework captured the hub's most salient effects on the BM, suggesting its usefulness as an assessment tool for other circular hubs.

Earlier literature recommends implementing IS by help of a circular hub and including IS and sustainability in the education [6, 9]. This study can add to this, showing that by *organizing the circular hub as a learning factory for pupils and other stakeholders in collaboration with local education institutions*, the hub can integrate CE principles into existing BM in an effective way.

While the lack of a culture of trust and cooperation between independent actors can be a significant barrier for IS implementation, the IS coordination and advancement by neutral actors such as the municipality and the local proximity of the actors are among the most important facilitators [6, 9]. This study supports earlier literature, showing that the *coordination of the learning factory by the municipality* (school management) appeared to have increased the stakeholders' trust (the local schools and manufacturer's potential IS partner) in the circular hub initiative.

However, during the first 6 months, the *hub initiative was* mainly *facilitated by the researchers*. The *researchers ensured that high-level circularity concepts were explored by the stakeholders*, such as 'extended product life-time' [1] (e.g. design for sustainability), while the other actors were more concerned with practicalities and tended to focus on lower-level circularity concepts (e.g. 'recycle' and 'recover' [12]).

The IS-hub was a combination of a 'self-organized' and a 'facilitated' initiative, as it arose through the facilitation of researchers in a publicly founded innovation project involving the manufacturer, in combination with the manufacturer's interest in a long-term IS and sales agreement with a large company. Thus, this study also supports the literature findings recommending *public financial support* as an IS facilitator [6, 9].

Salient barriers in the case included the complexity of sustainability assessments, and of establishing a system for monitoring and reporting results and for proving sustainability benefits, as well as a truly integrated, joint CBM for the manufacturer and schools. By applying the maturity model for circular hubs that is proposed by SPIRE [13], the circular hub in the case would be at an 'intermediate' level. The authors contend that the *network action learning principles and methods* that were introduced in Sect. 3 *should be investigated in future research*, with the aim of accelerating and taking to higher maturity levels ('advanced' and 'mature') and circularity levels (e.g. higher 'R' levels [12]) the transition from linear BM to CBM through circular hubs. In the studied case, the learning process started with programmed knowledge (P) through workshops where researchers presented CE and sustainability principles and methods. Then, it continued with a certain degree of questioning insight (Q) by reflecting on strategies such as 'design for sustainability' as individuals. Thereafter, the actors engaged in action learning activities (O) at organizational level through, for instance assessments of the opportunities and challenges with the hub initiative. However, the actors did not engage in significant action learning activities at inter-organizational level (IO). Thus, examples of additional learning activities that can be investigated at circular hubs and learning factories include IO activities such as extended value stream mapping for the stakeholder ecosystem [11], as well as Q activities such as visits at other circular hubs for inspiration [13].

To conclude, the purpose of this study was to investigate how circular hubs can facilitate the integration of CE principles into existing BMs. This topic was addressed through a longitudinal case study comprising 16 months of data about a circular hub, which appeared to be effective at integrating CE principles into the participants' BMs and strategies, and at easing the achievement of SDGs. The findings of this paper include a framework for the assessment of the impact of circular hubs on existing business models, and the following facilitators: (i) organizing the circular hub as a learning factory for pupils and other stakeholders in collaboration with local schools, (ii) the municipality coordinating the learning factory, (iii) researchers ensuring that high-level concepts of circularity are explored by the stakeholders, and (iv) public financial support. Proposed avenues of future research include investigating the role of network action learning principles and methods in achieving higher circularity and hub maturity levels.

Acknowledgements. The authors would like to thank to the Research Council of Norway and to the hub participants for their support and valuable contributions.

References

1. Nußholz, J.L.: Circular business models: defining a concept and framing an emerging research field. Sustainability 9(10), 1810–1820 (2016)

2. Vildåsen, S.S.: 29 Lessons learned from practice when developing a circular business model. Designing Circ. Econ. **1**, 21–31 (2018)
3. Bocken, N.M., De Pauw, I., Bakker, C., van der Grinter, B.: Product design and business model strategies for a circular economy. J. Ind. Prod. Eng. **33**(5), 308–320 (2016)
4. Antikainen, M., Valkokari, K.: A framework for sustainable circular business model innovation. Technol. Innov. Manag. Rev. **6**(7), 5–12 (2016)
5. Geissdoerfer, M., Pieroni, M.P., Pigosso, D.C., Soufani, K.: Circular business models: a review. J. Clean. Prod. **277**, 123741 (2020)
6. European Comission. https://ec.europa.eu/info/publications/study-and-portfolio-review-pro jects-industrial-symbiosis-dg-research-and-innovation-findings-and-recommendations_en, Accessed 03 Mar 2021
7. Yin, R.K.: Applications of Case Study Research, 3rd edn. Sage, California (2011)
8. European Committee for Standardisation and European Committee for Electrotechnical Standardisation. https://ftp.cencenelec.eu/EN/ResearchInnovation/CWA/CWA17354. pdf, Accessed 02 Feb 2021
9. Vahidzadeh, R., Bertanza, G., Sbaffoni, S., Vaccari, M.: Regional industrial symbiosis: a review based on social network analysis. J. Cleaner Prod. **280**(1), 124054 (2020)
10. Konietzko, J., Baldassarre, B., Brown, P., Bocken, N., Hultink, E.J.: Circular business model experimentation: demystifying assumptions. J. Cleaner Prod. **277**, 122 (2020)
11. Powell, D.J., Coughlan, P.: Rethinking lean supplier development as a learning system. Int. J. Oper. Prod. Manag. **40**(7/8), 921–943 (2020)
12. Kirchherr, J., Reike, D., Hekkert, M.: Conceptualizing the circular economy: an analysis of 114 definitions. Resour. Conserv. Recycl. **127**, 221–232 (2017)
13. A. SPIRE aisbl. https://www.spire2030.eu/sites/default/files/users/user85/spire-ccni_2050_ roadmap_draft_for_stakeholder_consultation.pdf, Accessed 03 Feb 2021

Crop Selection and Scheduling for Green Production with Intercropping and Rotation

Canan Pehlivan[1(✉)], Thomas G. Yeung[2],
and Aline Suzette Alvarado Munguia[2]

[1] Industrial Engineering Department, Yeditepe University, Istanbul, Turkey
canan.pehlivan@yeditepe.edu.tr
[2] IMT-Atlantique, Département Automatique, Productique et Informatique,
Nantes, France
thomas.yeung@imt-atlantique.fr

Abstract. In this study, we address a crop selection and scheduling problem employing two cropping systems, crop rotation and intercropping, simultaneously on a given parcel of land. Moreover, we also consider other ecological practices such as the use of fallow and green manure. We propose a 0–1 linear programming model to maximize revenue by determining the optimal combinations of crops in space (crops to be planted as neighbors) and in time (crop rotation schedule) while meeting the yearly demand of each crop. A realistic numerical example is presented to demonstrate the performance of the model.

Keywords: Sustainable agricultural production · Crop schedule · Crop rotation · Intercropping

1 Introduction

Conventional agricultural production systems are generally based on monoculture (i.e., growing only one crop) as this practice is generally lowest in production cost. However, monoculture often has important adverse side-effects that are not accounted for. These include the environmental costs of water contamination by pesticides and other polluting inputs, or the social costs associated with the exclusion of small farmers due to the large-scale capital requirement [5,12]. To avoid these adverse effects, more sustainable agricultural production systems are needed that are economically profitable, environmentally safe, and socially equitable. To this purpose, several strategies based on increasing spatial and temporal crop diversification have been proposed such as intercropping (combination in space), crop rotation (combination in time), agroforestry, composting, and green manuring [14,21].

To compete with monoculture, the proposed farming practices should be combined in such a way that fewer inputs and resources are used while yields

© IFIP International Federation for Information Processing 2021
Published by Springer Nature Switzerland AG 2021
A. Dolgui et al. (Eds.): APMS 2021, IFIP AICT 632, pp. 411–420, 2021.
https://doi.org/10.1007/978-3-030-85906-0_46

are not drastically reduced and may even be improved. This requires thorough planning and solving complex problems where, both technical and ecological production aspects of those farming practices need to be considered.

In this study, we address a crop selection and scheduling problem employing two cropping systems, crop rotation and intercropping, simultaneously on a given land, while considering other ecological practices such as the regular employment of fallows and green manures. Our objective is to determine the optimal combinations of crops in space (crops to be planted as neighbors) and in time (crop rotation schedule) to maximize revenue while meeting the yearly demand of each crop. We propose an integer linear programming (ILP) model to select the best combination of crops in space and time. A numerical experiment is conducted based on real crop data and an optimal crop schedule is provided to demonstrate the performance of the model.

In the next section, we first give a primer on sustainable cropping systems. In Sect. 3, we present the literature review and highlight the contribution of our work. In Sect. 4, we present the ILP formulation for our problem. Section 5 presents the numerical example followed by a conclusion.

2   Sustainable Agriculture Production Practices

Below we explain the sustainable agricultural practices that have been employed in this research. We present as well our assumptions, depending on the practical use of those practices.

Crop Rotation is the practice of planting different types of crops sequentially on the same plot of land to improve soil health, optimize nutrients in the soil, and combat pest and weed pressure [5]. It is generally undesirable to grow two crops of the same botanical family in sequence on the same piece of land to prohibit the propagation of pests [19]. Crop Rotations are most effective when combined with practices such as composting, intercropping, cover cropping, green manuring and short fallow periods [7].

Intercropping is the practice of growing two or more crops in the same field simultaneously or sequentially within the same season [5]. The key advantage of intercropping is the greater yield generated by the crop interactions. It has many other beneficial effects like increased biodiversity, nitrogen fixations by legumes, nutrient recycling in the soil, better control of pests and diseases, more efficient use of environmental sources, soil coverage and stable yields [15].

In this work, we limit intercropping to two crops for tractability and simplicity. There exist several types of intercropping systems. Most common ones such as mixed cropping, row intercropping, strip intercropping and relay intercropping are illustrated in Fig. 1. In this work, we consider *row intercropping* where different crops are grown at the same time in the same piece of land with a distinct row arrangement [6]. Within the row layout, we also employ *relay intercropping* where intercrops were sown when the first crop reach maturity but before being harvested. We choose to work with row intercropping due to its structured layout and suitability for a large-scale farming, and relay intercropping due to the time flexibility it provides.

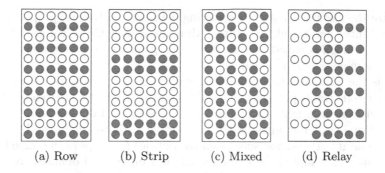

(a) Row   (b) Strip   (c) Mixed   (d) Relay

Fig. 1. Schematic illustrations of alternative intercropping systems

Green manuring is the practice of leaving uprooted or sown crop parts to wither on a field so that they serve as a mulch and soil amendment [5,12]. The function of a green manure crop is to add organic matter to the soil, increasing the nitrogen and nutrient supply of the soil thereby increasing its productivity.

In crop rotation, crops are categorized into three groups with respect to their nutrient demand. Green manures are heavy givers that provide necessary nutrients to heavy feeders or light feeders. Since heavy feeders consume most of the nutrient in soil, in our schedule, we consider employing green manure (planting a heavy giver) after a fixed number of heavy feeders, not necessarily sequential.

Fallow is the practice of leaving the land without being sown for one or more vegetative cycles to allow the land to recover and store organic matter and reduce pest damage [5,12].

3   Literature Review

The standard crop rotation problem is defined as determining the sequence of crops to plant, one after the other, in a given area to optimize a certain objective such as maximizing yield, profit, or minimizing area, etc. The problem is modeled as a linear program by many researchers such as [8,9,11,13]. However, none of them consider environmental concerns and sustainability practices.

In the recent literature, there exists a number of studies that address the problem in a sustainable development context, taking into account environmental constraints or objectives related with increasing soil quality, reducing the use of resources, increasing diversity. [10] developed a software program called ROTAT that generates all possible rotations for a given set of crops, however, they do not optimize the rotations. Later, a group of researchers, [2,19] focus on managing the area to be planted while satisfying the demand through reasonable crop schedules rather than optimizing the crop selection itself. [19] considered a sustainable vegetable crop demand supply problem. They determine the division of the available arable areas in plots and, for each plot, obtain an appropriate crop rotation schedule respecting ecological constraints. Their objective is to maximize the plots occupation considering demand constraints, proposing a 0–1 linear optimization model. [2] address Minimum-Space Crop Rotation Problem (MSCRP) which is defined as constructing crop rotations to minimize the total space area required to meet demand.

[20] is the first to introduce adjacency constraints in crop rotation problem. Adjacency constraints prevent crops of the same botanical family to be cultivated at the same time in neighboring plots. They propose a 0–1 optimization model for crop rotation in different areas, with an objective again to maximize the land use subject to neighborhood and succession restrictions for crops of the same botanic family. Later, [4] adapted the model of [20] and introduced demand constraints as well as an objective function which maximizes the profit of planted crops. Recently, [16] proposed some improvements in the model presented by [20] and [4] by considering both objectives of maximizing plot occupation and the profit.

We are the first to employ two cropping systems (crop rotation and intercropping) simultaneously to determine the crop schedule. Intercropping can be considered similar to adjacency constraints, but they differ in several key ways. In [4,20], and [16], adjacency relations are modeled as constraints which state adjacent plots cannot grow, simultaneously, crops belonging to the same botanical family. Thus, it defines strictly which group of crops cannot be planted, and ignore the yield information. This might be misleading considering that individual crops within the same family might have different effects on productivity when intercropped with a specific crop [15].

We consider both the family of crops (in determining the crop sequence) and the yield information (in determining the crops to intercrop). Additionally, intercropping involves dividing the land into many adjacent rows or strips and defines the two-way interaction between specific crops in terms of yield. Hence, our model chooses to plant the specific crops (not a family of crops) simultaneously or in sequence that have the highest positive outcome on the soil, and thus also on the yield. Moreover, [4,20] mainly focused on determining the area used for plantation or the best division of land to meet the demand through a feasible crop schedule. They do not address finding the optimal sequence of crops to be planted in a crop rotation problem.

4   Methodology

We consider a planning horizon of $|L|$ years, where the planning time unit is one month. We assume that each crop is planted at the beginning of a month. Each crop has a production time h_i, which includes the time required to sow, grow, and harvest. Each crop also has a suitable sowing (planting) time window. To disincentivize monocropping the highest revenue crop, we assume that there is a maximum and minimum annual demand (d_{il}^{max} and d_{il}^{min}) for each crop.

C is the set of crops that can be selected for planting, including the ones for green manuring and a hypothetical crop associated with fallow. Crops are also categorized according to their nutrient demands; the sets C_f, C_v and C_g correspond to the set of heavy feeders, heavy givers and cover crops (green

Parameters:	
S	Number of rows in the land
NF	Number of botanical families
p_i	Price (per kg) of crop i
h_i	Production time (in months) of crop i
y_i	Yield (kg) of crop i when grown as a sole crop
e_{ijk}	% effect of intercropping on the yield of crop i when crop j is planted k months before or after crop i
ω	Number of heavy feeders planted
d_{il}^{min}	Minimum expected demand for crop i in the year l
d_{il}^{max}	Maximum expected demand for crop i in the year l

Sets:	
L	Set of years indexed by $l = 1, 2, \ldots |L|$
T	Set of time periods (months) indexed by $t = 1, 2, \ldots |T|$
C	Set of crops indexed by $i, j = 1, 2, \ldots N$ where $i = N$ hypothetical crop associated with fallow
C_f	Set of heavy feeder crops
C_v	Set of heavy giver crops
C_g	Set of cover crops
$C_{m(t)}$	Set of crops which can be planted at each month t where $m(t) = (t-1)_{mod(12)} + 1$
$F(\delta)$	Set of crops of botanical family $\delta = 1, 2, \ldots NF$

Decision	Variables:
$x_{it}^a = 1$	If crop i is planted (sown) at time t at row a, 0 otherwise
$x_{it}^b = 1$	If crop i is planted (sown) at time t at row b, 0 otherwise
$z_{ijtk}^a = 1$	If crop i is planted in row a at time t and crop j is planted next to it k months before or after, 0 otherwise
$z_{ijtk}^b = 1$	If crop i is planted in row b at time t and crop j is planted next to it k months before or after, 0 otherwise

manure), respectively. Note that the sets C_v and C_g might contain the same crops, as heavy givers are generally also used as cover crops. However, cover crops differ in terms of production time in green manure (we assume half time) and they do not have any yield as they are not harvested.

To consider intercropping effects, the arable land is divided into S number of rows, consisting of an equal number $(S/2)$ of rows a and rows b. The parameter e_{ijk} models the intercropping effect on the yield which is dependent not only on the type of crops intercropped but also the timing of plantation. $x_{it}^a = 1$ $(x_{it}^b = 1)$ and $z_{ijtk}^a = 1$ $(z_{ijtk}^b = 1)$ are the binary decision variables described in the notation list.

The crop rotation problem consists in determining the types of crops to plant and their sequence at rows a and rows b over a finite planning horizon in order to maximize the revenue subject to ecological and demand constraints. The integer linear programming model formulation is given as:

$$\text{Maximize} \sum_{t=0}^{|T|} \left[\sum_{i=1}^{N} p_i y_i \left(x_{it}^a + x_{it}^b + \sum_{j=1}^{N} \sum_{k=-h_j+1}^{h_i-1} e_{ijk}(z_{ijtk}^a + z_{ijtk}^b) \right) \right] \tag{1}$$

subject to

$$\sum_{i \in C} \sum_{r=0}^{h_i-1} x_{i(t-r)}^\alpha \leq 1 \quad \alpha = \{a,b\} \quad \forall t \in T \tag{2}$$

$$\sum_{i \in C \backslash C_{m(t)}} x_{it}^\alpha = 0 \quad \alpha = \{a,b\} \quad \forall t \in T \tag{3}$$

$$\sum_{i \in F(\delta)} \sum_{r=0}^{h_i} x_{i(t-r)}^\alpha \leq 1 \quad \alpha = \{a,b\} \quad \forall t \in T \quad and \quad \delta = 1,2,\ldots NF \tag{4}$$

$$x_{it}^a + x_{j(t+k)}^b \geq 2z_{ijtk}^a \quad \forall i,j \in C, \quad \forall t \in T, \quad k = -h_j+1,\ldots,h_i-1 \tag{5}$$

$$x_{it}^a + x_{j(t+k)}^b - 1 \leq z_{ijtk}^a \quad \forall i,j \in C, \quad \forall t \in T, \quad k = -h_j+1,\ldots,h_i-1 \tag{6}$$

$$x_{it}^b + x_{j(t+k)}^a \geq 2z_{ijtk}^b \quad \forall i,j \in C, \quad \forall t \in T, \quad k = -h_j+1,\ldots,h_i-1 \tag{7}$$

$$x_{it}^b + x_{j(t+k)}^a - 1 \leq z_{ijtk}^b \quad \forall i,j \in C, \quad \forall t \in T, \quad k = -h_j+1,\ldots,h_i-1 \tag{8}$$

$$\sum_{r=0}^{t-1} \sum_{i \in C_f} x_{ir}^\alpha + x_{jt}^\alpha \leq \omega \sum_{r=0}^{t+h_j} \sum_{k \in C_g} x_{kr}^\alpha + (\omega - 1) \quad \alpha = a,b \quad \forall j \in C_f, \forall t \in T \tag{9}$$

$$\omega \sum_{r=0}^{t} \sum_{k \in C_g} x_{kr}^\alpha \leq \sum_{r=0}^{t} \sum_{i \in C_f} x_{ir}^\alpha \quad \alpha = \{a,b\}, \quad \forall t \in T \tag{10}$$

$$\sum_{r=t-6}^{t+6} \left(x_{Nr}^\alpha + \sum_{k \in C_g} x_{kr}^\alpha \right) \geq 1 \quad \alpha = \{a,b\}, \quad t = 6,\ldots,|T|-6 \tag{11}$$

$$d_{il}^{min} \leq \sum_{t=12(l-1)+1}^{12l} \left[\frac{S}{2} y_i \left(x_{it}^a + \sum_{j=1}^{N} \sum_{k=-h_j+1}^{h_i-1} e_{ijk} z_{ijtk}^a \right. \right.$$

$$\left. \left. + x_{it}^b + \sum_{j=1}^{N} \sum_{k=-h_j+1}^{h_i-1} e_{ijk} z_{ijtk}^b \right) \right] \leq d_{il}^{max} \quad \forall i \in C \quad and \quad \forall l \in L \tag{12}$$

In the objective function, we maximize the total revenue obtained from each crop pair throughout the planning horizon. Constraint (2) ensure that at most one crop is planted at a given time t in rows a and b. Additionally, constraints do not allow to plant any other crop during the production time (h_i) of the cultivated crop i. Constraint (3) ensure only the crops that are possible to be

Table 1. Crop data

	Crops	Botanical family	Nutrition demand	Plantation periods	Prod. time (months)	Yield (kg/row)	Price (€/kg)	Demand (min,max)
1	Onion	Allium	Light Feeder	2–3, 5–6, 8–11	4	40	160	(0, 100)
2	Coriander	Apiaceae	Light Feeder	6–7, 10–11	2	7	25000	(0, 7)
3	Beans	Fabaceae	Heavy Giver	2–3, 5–6	3	1,75	2430	(1, 100)
4	Soybeans	Fabaceae	Heavy Giver	6–7, 2–3	4	2	344	(0, 100)
5	Groundnut	Fabaceae	Heavy Giver	6, 10-1	4	2,5	1410	(0, 100)
6	Maize	Poaceae	Heavy Feeder	6–7, 10–11, 2	3	7,5	160	(0, 100)
7	Tomatoes	Solanaceae	Heavy Feeder	All year	4	55	1120	(0, 55)
8	Chilli	Solanaceae	Heavy Feeder	1–2, 5–6, 9–10	4	12,5	1700	(12, 100)
9	Eggplant	Solanaceae	Heavy Feeder	5–6, 8–9, 12-1	4	22,5	2170	(0, 25)
10	Potato	Solanaceae	Heavy Feeder	6–7, 10–11	4	20	130	(0, 100)
11	Ginger	Zingiberaceae	Heavy Feeder	2, 3, 5	6	14,08	2300	(0, 20)

planted during that month are planted. Constraint (4) forbid crops of the same botanic family to be planted in sequence (immediately one after the other). Constraints (5,6) and (7,8) keep the intercropping information for the crops in rows a and rows b, respectively. Constraint (9) force a green manure after ω heavy feeders are planted in rows a and b (regardless if they are consecutive or not). Constraint (10) ensure that green manures are not done preemptively to allow successive heavy feeders greater than ω. Constraints (11) ensure that we do either fallow (the crop N is fallow) or green manure in a 12-month rolling time intervals. The last constraint enforces the minimum and maximum demands.

5 Numerical Example

We demonstrate our model on a hypothetical tropical land based on real data as research in agro-ecology and intercropping is very popular in the regions with this climate. In our numerical example, we consider 11 crops grown in tropical regions, e.g. Brazil and India. Table 1 presents the type of crops and their parameters. The yield of sole-planted crops is obtained from FAO Statistics [1]. The price of the crops are determined based on average prices in France in 2020. Table 2 presents the percentage yield effect of intercropping one crop with another. The intercropping data is obtained through extensive literature review; some of the references are [3,17] and [18]. A value of 0 indicates no effect, while a value of -100 denotes the crops are not compatible for intercropping and thus forbidden.

We consider a planning horizon of two years ($|L| = 2$), divided into months ($|T| = 24$). We set $\omega = 2$ to allow only two heavy feeders before forcing a green manure to heal the soil.

The model is implemented in the PuLP library for Python and solved using ILOG CPLEX 12.10. The example was run on a PC with an Intel(R) Core (TM) i7-10510U CPU @ 1.80 GHz with 16 GB of RAM. The problem was solved to optimality in 2134 s yielding the policy in Fig. 2 with an objective value of 615,797.33. Alternate shading of light and dark grey is used for successive crops

Table 2. Percentage yield effect (e_{ij}) of intercropping crop $i \in C$ with $j \in C$

	1	2	3	4	5	6	7	8	9	10	11
1	0	0	−100	−100	0	−82,67	−3,22	−24,9	−75,81	−100	0
2	0	0	−100	−100	−24,74	−90,85	−73,54	0	−65,72	−100	0
3	−100	−100	0	0	−100	−58	−25	0	13	−100	27,42
4	−100	−100	0	0	−100	−13,25	0	−26,31	0	−100	0
5	0	−14,43	−100	−100	0	−55,55	0	0	−63,92	−100	−100
6	−8,84	−3,3	9,25	−20,39	−2,29	0	−13,96	−21,49	−28,51	−44,68	79,27
7	−15,16	−16,71	−3	0	0	−52,3	0	−100	−100	−100	−12,83
8	−73,51	0	0	−40	0	−42,96	−100	0	−100	−100	−100
9	−0,46	−21,58	−16,25	0	20,97	2	−100	−100	0	−100	−100
10	−100	−100	−100	−100	−100	−61,72	−100	−100	−100	0	−100
11	0	0	27,2	0	−100	−23,01	−18,64	−100	−100	−100	0

with white space corresponding to nothing planted at the time. The solid black shows a forced fallow period. Green manure are diagonally hatched.

Table 1 reveals that the highest revenue per row (yield x price) comes from Coriander, Tomatoes, Eggplant, Ginger and Chilli, respectively, with Coriander almost three times the revenue of Tomatoes. The model would normally seek to plant Coriander whenever possible, however we limit it to once per year by setting its demand equal to its yield. We similarly limit Tomatoes and Eggplant to once per year by limiting their demand. To promote the planting of Chilli and Beans which have comparatively lower revenues, we set a minimum demand to be met. The example policy shows that the highest revenue crops are indeed selected as much as possible, while respecting all of their constraints regarding placement and scheduling.

Constraint (1) is obviously respected as two crops are never planted at the same time and Constraint (2) is respected by only planting crops in the period in which they are allowed. Constraint (3) is seen through the spacing (fallow) between Chilli and Eggplant and then between Chilli and Tomatoes in Row B as they are from the same botanical family and can not be planted immediately following one another. Since this is not a forced fallow due to Constraint (10), but for family scheduling purposes, it is shown as white space. Constraints (8) and (9) are respected by forcing a green manure (Groundnut_GM) after the two heavy feeders Eggplant and Chilli in Row B and again after Tomatoes and Eggplant in Row A. Constraint (10) is seen in Row A where a Fallow is forced at $t = 8$ and $t = 17$ as there is no green manure in Row A until the very end and we must have at least one fallow within any 12-month interval.

A strong impact of intercropping effects can also be seen in this policy. Eggplant planted with beans will decrease its yield by 16.25%, which is unfortunate, but is chosen by the model as it is still highly desirable due to its still high revenue with respect to the other crops, and beans are required by the demand constraints. Beans will, however, receive a 13% increase in yield which will help to offset the yield loss of Eggplant. Eggplant is also forbidden to be planted with

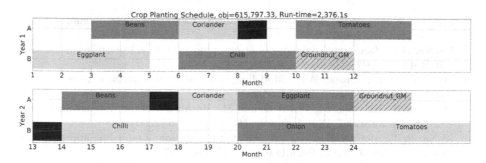

Fig. 2. Optimal crop schedule

Chilli (−100 intercropping effect) which also has a minimum demand to be met. The policy is able to satisfy these intercropping constraints.

6   Conclusion and Future Work

We have formulated a 0–1 linear program to optimize crop selection and scheduling while considering ecological aspects such as intercropping and rotation. This model is an initial work in trying to promote (economically, ecologically, and socially) a combination of green agro-ecology principles in a practical way. It will be a valuable tool in moving away from destructive monoculture habits that currently widely exist in large-scale agriculture. While the model is efficient for small sizes, it quickly becomes intractable for CPLEX as the number of crops and the time horizon increases. Specialized algorithms and/or heuristics will need to be developed to solve larger instances to (near) optimality. Moreover, the structure of the policies could be studied and demonstrated to develop more efficient solution procedures.

References

1. FAO Statistics. http://www.fao.org/land-water/databases-and-software/crop-information/en/, Accessed 10 Apr 2021
2. Alfandari, L., Plateau, A., Schepler, X.: A branch-and-price-and-cut approach for sustainable crop rotation planning. EJOR **241**(3), 872–879 (2015)
3. Ali, M., Rahman, M., Asaduzzaman, M., Hossain, M., Mannan, M.: Intercropping maize with different vegetables. Bang. Agron. J. **18**(1), 49–52 (2015)
4. Aliano Filho, A., de Oliveira Florentino, H., Vaz Pato, M.: Metaheuristics for a crop rotation problem. Int. J. Metaheurist. **3**(3), 199–222 (2014)
5. Altieri, M.A.: Agroecology: the science of sustainable agriculture. Boulder. Part three: development, climate and rights, vol. 238, pp. 12052–12057. Westview Press (1995)
6. Andrews, D., Kassam, A.: The importance of multiple cropping in increasing world food supplies. Multiple Crop. **27**, 1–10 (1976)

7. Baldwin, K.R.: Crop rotations on organic farms. Center for environmental farming systems, vol. 16 (2006)
8. Clarke, H.R.: Combinatorial aspects of cropping pattern selection in agriculture. EJOR **40**(1), 70–77 (1989)
9. Detlefsen, N.K., Jensen, A.L.: Modelling optimal crop sequences using network flows. Agric. Syst. **94**(2), 566–572 (2007)
10. Dogliotti, S., Rossing, W., Van Ittersum, M.: Rotat, a tool for systematically generating crop rotations. Eur. J. Agron. **19**(2), 239–250 (2003)
11. El-Nazer, T., McCarl, B.A.: The choice of crop rotation: a modeling approach and case study. Am. J. Agric. Econ.D **68**(1), 127–136 (1986)
12. Gliessman, S.R., Engles, E., Krieger, R.: Agroecology: Ecological Processes in Sustainable griculture. CRC Press, Boca Raton (1998)
13. Haneveld, W.K., Stegeman, A.W.: Crop succession requirements in agricultural production planning. EJOR **166**(2), 406–429 (2005)
14. Lichtfouse, E., Navarrete, M., Debaeke, P., Souchère, V., Alberola, C., Ménassieu, J.: Agronomy for sustainable agriculture: a review. In: Sustainable Agriculture, pp. 1–7. Springer, Heidelberg (2009). https://doi.org/10.1007/978-90-481-2666-8_1
15. Lithourgidis, A., Dordas, C., Damalas, C.A., Vlachostergios, D.: Annual intercrops: an alternative pathway for sustainable agriculture. Aust. J. Crop Sci. **5**(4), 396–410 (2011)
16. Mauri, G.R.: Improved mathematical model and bounds for the crop rotation scheduling problem with adjacency constraints. EJOR **278**(1), 120–135 (2019)
17. Monim, M., Islam, A., Rahman, A., Monim, A., Quddus, M.: Effect of intercropping different vegetables with groundnut. J. Agrofor. Environ. **4**(1), 27–30 (2010)
18. Raji, J.: Intercropping soybean and maize in a derived savanna ecology. Afr. J. Biotechnol. **6**(16) (2007)
19. dos Santos, L.M.R., Costa, A.M., Arenales, M.N., Santos, R.H.S.: Sustainable vegetable crop supply problem. EJOR **204**(3), 639–647 (2010)
20. dos Santos, L.M.R., Michelon, P., Arenales, M.N., Santos, R.H.S.: Crop rotation scheduling with adjacency constraints. Ann. Oper. Res. **190**(1), 165–180 (2011)
21. Vandermeer, J., van Noordwijk, M., Anderson, J., Ong, C., Perfecto, I.: Global change and multi-species agroecosystems: concepts and issues. Agric. Ecosyst. Environ. **67**(1), 1–22 (1998)

Improvement Models and Methods for Green and Innovative Systems

Generation Y – Modularity Enabling Radical Innovation

Bjørnar Henriksen$^{(\boxtimes)}$ and Carl Christian Røstad

SINTEF Technology Management, S.P. Andersens vei 5, 7465 Trondheim, Norway
bjornar.henriksen@sintef.no

Abstract. SMEs, in particular, have challenges working purposefully with inno-vation and development, as this is in a continuous conflict with day-to-day opera-tions. The innovation work is therefore often random and characterized by further development of existing product/production, or with technology suppliers setting the agenda. Traditionally, a distinction is made between stepwise/incremental and radical innovations. The latter involves creating new products, services, processes or mindsets (Generation Y) that can outdate existing ones (Generation X). Radi-cal innovations require conceptual and long-term thinking, and often require large amounts of resources that make it challenging to succeed. Incremental innovations, often via further development/improvement of existing products and pro-duction systems, occur far more frequently, and the overall effect of gradual innovations can be significant. But the step-by-step innovations can be unstructured and do not necessarily contribute in a direction that ensures long-term competitiveness in relation to Generation Y. Through three different (but connected) pro-jects, we have approached different aspects of aiming to enable a more modular, but radi-cal innovation process. This involves the development of solutions to concretize the future concepts for product/production through reference models, define the various innovation steps (modules), and solutions to follow up the path towards radical innovation (Generation Y).

Keywords: Innovation · Modularization · Concepts

1 Introduction

1.1 Drivers for Innovation

We live in the era of constant transformations where e.g. technological, product and process innovations have altered manufacturing for decades. The ability to be flexible and agile have been key qualities for success. It goes without saying that the future will witness even more breathtaking technological disruptions, as research around nan-otechnology and big-data analytics start to impact numerous manufacturing applications. The report "Remaking of Industries" [1], identifies six drivers for industrial changes; the always-on, hyperconnected consumer's search for personalized products and experi-ences; growing imperative for higher productivity and to do more with less; the challenge

A. Dolgui et al. (Eds.): APMS 2021, IFIP AICT 632, pp. 423–429, 2021.
https://doi.org/10.1007/978-3-030-85906-0_47

of digital disruption, which is blurring industry boundaries and upending markets at a rapid pace; the drumbeat to "go green", long a mantra but now increasingly a reality; evolution of business ecosystems, where established companies must work with, not against, start-ups, competitors and customers; the politics of economics, in which long-held views on trade and internationalism are strongly challenged resulting in new regulations.

These forces do not exist in a vacuum but collide in ways that increase their power and keep companies scrambling to keep up. How do you build for tomorrow without risking all that you do today? How do you keep pace in what may be an older but still-strong core business, alongside a new core that has lots of running room left and new businesses that are taking shape but face great uncertainty? Only strong players will get a chance to fulfil established goals, provide goods and services for untapped markets, and, finally, to stay ahead of the competition.

According to the BCG's Global Innovation Survey 2020 [2], the most innovative companies are those that view the need to constantly innovate as a top-priority and support this approach with a coherent strategy and sufficient investment. This group accounts for 45% of the more than 1.000 companies taking part in the Innovation Survey, which results in the top 50 innovator list. At the other end of the scale, 30% of companies in the survey were categorized as "skeptical innovators," placing little importance on defining a clear innovation strategy or committing investment. 25% of companies sit in the middle ground, exhibiting an inconsistent or indifferent approach to innovation and its importance to their business. This clearly states that companies need some kind of vision of the future superior products and processes.

Norwegian and international surveys show that 80–90% of managers see the ability to innovate as crucial for value creation and competitiveness. However, more than half of the managers are also unsure whether the company has enough innovation capacity and resources to succeed in innovations.

1.2 Scope

The paper is conceptual as it aims to describe how in particular SMEs could increase their innovation pace through a stepwise, modular approach, at the same time as they head for radical innovation. The paper presents different elements of modularization and prerequisites for such an approach to innovation, including enablers and methodologies for modular innovation. Section 2 describes the theoretical aspects, while Sect. 3 presents the use-cases/projects the paper is based upon. Section 4 goes into the different elements of our approach for modular innovation.

1.3 Research Approach

This paper is based on the research in four R&D projects in medium sized manufacturing companies in Europe. A common denominator for the projects is the objective on improving product development. The 3- to 4-years projects have several of the same partners, hence the R&D-work has been fertilized between the projects. One is funded by EUs H2020, while three are co-funded by the Norwegian Research Council (NRC). The action-oriented approach means that the researchers have actively worked out solutions the companies can use and possibly implement – in line with traditional action research methodology.

2   Theoretical Perspectives

2.1   Towards Radical Innovation

Radical innovation can change our everyday lives and improve sustainability through, e.g. new technology that gives us new products, radical improvement in performance, quality and/or price. Incremental innovation builds on and optimizes existing products/services, technologies, processes. As shown in Fig. 1, one can group innovation in relation to the extent to which the product and/or production concept itself is changed, and whether the innovation involves a change in whether the various components are connected in a new way. This gives us two more models for innovation, "architectural innovation" and "modular innovation".

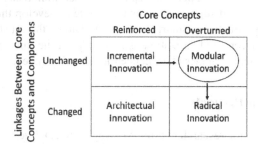

Fig. 1. Radical innovation through modularity [3]

Lack of resources, focus and/or knowledge can lead to a lack of innovation. By combining radical and incremental innovation in a systematic way, it will be possible to accumulate knowledge and product/process properties which means that, even in the improvement of an existing portfolio, the company's resources are purposefully utilized. However, there are few wide-spread, or rather no, good SME-adapted approaches, methodologies or practical solutions to achieve this. Therefore, there is a significant research need that is the starting point for Generation Y.

Recent innovation theory emphasizes interactive processes in which companies in most innovation activities interact and are dependent on actors in the organization's environment [4]. A key challenge, however, is to set these processes in a future, radical perspective, where known and traditional incremental techniques in e.g. Total Quality Management (TQM), Lean Product Development (LPD), Business Model Canvas [5], and others, must be set in a future perspective so that, for example, a redesign of a component and the accompanying process change (incremental Generation X innovation) takes into account that this can be used as an element (module) for the future Generation Y product/service/process. To succeed, one must work from a modular approach, but this is challenging if this is not the basis for Generation X and must be solved so that this work contributes. There are also great challenges in drawing a clear picture of the future product and production concepts that, among other things, manage to capture e.g. technological change and sustainability issues.

2.2 Modularization – Enabler for Innovation

With a holistic approach, module-based development/innovation will relate to mod-ule-based products with associated module-based production. This is the basis for various forms of module-based knowledge. Modularization usually yields gains in connection with. time, cost, quality, but the flexibility in modularization can also lead to development races that take us away from where we want to be in terms of strategy and radical innovation [6].

The concept descriptions for Generation Y must make it possible to think modularization and different time cycles for incremental innovation steps. Important premises for the module structure are service life, potential/risk of change in special technology, and user/market needs. This requires a form of innovation agenda and solutions that dynamically connect the opportunity space to Generation Y. In practice, this means having good processes and support systems to be able to develop the various elements (modules) of smart products and smart factories. A state-of-the-art study [7] from 2019 shows little link between modularization as a concept in the innovation literature and the more industry-oriented approaches, hence the focus is needed.

3 The Research Projects

This paper is based on the research in three Norwegian R&D 4-years projects co-funded by the Norwegian Research Council (NRC) in medium sized manufacturing companies, and one EU-funded H2020-project. A common denominator for the projects is the objective on improving product development and innovation capabilities. The projects emphasize how digitalization could enable process improvements and more fact-based decisions also at a strategic level.

RIT (NRC): 2018–2022, 3 industrial- and 3 R&D partners. The main objective is to develop a Design Dashboard where large data volumes are analyzed/presented together with other types of data according to product requirements in the leisure boat industry.

RADDIS (NRC): 2018–2022, 4 industrial- and 2 R&D partners. The main objective is the reduction of physical work using enabling technologies within visualization, product digital twins and simulation. The project also aims to find more proactive ways to deal with regulations within the leisure boat industry.

WRAPID (NRC): 2018–2022, 2 industrial- and 2 R&D partners. The main objective is to develop solutions for fact-based modularized product design for heavy machinery for agricultural and industrial applications.

LINCOLN (H2020): 2016–2019. 3 industrials and 13 R&D partners. The main objective was to develop three radical new boat/ship-concepts for aquaculture, coastal surveillance and search- and rescue operations.

4 Modular Innovation – The Conceptual Model

4.1 Challenges Experienced

For the projects' case-companies, the picture drawn in Sect. 1 (introduction) describes the situation they experience. The companies feel pressures for change and innovations, but have challenges in prioritizing among projects, finding resources (financial, but also people, equipment etc.) for the bigger innovation projects.

It often looks like a kind of "muddling through" where projects are brought to the decision table often based on outside initiatives (equipment companies, or consultants) and not based on strategic processes/considerations. Another well-known challenge that the SMEs face is the problems of keeping continuity in their projects as the day-to-day activities and operations often must be prioritized, capturing key personnel and resources from the development and innovation activities.

In all four projects different approaches to improve the development and innovation processes have been introduced. Some of them includes different tools for a more fact-based processes, while we in other cases have put more focus on project models and checklists. However, a common imperative has been to find ways that enable a dynamic and adaptive approach to innovation linked to a long-term strategy or vision. In all the projects modularization in products, production and product development has been tested and to some extent implemented. The research activities have enlightened modularization as a key for a new approach to innovation.

4.2 Generation Y

As the companies improved their efforts towards modularization, the perspectives towards innovation became clearer and a more innovation-oriented modularization process was discussed and conceptualized as illustrated in Fig. 2.

What we are heading for through the Generation Y-concept is to put innovation in a concrete industrial context and develop the practical approaches and solutions that increase the success rate. This involves moving from the theoretical models as de-scribed in Fig. 1 into an innovation context where one is able to create the robust images of what it is desirable to realistically move towards, and which one is at the same time able to relate to on an ongoing basis. Findings from the projects has shown that this must be enabled without a rigid control system. Moving in this way from the theoretical innovation models to practical fact-based solutions that are also feasible is very demanding and we have only made initial attempts at this in our cases, but with great promising results.

Radical innovation is usually about new products, services, processes and systems based on a completely new technology that gives us a dramatic improvement. Drivers for radical innovations can also be from the needs and user side where there is experience and competence the manufacturer does not have – i.e. user-driven innovation [8]. Establishing concepts that are radical and robust in relation to the future is both demanding and risky as the future is largely unpredictable, (ref. Corona crisis 2020/2021). At the same time, the description/conceptualization of Generation Y, must be so specific that it is possible to manage the ongoing development activities accordingly. Consequently, there are challenges associated with processes and methods for establishing the radical

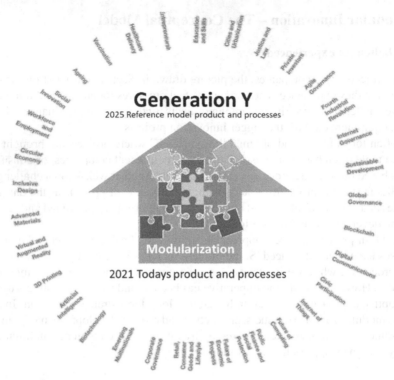

Fig. 2. Generation Y – A concept for modular innovation

product and production concepts. In the WRAPID project we emphasized the gathering of facts from the market department and sales forces especially on trends and customer expectations on what the future products could be like. This was then merged with the technology window defined through technology workshops.

After defining the reference Generation Y, an innovation agenda of which areas to be develop/focused in order to achieve Generation Y must be defined. In practice, this means having good processes and support systems to be able to develop a platform for sustainability, and the various elements (modules) of smart products and/or smart factories. In the LINCOLN, RIT and RADDIS projects different systems for simulation and onboard data-gathering and transfer were used for different kinds of analytics in the product design to get a picture of to which extent our innovations were coming together towards Generation Y. A further focus on modularization in all cases did substantiate this process.

Generation Y must be sufficiently concrete and measurable so that we can follow development work in relation to them at all times. Innovation barometers [9] can be used, but these are of a general nature and as snapshots, for example in an industry. Good monitoring solutions for ongoing follow-up of innovation work in SMEs over time are to a small extent available, but some are available e.g. Balanced Scorecard (BSC), with a sharper focus on strategy and learning [10]. All four research projects focus on fact-based product design to make our decisions in product design as robust as possible.

Especially, the RADDIS project aims to visualize and show a dynamic picture of our products and production through avatar solutions. In the roadmap towards Generation Y we also need to keep a close eye on critical measures for the products/concepts. These measures need to be as concrete and realistic as possible. The BEEM- methodology (Business Effects Evaluation Methodology) [11] is a such method defining objectives and measures, which was used in all use cases in our four projects. BEEM sets targets and enables measuring several dimensions: 1) product-/service – quality, 2) cost and profitability, 3) growth, 4) sustainability, 5) company specific. This makes it easier not only to establish a roadmap towards Generation Y, but also to see if we are following the right path.

5 Conclusions

Modular Innovation as a theoretical approach makes sense as a way for companies to head for radical innovations, as incremental innovation in e.g. today's product portfolio can dramatically contribute towards the radical if done in a context. Modularity on product and processes has gained a lot of popularity, which we also have experienced through our research projects. Bringing modularity into the innovation-fields as in our Generation Y concept requires a lot more research to be holistic and provide complete tools for companies. In our research projects, we will continue to explore and exploit different elements of it. However, we already see that modular innovation works in practice. In this way, especially SMEs, could gain a lot through a more efficient use of resources, capabilities and knowledge. This gain could be both in economical terms, but also in speed and the actual innovations and competitive-ness coming out of these processes.

References

1. Accenture Hompepage. https://www.accenture.com/us-en/insights/industry-x-0/reinvention-of-industries. Accessed 18 July 2021.
2. The World Economic Forum Homepage. https://www.weforum.org/agenda/2020/07/most-innovative-companies-bcg-survey-apple-amazon-alphabet/. Aaccessed 18 Jul 2021
3. Henderson, R.M., Clark, K.B.: Architectural Innovation. In: Tushman. M.L., Anderson, P. (eds.) Managing Strategic Innovation and Change. Oxford University Press (2004)
4. Jensen, M.B., Johnson, B., Lorenz, E., Lundvall B.Å.: Forms of knowledge and modes of innovation. Res. Policy 36(5), 680–693 (2007)
5. Osterwalder, A., Pigneur, Y.: Business Model Generation. John Wiley and Sons Inc., Hoboken (2016)
6. Henriksen, B., Røstad, C.C.: Paths for modularization. In: Grabot, B., Vallespir, B., Gomes, S., Bouras, A., Kiritsis, D. (eds.) APMS 2014. IAICT, vol. 440, pp. 272–279. Springer, Heidelberg (2014). https://doi.org/10.1007/978-3-662-44733-8_34
7. Micheli, G.J.L., Trucco, P., Sabri, Y., Mancini, M.: Modularization as a system life cycle management strategy: drivers, barriers, mechanisms and impacts. Int. J. Eng. Bus. Manage. 11, 1–23 (2019)
8. Hoholm, T., Huse, M.: Brukerdrevet innovasjon i Norge. Magma no 5, (2008)
9. Cramo Homepage. https://www.innovasjonsbarometeret.no/. Accessed 18 Jul 2021
10. Madsen, D.Ø., Stenheim, T.: Balansert målstyring. Magma 4, 22–33 (2014)
11. Henriksen, B., Røstad, C.C.: Evaluating and prioritizing projects – setting targets. the business effect evaluation methodology BEEM. Int. J. Managing Projects Bus. 3(2), 275–291 (2010)

Disassembly Line Balancing Using Recursive Optimization in Presence of Task-Failure

Rakshit Kumar Singh$^{(\boxtimes)}$ [ID], Amit Raj Singh [ID], and Ravindra Kumar Yadav

Department of Mechanical Engineering, National Institute of Technology Raipur, G.E. Road, Raipur 492010, Chhattisgarh, India

Abstract. Disassembly lines have to face task-failure situations due to the variability in quality of incoming product. Such failure violates the precedence relationship for the remaining task at downstream stations. Therefore, task failure requires corrective measure to improve the profitability of disassembly line. In this paper, a recursive optimization approach has been proposed to improve the profitability of disassembly lines, which takes corrective measure to determine optimal sequence of tasks. For this purpose, Teaching Learning Based Optimization (TLBO) algorithm has been used to find optimal sequences before and after task failure. To reduce the computational time required during recursion, the proposed solution approach is equipped with memoized list for finding corrective measure. A numerical illustration has been used to demonstrate the applicability of proposed solution approach which is capable to handle high variability in quality of incoming products.

Keywords: Disassembly · Task failure · Probability-based stacking · Line balancing

1 Introduction

Product recovery aims to retrieve parts and components from old or outdated products by disassembling products facing their end-of-life cycle into its constituent parts and components [1]. The disassembled parts face three end-of-life choices: recycling, remanufacturing and disposal. These end-of-life choices are made based on different objectives such as market demand for certain component, extraction of hazardous parts, retrieving parts and storing them in inventory for future use [2]. Thus, one decisive component of product recovery is disassembly which makes it crucial to perform disassembly in a way that meets various economic and environmental objectives for making product recovery sustainable. There are various settings of resources to perform disassembly such as single workstation (for high flexibility and low processing rate), disassembly cell (for moderate throughput and flexibility), and disassembly lines (for high disassembly rate and low flexibility).

Disassembly lines are very desirable in scenarios requiring high production rate, they also have certain associated benefits such as economies of scale, division of labor

Published by Springer Nature Switzerland AG 2021
A. Dolgui et al. (Eds.): APMS 2021, IFIP AICT 632, pp. 430–440, 2021.
https://doi.org/10.1007/978-3-030-85906-0_48

etc. [3]. The sequence in which various disassembly tasks are to be performed is critical to optimize the utilization of disassembly line resources, this problem is referred to as Disassembly Line Balancing Problem (DLBP) in the literature. The sequence of task assignment for line balancing can be obtained using exact solution approaches such as linear programming [4], Mixed Integer programming [5], second order cone programming [6]. DLBP belongs to NP-hard complexity of combinatorial optimization problem and, as the problem size increases it becomes time consuming to solve it using exact solution approaches [7]. Several authors have also made use of heuristics and meta-heuristics for solving DLBP under different scenarios such as ant colony optimization [8], simulated annealing [9], genetic algorithm [10], and particle fish swarm algorithm [11].

Although DLBP is similar to Assembly Line Balancing Problem (ALBP), DLBP has some additional complications such as operational considerations arising out of variations in incoming quality of the product [1]. Due to variability in quality of incoming product it might not be possible to perform some task on a given core (the product being disassembled). This situation is referred to as task-failure in DLBP literature and it can prevent the execution of other tasks on downstream workstations due to precedence relations of failed tasks and its successors. This variation in incoming quality of the product makes optimizing the utilization of disassembly line resources even more complicated. The first solution attempt in task-failure environment was provided by Gungor and Gupta [1]. They used weighted state network to find optimal disassembly sequence using Dijkstra's shortest path algorithm, the model was generated with the assumption of complete disassembly if possible, and the probability of task failures were assumed to be known and deterministic. The only other study in presence of task failure was done by [12], in their work authors attempted to improve the profitability of a disassembly line under task failure environment by introducing reactive rebalancing whenever a task failed. This reactive rebalancing was done on a sequence generated using predictive balancing, under predictive balancing solution approach a solution was found for given number of workstations to find optimal profit without considering task failure. Then the tasks in optimal sequence were failed one by one and a new optimal sequence was generated onward from the failed task under reactive line balancing scheme by relaxing cycle time constraint for the downstream workstations. Relaxing cycle time to generate reactive balance violates the necessary condition for paced line and introduces additional inefficiency in line resource utilization. Since the reactive balancing is done for only one optimal sequence obtained by predictive balance, it's a possibility that the solution obtained might be inferior to a solution having lower objective values in predictive balance and yet produce better overall results after task failure.

Considering the lacunae of the disassembly setting and solution strategy mentioned above, this article aims to provide a novel solution approach for optimizing the DLBP under task failure environment. For this purpose, Teaching Learning Based optimization (TLBO) meta-heuristic algorithm is utilized in recursive fashion to generate optimal disassembly sequence without violating the cycle time constraint. To reduce the time for reactive balancing during recursion, memoization of optimal reactive sequence is incorporated thereby, reducing the overall execution time of the algorithm.

The remaining paper is organized as follows: In Sect. 2 notations and problem definition for DLBP under task failure are provided. in Sect. 3, the proposed algorithm utilizing TLBO for optimizing DLBP under task failure environment is described. Numerical illustration along with results of computational experiments are given in Sect. 4, finally the conclusion and future scope are provided in Sect. 5.

2   Problem Description/Formulation

The focus of this work is on determining disassembly sequence of tasks for a single product to maximize profit on a straight line, and complete disassembly is targeted. However, partial disassembly is allowed only after a task in a given disassembly sequence has failed. It is assumed that the incoming product supply is infinite, and parts released upon performing any given task in each product are known, the retrieved components are accepted in their current condition by demand source, only one product is disassembled on each parallel line, operators are multi-skilled. Other disassembly parameters such as task time, revenue generated are known and deterministic. The probabilities of task failure are known and deterministic. For failed tasks, task completion time and costs are fully incurred. Every station has a buffer space meant to store subassemblies (to facilitate stacking of work stations). Partial disassembly is allowed (by adding dummy task) only after a task fails in the disassembly sequence.

The notations for formulating DLBP under task failure and TLBO are as follows:

n	Total number of tasks of product.
a	Total number of possible subassemblies.
i	Task index.
prt_i	List of parts released by task i.
CT	Cycle time.
$cost_i$	Costs of performing task i.
rev_j	Revenue generated by releasing part j.
TS_k	Tasks that can be performed on subassembly k.
ST_i	List of subassemblies activated upon performing task i.
t_i	Time required to perform task i.
scc	Station cost coefficient.
pf_i	Probability of failure of task i.
$'ca$	Set of currently activated subassembly for a solution string.
cdt	Updated set of candidate tasks based on precedence relationship and ca.
gen	Current iteration number of algorithm.
m	Population size for TLBO (common to main and failed optimization stages).
c_t	Teaching coefficient for teaching phase.
XC_l	Continuous decision vector: $|XC| = m$, $|XC_l| = n$.
XD_l	Discrete sequences of tasks generated using XC.
$XCF_{l,k}$	Continuous decision vector generated after sequentially failing tasks in $|XCF_{l,k}| = n + 1$($\because$ dummy task included), $\forall l \in (1, m)$, $\forall k \in (1, |XD_l|)$
$XDFp_{l,k}$	List of completed tasks before a task failed (includes the failed task).
$XDFa_{l,k}$	Sequence of tasks performable corresponding to failed sequence $XDFp_{l,k}$.

xdf^* Optimal sequence of tasks corresponding to $XDFp_{l,k}$.

ML Memoization list containing xdf^* found corresponding to every $XDFp_{l,k}$.

$eval$ List containing evaluated values for every sequence in XD.

$evalf$ List containing evaluated values for every sequence $XDFa_{l,k}$.

P_{XDFa} Probability of completing sequence $XDFa_{l,k}$.

P_{cXDFa} Conditional probability of completing sequence $XDFa_{l,k}$ given that one of the sequence in $XDFa_{l,k}$, $\forall k \in (1, |XD_l|)$ will happen.

WS_l Total number of work stations after probability-based stacking ($\forall l \in (1, m)$).

$wsc_{l,w}$ List containing tasks assigned to station w in disassembly sequence XD_l.

T_f Task index of failed task.

To provide visual representation for precedence relationship, diagrams or graphs are used in DLBP. The two main types of diagrams used in the literature are part-based precedence (PPD) and task-based precedence diagram (TPD). The part-based precedence diagram provides parts' order based on their immediate predecessor [13] while TPD represents the order of tasks based on their immediate predecessors. Executing any given task in a TPD results in removal of one or more subassemblies or parts. By using either TPD or PPD multiple disassembly sequences can be generated. However, TPD representation is more clear and easier to use for generating solution strings, for this reason we used Transformed AND/OR graph (TAOG) based TPD representation developed by Koç et al. [14]. In TAOG representation the subassemblies are represented by artificial nodes (A_i) and tasks are represented using normal nodes (B_i). These nodes are connected using two types of arcs, for any given node only one predecessor and one successor should be selected for execution. The arcs in TAOG represent two types of relationships, the arcs connected by a semicircle indicate an OR type relationship and the normal arcs indicate a normal type relationship.

3   Recursive Optimization Using TLBO

Most optimization algorithms have some algorithm-specific parameters, the improper tuning of these parameters may increase the computation time or yield a local optimal solution. Considering this fact, we make use of TLBO proposed by Rao et al. [15] as it does not need any algorithm-specific parameters apart from common control parameters like number of generations and population size. The pseudocode for the TLBO algorithm is provided below where the variable 'r' is a real number generated randomly in the range (0, 1):

Algorithm 1. Procedure of TLBO algorithm

Input: $eval, m, \max\_gen, lb, lbc, ubc$
Initialize random population: $XC = [[ ] for j \ in \ range \ (m)]$
i=0
while $t < max\_gen$:
    for $i = 1 \ to \ m$:
        choose XC_best based on eval
        determine XC_mean
        $XC_{i_{new}} = XC_i + r(XC_{best} - c_t XC\_mean)$
        Evaluate XC_new
        If $eval(XC\_new)$ is better than $eval(XC_i)$
            Replace XC_i with XC_new
        Randomly choose a solution XC_r
        If $eval(XC_i) < eval(XC_r)$
            $XC_{i_{new}} = XC_i + r(XC_i - XC_r)$
        else:
            $XC_{i_{new}} = XC_i - r(XC_i - XC_r)$
        Evaluate $XC_{i_{new}}$
        If $eval(XC_{i_{new}}) > eval(XC_i)$
            Replace XC_i with $XC_{i_{new}}$
    t+=1
output: $XC\_best, eval(XC\_best)$

The TLBO is inspired by the teaching-learning dynamics and is based on the influential effect of teacher on the learning output of a class. The algorithm involves two modes of evolution: first mode is through teacher and is known as teacher phase and second mode is through learners interacting with other learners and is therefore termed as learner phase. In TLBO the population consists of a group of learners and different design variables are analogous to different courses being offered to learners. The fitness value is analogous to the performance of learners in various courses. After initialization, best solution in the population is assigned the role of teacher. After determining the teacher, teaching and learning phases are executed for each solution string. At the end of each iteration, average performance and the teacher are updated.

TLBO for disassembly operates on real coded continuous decision vector XC_l of length equal to number of tasks in the precedence diagram. Based on sorted priority of continuous representation a discrete set of tasks XD_l is generated in accordance with precedence constraints. The tasks in XD_l are then assigned sequentially to work-stations without violating cycle time constraint. If the cycle time constraint is violated, a new workstation is opened and the task is assigned to it. For n part problem the random numbers needed for generating a continuous representation for a partial sequence are $n + 1$. The position of these numbers is associated with the task index and the n + 1 position is used for a dummy task, that can be assigned at any sequence with no resource requirement for a given product once a task in the given sequence fails. Once this dummy task for a product is assigned no other tasks can be performed on that product. The list of candidate tasks (cdt) is generated based on precedence constraint and the task with largest associated real number is assigned. This procedure is repeated until task $n + 1$ is assigned or until there are no more tasks in cdt.

Once XD for entire population is generated the sequences in XD are evaluated. Then, best performing solution string (XC_best) in XD is determined, for each member of the population teaching and learning phases are performed as stated in algorithm 1. After completion of teaching and learning phase of a population member the new solution is evaluated and accepted or rejected based on greedy selection and the best solution is updated. After all members of population go through teaching and learning phase, next iteration is started. The evaluation of a disassembly sequence in *XD* require additional steps due to inclusion of task failure. The flow diagram of the proposed recursive algorithm incorporates these steps as shown in Fig. 1.

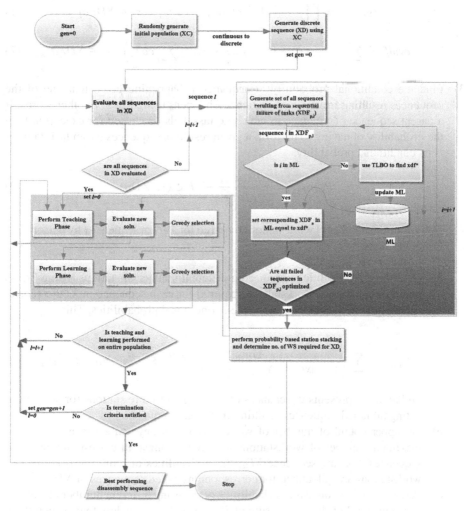

Fig. 1. Flowchart of recursive solution approach using memoization.

A sequence in *XD* is evaluated by performing the following steps,

1) The tasks of sequence XD_l are failed sequentially starting from the last task and then we start by searching optimal sequence in memoized list (ML) for each failed

sequence (*XDFp*). If *XDFp* does not exist in ML then a new optimal sequence (*xdf**) is obtained using TLBO corresponding to *XDFp* and the new found optimal solution corresponding to *XDFp* is stored in ML.

2) For a given sequence in XD_l once all tasks are failed the resulting sequences (*XDFa*) are assigned to work stations based on task based-assignment strategy, the probability of occurrence of each sequence (Eq. 1) is calculated along with the associated profit of each sequence (Eq. 2).

$$P_{XDFa_{l,k}} = \prod_{i, i \neq T_f} \left(1 - pf_{XDFa_{l,k,i}}\right) * pf_{T_f}, \ \forall i \in XDFa_{l,k} \qquad (1)$$

$$evalf = \sum_i rev_{i, i \neq T_f} - \left(scc * CT * ws + \sum_i cost_i\right), \ \forall i \in XDFa_{l,k} \qquad (2)$$

3) Find the conditional probability of sequence k happening given that one of the sequences resulting from parent sequence l happens using Eq. 3. In other words, if a parent sequence l (sequence in which no task fails) is chosen for execution then the probability of having to perform a given resulting sequences (from task failure) is its conditional probability.

$$P_{cXDF_{l,k}} = \frac{P_{XDFa_{l,k}}}{\sum_k P_{XDFa_{l,k}}}, \ k \in (1, |XD_l|) \qquad (3)$$

4) Determine the number of work stations required for a given sequence l by performing following steps:

a) Determine probabilities of requiring different number of stations (using Eq. 4) based on number of workstations required for each sequence in *XDFa* (corresponding to XD_l) and their associated conditional probabilities. This

$$P_{ws_q,l} = \sum_{k,k \in (1, |XD_l|)} \begin{cases} P_{cXDFa_{l,k}}, & if \ ws_{cXDFa_{l,k}} \geq q \\ 0, & else \end{cases}, \ \forall q \in (1, ws_{ub}) \qquad (4)$$

probability represents the chances of needing q or more stations for accommodating all failed sequences resulting from main sequence l.

b) Set upper bound of number of work stations for any sequence in XD_l as the maximum number of workstations required amongst all corresponding failed sequences. For any sequence XD_l, the probabilities of requiring q number of workstations are calculated for corresponding failed sequences of XD_l.

c) Perform stacking once the probabilities of requiring different number of stations is calculated. For this, if the sum of $P_{ws_{ub}}$ and $P_{ws_{ub-1}}$ is less than 1 then these stations are stacked and upper bound on station is set to upper bound minus one. If the stations are stacked then the probability of needing $q - 1$ stations is updated as the sum of probabilities P_{ws_q} and $P_{ws_{q-1}}$.

d) Perform stacking of workstations for a sequence XD_l iteratively until the probability of requiring last open work station exceeds 1.

5) Once stacking terminates, evaluate the fitness of XD_l as per Eq. 5.

$$eval_l = \sum_{k \in (1, |XD_l|)} \left(P_{XDFa_{l,k}} * \sum_{\forall i \in XDFa_{l,k}} \left(rev_{i, i \neq T_f} - cost_i \right) \right) - scc * WS_l$$

(5)

The first term in Eq. 5 represents the total profit without considering the cost of opening a workstation, the next term determines the station opening cost based on total number of stations required after stacking.

4 Numerical Illustration

The application of the proposed solution approach is demonstrated by using an example of an automatic pencil for balancing disassembly line in presence of task failure. The joint precedence diagram of the automatic pencil along with task times and task costs is provided in Fig. 2.

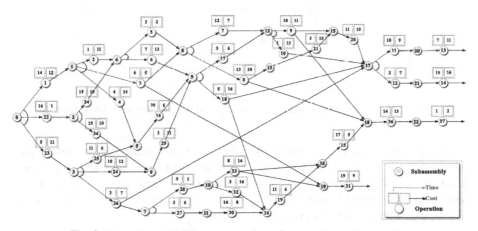

Fig. 2. Precedence TAOG representation of automatic pencil example.

The recursive TLBO algorithm was coded in python and was run on Intel i5 4.2 GHz processor with 6-GB RAM. The input data for the problem instance such as revenues for released parts and probabilities of task failure are generated randomly. The remaining data for the problem instance is provided in Table 1. The task failure rates were generated in the range $(0, 0.1)$ and scc was assumed to be 7, the problem is solved for a cycle time of 30 s.

The optimal sequence and resulting optimal sequences due to failed tasks are given in Fig. 3. The expected profit by the optimal sequence is 1379.61. The optimal sequence comprises of five workstations after stacking. The average execution time for finding the optimal disassembly sequence was recorded to be 198 s over 30 different runs for $m = 20$ and termination condition set as 100 iterations for TLBO.

Table 1. Problem data for automatic pencil example

Part index (j)	1	2	3	4	5	6	7	8	9	10	11
Task releasing part j	22, 28, 29, 30, 34	5, 17, 19, 3	2, 6, 22, 24, 27, 31	10, 15, 20	36	37	37	11, 14	13, 14	12, 13	4, 6, 7, 21, 23, 35
Revenue	580	470	510	46	47	52	40	54	54	43	560

	Failed task	WS 1	WS 2	WS 3	WS 4	WS 5	WS 6	Sequence probability	profit
Optimal XD	None	22	34,6,18	19,15	36,37	11,13	---	0.3329	3398
pdf	22	22,23,26,12,27	30,19	15	36,14,37	---	---	0.0495	2358
	34	22	34,35	29,18,19	15,12	36,37,14	---	0.0481	2919
	6	22	34,6,5	7,9	20,12,14	36,37	---	0.0071	2930
	18	22	34,6,18,17	9	36,37,20,12	14	---	0.0010	3427
	19	22	34,6,18,17	19	---	---	---	0.0832	2688
	15	22	34,6,18,17	19,15	---	---	---	0.0806	3153
	36	22	34,6,18,17	19,15	36	---	---	0.0339	3182
	37	22	34,6,18,17	19,15	36,37	---	---	0.0880	3227
	11	22	34,6,18,17	19,15	36,37	11,12	14	0.0381	3430
	13	22	34,6,18,17	19,15	36,37	11,13	---	0.0097	3359
Workstation stacking probabilities	Iteration 1	1	1	1	0.7861	0.5623	0.0497	Expected profit =1379.61	
	Iteration 2	1	1	1	0.7861	0.6120	---		

Number of workstations needed after stacking=5

Fig. 3. Optimal sequence and corresponding optimal sequences for failed tasks.

This execution time is significantly higher than the time consumed by reactive balancing strategy, but unlike reactive balancing the computation for finding optimal sequence is not performed every time a task fails in real time, instead all the calculations are performed only once and a solution sequence is generated for every scenario (in case of task-failure) without violating cycle time constraint.

5   Conclusion and Future Scope

In this paper, a recursive TLBO solution approach is developed to find a disassembly solution for optimizing expected profit, without violating the cycle time constraint as a reaction to task failure. To prevent the violation of cycle time constraint in event of a task failure, the number of workstations were determined for every sequence and then probability-based stacking of workstations was performed to determine number of workstations needed (which was required for expected profit evaluation). To reduce the time consumption of the recursive TLBO, memoization strategy was adopted and optimal sequences resulting from a failed task of parent sequence were stored and called whenever needed further down the iterative process. The proposed model was illustrated using an example of disassembly of automatic pencil. The result indicates that the proposed algorithm is able to find a near optimal solution within reasonable amount of time (average execution time of 3 min 18 s for thirty runs). As a future research direction, the proposed algorithm can be tested on a wide range of data set under different task failure rates and the effect of proposed solution strategy can be compared with that of a system in which predictive and reactive balancing are done separately. As another possible extension, the proposed solution approach can be tested under different line settings (such as parallel lines) to dampen the effect of uncertainty in quality of incoming product. Further, to reduce the problem complexity, only single task-failure was considered. Thus, for a more comprehensive analysis multiple task-failure setting can be studied.

References

1. Güngör, A., Gupta, S.M.: A solution approach to the disassembly line balancing problem in the presence of task failures. Int. J. Prod. Res. **39**(7), 1427–1467 (2001). https://doi.org/10.1080/00207540110052157
2. Gungor, A., Gupta, S.M.: Issues in environmentally conscious manufacturing and product recovery: a survey. Comput. Ind. Eng. **36**(4), 811–853 (1999). https://doi.org/10.1016/S0360-8352(99)00167-9
3. Das, S.K., Caudill, R.: The design of high volume disassembly lines. In: Demanufacturing of Electronic Equipment for Reuse and Recycling Information Exchange Meeting Archives, pp. 25–26 (1999)
4. Lambert, A.J.D.: Linear programming in disassembly/clustering sequence generation. Comput. Ind. Eng. **36**(4), 723–738 (1999). https://doi.org/10.1016/S0360-8352(99)00162-X
5. Altekin, F.T., Bayındır, Z.P., Gümüşkaya, V.: Remedial actions for disassembly lines with stochastic task times. Comput. Ind. Eng. **99**, 78–96 (2016). https://doi.org/10.1016/j.cie.2016.06.027
6. Bentaha, M.L., Battaïa, O., Dolgui, A., Hu, S.J.: Second order conic approximation for disassembly line design with joint probabilistic constraints. Eur. J. Oper. Res. **247**(3), 957–967 (2015). https://doi.org/10.1016/j.ejor.2015.06.019
7. Gupta, S.M., Lambert, A.J.D.: Disassembly line balancing, 1st edn. In: Environment Conscious Manufacturing. CRC Press (2007). https://doi.org/10.1201/9781420018790
8. Kalayci, C.B., Gupta, S.M.: Ant colony optimization for sequence-dependent disassembly line balancing problem. J. Manuf. Technol. Manag. **24**(3), 413–427 (2013). https://doi.org/10.1108/17410381311318909
9. Kalayci, C.B., Gupta, S.M.: Simulated annealing algorithm for solving sequence-dependent disassembly line balancing problem. IFAC Proc. Vol. **46**(9), 93–98 (2013). https://doi.org/10.3182/20130619-3-RU-3018.00064
10. Seidi, M., Saghari, S.: The balancing of disassembly line of automobile engine using Genetic Algorithm (GA) in fuzzy environment. Ind. Eng. Manag. Syst. **15**(4), 364–373 (2016). https://doi.org/10.7232/iems.2016.15.4.364
11. Zhang, Z., Wang, K., Zhu, L., Wang, Y.: A Pareto improved artificial fish swarm algorithm for solving a multi-objective fuzzy disassembly line balancing problem. Exp. Syst. Appl. **86**, 1339–1351 (2017). https://doi.org/10.1016/j.eswa.2017.05.053
12. Altekin, F.T., Akkan, C.: Task-failure-driven rebalancing of disassembly lines. Int. J. Prod. Res. **50**(18), 4955–4976 (2012). https://doi.org/10.1080/00207543.2011.616915
13. McGovern, S.M., Gupta, S.M.: Disassembly Line: Balancing and Modeling. McGraw-Hill Education (2011)

14. Koc, A., Sabuncuoglu, I., Erel, E.: Two exact formulations for disassembly line balancing problems with task precedence diagram construction using an AND/OR graph. IIE Trans. **41**(10), 866–881 (2009). https://doi.org/10.1080/07408170802510390
15. Rao, R.V., Savsani, V.J., Vakharia, D.P.: Teaching–learning-based optimization: a novel method for constrained mechanical design optimization problems. Comput. Des. **43**(3), 303–315 (2011). https://doi.org/10.1016/j.cad.2010.12.015

Quantity-Flexibility Contract Models for the Supply Chain with Green-Sensitive Demand in the Automotive Manufacturing Industry

Zhe Yuan[1]($\boxtimes$) (iD), Yeming Gong[2] (iD), and Mingyang Chen[3] (iD)

[1] Leonard de Vinci Pôle Universitaire, Research Center,
Paris La Defense 92 916, France
zhe.yuan@devinci.fr
[2] EMLYON Business School, 23 Avenue Guy de Collongue, Écully 09130, France
GONG@em-lyon.fr
[3] Business School, Henan University, Kaifeng 475000, China
mychen@henu.edu.cn

Abstract. This paper considers a quantity-flexibility contract with green-sensitive demand in the automotive industry. The automobile manufacturer determines the green level, and the retailer determines the retail price. The authors apply game theory to build the models, optimize the green level for maximizing the automobile manufacturer's profit, and optimize the retail price for maximizing the retailer's profit. We consider the equilibrium decision between the green level and the retail price to maximize the supply chain's profit. Furthermore, we conduct experiments to verify our analysis results. Interestingly, this study finds that it is optimal for the retailer in the decentralized case to charge a higher price when the green sensitivity increases. However, the optimal price in the centralized case is not necessarily monotonic when the demand is lower. The manufacturer should set a higher green level as the greening investment parameter increases.

Keywords: Sustainable supply chain · Quantity-flexibility contract · Green-sensitive demand · Game theory

1 Introduction

In Paris, the government divides vehicles into six environmental classes. The air quality certificate increases customers' demand for green automobiles, including electric vehicles, natural gas vehicles, or hybrid vehicles. This phenomenon can reflect that more customers prefer buying environmentally-friendly automobiles

---

Y. Gong—Partially supported by Business Intelligence Center (BIC) and AIM Institute of EMLYON.

and are sensitive to green products, which results in many automobile manufacturers and retailers begin to produce and sell green automobiles to meet customers' needs. Meanwhile, retailers require their automobile manufacturers to participate in carbon reduction disclosure projects, primarily from the necessary environmental certifications [10]. Therefore, facing the green-conscious consumer market, retailers cooperate with automobile manufacturers to initiate green product and process changes. This paper is motivated by this evidence and considers an automotive supply chain, including an automobile manufacturer and a retailer with green-sensitive customers' demand, and explores the influences of green-sensitive consumer demand on the supply chain members and the collaboration among them.

The greening improvement of green automobiles implies some attribute modifications, such as the use of electric or hydrogen-powered, and the combination of an internal combustion engine and an electric engine that reduces CO_2 emissions compared with the traditional gasoline or diesel automobiles [3]. After the air quality certificate starts working to raise the green level through green innovation, traditional automobile manufacturers need to invest in new technologies to produce plug-in hybrid automobiles as the green level improves. For example, producing 100% pure electric or hydrogen automobiles requires more managerial and technological investment to improve the green level. The automobile manufacturer may charge a green level and a higher unit cost than the condition where the order quantity is constant over time. The retailer must balance between the purchase, inventory holding, and shortage costs.

Automotive industries commonly use quantity-flexibility contracting as a necessary mechanism because the quantity-flexibility contract is a downstream protection contract, which can share the retailer's risk and increase the order quantities. Furthermore, the quantity-flexibility contract can coordinate the green supply chain of automotive manufacturing [8,9,14]. For example, Toyota Motor Corporation [6] currently uses the quantity-flexibility contract to deal with the variability in its production [12]. Although more practice about quantity-flexibility contracts appears in the automotive industries, few scholars research quantity-flexibility contracts in the green supply chain [4,5,13]. In this work, we propose the research question: How to optimize the green level and the retail price with green-sensitive demand to maximize the profits in the automotive industry?

To answer this question, we model a quantity-flexibility contract with green-sensitive demand between an automobile manufacturer and a retailer in the decentralized and centralized decision-making supply chain. Our work makes several contributions: First, this is one of the earliest researches to study quantity-flexibility contracts considering green-sensitive customers since a few previous studies have considered. Second, we combine quantity-flexibility contracts with green problems in the automobile industry because few types of research consider quantity-flexibility contracts in the automotive industry. Third, we find it optimal for the retailer in the decentralized case to charge a higher price when the green sensitivity increases. However, the optimal price in the centralized case is not necessarily monotonic when the demand is lower.

2   The Model

We consider a practical problem between an automobile manufacturer and a retailer. The production plans of the assembly lines determine the demand for a component. However, the production plans may vary due to green-sensitive customer demand. The automobile manufacturer and retailer establish a quantity-flexibility contract in the green supply chain. Two key parameters of such a contract are nominal quantity Q and variation rate $\beta \in (0,1)$, where $\beta = 0$ represents the inflexibility contract, and we also analyze this contract to validate the model, and Q is the quantity reserved by the retailer [11]. These parameters determine the interval $[Q(1-\beta), Q(1+\beta)]$ that the actual order quantities from the retailer must in [1]. When the order quantities are within this interval, the automobile manufacturer is committed to fulfilling them. The retailer commits herself to purchase, and the allowable range is determined as $[Q(1-\beta), Q(1+\beta)]$. According to Fig. 1, we provide the sequence of events and decisions as follows: First, the automobile manufacturer offers the retailer a quantity-flexibility contract, and the retailer decides whether to accept it or not. Second, the retailer makes a nominal order quantity of green automobiles Q before the period starts if she accepts this contract. Then, she determines the retail price p. Third, the nominal order becomes the basis for the automobile manufacturer to determine his green level, and he needs to decide the green level θ. In automotive manufacturing, retailers intend to release orders as close as possible to the demand because of the limited storage space in the assembly plant and the high holding cost. On the other hand, demand variability prevents them from ordering a constant quantity in every period. The unit purchase cost is a linear or piecewise linear convex function for the quantity-flexibility contract. We give the expression of the automobile manufacturer's unit wholesale price $w(\beta) = c_0 + c_1\beta$, where c_0 represents the minimal possible cost with zero flexibility and c_1 is a fixed rate [2]. We consider that the supply chain players' green-sensitive demand x is a linear function of retail price p and green level θ, where θ is a continuous variable. The demand function is $x = a - bp + \alpha\theta$ [4], where $a > 0$ expresses the potential market size of green automobiles and $b > 0$ denotes the customer sensitiveness to the retail price of green automobiles, and $\alpha > 0$ represents customer's sensitivity to greening improvement level of green automobiles.

Referring to [4], we use an increasing and convex function to represent the cost incurred in improving the green level. The cost of greening is $I\theta^2$, where I indicates the greening investment parameter of green automobiles. For example, after the air quality certificate starts, traditional automobile manufacturers need to invest in new technologies to produce plug-in hybrid automobiles (Crit'Air 1 sticker) to raise the green level through green innovation. As a result, the initial green investment is relatively costly, and then raising the green level might be relatively inexpensive. When the green level improves, more managerial and technological investment is required for further improvement in the green level, making it more expensive to reach the goal of a higher green level comparable with that at the early stage. To avoid trivial cases, let $I > \theta^2 - 4b$. In the view of consumers' sensitivity to greening and price, green innovation requires higher

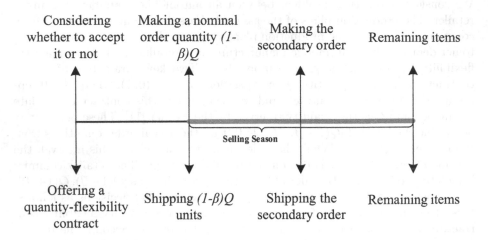

Fig. 1. Sequence of events under a quantity-flexibility contract

investment, consistent with the actual situation of product innovation [4]. The automobile manufacturer bears the cost of greening.

2.1   Decentralized Decision-Making Policy

In the decentralized decision-making supply chain, the automobile manufacturer chooses the product green level θ for his profit maximization using the retailer's response function. Then, the retailer decides the retail price p to maximize her profit given the green level.

If the demand of green-sensitive customers is less than $Q(1 - \beta)$, the retailer buys at the minimum commitment $Q(1 - \beta)$, and thus, the automobile manufacturer sells to the retailer. If the demand of green-sensitive customers is in the interval $[Q(1 - \beta), Q(1 + \beta)]$, the retailer buys green automobiles in quantity to the demand of affected areas. If the demand of green-sensitive customers is greater than $Q(1 + \beta)$, the retailer buys at maximum the automobile manufacturer's commitment level and will have $x - Q(1 + \beta)$ product shortage to satisfy. As $x = a - bp + \alpha\theta$, $b > 0$, and $p > 0$, we can get $x < a + \alpha\theta$. We give the order quantity in Eq. (1) by following the principle of quantity-flexibility contract.

$$
q = \begin{cases}
Q(1 - \beta), & 0 \leq x < Q(1 - \beta), \\
x, & Q(1 - \beta) \leq x \leq Q(1 + \beta), \\
Q(1 + \beta), & Q(1 + \beta) < x < a + \alpha\theta.
\end{cases} \tag{1}
$$

According to Eq. (1), we can get the profit of the automobile manufacturer as follows:

$$\pi_M(\theta) = \begin{cases} wQ(1-\beta) - (h_M + c_f + c_t + c_m + c_l)Q(1+\beta) - I\theta^2, & 0 \le x < Q(1-\beta), \\ wx - (h_M + c_f + c_t + c_m + c_l)Q(1+\beta) - I\theta^2, & Q(1-\beta) \le x \le Q(1+\beta), \\ wQ(1+\beta) - (h_M + c_f + c_t + c_m + c_l)Q(1+\beta) - I\theta^2, & Q(1+\beta) < x < a + \alpha\theta. \end{cases}$$
(2)

The first term of Eq. (2) is derived from demand satisfaction and the second term represents manufacturing and inventory costs for the automobile manufacturer, and the last term specifies the green cost of the automobile manufacturer. Then, the profit function of the retailer is:

$$\pi_R(p) = \begin{cases} px - wQ(1-\beta) - h_R[Q(1-\beta) - x], & 0 \le x < Q(1-\beta), \\ px - wx, & Q(1-\beta) \le x \le Q(1+\beta), \\ pQ(1+\beta) - wQ(1+\beta) - s[x - Q(1+\beta)], & Q(1+\beta) < x < a + \alpha\theta. \end{cases}$$
(3)

Similar to Eq. (2), the first term of the function is derived from demand satisfaction and the second term represents the retailer's purchasing cost, and the last term specifies the retailer's inventory or shortage cost.

First, the retailer determines the optimal retail price, and we can derive the following proposition:

Proposition 1. *If the demand is less than $Q(1-\beta)$, the retailer's profit function is concave with p, and the optimal p^* is $p = \frac{a+\alpha\theta-h_R b}{2b}$. If $Q(1-\beta) \le x \le Q(1+\beta)$, the retailer's profit function is concave with p and the optimal $p^* = \frac{a+\alpha\theta+(c_0+c_1\beta)b}{2b}$. If the demand is more than $Q(1+\beta)$, the retailer's profit is increasing in p and the optimal $p^* = \frac{a+\alpha\theta-Q(1+\beta)}{b}$.*

From Proposition 1, we find that when green-sensitive demand is less than $Q(1-\beta)$, the retailer must purchase $Q(1-\beta)$, which results in holding $Q(1-\beta)-x$ inventory. The profit is affected by the retail price, the green level, and unit inventory holding cost. So, we get the optimal $p^*(\theta) = \frac{a+\alpha\theta-h_R b}{2b}$. When green-sensitive demand is in the interval $[Q(1-\beta), Q(1+\beta)]$, the retailer can purchase automobiles to satisfy all demand without inventory holding cost. The profit is affected by the retail price, the green level, and the automobile manufacturer's wholesale price (the variation rate). So, we get the optimal $p^*(\theta) = \frac{a+\alpha\theta+(c_0+c_1\beta)b}{2b}$. When green-sensitive demand is more than $Q(1+\beta)$, since the maximum order quantity is $Q(1+\beta)$, the retailer's profit is increasing in p. However, the retail price is limited by the green level and the variation rate and the optimal $p^*(\theta) = \frac{a+\alpha\theta-Q(1+\beta)}{b}$.

Then, the retailer decides the retail price in line with Proposition 1. After getting this response, the automobile manufacturer optimizes his own profit and determines the optimal green level, as shown in the following proposition:

Proposition 2. *If the demand of green-sensitive customer $0 \le x < Q(1-\beta)$ or $Q(1+\beta) < x < a + \alpha\theta$, the automobile manufacturer's profit function is decreasing in θ. If the demand is less than $Q(1-\beta)$, the optimal $\theta^* = 0$. If* the demand is more than $Q(1 + \beta)$, the optimal $\theta^* = \frac{Q(1+\beta)-a+bp}{\alpha}$. If $Q(1 - \beta) \le x \le Q(1 + \beta)$, the profit function of the automobile manufacturer with θ is concave. The optimal θ is $\theta^* = \frac{\alpha(c_0+c_1\beta)}{2I}$ and the optimal retail price is $\frac{2Ia+(c_0+c_1\beta)(\alpha^2+2Ib)}{4Ib}$.

From Proposition 2, we know that when green-sensitive demand is less than $Q(1 - \beta)$ or more than $Q(1 + \beta)$, no need appears for the automobile manufacturer to increase the green level. Because when green-sensitive demand is less than $Q(1-\beta)$, customers are less sensitive to green automobiles, which increases that the green level will not attract more customers to purchase green automobiles and eventually leads to lower profits. When green-sensitive demand is more than $Q(1 + \beta)$, customers are more sensitive to green automobiles. However, due to the maximum order quantity is $Q(1 + \beta)$, the increase of the green level will not improve the profit but will increase the green investment cost. When green-sensitive demand is in the interval $[Q(1 - \beta), Q(1 + \beta)]$, the automobile manufacturer's profit will first increase and then decrease as the green level increases, and we get the optimal green level $\theta^* = \frac{\alpha(c_0+c_1\beta)}{2I}$.

2.2 Centralized Decision-Making Policy

In this centralized decision-making policy, we consider the automobile manufacturer and the retailer as a whole to maximize the channel profit by choosing the green level and the retail price. Thus, the profit function of the supply chain is as follows,

$$\pi_{SC}(\theta, p) = \begin{cases} px - (h_M + c_f + c_t + c_m + c_l)Q(1+\beta) - h_R[Q(1-\beta) - x] - I\theta^2, 0 \le x < Q(1-\beta), \\ px - (h_M + c_f + c_t + c_m + c_l)Q(1+\beta) - I\theta^2, Q(1-\beta) \le x \le Q(1+\beta), \\ pQ(1+\beta)-(h_M + c_f + c_t + c_m + c_l)Q(1+\beta)-s[x - Q(1+\beta)]-I\theta^2, Q(1+\beta)<x<a+\alpha\theta. \end{cases}$$

$$(4)$$

In the centralized decision-making supply chain, we solve the supply chain's profit function and get the following proposition:

Proposition 3. *If the demand of greens-sensitive customer is less than $Q(1 - \beta)$, the supply chain's profit function is jointly concave in θ and p, and the optimal $\theta^* = \frac{a\alpha}{4Ib-\alpha^2}$ and $p^* = \frac{2Ia-h_R\alpha^2-2Ih_Rb}{4Ib-\alpha^2}$. If the demand of green-sensitive customer is in $[Q(1 - \beta), Q(1+\beta)]$, the supply chain's profit function is jointly concave in θ and p, and the optimal $\theta^* = \frac{a\alpha}{4Ib-\alpha^2}$ and $p^* = \frac{2Ia}{4Ib-\alpha^2}$.*

From Proposition 3, we find that when green-sensitive demand is less than $Q(1 - \beta)$, customers are less sensitive to green automobiles, the retailer must purchase $Q(1-\beta)$, which results in holding $Q(1-\beta) - x$ inventory. The profit of the supply chain is affected by the retail price, the green level, and unit inventory holding cost. So, we get equilibrium values for the supply chain. The optimal $\theta^* = \frac{a\alpha}{4Ib-\alpha^2}$ and $p^* = \frac{2Ia-h_R\alpha^2-2Ih_Rb}{4Ib-\alpha^2}$. When green-sensitive demand is in the interval $[Q(1 - \beta), Q(1 + \beta)]$, the retailer can purchase automobiles to satisfy all demand without inventory holding cost. The profit is affected by the retail price, the green level, and the automobile manufacturer's wholesale price (the variation rate). The optimal $\theta^* = \frac{a\alpha}{4Ib-\alpha^2}$ and $p^* = \frac{2Ia}{4Ib-\alpha^2}$. When green-sensitive demand is more than $Q(1+\beta)$, the supply chain's profit function is decreasing in θ and increasing in p, and equilibrium values do not exist.

2.3 Equilibrium Analysis

In this subsection, we analyze the equilibrium strategies derived by Propositions 2 and 3, and find the condition that the optimal solutions can sustain. The primary purpose is to solve the coordination problem of the members in the supply chain. First, we can obtain the condition that the equilibrium strategies exist according to the demand function because the quantity in the centralized case must be not less than that in the decentralized case based on the principle of the members' coordination. Since the optimal quantity in the range of $Q(1-\beta) \le x < Q(1+\beta)$ under the decentralized decision-making policy is $q^* = \frac{2abI}{4bI-\alpha^2}$. By comparing the optimal quantities in the decentralized case and that in the centralized case, we can obtain the following proposition:

Proposition 4. When $c_0 + c_1\beta \ge \frac{2a\alpha^2 I}{-\alpha^4 - 8b^2 I^2 + 6\alpha^2 bI}$, the supply chain coordination can be sustained in the range of $x \in [Q(1-\beta), Q(1+\beta)]$, otherwise, the optimal solutions may not exist.

Then, we analyze the equilibrium strategies in the decentralized case. By computing these equilibrium solutions in Proposition 2, we can examine the impact of α, c, and I on the performance measures associated with different members and obtain the following proposition:

Proposition 5. As α or β increases, the optimal price p^* or the optimal green level θ^* also increases, i.e., $\frac{dp^*}{d\alpha} \ge 0$ and $\frac{dp^*}{d\beta} \ge 0$. Moreover, when c_0 or c_1 increases, the optimal green level θ^* increases, i.e., $\frac{d\theta^*}{dc_0} \ge 0$ and $\frac{d\theta^*}{dc_1} \ge 0$. When I increases, the optimal green level θ^* decreases, i.e., $\frac{d\theta^*}{dI} \le 0$.

For $\frac{dp^*}{d\alpha} \ge 0$ in Proposition 5, we find that both p^* and θ^* are increasing in α. The reason is that consumers are more sensitive to the green level in the automobile manufacturer with the increases of α, which indicates that they are willing to pay more for a higher greening improvement level and the manufacturer can set a higher price. For $\frac{d\theta^*}{dc_0} \ge 0$ and $\frac{d\theta^*}{dc_1} \ge 0$, we can explain them as follows: The optimal green level θ^* will be affected by the minimal possible cost with zero flexibility and the minimal possible cost with the fixed rate because the wholesale price includes them. Thus, the increased wholesale price means more investment and efforts for green automobiles, which improves the green level. The reason for $\frac{dp^*}{d\beta} \ge 0$ is similar to some explanations for $\frac{d\theta^*}{dc_0} \ge 0$ and $\frac{d\theta^*}{dc_1} \ge 0$ because the wholesale price is also increasing in β. Interestingly, from Proposition 5, we can find that $\frac{d\theta^*}{dI} \le 0$ represents that the manufacturer who has a lower marginal cost for any given quality in the quantity-flexibility contract is an inefficient firm [7].

Now, we turn to the equilibrium solutions in the centralized case. We can establish the following monotonicity results for the centralized decision-making policy after computing the optimal solutions in Proposition 3:

Proposition 6. *Under the centralized case, the optimal solutions exhibit the following characteristics:*

(i) *If the demand is less than $Q(1 - \beta)$, the optimal price p^* is nonmonotonic in α or b, i.e., $\frac{dp^*}{d\alpha} \leq 0$ when $a \in (0, 3bh_R)$ and $\frac{dp^*}{d\alpha} \geq 0$ when $a \geq 3bh_R$; $\frac{dp^*}{db} \leq 0$ when $a \geq \frac{3\alpha^2 h_R}{4I}$ and $\frac{dp^*}{db} \geq 0$ when $a \in (0, \frac{3\alpha^2 h_R}{4I})$. As I increases, the optimal green level θ^* decreases, i.e., $\frac{d\theta^*}{dI} \leq 0$.*

(ii) *Unlike $x < Q(1 - \beta)$, the optimal price p^* is increasing in α and decreasing in b if the demand is in the range of $[Q(1 - \beta), Q(1 + \beta)]$, i.e., $\frac{dp^*}{d\alpha} \geq 0$ and $\frac{dp^*}{db} \leq 0$.*

From Proposition 6(i), we can find that the optimal price p^* could first decrease and then increase in α given $a > 0$. This is because when the market potential is smaller, fewer consumers are concerned about EVs, which causes the retailer to lower the price to attract customers to buy. When the market potential is larger, more consumers are starting to pay attention to greenness. Thus, the retailer can raise the price to obtain more profits. The same explanation also applies to $\frac{dp^*}{db}$ and we also find that the optimal price p^* first increases and then decreases in b. The reason is that when the retailer is indifferent about the price-sensitivity of consumer when the market potential is smaller. When the market potential is larger, the retailer may lower the price because customers' higher price sensitivity means the higher demand reduction. Interestingly, Proposition 6 (ii) tells us that if $x \in [Q(1 - \beta), Q(1 + \beta)]$, the monotonicity of parameters α and b is different from that in $x < Q(1 - \beta)$. An important reason is that as the retailer's order quantity increases, the demand in the market also increases, which influences the market potential that is larger than $3bh_R$ or $\frac{3\alpha^2 h_R}{4I}$. So, the monotonicity of α and b has changed.

3   Concluding Remarks

This paper studies a quantity-flexibility contract between a manufacturer and a retailer with green-sensitive demand in the automotive industry. In a decentralized supply chain, we use game theory to solve the problem. The automobile manufacturer acts as the Stackelberg leader to set the green level, and the retailer acts as the follower to set the retail price. We determine the optimal green level to maximize the automobile manufacturer's profit and the retail price to maximize the retailer's profit. Under centralized decision-making, we consider the equilibrium decision between the automobile manufacturer and the retailer. We use the game theory to analyze the model to maximize the supply chain's profit. We analyze the equilibrium strategies and find the condition that the optimal solutions can sustain. This paper is one of the first researches to study quantity-flexibility contract considering green-sensitive customers. We propose a novel collaboration model in quantity-flexibility contract considering green issues. It is optimal for the retailer in the decentralized case to charge a higher price when green-sensitivity increases; however, the optimal price in the centralized case is not necessarily monotonic when the market potential is low. Interestingly, we also find that the supply chain with the quantity-flexibility contract does not always generate more profits than its inflexibility counterpart; it mainly depends on the retail price and greenness improvement level. Our results can be applied to maximize the profits on both upstream and downstream partners with quantity-flexibility contracts in the green supply chain.

References

1. Barnes-Schuster, D., Bassok, Y., Anupindi, R.: Coordination and flexibility in supply contracts with options. Manuf. Serv. Oper. Manage. **4**(3), 171–207 (2002)
2. Chu, C., Longomo, E.E., Song, X., Ouelhaj, D.: Flexibility analysis on a supply chain contract using a parametric linear programming model. In: 2014 IEEE International Conference on Automation Science and Engineering (CASE), pp. 704–709. IEEE (2014)
3. Emadi, A., Williamson, S.: Fuel cell vehicles: opportunities and challenges. In: 2004 IEEE Power Engineering Society General Meeting, pp. 1640–1645. IEEE (2004)
4. Ghosh, D., Shah, J.: Supply chain analysis under green sensitive consumer demand and cost sharing contract. Int. J. Prod. Econ. **164**, 319–329 (2015)
5. Giri, B., Mondal, C., Maiti, T.: Analysing a closed-loop supply chain with selling price, warranty period and green sensitive consumer demand under revenue sharing contract. J. Clean. Prod. **190**, 822–837 (2018)
6. Höhn, M.I.: Relational Supply Contracts: Optimal Concessions in Return Policies for Continuous Quality Improvements, vol. 629. Springer, Heidelberg (2009). https://doi.org/10.1007/978-3-642-02791-8
7. Jiang, B., Yang, B.: Quality and pricing decisions in a market with consumer information sharing. Manage. Sci. **65**(1), 272–285 (2018)
8. Kim, W.S.: Order quantity flexibility as a form of customer service in a supply chain contract model. Flex. Serv. Manuf. J. **23**(3), 290–315 (2011)
9. Knoblich, K., Ehm, H., Heavey, C., Williams, P.: Modeling supply contracts in semiconductor supply chains. In: Proceedings of the 2011 Winter Simulation Conference (WSC), pp. 2108–2118. IEEE (2011)
10. Lee, S.Y.: Corporate carbon strategies in responding to climate change. Bus. Strateg. Environ. **21**(1), 33–48 (2012)
11. Li, J., Luo, X., Wang, Q., Zhou, W.: Supply chain coordination through capacity reservation contract and quantity flexibility contract. Omega **99**, 102195 (2021)
12. Niemann, J., Seisenberger, S., Schlegel, A., Putz, M.: Development of a method to increase flexibility and changeability of supply contracts in the automotive industry. Procedia CIRP **81**, 258–263 (2019)
13. Song, H., Gao, X.: Green supply chain game model and analysis under revenue-sharing contract. J. Clean. Prod. **170**, 183–192 (2018)
14. Tsay, A.A., Lovejoy, W.S.: Quantity flexibility contracts and supply chain performance. Manuf. Serv. Oper. Manage. **1**(2), 89–111 (1999)

How Much Green Investments Are Efficient for a Smart Production System?

Rekha Guchhait[1], Mitali Sarkar[2], and Biswajit Sarkar[1]([envelope])

[1] Department of Industrial Engineering, Yonsei University, 50 Yonsei-ro,
Sinchon-dong, Seodaemun-gu, Seoul 03722, South Korea
[2] Information Technology Research Center, Chung-Ang University,
Seoul 06974, South Korea

Abstract. The increasing global warming effect on the environment is massive nowadays and the production industry is trying to reduce carbon emission to the minimum level. This study investigates the effect of green investment in a smart production system under the effect of energy. The effect of the green movement is depicted on the customer satisfaction level. The machine produces imperfect products at a random time and gets reworked within the same cycle. The system failure rate relates the imperfect production with reliability. The mathematical model is solved by the classical optimization procedure and found the global optimum solution. Managerial insights are provided to show the applicability of the model. Results find that the carbon reduction due to the green investment and customer satisfaction holds a wide margin of the profit.

Keywords: Smart production · Green investment · Customer satisfaction · System reliability · Imperfect production

1 Introduction

The changing relation of the production industry with the environment is the concern of this study. The carbon emission and energy consumption are obvious for a production-inventory system. The issue is the increasing rate of the average temperature of the earth, one of the main reasons is carbon emission. The carbon emission from the energy consumption of the system is high due to the use of fossil fuels as a resource. The failure rate within a production-inventory model is related to the working hours and the capacity of the machine. The fact is the prediction of the breakdown period is impossible and the consideration of the random time is more realistic than a fixed time interval. Then, it is common to produce imperfect during the breakdown period.

This research was supported by the Yonsei University Research Fund of 2020 (Project Number 2020-22-0509).

A. Dolgui et al. (Eds.): APMS 2021, IFIP AICT 632, pp. 450–459, 2021.
https://doi.org/10.1007/978-3-030-85906-0_50

There are several studies discussing the machine breakdown and its consequences. A random defective rate of production was investigated by Sana [15]. The warranty policy is one of the business strategies for imperfect products. The rework process for the imperfect products was discussed by Kang et al. [10]. Now, the quality improvement for the products was considered by Guchhait et al. [7]. They discussed the setup cost reduction and warranty policy. Iqbal et al. [9] discussed the preservation technology for deteriorating products. Sarkar et al. [13, 14] discussed a variable production model. Gong et al. [6] studied a green production system with the workers' flexibility. The system was energy-efficient and an evolutionary algorithm was used to solve the mathematical problem. These studies are about the traditional imperfect production system with no effect on energy.

There are very few studies that admit the energy consumption issue of the production quantity model or the supply chain model. Sun et al. [16] discussed the electricity demand reduction between the energy-saving things and the production loss. They tried to find out the inventory control policy with reduced electricity demand. But, Bhuniya et al. [3] studied the energy utilization within the traditional production-inventory model for variable market demand. Toptal et al. [17] discussed the emission reduction by another investment under emission regulations. The integrated inventory management is now turned towards the greening (Raza et al. [11]) process and other traditional enforcements. The carbon emission scenario for the defective production system was studied by Sangal et al. [12]. Thus, the economic perspective of an industry is changed now (Adhikari and Bisi [1]) based on green involvement in terms of collaboration and bargaining. Dong et al. [5] illustrated some strategic investments for green development.

The above discussions give ideas on how demand varies with the greening factor and emission from the production system. This study finds out the economic benefits of greening technology. Meanwhile, the greening process has some effect on customers. The following questions are addressed here: (i) The industry tries to reduce the emission from the system due to the energy consumption. How customer will react to this initiative of the industry? (ii) What will be the customer satisfaction level? (iii) How does the industry make a profit by carbon reduction strategy? The rest of the study is decorated as Sect. 2 provides the problem definition and mathematical model. Section 3 gives the theoretical and numerical results. Discussion about the sensitivity analysis and the managerial insights are described in Sect. 4. Section 5 gives the conclusions about the study.

2 Methods

This section gives the problem definition and detail of the study.

2.1 Problem Definition

Green investment and customer satisfaction are discussed within an imperfect production system. The imperfect production system encounters the failure rate of the system which is proportional to the system reliability. Multiple products are produced from the system and the system goes to the *out-of-control* state at a random time ν_i, i stands for the multiple products. The production system is complex in nature as the reworking process occurs within the same cycle. The imperfect products are found by an error-free automated inspection process and sent for reworking. The perfect products are sent to the market directly and imperfect products are sent to the market after reworking. Each stage of the production consumes energy and emits carbon dioxide. Thus, all the costs related to the production system are under the effect of energy. The defective rate is random as it depends upon the random ν_i.

2.2   Mathematical Modelling

A mathematical model for a production-inventory system is derived here for multiple types of products that are the single production system produces n types of different products. The production system goes to the *out-of-control* state at a random time ν_i and starts to produce imperfect products. The production rate is $P_i(P_i > \Delta_i)$ and the lot size is q_i at time t_i. Therefore, $t_i = \frac{q_i}{P_i}$. For no system failure, the production continues up to the time $\frac{q_i}{P_i}$. Here, one failure occurs during the time duration of $\frac{q_i}{P_i}$ and the inventory accumulates at a rate $P_i - \Delta_i$. The breakdown starts a point M and the reworking process starts at a time t_{1i}. After t_{1i}, the inventory deploy rate is Δ_i. The governing differential equations of the inventory are

$$\frac{dI_i^1(t_i)}{dt_i} = P_i - \Delta_i, 0 \le t_i \le t_{1i} \text{ with the initial condition } I_i^1(0) = 0, \text{ and}$$

$$\frac{dI_i^2(t_i)}{dt_i} = -\Delta_i, \ t_{1i} < t_i \le \text{ with the boundary condition } I_i^2(T) = 0.$$

The on-hand inventory at the time t_i is

$$I_i^1(t_i) = (P_i - \Delta_i) t_i, 0 \le t_i \le t_{1i}, \text{ and } I_i^2(t_i) = \Delta_i (T - t_i), t_{1i} < t_i \le T.$$

The relation between T and t_{1i} is $t_{1i} = \frac{\Delta_i T}{P_i}$.

The demand is variable and dependent upon the price and customer satisfaction. Then, the demand of the product i is $\Delta_i = \frac{p_{max} - p_i}{p_i - p_{min}} + \eta y_i^\mu$, where y_i is the customer satisfaction, p_i is the unit selling price of the product i, p_{max} is the maximum selling price of the product i, and p_{min} is the minimum selling price of the product i, i.e., $p_i \in [p_{min}, p_{max}]$. Then, the revenue is $p_i \Delta_i = p_i \left(\frac{p_{max} - p_i}{p_i - p_{min}} + \eta y_i^\mu \right)$. The carbon reduction function for green investment (GI_c) is $GI_c = \alpha \phi_i - \beta \phi_i^2$. ϕ_i is the investment for the greening of the environment for product i. The investment $\alpha \phi_i$ is used for carbon emission reduction. $\beta \phi_i^2$ is used for the carbon emission due to consumed energy within the system. GI_c is an increasing quadratic function. If e is the unit carbon emission cost, then the savings from the carbon emission reduction is $e \left(\alpha \phi_i - \beta \phi_i^2 \right)$. If the investment for the customer satisfaction for the product i is x for satisfaction y_i, then the investment function for the customer satisfaction for all products is $\sum_{i=1}^n \frac{x y_i^2}{2}$.

The carbon emission from the production system is one of the causes of the global warming issue. All the cost components are therefore bared a carbon emission cost under the effect of energy. If the unit setup cost for the product i is S_i^c, unit energy consumption cost is S_i^e, and the unit carbon emission cost for the system is e, then the setup cost of all product for each cycle is $\sum_{i=1}^{n} (S_i^c + S_i^e + e) \frac{\Delta_i}{q_i}$. All products are going through the automated inspection process which ensures the error-free result that is inspection error is negligible. The imperfect products are sent for the reworking. The production cost $S(\tau, P_i)$ is dependent upon the system reliability, production rate, and the development cost $A(\tau)$, where the development cost is system reliability dependent. The system reliability parameter τ is defined as $\tau = \frac{\text{number of failure}}{\text{total number of working hours}}$. τ has its upper and lower limit as τ_{max} is the maximum value and τ_{min} is the minimum value of the τ. The development cost $A_i(\tau)$ of the system is $A_i(\tau) = (L^c + L^e) + B_i e^{u \frac{\tau_{max} - \tau}{\tau - \tau_{min}}}$, where L^c and L^e are the fixed costs for labor and energy, u is the parameter for the difficulties of the reliability, and B_i is the resource cost for the corresponding product i. $A_i(\tau)$ is inversely proportional to the system reliability τ i.e., the development cost is maximum when $\tau = \tau_{min}$ and is minimum when $\tau = \tau_{max}$. The minimum development cost is $(L^c + L^e) + B_i$. The unit production cost is $S(\tau, P_i) = (M_i + e) + \frac{A_i(\tau)}{P_i} + \zeta P_i^\omega$, where M_i is the per unit material cost of product i, $A_i(\tau)$ is the development cost, ζ is the tool/die variation constant, and P_i is the production rate. From the second term, it is found that the production cost is proportional to the development cost and the distribution cost is distributed over the production at time t_i. The third term represents the tool/die cost of the production system. The production cost for all products per cycle is $\sum_{i=1}^{n} \left[(M_i + e) + \frac{A_i(\tau)}{P_i} + \zeta P_i^\omega \right] \Delta_i$.

The average inventory within the interval $[0, T]$ is

$$\sum_{i=1}^{n} \frac{\int_0^{t_{i1}} I_i^1(t_i) dt_i + \int_{t_{i1}}^{T} I_i^2(t_i) dt_i}{T}.$$

If the unit holding cost per unit time is H_i^c for product i and the energy cost is H_i^e, then the total holding cost of all products is given by $\sum_{i=1}^{n} \frac{(H_i^c + H_i^e + e) q_i}{2} \left(1 - \frac{\Delta_i}{P_i}\right)$. The machine produces imperfect products at a random time ν_i. If the unit inspection cost for the product i is C_i^c and the energy cost is C_i^e, then the total inspection cost is $\sum_{i=1}^{n} (C_i^c + C_i^e + e) \Delta_i$. After inspection, imperfect products are sent to the reworking process to make those as perfect. The duration of the imperfect production is $[\nu_i, t_{1i}]$ for the product i. After detecting the imperfect products, the reworking process starts immediately and continued until the time t_{1i}. t_{1i} is the maximum time of the production as well as reworking. After t_{1i}, the system goes through corrective maintenance until the time T and the maintenance is completed during the time $\frac{(P_i - \Delta_i) q_i}{P_i \Delta_i}$. As there is no imperfect production during $[0, \nu_i]$, therefore the total imperfect inventory IN_i of product i is $\left(\frac{\theta}{\xi+1}\right) P_i^{\lambda+1} (t_{1i} - \nu_i)^{\xi+1}$. Now, the random time ν_i has a random variable X_i which follows the exponential distribution i.e., $X_i \sim Exp(\tau)$. As the reworking process occurs within the same cycle, the time for the reworking is $[0, t_{1i}]$. Thus, the total number of imperfect products for reworking is

$$\sum_{i=1}^{n} INT_i(\tau, q_i, P_i) = \sum_{i=1}^{n} \left(\frac{\tau\theta}{\xi+1}\right) P_i^{\lambda+1} e^{\frac{-\tau q_i}{P_i}} \Psi_i(\tau, q_i, P_i), t_{1i} = \frac{q_i}{P_i}, \text{where}$$

$$\Psi_i(\tau, q_i, P_i) = \sum_{j=1}^{\infty} \frac{\tau^{j-1} t_{1i}^{\xi+j+1}}{(j-1)!(\xi+j+1)}.$$

If the unit reworking cost is R_i^c for the product i and the energy cost is R_i^e, then the total reworking cost of all products is $\sum_{i=1}^{n} \frac{(R_i^c + R_i^e + e)\Delta_i INT_i(\tau, q_i, P_i)}{q_i}$.

There the total profit of the system is given by subtracting all costs from the revenue, i.e.,

$$ETP(P_i, p_i, q_i, y_i, \tau, \phi_i) = \sum_{i=1}^{n} \Delta_i [p_i - S(\tau, P_i)] + e\left(\alpha\phi_i - \beta\phi_i^2\right) - \phi_i - \frac{xy_i^2}{2}$$

$$- \frac{(S_i^c + S_i^e + e)}{q_i}\Delta_i - \frac{(H_i^c + H_i^e + e)q_i}{2}\left(1 - \frac{\Delta_i}{P_i}\right) - (C_i^c + C_i^e + e)\Delta_i$$

$$- \frac{(R_i^c + R_i^e + e)\Delta_i INT_i(\tau, q_i, P_i)}{q_i}.$$

3   Results

This section provides the theoretical and numerical results of the objective function which is a profit function.

3.1   Solution Methodology

The objective function is a complex non-linear function that is solved by the classical optimization technique. The optimum values are in quasi-closed form. The values are

$$q_i^* = \frac{A_i}{Y_i}, P^* = \left(\frac{Z_i}{\omega\zeta}\right)^{\omega-1}, p_i^* = p_{min} + \sqrt{\frac{E_i}{\Delta_i}}, y_i^* = \left(\frac{x}{\eta\mu F_i}\right)^{\frac{1}{\mu-2}},$$

$$\tau^* = \tau_{min} + \sqrt{\frac{H_i}{J_i}}, \phi_i^* = \frac{e\alpha - 1}{2\beta e}.$$

[See Appendix for the value of $A_i, Y_i, E_i, F_i, H_i,$ and J_i]. * stands for the optimal value.

Lemma 1. *The selling price p_i^* of the product i exits if $\frac{E_i}{\Delta_i} \geq 0$. τ^* gives the value of the system reliability if $\frac{H_i}{J_i} > 0$ and $J_i \neq 0$.*

Proposition 1. *The total profit ETP at $P_i^*, p_i^*, q_i^*, y_i^*, \tau^*,$ and ϕ_i^* will be optimum if all the principal minors of the Hessian matrix of order 7×7 are alternative in sign.*

3.2   Numerical Experiment

This section provides the numerical study and its results. Table 1 provides the corresponding values of the parameters.

Table 1. Values of parameters.

Parameters	Values	Parameters	Values	Parameters	Values
p_{max}, p_{min}	$2,000, $300 (/unit)	n, λ	2, 0.8	R_1^e, R_2^e	$0.2, $0.2 (/unit)
x	$1,000,	η, μ	10, 0.185	R_1^c, R_2^c	$9.7, $14.7 (/unit)
S_1^c, S_2^c	$599.9, $499.9 (/setup)	α, β	18, 0.13	H_1^c, H_2^c	$1.9, $2.95 (/unit/unit time)
S_1^e, S_2^e	$0.2, $0.2 (/setup)	u	0.06	M_1, M_2	$99.8, $101.8 (/unit)
L^c, L^e	$199.8, $0.2	ζ, ω	0.2, 0.7	τ_{max}, τ_{min}	0.9, 0.1
B_1, B_2	$30, $32 (/unit)	θ, ξ	0.05, 3	C_1^c, C_2^c	$0.9, $1.5 (/unit)
e	$0.1	C_1^e, C_2^e	$0.2, $0.2 (/unit)	H_1^e, H_2^e	$0.2, $0.2 (/unit/unit time)

The optimum values of the decision variable and the total profit are given in Table 2. The total profit of the system is $12,476.1 per cycle. Two types of products are considered for the testing of the mathematical model.

Table 2. Optimum values of decision variables.

Decision variables	Values	Decision variables	Values	Decision variables	Values
p_1^*, p_2^*	$493.81, $492.35 (/unit)	q_1^*, q_2^*	100.38, 76.13 units/year	P_1^*, P_2^*	229.94, 201.51 units/year
y_1^*, y_2^*	0.83, 0.82	τ^*	0.47	ϕ_1^*, ϕ_2^*	$30.77, $30.77

4   Discussion

The revenue from the carbon reduction facility for green technology GI_c is $86.1. If only the investment exists in the system as general investment and there could not a specific carbon reduction strategy based on the green investment ϕ_i, then the profit of the system could be less than the present profit by $86.1 i.e., $12,390. This means not only the investment is important but also the execution in a proper way is important. This profit is made by the general carbon emission reduction and carbon emission reduction from the energy sources, as it is considered that the entire production-inventory system is measured under the energy effect.

4.1   No Investment for Customer Satisfaction

If the system only consists of the green investment and the reduction of carbon and carbon from energy consumption, there is no customer satisfaction, then $\eta = 0$ and $\gamma = 0$. Then the total profit is $ETP_1 = $23.84, which is 99.8% less than the original profit ETP of the system. That is the system survives anyhow and capable to pretend the loss. That is, without this investment, the production system able to maintain the revenue of the system instead of the profit.

4.2 Managerial Insights

The major benefit of this research to the industry is that the green investment for the carbon emission will save the carbon emission cost and add more revenue to the system. This serves two advantages at a time: reduction of the carbon from the system which is an environmental benefit and revenue generation which is an economical benefit. Thus, it establishes beneficial for the industry. The greening process of the industry faces several burdens and one of the reasons is customer feedback. The product which is launched by the industry should be acceptable by the customers. Thus, customer satisfaction feedback is important for the industry manager. From the special case of the discussion, it is found that if the industry manager wants to discard the customer satisfaction investment, then the profit of the system is significantly low. As the random breakdown time exists within the system, the industry manager needs to take precautions about the delivery time and the quantity.

Table 3. Sensitivity of cost parameters.

Decision variables	Changes (%)	Changes in ETP	Decision variables	Changes (%)	Changes in ETP
x	+50	−2.19	L^c	+50	−0.11
	+25	−1.21		+25	−0.06
	−25	+1.59		−25	+0.07
	−50	+3.90		−50	N.A.
H_1^c	+50	−0.48	R_1^c	+50	−0.002
	+25	−0.41		+25	−0.001
	−25	−0.26		−25	+0.001
	−50	−0.18		−50	+0.003
S_1^c	+50	−0.38	B_1^c	+50	−0.009
	+25	−0.20		+25	−0.005
	−25	+0.22		−25	+0.005
	−50	+0.49		−50	+0.010

4.3 Sensitivity Analysis

From the sensitivity analysis of key parameters, it has been found that the investment for customer satisfaction is the most sensitive parameter for the total profit of the system (Table 3). Whenever the system cost reduces due to reduction of the investment by 50%, total profit increases 3.90%. The negative percentage changes are less than the positive changes. Setup cost, labor cost, reworking cost, and resource cost have a similar pattern that the profit increases whenever the cost decreases. Changing of holding cost during −50% to +50% changes never gives more profit than the global optimum profit. If the holding cost decreases 51% or more than that, the total profit increases 0.44% or more.

5 Conclusions

An imperfect production system with random breakdown was discussed under the effect of energy and greening effect. Green investment and carbon emission reduction were explained in detail. The improvement of environmental health took equal priority as the economic benefit. Results found that the investment cost for the emission reduction from both the system and energy is beneficial for the system as it could save the emission cost and ultimately increased the profit of the system. The development cost, as well as the production cost, could be readjusted and the production rate also, based on the value of the reliability parameter. The mathematical model can be extended by assuming all reworked products are brand new and thus, the secondary market concept and warehouse are possible ways. Another possible extension is to use a different cycle for the reworking of defective products. The recycling of used products is very phenomenal to the recent time of era which can be introduced within the production system.

Appendix

$$A_i = q_i^2 \frac{(H_i^c + H_i^e + e)}{2} \left(1 - \frac{\Delta_i}{P_i}\right) + (R_i^c + R_i^e + e) P_i^{\lambda+1} \frac{\tau\theta}{\xi+1}$$

$$\sum_{j=1}^{\infty} \frac{\tau^{j-1}(\xi+j+1)q_i^{\xi+j+1}}{(j-1)!(\xi+j+1)P_i^{j+\xi+1}} - \{(S_i^c + S_i^e + e) + (R_i^c + R_i^e + e)$$

$$INT_i(\tau, q_i, P_i)\} \Delta_i$$

$$Y_i = (R_i^c + R_i^e + e) P_i^{\lambda+1} \frac{\tau\theta\tau}{(\xi+1)P_i} e^{\frac{-\tau q_i}{P_i}} \Psi_i(\tau, q_i, P_i)$$

$$Z_i = A_i(\tau) - \frac{H_i^c + H_i^e + e}{2} + \frac{R_i^c + R_i^e + e}{q_i} \frac{\tau\theta}{\xi+1} \left[e^{\frac{-\tau q_i}{P_i}} P_i^{\lambda+2} \Psi_i(\tau, q_i, P_i)\right.$$

$$+\Psi_i(\tau, q_i, P_i) P_i^{\lambda+1} \tau q_i e^{\frac{-\tau q_i}{P_i}} + e^{\frac{-\tau q_i}{P_i}} P_i^{\lambda+3}$$

$$\left. + \sum_{j=1}^{\infty} \frac{\tau^{j-1}(\xi+j+1)q_i^{\xi+j+1}}{(j-1)!(-1)(\xi+j+1)P_i^{\xi+j+2}}\right]$$

$$E_i = (p_{max} - p_{min}) \left[p_i - S_i(\tau, P_i) - \frac{S_i^c + S_i^e + e}{q_i} + \frac{(H_i^c + H_i^e + e) q_i}{2P_i}\right.$$

$$\left. - (C_i^c + C_i^e + e) - \frac{R_i^c + R_i^e + e}{q_i} P_i^{\lambda+1} \frac{\tau\theta}{\xi+1} e^{\frac{-\tau q_i}{P_i}} \Psi_i(\tau, q_i, P_i)\right]$$

$$F_i = p_i - S_i(\tau, P_i) - \frac{S_i^c + S_i^e + e}{q_i} + \frac{(H_i^c + H_i^e + e)\,q_i}{2P_i} - (C_i^c + C_i^e + e)$$

$$- \frac{R_i^c + R_i^e + e}{q_i} P_i^{\lambda+1} e^{\frac{-\tau q_i}{P_i}} \frac{\tau\theta}{\xi+1} \Psi_i(\tau, q_i, P_i)$$

$$H_i = \frac{uB_i}{P_i} (\tau_{max} - \tau_{min}) e^{u\frac{\tau_{max}-\tau}{\tau - \tau_{min}}}$$

$$J_i = \frac{R_i^c + R_i^e + e}{q_i} P_i^{\lambda+1} \left[e^{\frac{-\tau q_i}{P_i}} \frac{\theta}{\xi+1} \Psi_i(\tau, q_i, P_i) - \frac{\theta \tau q_i}{(\xi+1)P_i} e^{\frac{-\tau q_i}{P_i}} \Psi_i(\tau, q_i, P_i) \right.$$

$$\left. + e^{\frac{-\tau q_i}{P_i}} \Psi_i(\tau, q_i, P_i) \sum_{j=1}^{\infty} \frac{\left(\frac{q_i}{P_i}\right)^{j+\xi+1} (j-1)\tau^{j-2}}{(j-1)!(\xi+j+1)} \right].$$

References

1. Adhikari, A., Bisi, A.: Collaboration, bargaining, and fairness concern for a green apparel supply chain: an emerging economy perspective. Transp. Res. Part E Logistics Transp. Rev. **135**, 101863 (2020)
2. Bohlayer, M., Fleschutz, M., Braun, M., Zöttl, G.: Energy-intense production-inventory planning with participation in sequential energy market. Appl. Energy **258**, 113954 (2020)
3. Bhuniya, S., Sarkar, B., Pareek, S.: Multi-product production system with the reduced failure rate and the optimum energy consumption under variable demand. Mathematics **7**(5), 465 (2019)
4. Cárdenas-Barrón, L.E.: Optimal manufacturing batch size with rework in a single-stage production system-a simple derivation. Comput. Ind. Eng. **55**(4), 758–765 (2018)
5. Dong, C., Liu, Q., Shen, B.: To be or not to be green? Strategic investment for green product development in a supply chain. Transp. Res. Part E Logistics Transp. Rev. **131**, 193–227 (2019)
6. Gong, G., et al.: Energy-efficient flexible flow shop scheduling with worker flexibility. Expert Syst. Appl. **141**, 112902 (2020)
7. Guchhait, R., et al.: Investment for process quality improvement and setup cost reduction in an imperfect production process with warranty policy and shortages. RAIRO-Oper. Res. **54**(1), 251–266 (2020)
8. Huang, Y., Fang, C., Lin, Y.: Inventory management in supply chains with consideration of logistics, green investment and different carbon emissions policies. Comput. Ind. Eng. **139**, 106207 (2020)
9. Iqbal, M.W., Sarkar, B., Sarkar, M., Guchhait, R., Sardar, S.K.: Supply chain model for deteriorating products with advanced preservation policy. In: 2nd IEOM European Conference, Proceedings of the International Conference on Industrial Engineering and Operations Management, Paris, France (2018)
10. Kang, C.W., Ullah, M., Sarkar, M., Omair, M., Sarkar, B.: A single-stage manufacturing model with imperfect items, inspections, rework, and planned backorders. Mathematics **7**(5), 446 (2019)
11. Raza, S.A., Rathinam, S., Turiac, M., Kerbache, L.: An integrated revenue management framework for a firm's greening, pricing and inventory decisions. Int. J. Prod. Econ. **195**, 373–390 (2018)

12. Sangal, I., Shaw, B.K., Sarkar, B., Guchhait, R.: A joint inventory model with reliability, carbon emission, and inspection errors in a defective production system. Yugoslav J. Oper. Res. **30**(3), 381–398 (2020)
13. Sarkar, M., Do Chung, B.: Controllable production rate and quality improvement in a two-echelon supply chain model. In: Moon, I., Lee, G.M., Park, J., Kiritsis, D., von Cieminski, G. (eds.) APMS 2018. IAICT, vol. 535, pp. 238–245. Springer, Cham (2018). https://doi.org/10.1007/978-3-319-99704-9_29
14. Sarkar, M., Guchhait, R., Sarkar, B.: Modelling for service solution of a closed-loop supply chain with the presence of third party logistics. In: Moon, I., Lee, G.M., Park, J., Kiritsis, D., von Cieminski, G. (eds.) APMS 2018. IAICT, vol. 535, pp. 320–327. Springer, Cham (2018). https://doi.org/10.1007/978-3-319-99704-9_39
15. Sana, S.: A production-inventory model in an imperfect production process. Eur. J. Oper. Res. **200**(2), 451–464 (2010)
16. Sun, Z., Li, L., Fernandez, M., Wang, J.: Inventory control for peak electricity demand reduction of manufacturing systems considering the tradeoff between production loss and energy savings. J. Cleaner Prod. **82**, 84 93 (2014)
17. Toptal, A., Özlü, H., Konur, D.: Joint decisions on inventory replenishment and emission reduction investment under different emission regulations. Int. J. Prod. Res. **52**(1), 243–269 (2013)

Demand Driven Material Requirements Planning Buffer Positioning Considering Carbon Emissions

Achergui Abdelhalim[(✉)], Allaoui Hamid, and Hsu Tiente

Univ. Artois, UR 3926, Laboratoire de Genie Informatique et d'Automatique de l'Artois (LGI2A), 62400 Bethune, France
{abdelhalim.achergui,hamid.allaoui,tiente.hsu}@univ-artois.fr

Abstract. Firms are more and more interested in reducing the carbon footprint related to their activity. Their supply chain remains one of the main sources of carbon emissions. Better operational routines and planning adjustments have proven to be an effective way to reduce the carbon emissions but not enough. In this paper, the carbon footprint is taken into consideration in the Demand Driven Material Requirements Planning (DDMRP) strategic buffer positioning problem. The focus is put on the storing activities and transportation, for which a function was proposed to quantify the associated emissions. Two environmental regulations are simulated: carbon emissions tax and carbon emissions cap. These approaches have been implemented in a buffer positioning model with a cost minimization objective function. The resulting models were solved using CPLEX solver for multiple instances. The numerical results provide a better measurement of the buffer positioning impact on the carbon emissions. The observed sensibility of the problem to the environment parameters would give insights for further research work.

Keywords: Buffer positioning problem · DDMRP · Carbon footprint

1 Introduction

The optimization of logistics and production activities has been based only on economic criteria (cost minimization or profit maximization) over a long period of time, regardless of the negative impacts these activities may have on the environment, mainly in terms of carbon emissions [1]. Over the past decade, environmental concerns have become increasingly relevant to businesses as government environmental policies have become stricter and customer awareness of the environment has increased. As a result, many traditional logistics and production management issues have been re-examined with the environmental considerations [2].

Besides, many research projects were engaged recently to try to measure, minimize or completely substitute the polluting supply chain activities. Some

© IFIP International Federation for Information Processing 2021
Published by Springer Nature Switzerland AG 2021
A. Dolgui et al. (Eds.): APMS 2021, IFIP AICT 632, pp. 460–468, 2021.
https://doi.org/10.1007/978-3-030-85906-0_51

researches focused their work on specific supply chain configurations. Hong et al. [3] studied the carbon emissions problem for a green product type with a stochastic demand in a guaranteed service time configuration with carbon cap strategy. They optimized the service time and option selection decisions while minimizing the costs. Tiwari et al. [4] studied the same problem for a deteriorating product integrated in a single-vendor single-buyer inventory model. Their model minimized the inventory level and the carbon emissions through a better product delivery planning. Hovelaque and Bironneau [5] linked the carbon emissions to the price and environmental dependant demands for an inventory with Economic Order Quantity (EOQ) policy, providing the order quantity that minimizes the holding costs and ordering costs, maximizing in consequence the profits. Ni and Shu [6] presented a formal presentation of a carbon emission function to optimize the safety stock placement in a multi-echelon supply chain with guaranteed service model. Their work finds a trade-off between service time and carbon emissions to position safety stocks. They show that a potential increase in the inventory levels may reduce the emissions with the proper carbon cap or carbon tax price. Hammami et al. [7] and Manupati et al. [8] generalized the problem to a multi-echelon setting. Our work fills the gap of the carbon emissions problem for a DDMRP [9] setting with guaranteed service configuration.

In this article, we present a model of buffer positioning with an ecological aspect. The installation of a buffer leads to the setting of a stock and thus adds a source of CO_2 emissions. However, the frequency of replenishment orders is considerably reduced, thus intriguing a production mode with much lower emissions. To study this problem, we introduce the parameters and the settings of the environment in Sect. 2. In Sect. 3, two strategies are implemented, that of the carbon tax and that of the authorized emissions limit. The first one translates the emissions in terms of budget which is added to the objective function formula representing the sum of the costs. The second one sets a cap on emissions not to be exceeded during production, thus adding a constraint to our model. The experimentation results are presented in Sect. 4 with a related analysis of the deduced observations. A conclusion is made in Sect. 5 with the perspectives of our future research work.

2 Model Setting and Assumptions

For a better accuracy, the simulated environment should be well set and defined. We present in the next paragraphs the different parameters on which the proposed research is based and where our model would be tested and simulated. In addition to the approach strategies to carbon emissions sources and regulations that would be discussed.

To set the **supply chain configuration** for this paper, we consider a single echelon Supply Chain with a guaranteed service approach [10]. A standard case of a firm with a set of manufacturing facilities and suppliers are represented by a Bill of Materials (BOM). The nodes represent the flowing products of the Supply Chain: the raw materials, the intermediate products, and the final product.

A fictional root node representing the end customer is also added to the structure of the BOM, as seen in our previous work [11]. It would be referred to as node $i = 0$. The following modeling assumptions are considered:

- Lead times are considered to be deterministic for the parts of the BOM.
- A separate BOM is considered for each final product for which the firm satisfies the internal and external demand.
- A component may serve only one downstream node.

Carbon Emissions Function is introduced to simulate the carbon emissions generated by the supply chain. The following approach is considered. We start by determining the different sources of CO2 along the processes of the production line. Mainly the emissions are due to transportation and inventory settings. We would focus on these two major sources, as they also are impacted by the decision of the buffer positioning process. The Carbon Emissions function is then the sum of the emissions for an average flowing quantity (avg_i) of every item i. With $X = \{x_i\}, \forall i \in N$ the decision variable of the problem indicating whether the item i is buffered or not, the Carbon Emissions function E would be formulated as:

$$E(X) = \sum_{\forall i \in N} E(x_i) \tag{1}$$

Transportation is a key element of the supply chain, as it is needed to complete the gap between the nodes of the BOM when it is the case as in between raw material suppliers and the first processing site. We consider that each item i has a quantity of emissions β_i due to its transportation along the factory premises. We suppose in this article, that the same type of vehicles is used, and that all items average the same quantity of transportation emissions TE for the whole activity cycle, equal to $\beta = 1500 \, gCO2/unit$. By simulation of the buffer positioning model in our previous paper [11], it is observed that buffered items have a low frequency of replenishment orders compared to non-buffered items that needs daily deliveries in the absence of inventory. It considered for this work that the transportation emissions, related to the replenishment activity, is lowered by 3. While all items are supposed to average the same quantity of transportation emissions, the buffered items transportation emissions would be equal to $\beta^* = \beta/3$. These emissions of an item i would be expressed as follows :

$$TE(x_i) = \beta^* \cdot avg_i \cdot x_i + \beta \cdot avg_i \cdot (1 - x_i) \tag{2}$$

Inventory Settings are crucial in case of buffered items. Setting up an inventory, brings two types of emissions: the constant emissions and the variable emissions, that would represent its Inventory Emissions IE. The constant emissions α_0 are due to the facility or the warehouse fixed running resources, as in the consumed energy and the needed human resources. Its amount is supposed to be the same for all the items, as we consider the same storing conditions.

It could be product specific in case of condition-sensitive products, as they require special facilities. The variable emissions, $\alpha_i \quad \forall i \in N$, are due to the amount of products stored on site. Each product represents a percentage of potential waste that can, in addition to its handling operations, take part in its carbon footprint. These emissions would be formulated as follows:

$$IE(x_i) = (\alpha_0 + \alpha_i \cdot avg_i) \cdot x_i \tag{3}$$

For non buffered items, these emissions are not considered.

Carbon Tax Strategy consists in simulating government CO2 tax rates. Their cost comes as a compensation to allow firms to adapt their configuration for better performance. To integrate these potential taxes in the total cost of the supply chain, we consider an average tax compensation price e_i for every quantity gCO2 of carbon emissions resulting from the activities of the site. The objective function gets new terms, besides the holding costs, representing the carbon emissions tax cost of every item.

Carbon Cap Strategy consists in simulating the regulation of emissions target caps. The carbon emissions function is used to sum the emissions of all the items in the BOM, and then added in the model as a constraint limiting its value to the restricted emissions target cap noted as $ECap$.

3   Model Formulation

Based on the model from our previous work [11], the two strategies are implemented to take into consideration the carbon emissions into the DDMRP buffer positioning model. The models are tested separately on different instances generated to simulate the market data. The notations used for the considered model are presented in Table 1:

Table 1. The modelization notations.

Variable	Signification
a_i	Lead time of the ith part
SvT	Customer service time
adu	Final product average daily usage
$rqtf_i$	Needed quantity of the ith part to produce the final product
TC	Total of Storing costs
u_p_i	Unit price of the ith part
aih_cost_i	Average inventory holding cost rate of the ith part
lt_f_i	Lead time factor of ith part
var_f_i	Variability factor of ith part

The Carbon Emissions Function would be written as follows:

$$E(X) = \sum_{\forall i \in N} [IE(x_i) + TE(x_i)] \tag{4}$$

which would be expressed after factoring the decision variable:

$$E(X) = \sum_{\forall i \in N} (\alpha_0 + \alpha_i \cdot avg_i + \beta^* \cdot avg_i - \beta \cdot avg_i) \cdot x_i + \beta \cdot avg_i \tag{5}$$

For the **Carbon Tax Model** strategy, we include the emission compensation costs in the objective function. It would be minimised in parallel to inventory holding costs of positioned buffers. The model would be formulated as follows:

Minimize

$$TC = \sum_{\forall i \in N} u\_p_i \cdot aih\_cost_i \cdot (1,5 + var\_f_i) \cdot lt\_f_i \cdot adu \cdot rqtf_i \cdot a_i \cdot x_i + e_i \cdot E_i(x_i) \tag{6}$$

s.t.

$$a_0 \leq SvT$$

For the **Carbon Cap Model** strategy, the total emissions are limited to $ECap$. It would be a second constraint beside the service time constraint to our problem. This limit is expected to be reasonable and allows the manufacturing process to progress. The model would be formulated as follows:

Minimize

$$TC = \sum_{\forall i \in N} u\_p_i \cdot aih\_cost_i \cdot (1,5 + var\_f_i) \cdot lt\_f_i \cdot adu \cdot rqtf_i \cdot a_i \cdot x_i \tag{7}$$

s.t.

$$a_0 \leq SvT$$
$$E \leq ECap$$

4   Experimental Analysis

According to our research settings, many sets of instances are generated to test the model with its both strategies. Each set is composed of a BOM with a different number of items tested to a selection of service times. The parameters of the items were generated following the logic of an assembly line where the final product is more expensive, more complicated to store and more polluting. The lead time and variability factors are parameters related to the DDMRP method, they were calculated following the rules in the book [9]. Some of these parameters are considered the same for all items for simplification purposes. The model has been run on the version 12.8.0 of CPLEX solver on a machine with Intel i7-4700MQ 2.40 GHz with 8 GB of RAM, with a Windows 8.1 operating system. The instances were generated using a Typescript program, as it is on an online user-ready platform.

Results and Analysis

The results of the strategic DDMRP buffer positioning model and its green variant with both carbon cap and carbon tax strategies are listed in Table 2.

Table 2. Total cost and carbon emissions comparison.

Instance	SvT	No buffer emissions (KgCO2)	Strategic buffer positioning			Carbon cap strategy				Carbon tax strategy			
			TC	Emis (KgCO2)	Comp time(s)	Cap (KgCO2)	TC	Emis (KgCO2)	Comp	Tax	TC	Emis (KgCO2)	Comp time(s)
5	6	8110	15600	1507	0,21	1200	33280	1097,6	0,26	0,03	58416	1251,2	0,1
						1300	20880	1251,2	0,16	0,01	30672	1507,2	0,16
13	6	23448	66912	18592	1,07	18500	67232	18337	0,15	0,03	404780	10190	0,21
						17000	70036	16282	0,18	0,01	197680	10604	0,16
	15		39040	19625	1,08	19000	39120	15104	0,21	0,03	387610	10725	0,13
						15000	40272	14511	0,24	0,01	162430	11615	0,22
26	10	26256	568240	27467	1,1	26000	572160	25915	0,41	0,03	1313500	23132	0,27
						20000	905760	19990	0,33	0,01	831310	25915	0,22
	20		369840	25779	1,04	24000	436880	23976	0,26	0,03	1123200	24142	0,22
						20000	778480	19928	0,36	0,01	627630	25779	0,25
50	10	172460	776560	178560	1,06	170000	837360	137430	0,79	0,03	4429700	99121	0,33
						120000	1046600	117120	0,51	0,01	2206300	131130	0,3
	20		627120	125370	1,06	100000	816960	96596	0,31	0,03	3699400	94354	0,27
						85000	1338100	84990	0,57	0,01	1782900	96596	0,34
80	6	1101400	888800	1120200	1,19	1000000	1328000	999900	0,41	0,03	22311000	557790	0,5
						800000	2057600	799210	0,41	0,01	9744700	740150	0,46
	30		443520	1100500	0,93	600000	3753600	584460	0,4	0,03	21092000	541990	0,42
						500000	6432200	499900	0,54	0,01	8973400	719930	0,42
	34		224640	1104200	1,16	400000	11234000	399990	0,73	0,03	21092000	541990	0,43
						380000	12941000	379850	0,53	0,01	8790600	723540	0,44
123	6	270380	1374480	321120	1,32	300000	1513200	299910	0,96	0,03	9468200	188710	1,79
						260000	2005800	259710	1,84	0,01	4474600	283420	1
	30		132160	263600	1,14	250000	248960	249610	0,78	0,03	7136800	188940	0,6
						200000	1188200	199970	0,67	0,01	2743800	247900	0,72
140	6	2077200	18556960	1014100	0,08	1000000	18576000	894170	0,75	0,03	43665000	781090	0,76
						800000	20168000	799910	0,8	0,01	27428000	879510	0,7
	15		12460200	980020	0,11	800000	14043000	799270	1,12	0,03	36636000	749970	0,69
						650000	30753000	646650	3,85	0,01	21021000	848390	0,71
160	6	11415000	184320248	2868700	0,17	2800000	184340000	2799000	0,76	0,03	2,64E+08	2648500	0,82
						2700000	184820000	2699900	0,83	0,01	2,11E+08	2649000	0,94
	15		88211448	2832900	0,23	2800000	88221000	2798200	1,74	0,03	1,67E+08	2616000	0,71
						2700000	88299000	2698600	1,15	0,01	1,15E+08	2616300	0,72
200	6	5472200	49082048	2825400	0,11	2800000	49086656	2756000	0,85	0,03	1,06E+08	1899400	1,64
						2600000	49082048	2559000	0,83	0,01	68303000	1913600	0,97
	15		19062360	2717200	0,34	2500000	19062000	2450800	1,12	0,03	73801000	1819500	1
						2000000	19067000	1853900	1,08	0,01	37369000	1827400	1,03

The instances are sorted by the number of items in the BOM. Every instance has its no buffer emissions, which is the working scenario where the BOM is not decoupled and we have no DDMRP applied to our supply chain. Then the emissions of the strategic buffer positioning model with no carbon emissions restrictions is given next. For each set of service times, two capacities and two carbon compensation tax prices were tested to measure the sensibility of the parameters. This also allows to measure the impact of the two strategies. The performance of the linearized model, for both variants, is remarkable as we obtain results in very short times.

With the carbon cap strategy, the model repositions buffers along the BOM to satisfy the emissions limit. In some cases, like the instance of 80 items for a service time of 30, the total cost dropped by 42% for an easier emission cap. Even though, the product takes the same time to be produced. This is because the model changed the buffers for more expensive ones but less polluting. In better cases, like the instance of 5 items, the more strict emission constraint, allowed the product to be produced in a better time all while reducing the carbon footprint of the process. However, a much lower emissions cap would push the model to a non feasible solution in case no possible buffer configuration could produce that little emissions.

The carbon tax strategy, appears to be a more expensive option by an average of 52%. With some exceptions where we have a better cost minimization but for a higher carbon emissions quantity, the case of the instances: the BOM of 26 items when the tax price is set to 0.01, the BOM of 80 items for a service time of 34 when the tax price is 0.01 and the BOM of 140 items for a service time of 15 when the tax price is 0.01. It is though more efficient in terms of the carbon footprint reduction by an average improvement of 45%. The model is also sensitive to the tax compensation price. The appropriate pricing would be crucial to find the optimal compromise between setting a buffer and relying more on transportation.

The performance of the two strategies is compared to the strategic buffer positioning model with no restriction in Fig. 1. An adapted carbon cap is considered for each instance and a carbon tax of 0.03 is considered for all of them. Each instance has its own behaviour as they were independently generated. The graphs show

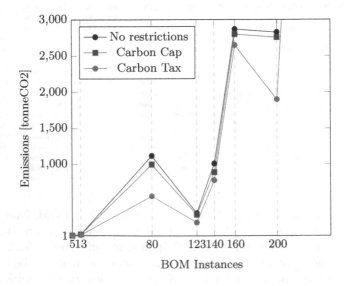

Fig. 1. Carbon emissions by strategy

that the carbon tax strategy is better performing in term of minimizing the carbon emissions, followed by the carbon cap strategy.

5   Conclusion and Perspectives

In this paper, the carbon footprint aspect was considered in a DDMRP buffer positioning problem with client service time constraint. Two strategies have been adopted to simulate the environmental regulations: carbon emissions cap and carbon emissions tax. A function has been proposed for modeling these emissions that are mainly related to storing activities and transportation. The numerical results showed the impact of buffers positioning on the amount of generated emissions. Hence, the usefulness of our model is to find out which of the buffer settings is the most suitable for both economical and ecological aspects. Transportation was considered brief and standard in this work, adding distance variability and transportation costs to the equation would make the problem more complicated. A hybrid version of the two carbon emission strategies may be considered in the future. The impact of buffered items on the replenishment frequency and its transportation emissions minimization could be considered at a future tactical study of the DDMRP method. The difference of carbon tax pricing from a region to an other may rise the question of inventory location for multi-echelon supply chain.

Acknowledgments. This work is a part of the ELSAT 2020 project. It was performed in collaboration with the "Pole d'excellence Logistique & Supply Chain en Hauts-de-France Euralogistic". ELSAT is co-financed by the European Union with the European Regional Development Fund, the French state and the Council of Hauts-de-France Region. The support of ELSAT 2020 and Euralogistic is gratefully acknowledged.

References

1. Allaoui, H., Guo, Y., Sarkis, J.: Decision support for collaboration planning in sustainable supply chains. J. Cleaner Prod. **229**, 761–774 (2019). https://doi.org/10.1016/j.jclepro.2019.04.367
2. Eskandarpour, M., Dejax, P., Miemezyk, J., Peton, O.: Sustainable supply chain network design: an optimization-oriented review. Omega **54**, 11–32 (2015). https://doi.org/10.1016/j.omega.2015.01.006
3. Hong, Z., Dai, W., Luh, H., Yang, C.: Optimal configuration of a green product supply chain with guaranteed service time and emission constraints. Eur. J. Oper. Res. **266**, 663–677 (2018). https://doi.org/10.1016/j.ejor.2017.09.046
4. Tiwari, S., Daryanto, Y., Wee, H.M.: Sustainable inventory management with deteriorating and imperfect quality items considering carbon emission. J. Cleaner Prod. **192**, 281–292 (2018). https://doi.org/10.1016/j.jclepro.2018.04.261
5. Hovelaque, V., Bironneau, L.: The carbon-constrained EOQ model with carbon emission dependent demand. Int. J. Prod. Econ. **164**, 285–291 (2015). https://doi.org/10.1016/j.ijpe.2014.11.022

6. Ni, W., Shu, J.: Trade-off between service time and carbon emissions for safety stock placement in multi-echelon supply chains. Int. J. Prod. Res. **53**(22), 6701–6718 (2015). https://doi.org/10.1080/00207543.2015.1056319
7. Hammami, R., Nouira, I., Frein, Y.: Carbon emissions in a multi-echelon production-inventory model with lead time constraints. Int. J. Prod. Econ. **164**, 292–307 (2015). https://doi.org/10.1016/j.ijpe.2014.12.017
8. Manupati, V.K., Jedidah, S.J., Gupta, S., Bhandari, A., Ramkumar, M.: Optimization of a multi-echelon sustainable production-distribution supply chain system with lead time consideration under carbon emission policies. Comput. Ind. Eng. **135**, 1312–1323 (2019). https://doi.org/10.1016/j.cie.2018.10.010
9. Ptak, C., Smith, C.: Demand Driven Material Requirements Planning, 3rd edn. Industrial Press, Inc., New York (2019)
10. Simpson, Jr., K.F.: In-process inventories. Oper. Res. **6**(6), 863–873 (1958)
11. Achergui, A., Allaoui, H., Hsu, T.: Strategic DDMRP's buffer positioning for hybrid MTO/MTS manufacturing. In: 2020 IEEE International Conference on Technology Management, Operations and Decisions (ICTMOD), Marrakech, Morocco, pp. 1–8 (2020). https://doi.org/10.1109/ICTMOD49425.2020.9380588

Supply Chain and Routing Management

Reinforcement Learning for Layout Planning – Modelling the Layout Problem as MDP

Hendrik Unger$^{(\boxtimes)}$ (iD) and Frank Börner

Technische Universität Chemnitz, Erfenschlager Straße 73, 09125 Chemnitz, Germany
`hendrik.unger@mb.tu-chemnitz.de`

Abstract. The layout problem has been a focus point of research in factory planning for over six decades. Several newly emerging techniques for example genetic algorithms have been applied to the problem to generate better solutions closer to practical application. Nevertheless, solving the layout problem without considerable simplification of the base problem still presents a challenge. This publication shows how to model the layout problem in the framework of Markov decision processes (MDP) to apply reinforcement learning as a novel approach for generating layouts. Reinforcement learning (RF) has previously not been applied to the layout problem to the best knowledge of the author. Research in other fields of study shows the enormous potential of RF and the capability to reach superhuman performance in a variety of tasks. Although RF may not provide a better solution for finding the global optimum in the layout problem than genetic algorithms or dynamic programming, we hope to be able to include more constrains that matter for real world planning applications while keeping the calculation time feasibility short for practical application.

Keywords: Layout problem · Reinforcement learning · Artificial intelligence

1 Motivation

A challenge in factory planning, which must be solved in every planning job, is the layout problem. This is the task of arranging the elements and subsystems contained in a production system, such as production machines and transport routes, optimally in a defined solution space within a coordinate system according to certain target criteria (usually based on the material flow) resulting in a definition of the target function. Classically, ideal layout planning is performed first, without existing external constrains for the solution space in the coordinate system. Then, the solution generated in this way is adapted to the real layout planning to the constraints that exist in the real project [1, p. 335], [2, p. 13ff], [3, p. 317f].

Central factors influencing the complexity of the layout problem are the number and the shape of the elements to be arranged. In the simplest case, only rectangular (2D planning) or cuboid-shaped (3D planning) elements are placed, which leads to a faster solution, but one that is further away from practical planning reality. Considering

© IFIP International Federation for Information Processing 2021
Published by Springer Nature Switzerland AG 2021
A. Dolgui et al. (Eds.): APMS 2021, IFIP AICT 632, pp. 471–479, 2021.
https://doi.org/10.1007/978-3-030-85906-0_52

real machine floor plans where logistics and working areas need to be placed, much more complex geometries emerge in practical application cases. Thus, solutions created with previous methods usually must be reworked by a planner [4, p. 427]. Another factor that complicates the solution of the layout problem is the optimality criterion. Classically, the material flow between the arranged elements is determined to achieve a global minimum [1, p. 323], [5, 6]. An efficient material flow correlates strongly with an efficient factory and accordingly lower operating costs of the factory life cycle [7, p. 200], [8, p. 348]. Nevertheless, there are numerous other influencing factors that must be considered in real planning. These include information flows, energy flows, media availability (compressed air, electricity, process gases, …), the load-bearing capacity of the floor slab, the necessary illumination of the workplaces, as well as requirements for air purity, vibration behaviour, temperature stability and the influence of other system elements based on these factors. While optimization, considering several of these criteria usually leads to a conflict of objectives due to the mutually contradictory target criteria. Even using simple object contours and only the material flow as optimization criteria, the complexity of the problem and its solution space increases exponentially to the point where no optimal solution can be found in a reasonable time even with current computational technology - the layout problem is classified as NP-hard. In particular, the objective of arranging several elements in the order of magnitude of a real planning problem leads to the fact that many of the known solution algorithms and heuristics are no longer usefully applicable, because no solution can be found, or the computational effort is no longer economically justifiable. To be able to find usable solutions at all, it is common to reduce the existing complexity by reducing restrictions in the described target criteria. Thus, known important influencing variables are either disregarded or evaluated in a downstream step only. A local optimization takes place in many other procedures as well, so the quality of the final solution depends on the starting point of the algorithm.

In conclusion, it can be stated that the computation time contributes a huge importance in the solution of the layout problem in practice, so many of the present algorithms may not be used in an economic application. In addition, in most cases not all relevant influencing factors of the problem are included in the optimization. Finally, a large part of the planning process is performed by humans based on empirical knowledge and domain-specific expertise. The simultaneous consideration of several objective criteria is limited by the cognitive abilities of the planner.

Our research goal is to apply reinforcement learning to the layout problem and evaluate its performance against other state of the art solution algorithms. This contribution shows our approach to formulating the layout problem in a way suitable to be solved by reinforcement learning algorithms.

2 Background

AlphaGo, AlphaGo Zero, and AlphaZero [9–11] achieved performances above that of reigning world champions in the extremely complex game of Go. AlphaZero was transferred to other complex games such as shogi and chess and was able to outperform humans there as well. Another machine learning success is represented by Agent57

[12], an artificial intelligence that solves all 57 different games in the Atari benchmark [13]. These examples highlight the potential of reinforcement learning technology. In another domain, a problem closely related to the layout problem – the floor planning problem on microchips - has been successfully solved by RF [14], which increases the motivation for applying similar methods to the layout problem as well.

The underlying mathematical theory used is the Markov decision processes (MDP) [15]. Depending on how well the process can be modelled there are different possible approaches for finding a solution. If all parameters are well known and well modelled, an optimal solution can be determined using dynamic programming and optimization. Obtaining and solving a complete model of the layout problem is not always possible or economically feasible, as described in the previous section. RF is applicable without the full model of the MDP. The basic principle is shown in Fig. 1.

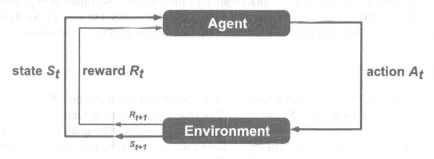

Fig. 1. Reinforcement learning cycle [16]

A learning agent interacts with an environment by selecting actions. The environment simulates the problem to be solved and provides feedback on the quality of the action according to the reward function as well as the new state of the environment. Based on this information, the agent selects a new action. The agent continuously learns from the interactions by exploring and tries to optimize its behavior in such a way that it receives the best possible reward. Considering the reward function there are several possible approaches for the design. The easiest solution would be to reward the action leading to the intended outcome of the problem with maximum reward and every other action with no or negative reward. Such an approach provides a particularly challenging problem to solve for the agent and would result in failure to learn anything for more complex environment due to the agent never achieving a positive reward. There are solutions to improve learning in such sparse reward environments in literature, e.g. curiosity [17] or attention [18]. The reward function can also supply additional smaller rewards for subgoals or behaviors that are considered well suited towards solving the bigger problem by the programmer. This results in easier learnable environments but also requires domain knowledge of the problem to be solved. Defining sub rewards can push the agent into a predefined behavior, instead of creating a new and not previously known solution from scratch. Such a reward design needs to be carried out very carefully otherwise there is a risk of the agent not developing the desired behavior. Instead, a behavior coined "reward gaming" can emerge, which results for example in choosing an action leading to an easy achievable low reward instead of a (desired) more complex action leading to a higher reward.

To be able to solve the layout problem it must be modelled as an MDP. A possible solution how this can be achieved is described in the next section.

3 Modelling the Layout Problem as MDP

According to [19, p. 10ff], an MDP consists of states, actions, action model and a reward function. In addition, there is an agent that makes decisions and learns from their results. All elements that are not part of or directly influenceable by the agent are called environment. The boundary between agent and environment is not always firmly defined in the literature and can be determined in the context of modeling a problem [16, p. 37ff]. The solution approach RF, as a representative of model-free algorithms, only requires states S, possible actions A and a reward for the last action as input since the information about the model is collected and learned during interaction with the environment.

3.1 State

States in the MDP capture all relevant aspects of the environment and therefore describe the available solution space for the agent. The relevant influencing factors in practical layout planning applications must be reflected in the states. The quality of the final layout depends on the fulfilment of the requirements for every individual influence factor and is considered in the reward function. Since not all influence factors are relevant in every planning project, a mechanism is required to ignore irrelevant influences in the environment. Nevertheless, during the training process, the agent must learn how to deal with all potential influencing variables. In addition, the number of system elements to be arranged is not constant in the layout problem. From planning case to planning case, different numbers of workstations/machines must be placed in a layout. Almost all algorithms that can act as agents expect a constant size of the state space as input. In terms of a practical solution, it is not possible to train a variant of the agent for different numbers of system elements.

To meet the requirements described above, the states of the environment are encoded as images or image stacks. Depending on the requirements, colored images (RBG), greyscale images or a combination of both can be used. In principle, colored images allow more information to be contained, but they also place higher demands on the available resources for executing the environment. The agent is not always able to use the additional information effectively [20]. To reduce memory consumption and speed up computation, it is advisable to encode as many environmental states as possible in greyscale images. The actual resolution of the images is defined as a hyperparameter of the environment. This parameter has a significant influence on the resource requirements and calculation time of both the agent and the environment and should be kept reasonably low. Many algorithms acting as an agent employ neural networks internally. The size of the state space often defines the number of used neurons. With a larger number of neurons, more complex relationships can be modelled [21], so there may also be a correlation between the potential learning ability of the agent and the resolution of the environmental state, which has to be explored in an subsequent publication.

An example of the described architecture of an environmental state stack is shown in Fig. 2.

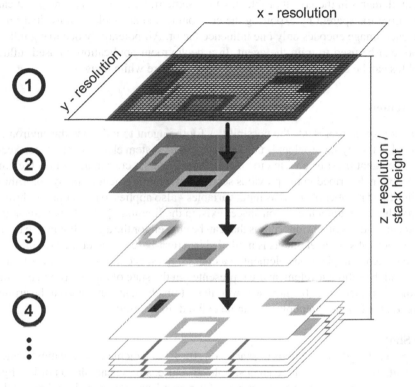

Fig. 2. Principle representation of an environmental state stack

While the resolution in x - and y - direction is defined by the hyperparameter mentioned above, stack height is derived from the selected influence factors of the layout problem. Each level of the environment state stack defines the need for a certain influence factor as well as the corresponding degree of fulfilment of the system elements that are going to be arranged. Greyscale images with 8-bit encoding result in a subdivision into 256 units, so that complex dependencies can be represented. The darker an element is drawn, the higher the requirement or degree of fulfilment. The background/free space of the layout is also colored according to the requirement or degree of fulfilment in the space at this point. In Fig. 2, Level 1 represents the basic layout, all interior and exterior walls and whether collisions occur between system elements and walls. Due to the complexity of this information, a colored representation was chosen. Level 2 encodes the foundation support load requirements of the individual system elements. The left part of the space has a reinforced floor slab, which is represented by darker color at this position in the greyscale image. Level 3 represents the emission of vibrations of the individual machines and their respective sensitivity to vibrations. These are arbitrary examples; the order of the influence factors can be chosen freely but must remain consistently after initial definition and training.

With the help of the described stacking system, an arbitrary but fixed set of influence factors can be represented with simultaneous flexibility regarding to the number of system elements in the layout problem. At the same time, decisions of the agent can be made more transparent by exporting the environment state stack as individual images, since each image encodes only one influence factor. All potentially occurring influence factors can be used to train the agent. In a deployment application, unused influence variables can be declared as "no requirements" by pure white images.

3.2 Actions

The action space represents the possibilities for the agent to influence the environment. The goal in the layout problem is the arrangement of system elements on plane. Accordingly, the agent must be enabled to change the x - and y - coordinates of each element. The problem described in the previous section – the requirement of many algorithms to obtain a fixed number of states as input variables - also applies to the output of the agent. Approaches for parametric action spaces exist in the literature [22, 23], but this imposes serious limitations on the algorithms that can be chosen for the agent. For this reason, the arrangement of system elements is modelled in a turn-based manner. In each interaction step, the agent can place one element in a continuous space in x - and y - direction. The active and the following element are represented in the state of the environment. Then, a turn then corresponds to the iteration over all system elements, that need to be arranged. However, the length of an episode can be defined differently:

One Shot

The episode length corresponds to exactly one turn. Each element is only moved once by the agent. The advantages here are a simple structure, simple calculation of key figures for agent performance and low potential for reward gaming. On the other hand, the learning task at the beginning of the training is difficult for the agent. If a state with an occurring reward does not arise during the random exploration phase, then a training run may end without learning success.

Objective Function Change Threshold

The end of the episode occurs when a defined objective function, or the reward function experiences a change below a specified threshold. This option, similar to the termination criterion in an optimization task, allows the agent to improve its initial solution and offers good potential for successful training. The risk for reward gaming is exceedingly high. A scenario in which the agent learns the termination threshold and then continually moves system elements just enough to obtain a positive reward each iteration is possible.

Fixed Number of Turns

This is a compromise between the two previous alternatives. The episode length is fixed, but multiple turns are allowed. It offers potential for optimizing the solution without creating too much risk for reward gaming. A fixed episode length simplifies the calculation of key figures of agent performance and the quantification of the training progress.

Termination by Agent
The agent is given an additional binary action to choose from to end an episode. This approach can in principle be combined with any of the previous ones but requires a specific formulation of the reward function. To prevent infinite episodes, a punishment factor must be modelled that correlates with the episode length.

In the current state of research, the best approach for the action space cannot be determined yet and needs further experimentation.

4   Conclusion and Further Research

In this paper we described our modelling approach for the layout problem tailored to the requirements of reinforcement learning as a solution algorithm. To check the plausibility and feasibility of the described model approach, a proof-of-concept implementation was created. In the process, the layout problem was simplified to central core aspects to achieve an executable state for a concept study more quickly. Only the material flow was used as an evaluation criterion for the quality of a layout and the reward. In addition, some constraints had to be implemented to obtain valid solutions. The most important aspect was the avoidance of collisions between the arranged objects and layout boundaries as well as within the objects themselves. The prototype already provides a simple interface for data transfer via Industry Foundation Classes (IFC) standard, result visualisation and the integration interface for state-of-the-art reinforcement learning algorithms. In the tests already conducted, a learning behaviour of the algorithms used so far, Proximal Policy Optimisation, [24] and Actor Critic using Kronecker-Factored Trust Region [25] could be observed. Depending on the formulation of the reward function and action space behaviours resembling other simple heuristics for graphically solving the layout problem like Schwerdtfegers's heuristic [26, p. 149ff], could be observed after training the model for 20–40 CPU hours. This result shows that an easy formulation of the layout problem can in fact be solved by reinforcement learning.

The next steps for research include the incorporation of additional influence factors to the layout problem to achieve a complexity closer to a real-world planning task in factory planning. After transitioning the environment to an architecture that enables computation on clusters, the performance of additional reinforcement learning algorithms on this problem will be evaluated. Finally, the best performing solution will be tuned to maximum performance and benchmarked against other solution approaches for the layout problem.

References

1. Wirth, S., Schenk, M., Müller, E.: Fabrikplanung und Fabrikbetrieb (2014)
2. VDI 5200 Blatt 1, VDI 5200 Blatt 1, pp. 1–24 (2011)
3. Arnold, D., Isermann, H., Kuhn, A., Tempelmeier, H., Furmans, K.: Handbuch Logistik (2008)

4. Singh, S.P., Sharma, R.R.K.: A review of different approaches to the facility layout problems. Int. J. Adv. Manuf. Technol. **30**(5–6), 425–433 (2006). https://doi.org/10.1007/s00170-005-0087-9

5. Kusiak, A., Heragu, S.S.: The facility layout problem. Eur. J. Oper. Res. **29**(3), 229–251 (1987). https://doi.org/10.1016/0377-2217(87)90238-4

6. Bozer, Y.A., Meller, R.D.: A reexamination of the distance-based facility layout problem. IIE Trans. (Institute Ind. Eng. **29**(7), 549–560 (1997). https://doi.org/10.1080/074081797089 66365.

7. Bracht, U., Dahlbeck, M., Fischer, A., Krüger, T.: Combining simulation and optimization for extended double row facility layout problems in factory planning (2018). https://doi.org/10.1007/978-3-319-96271-9_3

8. Hawer, S., Ilmer, P., Reinhart, G.: Klassifizierung unscharfer Planungsdaten in der Fabrikplanung. ZWF Zeitschrift fuer Wirtschaftlichen Fabrikbetr. (2015). https://doi.org/10.3139/104.111339

9. Silver, D., et al.: Mastering the game of Go with deep neural networks and tree search. Nature (2016). https://doi.org/10.1038/nature16961

10. Silver, D., et al.: Mastering the game of Go without human knowledge. Nature (2017). https://doi.org/10.1038/nature24270

11. Silver, D., et al.: A general reinforcement learning algorithm that masters chess, shogi, and go through self-play. Science (80-) (2018). https://doi.org/10.1126/science.aar6404

12. Badia, A.P., et al.: Agent57: Outperforming the Atari Human Benchmark March 2020. Accessed 30 October 2020. https://arxiv.org/abs/2003.13350

13. Bellemare, M.G., Naddaf, Y., Veness, J., Bowling, M.: The arcade learning environment: an evaluation platform for general agents. J. Artif. Intell. Res. (2013). https://doi.org/10.1613/jair.3912

14. Mirhoseini, A., et al.: Chip Placement with Deep Reinforcement Learning April 2020. Accessed 30 October 2020. http://arxiv.org/abs/2004.10746

15. Bellman, R.: Dynamic Programming. Princeton University Press, Princeton (1956)

16. Sutton, R.S., Barto, A.: Reinforcement learning: an introduction (2018)

17. Pathak, D., Agrawal, P., Efros, A.A., Darrell, T.: Curiosity-driven exploration by self-supervised prediction. In: 34th International Conference on Machine Learning ICML 2017, vol. 6, pp. 4261–4270 (2017)

18. Vaswani, A., et al.: Attention is all you need (2017)

19. van Otterlo, M., Wiering, M.: Reinforcement Learning and Markov Decision Processes BT - Reinforcement Learning: State-of-the-Art. Springer Berlin Heidelberg (2012). https://doi.org/10.1007/978-3-642-27645-3_1

20. Ng, C.B., Tay, Y.H., Goi, B.M.: Comparing image representations for training a convolutional neural network to classify gender. In: Proceedings - 1st International Conference on Artificial Intelligence Modelling Simulation, AIMS 2013, pp. 29–33 (2014). https://doi.org/10.1109/AIMS.2013.13

21. Hornik, K.: Approximation capabilities of multilayer neural network. Neural Networks **4**(1991), 251–257 (1991)

22. Hausknecht, M., Stone, P.: Deep reinforcement learning in parameterized action space. In: 4th International Conference on Learning Representations ICLR 2016 - Conference Track Proceedings, pp. 1–12 (2016)

23. Masson, W., Ranchod, P., Konidaris, G.: Reinforcement learning with parameterized actions. In: 30th AAAI Conference Artificial Intelligence AAAI 2016, pp. 1934–1940 (2016)

24. Schulman, J., Wolski, F., Dhariwal, P., Radford, A., Klimov, O.: Proximal Policy Optimization Algorithms, pp. 1–12 (2017). http://arxiv.org/abs/1707.06347

25. Wu, Y., Mansimov, E., Liao, S., Grosse, R., Ba, J.: Scalable trust-region method for deep reinforcement learning using Kronecker-factored approximation. Adv. Neural Inf. Process. Syst. 2017-Decem, 5280–5289 (2017)
26. Grundig, C.-G.: Fabrikplanung: Planungssystematik - Methoden - Anwendungen 5, aktualisierte Auflage (2018)

Supply Chain Management by Blockchain

Gianfranco Genta[1]([⊠]) [iD], Agostino Villa[2], and Gianni Piero Perrone[3]

[1] Department of Management and Production Engineering, Politecnico di Torino,
Corso Duca degli Abruzzi 24, 10129 Turin, Italy
gianfranco.genta@polito.it
[2] Politecnico di Torino, Corso Duca degli Abruzzi 24, 10129 Turin, Italy
[3] Perrone Informatica, Corso Venezia 53, 14100 Asti, Italy

Abstract. This paper first presents a formal model of the transactions activated in a blockchain used to manage a supply chain composed by Small-Mid Enterprises (SME). Such a formal model is based on a correspondence between the decision to be taken by a SME each time a new order is arrived from a downstream stage of the supply chain, and the formulation of a transaction in a blockchain. Based on this correspondence, a model of the blockchain management of all SMEs included in a supply chain is formulated according to the basic concepts of an event-driven production scheduling problem. The resulting blockchain model can be represented by a table showing the interactions between a provider and a consumer in terms of smart contract, thus connecting two stages of the supply chain. The transaction security is assured by secret codes of both the contract and the two actors, namely the provider and the consumer. Applications of blockchain to two SMEs operating in the agro-food sector is briefly described, thus showing the real impact of blockchain-based management in practice situations.

Keywords: Supply chain management · Event-driven scheduling · Blockchain

1 Introduction

Recently, blockchain application appears to be a powerful tool for management in industrial sectors of particular importance for the industrial world, mainly if applied to Small-Mid Enterprises (SMEs) supply chain management. The reason for the growing industrial interest for this blockchain application is that in a supply chain a huge number of movements of materials and information take place within a network of pairs of actors, being the upstream one the "provider or supplier" and the downstream one the "customers", and daily transactions must be managed via a very large number of contracts [1, 2]. Blockchain should guarantee the safe management of this mass of movements and relations among said actors [3].

In order to have a clear view of the two types of applications mentioned above, first it is necessary to recognize and state an industry-oriented model of how a SME, included in a supply chain, takes decisions concerning the schedule of orders received from other SMEs belonging to the downstream stages of the supply chain itself. According

© IFIP International Federation for Information Processing 2021
Published by Springer Nature Switzerland AG 2021
A. Dolgui et al. (Eds.): APMS 2021, IFIP AICT 632, pp. 480–488, 2021.
https://doi.org/10.1007/978-3-030-85906-0_53

to a theoretical point of view, the considered SME decision problem corresponds to an "event-driven production scheduling" one [4].

Then, a model of the blockchain transactions between two considered SMEs in the supply chain, based on the concept of digital ledgers, as well as a model of data and contract transfer in a network of SMEs (i.e., blockchain nodes) must be stated and its application be analyzed.

These two statements introduce a strong correspondence between event-driven scheduling at a SME inside a supply chain stage, and the management of the nodes of a blockchain.

Based on this correspondence, the following Sect. 2 will describe the event-driven scheduling problem to be solved by a SME at the arrival of a new order (i.e. from the supply chain downstream stage), when some previous orders (now denoted "jobs") are under processing; some jobs have already been finished; other jobs are waiting to be loaded for work. Then, at the arrival of a new order, the SME has to decide which order - among those queueing - must be completed and delivered to downstream stage: this means which transaction must be activated with a downstream SME.

This aspect, in the development of any blockchain oriented to a simple application, is of particular importance, because it refers to the identification, even if approximate, of the critical reaction time for a given event [5]. In addition, the difficulty of this evaluation is increased by the desire of the blockchain manager to tend to the imple-mentation of a zero-defect production or delivery strategy, particularly in the case of multi-stage productions [6].

Section 3 gives a new simple model of the "transaction" between a consumer and the provider. For sake of presenting a scheme of transaction easily understood by SME manager, first a basic comparison between a traditional ledger and a blockchain-used ledger is illustrated. Then, a new detailed scheme of a transaction between the two above mentioned actors is shown.

Since a blockchain transaction is represented on-line by a "block", Sect. 4 will give a simplified scheme of the block transfer in the network, its approval and its linkage to a chain, such that the transaction will be registered and remain protected and permanently in the blockchain.

Section 5 discusses how the blockchain can impact supply chains by referring to two types of applications, by which a brief analysis the main problems that may arise in real situations of blockchain utilization will be shown.

Finally, Sect. 6 will outline some remark on the interest – but also the difficulty – of applying blockchain in industrial practice.

2   Simplified Model of the Event-Driven Scheduling at a SME in a Supply Chain Stage

In industrial practice, a SME belonging to a supply chain stage has to satisfy the orders of downstream stage customers as soon as possible, mainly taking into account the "importance" of each customer itself. Then, it must be able to assure prompt product delivery by an effective event-driven re-scheduling of production, but without any information on the occurrence of the next event, i.e. the acceptance of customer orders for any type of products that the SME is able to manufacture. This is the case of the problem widely discussed in the paper [7], to address the re-scheduling caused by unexpected events, as well as in the paper [8], discussing re-scheduling in semi-automated assembling lines in front of rush orders events. In this second case, it would be really important to have at disposal a good procedure for predicting rush orders, such as the possibility of regulating the capacity reservation mechanism in advance [9].

Indeed, since the production of any order (denoted also job) from downstream in the supply chain requires the execution of a sequence of operations by the production resources, at the arrival time of a new order only some operations of a job have already been completed. Therefore, at that time, the "state" of any job has to be updated, where the term "job state" indicates the number of operations to be still executed to complete the job itself.

At each event time, the production reorganization at the considered SME has to be based on the new state of each jobs, then characterizing the event-driven dynamics of the production scheduling problem, as formally stated in [4].

Given any job under processing (i.e., order already received):

- to the operations already started and completed for this same job, an operation time equal to zero will be assigned;
- for the set of all the other operations, both the ones previously scheduled but not yet completed and the ones required to complete the new job, a new re-scheduling problem must be solved.

The difficulty to apply a job-shop rescheduling procedure in a SME pushes any manager to allocate jobs in the production plant by using very simplified logic, whose application seems him to be apparently useful and clear, even if frequently inefficient.

From the analysis of about 100 SMEs, settled in different Italian regions, within the PMInnova Program [10], it has been recognized the following event-driven scheduling rule [4]. Any arrival of a new order forces the manager to re-schedule by adopting one of the following criteria:

1. to decide to not modify the schedule under use, and insert the new job as the last in the queue to be processed; this rule is usually mentioned by SME managers as "weighted FIFO" or simply "FIFO" and, in some cases, as "JIT-type", if their internal movements of parts are managed by using cards;
2. to insert the new job as soon as one of those under processing will be completed, if the customer has a good level of importance; this is denoted as "weighted clients";
3. to allocate only biggest jobs, also considering some weights depending on the client importance and include smaller lots in a random way (denoted "random entry of new orders").

Each one of these decision-making criteria corresponds to a type of formulating a transaction in a blockchain used to manage order-driven interactions between two stages of the supply chain.

3   Model of a Blockchain Transaction Based on Digital Ledger

In practice, blockchain is a single master book for collecting and storing the transactions of a large number of Providers (upstream stage SMEs) and Consumers (downstream stage SMEs).

Traditionally, each pair of Providers and Consumers recorded the transaction that remained indefinitely in each book on their personal ledger. In the blockchain managing a supply chain, this happens for the unique decentralized distributed "Ledger of Blockchain" with the condition that each transaction (which became a block) is associated with the Provider & Consumer pair.

An individual traditional ledger will include, for any transaction, all data referred to a purchase or a sale. A unique general Ledger managed by a blockchain will contain, besides the transaction data, also a number of keys and signatures of both the Consumer and the Provider, as well as "secret key" associated to the transaction/contract itself.

The following Table 1 illustrates a comparison between the traditional ledger of either the consumer or the provider (in the left column), and the unique ledger managed by blockchain (in the right column).

Table 1. Comparison of transaction data registered in a traditional Ledger, and data/info's detailed in a transaction in a Blockchain.

Transaction's information and data contained in...	
Traditional Ledger	Blockchain-used Ledger
N° transaction	Transaction code
N° document	Contract code to be stored in the blockchain
Date Paid Received gain	Data set
Transaction description/type	Transaction type
Balance (everyone has their own)	Transaction balance:
	A. Provider and Consumer **public keys**, as actors operating on the unique ledger B. Provider and Consumer **signatures** to identify a one-to-one transaction **C. Secret key (Hash)** computed by Provider, to make the transaction readable by the Consumer

The following Table 2 is represented in a form similar to a flow chart, where the arrows illustrate the sequence of interactions between Consumer (C) and Provider (P) for activating a transaction in a blockchain.

Specifically, each arrow represents a transfer of information from one to the other actor of the transaction, thus showing the interaction between the Consumer C and a Provider P in stipulating a smart contract [11], with the additional scope of loading their

484   G. Genta et al.

Table 2. Interactions between Consumer (C) and Provider (P) for activating a transaction in a blockchain.

Consumer (C)	Provider (P)
Once the desired service and the Provider have been selected by the Consumer:	
C creates: - its Signature **SigC** and its Public key **PubC**	Provider creates its Public key **PubB** and the digital signature **SigP**
1) C sends its Public Key → **PubC** to P	2)Provider P creates a _smart contract_ (SCo) 2a) and P creates a Secret Key of the contract (**K**)
	3)**Then, Provider P** compute the hash (**SH**) used for authentication of consumer feedback
SH is the commitment to the consumer to verify the correctness of the transaction ←	4)Provider P sends SH to the consumer
	5)Provider P creates the message **mc (PubC, SigP, SH)** 6)Then, P appends the smart contract SCo and the message **mc** into the blockchain
Blockchain: Please note: This step notifies to all the other nodes of the blockchain that Consumer C asks for the service defined by the small contract SCo	
7)Consumer C checks the smart contract and approve it, by recognizing the smart contract by using **mc**	
	8)Provider P sees that the Smart Contract SCo is approved and send Secret Key (**K**) associated to the smart contract SCo
9)The contract's service type can be read, and a feedback message is created **fmc (K, PubP, SH, FV)**, where **FV** is the feedback value created together with **SigC**)	
10)Then, Consumer C sends the feedback value **Fv** for the service supplied by the smart contract SCo to the Provider P →	11)Provider P receives the feedback value **Fv**
Blockchain: For the Smart Contract SCo **it will be** verified: • The transactions indexed by **SH**; • The signatures **SigC** and **SigP** And the feedback transaction is included in the Blockchain, together a time mark (**Timestamp**), being represented on line as a "**block**" • The smart contract SCo is closed.	

contract on a unique distributed ledger, thus assuring their security through use of keys. The transaction is represented online as a "block".

The question now is how to manage a very large number of blocks, assuring them security and immutability.

4   Models of Blocks Transfer in Network of Blockchain Nodes

Blockchain is a set of blocks, each one archiving a set of validated and timestamp related transactions. Each block includes its own hash, i.e., a non-invertible algorithmic computer function that uniquely identifies the block and allows connection with the previous block by identifying the latter.

Each transaction can be practically managed by a Smart Contract (SCo) between a Consumer and a Provider, sent to blockchain as illustrated in Table 2, and reported in the following steps:

A.   a new block to be chained is created upon the execution of the smart contract SCo;
B.   this block (i) is chained to a previous one and includes:

- the previous block hash BH(i-1);
- the timestamp of the transactions contained in the block;
- the transaction;
- the hash of the transactions (SH) referred to the Smart Contract and the book sign, i.e., BH(i) done by the block creator.

C.   the inclusion of a new block into the Blockchain it must be approved.

A simplified scheme of the transaction approval in the blockchain, as well as of the block connection to other blocks, such to create a "blockchain", is the following:

1.   Customer C wants to pay a desired service to the Provider P for the considered smart contract SCo.
2.   The transaction is represented as a "block" (which could also contain other transactions to be verified and accepted in the blockchain).
3.   The block is broadcast to several other "nodes" of an internet network; each node could be a server or a simple computer, all connected.
4.   A selected group of nodes, or the majority of nodes in the network, will approve (or not) if the transition is valid.
5.   The considered block is then added to other blocks, previously created, thus obtaining a secure record of transactions, denoted "blockchain".
6.   Provider P will then receive the payment for the transaction.

5   Blockchain Applications in Real Supply Chains

According to the previous Section, blockchain applications have undoubtedly the potential to improve the supply chain sector because they provide an infrastructure that records, certifies and maps an asset that is transferred between often distant parts, connected between them through a chain of distribution between parties that are not necessarily bound by a bond of trust [12]. In this way, assets would be pawns that can be transferred along a chain of control that verifies over time, in an encrypted and transparent process, a transaction. The terms of each transaction would remain irrevocable and immutable, open to the control of anyone or only authorized users.

This has been verified by the blockchain application for two Small-Mid Enterprises (SME) operating in the agri-food sector, registered in the PMInnova Program [10]. For the two companies AGROCOMPANY (www.agrocompany.it) and the Consorzio dei Produttori di Piccoli Frutti (www.ciacuneo.org/frutta_verdura_piccoli_frutti.htm), the main problem is to manage a "short" supply chain to be able to implement a retail sale via e-commerce, but with a large number of small transactions.

On the other hand, if many analyses believe that one of the sectors that will benefit the most from the point of view of the consumer is the food industry, unfortunately there are examples of cases of mass contamination of food chains due to poor control on suppliers and other reasons related to production, such as excessive use of herbicides, fertilizers and various ways of storing products through incorrect freezing.

One of the most interesting initiatives to create transparent supply chains for food products in every part of their life cycle is the company Project Provenance Ltd (https://www.provenance.org/), which is developing a platform that, for each product or component it manages, at each point in the supply chain it details the nature (what it is), the quantity, the quality and the property [13].

With reference to the above mentioned two Italian SMEs, producing valuable agri-food products, those with a "controlled designation of origin - DOC", the applied blockchain could help to counter frauds in the sale of controlled-source Italian goods. An accurate product record could also make the managed supply chain more efficient and send food to stores faster, thus reducing waste and waste, especially by using "smart contracts" [13].

6 Concluding Remarks

The blockchain represents a new system of data distribution, extremely innovative and still little used as it is little known and detailed without a real standard, if not that of the bitcoins that have made it known. Although it is an innovative concept, it presents limits due to the lack of standards and, moreover, uses cryptographic systems that are dated and need to be evolved. Today, the cryptography of twenty years ago is still used, and the real problem is not its vulnerability but rather recognizing its authenticity of origin. In fact, it is almost impossible to attack a blockchain, but it is possible to create a false one. The problem of web security has never grown like the power of the web itself. Blockchain could distort the current concept of many servers also replicated that still contain data that are centralized and therefore very vulnerable.

However, there are some resistances to the adoption of this technology. What seems to be the biggest concern on the part of business owners is the fact that this technology is based on a public and shared ledger, which means that companies must freely allow others to have access to information. But the fact that there is a public register does not mean that one must necessarily share everything with everyone. Blockchain technology allows to manage information in a private way, making only the directly involved parties participate. Only those authorized can access the information of a contract. Furthermore, the blockchain is a chain where the past is always a recognizable trace ("inviolability of the past"), and the blocks are always sequential and maintain the history of the whole chain ("ordering of events"), as well as being available in each node and therefore also replicated ("competition and information retrieval").

It must also be said that there is currently no standard and perhaps it is the main problem of the blockchain. It will take years, and in the meantime, each application will follow a proprietary path by dirtying the data network. To protect the privacy of the chains, the risk is of overload of the transport band and one will have to think also of a useless or obsolete chain cleaning system. The comparison that comes to mind is that of plastic: a beautiful invention but people must be able to dispose of it.

Within few years, many communication technologies will disappear, will change the professionalism, and will change the life of man as well as it has happened from the 90s to today with the introduction of the World Wide Web (www). We must remember that technology is ready: blockchain is an integral part of this technology. Keep in mind that even today a small or large reality that is without connection presents very large problems. In the near future, the connection will be essential for any small or large business, so the hope is that it is powerful but, above all, safe.

Acknowledgments. This paper has been developed within the official agreement between Politecnico di Torino and Gruppo Banca di Asti, under the initiative Programma PMInnova - Promote innovation and development in SMEs.

References

1. Zheng, Z., Xie, S., Dai, H.-N., Chen, X., Wang, H.: Blockchain challenges and opportunities: a survey. Int. J. Web Grid Serv. **14**(4), 352–375 (2018)
2. Antonelli, D., Bruno, G., Taurino, T., Villa, A.: Graph-based models to classify effective collaboration in SME networks. Int. J. Prod. Res. **53**(20), 6198–6209 (2015)
3. Kehrli, J.: Blockchain explained. https://www.niceideas.ch/blockchain_explained.pdf. Accessed 20 Mar 2021
4. Villa, A., Taurino, T.: Event-driven production scheduling in SME. Prod. Plan. Control **29**(4), 271–279 (2017)
5. Leitão, P., Barbosa, J., Geraldes, C., Coelho, J.: Multi-agent system architecture for Zero Defect multi-stage manufacturing. In: Borangiu, T., Trentesaux, D., Thomas, A., Cardin, O. (eds.) Service Orientation in Holonic and Multi-Agent Manufacturing. SCI, vol. 762, pp. 13–26. Springer, Cham (2018). https://doi.org/10.1007/978-3-319-73751-5_2
6. Barbosa, J., Leitao, P., Ferreira, A., Queiroz, J., Geraldes, C.A.S., Coelho, J.P.: Implementation of a multi-agent system to support ZDM strategies in multi-stage environments. In: Proceedings of 2018 IEEE 16th International Conference on Industrial Informatics (INDIN), pp. 822–827 (2018)
7. Psarommatis, F., Gharaei, A., Kiritsis, D.: Identification of the critical reaction times for rescheduling flexible job shops for different types of unexpected events. Procedia CIRP **93**, 903–908 (2020)
8. Psarommatis, F., Zheng, X., Kiritsis, D.: A two-layer criteria evaluation approach for rescheduling efficiently semi-automated assembly lines with high number of rush orders. Procedia CIRP **97**, 172–177 (2021)

9. Wang, W.-P., Chen, Z.: A neuro-fuzzy based forecasting approach for rush order control applications. Expert Syst. Appl. **35**(1–2), 223–234 (2008)
10. Villa, A.: Scientific Coordinator, PMInnova Program, Official agreement between Politecnico di Torino and Gruppo Banca di Asti. https://www.pminnova.eu/. Accessed 20 Mar 2021
11. De Caria, R.: The legal meaning of smart contract. Eur. Rev. Private Law **6**, 731–752 (2019)
12. Saberi, S., Kouhizadeh, M., Sarkis, J., Shen, L.: Blockchain technology and its relationships to sustainable supply chain management. Int. J. Prod. Res. **57**(7), 2117–2135 (2019)
13. Kim, H.M., Laskowski, M.: Toward an ontology - driven blockchain design for supply-chain provenance. Intell. Syst. Account. Finance Manag. **25**(1), 18–27 (2018)

Optimization of Hierarchical Production Planning with Setup Time Feasibility for Effective Supply Chain Management

Guisen Xue[✉] [iD] and O. Felix Offodile [iD]

College of Business Administration, Kent State University, Kent, OH 44242, USA
gxue@kent.edu

Abstract. In this paper, we propose a two-tier mixed integer linear programming (MILP) model, composed of aggregate production planning (APP) and family dis-aggregation planning (FDP), to solve the hierarchical production planning (HPP) problem with nontrivial setup times. In addition to disaggregating the aggregate plan in the first period into detailed lot sizing plans as traditional models do, the proposed FDP model optimally adjusts the aggregate plan and eliminates infeasibility arising from the positive setup times. The performance of the proposed model is validated with a case study. Results of the validation show that the proposed model leads to significant cost savings and efficiencies in the supply chain compared to traditional HPP models.

Keywords: Hierarchical production planning · Aggregate production planning · Setup time · Supply chain management · Prescriptive analytics

1 Introduction

In the past few decades, companies have increased their product variety to satisfy customized demands and enhance competitiveness. Unfortunately, increases in product variety create negative effects on operations, such as high inventory level, demand forecasting bias [1], buffer capacity, frequent changeover, and workforce fluctuations. To face challenges of a volatile and smart market demand characterized by customization in the era of Industry 4.0 [2], manufacturers have to elaborately plan their production using modern systems such as *Seru*, Cellular Manufacturing, and Toyota Production System. With higher product variety, shorter product life cycles, and faster responsiveness, mixed-model and small-batch production continue to dominate the production strategy in the supply chain of modern manufacturing companies. Therefore, the production planning problem (PPP) becomes too complex to be solved easily.

Two approaches are traditionally used to model the PPP: monolithic and hierarchical. The monolithic approach produces more accurate results for individual items, but the time-consuming and expensive forecasts for the sporadic demand of thousands of items and the solution of the large-scale monolithic model discourage its wide application. This approach has long been rejected in the literature [3, 4]. On the other hand,

© IFIP International Federation for Information Processing 2021
Published by Springer Nature Switzerland AG 2021
A. Dolgui et al. (Eds.): APMS 2021, IFIP AICT 632, pp. 489–498, 2021.
https://doi.org/10.1007/978-3-030-85906-0_54

the hierarchical approach decomposes PPP into several layers of sub-problems that are easier to solve. Proper product aggregation can reduce the forecast bias and variability for the highly volatile and smart product demands. In most studies on HPP the information flow between two consecutive levels is hierarchical, with the APP model imposing constraints on the FDP model. Traditional HPP systems [4–6] employ the rolling horizon procedure to coordinate the interaction between them at the end of current period when the completion condition of the aggregate plan in the period has been determined. However, the feedback information cannot be capitalized on to adjust the APP in the current period, missing an opportunity to globally optimize the production plans in the planning horizon. Furthermore, the aggregate plan becomes infeasible after considering setup times in the FDP model, since the setup times consume some capacity.

In this study, a novel iterative optimization mechanism is proposed to optimally adjust the aggregate plan in the current period with the feedforward information from the FDP model and further optimize the production plan in the planning horizon. The mechanism also eliminates the infeasibility brought about by the non-trivial family setup times, which consume production capacity but are often ignored in the APP.

2 Literature Review

The theoretical and practical benefits of the HPP approach have been documented in the literature [3, 4, 6–9]. These HPP systems belong to the classical hierarchical class of models since they observe a strict top-down open loop solution procedure without regard to the interaction between the production tiers. However, efficient feedback procedures for anticipating the influence of lower planning levels on higher ones can improve information accuracy and bridge the production asymmetry between the two levels of HPP systems.

In order to optimize the performance of hierarchical systems, Schneeweiss [9] proposes an interaction scheme that considers feedback from and anticipation of the lower-level system. The interaction scheme is widely applied to HPP and other hierarchical systems, such as supply chain [10]. In the HPP system proposed by Qiu et al. [11], the concept of expected setup costs and anticipation of lower-level decision are incorporated into the aggregate planning level resulting in better production decisions than the traditional HPP system [12]. The feedback from lower-level systems is achieved through inaccurate anticipation, and therefore the effectiveness of the iterative optimization is questionable. Moreover, the influence of nontrivial setup times on aggregate plans is not considered in these HPP systems.

Omar and Teo [8] propose a three-level HPP and scheduling approach considering production planning and setup activities for each family, but the solution complexity of the model is large due to the inclusion of setups in all periods of the planning horizon. Jozefowska and Zimniak [13] propose a decision support system for short-term production planning and scheduling. The setup times occupy production capacity in the model, but their effects on the upper-level decision are not considered.

In HPP system [4], the capacity and inventory levels generated in APP impose constraints on the production and inventory in master production scheduling (MPS). In MPS model, setup times are included, but overtime is required to extend the production capacity, losing the opportunity of making the optimal adjustment resulting from setup times in the APP. Alvarez et al. [7] focus on improving the consistency in their hierarchical tactical and operational planning models, and ignores the infeasibility brought about by setup times.

Xue et al. [14] propose a full-space method that optimally integrates APP and FDP, with consideration for sequence-dependent family setup times. Xue et al. [15] also incorporate their integrated model in the dynamic cellular manufacturing setting to generate the optimal production plan and cell formation in each period. However, the solution complexity and customized algorithm for this model may not meet the managers' need for lower solution efforts, thereby encumbering its efficacy.

Therefore, an iterative optimization of HPP systems which considers the influence of family setup times on the feasibility of aggregate plans, adjusts the aggregate plan in the current period with the feedback information from FDP model for global optima, and considers the need of lower solution efforts in comparison with full-space method, is needed. This paper bridges this gap in the HPP literature.

3   The Proposed HPP System

3.1   The Traditional APP Model

The traditional APP model considers most mid-term decisions, with the objective of minimizing the total cost related to the lower-level decisions. Legend for all notations is summarized as follows:

Indices
$m = 1,..., M$ type.
$t = 1,...,T$ period.
$i = 1,...,I$ family.
Parameters
d_{mt} net demand of type m in period t.
ut_m unit processing time of type m.
A capacity allowance percentage (used for breakdowns, rest, absenteeism, etc.).
po percentage of overtime hours permitted (used to limit maximum overtime hours).
pu percentage of underutilization.
ua_m space occupied by a unit of type m.
$J(m)$ families pertaining to type m.
st_i setup time of family i.
sl_m fill rate (β service level) of type m.
OS total available space for inventory storage.
V a large number.
sc cost per unit setup time.
h_{mt} unit inventory holding cost of type m in period t.
c_{mt} unit production cost (labor cost excluded) of type m in period t.
cr_t, co_t regular time and overtime cost per man hour in period t.
cs_{mt}, cb_{mt} unit subcontracting and backordering cost of type m in period t.
ch_t, cf_t cost of hiring and laying off one man hour in period t.
CAS_{mt} maximum subcontracting capacity of type m in period t.

α_{it}, β_{it} lower and upper proportions of family i to its type in period t.

Decision variables

X_{mt} production level of type m in period t.

I_{mt} inventory level of product type m at the end of period t.

R_{mt}, O_{mt} regular time and overtime hours consumed for type m in period t.

S_{mt}, B_{mt} subcontracting and backordering quantity of type m in period t.

H_t, F_t man hours hired and laid off in period t.

P_{it} production quantity of family i in period t.

AR_t, AO_t added regular time and overtime hours in period t.

AS_{mt}, AB_{mt} added subcontracting and backordering quantity of type m in period t.

Auxiliary variables

TR_t, TO_t total regular time and overtime hours in period t.

The APP model, which is a mixed integer linear programming (MILP) model, can be formulated as follows:

$$Min \sum_{t=1}^{T} \left[ch_t H_t + cf_t F_t + \sum_{m=1}^{M} (c_{mt} X_{mt} + h_{mt} I_{mt} + cb_{mt} B_{mt} + cr_t R_{mt} + co_t O_{mt} + cs_{mt} S_{mt}) \right] \tag{1}$$

s.t.

$$I_{m,t-1} + X_{mt} + S_{mt} - I_{mt} + B_{mt} - B_{m,t-1} = d_{mt} \quad \forall m, t \tag{2}$$

$$\sum_{m=1}^{M} ut_m X_{mt} \leq (TR_t + TO_t) \cdot A \quad \forall t \tag{3}$$

$$\sum_{m=1}^{M} ut_m X_{mt} \geq (1 - pu) TR_t \quad \forall t \tag{4}$$

$$ut_m X_{mt} = R_{mt} + O_{mt} \quad \forall m, t \tag{5}$$

$$\sum_{m=1}^{M} R_{mt} \leq TR_t \cdot A \quad \forall t \tag{6}$$

$$S_{mt} \leq CAS_{mt} \quad \forall m, t \tag{7}$$

$$B_{mt} \leq (1 - sl_m) d_{mt} \quad \forall m, t \tag{8}$$

$$TR_t - TR_{t-1} = H_t - F_t \quad \forall t \tag{9}$$

$$\sum_{m=1}^{M} ua_m I_{mt} \leq OS \quad \forall t \tag{10}$$

$$X_{mt}, I_{mt}, B_{mt}, S_{mt} \geq 0 \text{ and integer } \forall m, t \tag{11}$$

$$R_{mt}, O_{mt}, H_t, F_t \geq 0 \quad \forall m, t \tag{12}$$

In the model, constraints (2) are the inventory balance equations. Constraints (3) are regular time and overtime capacity limits. In order to balance production in different periods, constraints (4) set lower bounds for the utilization of available capacity. In constraints (5), the total capacity consumed by each type in each period is defined. The consumed total regular time will not exceed the available regular time capacity in constraints (6). Constraints (7) and (8) are subcontracting and backordering limits. Constraints (9) are the balance equations for the relationship between the change in available regular time in two adjacent periods and the fluctuation value arising from hiring or laying off man-hours. Constraints (10) are the inventory limits.

3.2 The FDP Model

In the FDP model proposed in this paper the optimal scheme to adjust the aggregate plan in the first period is integrated. The model (1) determines the optimal production quantity of each family, (2) minimizes the sum of setup costs and extra costs including labor costs, subcontracting and backordering costs, arising from the adjustment of the aggregate plan in the first period, and (3) transforms the infeasible aggregate plan to feasibility. Furthermore, X_{m1}, TR_1, TO_1, R_{m1}, O_{m1}, CAS_{m1}, S_{m1}, and B_{m1} obtained from the APP model facilitate the solution of the FDP model.

The FDP model can be formulated as follows:

$$Min \sum_{i=1}^{I} (sc \cdot st_i Z_{i1}) + cr_1 AR_1 + co_1 AO_1 + \sum_{m=1}^{M} [(cs_{m1} - c_{m1})AS_{m1} + (cb_{m1} - c_{m1})AB_{m1}] \quad (13)$$

s.t.

$$\sum_{i \in J(m)} P_{i1} = X_{m1} - AS_{m1} - AB_{m1} \quad \forall m \quad (14)$$

$$\sum_{i=1}^{I} st_i Z_{i1} = AR_1 + AO_1 + \sum_{m=1}^{M} ut_m (AS_{m1} + AB_{m1}) \quad (15)$$

$$AR_1 \leq TR_1 \cdot A - \sum_{m=1}^{M} R_{m1} \quad (16)$$

$$AO_1 \leq TO_1 \cdot A - \sum_{m=1}^{M} O_{m1} \quad (17)$$

$$AS_{m1} \leq CAS_{m1} - S_{m1} \quad \forall m \quad (18)$$

$$AB_{m1} \leq (1 - sl_m)d_{m1} - B_{m1} \quad \forall m \quad (19)$$

$$\alpha_{i1} X_{m1} \leq P_{i1} \leq \beta_{i1} X_{m1} \quad \forall i \in J(m), \forall m \quad (20)$$

$$Z_{i1} \leq P_{i1} \leq Z_{i1} \cdot V \quad \forall i \quad (21)$$

$$Z_{i1} \in \{0, 1\}, P_{i1}, S_{m1}, AB_{m1} \geq 0 \text{ and integer } \forall i, m \quad (22)$$

$$AR_1, AO_1 \geq 0 \tag{23}$$

In the model, constraints (14) indicate that the production quantity of a type in the first period is not necessarily disaggregated into that of the families within the type because some may be subcontracted or backordered. Constraints (15) show the options to absorb setup times. Constraints (16) and (17) are the maximum idle regular time and overtime in the first period. Constraints (18) and (19) are the maximum permitted subcontracting and backlogging quantities. Constraints (20) set the lower and upper bounds of the production quantity of each family in the first period. Constraints (21) ensure that when family i is not produced in the first period, binary variable Z_{i1} is zero; otherwise, Z_{i1} is 1.

There are four options to absorb the influences of family setup times: idle regular time AR_1, idle overtime AO_1, or the released capacity resulting from added subcontracting quantities AS_{m1}, and added backordering quantities AB_{m1}. Therefore, the aggregate plan in the first period is adjusted and becomes feasible to implement.

4   Solution Heuristics

The APP model is solved first for types in order to obtain the production plans in the planning horizon and the production plan in the first period is implemented. Then, the proposed FDP model is solved with the adjustment feedback to the obtained production plan in the first period. The inherent adjustment rule heuristics used on the unconsumed capacity for single-type FDP model is summarized in Table 1. The assumption for the heuristics is that the added regular time cost is less than the added overtime cost, which is less than the added subcontracting cost and backlogging cost. These assumptions are is prevalent in practice.

In order to simplify the expression, the consumed total regular time and overtime are denoted as $TR'_t = \sum_{m=1}^{M} R_{mt}$ and $TO'_t = \sum_{m=1}^{M} O_{mt}$ respectively, while the total capacity consumed by the production of all types and setups between all families is set to be $TSP_t = \sum_{m=1}^{M} \left(ut_{mt} X_{mt} + \sum_{i=1}^{I} \sum_{j \in J(m)} \sum_{k=1}^{I} st_{ij} Y_{ijkt} \right)$. The inherent logic of the heuristics is as follows:

Case I: when $TSP_t \leq AR_t \cdot A$, that is, the idle regular time capacity is enough to absorb the setup times, $TSP_t - TR'_t$ units of extra regular time and no overtime will result. Since employing idle regular time is the most cost-saving option among the four options, the idle regular time is first used to absorb the setup times.

Case II: when TSP_t is between available regular time and total capacity, all idle regular time capacity $\left(AR_t \cdot A - TR'_t \right)$ and part of overtime capacity $\left(TSP_t - TR_t \cdot A - TO'_t \right)$ are employed to absorb the setup times since overtime is the second most cost-saving option except for regular time. Besides setup cost, the added costs include the labor costs of all idle regular time and part of the idle overtime necessary to replenish the capacity occupied by setup times.

Case III: when TSP_t is larger than total capacity, all idle regular time capacity $\left(TR_t \cdot A - TR'_t \right)$ and overtime capacity $\left(TO_t \cdot A - TO'_t \right)$ are not enough to absorb the

Table 1. Adjustment to the obtained aggregate plans with FDP results.

In any period, if:	$TSP_t \leq TR_t \cdot A$	$TR_t \cdot A < TSP_t \leq (TR_t + TO_t) \cdot A$	$TSP_t > (TR_t + TO_t) \cdot A$
Added regular time	$TSP_t - TR'_t$	$TR_t \cdot A - TR'_t$	$TR_t \cdot A - TR'_t$
Added overtime	0	$TSP_t - TR_t \cdot A - TO'_t$	$TO_t \cdot A - TO'_t$
Added total cost	$cr_t\left(TSP_t - TR'_t\right)$	$cr_t\left(TR_t - TR'_t\right) + co_t\left(TSP_t - TR_t \cdot A - TO'_t\right)$	$cr_t\left(TR_t - TR'_t\right) + co_t\left(TO_t \cdot A - TO'_t\right) + \sum_{m=1}^{M} \left[\left(cs_{mt} - c_{mt}\right)AS_{mt} + \left(cb_{mt} - c_{mt}\right)AB_{mt}\right]$

setup times, and some of the setup times are absorbed by the capacity released by sub-contracting or backordering some families scheduled for production. Besides the added labor costs of regular time and overtime, the added subcontracting (backordering) costs are the subcontracting (backordering) quantity multiplied by the difference between unit subcontracting (backordering) cost and unit production cost. Since the unit subcontract-ing costs are generally less than the unit backordering costs, subcontracting is preferred to backordering for absorbing the family setup times.

Finally, the feedback information from the FDP model is used to adjust the production plan in the first period and obtain the feasible and optimally adjusted production plan for the period. Then the HPP system is implemented on a rolling horizon basis and a new solution cycle starts at the end of the first period when updated information are available to plan production in the following planning horizon.

However, it is nontrivial to solve the FDP model with the above heuristics in a mul-tiple product production environment due to the different cost structures of the product types. Moreover, the disaggregation function of the FDP also hampers its quick solution. Therefore, some other optimizaiton method has to be introduced for the model. In this paper, branch-and-bound approach in LINGO 8 [16] is used to solve the FDP model.

5   Case Study

The manufacturing system for our test plant is a typical multi-product, small-batch and make-to-stock operation. Using data from the mold manufacturing plant, the APP model in the planning horizon of 12 months and the proposed FDP model in the first month are solved on a DELL OptiPlex GX-620 computer with 2.0 GHz RAM, W8400 Processor 80,547, Pentium 4 Prescott Dt 630. The integrated model proposed by Xue et al. [14] contains 3207 variables (3099 integer variables) and 4103 constraints. However, the integrated model could not reach optimality within a reasonable time frame.

In the MILP APP model proposed in this paper, there are 195 variables (96 integer variables), and 170 constraints. Since the APP model only plans the production of two types, its solution scale is drastically reduced and can be solved within 2 s. In the proposed MILP FDP model, only the production plan in the first month is disaggregated. The FDP model only needs 22 variables (14 integer variables) and 31 constraints to optimally adjust the aggregate plan in the first period and can be solved within 1 s.

From the solution, the aggregate plans for Types 1 and 2 in the first period, and the disaggregation and adjustment results are summarized in Table 2. The objective function of FDP model is $28,670, where the total setup cost is $1,220. In the production plan in the first period, the available regular time and overtime that can be used to absorb family setup times are 0 and 1364 h, respectively. Since the total family setup time is 61 h, the 1364-h overtime is enough to absorb the family setup times, which is also the result of the FDP model. Therefore, the production plan in the first period, which is infeasible due to the setup times, can be adjusted by using 61 h more of overtime in the first period.

In traditional HPP systems the extra cost resulting from the setup times is fixed at $53,460, nearly two times that of the results in this paper. Therefore, the proposed FDP model can adjust the aggregate plan in the first period to realize more cost savings.

Table 2. The aggregate plan in the first period and its adjustment.

Aggregate plan in the first period

Total regular time	Total overtime	Type 1	Type 2	Type 1	Type 2	Type 1	Type 2
		Subcontracting quantity		Backordering quantity		Production quantity	
3789	1516	0	0	0	0	125	82
Consumed regular time	Consumed overtime	Subcontracting capacity		Maximum backordering quantity		Inventory quantity	
3410	0	15	10	9	9	0	2

Input data for FDP model

Available regular time	Available overtime	Available subcontracting quantity		Available backordering quantity			
0	1364	15	10	9	9		

FDP model results

Added regular time	Added overtime	Added subcontracting quantity		Added backordering quantity		Total setup time	
0	61	0	0	0	0	61	

6 Conclusions and Future Research

This paper presents an iterative optimization approach of traditional HPP systems considering the feedback information from the FDP model. The proposed novel FDP model minimizes the family setup costs and extra costs arising from the adjustment of aggregate plans due to the existence of nontrivial family setup times. As is the case in most FDP models the proposed FDP model disaggregates the aggregate plan of types in the first period into detailed plans of families within the type. However, unlike other FDP models, the proposed FDP model also eliminates the infeasibility of the aggregate plan when setup times are nontrivial, and optimally adjusts the aggregate plan in the first period. Moreover, the proposed iterative optimization mechanism based on HPP system consummates the application of iterative method to the decomposition scenario of HPP problems.

Data from a mold manufacturing plant is used to validate the performance of the proposed FDP model. The results indicate that the proposed FDP model can optimally adjust the corresponding aggregate plan in the first period and eliminate the infeasibility arising from positive family setup times. The higher family setup times result in more cost savings over the traditional HPP systems. Moreover, compared with traditional HPP systems, the iterative optimization mechanism proposed in this paper can save over 37% of its setup and adjustment costs for each problem set.

This paper can be extended in two ways. First, the integration of APP and FDP models can lead to real optimization of the HPP system. Although the FDP model adjusts the aggregate plan optimally, the essence of sequential decisions of the two models impedes the achievement of true optimization. Therefore, an integrated model of APP and family disaggregation problems is worthy of further study. Second, the sequence dependency of family setup times and the lot sizes of each family can be integrated into the FDP model in the first period, since only sequence-independent setup times are considered in this paper.

References

1. Wan, X., Sanders, N.R.: The negative impact of product variety: forecast bias, inventory levels, and the role of vertical integration. Int. J. Prod. Econ. **186**, 123–131 (2017)
2. Yin, Y., Stecke, K.E., Li, D.: The evolution of production systems from Industry 2.0 through Industry 4.0. Int. J. Prod. Res. **56**(1–2), 848–861 (2018)
3. Sawik, T.: Monolithic versus hierarchical approach to integrated scheduling in a supply chain. Int. J. Prod. Res. **47**(21), 5881–5910 (2009)
4. Vogel, T., Almada-Lobo, B., Almeder, C.: Integrated versus hierarchical approach to aggregate production planning and master production scheduling. OR Spectrum **39**(1), 193–229 (2016). https://doi.org/10.1007/s00291-016-0450-2
5. Bitran, G.R., Haas, E.A., Hax, A.C.: Hierarchical production planning: a single stage system. Oper. Res. **29**(4), 717–743 (1981)
6. Selcuk, B., Fransoo, A.G., De Kok, A.G.: The effect of updating lead times on the performance of hierarchical planning systems. Int. J. Prod. Econ. **104**, 427–440 (2006)
7. Alvarez, P.P., Espinoza, A., Maturana, S., Vera, J.: Improving consistency in hierarchical tactical and operational planning using robust optimization. Comput. Ind. Eng. **139**, 106–112 (2020)
8. Omar, M.K., Teo, S.C.: Hierarchical production planning and scheduling in a multi-product, batch process environment. Int. J. Prod. Res. **45**(5), 1029–1047 (2007)
9. Schneeweiss, C.: Hierarchical planning in organizations: elements of a general theory. Int. J. Prod. Econ. **56–57**, 547–556 (1998)
10. Schneeweiss, C., Zimmer, K.: Hierarchical coordination mechanisms within the supply chain. Eur. J. Oper. Res. **152**, 687–703 (2004)
11. Qiu, M.M., Fredendall, L.D., Zhu, Z.: Application of hierarchical production planning in a multiproduct, multimachine environment. Int. J. Prod. Res. **39**(13), 2803–2816 (2001)
12. Bowers, M.R., Jarvis, J.P.: A hierarchical production planning and scheduling model. Decis. Sci. **23**, 144–159 (1992)
13. Jozefowska, J., Zimniak, A.: Optimization tool for short-term production planning and scheduling. Int. J. Prod. Econ. **112**, 109–120 (2008)
14. Xue, G., Offodile, O.F., Zhou, H., Troutt, M.D.: Integrated production planning with sequence dependent family setup times. Int. J. Prod. Econ. **131**, 674–681 (2011)
15. Xue, G., Offodile, O.F.: Integrated optimization of dynamic cell formation and hierarchical production planning problems. Comput. Ind. Eng. **139**, 106155 (2020)
16. LINDO User's Manual. Lindo Systems Inc., Chicago, IL (2003)

Integrated Planning of IoT-Based Smart Bin Allocation and Vehicle Routing in Solid Waste Management

Arindam Roy[1,3], Apurba Manna[2], Jungmin Kim[3], and Ilkyeong Moon[3,4(✉)]

[1] Department of Computer Science and Application, Prabhat Kumar College,
Contai 721404, India
[2] Research Centre in Natural Sciences, Raja N L Khan Women's College,
Medinipur 721102, India
[3] Department of Industrial Engineering, Seoul National University,
Seoul 08826, Korea
ikmoon@snu.ac.kr
[4] Institute of Industrial Systems Innovation, Seoul National University,
Seoul 08826, Korea

Abstract. The internet of things (IoT) is a prominent modern technology that offers robust solutions to modernizing consecutive systems. It accords controlled and calibrated outcomes to streamline smart cities, smart homes, smart industries, and smart environments. In this study, an ultrasonic sensor-based waste filling level is considered on IoT-based waste bins to optimize dynamic routes instead of fixed routes, such that the efficiency of waste collection and transportation can be improved. This article illustrates the time-dependent penalty concept to waste management authorities if these smart bins are not emptied in time after becoming full. This article presents a smart waste management model for smart cities that takes into account both bin allocation costs and routing costs. An innovative meta-heuristic neighborhood search technique is developed to solve the above model. The proposed model is illustrated with some numerical data, and a sensitivity analysis is performed with some parameters. After the waste from smart waste bins is collected, some waste products are recycled and reused through application of the game-theoretic concept involving the South Korean aspect of waste management.

Keywords: Smart bin · Neighbourhood search · Vehicle routing

1 Introduction

Due to rapid urbanization, waste management is becoming a vital issue in today's developed and developing countries. In South Korea, a rapid transition to urbanization and industrialization has changed both solid waste characteristics and management techniques. The generation of municipal solid waste (MSW) has

© IFIP International Federation for Information Processing 2021
Published by Springer Nature Switzerland AG 2021
A. Dolgui et al. (Eds.): APMS 2021, IFIP AICT 632, pp. 499–509, 2021.
https://doi.org/10.1007/978-3-030-85906-0_55

increased many times over the past few years in urban areas. Hence, the collection and treatment of waste are twin headaches that present vital problems to waste management authorities. Traditionally, waste bins are cleaned at certain intervals by cleaners. But, this process has plenty of drawbacks. Continuous monitoring is required to control the overflow of waste bins for a healthy and clean environment. Sometimes in specific areas, waste bins are filled up faster, due to various factors like festive seasons and unexpected overloads. The situation gets worse in the monsoon season, when rainwater enters waste bins, leading to the decomposition of waste by bacteria and insects that in turn increase the release of bad odors.

Nowadays, both municipal and private authorities are giving serious consideration to the use of advanced technologies, such as computerized vehicles, that make decisions on optimal route planning and scheduling for collecting waste, as described by Huang and Lin [8]. The mathematical model most often used for vehicle routing to collect municipal solid waste was presented by Beltrami and Bodin [4]. Angelelli and Speranza [2] considered a model in which collection vehicles use immediate facilities for unloading along their routes. In another research paper, Angelelli and Speranza [3] considered an algorithm that was used to measure the operating costs of three different waste-collection systems. Hemmelmayr et al. [7] presented one research paper on integrated waste bin allocation and vehicle routing in solid waste management. In that paper, however, they considered bin allocation cost and routing cost separately and did not consider smart waste bins. Nuortio et al. [9] and Vicentini et al. [11] developed sensitized waste collection containers for content estimation and collection optimization, but have not considered any other new advanced web-based information systems. Today, advanced IoT algorithms can boost information technology to a large extent. Sinha, Kumar, and Saisharan [10] proposed a smart waste bin that can contribute to a clean and hygienic environment to build a smart city. In our proposed model, we consider the smart waste bin system, which therefore has the potential for detecting the overflow of waste through an ultrasonic sensor. A smart waste bin can send a message to a central monitoring system (CMS) to clean the waste bin. Using our Vehicle Routing technique, we can clean the bin as early and efficiently as possible. A time-dependent penalty is considered if the filled (100%) bins are not emptied in time. Our study also highlights the game-theoretic approach of private and public waste collection and the ways in which waste is properly utilized for different purposes in South Korean society.

2   Smart Bin

Our proposed model of an IoT-based smart bin system has the potential for remotely detecting overflow of waste bins. Given this potential, it also has the potential to alert waste management authorities regarding the cleaning of waste bins in case of overflows above a set threshold fill level (TFL).

Detail Configuration

Ultrasonic Sensors (USs): Ultrasonic sensors sense the distance between the closing lid of the smart bin and the level of waste within it. The continuously recorded data by USs is sent to a Wi-Fi module through the ARDUINO UNO system in real-time data from the smart bin's US sensor and is transmitted through the wireless module to a smart waste management application platform. The ARDUINO UNO system is an automation system derived from the use of an ARDUINO UNO board; automation refers to the entire self-functioning system. The board itself acts as the "brain" or the central processing unit (CPU) for the entire apparatus. It controls the various interactions and synchronizations of the sensors.

Wi-Fi Module: Internet access, through Wi-Fi, will be allocated to our system by DSP8206, which is known as a Wi-Fi module. The Wi-Fi module can communicate with any kind of micro-controller and can help in making the system wireless for remote access. The Arduino technology is among the leading transmitting devices in the IoT platform.

Working Principle: Through the use of an Arduino board and the sensors, we can automate the function of a normal bin, thereby turning it into a smart bin. By using the US, the smart bin can measure the amount of waste, and detailed information on it can be sent to the Arduino board. As soon as the waste reaches a particular level set by the waste management authorities, the smart bin sends a notification to the municipal corporation for immediate cleaning of the bin. The Wi-Fi module is triggered from the Arduino board and sends the real-time data to the central monitoring system to analyze the amount of waste that is within the bin.

3   Problem Description and Mathematical Formulation

We present the smart waste collection problem occurring in a smart city where some IoT-based smart bins are placed in different places around the city. Our problem consists of integrating the IoT-based smart bin allocation with vehicle routing for waste collection. This problem is called the waste bin allocation and routing problem (WBARP) and requires a balance between bin allocation costs and vehicle routing costs in an optimum measure. In our proposed model IoT-based smart bins are sending alerts to cleaning authorities when smart bins are filled to a predefined threshold fill level, say, 90%. A time-dependent penalty cost to the waste management authorities is considered if smart bins are not emptied in time after filling full (100%). We developed a virgin neighborhood searching technique, which will search the filled (90%) bins and nearest neighbor bin's status at the time of cleaning of the last filled bin. The nearest neighbor bin will be cleaned when its waste filling status is less than TFL and sufficient space is available to hold the waste.

In our proposed model, a vehicle starts its journey from a depot and collects waste from a set of bins, and then unloads the waste into the nearest disposal center. Finally, the vehicle returns to the depot. To achieve the objective of this waste management model, some assumptions, notations are considered to make the model more realistic. These are given below:

Assumptions

- All the empty vehicles start from the depot and collect waste from all filled ($\geq 90\%$) waste bins and their neighbor waste bins and carry the collected accumulated waste to the nearest disposal center and return to the depot.
- The CMS sends a vehicle from the depot when some waste bins are filled ($\geq 90\%$).
- The cumulative waste of all the filled waste bins of a route must not exceed the maximum vehicle capacity of that vehicle assigned for that route.
- The capacities of waste bins are homogeneous.
- The capacities of vehicles are homogeneous.
- The average uniform speed of all vehicles is considered throughout the routing to avoid traffic congestion.

Notations

B Set of waste bins $B = \{b_1, b_2, b_3, \cdots, b_n\}$

V Set of vehicles $V = \{v_1, v_2, v_3, \cdots, v_m\}$

d_0 Depot of vehicles.

B_f Set of all bins filled $\geq TFL$, $B_f \subseteq B$

$N[b_i]$ Neighbor of b_i $\{b_x : b_x \in B,\ b_i \in B_f$ and $d(b_x, b_i) \leq K$, K is a fixed positive number, d denotes the euclidean distance; where filling level of $b_x < $ TFL$\}$ including b_i.

B_p Set of all bins initiated for a penalty, $B_p \subseteq B_f$.

D Set of disposal center.

B^+ ($\{d_0\} \cup B \cup D$); consider $G^+ = (B^+, E^+)$ to be the undirected graph. where B^+ is the vertex set and $E^+ = \{(i,j) : i,j \in B^+, i \neq j\}$ is the edge set.

B_f^+ ($\{d_0\} \cup B_f \cup D$); consider $G_f^+ = (B_f^+, E_f^+)$ to be the undirected graph where B_f^+ is the vertex set and $E_f^+ = \{(i,j) : i,j \in B_f^+, i \neq j\}$ is the edge set.

$N^+[b_i]$ ($\{d_0\} \cup N[b_i] \cup D$) consider $G_N^+ = (N^+[b_i], E_N^+)$ to be the undirected graph where $N^+[b_i]$ is the vertex set and $E_N^+ = \{(i,j) : i,j \in N^+[b_i], i \neq j\}$ is the edge set.

r_h Unit traveling cost of the vehicle type h per unit distance.

C_b Unit bin allocation cost.

$x_{ijh} = 1$, if a route visited between the ith node to j^{th} node in the undirected graph using the vehicle h; 0, otherwise.

d_{ij} Distance between the ith node to j^{th} node in the undirected graph, for simplicity, $d_{ij} = d_{ji} \forall i, j$

$\beta_1 = 1$ if $N[b_i] \neq \phi$ else $\beta_1 = 0$, $\forall b_i \in B$

$\beta_2 = 1$ if $B_f \neq \phi$ else $\beta_2 = 0$

$\beta_3 = 1$ if $B_p \neq \phi$ else $\beta_3 = 0$

$P_i(t)$ Penalty cost of waste bin b_i, after filling 100% waste at time t, $b_i \in B_p$.

lb_i Amount of waste at bin b_i at the time of visit.

L_h Maximum load capacity of the vehicle h.

l_{ijh} Load of vehicle h; when visited between node i to node j in the undirected graph G^+.

In our proposed waste bin allocation and routing problem (WBARP), a vehicle starts its journey from the depot after receiving the signal from the CMS to clean the filled bins, neighbor bins, and unload the waste to the nearest disposal center, while maintaining a minimum travel distance. Here, vehicles follow the shortest path using our developed neighborhood search technique. The mathematical formulation of the above-proposed model is given below.

Routing cost for collecting waste from filled bins

$$Z_2 = \beta_2 * \sum_{i=1}^{|B_f^+|} \sum_{j-1}^{|B_f^+|} \sum_{h=1}^{|V|} x_{ijh} * d_{ij} * r_h \tag{1}$$

Routing cost for collecting waste from neighboring bins

$$Z_1 = \beta_1 * \sum_{i=1}^{|N^+[b_i]|} \sum_{j=1}^{|N^+[b_j]|} \sum_{h=1}^{|V|} x_{ijh} * d_{ij} * r_h \tag{2}$$

Penalty cost of waste bin b_i, after filling 100% waste at time t

$$P_i(t) = a + bt, \qquad a, b, t > 0, \quad \forall\, i = 1, 2, \ldots, |B_p| \tag{3}$$

In Eq. (3), a penalty cost of a waste bin means if a waste bin is filled above 100%, waste management authority should pay a penalty for that. The formula for penalty is a plus bt, and both a and b are two positive constants. A is the fixed part, i.e., the minimum cost of the penalty, and the penalty cost is linearly increasing with time (t). The objective function is to minimize the bin allocation cost, transportation cost, and penalty cost as follows:

$$Z = C_b * |B| + Z_1 + Z_2 + \beta_3 * \sum_{i=1}^{|B_p|} P_i \tag{4}$$

subject to:

$$\sum_{i(b_i \in B_f)} x_{d_0 ih} = 1, \quad \forall\, h \in V \tag{5}$$

$$\sum_{i(b_i \in B_f)} l_{d_0 ih} = 0, \quad \forall\, h \in V \tag{6}$$

$$\sum_{i(b_i \in B_f \cup N[b_l])} lb_i \le L_h, \quad b_l \in B_f, \ \forall\, h \in V \tag{7}$$

$$x_{ijh} \in \{0, 1\}, \ i \ne j, \ (\forall\, i, j : b_i, b_j \in B_f \cup N[b_l]), \ b_l \in B_f, \ \forall\, h \in V \tag{8}$$

In Eq. (7) and in Eq. (8), b_l indicates the last filled bin being visited. Equation (5) confirms that each vehicle starts its journey from a depot. Equation (6) ensures that h^{th} vehicle will start its journey from the depot without any load. Equation (7) states that the total collected waste from a set of filled waste bins and its neighbor waste bins must not exceed the maximum load capacity of a vehicle. Equation (8) represents some binary variables.

4   Neighborhood Search Algorithm (NSA)

The vehicle routing problem (VRP) is a well-known optimization problem. Akhtar et al. [1] used the backtracking search algorithm (BSA) to solve the capacitated VRP. Our proposed algorithm finds the nearest set of bins from the current bin being visited. The nearest set of bins will be visited if they fulfill the pre-specified TFL. The proposed neighborhood search algorithm (NSA) is as follows.

Algorithm 1 Neighborhood search algorithm

Require: A set of given waste bins, B, with their current status.
Ensure: An optimum path for waste collection and transportation.

1:     **Begin**
2:         initialize the set of bins, (B_f), that have to be visited based on the report from CMS;
3:         a vehicle h starts its journey from the depot, (d_0);
4:         find the nearest bin, b_i, from the depot and visit b_i, $b_i \in B_f$;
5:     **while($|B_f| > 1$)**
6:         find the nearest neighboring bin from b_i with pre-specified TFL;
7:         visit the nearest neighboring bin, b_j, from b_i, if vehicle waste load $\leq L_h$, $b_j \in B_f$;
8:         randomly select a bin, b_k, $b_k \in B_f$;
9:         create an alternate route, starting from b_k;
10:        find the nearest neighboring bin from b_k with pre-specified TFL;
11:        visit the nearest neighboring bin, b_m, from b_k, if vehicle waste load $\leq L_h$, $b_m \in B_f$;
12:        $b_i = b_m$;
13:     **end while**
14:     **if $|B_f| = 1$**
15:        repeat the above searching technique from the current position for a set of neighbour bins $N[b_i]$; visit the neighboring bins $\in N[b_i]$, if vehicle waste load $\leq L_h$;
16:     **end if**
17:        finally, find the shortest path to collect waste from bins and unload the collected waste into the nearest disposal center;
18:        vehicle returns to it's depot (d_0);
19:     **End**

---

5   Computational Experiments and Discussion

Our proposed algorithm was created in Python on a PC with an Intel Core i3 processor running at 3.0 GHz and 8 GB of RAM. In this study, the proposed NSA algorithm is our developed search algorithm. This algorithm depends on only one parameter. The routing of a vehicle always depends on the current report from the CMS. The goal of our present study is to fulfill the main objective of optimizing the waste collection and transportation route by allocating the ideal number of smart waste bins. In Fig. 1(a), we consider seven cases according to the number of bins considered. In Case 1, the number of bins is 16; in Case 2, the number of bins is 15; and in this way in Case 7, the number of bins is 10. Here, Case 6 presents with low cost and Case 4 is near about Case 6. In Case 4, the number of bins allocated and the corresponding cost is higher than it is in Case 6, but the vehicle routing cost is lower than in Case 6. Figure 1(b) presents a comparative study of total costs along with routing costs and allocation costs. A sensitivity analysis is performed on Case 6 for the minimum total cost (Z) concerning different values of the parameters, results are graphically presented in Fig. 2(a) and Fig. 2(b) respectively. It is observed that unit traveling cost slightly more cost-effective than unit bin allocation cost. Figure 3 shows the performance of our proposed NSA algorithm against the traditional genetic algorithm (GA) and it is clearly shown that the performance of NSA is better than GA.

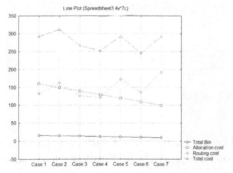

(a) Optimum number of bins to minimize the total cost.

(b) Routing cost vs allocation cost.

Fig. 1. Different costs vs optimum number of bins.

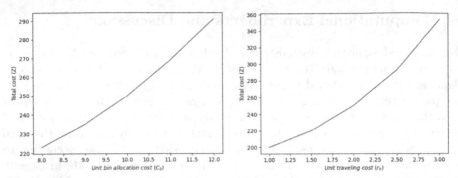

(a) Unit bin alloc. cost (C_b) vs Total cost (b) Unit traveling cost $(r_h, h = 1)$ vs Total (Z) for Case 6.   cost (Z) for Case 6.

Fig. 2. Unit bin allocation & traveling cost vs total cost for case 6.

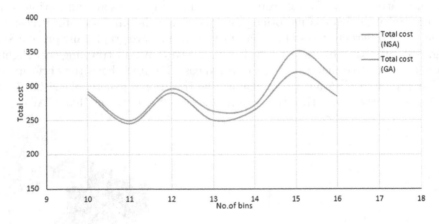

Fig. 3. NSA vs GA

Further extension of this study could be in clarifying the relationship between waste producers in light of the game-theoretic approach [5]. Suppose there exists cooperation between waste producers through communication. To be specific, there is a dominant waste producer, and the other waste producers are dependent on the dominant waste producer. This assumption is quite realistic, because there are two types of waste producers, public waste producers, and private waste producers, and their dominance is interrelated. Moreover, our concept also could be modeled as a Pareto optimization problem. Figure 4 shows that objectives are organized with multiple waste producers, thereby minimizing their total transportation costs, and with multiple wastes to energy(WtE) operators, thereby maximizing their profits. However, some of the waste producer's objectives might not necessarily be cost minimization. Rather, their main concern could be the utilization of waste collection vehicles. In this regard, checking the Pareto optimization in this problem could offer the possibility of improving supply chain value in waste management [6]. Waste could be classified based on its recyclability. Figure 5 shows a possible effective flow of waste management in

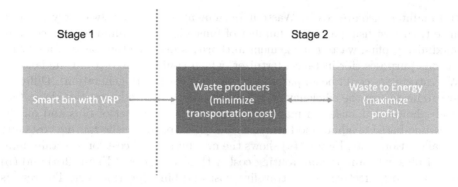

Fig. 4. A two-stage approach in waste management

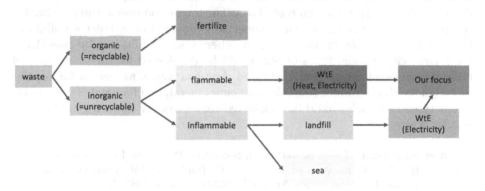

Fig. 5. Waste management in South Korea

Korea. If the waste is recyclable, then this waste could be recycled in several ways, e.g., fermentation to make additional utilization. However, if the waste is not recyclable then we need to decide whether to incinerate the waste. Inflammable waste could be disposed of at landfills or allocated sea areas. At the landfills, we could generate electricity through gas produced from waste, which is called the WtE process. But if the waste is flammable, there is also another WtE process available through the incinerator, which could provide both heat and electricity.

6   Conclusions

The present study represents a dynamic vehicle routing problem for smart bin waste management. The system is configured for IoT-based smart bins. All bins' monitoring processes are controlled through CMS. All vehicles start their journeys from a common depot to serve a set of bins reported by the CMS. The main goal of this paper is to minimize the routing cost for waste collection and transportation using an optimum number of bins because IoT-based bin allocation and maintenance are costly. Waste management authorities always try to minimize their cost using a certain number of bins with a minimum routing cost. To maximize profits, waste management authorities may use the waste of a city for various purposes (for instance, fertilizer, which could be used to fill the land, or WtE strategies could be employed for heat and electricity generation). Different researchers show the efficiency of IoT-based smart bins to keep cities clean. Our study, however, focuses on maintaining an efficient number of bins and on the real-time-based neighborhood search technique to optimize the routing costs and bin allocation costs. Figure 1(a) shows the minimum total cost for a certain number of bins with a minimum routing cost within seven cases. Figure 2(a) and (b) show the cost-effectiveness on traveling cost and bin allocation cost. The results of our study show the efficiency. The best waste management system has two wings. One is quick and efficient waste collection and transportation up to the disposal center with minimum cost. The other focuses on maximizing profits for reusing waste. Proper waste management is necessary to construct a pollution-free smart city. In the future, a large number of smart bins can be considered for a large city. Special types of bins could be considered for different types of critical waste such as medical waste and chemical waste, as well as for regular household and other waste (organic, inorganic, metal, and flammable). Also, different types of vehicles could be considered for separately removing critical and regular waste.

Acknowledgement. This research is supported by the Brain Pool Program of the National Research Foundation of Korea (NRF) funded by the Ministry of Science, ICT, and Future Planning [Grant No. NRF-2020H1D3A2A01085443].

References

1. Akhtar, M., Hannan, M.A., Begum, R.A., Basri, H., Scavino, E.: Backtracking search algorithm in CVRP models for efficient solid waste collection and route optimization. Waste Manage. **61**, 117–128 (2017)
2. Angelelli, E., Speranza, M.G.: The application of a vehicle routing model to a waste collection problem: two case studies. In: Klose, A., Speranza, M.G., Van Wassenhove, L.N. (eds.) Quantitative Approaches to Distribution Logistics and Supply Chain Management. Lecture Notes in Economics and Mathematical Systems, vol. 519, pp. 269–286. Springer, Heidelberg (2002). https://doi.org/10.1007/978-3-642-56183-2_16
3. Angelelli, E., Speranza, M.G.: The periodic vehicle routing problem with intermediate facilities. Eur. J. Oper. Res. **137**(2), 233–247 (2002)
4. Beltrami, E.J., Bodin, L.D.: Networks and vehicle routing for municipal waste collection. Networks **4**(1), 65–94 (1974)
5. Eryganov, I., Šomplák, R., Nevrlý, V., Smejkalová, V., Hrabec, D., Haugen, K.K.: Application of cooperative game theory in waste management. Chem. Eng. Trans. 887–882 (2020)
6. Govindan, K., Soleimani, H., Kannan, D.: Reverse logistics and closed-loop supply chain: a comprehensive review to explore the future. Eur. J. Oper. Res. **240**(3), 603–626 (2015)

7. Hemmelmayr, V.C., Doerner, K.F., Hartl, R.F., Vigo, D.: Models and algorithms for the integrated planning of bin allocation and vehicle routing in solid waste management. Transp. Sci. **48**(1), 103–120 (2014)
8. Huang, S.H., Lin, P.C.: Vehicle routing-scheduling for municipal waste collection system under the "Keep Trash off the Ground" policy. Omega **55**, 24–37 (2015)
9. Nuortio, T., Kytöjoki, J., Niska, H., Bräysy, O.: Improved route planning and scheduling of waste collection and transport. Expert Syst. Appl. **30**(2), 223–232 (2006)
10. Sinha, T., Kumar, K.M., Saisharan, P.: Smart dustbin. Int. J. Ind. Electron. Electrical Eng. **3**(5), 101–104 (2015)
11. Vicentini, F., et al.: Sensorized waste collection container for content estimation and collection optimization. Waste Manage. **29**(5), 1467–1472 (2009)

Smart Contracts Implementation in the Allocation of Covid-19 Vaccines

Mohammad Amin Yazdani$^{(\boxtimes)}$ (ID), Daniel Roy (ID), and Sophie Hennequin (ID)

LGIPM, University of Lorraine, Metz, France
mohammad-amin.yazdani@univ-lorraine.fr

Abstract. The need for a good supply chain distribution of vaccines in disasters is critical in today's world. This paper targets the vaccines' allocation in several periods for various and separated demand zones. To discover and make the allocation network more efficient and help the policymaker decide more wisely, we implement a smart contract to suggest product allocation in different cases taking into account dynamical changes. Our smart contract tries to decrease the uncovered demands and facilitate the governments' prediction of the demands and evolution of a disease in demand zones. In this manner, several reactions of the smart contract are considered through different scenarios that can happen in the pandemics. The cases are sudden increase, sudden decrease, and steady demands. Moreover, we discuss the validity of the proposed smart contract and its benefits. Finally, we discuss the future aspects of our work and other objectives that can be useful in the proposed problem.

Keywords: Vaccine supply chain · Allocation problem · Smart contract

1 Introduction

Several phenomena lead to significant losses in human beings' lives and damaged nations' economies, environments, and societies. The causes can be earthquakes, flooding, etc. According to World Health Organization, the COVID-19 had several features that make it easier to spray and damage people's lives [1]. According to the statistics, a year and a half after the appearance of Covid-19, the total number of affected cases was 173 million people, with 3.73 million death cases all over the world. After several months, some companies from different countries were able to produce vaccines to protect people from the virus. The problem is that the number of vaccines is not enough for all people. Therefore, an important task is to assign vaccines to priority groups, such as older people, medical staff, and so on [2]. In this manner, proposing a vaccine supply chain (VSC) that can supply vaccines well and help rulers and health organizations for allocating the vaccines more efficiently is crucial. Ozdamar *et al.* [3] introduced the distribution of various commodities problems in an emergency time. They proposed a multi-period multi-commodity model for material flows from supply centers towards distribution centers. They tried to minimize unsatisfied demands.

© IFIP International Federation for Information Processing 2021
Published by Springer Nature Switzerland AG 2021
A. Dolgui et al. (Eds.): APMS 2021, IFIP AICT 632, pp. 510–520, 2021.
https://doi.org/10.1007/978-3-030-85906-0_56

Several papers exist in the context of the uncertain and changing environment. In most cases, demand is an uncertain and changeable parameter. Abazari *et al.* [4] introduced a humanitarian supply chain (SC) for distributing relief items. They tried to minimize distance traveled by the reliefs' item, minimizing costs, traveling time and total perished items quantity. More information about the uncertainty in the VSC exist in [5]. One of the other important aspects of the demand is that it cannot stay fixed over time. Sarkar *et al.* [6] considered the cost of the products as the most important factor in changing demand over time. Pramanik *et al.* [7] considered the demand as a changeable parameter that is dependent on the selling price for the customers, credit period offers by the retailer, and credit amount.

It is necessary to discretize time into different periods, to take into account these potential changes and consider an uncertain demand of the humanitarian SC, which make the decision-making more challenging [8]. Therefore, it is vital to distribute vaccines optimally and predict the critical and dynamical demands more wisely. The distribution of vaccines could be complex since countries' strategy is different, and the different types of vaccines have various constraints. These problems brought the idea to propose a VSC that can well distribute vaccines and help the decision-maker to better allocate the limited vaccines quantities by a dynamic protocol based on smart contracts.

One of the first definitions of the smart contract by Szabo[1], which came long before Bitcoin and blockchain technology, is "a computerized transaction protocol that executes the terms of a contract." The other definition of smart contracts by Delmolino *et al.* [9] is "Smart contracts as computer protocols designed to oversee, enforce, or verify performances or negotiations of contracts." Regarding that, there will be no third party during all transactions. In addition to the irreversibility and documentation of all records, these protocols can prove their reliability and credibility [10]. Considering SC, smart contracts may be useful in several aspects and we can cite Dolgui *et al.* [11] who have implemented a smart contract on a SC. The decision-making of the scheduling problem according to the smart contracts has three roles. Rely on the completion time of the operations. Hasan *et al.* [12], considered the usage of smart contracts for shipment tracking and delivery. They consider the multi-echelon and multi-party setting.

In this paper, the proposed smart contract will suggest different vaccine allocations according to the evolution of the disease (which affects the demands) to the policymakers. The propositions are the vaccines' constraints and the real needs in a specific area at a given time. The policymaker will be able to define his allocation strategy according to the smart contract's allocation and other strategic data such as his health security strategy, economy, etc. The main interest of our work is to offer a tool that will allow integrating dynamic evolutions and allow the decision-makers to be more reactive in their strategy. In this paper, we only present the first step of our tool, which concerns the proposal of allocation in a short time. The second step of our work will be more appliances of the smart contract in the proposed SC.

The rest of the paper is as follows: Sect. 2 defines the problem. Section 3 proposes the mathematical formulation. Section 4 brings the results and discussions. Finally, Sect. 5 gives the conclusion and perspectives to our work.

---

[1] Szabo, N. (1994). Smart contracts. Unpublished manuscript, 26.

2 Problem Description

In this paper, we consider the distribution part of a VSC with two types of main actors: customers who are the representatives of a country (government, decision centers, etc.) and vaccine distributors. The first one is identified by demand zones (denoted DZs, DZs correspond to regional zones defined by the representatives of a country), and warehouses represent the second one (in this paper, we only consider the distribution part of the global VSC). The vaccines are COVID-19 vaccines that are vital to vaccine all the community and cover all demands in several periods. A period is a time duration defined by a government that will vaccine special group of people in each one of them. According to the strategy chosen by the government, the objective is to maximize the number of vaccinated people at a given final date (finite time horizon) to reach a collective immunity sufficient to face the virus.

The actors of this SC cooperate to optimize the distribution of products (vaccines). These actors are government and more precisely, policymakers (the customers), the pharmaceutical groups that are marketing the vaccines (suppliers), a 3PL-type service provider that ensures the distribution of the vaccines (the company that defines and manages the smart contract), this provider being able to call upon transport and warehouse suppliers, and finally the DZs in which doctors will carry out the vaccines, nurses, and any person defined in the government's strategy. The cooperation between actors is facilitated by the use of a smart contract that allows modifications to the initial defined contract to consider dynamic changes that may occur.

The products (COVID-19 vaccines) are stored in warehouses. We suppose that the sum of all distributed products for the finite time horizon (i.e. sum of all considered periods) of study is sufficient to cover the sum of all the demands in this finite time horizon (i.e. the objective define by the government to obtain the collective immunity to face the virus). Moreover, not all types of products are guaranteed to be available for all periods (the competition is very strong between the different countries wishing to vaccinate as soon as possible). In addition, the vaccination strategy for a given type of vaccine may change depending on the problems detected during vaccination (the testing phase have been shortened to the maximum). Consequently, products may be missing or not all be usable in the same way in a considered period. In parallel, new vaccines may appear and increase the availability of products. These changes may lead to changes in the vaccine strategy and subsequently the distribution of demand by period (new people could be vaccinated or not). The disease also evolves rapidly according to the mutations of the virus, causing increases in contamination and mortality in certain geographical areas, which can also vary the vaccination strategy. Therefore, the demand for a given period in a DZ could change.

When a country's government defines its initial vaccine strategy, usually defined according to the population's age and its specificities/functions, such as caregivers, the country's government defines pre-allocation of some vaccines to a given DZ at a given period. In this paper, we only propose the model for a country; we do not consider the market nor the competition. The total demand on the time horizon is known. Of course, depending on the evolution of the disease, this total demand may vary a little. Still, if we consider the case of covid-19, the mortality rate does not exceed 0.5% of the total population for each country in the world[2]. Therefore, the policymaker of a government defines its own vaccine strategy by defining periods and the DZs, and for each DZ i and each period f the demand dem_{pfi} for a given product p[3]. However, as described above, these government strategies may change over time depending on the number and characteristics of the products offered by the pharmaceutical groups and on the evolution of the epidemic. Besides, some DZs could have crucial periods and need more or fewer vaccines. The total demand over the finite time horizon is the same, but its distribution at the DZs and periods can change that is uncertain.

In the proposed problem, two types of material flows exist: from warehouses to DZs at the beginning of a considered period, and from a DZ to another DZ. In this case, it depends on the current travel time from a given DZ to another DZ. Indeed, this flow will not exist if the distance is too far (because of transport and storage constraints for some vaccines). These material flows will be allocated with the help of smart contracts, which allow integrating many changes as the demand for a given period, the availability of a product, the arrival of a new product, a change in vaccine strategy, etc. In the first step, the smart contract will propose an optimal allocation according to the changes (this allocation may or may not be retained by the political decision-maker). The second step that is not presented in this paper, the smart contract will propose an optimal location-allocation of the products to the different DZs, taking into account the strong constraints of the products (at the level of transport, storage, and duration of use).

The material flow should be according to the pre-allocated products and demands of the DZs. Regarding the first step, our smart contract must take into consideration the different changes that may occur in a given period and for a DZ. To do the mentioned task, we decompose our time period into sub-periods of the same size (Fig. 1). As it can be seen, each period is divided in several checking points according to some parameters such as the importance of the targeted population in that period, government strategy, etc. The number of checking points for a given period is known that it is the results of the calculations made before the beginning of the period by the organism and gave it as a parameter to the smart contract or directly determined by the smart contract itself, based on contextual parameters and government's strategy. It should not be too large because the policymaker will not want to change strategies too often, nor too small, in order to take into account enough changes. For example, in France, the vaccine strategy is revised every week, so we can define the same number of checkpoints for all periods equals one week (which allows the government to get enough information about the positive or negative evolution of its vaccine strategy). Another country may decide to schedule a different number of checkpoints by period, considering that some population groups are more or less subject to evolutions. The calculation of the allocation happens at the beginning of each period and checkpoints.

After determining the products' optimum material flow, our smart contract will check the differences between the demands (initial demands and real demands) and the existing materials in the DZs at different checking points (Fig. 1). Indeed, the virus can spread and increase the number of the affected people over time. Therefore, it will be necessary to cover the new and unpredicted demands at each checking point during each period. On the

---

[2] https://ourworldindata.org/coronavirus data base for covid-19.

[3] https://covidtracker.fr/ data base for covid-19 in France and in the world.

other hand, some communities will need fewer vaccines after injecting the vaccines. Then we can send the vaccines to other DZs to save more lives. According to the mentioned reasons, our smart contract will calculate the differences between the demands and determine the best possible products' flow in the checking points.

Real demand depends strongly on the evolution of the epidemic. It can be estimated from the rates (incidence rate, positivity rate and reproductively rate) and hospital tension (these data could be obtained with database) and from epidemiological models that are good estimators of the spread of the SARS-CoV-2 virus within a population [13].

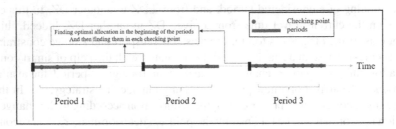

Fig. 1. Smart contract checking points and periods.

Besides, the main difference between the two types of material flows in the first of each period and checking points is that it is only from the warehouses toward the DZs at the beginning of the periods, and at checking points, it could be between DZs to each other and warehouses to DZs.

According to the real worlds' constraints, some DZs cannot send the products to each other because of some limitations such as the far distances and more traveling time. In what follows, we present the mathematical model of this allocation proposal.

3   Mathematical Formulation

The model assumptions are as follows:

1. There are multiple vaccines with different characteristics Because, in some cases, the usage of a product can be more useful than the other at several periods
2. Products carry in special conditions that are well respected without decay and harm
3. Each period includes several checking
4. The sum of products in the warehouses can answer all the demands
5. Real demand is reported by the organism and Covid-19 tracker at the checking points.

The notations, parameters and variables are given below:

i, i'	Set of DZs $\in \{1\ldots I\}$
p	Set of products $\in \{1\ldots P\}$
t	Set of checking points $\in \{1\ldots T\}$
f	Set of periods $\in \{1\ldots F\}$
w	Set of warehouses $\in \{1\ldots W\}$
a_{pfi}	Pre-allocated products p in the period f to the DZ i
$b_{pii'}$	1: if the product p from DZ i can be sent to the other DZ i' 0: otherwise
dem_{pfi}	The demand of the product p in the period f in the DZ i
Δdem_{pti}	The differences of the demands of the product p in the checking point t of the period f in the DZ i from the previous checking point
$Realdem_{pti}^{f}$	The real demand of the product p in the checking point t which belongs to the period f in the DZ i
θ_{pti}^{f}	The minimum percentage of uncovered demand of the product p in the checking point t which belongs to the period f in the DZ i
TC_{pwi}	The cost of transferring product p between warehouse w and DZ i
$RDZ_{pii'}$	The cost of sending product p from a DZ i to the other DZ
Z	The objective function
q_{pfwi}	The quantity of product p in the period f that send from the warehouse w to the DZ i
$qp_{ptii'}$	The quantity of product p in the checking point t of the period f that send from the DZ i to the other DZ i'
qt_{ptwi}	The quantity of product p in the checking point t of the period f that send from the warehouse w to the DZ i
s_{pti}	Not covered demand of product p in the checking point t of the period f in the DZ i

The difference between the real demands and predicted demands is given by formula (1). Formula (2) determines not answered demands rely on the real demands.

$$\Delta dem_{pti} = Realdem_{pti}^{f} - dem_{pfi} \quad \begin{array}{l} \forall p \in \{1\ldots P\} \\ \forall f \in \{1\ldots F\}, \quad \forall t \in F \\ \forall i \in \{1\ldots I\} \end{array} \tag{1}$$

$$s_{pti} = Realdem_{pti}^{f} - \left(\sum_{w} q_{pfwi} + \sum_{i'} b_{pii'} qp_{ptii'} + \sum_{w} qt_{ptwi} \right) \quad \begin{array}{l} \forall p \in \{1\ldots P\} \\ \forall f \in \{1\ldots F\}, \quad \forall t \in F \\ \forall i \in \{1\ldots I\} \end{array} \tag{2}$$

The objective function and constraints are as follows:

$$\min Z = \sum_{p}\sum_{f}\sum_{w}\sum_{i} TC_{pwi} q_{pfwi} + \sum_{p}\sum_{t}\sum_{i}\sum_{i'} RDZ_{pii'} qp_{ptii'}$$
$$+ \sum_{p}\sum_{t}\sum_{w}\sum_{i} TC_{pwi} qt_{ptwi} \tag{3}$$

Subject to:

$$a_{pfi} \le \sum_w q_{pfwi} \quad \begin{matrix} \forall p \in \{1 \dots P\} \\ \forall f \in \{1 \dots F\} \\ \forall i \in \{1 \dots I\} \end{matrix} \tag{4}$$

$$dem_{pfi} \le \sum_w q_{pfwi} \quad \begin{matrix} \forall p \in \{1 \dots P\} \\ \forall f \in \{1 \dots F\} \\ \forall i \in \{1 \dots I\} \end{matrix} \tag{5}$$

$$-\Delta dem_{pti} \le \sum_{i'} b_{pii'} qp_{ptii'} \quad \begin{matrix} \forall p \in \{1 \dots P\} \\ \forall t \in \{1 \dots T\} \\ \forall i \in \{1 \dots I\} \end{matrix} \tag{6}$$

$$\Delta dem_{pti} \le \sum_{i'} b_{pii'} qp_{ptii'} + \sum_w qt_{ptwi} \quad \begin{matrix} \forall p \in \{1 \dots P\} \\ \forall t \in \{1 \dots T\} \\ \forall i \in \{1 \dots I\} \end{matrix} \tag{7}$$

$$s_{pti} \le \theta^f_{pti} Realdem^f_{pti} \quad \begin{matrix} \forall p \in \{1 \dots P\} \\ \forall f \in \{1 \dots F\}, \forall t \in F \\ \forall i \in \{1 \dots I\} \end{matrix} \tag{8}$$

$$q_{pfwi}, qp_{ptii'}, qt_{ptwi}, rq_{ptiw} \ge 0 \quad \begin{matrix} \forall p \in \{1 \dots P\} \\ \forall f \in \{1 \dots F\}, \forall t \in F \\ \forall i \in \{1 \dots I\} \end{matrix} \tag{9}$$

Equation (3) is the cost function. This cost includes transferring the products at the starting of the periods and checking times between warehouses and DZs. Constraint (4) pre-allocates the products to the DZs according to the governments' point of view. It means that the flow of products should meet at least a considered lower bound. Constraint (5) represents that it is essential to answer all the demands in each period for the DZs. Constraint (6) ensures that if the demand is changed before the checking time and the amount of the products are more than need, the products can be sent to the other DZs that need the products. Constraint (7) depicts that when a DZ needs more products according to the checking time, it is necessary to answer it by other DZs or warehouses. Constraint (8) limits the uncovered demands. Constraint (9) determines the types of variables.

4   Results and Discussion

In this section, we will define the procedure of the smart contract and present several possible scenarios. Then we will solve a test problem, and we will discuss the managerial insights.

The proposed smart contract will consider several cases that can happen and bring the results. First, it will calculate the best allocations, and then it will discover allocation in the possibility of several cases. In the end, it will suggest the best decisions in each period. This procedure makes our proposed smart contract dynamic. Figure 2 shows the procedure of the proposed smart contract.

Several possible scenarios exist according to the virus behavior in different communities. The three most common scenarios are sudden increase, sudden decrease, and normal spray during a period. In the increased scenario, health organisms will inform the smart contract about the need for more products. Therefore, smart contracts try to reduce the shortage as much as possible and satisfy the demands by asking more products from suppliers. In the sudden decrease that mostly happens after the vaccination of most people of the society, the smart contract will try to help other DZs by using the existing products. In the normal situation, it is about supplying well from the warehouses and reducing the shortages.

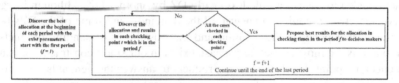

Fig. 2. The procedure of the proposed smart contract

Then, we will try to show the appliance of the smart contract by solving a test problem. Table 1 shows the random parameters.

Table 1. Data generation of the proposed problem.

Parameters	Value	Parameters	Value
a_{pfi}	Uniform-integer (100, 200)	Δdem_{pti}	Uniform-integer (−5, +5)
$b_{pii'}$	[0, 1]	TC_{pwi}	Uniform (2, 8)
dem_{pfi}	Uniform-integer (100, 200)	$RDZ_{pii'}$	Uniform (1, 15)

For the test problem, we considered two periods (F = 2). Each period includes two checking points, and the total number of checking points in the problem is four (T = 4). Number of warehouses, products, and DZs are respectively three, two, and nine (W = 3, P = 2, I = 9). To make the proposed smart contract's innovation clearer, we try to observe its behavior in a checking point through several cases by the numerical results. Table 2 shows the result of the smart contract in the checking point 1 in the period 1 according to the four different cases. All the values in the table are sum of the products.

In case 1, most of the DZs needed are fewer products than the considered from the first of period in the first checking point. Therefore, it was possible to answer most of the new demands in a less costly way. As it can be seen, the total changes of the demands have a positive value, which is 8, which means in more cases, the quantity of products

Table 2. The results of the smart contract (period 1 - checking point 1) through different cases.

	Total Δdem_{pti}	Total s_{pti}	Total $qp_{ptii'}$	Total qt_{ptwi}	Total cost
Case 1	8	10	20	24	17463 $
Case 2	−10	15	24	26	21350 $
Case 3	−20	19	16	16	22992 $
Case 4	24	4	22	30	21502 $

is more than the needed and can send products to the others. Besides, in this case, the DZs had the chance to answer the closer ones' demands. Therefore, the pro-posed smart contract decided to answer all the less costly DZ by another DZ. Although it was able to be cost-efficient, it could not answer all the demands, and some of the DZs became uncovered that depend on the location and the possibility of sending products. The reason that it is the most cost-effective case exists in our smart con-tract. For example, in the checking point, DZ 1 needs two products to answer the demands. According to the predictions and answering them, it was unexpected changes too complicated and costly at that moment. Hence, our smart contract decided to send one product from the closest to the DZ 1, DZ 2 and leave one of the products uncovered because it was other priorities to answer other demands.

Case 2 and Case 3 both show the drastic increase in the demands. They can be considered the critical time of a virus. On these occasions, according to the proposed smart contract, the amount of unsatisfied demand will rise, and the cost of the system is high. If the rulers consider predictions and use the proposed smart contract, they can decrease the speed of the spray of the virus in several ways. For example, according to our smart contract, we allocated more pre-allocated products to a DZ that could spread and assign more products to the DZ, less accessible for the warehouses and other DZs. For responding to unpredicted increases, the smart contract tries to balance the warehouses, and DZs material flows to answer the needed demands. For example, it sends products from the DZs that have more products than they wanted to the closest one and from warehouses to the DZs, which is unreachable for the other DZs. Rely on this point of view; it will be able to respond as fast as possible and be cost-effective. As an example, DZ 5 is the most unreachable for the other DZs. Therefore, the warehouses will cover all the needed demands at the checking point. On the other hand, DZ 3 is accessible to DZ 1 and DZ 2, and the exceeded products of DZ 1 and DZ 2 will be sent to DZ 3.

Case 4 can consider as the quarantine time in the pandemics or the time after several vaccination periods when considerable improvements are achieved. In this case, the lowest amount of unsatisfied demands will happen. The reason is that the total amount of demands is less than the predictions. Therefore, many products to answer other demands exist in this scenario. The smart contract in this section tries to answer all the demands and make the uncovered demands as small as possible by flowing materials from both warehouses and DZs. By studying four different cases, it is possible to have better choices and predict several aspects of the problem by passing times. Besides, all these results and the logical behavior show the validation of the smart contract.

As one of the digital SC enablers, our smart contract can work well and shows its appliances and validity. According to the previous studies in the introduction, other authors tried to use a smart contract appliance to track the vehicles and shipment of the vaccines. However, the main difference of this paper is in introducing a smart contract as a decision-maker tool in the VSC allocation problem in the condition that the demands should be calculated in the checking points and changeable scenarios. Several advantages and novelty exist in the proposed paper from the managerial point of view and remove the global SC barriers. Implementing a decision-making tool like the smart contract in a SC can help the rulers and health care organisms be more responsive and faster during the unpredicted changes. For example, the mentioned smart contract might be able to discover optimum allocation in all situations. Nevertheless, if the policymaker could not respond well through the changes of the situations, it could cause many deaths for the society, especially during a pandemic like Covid-19. Besides, the implemented smart contract can work when the number of nodes (such as DZs and warehouses) is large. Therefore, it is helpful to manage the real-world problems by implementing the mentioned smart contract in a vaccine distribution system.

5 Conclusion

In this paper, we considered a SC managed with the help of a smart contract that can be useful for COVID-19. The problem proposed the best allocation of the vaccines during several periods to cover all the possible demands. Then, to make the model more dynamic and help the decision-makers, we implemented a smart contract that optimize all the material flows in the checking points and periods. By implementing our smart contract, we discuss about several possible scenarios during periods such as sudden increase and decrease of the demands.

Future research is highly suggested to propose other smart contract structure objectives and bring the results according to the real case data. Data collection is an essential point, and control points are defined to ensure that the smart contract options are correct. A negotiation phase between decision-makers and suppliers must be integrated into our smart contract to facilitate SC management. The next step will be to define a real-time location-allocation problem considering the different events that can happen.

References

1. Behnam, A., Jahanmahin, R.: A data analytics approach for COVID-19 spread and end prediction (with a case study in Iran). Model. Earth Syst. Environ., 1–11 (2021). https://doi.org/10.1007/s40808-021-01086-8
2. Peeples, L.: News Feature: Avoiding pitfalls in the pursuit of a COVID-19 vaccine. Proc. Natl. Acad. Sci. **117**(15), 8218–8221 (2020)
3. Özdamar, L., Ekinci, E., Küçükyazici, B.: Emergency logistics planning in natural disasters. Ann. Oper. Res. **129**(1), 217–245 (2004)
4. Abazari, S.R., Aghsami, A., Rabbani, M.: Prepositioning and distributing relief items in humanitarian logistics with uncertain parameters. Socio-Econ. Plan. Sci. **74**, 100933 (2021)

5. Duijzer, L.E., van Jaarsveld, W., Dekker, R.: Literature review: the vaccine supply chain. Eur. J. Oper. Res. **268**(1), 174–192 (2018)
6. Sarkar, B., Dey, B.K., Sarkar, M., AlArjani, A.: A sustainable online-to-offline (O2O) retailing strategy for a supply chain management under controllable lead time and variable demand. Sustainability **13**(4), 1756 (2021)
7. Pramanik, P., Maiti, M.K., Maiti, M.: A supply chain with variable demand under three level trade credit policy. Comput. Ind. Eng. **106**, 205–221 (2017)
8. Cao, C., Liu, Y., Tang, O., Gao, X.: A fuzzy bi-level optimization model for multi-period post-disaster relief distribution in sustainable humanitarian supply chains. Int. J. Prod. Econ. **235**, 108081 (2021)
9. Delmolino, K., Arnett, M., Kosba, A., Miller, A., Shi, E.: Step by step towards creating a safe smart contract: lessons and insights from a cryptocurrency lab. In: Clark, J., Meiklejohn, S., Ryan, P.Y.A., Wallach, D., Brenner, M., Rohloff, K. (eds.) Financial Cryptography and Data Security, pp. 79–94. Springer , Berlin (2016). https://doi.org/10.1007/978-3-662-53357-4_6
10. Almasoud, A.S., Hussain, F.K., Hussain, O.K.: Smart contracts for block-chain-based reputation systems: a systematic literature review. J. Netw. Comput. Appl. **170**, 102814 (2020)
11. Dolgui, A., Ivanov, D., Potryasaev, S., Sokolov, B., Ivanova, M., Werner, F.: Blockchain-oriented dynamic modelling of smart contract design and execution in the supply chain. Int. J. Prod. Res. **58**(7), 2184–2199 (2020)
12. Hasan, H., AlHadhrami, E., AlDhaheri, A., Salah, K., Jayaraman, R.: Smart contract-based approach for efficient shipment management. Comput. Ind. Eng. **136**, 149–159 (2019)
13. Amaro, J.E., Dudouet, J., Orce, J.N.: Global analysis of the COVID-19 pandemic using simple epidemiological models. Appl. Math. Modell. **90**, 995–1008 (2021)

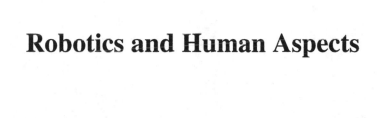

Robotics and Human Aspects

Methods of Forecasting Environmental Stress and Strain on Working Humans in the Digital Factory

Gert Zülch(✉)

Karlsruhe Institute of Technology, Karlsruhe, Germany
gert.zuelch@gefora-beratung.de

Abstract. According to the stress-strain concept of ergonomics, a distinction must be made between the stress on the working human and the resulting individual strain. Furthermore, it must be taken into account whether several influences act simultaneously or one of them acts successively. Therefore, point in time-related and period-related influences are to be considered, whereby in the latter case a connection to discrete event-driven simulation is necessary. It has been known for many years that simulation methods can be used to analyze stress on the human caused by the work task itself, at least in macro-ergonomic terms with regard to time utilization. In addition, anthropometric and work-physiological aspects of the work task can be analyzed using digital human models. The evaluation and assessment of influences from the indoor working environment are more difficult. In this case, both micro- and macro-ergonomic analyzes can be performed. In the following, it is explained in more detail to what extent such forecasts can already be carried out in Digital Factory tools. The result shows that there are still a lot of research and development tasks to be solved before a comprehensive forecast of ergonomic influences can be carried out.

Keywords: Stress-Strain concept · Indoor work area · Time-related analyzes · Evaluation · Assessment

1 Problem Statement and Relation to Associated Guidelines

The computer-aided planning of production systems involving working humans takes place over several levels of detail. It ranges from the human supported material and information flow concepts to the planning of personnel deployment in a certain operational area to methods' design at individual workplaces. The last two levels of detail mentioned have been already reported at this conference: The personnel deployment planning is performed using event-driven simulation procedures that have also been considering service companies for some time [1]. The planning of work methods is already realized nowadays by Digital Factory tools, which not only include time management, but also enable ergonomic issues to some extent [2].

© IFIP International Federation for Information Processing 2021
Published by Springer Nature Switzerland AG 2021
A. Dolgui et al. (Eds.): APMS 2021, IFIP AICT 632, pp. 523–532, 2021.
https://doi.org/10.1007/978-3-030-85906-0_57

The associated software procedures have been the subject of several guidelines of the Association of German Engineers (VDI) for many years: In VDI Guideline 3633 Part 6 [3], the state of the art for ergonomic analyses of working humans in simulation procedures is regarded (see also [4]). For this purpose, it is shown how the temporal workload and other macro-ergonomic aspects can be dealt with in existing software procedures. Furthermore, from a micro-ergonomic point of view, methods for anthropometric and work-physiological work design in Digital Factory tools are addressed. They are presented in VDI Guideline 4499 Part 4 ([5]; see also [6] for an overview).

Following the stress-strain concept according to Rohmert [7], the two VDI guideline parts mentioned only deal with one ergonomic aspect, namely the effects on the working human through the work task itself. So what is still missing is how stress from the work environment and the resulting strain on the individual human can be taken up in Digital Factory tools.

This question is investigated in this paper referring to the Guideline Project VDI 4499 Part 5 (see for this project [8]). Since this guideline part is currently in the final phase of its publication, only some methodological points can be discussed here. It is also shown which role the simulation plays in the prognosis of environmental influences in an indoor work area.

In the new guideline VDI 4499 Part 5, the environmental influences affecting humans working in an indoor work area are dealt with. According to the stress-strain concept, each of the treated influences is differentiated according to the effective stress and the resulting strain on the individual human. A further distinction is made according to their evaluation, i.e. the assignment of a numerical value, and the assessment using legally binding comparison values. Furthermore, a distinction can be made between person-related and location-related as well as between point in time-related and period-related forecasts in the Digital Factory.

2   State of the Art of Forecasting Environmental Influences

Thus, this guideline part supplements the previous ones, which deal with the inclusion of working humans in simulation procedures and Digital Factory tools. In addition, it can be stated that there is extensive knowledge about the effects of the work environment and about existing legal requirements. This comes in part from occupational health and safety regulations (see the required risk assessment in the German Act on the Implementation of Measures of Occupational Safety and Health [9], § 5 p.).

In Germany, software procedures are also available for forecasting purposes, but apart from one exception detailed below, these are not included in the Digital Factory. The existing methods not only come from the ergonomic field, but also to a large extent from building physics and planning. In this respect, the prognosis of environmental influences on working humans represents a new field of the Digital Factory.

Almost no corresponding forecasting methods are known on the international level. In the International Ergonomics Association there is a Technical Committee "Digital Human Modeling and Simulation", but this specialists' group primarily deals with human modeling, primarily in an anthropometric and work-physiological sense (see e.g. [10]). Also in international ergonomics congresses (see e.g. [11]) and in more recent English-language publications (see e.g. [12]) there is hardly any reference to this. Also in the

German-speaking countries there are only a few publications that indicate the importance of the prognosis of environmental influences (for one exception see [13]).

3 Simulation Application for Period-Related Forecasts and Its Validity

3.1 The EPRI Method

For the period-related prognosis of environmental influences, a connection with a discrete event-driven simulation procedure is necessary, but as far as the author is aware, only actually implemented in one specific example: Fig. 1 shows the coupling of such a simulation procedure with the prognosis of a temporally constant gamma radiation in a work area [14]. In order to limit the radiation exposure of the maintenance staff, two workers are deployed and their exposures are monitored by virtual dosimeters. The attached Gantt chart shows when it will be necessary to replace the active by the stand-by worker.

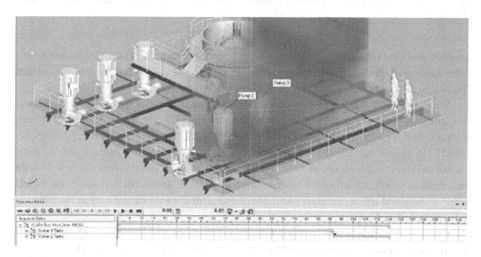

Fig. 1. Work area with calculated radioactive load and two workers deployed (Source: [15])

In this example there is no shield between the radiation source and the maintenance worker active in the area. The calculation method used by the American Electric Power Research Institute (EPRI; [16]) also provides for such shielding: In addition to the radiation strength of the source and the absorption value of the shielding material, at least one real measured value at a point in the work area must be known (Fig. 2). On this basis, the method then calculates the radiation loads at other calculation points therein.

3.2 Validation Studies

The algorithm developed was validated in several studies by the EPRI, initially under ideal conditions in a laboratory test ([16], pp. 2–6). Two directly shielded radiation

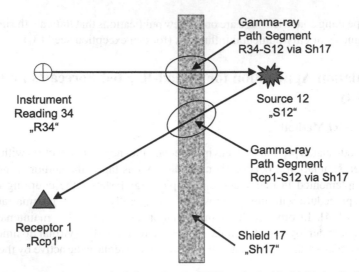

Fig. 2. Scheme of the forecast calculation using the EPRI method with shielded radiation (Source: [16], p. 2)

sources and two measuring points were used for this purpose. The real exposure rates were measured on these positions and compared with the calculated algorithmic values. The validation exhibits deviations of 2% and −15%, respectively.

Supplementary field studies were carried out in a nuclear power plant with the participation of software developers, in whose software procedures the spatial geometry, the radiation sources and the measured exposure rates were entered ([16], pp. 2–8; see also [17]). In one case, a room with three high-pressure charging pumps and the associated radioactive pipelines as well as 19 real measuring points was chosen. For the maintenance staff, a total of 24 calculation points were assumed, for which the values were determined using the algorithm. The validation showed deviations in the range of approximately ±55%.

Compared to maintenance work actually carried out and monitored by dosimeters, this result was nevertheless described as relatively good ([16], pp. 4–11). The deviations were attributed to differences in the work durations and locations of the real maintenance activities. In particular, approximately the same values resulted between the forecasts of the algorithm and manually calculated estimates.

For further validation studies in this field of investigation, reference must be made to the publication mentioned. Overall, it can be seen that validation studies for forecasting methods can only very rarely be found in the literature. Another validation study of environmental prognoses for lighting and noise in a workshop for tool production has been reported elsewhere ([18], p. 156) with promising results.

4   Challenges for Data Modeling

In the following, two essential challenges to the information technology modeling of environmental influences and their evaluation and assessment in tools of the Digital

Factory will be discussed. This involves, on the one hand, avoiding redundant entries in corresponding data models, and on the other hand, the issue of providing comparison values so that assessments can also be derived from legally binding information. Both topics are not only important for the modeling of environmental influences, they also concern the modeling of ergonomically relevant data in general.

4.1 Object-Oriented Data Modeling

Keller ([18], p. 83) has already pointed out that it makes sense to use an object-oriented approach for data modeling of environmental influences in an indoor work area (see also [19]). For this he used the notation of the Unified Modeling Language (UML [20]). Figure 3 shows the object-oriented model of the stress situation at a work place. The basic elements for modeling all objects in the work area are 3D objects, which in turn consist of polygons.

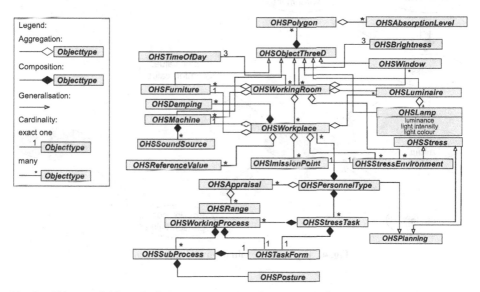

Fig. 3. Object model for calculating the stress situation at a workplace (according to [18], p. 140)

The use of this object-oriented approach offers considerable advantages when modeling occupational health and safety (OHS) data as it occurs when there are environmental influences. It gives a logical structure to the complex relationships and avoids redundancy of data entries. With the principles of inheritance and composition, hierarchically structured data models and complex functionalities can be implemented. In addition, methods for calculating stress situations can be integrated into this data model.

Each object class is described by attributes and applicable methods as well as the relationships between object classes by associations. The "workplace" object class can, for example, contain several elements of the "lighting" object class. The data relevant to occupational health and safety are integrated into the data model as attributes of the related objects. The "lamp" object contains, for example, the attributes "lamp type", "luminance", "light intensity" and "light color". The methods for calculating environmental stress are specializations of the object class "environmental stress" and are linked to all object data required for their calculation. This then ensures that a change in the property data leads to an update of the calculated stress situation.

Object-oriented three-dimensional building models are increasingly being used in building planning. Building Information Modeling (BIM [21]) is used for data storage and, in particular, for data exchange between manufacturers. The so-called Industry Foundation Classes (IFC), which are standardized in ISO 16739-1:2018 [22], are used as an open data standard. This data modeling was originally developed for building construction, later also for civil engineering. It is to be expected that this approach will also be used in the future for modeling objects in work areas.

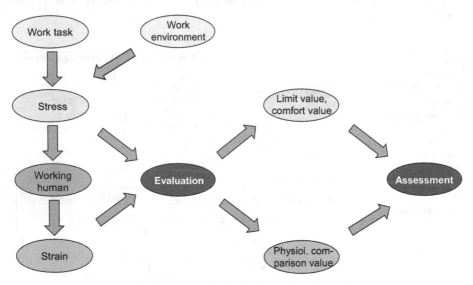

Fig. 4. Ergonomic evaluation and assessment

4.2   IT Provision of Comparison Values for Assessment Purposes

A special problem is the assessment of a determined stress or strain value (Fig. 4). For this purpose, a comparison value is necessary, which may be available in the form of a limit and occasionally a comfort value. Such values may be found in an ordinance, standard or as a recommendation with regard to a certain type of exposure (see e.g. comfort values at [23]). For types of strain, physiological comparison values are required in an analogous manner. However, such information is only available in text form, if at all.

In the case of a point in time-related prognosis in the Digital Factory, first the stress value (more rarely a strain value) is usually determined first at a calculation point. A corresponding comparison value is then manually taken from a regulation or another source, which is often achieved today through research on the Internet. An assessment of the determined value is then carried out, taking into account the task at hand. Ultimately, this requires a process performed by personnel.

Accordingly, there is no automized IT provision of the comparison values together with the associated context data. In order to achieve this, existing sources would first have to be processed into a structured knowledge base using IT (Fig. 5). This can be done through text and data mining.

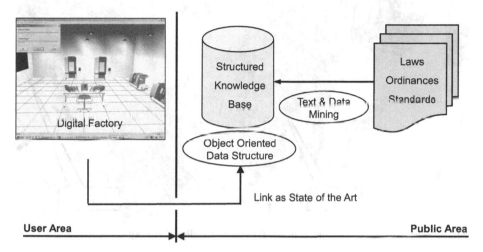

Fig. 5. Development of an occupational health and safety knowledge base

The problem with such a publicly available data is that many sources (e.g. guidelines and standards) are not provided free of charge. If possible at all, the user could take the evaluation data from the Digital Factory to access the public knowledge base in a structured manner and finally derive the assessment algorithmically from it. Such a concept would certainly simplify and improve the use of occupational health and safety regulations considerably. As far as the author is aware, this approach has not yet been pursued through research funding.

5 Further Development of Environmental Forecasts in the Digital Factory

A major number of calculation methods are already available for the prognosis of environmental influences. However, these mainly relate to a certain type of stress; the associated software procedures are (with a few exceptions) not integrated into the Digital Factory. With regard to the resulting strain on the working human, first methods and software procedures are available.

In addition, the existing methods usually concern time-related evaluations, and they are often no suitable methods for period-related influences. Only a few examples of successive exposure to a single environmental influence are available. In this regard, reference can be made to the calculation method for evaluating a fluctuating sound

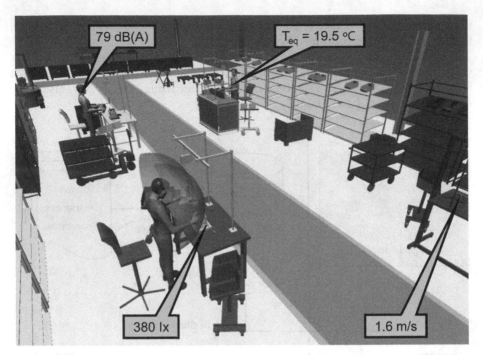

Fig. 6. Vision of forecasting environmental stress in the digital factory (Layout Graphics [27])

pressure level (person-related daily noise exposure level according to the German Noise and Vibrations Occupational Safety and Health Ordinance ([24], § 2 (2)).

Even more there is a lack of evaluation methods and procedures for simultaneously acting environmental influences, and this also for combinations of different types of stress caused by the work task and the work environment. A counterexample is the evaluation of energetic heat work (see e.g. [25], p. 14). In this respect a lack of integrating methods can be stated. The lexicographical approach developed for this purpose for simultaneously acting influences ([26], p. 42) can only represent a workaround.

All of this shows that there are an important number of open questions about the prognosis of environmental influences in the Digital Factory. Thus, multiple research efforts are required before a comprehensive prognosis can be made (Fig. 6).

References

1. Zülch, G., Stock, P., Hrdina, J.: Working time configuration in hospitals using personnel-oriented simulation. In: Koch, T. (ed.) APMS 2006. ITIFIP, vol. 257, pp. 493–501. Springer, Boston, MA (2008). https://doi.org/10.1007/978-0-387-77249-3_51
2. Zülch, G.: Evaluating human work in the digital factory - a new German guideline. In: Grabot, B., Vallespir, B., Gomes, S., Bouras, A., Kiritsis, D. (eds.) APMS 2014. IAICT, vol. 440, pp. 35–42. Springer, Heidelberg (2014). https://doi.org/10.1007/978-3-662-44733-8_5
3. VDI 3633-6:2001-10: Simulation of systems in materials handling, logistics and production – Representation of human resources in simulation models. Beuth, Berlin (2001). https://www.beuth.de/en/technical-rule/vdi-3633-blatt-6/44890290. Accessed 20 Jan 2021

4. Zülch, G.: Development and status of personnel deployment simulation and its inclusion into the digital factory. SNE Simul. Notes Eur. **30**, 197–202 (2020)
5. VDI 4499-4:2015-03: Digital factory - Ergonomic representation of humans in the digital factory. Beuth, Berlin (2015). https://www.beuth.de/en/technical-rule/vdi-4499-blatt-4/222 813009. Accessed 18 Mar 2021
6. Zülch, G.: Ergonomische Abbildung des Menschen in der Digitalen Fabrik – Die neue VDI–Richtlinie 4499-4. In: Dangelmaier, W., Laroque, C., Klaas, A. (eds) Simulation in Produktion und Logistik 2013: Entscheidungsunterstützung von der Planung bis zur Steuerung. ASIM-Mitteilung Nr. 147. HNI-Verlagsschriftenreihe, Paderborn, pp. 53–60 (2013). http://www.asim-fachtagung-spl.de/asim2013/papers/Proof_165_Zuelch.pdf. Accessed 09 Mar 2021
7. Rohmert, W.: Ergonomics: concept of work, stress and strain. Appl. Psychol. **35**(2), 159–181 (1986). https://doi.org/10.1111/j.1464-0597.1986.tb00911.x. Accessed 20 Jan 2021
8. VDI: VDI 4499-5 - Projekt. Digitale Fabrik: Prognose von Umgebungseinflüssen auf den arbeitenden Menschen. Beuth, Berlin (2020). https://www.vdi.de/richtlinien/details/vdi-4499-blatt-5-digitale-fabrik-prognose-von-umgebungseinfluoocn-auf-den-arbeitenden-men schen. Accessed 26 Jan 2021
9. ArbSchG: Act on the Implementation of Measures of Occupational Safety and Health to Encourage Improvements in the Safety and Health Protection of Workers at Work (Arbeits-schutzgesetz, ArbSchG). Occupational Safety and Health Act of 07.08.1996. Federal Law Gazette I, p. 1246, as amended by the Second Data Protection Adjustment and Implemen-tation ActEUof 20.11.2019 (2019). http://www.gesetze-im-internet.de/englisch_arbschg/eng lisch_arbschg.pdf. Accessed 16 Mar 2021
10. Briceno, L., Paul, G.: MakeHuman: a review of the modelling framework. In: Bagnara, S., Tartaglia, R., Albolino, S., Alexander, T., Fujita, Y. (eds.) IEA 2018. AISC, vol. 822, pp. 224–232. Springer, Cham (2019). https://doi.org/10.1007/978-3-319-96077-7_23
11. Nunes, I.L. (ed.): AHFE 2018. AISC, vol. 781. Springer, Cham (2019). https://doi.org/10.1007/978-3-319-94334-3
12. Neumann, W.P., Winkelhaus, S., Grosse, E.H., Glock, C.H.: Industry 4.0 and the human factor–a systems framework and analysis methodology for successful development. Int. J. Prod. Econ. **233**, 107992 (2021). https://doi.org/10.1016/j.ijpe.2020.107992
13. Illmann, B., Fritzsche, L., Ullmann, S., Leidholdt, W.: Ganzheitliche Gefährdungsbeurteilung mit digitalen Menschmodellen – Die Integration von Umgebungsbedingungen in die Digitale Fabrik. In: Gesellschaft für Arbeitswissenschaft (ed) VerANTWORTung für die Arbeit der Zukunft. GfA Press, Dortmund (2015). http://gfa2015.gesellschaft-fuer-arbeitswissenschaft.de/inhalt/A.2.7.pdf. Accessed 18 Mar 2021
14. Ribon, N.: 3D ALARA Planning Overview. Presentation, 13.01.2017. Siemens PLM Software, Fellbach (2013)
15. Brinkmeier, B.: Personal communication, 13.01.2017. Siemens Industry Software, Fellbach (2017)
16. Electric Power Research Institute: Demonstration of Advanced 3D ALARA Planning Proto-types for Dose Reduction. 1025310, Final Report. EPRI, Palo Alto, CA (2012). https://www.epri.com/research/products/000000000001025310. Accessed 02 Jun 2021
17. PennWell: ALARA planning: Siemens PLM Software and Microsoft engineer a partnership to ensure employee health and safety (n.d.). http://download.microsoft.com/download/F/0/D/F0D0F18A-D6BE-4214-B14D-1B52F8075135/ALARA%20Planning%20with%20Siem ens%20PLM%20and%20Microsoft.pdf. Accessed 20 Jan 2021
18. Keller, V.: Ansatz zur objektorientierten Modellierung betrieblicher Arbeitsschutzdaten. Shaker, Aachen (2002)

19. Zülch, G., Grieger, T., Keller, V.: Object-oriented modelling and prognosis of occupational health and safety-related data. In: Safety and Health, Proceedings Volume 5: Proceedings of the XVth Triennial Congress of the International Ergonomics, 24–30 August 2003, pp. 399–402. Ergonomics Society of Korea, Seoul (2003)

20. Alhir, S.S.: UML in a Nutshell. O'Reilly & Associates, Cambridge, MA (1998). UML 2.0 in a Nutshell. O'Reilly & Associates, Sebastopol, CA (2005)

21. Wikipedia: Building Informations Modeling (2021). https://en.wikipedia.org/wiki/Building_information_modeling. Accessed 04 Jun 2021

22. ISO 16739-1:2018: Industry Foundation Classes (IFC) for data sharing in the construction and facility management industries—Part 1: Data schema (2018). https://www.iso.org/standard/70303.html. Accessed 11 Mar 2021

23. Fraunhofer-Institut für Bauphysik (IBP): BNB-Tool Thermischer Komfort. Fraunhofer IBP, Holzkirchen (2014). https://www.ibp.fraunhofer.de/content/dam/ibp/ibp-neu/de/dokumente/produktblaetter/eer/produktblatt-bnb-tool.pdf. Accessed 16Mar 2021

24. LärmVibrationsArbSchV: Verordnung zum Schutz der Beschäftigten vor Gefährdungen durch Lärm und Vibrationen. Lärm- und Vibrations-Arbeitsschutzverordnung – LärmVibrationsArbSchV. Date of issue: 06.03.2007. Federal Law Gazette I p. 261. Last amended by Article 3 of the Ordinance of 19.07.2010. Federal Law Gazette I, p. 960 (2017)

25. Berufsgenossenschaft Holz und Metall (BGHM): Hitzearbeit erkennen – beurteilen – schützen. BGI 579. BGHM, Mainz (2013). https://publikationen.dguv.de/widgets/pdf/download/article/340. Accessed 16 Mar 2021

26. Zülch, M., Zülch, G.: Production logistics and ergonomic evaluation of U-shaped assembly systems. Int. J. Prod. Econ. **190**, 37–44 (2017). https://doi.org/10.1016/j.ijpe.2017.01.004. Accessed 16 Mar 2021

27. Schneck, M.: Personal communication, 11.07.2009. Delmia Systemes, Fellbach (2009)

Paraconsistent Annotated Evidential Logic Eτ Applied to Autonomous Robots in Logistic Center

Flávio Amadeu Bernardini(✉) ⓘ, Marcia Terra da Silva(✉) ⓘ, Jair Minoro Abe(✉) ⓘ, and Luiz Antonio de Lima(✉) ⓘ

Graduate Program in Production Engineering, Paulista Univesity, Sao Paulo, Brazil
flavio.bernardini@stricto.unip.br, {marcia.silva,
jair.abe}@docente.unip.br, luizlima@unip.br

Abstract. Due to the momentum of Industry 4.0 in various product and service sectors, academic and business investments in the development of new technologies in the logistics sector also stand out. Based on these trends, bibliographical research was carried out of articles dedicated to robotics with application in the logistics sector. Based on the bibliographic survey results, this work proposes a prototype of an autonomous terrestrial mobile robot that must go through corridors in specific layouts in logistics centres focusing on the aid of control tasks and management information for decision making. The main contribution is testing a para-analyzer algorithm based on non-classical logic such as Paraconsistent Annotated Logic Eτ, as the decision-making tool to avoid obstacles.

Keywords: Autonomous technology · Non-classic logic · Paraconsistent logic

1 Introduction

The "Digital Transformation" driven by Industry 4.0 is about to change countless companies and organizational models profoundly. This also applies in the manufacturing sector, where many companies will face various challenges from different perspectives, which four key components will govern: CPS (Cyber-Physical Systems), IoT (Internet of Things), Internet of Services, Intelligent Factory [1].

For all this, an increasing number of companies seek to automate their production lines, streamline processes, improve the transportation of inputs in the productive sector, streamline all logistics processes, and reduce costs.

AGV (Automatically Guided Vehicles) is an excellent example used in large logistics centres, implemented by already well-established technologies. In research carried out in this work, it was found that several lines of research seek to enable the implementation of these technologies both in the logistics sector and in the manufacturing sector.

Because of this scenario, the authors [2] conducted bibliographic research on multi-robot localization in a highly symmetrical environment. A team of robots, adequately coordinated, can perform complex tasks such as surveillance, monitoring, mapping, etc.

© IFIP International Federation for Information Processing 2021
Published by Springer Nature Switzerland AG 2021
A. Dolgui et al. (Eds.): APMS 2021, IFIP AICT 632, pp. 533–540, 2021.
https://doi.org/10.1007/978-3-030-85906-0_58

The correct and reliable location concerning a known map is essential in these tasks and represents one of the most significant mobile robotics challenges. They have done several studies on emerging technologies for the location and displacement of multi robots and propose a solution free of external locators such as GPS, as they highlight the possibility of interrupting this communication indoors. For the multi-robot locomotion solution, the authors propose to perform small asymmetric markings in an environment of symmetrical corridors, such as in a logistics centre. These markings are the references used by an algorithm based on Cartesian information about the site. They used the Pioneer P3DX differential robot prototype equipped with ultrasonic sensors to avoid obstacles.

Regarding navigation techniques, the authors [3] used a differential robot proto-type equipped with three front ultrasonic sensors and, through an algorithm based on Fuzzy logic, controls displacement and avoids collision with obstacles. According to the authors, the robot's direction is controlled by the rotation of the front wheels, and the rear freewheel serves only as support. The front wheels are also equipped with sensors whose information is transformed into the robot's angular and linear speed, which are necessary for positioning in a Cartesian system.

This article proposes applying the Paraconsistent Annotated Evidential Logic Eτ in a terrestrial mobile robot's navigation system in corridors of logistics centres and warehouses. This work's main objective is to develop a paraconsistent algorithm capable of avoiding obstacles and the possibility of integration with other navigation systems.

1.1 Paraconsistent Annotated Evidential Logic Eτ Applied in Robotics

The Paraconsistent Annotated Evidential Logic Eτ is a non-classical logics known as paraconsistent logics. Roughly, paraconsistent logic is a logic that serves as underlying logic for inconsistent but non-trivial theories. It has as atomic formulas propositions of the type $p(\mu, \lambda)$, where p is a proposition in a usual sense, and $\mu, \lambda \in [0, 1]$ (closed real unitary interval). The remaining formulas are obtained through Boolean combinations of connectives of the logic. Intuitively, μ indicates the degree of favourable evidence of p, and λ indicates the degree of unfavourable evidence of p. The reading of the μ, λ, depends on the most diverse applications considered and may change.

With these applications' effect, μ may be the degree of favourable belief, and λ may be the degree of belief contrary to proposition p. In some specific applications, μ may also indicate the probability expressed by p occurring and λ, the improbability expressed by p of occurring and other readings. An order relation is defined in $[0, 1]^2$: $(\mu_1, \lambda_1) \le (\mu_2, \lambda_2) \Leftrightarrow \mu_1 \le \mu_2$ and $\lambda_2 \le \lambda_1$, forming a lattice, symbolized by τ, which is represented in Fig. 1 [4].

Concerning the Paraconsistent Logic application, in 1999, the Emmy I autonomous mobile robot was built consisting of a mobile tower with a circular aluminium base of 30 cm diameter and 60 cm in height. The robot was designed on four overlapping electronic circuit boards separated by function in the control system to facilitate the visualization of each module's action in the robot's movement control [5]. The authors used two ultrasonic devices called Parasonic in front of the mobile robot to detect possible obstacles.

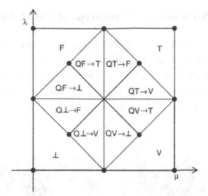

Fig. 1. The Lattice τ of decision-making

Despite technical difficulties such as braking, lack of multi-speed and rotational timings between engines, they claim that the tests performed show that Paracontrol performed well to solve problems related to robot navigation. The system demonstrated a good ability to modify the robot's behaviour when unexpected changes occur in environmental conditions.

In 2004 the Emmy II appeared with a significant reduction in the robot structure's height and with a diameter of 25 cm. Similarly, its predecessor also used two ultrasonic sensors to detect obstacles and programming based on the Annotated Paraconsistent Logic [6, 7]. According to the authors, the modifications made both in the structural parts and in the electronic circuit of the autonomous mobile robot allowed a significant improvement in the performance of the robot's movement. To show it, the robot was submitted to four performance tests in a square environment with a side of 3.3 m and with three internal obstacles. The authors recorded an average of 10 collisions per test and claimed that most were because of a deficiency of ultrasonic sensors, especially when obstacles are too close to the robot.

A more advanced version emerged in 2009 with the Emmy III prototype, whose design was divided into three parts: mechanical subsystem, path planning and sensing. The authors' main idea was to improve this version to expand the navigation capabilities of the robot through a task with an origin and a destination to be fulfilled as a goal.

For this, they developed a computer system that receives information from sensors distributed in the environment, maps the environment by coordinates, and transmits commands to the robot's mechanical system during displacement. With the use of Paraconsistent Evidential Logic, the proposed sensing system aims to generate a degree of favourable evidence in each environmental position. The degree of favourable evidence is related to the sentence: "There is an obstacle in the position analyzed." Thus, through the input information of the ultrasonic sensor, the distance between the sensor and the obstacle, the angle between the horizontal axis of the environment and the direction to the front of the sensor, the coordinate (X, Y) where the robot is about the environment is determined. The authors performed three system performance tests and presented Cartesian graphs with variations in the degree of favourable evidence, which prove the correct functioning of the algorithm [8, 9].

1.2 Project Proposal Structure and Prototype of the Mobile Robot

To develop the autonomous terrestrial robot project, a structure consisting of corridors was elaborated to simulate a production line's environment. Based on proportional relationships was defined width of 80 cm for corridors of the production line. Figure 2 shows the prototype of the robot in the simulation environment. The simulation of the robot navigation performance in this environment was significant for the tests foreseen in the project.

Fig. 2. Terrestrial autonomous robot in a logistic centre

The project proposal is to build a prototype of an autonomous terrestrial mobile robot that will go through corridors of production lines, which will perform monitoring, tracking, and transport of materials. Figure 3 shows the overall structure and all the electrical and electronic devices that were used. Two front ultrasonic sensors monitor the robot that sends signals to the microcontroller, warning of possible obstacles. The left and right side sensors inform the lateral distances so that the robot maintains a central position in the corridor during displacement.

Fig. 3. Prototype of the terrestrial robot

The Atmega 2560 microcontroller will be programmed in C language, with technology embedded in the concepts of the Paraconsistent Annotated Evidential Logic Eτ. After receiving the information from the sensors, the paraconsistent algorithm will assist in decision-making. This information will be transformed into electrical signals and sent to the control devices of the traction motors and the servo motor that will control the direction of the autonomous terrestrial mobile robot, thus avoiding collisions during displacement. A differential of this prototype will be installing an LCD for monitoring sensor readings and the angle of the steering control servo motor. During the mobile robot's trajectory, these variables will be observed to make the necessary adjustments in the programming of the paraconsistent algorithm. We opted for a Lithium battery to equip the prototype because it is very light and with considerable energy storage capacity.

2 Methodology

Initially, the concepts of Paraconsistent Annotated Evidential Logic Eτ, through a built-in paraconsistent algorithm, will play a fundamental role in decision-making assistance [10].

Then, based on the lattice properties represented in Fig. 1 and on the proposition: "The front of the robot is free", Table 1 was elaborated. The distances measured by the left and right sensors were converted, respectively, by the μ and λ, through a normalization calculation of these values.

Table 1. Paraconsistent algorithm values.

Front sensors					Degree of uncertainty	Setpoint (°)
Situation	Left (cm)	μ	Right (cm)	λ		
1	20	0,1	200	0	−0,9	−85,23
2	40	0,2	180	0,1	−0,7	−66,29
3	60	0,3	160	0,2	−0,5	−47,35
4	80	0,4	140	0,3	−0,3	−28,41
5	100	0,5	120	0,4	−0,1	−9,47
6	120	0,6	100	0,5	0,1	9,47
7	140	0,7	80	0,6	0,3	28,41
8	160	0,8	60	0,7	0,5	47,35
9	180	0,9	40	0,8	0,7	66,29
10·	200	1	20	0,9	0,9	85,23

Then, the degree of uncertainty was calculated through the concepts of Paraconsistent Logic and provided precise and decisive values to determine the servo motor's correct position for each situation under the presence of obstacles. In the last column of Table 1, the setpoint values of the servo motor already calculated are observed.

The following is presenting a programming excerpt performed in C language, which was divided into three main blocks. Frontal paraconsistent logic, lateral paraconsistent logic, and servo motor control. In the first block, the variables perceived by the left and right frontal sensors (sr_lf and sr_rf) have already gone through the normalization process and follow the concepts of paraconsistent logic. These values were converted into the variables (mi1 and la1) respectively in μ_1 and λ_1, as described in the Lattice of Fig. 1. Next, the degree of uncertainty of the frontal decision was calculated and stored in the variable (deg_unc1). In the second block, the same process is repeated for the values read by the left and right side sensors and converted to (mi2 and la2), respectively μ_2 and λ_2. Then, the degree of uncertainty of the lateral decision is stored in the variable (deg_unc2). The third block constantly receives the values of the degree of frontal and lateral uncertainty variables, so the microcontroller, through logical constraints, controls the variable (sv_set_pt) of decision-making of the steering servo of the autonomous terrestrial robot

```
// frontal paraconsistent logic//
mi1 = (sr_lf/50); // conversion of left front sensor reading into mi1 variable
la1 = (1-(sr_rf*0.02)); // conversion of right front sensor reading into la1variable
deg_unc1 = ((mi1 + la1)-1); // calculation of the degree of uncertainty of the frontal
sensors
//sv_set_pt = 538.42*gra_unc + 551.5;// determination of the servo motor set point
sv_set_pt = 300*gra_unc1 + 511.5;
// lateral paraconsistent logic//
mi2 = (sr_ls/80); // conversion of left lateral side reading into mi2 variable
la2 = (1-(sr_rs*0.0125)); // conversion of right side sensor reading into la1variable
deg_unc2 = ((mi2 + la2)-1)); // calculation of the degree of uncertainty of the lateral
sensors
//sv_set_pt = 538.42*gra_unc + 551.5; // determination of the servo motor set point
sv_set_pt = 200*gra_unc2 + 511.5;
// servo motor control//
valor_motor = map(sv_set_pt, 0, 1023, 0, 180); // servo motor control
servo.write (valor_motor);
ang_sv = gra_inc1*95; // calculation of the angle of the servo motor
```

3 Experiments and Results

According to the project's initial proposal, the next step was to perform the physical tests and submit the terrestrial robot autonomous to move in a structured environment. This environment has an 80 cm wide corridor and 3 m long, which simulates a supposed production environment. Table 2 shows the tests were repeated ten times at each of the three standardized speeds to verify performance and possible collisions with obstacles or collisions with the side barriers.

The robot will be able to perform tasks such as providing components for these product lines. Figure 4 shows this test with an obstacle on the robot's right side, perceived by the right front sensor (Sensor λ_1).

Table 2. Robot performance tests

Number of collisions X speed			Type of obstacle
0.25 m/s	0.5 m/s	0.75 m/s	
0	3	2	Left side boundary
0	1	3	Right side boundary
0	4	5	Rectangular obstacle object

Fig. 4. Robot navigation test in a structured environment (Color figure online)

At point A of the red line, there is a tendency to deviate to the left, and at point B, there is already a perception of the proximity to the left lateral limit by the left lateral sensor (Sensor μ_2). At point C, the two lateral sensors (Sensor μ_2 and λ_2) are responsible for maintaining the robot's rectilinear trajectory and maintaining the robot's displacement in the middle of the corridor. This test was also performed with an obstacle on the robot's left side, which similarly swerved to correct its trajectory.

4 Discussion

The authors [2] conducted studies on emerging technologies in robotic navigation and researched multi-robot use in structured and highly symmetrical environments, such as logistics centres and industrial production lines. The GPS robotic navigation technology researched by the authors showed some deficiencies in internal communication. In such cases of lack of communication, the navigation system with a paraconsistent algorithm could be used in conjunction with GPS and avoid collisions with obstacles. In other studies, the authors [3] and the authors [8] built prototypes of differential robots with a free rear wheel only as support. In these cases, the steering is determined by the difference in the rotation of the traction wheels. This type of prototype is very subject to inaccuracies because of slippages. With the placement of the servomotor instead of the freewheel, as in the case of this work, there is a better performance in the movement of the robot's prototype due to the accuracy of the servomotor combined with the paraconsistent algorithm. The results obtained in the tests at a speed of 0.25 m/s without collisions with obstacles or collisions with the lateral limits showed to be very promising.

5 Conclusion

This article began with the proposal to apply paraconsistent logic to control an autonomous terrestrial mobile robot. Historically, research has revealed numerous studies with the application of the Paraconsistent Annotated Evidential Logic Eτ in the development of robotic navigation systems. The paraconsistent algorithm developed in the C language showed the possibility of integration with other robotic navigation systems to act in symmetrical environments, such as logistics centres and industrial production lines. Another observation of this work was using a servomotor for robot steering control to improve the accuracy of movements. As future work, Paraconsistent Logic can be integrated with other navigation systems, such as odometric navigation. The algorithm developed showed the possibility of implementing the prototype in logistic centres, performing component transport and monitoring tasks.

Acknowledgements. "This study was financed in part by the Coordenação de Aperfeiçoamento de Pessoal de Nível Superior - Brasil (CAPES) -Finance Code 001".

References

1. Preindl, R., Nikolopoulos, K., Litsiou, K.: Transformation strategies for the supply chain: the impact of industry 4.0 and digital transformation. Supply Chain Forum: Int. J., 1–9. Taylor & Francis (2020)
2. Abrate, F., Bona, B., Indri, M., Rosa, S., Tibaldi, F.: Multirobot localization in highly symmetrical environments. J. Intell. Rob. Syst. **71**(3–4), 403–421 (2013)
3. Chen, Y.S., Juang, J.G.: Intelligent obstacle avoidance control strategy for wheeled mobile robot. In: 2009 ICCAS-SICE, pp. 3199–3204. IEEE (2009)
4. Abe, J.M. Silva Filho, J.I.d., Celestino, U., Araújo, H.C.d.: Lógica Paraconsistente Anotada Evidencial Eτ. Comunicar (2011)
5. Da Silva Filho, J.I., et al:. Emmy: robô móvel autônomo paraconsistente-protótipo 1. Coleção Documentos, Série Lógica e Teoria da Ciência, IEA-USP (1999)
6. Torres, C.R, Abe, J.M., Torres, G.L.: Sistema inteligente paraconsistente para controle de robôs móveis autônomos. Portuguese, MSc Dissertation, Universidade Federal de Itajubá–UNIFEI, Itajubá (2004)
7. Abe, J.M., Nakamatsu, K., Akama, S., Ahrary, A.: Handling paraconsistency and paracompleteness in robotics. In: 2018 Innovations in Intelligent Systems and Applications (INISTA), pp. 1–7. IEEE (2018)
8. Torres, C.R., Abe, J.M., Lambert-Torres, G., da Silva Filho, J.I., Martins, H.G.: Autonomous mobile robot Emmy III. In: New Advances in Intelligent Decision Technologies, pp. 317–327. Springer, Berlin (2009). https://doi.org/10.1007/978-3-642-00909-9_31
9. Torres, C.R., Lambert-Torres, G., Abe, J.M., da Silva Filho, J.I.: The sensing system for the autonomous mobile robot Emmy III. In: 2011 IEEE International Conference on Fuzzy Systems (FUZZ-IEEE 2011), pp. 2928–2933. IEEE. (2011)
10. Abe, J.M., Akama, S., Nakamatsu, K.: Introduction to Annotated Logics: Foundations for Paracomplete and Paraconsistent Reasoning, vol. 88. Springer, Cham (2015). https://doi.org/10.1007/978-3-319-17912-4

Human Aspects in Collaborative Order Picking – What if Robots Learned How to Give Humans a Break?

Yaxu Niu[1,2] and Frederik Schulte[2(✉)]

[1] Beijing University of Chemical Technology, Beijing 100029, China
2017400145@mail.buct.edu.cn
[2] Delft University of Technology, 2628 Delft, CD, The Netherlands
F.Schulte@tudelft.nl

Abstract. Human aspects in collaboration of humans and robots, as common in warehousing, are considered increasingly important objectives in operations management. In this work, we let robots learn about human stress levels based on sensor data in collaborative order picking of robotic mobile fulfillment systems. To this end, we develop a multi-agent reinforcement (MARL) approach that considers human stress levels and recovery behavior next to traditional performance objectives in the reward function of robotic agents. We assume a human-oriented assignment problem in which the robotic agents assign orders and short breaks to human workers based on their stress/recovery states. We find that the proposed MARL policy reduces the human stress time by up 50% in comparison to the applied benchmark policies and maintains system efficiency at a comparable level. While the results may need to be confirmed in different settings considering different types of humans aspects and efficiency objectives, they also show a practicable pathway to control stress levels and recovery for related problems of human-robot collaboration, inside and outside of warehousing.

Keywords: Order picking · Robotic mobile fulfillment systems · Human aspects · Multi-agent reinforcement learning · Human-robot collaboration · Sensor data · Recovery

1 Introduction

Human-oriented collaboration between humans and robots is widely considered one of the greatest challenges in the final steps of the 4th Industrial Revolution and an anticipated central question of the 5th Industrial Revolution. Order-picking in robotic mobile fulfillment systems (RMFS) is one of the applications in which human-robot collaboration is already a pivotal element of today's working reality. Various authors have recognized and addressed the issue with a respective

Thanks for the support of China Scholarship Council (CSC).

survey paper [1], a conceptual framework for the integration of humans aspects in planning approaches of ordering picking [2], or specific operational models (e.g., [3]). Niu et al. [4] have proposed a decision support approach that enables robots to learn a human-oriented assignment policy in collaborative order picking based on a discomfort model introduced by Larco et al. [5]. On top of that, Sedighi Maman et al. [6] have recently demonstrated how sensor data from wearable devices can be used to detect the stress levels and recovery of workers. Nonetheless, to leverage these findings for human well-being in collaborative operations, the two methods would need to be integrated in an approach that learns to take (assignment) decisions based on sensor data indicating human stress and recovery levels.

In RMFSs, most related works focus on different variants of operational assignment problems considering a general assignment between work stations and robots [7], shelves to storage assignment [8], order and storage assignment [3], velocity-based storage assignment [9], and robots to shelves assignment [10]. Apart from that, workstation location problems [11], pod travel times under different lane characteristics [12], fleet sizing [13], path planning [7], and order batching and shelf sequencing [14] are considered. The most common methods are statistical models, analytical and queuing models as well as optimization models. Only [13] propose a MARL negotiation scheme and apply it to an order picking example application, and [11] develop a discrete event simulation framework for RMFS. Among these references, only [7] consider human aspects using the proxy of the workers' handling speed.

In this work, we propose a multi-agent reinforcement learning (MARL) approach in which robotic agents effectively learn to consider human needs for recovery based on wearable sensor data, next to established objectives such as minimum processing times. This assumed human-oriented assignment with its sensor-based decisions is illustrated in Fig. 1 based on the layout of the underlying RMFS. The proposed policy considers short breaks for workers that are implemented via assignment decisions. For the conducted experimental study, this paper develops four different policies that are commonly deployed in order picking. The proposed MARL reduces the total stress time for humans by up 50 % during the collaborative order picking process without significantly compromising the system efficiency. While it appears probable that the evaluated policy can be further improved in terms of human aspects as well as operational efficiency, the experiments confirm that the MARL approach enables robotic learning with respect to human aspects and (multiple) other objectives. Since the general characteristics of the considered human-oriented assignment problem resemble many other operational problems including human-robot collaboration, the MARL approach also be adopted in different and new problem settings.

Subsequently, we present the human-oriented assignment problem in order picking of an RMFS (in Sect. 2), the proposed MARL approach (in Sect. 3), the experimental study with results (in Sect. 4), and a conclusion with open issues for future work (in Sect. 5).

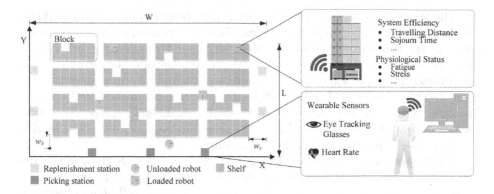

Fig. 1. Layout of the RMFS illustrating robotic assignment decision points in which human sensor data is considered

2 Problem Description

In this section, the underlying RMFS in this paper is described and the assumptions used are presented in Sect. 2.1. Then, in Sect. 2.2, the human-oriented robot assignment problem is defined, both considering system efficiency and human well-being objectives.

2.1 The Robotic Mobile Fulfillment System

The layout of RMFS is shown in Fig. 1, where shelves are organized as rectangular blocks in the storage area. The workstations are situated along the boundary of the warehouse. The available robot moves underneath the shelves from the dwell location toward the targeted shelf. Then robot lifts the movable shelf and transports it to the designated workstations along the aisles and cross-aisles, and queues for its turn if the worker is busy. Finally, the order is fulfilled and the robot transports the completed shelf to its previous storage position.

In order picking activities, pickers are engaged in intensive and repetitive manual handling activities, which will inevitably lead to the accumulation of physiological fatigue and the generation of stress, which will affect the efficiency of the system and may even endanger health. In RMFSs, frequent and repetitive item picking, handling, and packing activities will contribute to the accumulation of fatigue, which will result in a decrease in efficiency and an increase in reaction time. Besides, it has been demonstrated that heart rate monitoring has turned out to be an efficient way to realize fatigue detection. As presented in [6], fatigue detection is mainly comprised of the following steps: (1) selected sensors' data are preprocessed for feature generation; (2) then processed data are used to train the statistical and data analytic model for distinguishing between fatigue and non-fatigued state; (3) the trained models are evaluated based on accuracy, sensitivity, etc.; (4) finally, the best-trained model is evaluated.

The stress of the order pickers mainly results from the increase in workload or the occurrence of unexpected events. This article assumes that the generation of stress is caused by an excessive workload. Moreover, the relationship between stress and performance follows the Yerkes-Dodson law, represented as an inverted-U shape where high performance can only be guaranteed within a moderate stress level. It's interesting that if stress occurs, the PD tends to increase, on the contrary, the PD remains small [15]. Therefore, stress detection, in this paper, referred to an on-line stress detection approach proposed by [15], which processes pupil diameter derived features

This paper mainly focuses on seeking an intelligent robot assignment policy to cope with dynamic changes in pickers' efficiency due to fatigue, stress, and short-break recovery, balancing system efficiency, and human well-being objectives. The studied assignment problem assumes that the previous decision problems, such as order assignment and picking shelf selection, have been solved. Thus, the next target shelf has already been determined. For the model formulation, some assumptions, which are reasonable in real RMFS, are first listed as follows.

- It is assumed that all the robots are busy and there are always retrieval orders waiting in the external queue.
- Each robot in the system executes its tasks independently and only wirelessly communicates with workstations to obtain environmental information.
- Robots are scheduled based on the First-Come-First-Served (FCFS) policy.
- The orders are single-line orders, which are common and account for a large number of E-commerce orders.

2.2 Human-Oriented Assignment Problem of the Robot to Workstations

In a typical RMFS, there always exist numerous unfulfilled order tasks. Suppose that robots are dealing with $\mathbb{O}$ fixed sequence orders scattered among different shelves parking in different positions in the storage area, and then will be assigned to pickers with different handling speed T_{w_k} to fulfill the retrieval process. This robot assignment problem is modeled as a Markov Game model, in which all the robots make assignment decisions following a joint policy π, $\pi \in \Pi$ to service a sequence of order tasks.

The robot r_j at the dwell position receives an order task located at the position p_{o_i} and can realize retrieval transaction by assigned to one of the workstations. Let $A = [0, 1, ..., n_{w_l}]$ be the set of all the assignment decisions. When n_{w_k} is selected in the set $A^0 = [1, ..., n_{w_l}]$, it means the robot r_i is assigned to the corresponding workstation w_l, whereas 0 means that the robot is working on current order task not making assignment decisions at the moment. The available robot will make assignment decisions from two aspects: system efficiency and picker condition. On the one hand, the robot evaluates the expected time to reach all workstations based on the target shelf position, to measure the efficiency impact of selecting different workstations. On the other hand, the fatigue and stress level of each picker will be transmitted to the current robot via the wireless device after processing the physiological signal collected by the wearable device at the workstation. The picker status will be an important factor in robot decision-making to achieve a human-oriented assignment policy. Based on the picker's physiological signals, the robot will avoid selecting fatigued/stressed pickers to fulfilled the order task. At the same time, the current workload of each workstation, such as the length of the waiting queue and the number of shelves to the current workstation, is also an important basis for the assignment decision. It not only affects the sojourn time of the shelf at the workstation and therefore contributes to the efficiency of the system, but also affects the physiological state of the picker (over high and low workloads will lead to stressed-out and passive on picker respectively). Based on the information obtained above, the robot makes assignment decisions for balancing system efficiency and worker fatigue and stress. The assignment decision is based on the system state information that includes the robot state vector, order information vector, and human information vector. Figure 2 shows how robots and pickers cooperate to complete shared tasks.

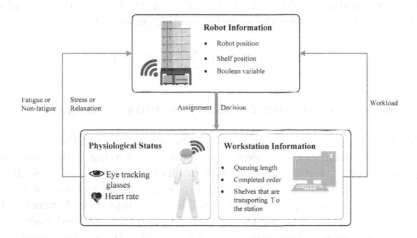

Fig. 2. The mechanism of robots and pickers cooperation for sharing tasks

Specifically, in the setting of this article, the robot can determine its current position p_{r_j} by scanning the QR code on the warehouse ground. Considering the current time step, the position can be expressed as $p_{r_j}^t$. For each robot, a boolean b is used to indicate task status. If the robot is working on the current order task, $b = 0$, otherwise $b = 1$. Each workstation information vector is defined as $WI_k = [N_{que}^k, N_{tran}^k, N_{comp}^k]$, where N_{tran}^k represents the number of orders completed within the time interval T_{int} between two assignment decisions time step recorded by the workstation. The workstation also records the current queue length N_{que}^k and the number of shelves being transported N_{tran}^k to the workstation. As shown in Fig. 1, based on the pickers' real-time physiological signals collected from wearable sensors, signal processing, and data analysis methods allow us to detect the current picker's stress state S_{stress} and fatigue state $S_{fatigue}$. Thus, each human information vector can be defined as $HI_k = [S_{stress}^k, S_{fatigue}^k]$. With all these required vectors, the system state at the time t is defined as $S_t = [RS_t, WI_t, HI_t]$, where $WI_t = [WI_0^t, ..., WI_l^t]$ and, $HI_t = [HI_0^t, ..., HI_l^t]$.

Based on the current system status, all robots follow the joint assignment policy, which will contribute to the total fulfilled orders and the stress level of the human picker who is assigned to complete the order task. Meanwhile, robots will receive the corresponding penalties on time cost and discomfort. Assuming time cost and discomfort penalties are linear, the penalty function at state S_t with joint action is given by

$$R_t(S_t, n_t) = -T_{int} - \beta T_{stress} \tag{1}$$

where β is the weight of the element to evaluate the importance of this item. This paper aims to determine the joint policy π^* for all robots which respond to the efficiency changes of pickers due to fatigue, stress, and short breaks, thereby contributing to system efficiency and worker well-being, namely realizing equilibrium, and maximizes the expected cumulative penalty.

$$J(\pi^*) = max_{\pi \in \Pi} (\sum_{o_i=0}^{m} R_t(S_t, n_t)) \tag{2}$$

3   Multi-agent Reinforcement Learning Approach

In this section, a robot-based multiagent reinforcement learning (MARL) method for the robot assignment problem that aims at obtaining a human-oriented assignment policy considering both system efficiency and the pickers' discomfort is presented. In the RMFS, learning in a multi-robot environment is inherently complex. In this paper, we propose a Value-Decomposition Network (VDN) approach to solve the assignment problem, which is a centralized training and decentralized execution framework, allowing the policy to use other agents' local information for training, and execute each robot's action only via individual observations [16]. The VDN value function for the system is estimated under the assumption that the value decomposition networks learn to decompose the total Q value function into value functions across agents that condition only on robot individual observations, namely

$$Q_{total}(S_t, n_t; \theta) = \sum_{j=0}^{n} Q_{r_j}(S_t^{r_j}, n_{w_k}; \theta^{r_j}) \tag{3}$$

where θ are the parameters of the neural network, which is introduced to deal with the "curse of dimensionality" caused by enumerating all the combinations of robot location, picker information, and workstation information. Finally, following the independent deep Q-learning rules, the problem is solved by minimizing the following loss function for VDN.

$$L(\theta) = \sum_{\omega=1}^{M} \sum_{j=0}^{n} (R_\omega + \gamma max_{n'_{w_k} \in \mathbb{A}} Q(S_\omega'^{r_j}, n'_{w_k}, \theta^-) - Q(S_\omega^{r_j}, n_{w_k}, \theta))^2 \qquad (4)$$

4 Experimental Results

In this section, the performance of the proposed human-oriented MARL assignment policy (HOAP) is compared with the other three traditional robot assignment policies, namely random assignment policy (RAP), nearest assignment policy (NAP), and shortest-queue assignment policy (SAP). The simulation experiments are performed on a warehouse equipped with 2 picking stations, investigating the system efficiency and human discomfort during 30 min work. Beside, if the size of the robot fleet exceeded the operator's capability, the operator will always face stress, contributing to a total stress time increase, while the size of the robot fleet is too small, unable to exert the operator's performance, resulting in a decrease in system efficiency. Therefore, in this article, we set 16 robots in the experiment which is a good equilibrium point(number of robots necessary compared to the number of operators). An aisle and two cross-aisles are deployed in the storage zone, dividing the zone into six 5×2 rectangle blocks. The handling speed of workstations w_0 and w_1 is set to 6 shelves/min and 10 shelves/min, respectively, to consider the different speeds for different pickers. Besides, at the beginning of the experiment, we assume that the picker working at station w_1 has been working for a while and will have a short break of 10 min after 5 min to get recovery.

During the experiment, the agents learn for 500 episodes with the discount factor is set to 0.95, and the exploration rate decreases from 1 to 0.01 in 6000 time steps. And the number of nodes of the one layer in the Q network is 128. Based on the learned policy, a comparison among all assignment policies in terms of total completed orders and stress time for 100 run when $t = 20$ min and $t = 200$ min are presented in Fig. 3 and Fig. 4.

It can be seen from the figures that the proposed human-oriented MARL policy and the shortest assignment policy always outperform the other two assignment policies, and have little difference in system efficiency, which both completed nearly 330 and 290 orders when $t = 20$ min and $t = 200$ min. Comparing Fig. 3 and Fig. 4, we can see that at $t = 200$ min, the efficiency of all policies is lower than that of their own performance at $t = 20$ min. This is because pickers can maintain a high working efficiency at $t = 20$ min, fatigue and stress do not have a significant impact on efficiency, while picker fatigue accumulates with the increase of working time and leads to a decrease in efficiency. Although in the experiment one of the pickers, w_1, arranged a short break to relieve fatigue and work stress, not enough to fully recover. In terms of the average total stress time, the proposed learning-based method has a great improvement in reducing pickers' stress time, whereas random assignment, nearest assignment, and shortest assignment have a higher total stress time. The total stress time of the learning-based policy is only 50% to 65% of the stress time of the other three policies. This phenomenon can be explained by the fact that these three policies only mechanically assign orders to the workstation based on rules, without considering the status of the pickers. However, the proposed policy, while considering the system efficiency, is also aware of the real-time status of pickers and makes assignment decisions to reduce the duration of total stress time. The MARL can greatly alleviate the stress of the order pickers without significantly sacrificing system efficiency. Therefore, compared with a traditional rule-based allocation method, the method proposed in this article not only considers the total amount of completed orders, but also comprehensively considers the fatigue and stress levels of the order pickers, achieving the bi-objective solution for the system efficiency and worker well-being.

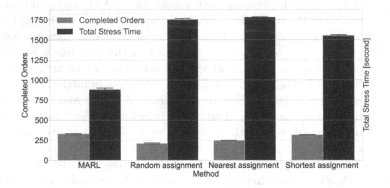

Fig. 3. Average completed orders and total stress time when $t = 20$ min

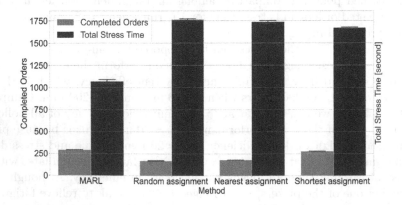

Fig. 4. Average completed orders and total stress time when $t = 200$ min

5   Conclusion

The consideration of human aspects in the collaboration between humans and robots has been widely recognized as one of the major challenges in the era of the 4th Industrial Revolution. Also, human aspects of order picking in warehousing have received significant attention in recent research. However, human well-being has hardly been considered in collaborative order picking (of humans and robots), as common in robotic mobile fulfillment systems. This work has proposed a multi-agent reinforcement learning approach that considers wearable sensor data to incorporate human stress levels and recovery behavior for a human-oriented assignment problem in robotic mobile fulfillment systems. The results show that the developed approach reduces human stress times by nearly 50 % and achieves a similar system efficiency as three considered benchmark policies. In this way, our research extends existing work on wearable sensors to detect human stress [6] and human aspects in collaborative order picking [4] by introducing a new method for robotic learning in RMFS and by considering short breaks to control human stress levels and recovery in order picking of RMFS. Learning this, robots grow into the role of caring colleagues for human co-workers who, for instance, tell humans when they need a break. Moreover, the underlying human-oriented assignment problem resembles a growing amount of related problems, and the proposed MARL approach may therefore also be adopted in those other domains. Nonetheless, there are a few extensions to be considered for a more coherent understanding of this new form of human-robot collaboration. In this work, two pickers are considered but an extension to more pickers will probably create more options to balance the workload. Similarly, the robots maybe also pause when all workers show elevated stress levels. Future work will, furthermore, define different options to connect the theory of sensor-based stress and recovery curves to collaborative operations research models. Finally, we also aim to explore further use cases in problems of multi human-robot collaboration, inside and outside of warehousing.

References

1. Grosse, E.H., Glock, C.H., Neumann, W.P.: Human factors in order picking: a content analysis of the literature. Int. J. Prod. Res. **55**(5), 1260–1276 (2017)
2. Grosse, E.H., Glock, C.H., Jaber, M.Y., Neumann, W.P.: Incorporating human factors in order picking planning models: framework and research opportunities. Int. J. Prod. Res. **53**(3), 695–717 (2015)
3. Merschformann, M., Lamballais, T., De Koster, M., Suhl, L.: Decision rules for robotic mobile fulfillment systems. Oper. Res. Perspect. **6**, 100128 (2019)
4. Niu, Y., Schulte, F., Negenborn, R.R.: Human aspects in collaborative order picking-letting robotic agents learn about human discomfort. Procedia Comput. Sci. **180**, 877–886 (2021)
5. Larco, J.A., De Koster, R., Roodbergen, K.J., Dul, J.: Managing warehouse efficiency and worker discomfort through enhanced storage assignment decisions. Int. J. Prod. Res. **55**(21), 6407–6422 (2017)

6. Maman, Z.S., Chen, Y.J., Baghdadi, A., Lombardo, S., Cavuoto, L.A., Megahed, F.M.: A data analytic framework for physical fatigue management using wearable sensors. Expert Syst. Appl. **155**, 113405 (2020)
7. Zou, B., Gong, Y., Xu, X., Yuan, Z.: Assignment rules in robotic mobile fulfilment systems for online retailers. Int. J. Prod. Res. **55**(20), 6175–6192 (2017)
8. Weidinger, F., Boysen, N., Briskorn, D.: Storage assignment with rack-moving mobile robots in kiva warehouses. Transp. Sci. **52**(6), 1479–1495 (2018)
9. Yuan, R., Graves, S.C., Cezik, T.: Velocity-based storage assignment in semi-automated storage systems. Prod. Oper. Manage. **28**(2), 354–373 (2019)
10. Roy, D., Nigam, S., de Koster, R., Adan, I., Resing, J.: Robot-storage zone assignment strategies in mobile fulfillment systems. Transp. Res. Part E Logistics Transp. Rev. **122**, 119–142 (2019)
11. Lamballais, T., Roy, D., De Koster, M.: Estimating performance in a robotic mobile fulfillment system. Eur. J. Oper. Res. **256**(3), 976–990 (2017)
12. Wang, K., Yang, Y., Li, R.: Travel time models for the rack-moving mobile robot system. Int. J. Prod. Res. **58**(14), 4367–4385 (2020)
13. Zhou, L., Yang, P., Chen, C., Gao, Y.: Multiagent reinforcement learning with sparse interactions by negotiation and knowledge transfer. IEEE Trans. Cybern. **47**(5), 1238–1250 (2016)
14. Boysen, N., Briskorn, D., Emde, S.: Parts-to-picker based order processing in a rack-moving mobile robots environment. Eur. J. Oper. Res. **262**(2), 550–562 (2017)
15. Ren, P., Barreto, A., Huang, J., Gao, Y., Ortega, F.R., Adjouadi, M.: Off-line and on-line stress detection through processing of the pupil diameter signal. Ann. Biomed. Eng. **42**(1), 162–176 (2014)
16. Sunehag, P., et al.: Value-decomposition networks for cooperative multi-agent learning. arXiv preprint arXiv:1706.05296 (2017)

Assembly System 4.0: Human-Robot Collaboration in Assembly Operations

Gursel A. Suer[1]($\boxtimes$), Najat Almasarwah[2]($\boxtimes$), Jesus Pagan[3]($\boxtimes$), and Yuqiu You[3]($\boxtimes$)

[1] Industrial and Systems Engineering, Ohio University, Athens 45701, USA
Suer@Ohio.edu
[2] Department of Industrial Systems Engineering, Mutah University, Alkarak 61710, Jordan
Najat.eid@Mutah.edu.jo
[3] Russ College of Engineering and Technology, Ohio University, Athens 45701, USA
{Paganj,Youy}@Ohio.edu

Abstract. This study focuses on allocation of assembly tasks to the robot(s) and assembly worker(s) in human-robot collaboration assembly systems 4.0. A new method is proposed to allocate tasks of products to a robot and a worker (resources) to minimize the cycle time and hence maximize the output, the single workstation, where the safety issues are considered. Thus, it is not allowed for the worker and robot to process the same product simultaneously to avoid any direct contact between the resources. The proposed method starts with dividing the cycle time for a station into intervals with unknown and unequal lengths. Afterward, a COMSOAL heuristic is utilized to task allocation to resources. The results obtained illustrate the ability of the proposed method to minimize the workstation cycle time and improve productivity.

Keywords: Assembly system 4.0 · Assembly line · Safety issues · COMSOAL

1 Introduction

Manufacturing systems are going through rapid transformation in recent years as a result of various developments in the manufacturing processes, materials, and information technology and also as a result of increased globalization. Several new concepts have been used to capture these developments as advanced manufacturing, industry 4.0, smart manufacturing, cyber manufacturing among others. Most of these systems involve the Internet of Things (IoT), 3D printing, Wearable Robots, Human-Robot Collaboration, etc.

Cellular manufacturing is a manufacturing system, where dissimilar machines are grouped to process raw materials. The Assembly line is an integral part of most cellular manufacturing systems. It consists of various workstations in which the resources (e.g., robot(s), and or human worker(s)) use usually simple tools to assemble the products.

© IFIP International Federation for Information Processing 2021
Published by Springer Nature Switzerland AG 2021
A. Dolgui et al. (Eds.): APMS 2021, IFIP AICT 632, pp. 551–560, 2021.
https://doi.org/10.1007/978-3-030-85906-0_60

1.1 Assembly Line

Depending on the number of products assembled in the assembly lines, they can be categorized into single-model, mixed model and multi-model assembly lines [1, 2], as depicted in Fig. 1. A single product is assembled in the single-model assembly line. More than one product can be assembled in the mixed-model assembly line simultaneously [3, 4]. In this category, similar products are grouped, where the setup times, the changeover times between products, are negligible. Meanwhile, dissimilar products are assembled in the multi-model assembly line at different times based on the demand and processing times of tasks. In this study, two products are assembled in the line simultaneously (mixed-model assembly line).

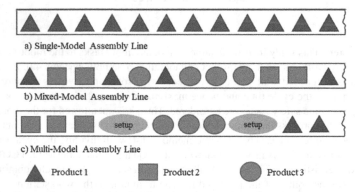

Fig. 1. Categories of assembly line based on the number of products on assembly line.

Typically, there are two essential problems in mixed-model assembly lines, which are balancing and scheduling [5]. Assembly line balancing problem is one of the main active research areas, where several methods have been emerged in the literature to assign the tasks into consecutive workstations depending on a sequential manner. It is divided into two types of problems. The first type (type I) aims to minimize the number of workstations since the cycle times, assembly tasks, and precedence requirements are known. The second type (type II) has a fixed number of workstations, and the performance measures are minimizing the cycle time, maximizing output rate, etc. The second problem is assembly line scheduling. This problem studies the starting and completion times of products and defines the sequence of products in the line [3]. On the other hand, different types of material handling equipment can be used to move the products among the workstations, such as a conveyor belt, forklift, *etc.*

1.2 Human-Robot Collaboration

Human-robot collaboration is studied in this paper, where a set $P = \{P_1, P_2, ..P_n\}$ of n products with different tasks is assigned to be assembled in a single station. In this case, resources work together to run the products in the workstation. Depending on the resources' skills, some tasks can be assembled by the worker(s), other tasks can be run by the robot(s), while other tasks can be assembled by either the worker(s) or robot(s). Furthermore, the task times vary based on the resources used to implement the task. However, it is assumed that the processing times of tasks by worker and robot are known in advance and constant.

The human-robot collaboration assembly line problems are theoretically attractive combinatorial optimization problems since they are NP-complete, i.e., no procedure can solve each problem instance in polynomial time. Over the years, different solution approaches to these problems have been developed. These approaches can be divided into two groups: exact and heuristic methods. Specific methods, which are mostly based on linear programming or enumeration approaches such as branch-and-bound or dynamic programming, can quickly become inefficient to solve the problem when the number of variables increases. Heuristic and metaheuristic procedures, on the other hand, are fast but do not guarantee convergence to an optimal solution. They produce well enough solutions or near-optimal solutions at a reasonable computational cost and time.

In this paper, COMSOAL heuristic propounded by [6] is modified to schedule the products in a station in mixed mode to minimize the cycle time and hence improve productivity, to determine the task allocation to resources (worker(s), and robot(s)) where the worker(s) and robot(s) are working side by side in the workstation. The strong motivation for the proposed method is to avoid any direct contact between the resources to preserve the resources' safety. Another motivation for the method is the use of human and robotic skills in combination simultaneously. Typically, people contribute dexterity and can react very flexibly to new situations, while robots are not. Furthermore, this method allows the implementation of partially automated manufacturing solutions, which would improve flexibility in face of small lot sizes, such as electrical circuits, etc.

This paper is organized as follows. Section 2 reviews the related works on assembly line balancing and scheduling. Section 3 describes the problem statement. Section 4 describes the methodology proposed. Section 5 briefly discusses the results. Finally, the paper is concluded, and future research possibilities are stated in Sect. 6.

2 Related Literature

The concept of the assembly line arose in the literature at the beginning of the 20th century by Henry Ford [7]. In each assembly line, a series of workstations processes a repetitive set of tasks of products. Each workstation in the line is responsible for certain tasks, these tasks can be done by robot(s), and or human worker(s) using simple equipment. Thus, lines can be labeled as manual, robotic, and human-robot collaboration assembly lines. Typically, the manual assembly line is classified by high labor cost, where the skilled worker(s) work/s in the line to perform the operations consecutively [8]. In some cases, at least one worker should be assigned to a workstation, where the worker is responsible to complete the tasks at a workstation [9]. In other cases, the worker should move from the workstation to others in the assembly line in order to complete the assembly process (*Seru*) [10, 11]. The flexibility and changeability of the assembly process in the manual assembly line are high [8]. Meanwhile, the robotic assembly line is used for faster assembly rates with high line efficiency, where certain tools, grippers are required to perform the tasks in the workstations by the robot(s). The variation between the established workplace and task performance is negligible; therefore, any breakdown that takes a place in workstation(s) reduces the line efficiency [12–14].

In the human-robot collaboration assembly line, the robots perform assembly tasks alongside a human in the workstation(s) based on their ability [15]. Allowing worker(s) and robot(s) to work in the same workstation guarantees more flexibility in production processes [16]. More importantly, the human-robot collaboration in the assembly field results in a new concept in an assembly line, which is assembly system 4.0 [17]. Several studies have covered the area of human-robot collaboration assembly line. For example, Bogner, Pferschy, Unterberger, and Zeiner, [18] studied scheduling and task allocation of printed circuit board assembly using integer linear programming model, and heuristic approaches to minimize the makespan. They assumed that the workers and robots are working together in a station to assemble the products.

Allowing workers and robots to work in the same workplace increases the interaction between them, and it does not comply with the safety condition (ISO 10218) [17, 19]. However, this research is proposed to study the optimal task allocation and scheduling in type II mixed-model assembly line balancing problem considering human-robot collaboration, where the worker and robot cannot perform assembly tasks on the same workstation simultaneously to maintain worker safety.

3   Problem Description

The layout of the workstation in this study is divided into five zones (Fig. 2). In *Zone A*, the materials required to build products 1 and 2 are moved from the inventory area at a predetermined feed rate to the end of Zone A by using a conveyor belt. Once the materials get close to *Zone D*, the worker or robot move them to *Zone D*. The next step involves assembling the products in *Zone D* by worker and robot using the required parts from *Zone B* and *Zone C*. *Zone B* shows the storage area of the robot and it has all parts needed by the robot. *Zone C* presents the worker's storage area, where all parts needed by the worker are found. Considering the safety issues, it is not allowed to the resources to work on the same product simultaneously. Thus, the conveyor belt is utilized in *Zone D* to move the products from the worker side to the robot side, and *vice versa*, until the desired products are assembled. Finally, a material handling system like a conveyor belt in *Zone E* moves the products to the finished product containers.

The problem considered in this study consists of two products that are assigned to be assembled in a single station. Their precedence relations are given in Fig. 3. Product 1 has tasks 1–7 and Product 2 has tasks 8–14. There is only one robot and one worker in the station. The task feasibility matrix with processing times is given in Table 1. Some tasks can only be performed by the assembly worker (tasks 3,7,8, and 12) while some others can only be performed by the robot (tasks 1,4,10, and 14) and the remaining tasks can be performed by either the robot or the worker (tasks 2,5,6,9,11, and 13). It is easy to notice that the robot can finish its tasks in a shorter time compared to the worker.

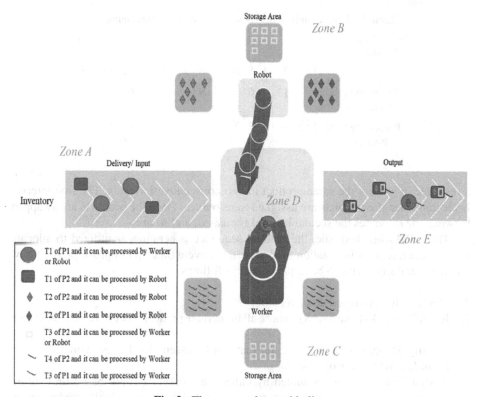

Fig. 2. The proposed assembly line.

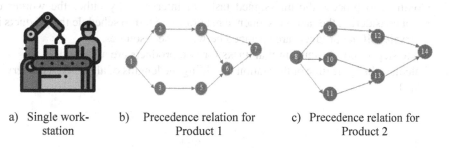

a) Single work-
station

b) Precedence relation for
Product 1

c) Precedence relation for
Product 2

Fig. 3. An example.

4 Methodology

This study assumes that ($i = 1..m$) tasks of products are assigned to be assembled on a single workstation by the resources (worker and robot). The cycle time of the station is divided into $m - 1$ intervals with unknown lengths, as depicted in Fig. 4. L_j is the length of interval#j. The lengths of intervals might be equal, or might not. It depends on the processing times of the tasks and the idle times at each interval. Each resource is dedicated to processing a single product in an interval, where it is not allowed for

Table 1. Task feasibility matrix with processing times (minutes).

Product	1							2						
Task	1	2	3	4	5	6	7	8	9	10	11	12	13	14
Processing time (worker)	–	6	13	–	6	12	4	9	5	–	4	6	7	–
Processing time (robot)	5	3	–	3	3	7	–	–	3	4	2	–	5	9

a resource to process the same product in two consecutive intervals. The first interval is created when the products are assigned to resources. Once the products are swapped between the resources the second interval is created, and *so on*.

The *COMSOAL* heuristic, the random sequence generation, is utilized to allocate tasks to the resources in a station to minimize the cycle time and improve productivity, where several steps have to be implemented as follows:

1. Identify all unassigned tasks, S_A
2. Identify all tasks from a set S_A, whose all immediate predecessors have been assigned, S_B.
3. Identify all operations from set S_B, that can be assembled by the worker S_W, the robot S_R, and worker or robot $S_{W\&R}$
4. Assign the task to be assembled by either the worker or robot based on random sequence generation, where each resource is dedicated to a single product in an interval.
5. Continue to process the unassigned tasks in interval#1 by either the worker or robot considering the random sequence generation. Start to schedule the products in interval#2, if the products are swapped between the resources.
6. Go to step 1 and continue until all tasks for two products are allocated.
7. Calculate the cycle time of the station by adding the lengths of all generated intervals (Eq. 1).

$$Cycle\ time = \sum_{j=1}^{m-1} L_j \tag{1}$$

A possible solution to the given example is illustrated in Fig. 5. In the interval of $0 \le t \le 13$, the robot assembles product 1, while the worker runs Product 2. At time 9, three tasks, T_3, T_9 & T_{11}, are available to be assembled in a station by a worker. Considering the COMSOAL heuristic, three periods are generated for scheduling purposes. The length of each period is 0.333, which equals 1 divided by the number of tasks available $\left(\frac{1}{3}\right)$. The first period is (0–0.333), and it is corresponding to T_3. The second period is (0.334–0.666), it is corresponding to T_9, and *so on*.

T_3	0–0.333
T_9	0.334–0.666
T_{11}	0.667–1.000

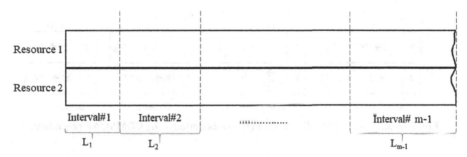

Fig. 4. Task allocations to two resources (robot & worker) in the station.

Having determined the number of periods, length of each period, and their corresponding tasks, the first random number (RN#1) is created. In this case, it is 0.823, and it is within the fourth period (0.667–1.00). Thus, T_{11} is assigned to be performed by the worker in the first interval because it belongs to product 2.

RN#1: 0.823			
	T_3	0 – 0.250	
	T_9	0.251-0.500	
0.823 ➔	T_{11}	0.751 – 1.00	∴ T_{11} is assigned to be assembled after T_8 by the worker

By the same token, two tasks, T_9 & T_{10}, are available to be assembled by the robot at time 11. These tasks belong to product 2. In this case, it is not allowed for the robot to perform any of them because product 2 is assembled by the worker. Therefore, the robot should stay idle till the worker finishes its current task (T_{11}). At time 13, two tasks, T_3 & T_9, are available to be performed by the worker; thus, two periods are created. The first period is (0–0.50), and it is corresponding to T_3. The second period is (0.501–1.000) and is corresponding to T_9. The generated random number is 0.231. Considering this, the products are swapped between the robot and the worker and they continue performing tasks until t = 26 min in the second interval when they swapped products again and *so on.*

The results obtained show that four intervals with different lengths are created. The length of the first two intervals is identical and equals 13 min, and the lengths of the third and fourth intervals are 10 and 9 min, respectively. The completion times of the worker and robot are 40 and 45 min, respectively. Therefore, the cycle time of the workstation is 45 min. The idle times for the worker and robot are 9, and 3 min, respectively.

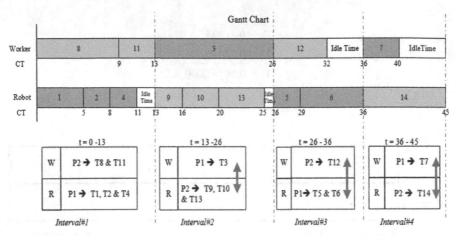

Fig. 5. Gantt chart: scheduling tasks in the workstation using COMSOAL procedure.

5   Analysis and Results

Three problems are developed to test the performance of the proposed method. In each problem, two products are assigned to be assembled in a station by either robot or worker. The number of tasks in problems 1, 2, and 3 is 10, 12, and 8, respectively. The processing times are constant and known in advance.

In Table 2, the results obtained are summarized. The minimum idle times in three problems are acquired by the worker, and equal 4, 0, and 10.02 min, respectively. Meanwhile, the idle times for the robot are 21, 19.97, and 9 min in problems 1, 2, and 3, respectively. The completion time for the worker and robot in problem 1 is identical and equals 42 min; thus, the cycle time for a workstation is 42 min. In problem 2, the completion times for worker and robot are 69.19, and 49.22 min, respectively. Therefore, the cycle time for a workstation is 69.19 min based on the maximum completion time in a workstation. Whereas, the completion times for the worker and robot in problem 3 are 37, and 32 min, respectively; thus, the cycle time for a workstation is 37 min. The cycle time for the workstation is determined based on the completion time for the worker. Based on the results found, the number of intervals and the lengths of them are different from one problem to another and they depend on the number of tasks and processing times of tasks and the resources' skills.

Table 2. The results for three problems.

	Problem 1		Problem 2		Problem 3	
	Idle time	Completion time	Idle time	Completion time	Idle time	Completion time
Worker	4	42	10.02	69.19	0	37
Robot	21	42	19.97	49.22	9	32

6   Conclusion

This paper introduced a new method for task allocations to the robot(s) and worker(s) in a single workstation to minimize the cycle time and hence maximize the output with known and constant processing times. This method depends on dividing the cycle time of the station into intervals with unknown lengths. Afterward, the COMSOAL heuristic is utilized to allocate tasks at each interval. Each resource is dedicated to processing a single product in an interval to avoid any direct contact between the resources. Any direct contact could lead to creating an unsafe work environment. The completion time (cycle time) for the station is calculated based on the maximum completion time of both resources. The results obtained illustrate that the number of products and their tasks, and the processing times of tasks affect the number of intervals created and their lengths and idle times of the resources.

Human-robot collaboration is one of the main research areas, where it plays a vital role in manufacturing systems, and it introduces to the industry 4.0. Even so, the human-robot collaboration leads to reduce to use of the workers in the system, which increases the unemployment rate.

Several issues should be taken into account for future research, such as developing meta-heuristics, heuristics, and mathematical models for solving different sizes of problems, considering the task allocation in the assembly line with the different number of workstations, and minimizing the idle times for the resources in the system.

References

1. Kumar, N., Mahto, D.: Assembly line balancing: a review of developments and trends in approach to industrial application. Glob. J. Res. Eng. **13**(2), 1–23 (2013)
2. Boysen, N., Fliedner, M., Scholl, A.: Assembly line balancing: which model to use when? Int. J. Prod. Econ. **111**(2), 509–528 (2008)
3. Öztürk, C., Tunalı, S., Hnich, B., Örnek, A.: Balancing and scheduling of flexible mixed model assembly lines with parallel stations. Int. J. Adv. Manuf. Technol. **67**(9–12), 2577–2591 (2013)
4. Mosadegh, H., Fatemi Ghomi, S.M.T., Süer, G.A.: Heuristic approaches for mixed-model sequencing problem with stochastic processing times. Int. J. Prod. Res. **55**(10), 2857–2880 (2017)
5. Hwang, R.K., Katayama, H., Gen, M.: U-shaped assembly line balancing problem with genetic algorithm. Int. J. Prod. Res. **46**(16), 4637–4649 (2008)
6. Arcus, A.L.: COMSOAL: A Computer Method of Sequencing Operations for Assembly Lines, I—The Problem in Simple Form, II–The Problem In Complex Form. Readings in Production and Operations Management. Wiley, New York (1966)
7. Ghutukade, S.T., Sawant, S.M.: Use of ranked position weighted method for assembly line balancing. Int. J. Adv. Eng. Res. Studies/II/IV/July-Sept., 1(03) (2013)
8. Scholl, A.: Balancing and Sequencing of Assembly Lines. Physica-Verlag, Heidelberg (1999)
9. Aboelfotoh, A., Süer, G., Abdullah, M.: Selection of assembly systems; assembly lines vs seru systems. Procedia Comput. Sci. **140**, 351–358 (2018)
10. Zhang, X., Liu, C., Li, W., Evans, S., Yin, Y.: Effects of key enabling technologies for seru production on sustainable performance. Omega **66**, 290–307 (2017)
11. Abdullah, M., Süer, G.A.: Consideration of skills in assembly lines and seru production systems. Asian J. Manage. Sci. Appl. **4**(2), 99–123 (2019)

12. Rubinovitz, J., Bukchin, J., Lenz, E.: RALB–a heuristic algorithm for design and balancing of robotic assembly lines. CIRP Ann. **42**(1), 497–500 (1993)
13. Becker, C., Scholl, A.: A survey on problems and methods in generalized assembly line balancing. Eur. J. Oper. Res. **168**(3), 694–715 (2006)
14. Kim, H., Park, S.: A strong cutting plane algorithm for the robotic assembly line balancing problem. Int. J. Prod. Res. **33**(8), 2311–2323 (1995)
15. Casalino, A., Zanchettin, A.M., Piroddi, L., Rocco, P.: Optimal scheduling of human-robot collaborative assembly operations with time petri nets. In: IEEE Transactions on Automation Science and Engineering (2019)
16. Faccio, M., Minto, R., Rosati, G., Bottin, M.: The influence of the product characteristics on human-robot collaboration: a model for the performance of collaborative robotic assembly. Int. J. Adv. Manuf. Technol. **106**(5), 2317–2331 (2020)
17. Bortolini, M., Ferrari, E., Gamberi, M., Pilati, F., Faccio, M.: Assembly system design in the industry 4.0 era: a general framework. IFAC-PapersOnLine **50**(1), 5700–5705 (2017)
18. Bogner, K., Pferschy, U., Unterberger, R., Zeiner, H.: Optimised scheduling in human–robot collaboration–a use case in the assembly of printed circuit boards. Int. J. Prod. Res. **56**(16), 5522–5540 (2018)
19. Vasic, M., Billard, A.: Safety issues in human-robot interactions. In: 2013 IEEE International Conference on Robotics and Automation, pp. 197–204. IEEE (May, 2013)

An Integrated QFD Approach for Industrial Robot Selection

Gülçin Büyüközkan$^{(\boxtimes)}$ ⓘ, Öykü Ilıcak ⓘ, and Orhan Feyzioğlu ⓘ

Galatasaray University, Istanbul 34349, Turkey
{gbuyukozkan,ofeyzioglu}@gsu.edu.tr

Abstract. Nowadays, where Industry 4.0 is discussed extensively, the selection of industrial robots has become an important issue. These robots enable production companies to produce higher quality products with high efficiency and in a cost-effective manner. However, an incorrect selection of those robots can cause significant losses for companies. Various factors need to be considered for the effective selection of industrial robots. In this study, a decision model is presented for industrial robot selection. Quality function deployment (QFD), a well-known and powerful tool that converts customer requirements into final design characteristics, is used in this study, with Group Decision Making (GDM) perspective. In GDM, decision-makers who have different backgrounds or ideas can state their preferences in various formats. The Multiple Preference Relations (MPR) technique is used to combine different assessments. Therefore, this study combines QFD with MPR to handle the different forms of information while calculating the customer requirements importance. Furthermore, the Complex Proportional Assessment (COPRAS) method is used to choose the most suitable industrial robot for the proposed study. The presented method was analyzed in a case study on the robot selection problem for the assembly line of a company operating in the manufacturing industry. The alternatives evaluated with the COPRAS method were also applied with the Technique for Order Preference by Similarity to Ideal Solution (TOPSIS) method. The results of both methods were compared and found to be consistent.

Keywords: Robot selection · QFD · Multiple preference relations · COPRAS

1 Introduction

The ability of businesses to maintain their positions in an internationally competitive environment depends on their transition to automation-based systems by changing their production structures [1]. Robots can perform repetitive and dangerous tasks and complete all processes much better, more accurately, and more efficiently [2]. Robotics-based automation changes and improves manufacturing applications. Customer choice (CRs) and technical requirements (DRs) should be analyzed correctly to select industrial robots. The Quality Function Deployment (QFD) approach, known as a customer-oriented systematic method that focuses on this analysis, was used in this study. QFD is also a Group

© IFIP International Federation for Information Processing 2021
Published by Springer Nature Switzerland AG 2021
A. Dolgui et al. (Eds.): APMS 2021, IFIP AICT 632, pp. 561–570, 2021.
https://doi.org/10.1007/978-3-030-85906-0_61

Decision Making (GDM) approach with many expert opinions. Considering the GDM approach, Decision Makers' (DMs) perspectives may differ from each other and may wish to evaluate in different formats. Multiple preference relations (MPR) are often applied to deal with varying forms of evaluations [3].

In this study, selecting an industrial robot to be used in the assembly line of ABC company is discussed. QFD approach was applied and integrated with the MPR technique to deal with evaluation structures in different formats in prioritizing the CRs. Then DRs were determined, and their weights were identified by the House of Quality (HoQ) relationship matrix. Finally, alternative robots were selected in line with DRs with the Complex Proportional Assessment (COPRAS) method. The alternatives were also evaluated with the Technique for Order Preference by Similarity to Ideal Solution (TOPSIS) method, and the results of both methods were compared.

This study continues with the following sections: In Sect. 2, a literature review is provided. Section 3 provides the methodology, Sect. 4 introduces the case study, and Sect. 5 gives results and discussion, while Sect. 6 concludes the study and offers future research directions.

2   Literature Review

Robots that are starting to enter the production environment with Industry 4.0 are more intelligent and secure. The selection of the correct robot is an important issue. When we examine the literature, it is seen that many studies have been performed on robot selection problems. Vahdani et al. [4] proposed a robot selection problem based on interval-valued fuzzy COPRAS. Pasawang et al. [5] presented a QFD technique to design an autonomous underwater robot. Sen et al. [6] used an extended PROMETHEE method to select the best robot by considering subjective and objective criteria. Yalçın and Uncu [7] applied the EDAS method for the robot selection problem. Fu et al. [8] proposed a GDM approach to handle multiple criteria robot selection problems. Nasrollahi et al. [9] solved a robot selection problem using fuzzy the best-worst method (BWM) with PROMETHEE. More recently, Ali and Rashid [10] used group BWM and group AHP method for robot selection. Another recent study, Rashid et al. [11], proposed a hybrid BWM-EDAS method, which is the first study that integrates BWM with the EDAS method for the proper selection of robots.

The literature review shows that several studies have been done about the robot selection problem. However, there are no such studies on evaluating industrial robots for an assembly line using an integrated QFD methodology with MPR and COPRAS.

3   Methodology

3.1   Quality Function Deployment (QFD)

QFD is a systematic method that helps to identify the customer's design needs to reflect the needs and expectations of the product/service [12]. The fundamental structure of the QFD is the HOQ. With HOQ, "What's" and "How's" can be defined in a short time. The HOQ matrix is shown in Fig. 1.

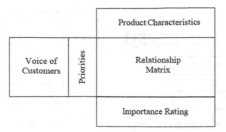

Fig. 1. HOQ matrix for the study

In this study, in the HOQ matrix, the voice of the customer will be the needs for the selection of industrial robots, priorities will be the importance of end-user needs, product characteristics will be technical requirements. The relationship matrix shows the relationship between needs and technical requirements.

3.2 Multiple Preference Relations (MPR)

In the GDM process, DMs can present evaluations in different ways. These can be linguistically, numerically, or by subsets according to their level of information. MPR allows DMs, having different backgrounds/perspectives, to submit their preferences in various ways. The advantages of this technique are: (1) It gives flexibility to DMs during the evaluation process. (2) It gives better solutions as it is based on GDM. (3) It allows collecting different types of assessments under a single group [13].

3.3 Complex Proportional Assessment (COPRAS)

This method is an MCDM method that can evaluate qualitative and quantitative criteria [14]. The advantages of the COPRAS method compared to other MCDM methods can be given as follows: (1) It compares the evaluated alternatives with each other, expresses how good or how bad it is from other alternatives as a percentage. (2) Since long binary comparisons are not made in this method, as in PROMETHEE and ELECTRE, the high number of alternatives does not complicate the process. (3) It gives easier and faster results than other MCDM methods such as ARAS, VIKOR or TOPSIS. It is possible to apply easily with Excel. One disadvantage of the method is that it cannot calculate criteria weights alone. This can be determined using different methods or depending on DMs [15].

3.4 Proposed Methodology

This study implements an improved QFD methodology by presenting a GDM approach that aggregates different preferences into a single group decision, consisting of the weighting of CRs using the MPR method followed by identification and prioritization of DRs, and ranking the alternatives using the COPRAS method. The framework of the proposed methodology is given in Fig. 2 and detailed below.

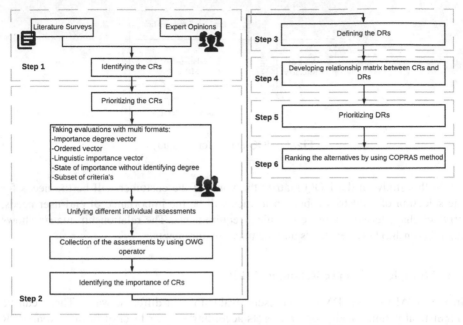

Fig. 2. The framework of the proposed methodology.

(i)   Step 1- Identifying the CRs: CRs are identified by benefiting from the detailed literature researches and expert opinions.

(ii) Step 2- Prioritizing the CRs: Here, the importance of CRs is determined by expert opinions. In this step, the MPR technique is utilized [13].

    (a)   Step 2.1- Unifying DMs evaluations: Opinions in different formats from DMs will be combined at this stage. DMs can give preferences in different formats as follows:

- An importance degree vector $(u_1, \ldots, u_N)$ where $u_i \in [0, 1]$ $i = 1, \ldots, N$. Closer to 1 means more important for u_i. With the formula below we can turn it to relevance of relative importance:

$$z_{ij} = u_i/u_j \text{ for all } 1 \le i \ne j \le N \tag{1}$$

- An ordered vector $(o(1), \ldots, o(N))$. Here, $o(i)$ represents the importance ranking of CR i, where the most important is 1 and the least important is N. With the formula below we can turn it to relevance of relative importance:

$$z_n = 9_i^{u} {}^{-u}_{j} \text{ for all } 1 \le i \ne j \le N \text{ where } u_i = (N - o(i))/(N - 1) \tag{2}$$

- DMs may present a linguistic importance vector. Given a fuzzy triangular number can be noted as (a_i, b_i, c_i) where b_i is the most common value. The membership functions of linguistic terms for fuzzy triangular quantification are: NI = (0.00, 0.00, 0.25), SI = (0.00, 0.25, 0.50), MI = (0.25, 0.50, 0.75), I = (0.50, 0.75, 1.00) and VI $= (0.75, 1.00, 1.00)$. With the formula below the linguistics importance vector can be transformed to relative importance relation.

$$z_n = 9_i^{b} {}_j^{-b} \text{ for all } 1 \le i \ne j \le N \tag{3}$$

- DMs may give the importance of criteria without degree explicitly. So,

$$z_{ij} = 9 \text{ and } z_{ij} = 1/9, \text{ if i is more important than j}$$
$$\text{and } z_{ij} = 1 \text{ if nothing mentioned.} \tag{4}$$

- DMs may choose just a subset of criteria (R'). So, for all $1 \le i \ne j \le N$, the preference relation can be given as,

$$z_{ij} = \begin{cases} 9, & i \in R', j \in R/R' \\ 1/9, & i \in R/R', j \in R' \\ 1, & \text{otherwise} \end{cases} \tag{5}$$

(b) Step 2.2- Aggregating the evaluations: Each evaluation is aggregated using the order weighted geometric (OWG) operator to define a common group decision in this step by the following formula:

$$\Phi^G\{(\overline{w} k1, p_{ij}^{k1}), \dots (\overline{w}kLk, p_{ij}^{kL_k})\} = \prod_{l=1}^{L_k}\left(p_{ij}^{k[l]}\right) \tag{6}$$

Here, $\{1, \dots, L_k\} \to \{1, \dots, L_k\}$ is a permutation such that $\overline{w}_{kl} \ge \overline{w}_k[1+1]$, $1 = \{1, \dots, L_{k-1}\}$, so $\overline{w} k1$ is the lth largest value in the set $(\overline{w}_{k1}, \dots, \overline{w}_{kLk})$. Proportional quantifiers, such as "most," "as many as possible," etc., can be represented by fuzzy subsets of the unit interval $[0,1]$. When the ratio t is suitable with the purpose of the quantifier it demonstrates then for any $t \in [0,1]$, $Q(t)$ indicates the degree. For a non-decreasing relative quantifier, Q, the weights can be acquired with the formula below:

$$W_k = Q(k/K) - (Q(k - 1)/K)k = 1, \dots, K \tag{7}$$

where Q(t) is described as;

$$Q(t) = \begin{cases} 0, & \text{if } t < s \\ \frac{t-s}{v-s}, & \text{if } s \le t \le v \\ 1, & \text{if } t \ge v \end{cases} \tag{8}$$

Note that s, t, $v \in [0,1]$ and $Q(t)$ indicates the degree to which the proportion t is compatible with the meaning of the quantifier it represents. Examples of the relative quantifiers in the literature are as follows; "most" $(0.3, 0.8)$, "at least half" $(0,0.5)$, and "as many as possible" $(0.5,1)$. When the fuzzy quantifier Q is used to calculate the OWG operator's weights Φ_W^G, it is represented by. Therefore, the collective multiplicative relative importance relation is obtained as follows:

Therefore, the collective multiplicative relative importance relation is obtained as follows:

$$p_{ij}^k = \Phi_Q^G\left(p_{ij}^{k1}, p_{ij}^{k2}, \dots, p_{ij}^{kL_k}\right), \ 1 \le i \ne j \le N \tag{9}$$

(c) Step 2.3- Identifying the importance of CRs: To define the importance weights of CRs, the evaluations of DM groups aggregated in the matrix P^k must be utilized. The element ij represent the relative importance of criterion i compared to criterion j. Then, calculate the quantifier guided importance degree (QGID) of each criterion, which quantifies the importance of one criterion compared to others in a fuzzy majority sense. With using the OWG operator, Φ_0^G, defined as follows:

$$QGID_i^k = 1/2\left(1 + \log_9 \phi_Q^G\left(p_{ij}^k : j = 1, \ldots, N\right)\right), \text{ for all } i = 1, \ldots, N \quad (10)$$

As a final step, the $QGID_i$ values should be normalized as below equation to obtain the importance degrees in percentage for the group k.

$$QGID_i^k = QGID_i^k / \sum_i QGID_i^k \quad (11)$$

(iii) Step 3- Identifying the DRs: DRs for robots have been introduced by benefiting from literature researches and expert opinions.
(iv) Step 4- Developing a relationship matrix between CRs and DRs: The relationship matrix is created to which the need influences each technical characteristic.
(v) Step 5- Prioritizing DRs: DRs are ranked according to their importance.
(vi) Step 6- Ranking the alternatives: After completing the QFD and determining the weights of the DRs, robot selection is made at this stage by using the COPRAS method.

(a) Step 6.1- Creating the decision matrix: The decision matrix includes alternatives in the rows and the criteria in the columns are created.
(b) Step 6.2- Normalizing the decision matrix: The normalized decision matrix is formed by applying the following formula to the entries of the decision matrix.

$$x_{ij}^* = \frac{x_{ij}}{\sum_{i=1}^m x_{ij}}, \ j = 1, 2, \ldots, n \quad (12)$$

(c) Step 6.3- Determining the weighted normalized decision matrix: A weighted decision matrix is formed by multiplying the entries in every column of the normalized decision matrix among the corresponding criteria weights.
(d) Step 6.4- Calculating weighted normalized indices: At this step, the sum of the weighted normalized decision matrix values is calculated for the decision problem's criteria.

• For the maximization (benefit) criteria:

$$S_{+i} = \sum_{j=1}^k d_{+ij}, \ j = 1, 2, \ldots, k \quad (13)$$

• For the minimization (cost) criteria:

$$S_{-i} = \sum_{j=k+1}^n d_{-ij}, \ j = k+1, \ k+2, \ldots, n \quad (14)$$

(e)   Step 6.5- Calculating the relative importance levels of alternatives: Q_i, which means relative importance for each decision alternative, is calculated as follows.

$$Q_i = S_{+i} + \frac{S_{-min} \sum_{i=1}^{m} S_{-i}}{S_{-i} * \sum_{i=1}^{m} \frac{S_{-min}}{S_{-i}}} \qquad (15)$$

(f)   Step 6.6- Calculating the performance index of decision alternatives: The index values are calculated with the formula below.

$$P_i = \frac{Q_i}{Q_{max}} * 100 \qquad (16)$$

4   Case Study

In this section, a case study is carried out in line with the proposed methodology for ABC company operating in the production sector. The company wishes to expand its production capacity by increasing the production speed and producing much more efficient and quality products. Thus, a robot is required for the company. It is aimed to perform assembly line operations by this robot, thus reducing the assembly times and increasing the production speed and improving the quality. A five-expert evaluation team of company executives (DM1, DM2, DM3, DM4, DM5) will evaluate six robot alternatives. These robots are Articulated robots (A1), Cartesian robots (A2), SCARA (A3), Delta robots (A4), Cylindrical Robots (A5), and Polar Robots (A6).

In this study, to evaluate the alternatives, three main criteria and ten sub-criteria are determined as CRs by benefiting from literature review and expert opinions [5, 15]. These criteria are: Configuration criteria (CR1) includes Payload capacity (CR11), Workspace (CR12), Accuracy (CR13), and Repeatability (CR14). The second main criteria are Functional criteria (CR2) includes Life expectancy (CR21), Programmable flexibility (CR22), and Safety and security (CR23). The last main criterion is Cost criteria (CR3) includes Purchase cost (CR31), Maintenance cost (CR32) and Operation cost (CR33). Five DMs assess the CRs and provide their evaluations in the forms of an "importance degree vector", "ordered vector", "linguistic importance vector", "importance of criteria without degree" and "subset of criteria", respectively. As an example, the evaluations for the main criteria are, (0.9, 0.7, 0.8) for DM1, (3, 1, 2) for DM2, (VI, I, I) for DM3. DM4 says {C1} > {C2} and {C2} > {C3} according to their importance and DM5 says that the C1 is more important. Then by operating Eq. (6)–(9), evaluations in different formats are combined under a single group view, and the group importance relation matrices are specified. Subsequently, with the help of Eq. (10)–(11), final evaluations are given in Table 1 for all primary and sub-criteria.

After identifying and prioritizing CRs, DRs were identified which are Weight of the robot (DR1), Speed of the robot (DR2), Geometrical dexterity (DR3), Path measuring system (DR4), Material of the robot (DR5), Size of the robot (DR6), Easy Programming (DR7), Drive system (DR8) [5, 16]. HoQ relation matrix for CRs and DRs and the final importance degrees of DR are given in Table 2.

Table 1. Final evaluations of CRs.

Main criteria	Priority	Sub-criteria	Local priority	Global priority
CR1	0.452	CR11	0.333	0.150
		CR12	0.186	0.084
		CR13	0.258	0.117
		CR14	0.223	0.101
CR2	0.348	CR21	0.391	0.136
		CR22	0.320	0.112
		CR23	0.289	0.100
CR3	0.201	CR31	0.377	0.076
		CR32	0.328	0.066
		CR33	0.296	0.059

Table 2. Final HoQ matrix.

CRs	DRs for the problem								
	Weights of CRs	DR1	DR2	DR3	DR4	DR5	DR6	DR7	DR8
CR11	0.150	S	M				M		S
CR12	0.084			S		L	L		
CR13	0.117			L	S			L	S
CR14	0.101	L	S	L					L
CR21	0.136					S			M
CR22	0.112	L	M	S	S			M	
CR23	0.100					M			
CR31	0.076		S			S	S		M
CR32	0.066					L			S
CR33	0.059					L	S		
Weights of DRs		1.497	2.050	1.935	1.875	2.258	1.687	0.396	3.870
Normalized Value		9.18%	12.57%	11.86%	11.50%	13.84%	10.35%	2.43%	23.73%

(Strong Relation (S) = 9; Medium Relation (M) = 3; Low Relation (L) = 1; Blank = 0)

At the last stage, alternatives are listed using the COPRAS and TOPSIS methods and results are given in Table 3. According to Table 3, it is seen that in the COPRAS method, A2 has the first priority when A1 the third. When we look at the TOPSIS method, it is the opposite, and it is seen that A1 has the first priority when A2 has the third.

Table 3. Rankings of alternatives by COPRAS and TOPSIS.

COPRAS method				TOPSIS method		
Alternatives	Q_i	P_i	Ranking	Alternatives	Weights	Ranking
A1	0.126	96.02	3	A1	0.729	1
A2	0.131	100.00	1	A2	0.588	3
A3	0.123	93.68	4	A3	0.495	4
A4	0.129	98.42	2	A4	0.699	2
A5	0.108	82.58	5	A5	0.267	5
A6	0.098	75.05	6	A6	0.253	6

5 Results and Discussion

Determining the relative importance of CRs is a significant challenge in QFD applications. In order to achieve success in QFD applications, there must be effective communication between DMs and a decision process that reflects the preferences of each. Therefore, the primary purpose of this study is to select an industrial robot for the assembly line by considering the QFD with the GDM approach. Because DMs have different education levels/different perspectives, they may want to express their preferences in various formats. Therefore, using the MPR technique in the GDM application allows us to get valuable results. Although the method may seem confusing and complicated, it can easily be implemented using Microsoft Excel, and results can be obtained quickly. Using such a detailed methodology for industrial robot selection will ensure that decision-making processes will be more transparent with higher quality. As a result of the study, the most essential CR is determined as "Payload capacity," and the most important DR is defined as "Drive system". In the final, alternatives are ranked with the COPRAS, and Cartesian robots (A2) seemed to have the highest importance among the other alternatives. Afterward, the alternatives were also evaluated with the TOPSIS method, and the results were compared with the COPRAS. The highest priority alternative identified as Articulated robots (A1) in TOPSIS. This shows that problems applying different evaluation approaches can lead to different decisions. The reason why the methods cause different results can be shown as the inability to extract the subjectivity that plays a role in the perception of objective world environments depending on the expertise of DMs.

6 Conclusion

Industry 4.0 is an essential issue from a robotics perspective. It enables a better understanding of how automation can improve process efficiency, quality, and safety. Choosing the right robot for the company is a strategic decision. Industrial robot selection is a GDM process that requires customer expectations and technical requirements to be well analyzed by multiple DMs. In this study, a QFD approach is presented to select industrial robots for use in the assembly line. QFD is integrated with MPR to deal with evaluations in different formats when evaluating the criteria, and COPRAS is used to assess the alternatives. In future studies, a more comprehensive study will be introduced by expanding the criteria and alternatives specified. Furthermore, incomplete preference relations will be used to reduce the uncertain nature of GDM.

Acknowledgments. The authors would like to express their sincere gratitude to the experts. This work has been supported by the Scientific Research Projects Commission of Galatasaray University.

References

1. Karsak, E.E., Sener, Z., Dursun, M.: Robot selection using a fuzzy regression-based decision-making approach. Int. J. Prod. Res. **50**, 6826–6834 (2012)
2. Bhattacharya, A., Sarkar, B., Mukherjee, S.K.: Integrating AHP with QFD for robot selection under requirement perspective. Int. J. Prod. Res. **43**, 3671–3685 (2005)
3. Büyüközkan, G., Feyzioğlu, O.: Group decision making to better respond customer needs in software development. Comput. Ind. Eng. **48**, 427–441 (2005)
4. Vahdani, B., Mousavi, S.M., Tavakkoli-Moghaddam, R., Ghodratnama, A., Mohammadi, M.: Robot selection by a multiple criteria complex proportional assessment method under an interval-valued fuzzy environment. Int. J. Adv. Manuf. Technol. **73**(5–8), 687–697 (2014). https://doi.org/10.1007/s00170-014-5849-9
5. Pasawang, T., Chatchanayuenyong, T., Sa-Ngiamvibool, W.: QFD-based conceptual design of an autonomous underwater robot. Songklanakarin J. Sci. Technol. **37**, 659–668 (2015)
6. Sen, D.K., Datta, S., Mahapatra, S.S.: Extension of PROMETHEE for robot selection decision making: simultaneous exploration of objective data and subjective (fuzzy) data. Benchmarking **23**, 983–1014 (2016)
7. Yalçın, N., Uncu, N.: Applying EDAS as an applicable MCDM method for industrial robot selection. Sigma J. Eng. Nat. Sci. **3**, 779–796 (2019)
8. Fu, Y., Li, M., Luo, H., Huang, G.Q.: Industrial robot selection using stochastic multicriteria acceptability analysis for group decision making. Robot. Auton. Syst. **122**, 103304 (2019)
9. Nasrollahi, M., Ramezani, J., Sadraei, M.: A FBWM-PROMETHEE approach for industrial robot selection. Heliyon **6**, e03859 (2020)
10. Ali, A., Rashid, T.: Best-worst method for robot selection. Soft Comput **25**, 563–583 (2021)
11. Rashid, T., Ali, A., Chu, Y.-M.: Hybrid BW-EDAS MCDM methodology for optimal industrial robot selection. PLoS One **16**, e0246738 (2021)
12. Chan, L.-K., Wu, M.-L.: Quality function deployment: a literature review. Eur. J. Oper. Res. **143**, 463–497 (2002)
13. Büyüközkan, G., Çifçi, G.: An extended quality function deployment incorporating fuzzy logic and GDM under different preference structures. Int. J. Comput. Intell. Syst. **8**, 438–454 (2015)
14. Zavadskas, E.K., Kaklauskas, A., Turskis, Z., Tamošaitienė, J.: Selection of the effective dwelling house walls by applying attributes values determined at intervals. J. Civ. Eng. Manag. **14**, 85–93 (2008)
15. Rishi Kanth, N., Srinath, A., Suresh Kumar, J.: Selection of industrial robots for automation applications in multiple attribute decision making environment using the analytical network process. IJET **7**, 392 (2018)
16. Mateo Ferrús, R., Domínguez Somonte, M.: Design in robotics based in the voice of the customer of household robots. Robot. Auton. Syst. **79**, 99–107 (2016)

Classification and Data Management Methods

Dissimilarity to Class Medoids as Features for 3D Point Cloud Classification

Sylvain Chabanet[(✉)] [iD], Valentin Chazelle, Philippe Thomas[iD],
and Hind Bril El-Haouzi[iD]

Université de Lorraine, CNRS, CRAN, 88000 Epinal, France
{sylvain.chabanet,valentin.chazelle,philippe.thomas,
hind.el-haouzi}@univ-lorraine.fr

Abstract. Several sawmill simulators exist in the forest-product indus
try. They are able to simulate the sawing of a log to generate the set of
lumbers that would be obtained by transforming a log at a sawmill. In
particular, such simulators are able to use a 3D scan of the exterior shape
of the logs as input for the simulation. However, it was observed that
they can be computationally intensive. Therefore, several authors have
proposed to use Artificial Intelligence metamodel, which, in general, can
make predictions extremely fast once trained. Such models can approximate the results of a simulator using a vector of descriptive features
representing a log, or, alternatively, the full 3D log scans. This paper proposes to use dissimilarity to representative log scans as features to train
a Machine Learning classifier. The concept of class Medoids as representative elements of a class will be presented, and a Similarity Discrimant
Analysis was chosen as a good candidate ML classier. This classifier will
be compared with two others models studied by the authors.

Keywords: Sawmill simulation · Artificial intelligence · Iterative
closest point dissimilarity · Medoids · Similarity discriminant analysis

1 Introduction

The integration of 3D point cloud based tools in decision support systems has
been gaining attention in the past decades with the development of reliable
acquisition devices like terrestrial or airborne Lidar. For example, [18] reviews
different usages of 3D point cloud processing in the construction industry from
2004 to 2018, from construction progress tracking to 3D model reconstruction.
Similarly, [13] proposes a method to automatically model complex industrial
installations from 3D scan scenes by segmenting and comparing individual elements with a model library. [16] proposes an application to industry 4.0 with

The authors gratefully acknowledge the financial support of the ANR-20-THIA-0010-
01 Projet LOR-AI (lorraine intellgence artificielle) and région Grand EST. We are also
extremely grateful to FPInnovation who gathered and processed the dataset we are
working with.

A. Dolgui et al. (Eds.): APMS 2021, IFIP AICT 632, pp. 573–581, 2021.
https://doi.org/10.1007/978-3-030-85906-0_62

the creation of facility digital twins. The point clouds would be acquired from mobile phones and processed on remote servers to be transformed into multiple 2D views of the scene and fed to Artificial intelligence (AI) classification models.

Diverse usages of 3D scans similarly exists in the forest-wood industry and in the related literature. For example, [12] proposes the use of 3D scans generated by a terrestrial Lidar to detect and classify defects on standing tree surfaces. Similarly, scans of wood logs have been used for a long time in the sawmilling industry, which has several simulators as its disposal to process these point clouds. The objective of these simulators is to simulate the sawing of the logs in a non destructive way and generate production data. For example, [11] proposes to use such scans and simulators to optimize the allocation of logs between several harvest sites and sawmills, using the simulated basket of products which would be obtained by transforming sampled logs at each possible sawmill. Since introducing new machinery to sawmills might require heavy investment, it additionally appears of particular interest to provide solutions using existing or low cost laser scanners.

Considering, however, that traditional point cloud processing methods can be extremely time consuming [13], AI based methods have been gaining attention in the literature. For example, multiple works have been published in the past few years proposing new deep learning models trained on huge CAD databases. The interested reader may refer to [6] for a survey on the field. The use of these neural networks to predict log basket of products has been studied recently by [8], with interesting results.

In this paper, we propose to rather use a variant of Naive Bayes classifiers which uses dissimilarity to class medoids as input features. This model is named Similarity Discriminant Analysis (SDA) [3] in the literature. Such a model has, indeed, the advantage of being trainable with relatively few data. Furthermore, training such a classifier doesn't require the extraction of knowledge based features and is, therefore, completely data driven. This methodology was tested on a dataset from the Canadian sawmilling industry.

This paper is structured as follow. Section 2 reviews previous works about the use of ML simulation metamodels in the wood industry. The SDA classifier is briefly explained in Sect. 3. Section 4 presents the experimental setup and simulation results. Section 5 will conclude and gives some perspectives.

2   Previous Works on Sawmill Simulation Metamodeling

Breaking a log into lumbers is a divergent process with co-production. Several different products are, indeed, simultaneously obtained from the sawing of one log. Additionally, these lumbers can have various dimensions and grades. For this reason, this process is sometime compared with a disassembly process. Due to the fact that this sawing process can be automatized, with online optimizers, and that logs are heterogeneous in terms of shape and quality, it is difficult to predict in advance the lumber output of a log. The sawmill industry, however, has numeric simulators at its disposal to compute the set of lumbers, called in this paper basket of products, which would be obtained by processing a specific log at a modeled sawmill. Such simulators can use 3D point clouds obtained by laser scanners. Examples are Optitek [5], Autosaw [17] or Sawsim [7], which, in particular, proposes the assessment of multiple sawmill designs as an example of typical use. Similarly, [19] proposes the use of a sawmill digital simulation to optimize a tactical production plan taking into consideration the acceptation of orders with unusual products. Indeed, to respond positively to such an order would have an impact on the whole lumber mix produced at the sawmill.

These simulators can, however, be computationally intensive. For example, depending on the simulation setting and log scan, computing the resulting basket of products for one log can take from a few seconds to 3 h and more using Optitek. Considering that fact, [10] proposed to approximate these simulators with AI metamodels. In particular, several Machine Learning (ML) classifiers are trained on results from past simulations. These models include k Nearest Neighbors (kNN) and Random Forest. The input features used as input of these classifiers are know-how features describing each log, like, for example, their length and volume. A further work, [9], considers the problem of logs allocation to sawmills. By using machine learning metamodels, this study demonstrates that it is possible to increase significantly the value of the objective function being optimized. While this objective function doesn't represent the actual benefit obtained at a real sawmill, their numeric experiments are promising. Considering, however, that contrary to sawmill simulators those classifiers only used six features describing the logs, [15] proposed to use a kNN based on a point cloud dissimilarity. A drawback of this method is that computing this dissimilarity involves the Iterative Closest Point (ICP) algorithm [2], which can be relatively computationally intensive, especially since multiple ICP are needed by the kNN to yield each prediction. Each new log has, indeed, to be compared with all known logs in an example database. [4] later proposed to reduce the number of ICP needed to yield a prediction by implementing a set of rules to filter out unnecessary comparisons. While this approach reduce in average by more than half the number of ICP comparisons needed for a prediction, several hundreds are still required. In this paper, another approach is considered, which is to use a dissimilarity as feature scheme [14]: a few representative logs are selected, and a new log is represented by its vector of dissimilarity to these features.

3   Similarity Discriminant Analysis

Following is a description of the SDA, a naive bayes classifier using similarity to medoids as features.

3.1   Medoids

As presented in [14], the use of an euclidean metric is central to numerous standard ML algorithms. Several methods have been proposed to adapt them when the data points are unstructured and cannot be easily considered member of a metric space, but are, instead, only known by comparison among themselves using a non metric similarity (or dissimilarity) measure. One of these methods considers the use of dissimilarity toward representative elements of the dataset as features. These features can then be used like any standard vector representation. [1] shows that under some theoretical conditions on the similarity function, a binary classifier with bounded error can be learned from a representation of data points as a vector of similarities to a subset of other randomly sampled points. Similarly, [3] proposed to use medoids as representative points.

Class medoids are, indeed, a natural choice for class representatives when the data points composing said class can't be easily averaged to form a class mean. Considers $x_1, x_2, ..., x_n$ the n elements of a class in a database, i.e., in this paper, the n logs sharing a particular basket of products. The class medoid μ is a central element of the class, i.e.:

$$\mu = \underset{j \in \{1,2,...,n\}}{\arg\min} \frac{1}{n} \sum_{i=1}^{n} d(x_j, x_i), \tag{1}$$

with d the ICP dissimilarity. The medoid is, therefore, the member of the class with minimal average dissimilarity with all the other class members. Contrary to the class mean, it is a real member of the database.

In this paper, the medoids of each p classes, $\mu_1, ..., \mu_p$ are used to represent log scans in the following way. Let x be a new log scan. It is represented by the p dimensional vector $(d(\mu_1, x), d(\mu_2, x), ..., d(\mu_n, x))$, i.e., the vector of dissimilarity between x and each medoid.

The dataset used in this paper contains numerous classes. Some of them are extremely rare, to the point of appearing only once or twice in the whole dataset. therefore, a medoid is considered only if the class it belongs to appears more than once in the dataset used for training the ML classifier. SDA parameters need, indeed, strictly more than one sample per class to be estimated. Therefore, when a class appears too rarely in the dataset, it isn't taken into consideration by the classifier. This also implies, however, that such a class can never be predicted correctly.

3.2   Similarity Discriminant Analysis

SDA is a generative classifier introduced by [3]. It is specifically tailored for cases where data inputs are only known from similarities or dissimilarities comparison among themselves. More particularly, considering a vector $T^x = (t_1^x, ..., t_p^x)$ of dissimilarities to the class medoids, the model aims at modeling the probability $\mathbf{P}(Y = j | T^x)$ for all possible classes $j \in \{1, ..., p\}$. The class predicted for x is then the class which minimize the expected misclassification cost, i.e.:

$$\hat{y} = \underset{j \in (1,...,p)}{\arg\min} \ \mathbf{E}_{\mathbf{P}(Y|T^x)}(\text{Cost}(j, Y)), \tag{2}$$

where $\text{Cost}(j, Y))$ represents the cost of predicting the class j for x, while its real class is Y.

[3] authors give an elegant argument based on Bayes theorem and entropy maximization to justify their proposed estimator for this quantity, leading to the following formula for the prediction $\hat{y}$:

$$\hat{y} = \arg\min_{\substack{i\in(1,\ldots,p)\\ j\in(1,\ldots,p)}} \sum \text{Cost}(i,j)(\prod_{k=1}^{p} \lambda_{jk} e^{-\lambda_{jk} t_k^x})\mathbf{P}(Y=j), \tag{3}$$

with $\frac{1}{\lambda_{jk}} = \frac{1}{|J|}\sum_{x \text{ with label } j} t_k^x$, $|J|$ the number of elements with label j in the training database. $\frac{1}{\lambda_{jk}}$ is, therefore, the average dissimilarity from the class j to the medoid μ_k. The probabilities $\mathbf{P}(Y=j)$ are, generally, unknown. They are, therefore, inferred from the training set. The Cost function used in this paper is $1 - s^{pre\times pro}$, with $s^{pre\times pro}$ defined in Sect. 4.

This model was implemented using the programming language Python.

4   Experiment

This section present our experiments on a logs 3D scan database. The results from the SDA models are compared with the results from two other models, previously studied in [4].

4.1   The Log Database

The database used in this paper was provided by the Canadian wood industry. It contains the scans of 1207 logs, and their associated baskets of products, computed by the sawing simulator Optitek. Each scan is a point cloud composed of a succession of ellipsoid which, together, sample the log surface. The original scans had empty sections, i.e. missing ellipsoids, leading to poor performances of the ICP algorithm when computing scan dissimilarities. This behavior had been corrected by repeating the ellipsoid immediately preceding an empty section to fill it. The database contains 19 types of lumbers. The basket of products y associated with a log x can, therefore, be represented by a vector of length 19. The ith element of this vector is then the number of lumbers of type i present in x basket of products. It might be noticed that no basket contains more than five different types of lumbers and that, therefore, the vectors y are sparse.

The database contains in total 105 different baskets, each being considered a class in our classification problem and is represented by a number from 1 to 105.

4.2   Evaluation Scores

When training ML classifiers, scores have to be introduced to measure and compare their performances. The most commonly used score is, probably, the 0–1 score, s^{01}, defined as (Fig. 1):

Fig. 1. Example of a log 3D scan

$$s^{01}(y, \hat{y}) = \begin{cases} 1, & \text{if } y = \hat{y} \\ 0, & \text{otherwise} \end{cases}, \tag{4}$$

with y the true label of a data point x, and $\hat{y}$ its predicted label. Such a score is then averaged over all the data points in a test dataset to estimate the probability for the classifier to predict the real class of any point x.

However, it might appear desirable for the cost of making a false prediction to vary depending on the true class label y and false prediction $\hat{y}$. The prediction-production score, $s^{pre \times pro}$, was specifically introduced in [10] for the problem of sawmill simulator metamodelling. Let y and $\hat{y}$ be once again the real and predicted baskets of products associated with a log x. Since these vectors are sparse, counting all the $(0,0)$ real/predicted pairs contained in these vectors would skew the scores optimistically, all such pairs are, therefore, removed. The new length of y and $\hat{y}$ is called l. the prediction score, s^{pre}, is defined as:

$$s^{pre} = \frac{1}{l} \sum_{i=1}^{l} \min(1, \frac{\hat{y}_i}{\max(\epsilon, y_i)}), \tag{5}$$

with ϵ a small value to avoid dividing by 0. Similarly, the prediction score, s^{pro}, is defined as:

$$s^{pro} = \frac{1}{l} \sum_{i=1}^{l} \min(1, \frac{y_i}{\max(\epsilon, \hat{y}_i)}). \tag{6}$$

s^{pre} can be interpreted as the proportion of real basket that was predicted, while s^{pro} is the proportion of the prediction that was effectively produced.

The prediction-production score is then naturally defined as:

$$s^{pre \times pro} = s^{pre} \times s^{pro}. \tag{7}$$

4.3 Results and Discussion

For training and testing the SDA, the log database was randomly separated 10 times into a train test of size 724, i.e., 60% of the database, and a test set of size 483, i.e., 40% of the database. The results from the SDA are, furthermore, compared with two other models from [4]. the first one is a classic k nearest neighbors algorithm. The second is a kNN which uses a set of rules to filter out unnecessary ICP comparisons. This model is named r-kNN in this section. The rules used to filter these comparisons are:

- If a log is shorter than the length of the smallest possible lumber, it is attributed an empty basket of product without performing any comparison.
- Since logs come in a few standard length, two logs are compared only if they have the same length.

For both of these models, k was fixed to 25 as in [4].

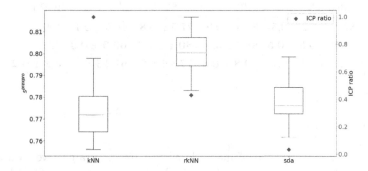

Fig. 2. Boxplots of the average prediction-production scores over the 10 train-test separations for each model. The averaged ratio of the number of ICP needed to yield a prediction over the total size of the train set are presented as well. The scores are in percent

The boxplots of the $s^{pre \times pro}$ scores of each model over the ten train-test are presented Fig. 2. As can be seen, r-kNN has the highest $s^{pre \times pro}$ scores among the three models, while kNN and SDA are comparable. What strongly counterbalance this lesser prediction performance for SDA, compared with r-kNN, is, however, an important reduction of the number of ICP comparisons needed to yield a prediction. While kNN needs to compare the new log with the whole training database and r-kNN with, in average, 40% of the database, SDA needs only to compare it with 3% of the database, i.e., only with the medoids. Additionally, while the number of comparisons needed would increase linearly in the size of the training database for r-kNN, it would remain constant for SDA as long as no new class appears in the dataset.

The average values of the compared models evaluation scores are further presented in Table 1. These evaluation scores are mean s^{pre}, mean s^{pro}, mean

$s^{pre \times pro}$ and mean s^{01}, averaged over the ten random separations in train and test sets. The highest scores among both models are set in bold. As previously, r-kNN has slightly higher evaluations scores than the SDA model, except for the production score. However, when comparing the 0–1 scores of r-kNN and SDA using a Mcnemar test, the minimum pvalue of the test among the ten experiments was 6 %. The error rate difference among the models can, therefore, never be considered significant at a 5% confidence level in any of our experiments. The difference in score is, indeed, only around 2% in average for both s^{01} and $s^{pre \times pro}$. To deem this difference acceptable or not would depend on the actual industrial application considered.

Table 1. Evaluation scores of SDA and r-kNN, averaged over ten random separations of the database into a train and a test set, as well as the averaged ratio of the number of ICP needed to yield a prediction over the total size of the train set. The scores are similarly presented in percent.

Model	s^{pre}	s^{pro}	$s^{pre \times pro}$	s^{01}	ICP ratio
kNN	89.2 ± 0.5	85.5 ± 0.9	77.5 ± 0.8	66.5 ± 0.1	100
r-kNN	$\mathbf{89.3 \pm 0.5}$	88.2 ± 0.6	$\mathbf{80.1 \pm 0.7}$	$\mathbf{69.0 \pm 0.9}$	42 ± 1
SDA	85.2 ± 0.7	$\mathbf{89.8 \pm 0.5}$	77.8 ± 0.7	67.2 ± 0.1	$\mathbf{3.2 \pm 0.2}$

5   Conclusion

This paper explores the use of medoids as features to train a well understood ML classifier to the task of predicting the baskets of products of 3D log scans. In particular, this method improves on previous works using kNN classifier by reducing drastically the number of ICP comparisons needed to compare a new log with a known database from 40% to 3% of the size of the training set, with a limited reduction in score.

A second advantage of this method is that it doesn't require complex feature extraction and, therefore, it would be of interest to generalize it to other point cloud applications.

Furthermore, while the SDA was specifically introduced for case with non metric similarities, the representation as a vector of dissimilarities to medoids could be used with other off the shelf ML classifiers. In particular, further works will consider using this representation with Random Forest classifiers and Multi Layer Perceptrons.

References

1. Balcan, M.F., Blum, A., Srebro, N.: Improved guarantees for learning via similarity functions (2008)

2. Besl, P.J., McKay, N.D.: A method for registration of 3-d shapes. IEEE Trans. Pattern Anal. Mach. Intell. **14**(2), 239–256 (1992)
3. Cazzanti, L.: Similarity Discriminant Analysis (01 2009)
4. Chabanet, S., Thomas, P., Bril El-Haouzi, H., Morin, M., Gaudreault, J.: A kNN approach based on ICP metrics for3d scans matching: an application to the sawing process. In: 17th IFAC Symposium on Information Control Problems in Manufacturing (2021)
5. Goulet, P.: Optitek: User's manual (2006)
6. Guo, Y., Wang, H., Hu, Q., Liu, H., Liu, L., Bennamoun, M.: Deep learning for 3d point clouds: A survey. IEEE Trans. Pattern Anal. Mach. Intell. (2020)
7. HALCO software systems ltd. : The sawsim sawmill simulation tool. https://www.halcosoftware.com/software-1-sawsim. Accessed June 2021
8. Martineau, V., Morin, M., Gaudreault, J., Thomas, P., Bril El-Haouzi, H.: Neural network architectures and feature extraction for lumber production prediction. In: The 34th Canadian Conference on Artificial Intelligence. Springer (2021)
9. Morin, M., et al.: Machine learning-based models of sawmills for better wood allocation planning. Int. J. Prod. Econ. **222**, 107508 (2020)
10. Morin, M., Paradis, F., Rolland, A., Wery, J., Laviolette, F., Laviolette, F.: Machine learning-based metamodels for sawing simulation. In: 2015 Winter Simulation Conference (WSC), pp. 2160–2171. IEEE (2015)
11. Morneau-Pereira, M., Arabi, M., Gaudreault, J., Nourelfath, M., Ouhimmou, M.: An optimization and simulation framework for integrated tactical planning of wood harvesting operations, wood allocation and lumber production. In: MOSIM 2014, 10eme Conférence Francophone de Modélisation, Optimisation et Simulation (2014)
12. Nguyen, V.T., et al.: Estimation de la qualité de bois ronds et d'arbres sur pied par Lidar terrestre. Ph.D. thesis, Paris, AgroParisTech (2018)
13. Pang, G., Qiu, R., Huang, J., You, S., Neumann, U.: Automatic 3d industrial point cloud modeling and recognition. In: 2015 14th IAPR international conference on machine vision applications (MVA), pp. 22–25. IEEE (2015)
14. Schleif, F.M., Tino, P.: Indefinite proximity learning: a review. Neural Comput. **27**(10), 2039–2096 (2015)
15. Selma, C., Bril El Haouzi, H., Thomas, P., Gaudreault, J., Morin, M.: An iterative closest point method for measuring the level of similarity of 3D log scans in wood industry. In: Borangiu, T., Trentesaux, D., Thomas, A., Cardin, O. (eds.) Service Orientation in Holonic and Multi-Agent Manufacturing. SCI, vol. 762, pp. 433–444. Springer, Cham (2018). https://doi.org/10.1007/978-3-319-73751-5_33
16. Stojanovic, V., Trapp, M., Richter, R., Hagedorn, B., Döllner, J.: Towards the generation of digital twins for facility management based on 3d point clouds. In: Proceeding of the 34th Annual ARCOM Conference, vol. 2018, pp. 270–279 (2018)
17. Todoroki, C., et al.: Autosaw system for sawing simulation. New Zealand J. For. Sci. **20**(3), 332–348 (1990)
18. Wang, Q., Kim, M.K.: Applications of 3d point cloud data in the construction industry: a fifteen-year review from 2004 to 2018. Adv. Eng. Inf. **39**, 306–319 (2019)
19. Wery, J., Gaudreault, J., Thomas, A., Marier, P.: Simulation-optimisation based framework for sales and operations planning taking into account new products opportunities in a co-production context. Comput. Ind. **94**, 41–51 (2018)

A Comparative Study of Classification Methods on the States of the USA Based on COVID-19 Indicators

İbrahim Miraç Eligüzel(✉) ⓘ and Eren Özceylan ⓘ

Industrial Engineering Department, Gaziantep University, 27100 Gaziantep, Turkey

Abstract. COVID-19 spreads across the world and specific pre-caution strategies are required for different regions depending on the current satiation. Therefore, proper region-specific pre-caution processes occupy a significant place to tackle with COVID-19 pandemic. During the COVID-19 pandemic, significant data are cumulated and these data can be utilized in order to cope with pandemic efficiently via providing a better understanding for decision-makers. In the aforementioned aspect, data related to the COVID-19 pandemic is used to decide on group states where the application of the same pre-caution processes has become efficient and effective. Therefore, COVID-19 indicators (e.g. number of deaths and infected) can be utilized to cluster the states, regions, countries, etc. In order to accomplish the underlined objective, data with seven features (rate of one dose, rate of two doses, number of cases, death, tests, recovered people, and percentage of positive tests) are retrieved for each of 50 states in the USA. After that, a dissimilarity matrix for cities is generated with respect to the corresponding seven features. Lastly, clustering methods (K-means, Agglomerative Hierarchical and BIRCH clustering, and P-median model) in literature are applied to gather clusters of states. In the proposed study, 50 states are taken into consideration and four different methods are applied to divide states into 6 subsets. The best result is gathered via the K-means application.

Keywords: Agglomerative hierarchical clustering · BIRCH clustering · COVID-19 · K-means clustering · P-median

1 Introduction

With the spread of COVID-19 through the world, authorities required to take necessary pre-cautions to avoid the public health crisis. In the world most of the countries, regions and states demonstrate the different trends of COVID-19 spread, number of deaths, cases and recoveries. Therefore, it is necessary to adopt differentiated procedures for different trends. In addition, quick response is required to handle COVID-19 with respect to trends and it requires efficient and effective decision making process. In this study our aim is to demonstrate applicability of clustering algorithms on problems in which, geographical classification occupies a crucial place. In addition, focus of this study is

© IFIP International Federation for Information Processing 2021
Published by Springer Nature Switzerland AG 2021
A. Dolgui et al. (Eds.): APMS 2021, IFIP AICT 632, pp. 582–590, 2021.
https://doi.org/10.1007/978-3-030-85906-0_63

to provide scientific approach for decision makers against the COVID-19 pandemic. Therefore, decision makers can determine the policies and apply them in accordance with the proposed geographical clusters.

Decisions comprehend travel and mobility restriction, social distancing and quarantine requirements, school and business closures, large scale testing, forbidding large crowd gatherings [1]. Moreover, there are organizations that generate indexes for countries and cluster them in accordance. For instance, Deep Knowledge Group conducted a study that focuses on COVID-19 regional safety assessment [2] and INFORM (Information Network Focus on Religious Movements) provides a report related to risk index for countries [3]. Results and methods of this study can be utilized in order to generate indexes as in explained above. There are several studies conducted to have deeper insight to COVID-19 pandemic due to developing strategies against it. In this manner, the study is conducted by using the fuzzy clustering for countries and Pearson correlation is applied find meaningful relation between the data features, in which strong correlation is detected between confirmed cases, dead cases and population size [4]. Another study that aims to support decision making process propose novel clustering algorithm adapted to make comparison of the various COVID time-series of different countries [5]. From the aforementioned perspective, it is also important to analyze spread of the COVID-19. Therefore, spatiotemporal distribution assessment and spread pattern analysis of COVID-19 is done by utilizing clustering algorithm and geographical information system [6]. Early detection of COVID-19 can also be thought as a crucial step of handling the pandemic. There are several ways to detect COVID-19. Chest X-ray CT-scan images are rather cheaper way to implement. In this aspect, a novel meta-heuristic feature selection method (Golden Ratio Optimizer) is proposed to extract features from images and it demonstrates outstanding performance with accuracies more than 99% [7]. Another study focuses on time series analysis which occupies a significant place to extract the dissimilarity in the COVID-19 spread in states and the establishment of models which can contribute analysis and prediction for transmission process of this infectious disease [8]. Relaxation of the restriction for COVID-19 is also important concern for economic and social life. The study is conducted to develop strategy to apply gradual relaxation by analyzing an epidemiological compartmental model with multi-objective genetic algorithm design optimization in order to make comparison on scenarios of strategy type [9]. As it is stated above, better understanding of COVID-19 spread is crucial to tackle pandemic. In this manner study is conducted to detect relation between living environment deprivation and spatial clustering of COVID-19 hotspots, and results show that living environment deprivation is significant determinant [10]. Social impact of the COVID-19 is taken into consideration during the pandemic. The best way to analyze the social impact is utilizing the social media. One of the studies uses Twitter hashtags and analyze them with multi-view clustering method and results demonstrates that some topical cluster of hash-tags stay consistent, while some of them shift during the pandemic [11]. Deciding on right protocol is a crucial step for the cases which require precision planning. Ramirez-Nafarrate et. al. conducted a study that includes the optimal planning for emergency departments to utilize ambulance diversion to ease congestion by requesting that ambulances bypass the ED and move patients to another location [12]. All in all, it can be concluded that having a deep insight of COVID-19 and application of right decisions for right place is very crucial to handle COVID-19 pandemic. In this study, it is aimed to gather clusters of states in USA to apply same pre-caution strategies on states in same cluster. Moreover, agglomerative hierarchical clustering, BIRCH clustering, K-means clustering and P-median are applied on the data-set that retrieved from Johns Hopkins Coronavirus Resource Center [13], The New York Times [14] and worldometer [15]. In the combined data-set seven features are gathered and used for generating dissimilarity matrix based on Euclidean distance. After that aforementioned methods applied and performance evaluation each method is done by total distances of cluster from its centroid. Therefore, efficient and effective application of strategies can be implemented and general view of current situation can be provided for decision makers. Also, proposed study differentiated from other studies by considering vaccine dose data in the dataset. The rest of the study is organized as follows: Sect. 2 introduces the methods; the experiments are given in Sect. 3. Section 4 presents the conclusion.

2 Methodology

Four methods are applied on retrieved data-set in order to cluster given 50 states with respect to data with seven features which are rate of one dose, rate of two doses, number of cases, number of deaths, number of tests, number of recovered people, and percentage of positive tests. After that Euclidean distance is calculated for each pair of feature to gather dissimilarity matrix. Then, agglomerative hierarchical clustering, BIRCH clustering, K-means clustering and P-median methods applied in order to gather group of states. Number of cluster is decided by elbow graph via K-means application and six clusters are generated by application of each method. There is also Silhoutte score to find the right number of clusters. Since, elbow method gives the result that close the optimal number of clusters [16], it is utilized in this study. Another reason to utilize elbow method is to identify K beyond which the inertia doesn't change much.

2.1 K-means Clustering

The algorithm works with a set of d-dimensional (feature) vectors, $D = \{x_i \mid i = 1,...,N\}$, where $x_i^{(k)}$ denotes the ith point and initialization of algorithm starts with selecting random k points in d as centroids to set them as the solution of clustering [17]. Also, c_j denotes center of cluster j. Objective function of K-means is given in Eq. (1).

$$\sum_{j=1}^{k} \sum_{j=1}^{k} \left(xi^{(k)} - cj\right)^2 \tag{1}$$

In order to apply K-means, "sklearn" library is used. In this library, K-means is applied with giving number of clusters, initialization procedure, maximum number iteration and randomness procedure. Number of clusters is decided by applying elbow method (see Fig. 1) and number of cluster is decided as 6 for four algorithms.

After the application of K-means, clusters are gathered and centroids of each cluster are found. Total distance for each cluster calculated with respect to Euclidean distance and total distances are summed in order to demonstrate the general performance of K-means.

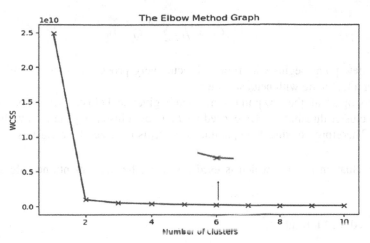

Fig. 1. Elbow method graph for deciding number of clusters

2.2 Agglomerative Hierarchical Clustering

The single linkage base method for agglomerative hierarchical clustering algorithm and the process of this algorithm consists of initialization which regards each point as a single cluster. Then, connection of a pair of clusters is implemented by aiming nearest members (states) with shortest distance and this procedure is repeated till only one cluster remains [18]. In addition, "ward" method is utilized in this algorithm. "Ward" method aims to minimize the variance for each cluster. Its difference from K-means is instead of minimizing within cluster sum of square, it focuses on minimizing the within-cluster variants. In order to perform this algorithm, "scipy" and "sklearn" Python libraries are utilized together.

2.3 BIRCH Clustering

BIRCH is an annotation for balanced iterative reducing and clustering using hierarchies and it is an unsupervised method which is grouping the given dataset into clusters. For this method "sklearn" Python library is utilized. BIRCH parameters can be expressed as the branching factor Br, the threshold T, and the cluster count k and the steps are given as follows [19]:

- When data is given to BIRCH, one of the trees which are a height-balanced, the cluster features, and CF of is generated.
- Each node indicates a subset in the cluster hierarchy, intermediate nodes present super-clusters and the leaf nodes are considered as actual clusters.
- The branching factor Br is the maximum number of offspring that allowable for a one which is a global parameter. Every node comprehends the information of the cluster which is the cluster features (CF). The cluster centers (C_i) and cluster radius (R_i) can be calculated, where $\{x_{ij}\}_{j=1}^{n}$ are the elements of the ith cluster. Formulas for C_i and R_i given in Eqs. (2) and (3), respectively.

$$R_i = \sqrt{1/n_i \sum_{j}^{n} (x_{ij} - C_i)^2} \qquad (2)$$

$$C_i = \frac{1}{n_i} \sum_j^n x_{ij} \tag{3}$$

- Every new point begins with root and recursively proceeds the tree, until the walk ends at a leaf node with nearest center.
- By arriving a leaf, the new point is included in given leaf cluster with respect to radius of the cluster threshold T. By exceeding T, a new cluster is generated with the new point. Therefore, the threshold parameter controls the size of the clusters.

By evaluation method which is used for two other aforementioned algorithms is applied.

2.4 P-median Method

The P-median problem and its variations has its crucial place to be applied on real life situations [19]. Considering a set L of m facilities, a set U of n users, and nxm matrix D indicates distances between two points d_{ij} in which i is demand from the facility j, for all $j \in L$ and $i \in U$ [19]. The objective function and variables are given below.

$$y_j = \begin{cases} 1, & \textit{if a center state is opened in } j \in L, \\ 0, & \textit{otherwise} \end{cases}$$

$$x_{ij} = \begin{cases} 1, & \textit{if state i is attended to center state } j \in L, \\ 0, & \textit{otherwise} \end{cases}$$

$$min \sum_i \sum_j d_{ij} x_{ij} \tag{4}$$

Subject to

$$\sum_j x_{ij} = 1, \forall_i, \tag{5}$$

$$x_{ij} \leq y_j, \forall_{i,j}, \tag{6}$$

$$\sum_j y_j = p, \tag{7}$$

$$x_{ij}, y_j \in \{0, 1\}. \tag{8}$$

The objective function (Eq. 4) aims to minimize total distance. In P-median model each state must be attended to only one subset (Eq. 5). Equation (6) ensures that if a center state is opened then a state can be assigned to that center. Equation (7) provides number of clusters do not exceed the pre-decided number of clusters. The signs of the decision variables are shown in Eq. (8). After applying P-median, centroid of each of six sub-sets are gathered by using the "numpy" Python library. Then, same evaluation with rest of the aforementioned algorithms is applied.

3 Clustering of the States

Utilized dataset consists of the seven features and features for is state is treated as dimensional vector to calculate dissimilarities. The illustration of dataset for states is given in Table 1. 1st and 2nd features are retrieved from The New York Times [14], 3rd, 4rd, 5th and 7th features are gathered from Johns Hopkins Coronavirus Resource Center [13] and 6th feature is taken from worldometer [15].

Table 1. Used dataset

#	State	Rate of one dose (in population)	Rate of two doses (in population)	Cases per 100k population	Deaths per 100k population	Tests per 100k population	Recovered people per 100k population	Percentage of positive tests
1	Alabama	10%	3.40%	9,879	192	93.3	5,613.60	21,22%
2	Arizona	13%	4.00%	11,034	210	394.4	1,556.19	5,52%
3	Arkansas	11%	4.70%	10,420	176	150.2	9,999.72	10.72%
...	...	...	...	...	...	...	...	...
48	West Virginia	14%	8.30%	7,185	125	493.9	6,497.01	3,78%
49	Wisconsin	13%	4.60%	10,478	117	429.7	9,300.49	3,07%
50	Wyoming	13%	5.20%	9,249	114	403.9	9,010.49	3,37%

For making comparison between aforementioned models and clustering algorithms, median of each cluster is found and total distance for each cluster is calculated with respect to medians to receive aggregate distance for each application via Euclidean distance. Therefore, evaluation of each application is implemented. Meanwhile, Python 3.7 libraries are utilized with a computer that has Intel Core i7 9750H CPU with 8 GB RAM features. In this study, total distances of applications which are K-means, agglomerative hierarchical clustering, BIRCH clustering and P-median are gathered as 82,914.43, 89,597.34, 89,597.34 and 85,225.59 respectively. Total distances are calculated with given equation below (Eq. 9).

$$\sqrt{\sum_{j}^{k} \sum_{i}^{n} \left(x_{ji} - c_j\right)^2} \tag{9}$$

Where x_{ji} indicates the data point "i" that attended to cluster "j" and c_j indicates the center point of cluster "j".

All in all, K-means shows better result compared to others, which is followed by P-median method. In addition, Agglomerative hierarchical clustering and BIRCH clustering show exactly the same performance. In nutshell, purpose of the study is to cluster the states in order to apply same procedure for each cluster of states against pandemic. Six clusters are gathered from aforementioned four methods. The best result is gathered from K-means application. Demonstrations of the results obtained by four methods are given in Fig. 2.

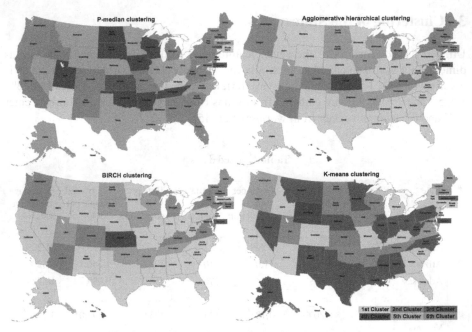

Fig. 2. The clustered states obtained by four methods

Clusters are represented by different colors in Fig. 2. Each cluster indicates the collection of states, where same strategic decisions can be applied against COVID-19 pandemic. For instance, cities significantly differ from each other by "percentage of positive tests", "tests per 100k population" and "rate of one dose" in 4th cluster and 2nd cluster for K-means application. However, there is no significant or consistent difference for rest of the attributes for cities. From the Fig. 2 it can be seen that Arkansas, Illinois, North Dakota, Oklahoma, South Dakota, Tennessee, Utah, and Wisconsin are assigned in the same cluster in all methods. Therefore, it can be concluded that same strategy against COVID-19 can be applied whole aforementioned eight states.

4   Conclusion

The main focus of study is to implement four clustering methods on USA states in order to cluster them with respect to COVID-19 via using extracted dissimilarity matrix from dataset with seven features. As a result, total distances of four applications (K-means, agglomerative hierarchical clustering, BIRCH clustering and P-median) are calculated as 82,914.43, 89,597.34, 89,597.34 and 85,225.59 in accordance. K-means gives the better results compared to rest of the applications. Benefit of proposed study is providing information for decision makers to have general view of current situation geographically by aiming application of specific protocol on a gathered cluster. Limitations of this study can be expressed as required time to obtain data and evaluating several different features to analyze their effects on clusters. For the feature work, effect of each feature on the result can be investigated. Therefore, effectiveness of application can be augmented. For the future study, a web-based dynamic system can be developed due to being updated because COVID-19 data is altering over time. Lastly, utilized methods can be improvement with some modifications to increase performance. This study conducted on COVID-19 data in order to demonstrate geographical relation in USA states to provide inside for decision makers. In aforementioned aspect, given approach can be generalized for the similar situations with cumulated data. In addition, it can be used for classifications of geographic regions for different concerns to develop strategies, such as crime, politics and other pandemics situations.

References

1. Campedelli, G.M., D'Orsogna, M.R.: Temporal clustering of disorder events during the COVID-19 pandemic. 1–32. arXiv preprint arXiv:2101 06458 (2021)
2. Deep Knowledge Group. http://analytics.dkv.global/covid-regional-assessment-200-regions/infographic-summary.pdf. Accessed 16 Mar 2021
3. INFORM.   https://reliefweb.int/sites/reliefweb.int/files/resources/INFORM%20COVID%20Risk%20Index%20V012%20Report.pdf. Accessed 16 Mar 2021
4. Mahmoudi, M.R., Baleanu, D., Mansor, Z., Tuan, B.A., Pho, K.H.: Fuzzy clustering method to compare the spread rate of COVID-19 in the high risks countries. Chaos, Solitons Fractals **140**, 1–9 (2020)
5. Zarikas, V., Poulopoulos, S.G., Gareiou, Z., Zervas, E.: Clustering analysis of countries using the COVID-19 cases dataset. Data Brief **31**, 105787, (2020)
6. Azarafza, M., Azarafza, M., Akgün, H.: Clustering method for spread pattern analysis of corona-virus (COVID-19) infection in Iran. medRxiv (2020)
7. Chattopadhyay, S., Dey, A., Singh, P.K., Geem, Z.W., Sarkar, R.: COVID-19 detection by optimizing deep residual features with improved clustering-based golden ratio optimizer. Diagnostics **11**(2), 315 (2021)
8. Rojas, F., Valenzuela, O., Rojas, I.: Estimation of COVID-19 dynamics in the different states of the United States using time-series clustering. medRxiv (2020)
9. Pinto Neto, O., et al.: Mathematical model of COVID-19 intervention scenarios for São Paulo—Brazil. Nat. Commun. **12**(1), 1–13, (2021)
10. Das, A., Ghosh, S., Das, K., Basu, T., Dutta, I., Das, M.: Living environment matters: Unravelling the spatial clustering of COVID-19 hotspots in Kolkata megacity, India. Sustain Cities Soc. **65**(October) 2020, 102577 (2021)
11. Cruickshank, I.J., Carley, K.M.: Characterizing communities of hashtag usage on twitter during the 2020 COVID-19 pandemic by multi-view clustering. Appl. Netw. Sci. **5**(66), 1–40 (2020)
12. Ramirez-Nafarrate, A., Hafizoglu, A.B., Gel, E.S., Fowler, J.W.: Optimal control policies for ambulance diversion. Eur. J. Oper. Res. **236**(1), 298–312 (2014)
13. Johns Hopkins University. https://coronavirus.jhu.edu/testing/states-comparison/testing-state-totals-bypop. Accessed 16 Mar 2021
14. New York Times. https://www.nytimes.com/interactive/2020/us/covid-19-vaccine-doses.html. Accessed 16 Mar 2021
15. Report Coronavirus Cases. https://www.worldometers.info/coronavirus/country/us/. Accessed 16 Mar 2021
16. Et-taleby, A., Boussetta, M., Benslimane, M.: Faults detection for photovoltaic field based on k-means, elbow, and average silhouette techniques through the segmentation of a thermal image. Int. J. Photoenergy **2020**, 7 (2020)

17. Wu, X., et al.: Top 10 algorithms in data mining. Knowl. Inf. Syst. **14**, 1–37 (2008)
18. Koga, H., Ishibashi, T., Watanabe, T.: Fast agglomerative hierarchical clustering algorithm using locality-sensitive hashing. Knowl. Inf. Syst. **12**(1), 25–53 (2007)
19. Lorbeer, B., Kosareva, A., Deva, B., Softić, D., Ruppel, P., Küpper, A.: Variations on the clustering algorithm BIRCH. Big Data Res. **11**, 44–53 (2018)
20. Dzator, M., Dzator, J.: An effective heuristic for the P-median problem with application to ambulance location. Opsearch **50**(1), 60–74 (2013)
21. Mladenović, N., Brimberg, J., Hansen, P., Moreno-Pérez, J.A.: The P-median problem: a survey of metaheuristic approaches. Eur. J. Oper. Res. **179**(3), 927–939 (2007)

Maintenance Data Management for Condition-Based Maintenance Implementation

Humberto Teixeira[(⊠)], Catarina Teixeira, and Isabel Lopes

ALGORITMI Research Centre, University of Minho, Guimarães, Portugal
b6440@algoritmi.uminho.pt

Abstract. The ability to rapidly obtain significant and accurate information from extensive data records is a key factor for companies' success in today's competitive environment. Different machine learning algorithms can be used to extract information from data. However, to enable their application appropriate data structures must be defined. In addition, the quality of data must be ensured to allow appropriate decisions to be made based on the resulting information. Condition-Based Maintenance (CBM) decisions usually result from the analysis of the combination of data monitored on equipment with events data, such as failures and preventive maintenance interventions. Thus, to enable CBM implementation, data from equipment maintenance history should be properly organized and systematized. This paper presents a study performed in a manufacturing plant with several production lines. A structure to properly organize the failure records data and an overall data structure, including data events and monitored data, were defined to enable the application of CBM. The information obtained based on the data structure for the failure records allowed prioritizing the failure modes of a machine for CBM implementation.

Keywords: Condition-Based Maintenance (CBM) · Maintenance data · Data management

1 Introduction

The effectiveness of physical asset management depends on the use of a wide variety of technical and business data arising from different areas of the company. In general, business data belong to categories, such as inventory, customers, suppliers, financial, etc. Whereas technical data are directly related to the assets. These data are usually associated with the condition, performance, criticality, risk, reliability, etc. If the existing data are properly processed, information to support decision-making can be obtained [1]. However, data can only truly become information when a context is assigned and if they are presented in a way that people can understand [2]. Moreover, the speed and success of the decision-making process depend on the existence of detailed and accurate information, and on means that make it immediately accessible [1, 3].

© IFIP International Federation for Information Processing 2021
Published by Springer Nature Switzerland AG 2021
A. Dolgui et al. (Eds.): APMS 2021, IFIP AICT 632, pp. 591–598, 2021.
https://doi.org/10.1007/978-3-030-85906-0_64

Although large amounts of data are generated in companies, the lack of visibility and control can originate distrust and discourage its use to support decisions. In addition, the users may not be able to translate the vast amount of data into meaningful information. Therefore, several decisions end up being made based on subjective judgments. Of such decisions, can result ineffective strategic options, increased costs, loss of revenue or, in some cases, failures with catastrophic consequences [1].

Condition-based Maintenance (CBM) is a maintenance strategy that aims to recommend maintenance decisions based on information acquired through condition monitoring [4]. When CBM is established, all potential failure modes that can result in economic losses must be considered [5]. The main goal is to determine the instant in which maintenance should be performed and defining the most appropriate action [6]. The data collected in a CBM program can be classified as event data or monitoring data.

According to Bokrantz et al. [7], data analytics and big data management will play a major role in supporting the maintenance function over the coming years. The application of machine learning algorithms in CBM domain is increasing due to the need of analyzing large amounts of data collected by sensors and combining them with data related to failure events. However, the existence of uniform and reliable failure records is a mandatory requirement for the application of machine learning algorithms and to automatically estimate maintenance indicators, such as Mean Time to Failure (MTTF). Furthermore, these data are useful for selecting the most appropriate maintenance policy [8], based on the failure mode impact, comparing the cost of different maintenance policies and optimizing decision criteria, such as cost and equipment availability.

The studies that propose machine learning algorithms for CBM are usually tested and validated using data from predefined datasets available online [9, 10], since it is difficult to obtain organized and consistent datasets in manufacturing plants. Moreover, these studies are mainly focused on demonstrating the effectiveness of the proposed algorithms. Thus, maintenance data management for enabling CBM implementation is a key issue, which has not received enough attention in the literature.

In this paper, a data structure aimed at organizing and systematizing the failure records data of a manufacturing plant and an overall data structure to combine events data and monitored data were defined. It was intended to enable the treatment and analysis of the failure records data for supporting CBM implementation. The paper is organized as follows. Section 2 describes how maintenance data were initially managed in the analyzed manufacturing plant. In Sect. 3, the methodology for defining the data structure for the failure records is presented. Section 4 describes the data structure for the failure records and the overall data structure. Finally, in Sect. 5 the conclusions derived from the study are presented.

2   The Manufacturing Plant and Maintenance Data Management

This study was performed in a company that produces electronics systems. Three categories of maintenance records were found in the company's information system: failure records, preventive actions records and improvement actions records.

Only the failure records are filled in the company's Computerized Maintenance Management System (CMMS). When a failure occurs, the operator sends a repair order to the corrective maintenance team to transmit information about the problem detected, the equipment location and the status of the production line. After the intervention, a report describing the action performed is filled in by the technician. The preventive actions records are performed in Systems Applications and Products (SAP) software, whereas the improvement actions records are filled in Excel files. Therefore, these records cannot be merged in an automatic manner with the failure records data, to obtain the complete sequence of events concerning a specific equipment. Moreover, the spare parts consumptions related to both corrective and preventive replacements are only registered in SAP and cannot be associated with the exact component location. This limitation is particularly relevant, since a machine can have several equal components.

Several flaws were identified in the failure records in the initial phase of the study. It was not possible to extract meaningful information, in a quick and direct manner, about the failure modes, particularly the associated component, causes, effects and frequency. The information was registered using different terms and expressions to describe similar events and actions. Furthermore, the information provided was often inaccurate, inconsistent or incomplete. Some fields were composed by predefined lists in which some elements were not in accordance with the subject of the respective list, since they were indiscriminately updated by different employees based on their subjective interpretation. This circumstance resulted in ambiguous and potentially misleading information. It was also found that certain corrective interventions in critical equipment and their subsequent follow-up were recorded by the technician in a paper form. Nevertheless, this information was not transferred to the CMMS.

3 Defining the Data Structure

To enable a cost-effective implementation of CBM, the existing data structure of the failure records needed to be reformulated. Subsequently, the failure records should be integrated with the preventive actions records, and easily combined with the monitored data within an overall structure. The methodology adopted for defining and applying the new data structure for the failure records comprises the following steps:

- *Defining objectives for restructuring the failure records:* A set of requirements to support the definition of a proper data structure for the failure records were established.
- *Defining the data structure for the failure records and the overall data structure:* A structure for properly organize the failure records data was defined. It was intended to overcome the existing gaps concerning the failure data records and to make use of the current fields of the CMMS, in order to avoid immediate modifications to the software. Afterwards, the overall data structure was defined. This structure aims to assist the integration of events data and their combination with the monitored data.
- *Defining the failure data recording process:* The data recording process was defined to ensure the data integrity, according to the existing technologies and resources.
- *Validating the defined failure records structure:* The failure records structure was validated with the corrective maintenance responsible, to prevent potential flaws.
- *Providing training on the failure data recording process:* The equipment operators and maintenance technicians received appropriate training about the recording process.

4 The Defined Data Structure

4.1 Requirements for Restructuring the Failure Data Records

The new data structure and the respective records aim to meet the following three requirements to continue to assure the functions of the previous one:

- *Prioritizing the maintenance action:* An accurate description of the production line status after failure should be provided.
- *Assigning responsibilities for performing the maintenance action:* The classification of the failure should be specified, in order to call a qualified technician.
- *Transmitting information to technicians:* The specific designation and/or code of the production line and machine should be identified, to easily locate the equipment to be serviced in the manufacturing plant.

Other requirements were established to organize the data for analysis, as detailed below.

- *Locating the failure event in the manufacturing equipment:* For each failure event, the records should provide the specific designation and/or code of the subset, component and socket. This information allows the determination of the MTTF of specific components and to perform reliability studies.
- *Providing a uniform designation for each machine failure mode:* It is intended to obtain a list of failure modes by component with appropriate designations to incorporate in the CMMS. The resulting information is useful to determine automatically the rate of occurrence of the failure mode.
- *Providing a clear and uniform description of the failure effect:* The failure effect should provide enough information to determine the nature of the failure (evident or hidden) and its consequences. For this purpose, the possible effect of the identified failures modes must be described, generating predefined descriptions. This information aims to assist the definition of the failure mode criticality, which will be represented by a category. Then, the most appropriate maintenance policy will be selected accordingly and priorities will be defined for the failure modes that are eligible for CBM.
- *Enabling the recording of the failure mode causes:* This information will be used to assist the definition of improvement actions and for identifying the failure mode hazard rate behavior (increasing or non-increasing).
- *Facilitating the combination of failure data with monitoring data:* The failure records should be structured to automatically link changes, patterns or trends in the values of the parameters measured by sensors with the initiation of specific failure modes.

4.2 Structure

The data structure for the failure records was defined based on the previously established objectives. Figure 1 represents the fields of the defined data structure and provides a practical example of a failure record for a machine type that is part of several lines of the manufacturing plant. The data structure is composed of five levels, namely: line, machine, subset, component and failure mode. The line has an associated status obtained through a predefined list of four options. Moreover, the location of the component and

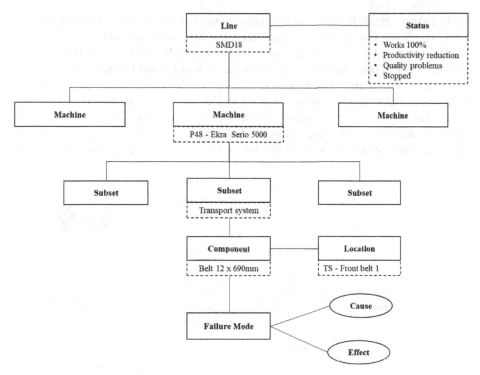

Fig. 1. Data structure for the failure records.

the causes and effects of the corresponding failure modes must be defined to provide predefined lists to the users (operator and maintenance technicians).

A work team was formed to define lists of failure modes associated with the components of each machine type, and lists of effects and causes related to each failure mode.

Table 1. Examples of components failure modes, and their effects and causes.

Component	Failure mode	Effect	Cause
Battery pack	Discharged	Stopped machine - UPS shutdown	Wear
Suction hose	Punctured	Stopped machine - Incorrect cleaning of the screen; Vacuum error	Wear due to the cleaning system movement
PPR valve	Air leak	Stopped machine - Solder paste printing performed incorrectly; Pressure error	Wear
VUVG valve	Damaged	Incorrect cleaning of the screen - The cleaning bar stops vibrating	Wear due to the high number of commutations

Table 1 shows examples of options included in the lists of the solder printing machine Ekra Serio 5000. For this machine type, complete lists are already defined.

The options of the predefined lists should be regularly updated, based on the operators and technicians' feedback. Furthermore, to detect possible errors or incomplete information, the records must be periodically revised by a qualified employee. For the components failure modes that are eligible for CBM, the failures data and the preventive events data should be easily combined with the monitored data. Thus, an overall data structure including events data and monitored data was defined. The main elements of the defined data structure and the relationships between them are represented in Fig. 2.

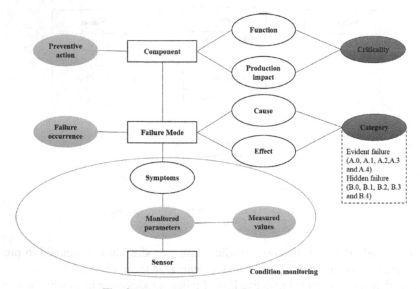

Fig. 2. Elements of the overall data structure.

The preventive actions data are associated with the component, whereas the failure occurrence is directly linked to the failure mode. The components criticality is determined based on their function and production impact [11]. This information is used to prioritize failure modes for CBM implementation. The failure modes are associated with the component and their category is derived from their effect, causes and hazard rate behavior. The information on the failure mode symptoms is used for identifying parameters to be monitored by sensors. The values of the parameters recorded during condition monitoring will be analyzed to predict or detect the failure mode occurrence.

4.3   Application

The organization and systematization of the failure records, according to the defined data structure, allowed prioritizing relevant failure modes to monitor for CBM implementation for the analyzed machine. Table 2 shows the first four priority failure modes, sorted in descending order. The presented failures modes were selected from the general list of critical failure modes of the analyzed machine based on two criteria: "increasing hazard rate with time" and "at least one associated symptom". The monitored parameters were then defined taking into account the information about the failure mode symptoms and techniques proposed in the literature. Finally, the failure modes priority was obtained by considering sequentially the following criteria: "sensors to measure the defined parameter already installed", "relationship between the parameter values and the failure mode development", "rate of occurrence of the failure mode", "component criticality" and "failure mode category".

Table 2. Failure modes prioritization for CBM implementation.

Component	Failure mode	Sensor	Relationship	Occurrence	Criticality	Category[a]
Battery pack	Discharged	Voltage; Current	Very strong	10	Vital	A.3
Suction hose	Punctured	Pressure	Very strong	3	Vital	A.3
PPR Valve	Air leak	Pressure	Very strong	1	Vital	A.3
VUVG Valve	Damaged	-	Very strong	5	Desirable	B.1

[a] A.3 – Sudden failure; B.1 – Quality losses

The relationship criterion was assessed based on scientific knowledge and technical experience from a team of engineers. Whereas the category was assigned to each failure mode, considering its impact both on the process and operating environment. Before this analysis, a predefined list of relevant categories was defined. The first three failure modes presented in Table 2 cause sudden stop of the machine and originate evident failures, whereas the fourth is likely to result in defective product and generates a hidden failure. The next step involves the feasibility study of CBM for each failure mode, according to the defined priorities.

5 Conclusion

In this study, a new data structure to organize and standardize the failure records of a manufacturing plant was defined. The main purpose was to provide a structure for facilitating CBM implementation, which enables the direct application of machine learning algorithms and other data analysis methods. Thus, the time required for data preparation will be significantly reduced or eliminated, and the accuracy and reliability of the data will be ensured.

The defined data structure was used for systematizing the failure records of a machine from the analyzed manufacturing plant and will be gradually applied to the failure records of the remaining machines. This analysis can be time-consuming, due to the need of standardizing terms and expressions. However, the time and effort invested enable the maintenance team to develop greater knowledge about the equipment and the associated problems. Therefore, it has a positive impact on the company's knowledge management, since the technical knowledge is often tacit and it is carried by a small number of people. Based on the existing data, relevant failure modes for CBM implementation were defined and priorities were established. Furthermore, an overall data structure which aims to support the integration of events data and their combination with the monitored data was established. This structure reveals key elements concerning the maintenance data and represents their relationships.

In companies, the data associated with maintenance activities are often dispersed and cannot be merged in an automatic manner. Moreover, the data are not always organized in a uniform format and their integrity is affected by several flaws in the recording process. This impedes real-time decision-making based on data. Thus, it is considered that the data structures defined in this study provide a relevant contribution to bridge these gaps and to enable the development of intelligent maintenance systems.

Acknowledgements. This work is supported by: European Structural and Investment Funds in the FEDER component, through the Operational Competitiveness and Internationalization Programme (COMPETE 2020) [Project n° 39479; Funding Reference: POCI-01–0247-FEDER-39479].

References

1. Koronios, A., Lin, S., Gao, J.: A data quality model for asset management in engineering organisations. In: Proceedings of the 10th International Conference on Information Quality (ICIQ 2005), Cambridge, MA, USA (2005)
2. Brous, P., Overtoom, I., Herder, P., Versluis, A., Janssen, M.: data infrastructures for asset management viewed as complex adaptive systems. Procedia Comput. Sci. **36**, 124–130 (2014)
3. Schuh, G., Prote, J.-P., Busam, T., Lorenz, R., Netland, T.H.: Using prescriptive analytics to support the continuous improvement process. In: Ameri, F., Stecke, K.E., von Cieminski, G., Kiritsis, D. (eds.) APMS 2019. IAICT, vol. 566, pp. 46–53. Springer, Cham (2019). https://doi.org/10.1007/978-3-030-30000-5_6
4. Jardine, A.K.S., Lin, D., Banjevic, D.: A review on machinery diagnostics and prognostics implementing condition-based maintenance. Mech. Syst. Signal Process. **20**, 1483–1510 (2006)
5. Al-Najjar, B.: On establishing cost-effective condition-based maintenance: exemplified for vibration-based maintenance in case companies. J. Qual. Maint. Eng. **18**, 401–416 (2012)
6. Ahmad, R., Kamaruddin, S.: A review of condition-based maintenance decision-making. Eur. J. Ind. Eng. **6**, 519–541 (2012)
7. Bokrantz, J., Skoogh, A., Berlin, C., Stahre, J.: Maintenance in digitalised manufacturing: Delphi-based scenarios for 2030. Int. J. Prod. Econ. **191**, 154–169 (2017)
8. Vilarinho, S., Lopes, I., Oliveira, J.A.: Preventive maintenance decisions through maintenance optimization models: a case study. Procedia Manuf. **11**, 1170–1177 (2017)
9. Kraus, M., Feuerriegel, S.: Forecasting remaining useful life: Interpretable deep learning approach via variational Bayesian inferences. Decis. Support Syst. **125**, 113100 (2019)
10. Su, C., Li, L., Wen, Z.: Remaining useful life prediction via a variational autoencoder and a time-window-based sequence neural network. Qual. Reliab. Eng. Int. **36**, 1639–1656 (2020)
11. Teixeira, C., Lopes, I., Figueiredo, M.: Classification methodology for spare parts management combining maintenance and logistics perspectives. J. Manag. Anal. **5**, 116–135 (2018)

A Machine Learning Based Health Indicator Construction in Implementing Predictive Maintenance: A Real World Industrial Application from Manufacturing

Harshad Kurrewar, Ebru Turanouglu Bekar$^{(\boxtimes)}$ ⓘ, Anders Skoogh ⓘ,
and Per Nyqvist

Chalmers University of Technology, Hörsalsvägen 7A, 412 96 Gothenburg, Sweden
ebru.ut@chalmers.se

Abstract. Predictive maintenance (PdM) using Machine learning (ML) is a top-rated business case with respect to the availability of data and potential business value for future sustainability and competitiveness in the manufacturing industry. However, applying ML within actual industrial practice of PdM is a complex and challenging task due to high dimensionality and lack of labeled data. To cope with this challenge, this paper presents a systematic framework based on an unsupervised ML approach by aiming to construct health indicators, which has a crucial impact on making the data meaningful and usable for monitoring machine performance (health) in PdM applications. The results are presented by using real-world industrial data coming from a manufacturing company. In conclusion, the designed health indicators can be used to monitor machine performance over time and further be used in a supervised setting for the purpose of prognostic like remaining useful life estimation in implementing PdM in the industry.

Keywords: Smart maintenance · Predictive maintenance · Health assessment · Machine learning · Feature selection and fusion · Real world industrial data

1 Introduction

Industrial digitalization is a key enabler of future competitiveness and sustainability in manufacturing companies. This allows for increased automation and data exchange through increased deployment of information and communication technologies (i.e., smart sensors) [1]. Recent studies have also shown that digital solutions in the maintenance field, specifically in Predictive Maintenance (PdM), have the highest potential to contribute towards industrial competitiveness with the vision of failure-free production [2]. Therefore, PdM research has a lot of

© IFIP International Federation for Information Processing 2021
Published by Springer Nature Switzerland AG 2021
A. Dolgui et al. (Eds.): APMS 2021, IFIP AICT 632, pp. 599–608, 2021.
https://doi.org/10.1007/978-3-030-85906-0_65

attention in industry and academy due to its potential benefits in terms of reliability, safety and maintenance costs, among many other benefits and has been started to be adopted by many manufacturing companies [3]. Machine Learning (ML), within Artificial Intelligence, has emerged as a powerful tool for developing intelligent predictive algorithms in many applications of manufacturing[4]. Therefore, ML provides powerful predictive approaches for implementing different PdM applications such as health indicators construction, (early) anomaly detection, and remaining useful life (RUL) estimation [5–7]. Although they have been successfully implemented to improve PdM capabilities, many of them follow a supervised learning approach. This perfectly works fine with experimental data sets, which means in the presence of a high amount of labelled data (i.e., the data is annotated with an actual machine health condition or the data contains examples of every possible fault type) [8]. However, the high amount of required labelled data for supervised prediction models in implementing PdM might not be available (partially/completely missing) in real-world industrial environments [9]. This shows that there still exists a gap, which most ML-based models for PdM are not designed with regard to actual industrial practice and are not validated with industrial data [9]. To overcome this gap, we propose a systematic framework to construct suitable health indicators that can be monitored and interpreted easily by practitioners in implementing PdM in real-world industrial environments. The main contribution of the proposed health indicator construction framework is that it gives significant insights into the implementation of unsupervised ML in PdM by identifying, cleaning, extracting, and selecting relevant features and fusing them as health indicators. Furthermore, it can also be effectively used with different condition monitoring data types with the extension of the framework in machine health assessment for PdM applications.

The remainder of the paper is structured according to the presented approach. In Sect. 2, related literature focuses on health indicator construction in PdM. Section 3 presents the framework by describing the steps of the designed approach. Section 4 presents the results from real-world industrial application. Finally, Sect. 5 concludes the paper with a summary and further research directions.

2   Related Literature

According to a systematic and comprehensive review done by [10], it was noted that ML algorithms have increasingly being applied for designing PdM applications especially handling the health status of industrial equipment and estimation of its RUL. Furthermore, a framework proposed by [11] for a data-driven based PdM generally covers three steps such as data acquisition and preprocessing, the construction of health indicator, and prognostics (i.e., prediction of a failure time). Among these steps, the construction of health indicators has a crucial impact on monitoring a system's performance evolution over time. Moreover, a health indicator can be even used to not just detect the deviation from the healthy system conditions but also by trending it to predict the RUL of the system [12]. Moreover, there are two significant steps for a health indicator construction in literature: feature extraction and the selection and feature fusion, where multidimensional features are transformed into a one-dimensional health indicator using ML algorithms [13]. For instance, [11] proposed a recurrent neural network (RNN) based health indicator to predict the RUL of bearings. The most sensitive features were selected from an original feature set based on monotonicity and correlation metrics and then fed into an RNN network to construct a health indicator, which was used RUL estimation of generator bearings from wind turbines. [14] also implemented RNN to fuse the selected sensitive features to construct a health indicator that incorporates mutual information of multiple features correlated with the damage and degradation of bearing. As one of the most popular unsupervised ML algorithm for dimension reduction, Principle component analysis (PCA) is often applied to fuse multiple features and construct health indicators for different systems such as bearings and cutting tools [13]. [15] recently presented a new approach for machine tool component health identification based on unsupervised ML. They trained different clustering models using time series feature extraction and demonstrated promising potential of the unsupervised techniques for machine tool supervision. Briefly, given the literature mentioned above, it is important to highlight that unsupervised ML approaches are particularly promising and need to be further developed for PdM applications in industries.

3   Methodology

To establish a systematic framework for health indicator construction, the cross-industry standard process for data mining (CRISP-DM) is followed as a reference model in this paper. It provides a structured methodology for planning and managing the data-driven knowledge discovery process in data mining projects [16]. The CRISP-DM methodology consists of six iterative phases such as business understanding, data understanding, data preparation, modelling, evaluation and deployment. With these phases, the data is ensured regarding its relevance with identified business objectives in the business understanding phase of the process. However, it should be noted that the CRISP-DM methodology is taken a basis in this study. Hence, it is adjusted for practical development and implementation of the proposed framework according to real-world industrial application requirements. To answer this study's data-related questions, some certain phases of CRISP-DM, which are business understanding, data understanding, data preparation, and modelling, are focused and adapted to construct health indicators in the proposed framework. Therefore, the proposed framework can differ from the CRISP-DM with the main focus of the feature selection part. A flow chart of the proposed framework is illustrated in Fig. 1.

Following understanding the industrial requirements (analysis goals) and exploring the current system and data, suitable data sources are chosen and preprocessed, including various data preprocessing tasks such as data cleaning and integration to get feature set. Afterwards, feature selection is performed to discard redundant features, which do not provide sufficient information related to the system performance (health) [11]. Therefore, the literature proposes some metrics such as monotonicity and trendability [13], which are used to select the most important features from the feature set as shown in the proposed framework. The monotonicity metric evaluates an increasing or decreasing trend of the features, and it is calculated by the formula as follows [17].

$$Monotonocity = mean\left(\left|\frac{positive(diff(x_i)) - negative(diff(x_i))}{n-1}\right|\right) \quad (1)$$

where n is measurement points with respect to time (cycles, i = 1,2,...n) and diff is the difference of consecutive measurement points for each feature.

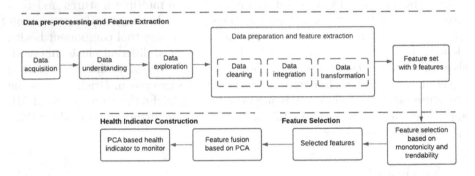

Fig. 1. A flow chart of the proposed framework for health indicator construction.

The trendability metric measures a linear correlation between features and operating time. It is calculated by the absolute minimum correlation in a population of the indicators using the formula as follows [17].

$$Trendability = min(|corrcoef(x_i, x_j)|); i = 1, 2, ...m, j = 1, 2, ...m \quad (2)$$

where m is the number of features of the system.

These two feature metrics are restricted to the range [0, 1], and they are positively associated with the feature performance accuracy, making them ideal as feature selection metrics. Therefore, the feature selection is performed based on a final feature importance score, which is computed as a linear combination of the above two metrics (considering each metric equally weighted) for each feature by using the formula as follows:

$$Final\_feature\_importance\_score = Monotonocity + Trendability \quad (3)$$

It should also be noted that the average value of these two metrics is computed for determining a threshold level to select the most important features.

In the final step of the proposed framework, the PCA is utilized to fuse the selected features for health indicator construction. PCA is a powerful unsupervised ML algorithm, which reduces the dimensionality of the data and retains most of the variation (information) in the data set [18]. To take advantages of mutual information from the selected features, they are fed to the PCA algorithm to estimate the number of principal components that cover a minimum 85% cumulative percentage of explained variance and satisfy the "rule of thumb" inertial shift through scree plot visualization of eigenvalues. Based on this principle, the selected principal components are determined as health indicators to be monitored for machine performance and further be used in the estimation of RUL. As a common acknowledgement, the individual case study requires a different approach. This refers to that no single algorithm is superior to the other, as they each serve a purpose and are case-dependent. Despite this, the efforts in this study have been invested in developing a structured approach to create and streamline the model for health indicator construction. Furthermore, to approach the real-world case application effectively, and also with acknowledgment that the PCA is the most well know and applied technique in the literature [19], any comparisons between the PCA and the other types of unsupervised dimensionality reduction techniques have not been focused in this study.

4   A Real-World Industrial Application from Manufacturing

This section will give the results according to each step of the proposed framework for health indicator construction. Python programming language and its libraries such as Matplotlib and Seaborn for data visualization, Numpy and Pandas for data preprocessing and Sci-kit learn for machine learning are used to apply the proposed framework.

4.1   Data Preprocessing and Feature Extraction

The two bottleneck machines from an engine component line in one of the leading manufacturing industry in Sweden is used as a real-world industrial application in this paper. The industrial high challenging data (high frequency and lack of labels) coming from sensors and control system of the machines (machine programmable logic controllers (PLCs)) are collected by agents, converted into understandable structures and stored in a database system. This database system contains four structured query language (SQL) tables, including "Process Data" and "Vibration Data" from sensors, as well as machine-motor data from the control systems' including "Machine_1" and "Machine_2" tables. According to production and maintenance domain experts, vibration data should be used to generate health indicators because it is significant information when assessing the machine's condition practically. With this information given by the domain experts, the "Process Data" table is not considered for further analysis in this study.

We have vibration measurements such as Acceleration_RMS, Velocity_RMS, and Acceleration_Peak, measured by different sensors on the spindle, spindle-motor, and gearbox of the machine, which is stored in the SQL table Vibration_Data. These measurements have been collected at each 1-s interval for more than one year. Machine-motor data is stored in the SQL databases of Machine_1 and Machine_2, including power consumption, torque drive, and motor temperature. These tables also contain some other values such as event_time, vibration_start_stop, and block_type as well. The scope of the data is given in Table 1. Here, Acceleration_peak (_A_Peak) is a time-domain feature while Acceleration_RMS (_A_RMS) and Velocity_RMS (_V_RMS) are frequency domain features. The difference between the maximum and minimum values of the given time-domain based signals is defined as the Peak [20]. The root mean square (RMS) is used to calculate the signal's overall energy and amplitude [20]. The data from PLCs are used for synchronization and preprocessing with the vibration data. Thereby, the vibration data is extracted at the beginning of each cycle, which means before the machining process starts by incorporating cycle start-stop information from PLCs. The domain experts suggest this period for analysis of the machine's condition without any loading.

After relationships between the measurements given in Table 1 are explored by using visualization techniques and trend analysis based on the average smoothing method, it is observed that the spindle motor acceleration RMS value shows a slightly positive trend. In contrast, gearbox acceleration RMS shows a slightly negative trend in terms of time (cycles). This analysis motivated us to further evaluate each feature based on monotonocity and trendability metrics. It should be noted that the feature set is also normalized before comparing them with each other due to unit differences of the features by using a proper normalization method which is called z-score [21].

Table 1. Data scope.

Number of machines	2
Vibration measurements	Spindle Spindlemotor Gearbox
Computed features(time and frequency domain)	Acceleration_RMS Velocity_RMS Acceleration_Peak
Number of sensor measurements	9
Data resolution	1-s
Period of interest	October 2019 - July 2020

4.2 Feature Selection

A good health indicator is characterized by monotonicity and trendability with respect to time (or cycles), as explained in the Methodology section of the paper. According to the final importance score computed from these two metrics, the features such as Spindle_A_Peak, Spindle_A_RMS, Spindlemotor_A_Peak, Spindlemotor_A_RMS and Gearbox_A_Peak are selected as the most important features for Machine_1. For Machine_2, Spindle_A_Peak, Spindle_A_RMS and Spindlemotor_A_RMS are chosen as the most important features. The feature selection is graphically shown in Fig. 2.

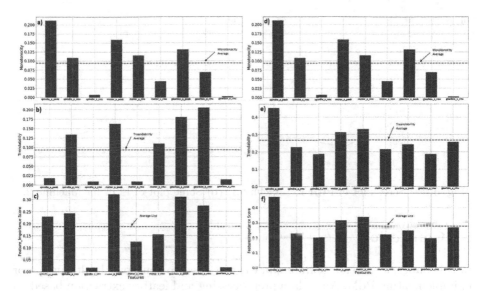

Fig. 2. (a), (d) Monotonocity (b), (e) Trendability and (c), (f) Final feature importance score of Machine_1 and Machine_2.

4.3 Heath Indicator Construction

In this section, the PCA algorithm is used to fuse the selected features for both machines to construct health indicators. In this algorithm, the data is mapped linearly into a lower dimension space to maximize the variance of the data. The covariance matrix for the data is constructed, and the eigenvectors and eigenvalues of the covariance matrix are calculated. Then, based on the inertia shift of the principal component, feasible components are selected. The inertial shift of the principal components can be seen in the scree plot in Fig. 3. The plot is calculated based on the eigenvalues on the ordinate and the number of components on the abscissa. Since there is an inertia shift after two principal components in the scree plot of Machine_1 and Machine_2 and the decay becomes more linear, two optimal components are selected, which explain more than 85% and 95% variation for Machine_1 and Machine_2, successively. Thus, the complex and high dimensional vibration data are simplified and scaled-down, two principal components to be used as health indicators for easily monitoring the performance of the machines over time (cycles). The robustness of the proposed framework is demonstrated in the results by identifying similar features in two identical machines from the same production line. This reflects the degree of assurance that a case-specific health indicator construction may maintain its effectiveness and applicability in real-world industrial settings. In addition, the proposed framework advises and supports practitioners in the decision-making of machine health by visualizing the health indicators in an illustrated manner.

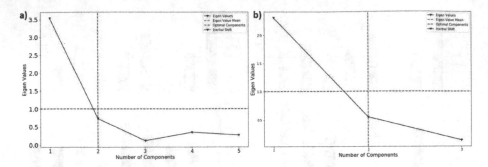

Fig. 3. (a) Scree plot of PCA for Machine_1. (b) Scree plot of PCA for Machine_2.

5   Conclusion

In this paper, a systematic framework is proposed to construct health indicator in implementing PdM. After data preprocessing and feature extraction based on industrial requirements, the most important (informative) features are selected based on their final feature importance score. These selected features are used as inputs into the PCA algorithm for designing suitable health indicators. We demonstrate our results from entirely real-world industrial data during the implementation of the proposed framework, which is a good contribution to fulfil the gap between research and actual industrial practice of PdM by dealing with the challenges such as high dimensionality and lack of labelled data. Therefore, this study would help practitioners in implementing PdM in real-world industrial environments. Further research is required to build predictive models for RUL estimation using the designed health indicators from this study.

Acknowledgement. The authors would like to thank the Production 2030 Strategic Innovation Program funded by VINNOVA for their funding of the research project SUMMIT - SUstainability, sMart Maintenance factory design Testbed (Grant No. 2017-04773), under which this research has been conducted. Thanks also to Anders Ramström and Robert Bergkvist, who supported real-time data from a real-world manufacturing system. This research has been conducted within the Sustainable Production Initiative and Production Area of Advance at the Chalmers University of Technology.

References

1. Bokrantz, J., Skoogh, A., Berlin, C., Wuest, T., Stahre, J.: Smart maintenance: A research agenda for industrial maintenance management. Int. J. Prod. Econ. **224**, 107547 (2020)
2. May, G., et al.: Predictive maintenance platform based on integrated strategies for increased operating life of factories. In: Moon, I., Lee, G.M., Park, J., Kiritsis, D., Cieminski, G.V. (eds.) APMS 2018. IFIP AICT, vol. 536, pp. 279–287. Springer, Cham (2018). https://doi.org/10.1007/978-3-319-99707-0

3. Lee, J., Ni, J., Singh, J., Jiang, B., Azamfar, M., Feng, J.: Intelligent maintenance systems and predictive manufacturing. ASME. J. Manuf. Sci. Eng. **142**(11), 1–23 (2020)
4. Wuest, T., Weimer, D., Irgens, C., Thoben, K.D.: Machine learning in manufacturing: advantages, challenges, and applications. Prod. Manuf. Res. **4**(1), 23–45 (2016)
5. Carvalho, T.P., Soares, F.A., Vita, R., Francisco, R.D.P., Basto, J.P., Alcalá, S.G.: A systematic literature review of machine learning methods applied to predictive maintenance. Comput. Ind. Eng. **137**, 106024 (2019)
6. Jimenez, J.J.M., Schwartz, S., Vingerhoeds, R., Grabot, B., Salaün, M.: Towards multi-model approaches to predictive maintenance: a systematic literature survey on diagnostics and prognostics. J. Manuf. Syst. **56**, 539–557 (2020)
7. Lughofer, E., Mouchaweh, S. M.: Predictive Maintenance in Dynamic Systems, 1st edn. Springer, Switzerland (2019). https://doi.org/10.1007/978-3-030-05645-2
8. Olesen, J.F., Shaker, H.R.: Predictive maintenance for pump systems and thermal power plants: state-of-the-art review, trends and challenges. Sensors **20**(8), 2425 (2020)
9. Zhai, S., Gehring, B., Reinhart, G.: Enabling predictive maintenance integrated production scheduling by operation-specific health prognostics with generative deep learning. J. Manuf. Syst. (2021)
10. Çınar, Z. M., Nuhu, A. A., Zeeshan, Q., Korhan, O., Asmael, M., Safael, B.: Machine learning in predictive maintenance towards sustainable smart manufacturing in industry 4.0. Sustainability **12**(19), 8211 (2020)
11. Guo, L., Li, N., Jia, F., Lei, Y., Lin, J.: A recurrent neural network based health indicator for remaining useful life prediction of bearings. Neurocomputing **240**(31), 98–109 (2017)
12. Fink, O.: Data-driven intelligent predictive maintenance of industrial assets. In: Smith A. (eds) Women in Industrial and Systems Engineering. Women in Engineering and Science, pp. 589–605. Springer, Cham (2019). https://doi.org/10.1007/978-3-030-11866-2_25
13. Lei, Y., Li, N., Guo, L., Li, N., Yan, T., Lin, J.: Machinery health prognostics: a systematic review from data acquisition to RUL prediction. Mech. Syst. Sig. Process. **104**(1), 799–834 (2018)
14. Ning, Y., Wang, G., Yu, J., Jiang, H.: A feature selection algorithm based on variable correlation and time correlation for predicting remaining useful life of equipment using RNN. In: Proceedings of the 2018 Condition Monitoring and Diagnosis (CMD), pp. 1–6. IEEE, Australia (2018)
15. Gittler, T., Scholze, S., Rupenyan, A., Wegener, K.: Machine tool component health identification with unsupervised learning. J. Manuf. Mater. Process. **4**(3), 86 (2020)
16. Schröer, C., Kruse, F., Gómez, J.M.: A systematic literature review on applying CRISP-DM process model. Procedia Comput. Sci. **181**, 526–534 (2021)
17. Saidi, L., Ali, J.B., Bechhoefer, E., Benbouzid, M.: Wind turbine high-speed shaft bearings health prognosis through a spectral Kurtosis-derived indices and SVR. Appl. Acoust. **120**, 1–8 (2020)
18. Bekar, E. T., Nyqvist, P., Skoogh, A.: An intelligent approach for data preprocessing and analysis in predictive maintenance with an industrial case study. Adv. Mech. Eng. **12**(5) (2020)
19. Tharwat, A.: Principal component analysis-a tutorial. Int. J. Appl. Pattern Recognit. **3**(3), 197–240 (2016)

20. Atamuradov, V., Medjaher, K., Camci, F., Zerhouni, N., Dersin, P., Lamoureux, B.: Machine health indicator construction framework for failure diagnostics and prognostics. J. Sign. Process. Syst. **92**, 591–609 (2020)
21. Jain, A., Nandakumar, K., Ross, A.: Score normalization in multimodal biometric systems. Pattern Recognit. **38**(12), 2270–2285 (2005)

Development of Convolutional Neural Network Architecture for Detecting Dangerous Goods for X-ray Aviation Security in Artificial Intelligence

Woong Kim[1] and Chulung Lee[2(✉)]

[1] Department of Industrial Management Engineering, Korea University,
Seoul, Republic of South Korea
woong2241@naver.com
[2] School of Industrial Management Engineering, Korea University,
Seoul, Republic of South Korea
leecu@korea.ac.kr

Abstract. Aviation-security X-ray equipment is used to screen objects, while human screeners re-examine baggage and travelers to detect prohibited objects. Artificial Intelligence technology is applied to increase the accuracy in searching guns and knives, considered the most dangerous in X-ray images at baggage and aviation security screening. Artificial intelligence aviation security X-ray detects objects, finds them rapidly, reducing screeners' labor, thereby providing better service to passengers. In this regard, neural networks based on machine learning have been continuously updated to develop such advanced equipment. In this study, the neural network O-Net is developed to improve object detection. O-Net is developed based on U-Net. The developed O-Net is tested for various neural networks, providing a wide range of experimental results.

Keywords: Artificial intelligence · Machine learning · Aviation security · X-ray detection

1 Introduction and Related Research

The main reason for improving aviation security was the 9/11 terrorist attack. As the attack carried the largest number of fatalities and shocks worldwide, countries began to increase their aviation security [1]. In order to build an intelligent security system, numerous data collection and computing technology concerning aviation security systems have been developed. Safe air freight transportation by restricting the transport of dangerous baggage using X-rays and preparing countermeasures against aircraft terrorism in various ways is being promoted [2]. Passenger safety has increased due to such reinforcement of aviation security. However, a thorough baggage inspection makes travel overseas difficult and causes losses to the airline industry, such as airport entry/exit costs

© IFIP International Federation for Information Processing 2021
Published by Springer Nature Switzerland AG 2021
A. Dolgui et al. (Eds.): APMS 2021, IFIP AICT 632, pp. 609–615, 2021.
https://doi.org/10.1007/978-3-030-85906-0_66

and flight schedule change costs [3, 4]. Particularly, although the security control system has been developed at a professional level, in practice, errors when identifying dangerous substances have been increased due to the increase in work stress and fatigue of aviation security personnel caused by exhaustive immigration controls [5]. In this regard, artificial intelligence has been developed to enable X-rays to reduce the workload of the aviation security personnel as much as possible [6]. In this study, we construct an algorithm for the automatic detection of dangerous goods from X-ray inspection images by applying an artificial neural network.

Aviation security equipment improves aviation services by detecting passengers' carry-on items, checked baggage, oversized baggage, and dangerous or hazardous substances. Artificial intelligence aviation security systems able to detect dangerous objects are constantly evolving, depending on the type of security service. While most equipment detects dangerous goods, X-ray scanning equipment can capture images of the contents inside the luggage. The screener can check for the presence of dangerous goods. Because mistakes occur during the human identification process, screeners have a high probability of error identification. Therefore, image recognition algorithms can help improve the aviation security process and detect dangerous objects from improved X-ray images [7].

X-ray images are expressed by the X-ray transmittance, which is related to density. When no object is present, or the density is low, the image displays white. In contrast, when an object is present, or the density is high, the image displays blue or red with high saturation are [8]. In a situation where objects overlap, the image displays a diagram according to the degree of transmission of X-rays. In addition, all information of the overlapping object is displayed as a visual picture through X-ray. Therefore, visual difficulty, complexity, and overlapping problems are characteristics of X-rays [9–11]. The "overlapping" phenomenon increases the stress of the screener. Thus, various studies considering U-Net structural changes have been developed. For instance, various studies represented the modification and preprocessing of the input image-processing step [12]. In this study, deep learning is implemented to detect dangerous objects such as guns and knives. Moreover, X-ray images that can accurately identify target objects are obtaining by overcoming the limitations of overlapping phenomena in X-ray images. That is, we designed two U-Nets in an O-Net to study the characteristics of the X-ray image.

2   Development of Convolutional Neural Network Architecture

2.1   Neural Network Structure Development: O-Net Structure

O-Net networks are usually composed of fully convolutional networks (FCN) based on the U-Net of semantic divisions. The structure of the encoder-decoder for image segmentation of the O-Net structure is shown in Fig. 1. The numerous layers are multi-channel feature maps. As the neural network layers deepen, the number of parameters can be significantly reduced, considering the characteristics of the layers. The most important step in the network is to copy and crop the 3×3 convolution kernel computed from the multi-channel functional map of the encoder part and connect it from the top to avoid loss of boundary pixels in each convolution process. The reason is that reducing and stretching the input image through the neural network prevents the loss of pixel information. Encoder and decoder reasons can specify the exact location of spatial information. The first image of the input value was a color image, and the second image was a grayscale image. The two images were each trained on a neural network, and the output image was a segmentation map representing the predicted class of each pixel.

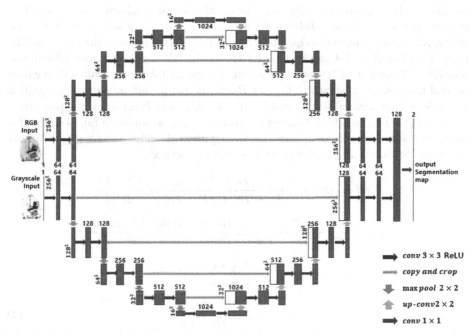

Fig. 1. The first image of the input value was a color image, and the second image was a grayscale image in O-Net structure (Color figure online).

2.2 Performance Measure

When evaluating a model, the *Confusion Matrix* is used to evaluate the precision of the model. How practical and accurate the model classified the image? The confusion matrix is shown in Table 1. Four values define the confusion matrix: True Positive (TP), False Positive (FP), False Negative (FN), and True Negative (TN). TP predicts a correct

Table 1. Confusion matrix

		Actual	
		Positive	Negative
Predicted	Positive	TP	FP
	Negative	FN	TN

answer as true, FP predicts a false answer as true, FN predicts a correct answer as false, and TN predicts a false answer as false [13].

In particular, because the proposed model quantifies the value for each pixel of the semantic segmentation, *Pixel Accuracy* and *m-IoU* evaluation scales are necessary. *Pixel Accuracy* refers to the number of pixels predicting successfully among all pixel classes as follows (1). The model's evaluation index evaluates the pixel-wise predicted values of *Intersection-over-Union (IoU)* as follows (2). *IoU metric*, also known as *Jaccard index*, is basically a method to quantify the percent overlap between the target and the prediction. Therefore, *IoU_i* are denoted by $TP + FP + FN = Ground\ truth \cup Prediction$ and $TP = Ground\ truth \cap Prediction$. *m-IoU* represents IoU as the arithmetic mean of several test images, as shown in Eq. (3). *Precision* and *Recall* are pattern recognition and information retrieval fields using binary classification. *Precision* is the proportion of results classified as relevant among the search results, as shown in Eq. (4). *Recall* is the percentage of items actually searched among items classified as relevant, as follows (5). Both *Precision* and *Recall* rely on measures of relevance.

$$Pixel\ Accuracy = \frac{TP + TN}{TP + TN + FP + FN} = \frac{TP + TN}{Total} \tag{1}$$

$$IoU_i = \frac{TP_i}{TP_i + FP_i + FN_i} = \frac{Ground\ truth \cap Prediction}{Ground\ truth \cup Prediction} \tag{2}$$

$$mIoU = \frac{1}{n}\sum_{i=1}^{n} IoU_i \tag{3}$$

$$Precision = \frac{TP}{TP + FP} \tag{4}$$

$$Recall = \frac{TP}{TP + FN} \tag{5}$$

3 Experiments

3.1 Dataset

The dataset considered image data generated by a large hub airport in Northeast Asia and an international hub airport in Asia. The datasets included dangerous goods and images of the baggage of ordinary passengers. Dataset images were acquired using a HI-SCAN 6040i X-ray machine and a HI-SCAN 6040-2is HR X-ray machine. The X-ray machine was manufactured by Smiths Detection GmbH (Germany). We also checked Realize, Comprehensive, and Randomize to ensure the accuracy of the data. The dataset used 2,000 RGB image data, and the aviation security process data in our study has a relatively large amount of data compared to other studies. The experiment was performed with a training set of 700 images and a validation set of 300 images, with 1,000 images of "Gun" and 1,000 images of "Knife." The experiment was conducted considering epoch 100 and batch size 8.

3.2 Experiment Results

This experiment is restricted to U-Net and O-Net, and the study analysis considers the *Pixel Accuracy, Accuracy, Loss, Precision, Recall*, and *m-IOU* values. The proposed O-Net model experiments related to the gun show a better *Pixel Accuracy* and *m-IoU*, 95.23% and 98.60%, respectively than the U-Net. The "Knife" experiment shows 97.92% pixel accuracy and 90.86% *m-IoU* (Tables 2 and 3).

Table 2. Comparative values of U-Net and O-Net in the Gun scenario

Gun			
Base model	Pixel accuracy	Loss	m-IOU
U-Net	0.9678	0.0172	0.8389
O-Net (proposed model)	**0.9860**	0.0165	**0.9523**

Table 3. Comparative values of U-Net and O-Net in the Knife scenario

Knife			
Base model	Pixel accuracy	Loss	m-IOU
U-Net	0.9522	0.0072	0.8251
O-Net (proposed model)	**0.9792**	0.0054	**0.9086**

Conversely, the O-Net performance index was improved compared to U-Net. In Gun detection, *Pixel Accuracy* and *Recall* increased by approximately 6% and 8%. In the knife detection scenario, the proposed method improved by approximately 7%, and 10%, respectively (Tables 4 and 5).

Table 4. Performance measure of U-Net and O-Net for the Gun scenario

Gun			
Base model	Accuracy	Precision	Recall
U-Net	0.9080	0.9578	0.8853
O-Net (proposed model)	**0.9692**	**0.9802**	**0.9671**

Therefore, the results shows that the proposed O-Net architecture has a very high detection rate of guns and knives with a very high accuracy. Figure 2 shows output results from the proposed model.

Table 5. Performance measure of U-Net and O-Net for the Knife scenario

Knife			
Base model	Accuracy	Precision	Recall
U-Net	0.8652	0.9223	0.8456
O-Net (proposed model)	**0.9352**	**0.9466**	**0.9462**

4 Conclusion

The proposed O-Net network was derived starting from the U-Net to improve its performance. The accuracy of O-Net was 6.56% higher than that of U-Net, showing the excellent performance of O-Net. As shown below, Fig. 2(a) is the original image file with a gun and knife, which are dangerous goods in the baggage, while Fig. 2(b) is the Ground Truth indicating the correct answer. Fig. 2(c) shows an experiment with the O-Net structure.

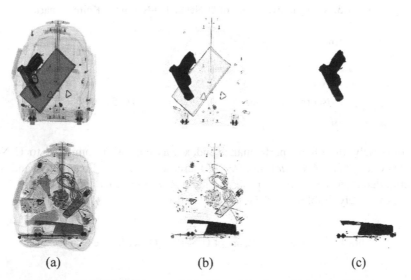

(a)   (b)   (c)

Fig. 2. (a) is Original image, (b) is Ground Truth, and (c) is the O-Net

References

1. The 9/11 Commission Report: The Final Report of the National Commission on Terrorist Attacks upon the United States. Barnes & Noble Publishing, Inc., New York, USA (2004)
2. Klenka, M.: Major incidents that shaped aviation security. J. Transp. Secur. **12**(1–2), 39–56 (2019). https://doi.org/10.1007/s12198-019-00201-2

3. Oum, T.H., Xiaowen, F.: Air transport security user charge pricing: an investigation of flat per-passenger charge vs ad valorem user charge schemes. Transp. Res. Part E Logistics Transp. Rev. **43**(3), 283–293 (2007)

4. Coughlin, C.C., Cohen, J.P., Khan, S.R.: Aviation security and terrorism: a review of the economic issues. Research Department, Federal Reserve Bank of St. Louis (2002)

5. Vagner, J., et al.: Fatigue and stress factors among aviation personel. Acta Avionica **20**, 1335–1947 (2018)

6. Demao, Y., et al.: An auxiliary intelligent identification system for contraband of x-ray machine. In: AOPC 2020, vol. 11565. International Society for Optics and Photonics (2020)

7. International Air Transport Association: IOSA Standards Manual (2019). https://www.iata.org/en/iata-repository/publications/iosa-audit-documentation/iosa-standards-manual-ism-ed-132/

8. Krug, K.D., Aitkenhead, W.F., Eilbert, R.F., Stillson, J.H., Stein J.A.: Detecting explosives or other contraband by employing transmitted and scattered X-rays, U.S. Patent 5 600 700, 4 February (1997)

9. Donnelly, N., Muhl-Richardson, A., Godwin, H., Cave, K.: Using eye movements to understand how security screeners search for threats in X-ray baggage. Vision **3**(2), 24 (2019)

10. Schwaninger, A., Hardmeier, D., Hofer, F.: Aviation security screeners visual abilities & visual knowledge measurement. IEEE Aerosp. Electr. Syst. Mag. **20**, 29–35 (2005)

11. Bolfing, A., Halbherr, T., Schwaninger, A.: How image based factors and human factors contribute to threat detection performance in X-ray aviation security screening. In: Holzinger, A. (ed.) USAB 2008. LNCS, vol. 5298, pp. 419–438. Springer, Heidelberg (2008). https://doi.org/10.1007/978-3-540-89350-9_30

12. Ronneberger, O., Fischer, P., Brox, T.: U-Net: convolutional networks for biomedical image segmentation. In: Navab, N., Hornegger, J., Wells, W.M., Frangi, A.F. (eds.) MICCAI 2015. LNCS, vol. 9351, pp. 234–241. Springer, Cham (2015). https://doi.org/10.1007/978-3-319-24574-4_28

13. Visa, S., Ramsay, B., Ralescu, A.L., Van Der Knaap, E.: Confusion matrix-based feature selection. In: MAICS, vol. 710, pp. 120–127 (2011)

Smart Supply Chain and Production in Society 5.0 Era

Coalition Analysis on Two Manufactures and Two Retailers Supply Chain via Cooperative Game Theory

Taiki Saso and Tatsushi Nishi[✉]

Okayama University, 3-1-1 Tsushima-naka, Kita-ku, Okayama City 700-8530, Japan
nishi.tatsushi@okayama-u.ac.jp

Abstract. In this study, we consider a coalition analysis on the pricing problem for a decentralized supply chain model in which two manufacturers and two retailers with price competitions. In the pricing game, we analyze the equilibrium solutions with perfect competition, grand coalition and partial cooperation between manufacturers and retailers. The results show the externality between coalitions for supply chain members. Therefore, the pricing game is represented as a partition function game. The stable profit allocation in each alliance structure is obtained based on cooperative game theory for the partition function game. We derive the new finding that if there are multiple partial alliances within the same alliance structure, the profit within the partial alliance is smaller than the profit when there is only one partial alliance. Then, it is shown that the pessimistic and optimistic Shapley values of the manufacturers are lower than the optimistic personal alliance value of the manufacturer when the product substitutability is lower and the store substitutability is higher.

Keywords: Supply chain management · Cooperative game theory · Shapley value · Partial coalition

1 Introduction

In recent years, coalition analysis for supply chain management has increased to realize an efficient optimization and collaboration of the entire supply chain. Game theoretical models for supply chain management have been used to analyze cooperation and competition between supply chain members. However, there are some cases that companies partially cooperation in the real world. In addition to the conventional examination of two manufacturers and one retailer, it is important to analyze coalitions for a supply chain consisting of multiple manufacturers and multiple retailers in consideration of competitions between retailers. In this study, we study a supply chain model in which two manufacturers and two retailers which has the minimum number of companies that can consider both competitions, rep- resented by product substitutability and represented by store

© IFIP International Federation for Information Processing 2021
Published by Springer Nature Switzerland AG 2021
A. Dolgui et al. (Eds.): APMS 2021, IFIP AICT 632, pp. 619–628, 2021.
https://doi.org/10.1007/978-3-030-85906-0_67

substitutability. In the pricing game, we analyze both equilibrium solutions with perfect competition and grand coalition and partial cooperation between companies. The stable profit allocation in each alliance structure is obtained based on the cooperative game theory.

Many game-theoretic approaches to supply chain management studies analyze only perfect competition and grand coalition. Conventional supply chain models are limited two manufacturers and one retailer. Choi (1991) studied a supply chain pricing problem for two manufacturers and one retailer, and the case of two producers and one seller become leaders, respectively [1]. Trivedi (1998) studied two manufacturers and two retailers, and the case of two manufacturers and two retailers become leaders, respectively [2]. Feng and Lu (2012) compared the results of the Stackelberg game with the results of the negotiation set for the case of changing the contract form in the case of two manufacturers and two retailers [3]. Chung and Lee (2016) discussed the strategic choices for two manufacturers and one retailer when changing the asymmetric leader-follower relationship structure between manufacturers and retailer [4]. Sakurai (2016) studied the changes in the profit due to changes in the leader-follower relationship structure in the case of two manufacturers and two retailers [5]. Hasegawa (2019) examines the changes in the profits of each company due to changes in the alliance structure in the case of two manufacturers and one retailer in the case of considering partial alliances between companies [6]. Granot and Sosic (2005) examined the changes in the profits of each company due to changes in the alliance structure in the case of three retailers and considering partial alliances between companies [7]. Since there are the supply chain models of two manufacturers and two retailers that considers partial alliances between companies, it is possible that there are a partial alliance between them in the supply chains consisting of multiple manufacturers and retailers in the real world. From the above past studies, it is considered that the profit and stable allocation between companies may change when changing the alliance structure in consideration of partial cooperation between companies. In this study, we extend the supply chain model to four companies from the work conducted by Hasegawa, which consist of two manufacturers and two retailers [6]. The total profit of partial cooperation between companies is examined due to changes in the alliance structure. Manufacturers sells differentiated product to both retailers. The model features both manufacturer competition represented by product substitution. The retail competition is represented by store substitution.

Supply chains with similarly structured two level competitions are commonly observed in practice. For example, both Calvin Klein and Ralph Lauren sell their products to Macy's and Lord and Taylor, two of the largest department stores. The analysis target is the supply chain model that was studied by Trivedi (1998), which also consists of four companies consisting of two manufacturers and two retailers with partial cooperation between companies. In this study, we analyze all possible alliance structures in this supply chain model to study the total profit between companies due to changes in the alliance structure. Also, from the perspective of the total profit of the entire supply chain, it is obvious that integrated decision making through a grand coalition is the most ideal relationship structure. However, when distributing the profits from the whole entity to each individual company, each company has to understand the distribution of the total profit. Therefore, in addition to the analysis of the equilibrium solution, we analyze the stable profit allocation for each company when forming a grand coalition by applying the idea of cooperative game theory. Game theory is explained in more detail in reference [8]. The objective of this study is to consider the stable allocation that can be finally obtained by using the core and Shapley values, which are typical solution concepts of the grand coalition.

2   Model

The supply chain model proposed by Trivedi (1998), which is the model target of this study, is introduced. We consider a pricing game in which a product produced by two competing manufacturers is sold at two competing retailers. See the reference of [9] for more information on the most basic models of the pricing games. In the following, two manufacturers are M1 and M2, and two retailers are R1 and R2. In addition, they may be referred to as M without distinction as manufacturers and R without distinction as retailers. The numbers for this company are for distinguishing between the two companies , and there is no difference in conditions between the two companies. The figure of the two manufacturers and two retailers' model is shown in Fig. 1, and the arrows indicate the flow to the product.

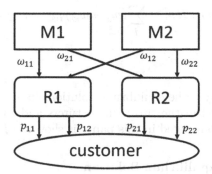

Fig. 1. Two manufacturers and two retailers' model

In this model, two manufacturers produce a different product. Each manufacturer can set a wholesale price to sell the product to two retailers. Two retailers can also set a selling price for each product purchased from a manufacturer to sell it to consumers. The demand of consumer is determined by the demand function described later. This model does not consider the cost of producing the product. The cost of transportation from the manufacturer to the retailer is negligible.

Also, since the demand is decisive, the cost which are the product inventory, raw material inventory, and inventory are stored is not taken into consideration. The products are produced according to the demand determined by the demand function, and all the produced products are supplied to the consumer. The decision variables are the following two types, w_{ij}: wholesale price determined by the manufacturer $(i = 1, 2; j = 1, 2)$, p_{ij}: The selling price determined by the retailer $(i = 1, 2; j = 1, 2)$. Also, the parameters are product substitutability is given $(0 \leq a < 1)$, store substitutability is given as $(0 \leq x < 1)$. Given the demand function and the profit function below that compose the model.

Demand

$$q_{ij} = 1 - p_{ij} + (1 - a)xp_{kj} + a(1 - x)p_{il} + axp_{kl} \tag{1}$$
$$(i = 1, 2; j = 1, 2; k = 3 - i; l = 3 - j)$$

Demand q_{ij}, that is the demand for a product produced by manufacturer j and sold by retailer i, can be seen to decrease as the selling price of the product p_{ij} increases. Also, since the parameters a and x take values from 0 to 1, $a, x, (1 - a), and (1 - x)$ each take a value of 0 or more. Therefore, it can be seen that the higher the selling prices of three types of products p_{il}, p_{kj}, p_{kl} which are sold from the same store and two types of products sold at different stores, the larger the demand q_{ij}.

Profit Function

$$Manufacturer : \Pi_{M_j} = \sum_i w_{ij} q_{ij} \quad (i, j = 1, 2) \tag{2}$$

$$Retailer : \Pi_{R_i} = \sum_j (p_{ij} - w_{ij}) q_{ij} \quad (i, j = 1, 2) \tag{3}$$

3 Analysis

In this study, we analyze the equilibrium solutions in all the alliance structures that can be considered in the two manufacturers and two retailers model. All coalition structures considered in this paper is shown in Fig. 2.

3.1 Analysis of Equilibrium Solution

By using the Nash equilibrium solution, the optimum coefficient and the equilibrium solution can be obtained for each company in the coalition. The procedure for analyzing the equilibrium solution is explained below.

STEP 1. If a partial cooperation exists, the sum of the objective functions of the companies participating in the cooperation is the objective function of the coalition group.

STEP 2. Find the Nash equilibrium solution by partially differentiating with the determinants of each company or group of companies and solving simultaneous equations.

Table 1. Definition of the profit function for each coalition structure

coalition structure	Profit function
MM-R-R	$\Pi_{MM}^{MM-R-R} + \Pi_{R}^{MM-R-R} + \Pi_{R}^{MM-R-R}$
M-M-RR	$\Pi_{RR}^{M-M-RR} + \Pi_{M}^{M-M-RR} + \Pi_{M}^{M-M-RR}$
MM-RR	$\Pi_{MM}^{MM-RR} + \Pi_{RR}^{MM-RR}$
MR-M-R	$\Pi_{MR}^{MR-M-R} + \Pi_{M}^{MR-M-R} + \Pi_{R}^{MR-M-R}$
MR-MR	$\Pi_{MR}^{MR-MR} + \Pi_{MR}^{MR-MR}$
MMR-R	$\Pi_{MMR}^{MMR-R} + \Pi_{R}^{MMR-R}$
M-MRR	$\Pi_{MRR}^{M-MRR} + \Pi_{M}^{M-MRR}$
MMRR	Π_{MMRR}^{MMRR}

The notation of the profit function for each coalition structure is shown in Table 1. The coalition structure MM-R-R means that manufacturer cooperation (MM) with two decentralized retailers R-R. In this case, the profit function of the two manufacturer MM in the sense of coalition MM-R-R is written by Π_{MM}^{MM-R-R} and the profit function for decentralized retailer is written by Π_{R}^{MM-R-R}. The total profit for the coalition structure is $\Pi_{MM}^{MM-R-R} + \Pi_{R}^{MM-R-R} + \Pi_{R}^{MM-R-R}$. The superscript of Π is the coalition structure of the game and the subscript of Π is the cooperating group companies or a single company.

3.2 Analytical Results

The following propositions can be mentioned as new findings obtained in this study.

[Proposition]

The following relationship holds for the equilibrium solution of the profits of companies that have the same alliance.

$$\hat{\Pi}_{MM}^{MM-R-R} \geq \hat{\Pi}_{MM}^{MM-RR} \tag{4}$$

$$\hat{\Pi}_{RR}^{M-M-RR} \geq \hat{\Pi}_{RR}^{MM-RR} \tag{5}$$

$$\hat{\Pi}_{MR}^{MR-M-R} \geq \hat{\Pi}_{MR}^{MR-MR} \tag{6}$$

where $\hat{\Pi}$ is the equilibrium solution.

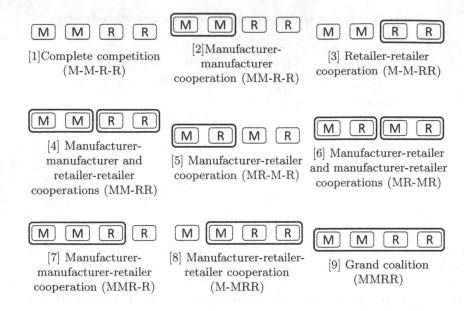

Fig. 2. All coalition structures

[Proof]

$$\hat{\Pi}_{MM}^{MM-R-R} - \hat{\Pi}_{MM}^{MM-RR} = \frac{4x(6ax - 6a - x + 6)}{9(ax - a - x + 1)(3ax - 3a - x + 3)^2} \geq 0 \quad (7)$$

(equality holds when $x = 0$)

$$\hat{\Pi}_{RR}^{M-M-RR} - \hat{\Pi}_{RR}^{MM-RR} = \frac{4a(6ax - a - 6x + 6)}{9(ax - a - x + 1)(3ax - a - 3x + 3)^2} \geq 0 \quad (8)$$

(equality holds when $a = 0$)

The calculated values of $\hat{\Pi}_{MR}^{MR-M-R} - \hat{\Pi}_{MR}^{MR-MR}$ are shown in Fig. 3. It can be seen that $\hat{\Pi}_{MR}^{MR-M-R} - \hat{\Pi}_{MR}^{MR-MR} \geq 0$ from Fig. 3. Accordingly,

$$\hat{\Pi}_{MR}^{MR-M-R} - \hat{\Pi}_{MR}^{MR-MR} = \cdots \geq 0$$

(equality holds when $a = 0, x = 0, \dots$ is omitted due to the huge number of expressions)

From the proposition, we obtained the new findings that could not be obtained in the two manufacturers and one retailer model that the profit within a partial cooperation is greater in a alliance structure that includes only one partial cooperation than in a alliance structure that includes multiple partial cooperations. From this, it is considered that the existence of multiple partial cooperations is disadvantageous for the companies within the partial coopera-tion.

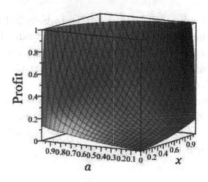

Fig. 3. $\hat{\Pi}_{MR}^{MR-M-R} - \hat{\Pi}_{MR}^{MR-MR}$

4   Allocation Analysis

Based on the equilibrium solution obtained in the analysis in the previous section, the idea of cooperative game theory is utilized to analyze the stable allocation in each alliance structure. We examine the stability of the allocation using the concept of the Shapley value, which is the allocation obtained from the contribution of the player and the core which is a collection of allocations that are not controlled by any allocation.

The core, Shapley value, and bargaining set are defined on the game of characteristic function and should be applied to the partition function game. When $v_{\min}^P(S) = \min\{v^P(S), P \ni S\}$, $v_{\max}^P(S) = \max\{v^P(S), P \ni S\}$, the core under pessimistic conjecture C^{pes} and the core under optimistic conjecture C^{opt} in the partition function game are given by the following equations, respectively.

$$C^{pes} = \{x| \sum_{i \in S} x_i \geq v_{\min}^P(S) \forall S \subset N, \sum_{i \in N} x_i = v^{P^N}(N)\} \tag{9}$$

$$C^{opt} = \{x| \sum_{i \in S} x_i \geq v_{\max}^P(S) \forall S \subset N, \sum_{i \in N} x_i = v^{P^N}(N)\} \tag{10}$$

The Shapley value in the game of characteristic function (N, v) is given by the following equation.

$$\phi_i = \sum_{S \subset N} \frac{(s-1)!(n-s)!}{n!} [v(S) - v(S - \{i\})] \tag{11}$$

The following results were obtained as new findings in this study. The Shapley values of pessimistic and optimistic manufacturers are shown in Fig. 4, and the analysis results of pessimistic core and Shapley values are shown in Fig. 5. The analysis results of optimistic core and Shapley value are shown in Fig. 6.

The Shapley value of pessimistic and optimistic manufacturers is shown in yellow, and the individual partnership value of optimistic manufacturers is shown in red.

Figure 4 shows that when a is small and x is large, the Shapley value of the pessimistic and optimistic manufacturer is lower than the optimistic personal alliance value. This means that the manufacturers have not made a sufficient contribution to the grand coalition. This is because there may be competition between retailers due to the fact that there are two retailers. Therefore, if the sellers are competing and the manufacturers are not competing (x is large, a is small), manufacturers can set higher wholesale prices, so their profits increase. Therefore, it is considered that the optimistic personal alliance value M^+ exceeds the Shapley value when a is small and x is large.

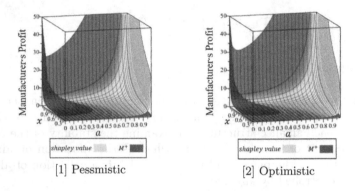

[1] Pessmistic   [2] Optimistic

Fig. 4. Shapley value of manufacturers (Color figure online)

In the graph below, M^- and R^- (red) is the lower limit of the core, M^+ and R^+ (blue) is the upper limit of the core, and yellow is the Shapley value.

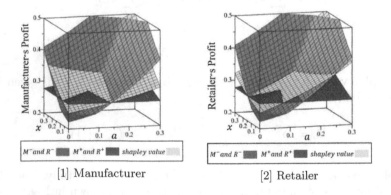

[1] Manufacturer   [2] Retailer

Fig. 5. Pessimistic core and Shapley value (Color figure online)

The analytical results of the pessimistic core and Shapley value of the manufacturer and the retailer are shown in Fig. 5. It can be confirmed that the core is

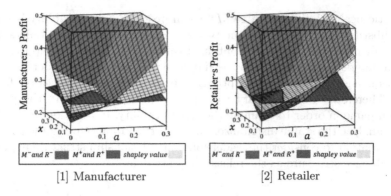

[1] Manufacturer   [2] Retailer

Fig. 6. Optimistic core and Shapley value (Color figure online)

not empty, when a and x are close to 0 in both the manufacturer and the retailer. In other words, it shows that when a grand coalition is formed, there is an allocation that allows all companies to make more profits than if they formed an alliance of two or a three companies. In other ranges, the core is empty because the magnitude relations of M^- and R^- and M^+ and R^+ are swapped. This means that there are some companies that can make more profits by forming an alliance of two or three companies than the allocation when forming a grand coalition. It can be seen that the Shapley value may exist outside the core in the region where both a and x are close to 0. In other words, profits based on the degree of contribution to the alliance cannot be a stable distribution in the core sense.

Then, the analysis results of the optimistic core and Shapley values of the manufacturer and the retailer are shown in Fig. 6. It has he same tendency as Fig. 5. In other words, it shows that when a grand coalition is formed, there is an allocation that allows all companies to make more profits than if they formed an alliance of two or a three companies alliance, and the profits based on the degree of contribution to the alliance cannot be a stable distribution in the core sense.

5   Conclusion

In this study, we analyzed the equilibrium solution of a supply chain consisting of two manufacturers and two retailers using a cooperative game theory. For all alliance structures, the changes of the total profit between companies due to changes in the alliance structure were examined. As a result, we have obtained a new finding that if there are multiple partial alliances within the same alliance structure, the profit within the partial alliance will be smaller than if there is only one partial alliance. Beside, the stable distribution that can be finally obtained was examined by using the concept of core and Shapley value, which is a typical solution concept of the grand coalition. As a result, we have a new finding that the Shapley value of pessimistic and optimistic manufacturers fall below the optimistic personal alliance value M^+ when product substitutability is low and store substitutability is high in the two manufacturers and two retailers model. The result of the Shapley value obtained this time is pseudo by applying it to the characteristic function game based on the idea of the core under pessimistic prediction and the core under optimistic prediction in the partition function game. Therefore, it is necessary to apply the Shapley value to the partition function game in order to examine the strict stability. In addition, it is a future task to analyze the stable distribution in the partial alliance using the concept of the negotiation to consider the leader-follower relationship structure in addition to the alliance structure as the relationship structure.

References

1. Choi, S.C.: Price competition in a channel structure with a common retailer. Mark. Sci. **10**(4), 271–296 (1991)
2. Trivedi, M.: Distribution channels: an extension of exclusive retailership. Manage. Sci. **44**(7), 896–909 (1998)
3. Feng, Q., Lu, L.X.: Supply chain contracting under competition: bilateral bargaining vs. stackelberg. Prod. Oper. Manag. **22**(3), 1–19 (2012)
4. Chung, H., Lee, E.: Asymmetric relationships with symmetric suppliers: strategic choice of supply chain price leadership in a competitive market. Eur. J. Oper. Res. **259**(2), 564–575 (2017)
5. Sakurai, S., Nishi, T.: Game theoretical analysis of supply chain configurations. In: Proceedings of 2016 International Conference on Industrial Engineering and Engineering Management, pp. 836–840 (2016)
6. Hasegawa, M.: Coalition analysis by cooperative game theory with partial coalition in two manufacturers and one common retailer. Master thesis, Graduate School of Engineering Science, Osaka University (2019)
7. Granot, D., Sosic, G.: Formation of alliances in internet-based supply exchanges. Manage. Sci. **51**(1), 92–105 (2005)
8. Suzuki, M.: "New Game Theory", Keiso Shobou (1994)
9. Kogan, K., Tapiero, C.S.: Supply Chain Games: Operations Management and Risk Valuation. Springer (2007). https://doi.org/10.1007/978-0-387-72776-9

Supply Chain Optimization Through Cooperative Negotiation by Using Backward Scheduling

Yoshitaka Tanimizu[1](✉) and Rika Kanbara[2]

[1] Waseda University, 3-4-1 Okubo Shinjuku-ku, Tokyo 169-8555, Japan
tanimizu@waseda.jp
[2] Osaka Prefecture University, 1-1 Gakuen-Cho Naka-ku, Sakai Osaka 599-8531, Japan

Abstract. In recent years, mass customization is an important issue in manufacturing industries. They may require a make-to-order (MTO) manufacturing system throughout the whole supply chain. Our previous researches proposed a basic three-layered supply chain model for dynamic configuration of supply chains including an MTO manufacturing system. The model consists of three model components named a client, a manufacturer, and a supplier. A negotiation process among the model components were proposed in order to enter into a lot of contracts. This paper presents a cooperative negation method between a manufacturer and a supplier. The objective is to provide a negotiation method for entering into a large amount of contracts with a client. A manufacturer adjusts the requirement of part order for a supplier by reallocating manufacturing operations backwards from the delivery time required by a client. We developed a prototype of simulation system for a three-layered supply chain. We carried out large number of computational experiments by changing experimental conditions and verified the effectiveness of the proposed negotiation method.

Keywords: Supply chain configuration · Make-to-Order (MTO) manufacturing · Job-shop scheduling · Backward scheduling · Cooperative negation

1 Introduction

Mass customization is attracting the attention of manufacturing industries, since customers need various products. Conversion from an MTS (make-to-stock) manufacturing system to an MTO (make-to-order) manufacturing system is required for not only a single company but also a group of companies in a supply chain. Recent advantages in Internet technology have enabled a dynamic configuration of supply chains [1]. Independent but cooperative relationships between manufacturing companies can make large profits in the supply network.

We developed a dynamic supply chain model including an MTO manufacturing system [2, 3]. Without a specific leader such as an automobile final assembly company, all the companies in a supply chain should be cooperatively negotiated with each other

© IFIP International Federation for Information Processing 2021
Published by Springer Nature Switzerland AG 2021
A. Dolgui et al. (Eds.): APMS 2021, IFIP AICT 632, pp. 629–636, 2021.
https://doi.org/10.1007/978-3-030-85906-0_68

in order for all the companies to obtain a large profit. The companies in a supply chain repeatedly send orders and offers to determine a suitable price and delivery time of the products which customers need.

Our previous researches proposed a negotiation method among the three model components. In this research, we improve the negotiation method between a supplier and a manufacturer in the supply chain model to obtain a large profit by entering into a lot of contracts. A manufacturer adjusts the required delivery time of parts by estimating a lower bound of the earliest starting time of manufacturing operations in the manufacturer's production schedule through backward scheduling.

2   Literature Review

Most of the existing researches about supply chain management deal with an MTS manufacturing system. In recent years, the supply chain models including an MTO manufacturing system are proposed by some researches, such as Robinson et al. [4], Sahin and Robinson [5], Li et al. [6], Aboolian et al. [7]. The MTO supply chain models proposed dynamic scheduling procedures. Decentralized negotiation processes control the entire supply chain without a specific leader company. A competitive negotiation approach such as a game theory is proposed to divide profits accurately in the supply chain. A cooperative negotiation approach should be considered not only to divide profits but also to increase profits for the entire supply chain.

3   Dynamic Supply Chain Model

3.1 Basic Model Components

In general, there are a large number of manufacturing companies in a supply network as shown in Fig. 1. Dynamic configuration of supply chains is considered for each order to create appropriate supply chains. Manufacturing companies, including MTO manufacturing systems, send and receive orders and offers of parts and products for entering into profitable contracts. Most companies in the supply network receive orders from lower-tier companies and create orders to higher-tier companies. On the other hand, the companies receive offers from higher-tier companies and make offers to lower-tier companies.

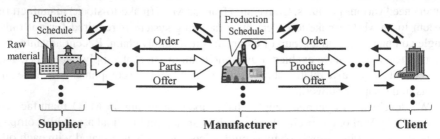

Fig. 1. A supply network includes a large number of manufacturing companies. Dynamic configuration of supply chains is considered for each order to create appropriate supply chains.

Our previous researches propose a basic dynamic supply chain model which consists three model components, those are a client, a manufacturer, and a supplier, as shown in Fig. 2. A client represents a customer which generates an order of a product. The order includes the information about the required delivery time and price of the product. It is sent to manufacturers. A manufacturer is a manufacturing company which machines and assemblies some parts to make a product. An order of a part is created based on the manufacturer's production schedule and the received order from a client. A supplier is a part manufacturing company which produce parts based on both its production schedule and the received orders from Manufactures.

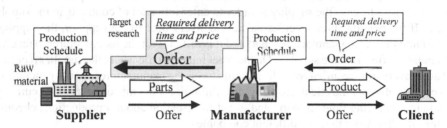

Fig. 2. A three-layered dynamic supply chain model consists of three kinds of model components which are a client, a manufacturer, and a client as a basic model.

3.2 Previous Negotiation Process Among Model Components

A client can enter into a contract with a manufacturer, when an offer sent from the manufacturer is satisfied with an order from the client. The offered price of a product is equal to or less than the required one. In addition, the offered delivery time of a product is equal to or shorter than the required one. When the client accepts the offer from the manufacturer, the Manufacture can also enter into a contract with the supplier. The manufacturer accepts the offer sent from the supplier. Both the Manufacture and the supplier make a profit by the contract.

The supplier can reject an order from the manufacturer, if the supplier evaluates that the order cannot be profitable. The supplier should pay a penalty charge for delays in the delivery time. The manufacturer permits a delay of a part but requires a penalty charge for the delay. If the required delivery time suggested from the manufacturer is too early for all suppliers, no offer from the suppliers can be received by the manufacturer. In this case, the manufacturer cannot generate an offer to the client, and loses the chance of a contract. The manufacturer and client need to determine the required delivery times of parts and products respectively in consideration of their production schedules accurately, and suggest the penalty charge due to delays.

The manufacture estimates a feasible delivery time when the supplier can generate and deliver a part to the manufacturer. The estimated feasible delivery time dt of a part is used as the required delivery time which sent to the supplier. Furthermore, the manufacturer uses the estimated feasible delivery time as the earliest starting time est of a product for optimizing the manufacturer's production schedule. No manufacturing operations of a product can be allocated before the earliest starting time in the production schedule. Our previous researches proposed the following equation for determining the feasible delivery time by using the sum of the estimated processing times *spt* of parts in the supplier. The parameter T means a present time. A coefficient value α represents the margin of delivery time.

$$dt_n = T + \alpha \times \sum_{j=1}^{J} spt_{n,j} \leq est_n \tag{1}$$

The appropriate delivery time of a part should be determined and required as an order by the manufacturer to the supplier in order to enter into a lot of contracts in the supply chain. If the manufacturer specifies an early delivery time to the supplier, the supplier loses enough time to manufacture a part and it is difficult for the manufacturer to receive a beneficial offer from the supplier. On the other hand, in case where the supplier receives a late delivery time required from the manufacturer, the manufacturer cannot generate an acceptable offer for the client. However, it is difficult for the manufacturer to accurately estimate processing times of parts and to get information about a production schedule of the supplier, since they are different companies.

3.3 Adjustment of the Required Delivery Time

This research proposes a negotiation method for creating a profitable order from a manufacturer to a supplier. The order includes a delivery time suitable for both a manufacturer and a supplier in order to enter into a lot of contracts and improve the profits of the whole supply chain.

A manufacturer tightens or relaxes the required delivery time of a part to the lower bound in its production schedule, after the production schedule is optimized through the scheduling process. The adjustment process of the required delivery time is summarized as follows.

1. When a manufacturer receives a new order of a product from a client, the manufacturer estimates an earliest starting time of the product based on Eq. 1 and makes a production schedule by using a genetic algorithm. All manufacturing operations of the product are assigned after the earliest starting time in the production schedule.
2. The manufacturing operations in the production schedule are reallocated backwards from the delivery time required by the client. When the latest finishing time of the product is later than the delivery time required by the client, the manufacturer moves the manufacturing operations forward and tightens the required delivery time of a part, as shown in Fig. 3. On the other hand, the latest finishing time of the product is earlier than the delivery time required by the client, the manufacturer moves the manufacturing operations backwards without changing the loading sequences of the manufacturing operations in the production schedule. Then, the required delivery time of a part are relaxed from the initial condition.
3. The earliest starting time is modified and estimated by the reallocated manufacturing operations. Then, it represents a new value of the required delivery time sent by the manufacturer to the supplier.

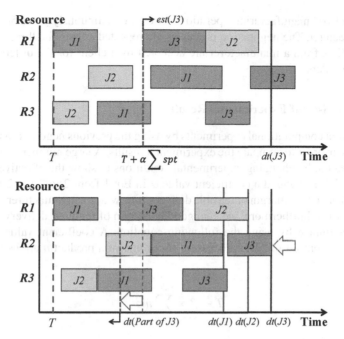

Fig. 3. A manufacturer's production schedule contains three jobs consisting of three manufacturing operations. After the schedule of the third job $J3$ is optimized, the manufacturing operations of $J3$ are moved forward from the delivery time required by the client.

When the delivery time required by the client is early, the manufacturer requires the supplier to deliver a part early. The supplier makes an effort to the requirement by improving its production schedule, and creates a beneficial offer for entering into a contract with the manufacturer. On the other hand, when the delivery time required by the client is late, the required delivery time of a part is relaxed by the manufacturer compared to the initial condition. The supplier can reduce the penalty charge for delay, and gain a profit. The manufacturer can receive a beneficial offer from the supplier, and enter into a lot of contracts with the client.

4 Computational Experiments

4.1 Development of a Supply Chain Simulation System

We developed a prototype of a supply chain simulation system by using an object-oriented language Smalltalk. The prototype system was implemented on a Windows-based personal computer having a 3.16 GHz Intel Core2 processor with 2 GB of RAM. Three model components, which were a supplier, a manufacturer, and a client, were described in the simulation system.

In the initial conditions, a manufacturer had a job-shop type production schedule consisting of 10 manufacturing resources, 20 jobs, and 200 manufacturing operations. A supplier had a job-shop type production schedule consisting of 5 manufacturing resources,

20 jobs, and 100 manufacturing operations. A client continuously gives 50 new orders to a manufacturer. The negotiation processes are repeated among the three components until the offers from a manufacturer are accepted by a client for the orders or a client cancels the orders.

4.2   Comparison of Experimental Results

We carried out computational experiments by using the previous negotiation method and the new one in order to compare the experimental results. A large number of experiments were carried out by changing experimental conditions to show the effectiveness of the new method. We changed a coefficient value α in Eq. 1 from 2 to 20 in 2 increments. Then, we changed the margin of feasible delivery time which a manufacturer estimated in the experiments. Furthermore, we changed the margin of required delivery time which a client determined by using the following equation. A coefficient value β in Eq. 2 was changed from 2 to 6. The processing times mpt of a product n are estimated by a manufacturer.

$$T + \beta \times \sum_{j=1}^{J} mpt_{n,j} \tag{2}$$

Experimental results of the previous negotiation method are summarized in a bar chart as shown in Fig. 4. The variation of α is arranged in the horizontal direction, and the variation of β is arranged in the depth direction. The vertical axis represents the average number of contracts which are additionally accepted by a client. Each bar shows the average number of contracts obtained by 10 experiments under each condition. The experimental results show that the number of contracts decrease as the coefficient value α increases especially when the coefficient value β is small. For example, most of the orders from the client cannot enter into contracts on the condition that α is about 20 and β is about 2. The reason is that the manufacturer has relaxed the requirements for delivery times of parts to the supplier, even though the client has shortened the required delivery times of products to the manufacturer. These results mean that the profit in the whole supply chain decreases when a manufacturer estimates the longer margin of processing times of a supplier.

Figure 5 summarizes experimental results of the newly proposed negotiation method. The average number of additional contracts through 10 times of experiments under each condition is represented on the vertical axis. The experimental results show that both the manufacturer and the supplier can enter into a lot of contracts independent of the variation of the coefficient value α. For example, even if the value α is about 20, many orders from the client can enter into contracts. These results mean that the profit in the whole supply chain is stable even if a manufacturer estimates the longer or shorter margin of processing times of a supplier without considering the processing times accurately. A manufacturer does not need to know the exact processing times of suppliers. This negotiation method can be one of the useful approach for operating an MTO decentralized supply chain which each company in the supply network can make decisions independently under the limited information sharing.

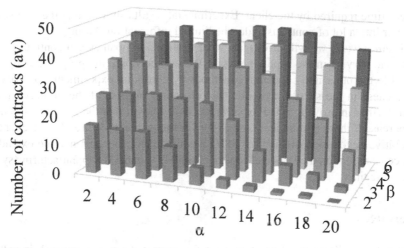

Fig. 4. This bar chart summarizes experimental results by using the previous negotiation method which determines the required delivery time of parts based on the sum of the estimated processing time of a supplier by a manufacturer.

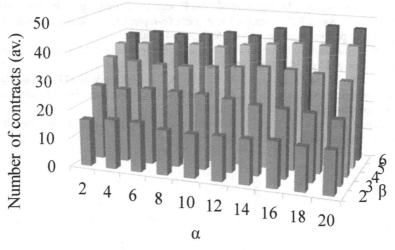

Fig. 5. This bar chart shows experimental results by using the proposed negotiation method which determines the required delivery time of a part by reallocating manufacturing operations backwards in the manufacturer's schedule from the required delivery time by the client.

5 Conclusion

This research proposed a cooperative negotiation method between a supplier and a manufacturer. A manufacturer adjusts the required delivery time of a part by reallocating manufacturing operations backwards in a manufacturer's production schedule from the delivery time required by the client. Experimental results showed that the supply chain can enter into a lot of contracts under the limited information sharing.

In future work, we will investigate what strategic companies can continue to make profits and survive in the supply network. We will compare the proposed cooperative method to the other non-cooperative methods by computer experiments to verify their effectiveness in the supply network. The relaxation process of the proposed method can be further improved, as the experiments have shown that the number of contracts can increase if there is sufficient time to deliver the product required by the client. The cooperative negotiation method for MTO manufacturing systems may be extended to advanced negotiation methods that consider both MTO and MTS manufacturing systems at the same time.

References

1. Piramuthu, S.: Knowledge-based framework for automated dynamic supply chain configuration. Eur. J. Oper. Res. **165**(1), 219–230 (2005)
2. Tanimizu, Y., et al.: Computational evaluation of order selection methods in dynamic supply chains. Procedia CIRP **3**, 281–286 (2012)
3. Tanimizu, Y.: Dynamic supply chain management for lean manufacturing. In: Handbook of Research on Design and Management of Lean Production Systems, pp. 358–388 (2014)
4. Robinson, E.P., Sahin, F., Li-Lian, G.: The impact of e-replenishment strategy on make-to-order supply chain performance. Decis. Sci. **36**(1), 33–64 (2005)
5. Sahin, F., Robinson, E.P.: Information sharing and coordination in make-to-order supply chains. J. Oper. Manag. **23**(6), 579–598 (2005)
6. Li, Y., Cheng, Y., Hu, Q., Zhou, S., Ma, L., Lim, K.: The influence of additive manufacturing on the configuration of make-to-order spare parts supply chain under heterogeneous demand. Int. J. Prod. Res. **57**(11), 3622–3641 (2019)
7. Aboolian, R., Berman, O., Wang, J.: Responsive make-to-order supply chain network design. Nav. Res. Logist. **68**(2), 241–258 (2020)

A Proposal of Scheduling Method Based on Decision Criteria Considering Electric Power Costs and Productivity

Masayuki Yabuuchi[1]([☒]), Toshiya Kaihara[1], Nobutada Fujii[1], Daisuke Kokuryo[1], Mio Nonaka[2], and Kotone Senju[2]

[1] Graduate School of System Informatics, Kobe University,
1-1 Rokkodai-cho, Nada, Kobe, Hyogo 657-8501, Japan
yabuuchi@kaede.cs.kobe-u.ac.jp, kaihara@kobe-u.ac.jp,
nfujii@phoenix.kobe-u.ac.jp, kokuryo@port.kobe-u.ac.jp
[2] Mitsubishi Electric Corporation, 8-1-1 Tsukaguchi-honmachi,
Amagasaki, Hyogo 661-0001, Japan
Nonaka.Mio@dc.MitsubishiElectric.co.jp,
Senju.Kotone@ak.MitsubishiElectric.co.jp

Abstract. In recent years, the price of electricity in Japan has increased, and then manufacturing industries are required to implement production plan in consideration of the electric power costs. In response to this demand, production scheduling has to be implemented in consideration of several decision criteria such as productivity and electric power costs. In this paper, we propose a production scheduling with satisficing trade-off method in order to maintain productivity and reduce electricity costs, and evaluate the effectiveness of the proposed method.

Keywords: Production scheduling · Electric power costs · Satisficing trade-off method

1 Introduction

In Japan, the price of electricity has increased due to the change in the ratio of thermal power generation since the Great East Japan Earthquake [1]. In the manufacturing industry, the production activities are performed in consideration of reduction of the electric power costs such as peak shifting. Furthermore, in order to reduce the electric power costs, the manufacturing industry is considering the introduction of Energy Management System (EMS), the renewal and installation of energy-efficient equipment, and the production scheduling for electricity cost saving [2]. We have so far focused on the relationship between productivity and electricity in production lines, and proposed an optimized scheduling method that considers the total weighted productivity and electricity [3]. However, it was not clear how to set the weighting factor for multiobjective optimization problem in consideration of the various decision criteria. In order to solve this issue, we focus on the Satisficing Trade-Off Method (STOM), which is one of the

© IFIP International Federation for Information Processing 2021
Published by Springer Nature Switzerland AG 2021
A. Dolgui et al. (Eds.): APMS 2021, IFIP AICT 632, pp. 637–645, 2021.
https://doi.org/10.1007/978-3-030-85906-0_69

multi-objective optimization technique. STOM is an optimization method that is satisfied with the multiple decision criteria [4], and is applied to scheduling problems and layout optimization problems [5, 6]. In this paper, we propose a scheduling method using STOM that can simultaneously consider to reduce electric power costs and to maintain productivity. The computational experiments are carried out to evaluate the performance of the proposed method.

2 Target Model

In this paper, our target model is a flexible flow shop type production line including EMS as shown in Fig. 1. The electric power costs are different depending on the time range. The length of planning period, the number of jobs and the processing time of each job are determined in advance as practical case. The features of the stage, job, and machine in this paper are described as follows:

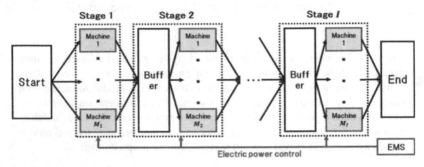

Fig. 1. A schematic diagram of the target model

Stage:

- There are multiple machines in each stage.
- There is no capacity of each buffer between connected stages.

Machine:

- All machines can be used from the start of production.
- Each machine can process all jobs, but the ability such as processing time and electric power consumption differs depending on the machine.
- During the planning period, the state of each machine is either processing or idle, and the electric power consumption differs depending on the state.
- No interruption occurs during job processing.
- No machine failure occurs.
- Setup time is not considered.

Job:

- All jobs are known at the beginning of the production.
- Each job is assigned to only one machine in each stage, and each machine can process at most one job at a time.
- The job in a certain stage is started after the processing completion time in the previous stage.

3 Proposal of Scheduling Method Based on Decision Criteria Considering Electric Power Costs and Productivity

In production scheduling, it is important to obtain the appropriate solution in practical time even if the optimal solution cannot be acquired. Thus, we propose the scheduling method applying STOM in considering of various decision criteria such as electric power costs and productivity [4]. In the proposed method, the ideal level, which consists of the ideal value of each decision criteria and the aspiration level which is the satisfaction solution of each decision criteria, are set, and a solution which is satisfied for aspiration level is obtained. The algorithm of proposed method is described in Sect. 3.2, and the formulation of scheduling within the algorithm is shown in Sect. 3.3.

3.1 Notation

The definition of the characters used in the formulation is as follows:
Parameters

- j, k : job number $(j, k = 1, \ldots, J)$
- i : stage number $(i = 1, \ldots, I)$
- l : machine number $(l = 1, \ldots, M_i)$
- t : timeslot number $(t = 0, \ldots, T - 1)$
- a : state number $(a = 1, \ldots, A)$

In this paper, there are two states: processing and idle, where $a = 1$ represents processing and $a = 2$ represents idle.

- P_{ilj} : processing time of job j at machine l on stage i
- EC_{ila} : electric power consumption of state a at machine l on stage i
- $Rate_t$: electricity charges at time t
- $f_{c_{max}}^{best}$: ideal level of makespan
- f_{cost}^{best} : ideal level of electric power costs
- $\bar{f}_{c_{max}}$: aspiration level of makespan
- $\bar{f}_{cost}$: aspiration level of electric power costs
- $w_{c_{max}} = \frac{1}{\bar{f}_{c_{max}} - f_{c_{max}}^{best}}$: weighting factor of makespan
- $w_{cost} = \frac{1}{\bar{f}_{cost} - f_{cost}^{best}}$: weighting factor of electric power costs
- α : weighting factor used for objective function
- $BigM$: large constant for constraints

Variables

- $C_{max} \in \mathbb{N} \cup \{0\}$: makespan (total time from the start time of the planning period to the end time of the last job)
- $Cost \in \mathbb{R}_0^+$: electric power costs
- $s_{ilj} \in \mathbb{N} \cup \{0\}$: start time of job j at machine l on stage i
- $c_{ilj} \in \mathbb{N} \cup \{0\}$: completion time of job j at machine l on stage i
- $e_t \in \mathbb{R}_0^+$: electric power consumption at time t
- x_{iljk} : $\begin{cases} 1 : \text{if job } j \text{ precedes job } k \text{ at machine } l \text{ on stage } i \\ 0 : \qquad\qquad\qquad \text{otherwise} \end{cases}$
- y_{iljt} : $\begin{cases} 1 : \text{if job } j \text{ starts to process at time } t \text{ at machine } l \text{ on stage } i \\ 0 : \qquad\qquad\qquad \text{otherwise} \end{cases}$
- ms_{ilat} : $\begin{cases} 1 : \text{if machine } l \text{ on stage } i \text{ is in state } a \text{ at time } t \\ 0 : \qquad\qquad\qquad \text{otherwise} \end{cases}$
- mp_{iljt} : $\begin{cases} 1 : \text{if job } j \text{ is processing at time } t \text{ at machine } l \text{ on stage } i \\ 0 : \qquad\qquad\qquad \text{otherwise} \end{cases}$
- $z \in \mathbb{R}$: auxiliary variable

In our proposed method, y_{iljt} is decision variable.

3.2 Algorithm of Proposed Method

In the proposed method using STOM, the purpose is to schedule based on the decision maker's value judgment, and obtain a schedule that the decision maker is satisfied with. The algorithm of proposed method is as follows.

STEP1. Set the ideal levels $f_{C_{max}}^{best}$ and f_{cost}^{best}, and show them to the decision maker. Each ideal level is set as the optimized solution in each single objective optimization problem.
STEP2. Decision maker determines the aspiration levels $\bar{f}_{C_{max}}$ and $\bar{f}_{cost}$. The aspiration level is the value the decision maker is satisfied.
STEP3. Solve the optimization problem shown in Sect. 3.3 and find the closest Pareto-optimal solution to the aspiration level given by the decision maker and show it to the decision maker.
STEP4. If the decision maker is satisfied with the shown schedule, the process ends. Otherwise, return to **STEP2** and reset the aspiration level.

3.3 Formulation

The scheduling problem in **STEP3** is formulated as follows:

$$\min \; OF = z + \alpha \left\{ w_{C_{max}} \left(C_{max} - \bar{f}_{C_{max}} \right) + w_{cost} \left(Cost - \bar{f}_{cost} \right) \right\} \tag{1}$$

$$\text{where } C_{max} = \max_{\forall i, \forall l, \forall j} \left\{ c_{ilj} \right\} \tag{2}$$

$$Cost = \sum_{\forall t} e_t \times Rate_t \tag{3}$$

$$e_t = \sum_{\forall i} \sum_{\forall l} \sum_{\forall a} ms_{ilat} \times EC_{ila}, \forall t \tag{4}$$

$$s.t. \sum_{\forall l} \sum_{\forall t} y_{iljt} = 1, \forall i, \forall j \tag{5}$$

$$s_{ilj} + c_{ilj} \leq BigM \times \sum_{\forall t} y_{iljt}, \forall i, \forall l, \forall j \tag{6}$$

$$c_{ilj} \geq s_{ilj} + P_{ilj} - BigM \left(1 - \sum_{\forall t} y_{iljt}\right), \forall i, \forall l, \forall j \tag{7}$$

$$\sum_{\forall l} s_{ilj} \geq \sum_{\forall l} c_{(i-1)lj}, \forall i \in \{I \setminus 1\}, \forall j \tag{8}$$

$$\sum_{\forall l} s_{ilj} = \sum_{\forall l} \sum_{\forall t} t \times y_{iljt}, \forall i, \forall j \tag{9}$$

$$\sum_{\forall l} c_{ilj} = \sum_{\forall l} \sum_{\forall t} (t + P_{ilj}) \times y_{iljt}, \forall i, \forall j \tag{10}$$

$$s_{ilk} \geq c_{ilj} - BigM (1 - x_{iljk}), \forall i, \forall l, \forall j, k, j \neq k \tag{11}$$

$$s_{ilj} \geq c_{ilk} - BigM \times x_{iljk}, \forall i, \forall l, \forall j, k, j \neq k \tag{12}$$

$$C_{max} \leq T \tag{13}$$

$$\sum_{\forall j} mp_{iljt} = ms_{il1t}, \forall i, \forall l, \forall t \tag{14}$$

$$\sum_{\forall a} ms_{ilat} = 1, \forall i, \forall l, \forall t \tag{15}$$

$$\sum_{\forall j} mp_{iljt} \leq 1, \forall i, \forall l, \forall t \tag{16}$$

$$P_{ilj} \times y_{iljt} \leq \sum_{q=t}^{t+P_{ilj}-1} mp_{iljq}, \forall i, \forall l, \forall j (if P_{ilj} > 0 \text{ and } T - t \geq P_{ilj}) \tag{17}$$

$$P_{ilj} \times \sum_{\forall t} y_{iljt} = \sum_{\forall t} mp_{iljt}, \forall i, \forall l, \forall j \tag{18}$$

$$w_{c_{max}} \left(C_{max} - \bar{f}_{c_{max}}\right) \leq z \tag{19}$$

$$w_{cost} \left(Cost - \bar{f}_{cost}\right) \leq z \tag{20}$$

Objective function (1) minimizes the sum of z and weighted dissatisfaction with both makespan and electric power costs. The auxiliary variable z represents the dissatisfaction levels for makespan and electric power costs. The dissatisfaction level for makespan and electric power costs are close as much as possible by minimizing z, and reduce the dissatisfaction with both makespan and electric power costs. The second term of the objective function is a correction term to prevent weak Pareto solutions, and the weighting factor α should be small enough to prevent the second term from becoming dominant [7]. Equations (5)–(20) are constraints. Equation (5) guarantees that a job is assigned to one machine in each stage. Equations (6)–(10) are constraints on the start and completion times. Equations (11) and (12) represents the precedence relation constraints for jobs. Equations (13) is a constraint that prevents the makespan from exceeding the planning period. Equations (14)–(16) are constraints on the allocation of machines and jobs. Equations (17) and (18) are constraints to determine the operating state of the machine. Equations (19) and (20) are inequalities that select the evaluation criteria with the weighted dissatisfaction levels for makespan and the electric power costs using the auxiliary variable z.

4 Computational Experiments

In order to evaluate the relationship between the ideal level and the aspiration level acquired the schedule, the computational experiments are performed with different conditions. In this paper, **STEP4** of Sect. 3.2 is not executed and the aspiration level is not reset as basic study. IBM ILOG CPLEX 12.9 [8] is used to solve the scheduling problem. The evaluation criteria are as follows:

- C_{max} : makespan
- $Cost$: electric power costs
- $MSNA = \frac{C_{max} - \bar{f}_{cmax}}{\bar{f}_{cmax} - f_{cmax}^{best}}$: the dissatisfaction degree of makespan
- $CONA = \frac{Cost - \bar{f}_{cost}}{\bar{f}_{cost} - f_{cost}^{best}}$: the dissatisfaction degree of electric power costs

4.1 Experimental Conditions

In general, each production machine differs the required manufacturing time and usage electric power for making the same product. In order to take into consideration these conditions, this experiment assumes that each stage has two type machines: Machine 1 in each stage has a high job processing speed but high power consumption, and Machine 2 in each stage has a slower job processing speed and lower electric power consumption than Machine 1. There are three price time range for electricity charges; high, middle and low. We set the experimental conditions to understand the characteristics of the proposed method as follows:

- Total number of jobs (J): 8
- Total number of stages (I): 2
- The number of machines in each stage (M_i): 2
- Total number of timeslots (T): 48
- Total number of states (A): 2 ($a = 1$, represents processing; $a = 2$, represents idle)
- Processing time of job j at machine 1 on stage $i (P_{i1j})$: $2(1 \leq j \leq 4), 3(5 \leq j \leq 8)$

- Processing time of job j at machine 2 on stage $i(P_{i2j})$: $4(1 \leq j \leq 4), 6(5 \leq j \leq 8)$
- Electric power consumption of state a at machine 1 on stage $i(EC_{i1a})$: $80(a = 1), 8(a = 2)$
- Electric power consumption of state a at machine 2 on stage $i(EC_{i2a})$: $10(a = 1,$ state is processing$), 1(a = 2,$ state is idle$)$
- Electricity charges $(Rate_t)$: $5(0 \leq t < 16), 10(16 \leq t < 32), 1(32 \leq t < 48)$
- BigM: 50000
- Weighting factor for the second term of the objective function (α): 1.0×10^{-3}

An appropriate α value is set by conducting a preliminary experiment.

Setting the Ideal and Aspiration Level of Makespan and Electric Power Costs
The ideal level of makespan $f_{C_{max}}^{best}$ and electric power costs f_{cost}^{best} are set the value acquired from the makespan and electric power costs minimization scheduling problem respectively as follows:

- Ideal level of makespan $\left(f_{C_{max}}^{best}\right)$: 17
- Ideal level of electric power costs $\left(f_{cost}^{best}\right)$: 6714

For setting the aspiration level of makespan and electric power costs, the four cases of aspiration level are used as shown in Table 1. In Case 1, the both aspiration levels are twice as many as the ideal levels. In Case 2, the aspiration level for electric power costs is increased from Case 1 as tougher requirement. In Case 3, the aspiration level for makespan is increased. In Case 4, the both aspiration level is 1.2 times as many as the ideal levels. In this time, Case 1 is loose aspiration level that gets a result that meets the aspiration level. Case 2–4 values are set to analyze how the scheduling result will be affected if the aspiration level of each evaluation criteria or all of them are increased.

Table 1. Aspiration level of makespan and electric power costs

Case	$\bar{f}_{C_{max}}$	$\bar{f}_{cost}$
1	34 $(f_{C_{max}}^{best} \times 2.0)$	13428 $(f_{cost}^{best} \times 2.0)$
2	34 $(f_{C_{max}}^{best} \times 2.0)$	**8057** $(f_{cost}^{best} \times 1.2)$
3	**20** $(f_{C_{max}}^{best} \times 1.2)$	13428 $(f_{cost}^{best} \times 2.0)$
4	**20** $(f_{C_{max}}^{best} \times 1.2)$	**8057** $(f_{cost}^{best} \times 1.2)$

4.2 Experimental Result

Table 2 shows the evaluation values acquired from solving the scheduling problem using proposed method with each case. The schedules acquired from Case 1 and Case 2 are shown in Fig. 2. The objective function value *OF* is less than or equal to zero when all aspiration levels are satisfied. In Case 1, the objective function value is negative and both the aspiration level of makespan and electric power costs are satisfied. On the other hand, in Cases 2 to 4, the objective function values are positive because the some aspiration levels are not satisfied. In Case 2, the aspiration level of electric power costs is increased, and then the electric power costs decrease as shown in Table 2. As shown in Fig. 2, Job 1 (Blue box) and Job 4 (Pink box) in Case 2 are processed in low price range to reduce the electric power costs. Thus, the result in Case 2 indicates that the proposed method can adjust the production schedule for satisfying the aspiration level. However, the aspiration level of electric power costs in Case 2 may be strict, so *CONA* in Case 2 is positive and then the *OF* and *MSNA* are positive. In Case 3, the aspiration level of electric power costs increase from the level in Case 1 though the aspiration level of makespan is satisfied. This indicates that the proposed method may adjust the schedule to satisfy the strict aspiration level of makespan. In Case 4, the both aspiration levels are increased so that the proposed method may acquire the schedule while adjusting *MSNA* and *CONA* to improve the both values. Therefore, these results indicate that it is possible to adjust the production schedule in consideration of *MSNA* and *CONA* using the proposed method.

Table 2. Results of Experiment

Case ($\bar{f}_{c_{max}}, \bar{f}_{cost}$)	*OF*	*MSNA*(C_{max})	*CONA*(*Cost*)
1 (34, 13428)	**−0.118**	**−0.1176 (32)**	**−0.1206 (12618)**
2 (34, 8057)	0.353	0.3529 (40)	0.1124 (8208)
3 (20, 13428)	0.174	**0.0 (20)**	0.1743 (14598)
4 (20, 8057)	3.67	3.333 (30)	3.664 (12978)

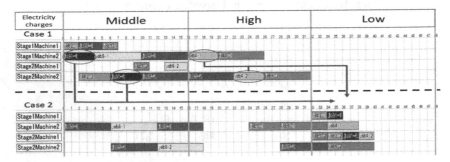

Fig. 2. Schedules obtained in Case 1 and Case 2. Red arrow: some jobs are scheduled in low price range in Case 2

5 Conclusion

In this paper, we proposed a scheduling method that can handle decision criteria of productivity and electric power costs in the flexible flow shop type production line with usage electric power. As a result of the experiment, we have confirmed that the proposed method can adjust the production schedule in consideration of the various decision criteria such as productivity and electric power costs. In future work, we will implement the adjustment mechanism of aspiration level autonomously and consider how to set the aspiration level to satisfy decision makers. Then, with the aim of applying it to the realization field, we will investigate the characteristics of the proposed method such as the calculation time and the scale of the problem that can obtain the optimum result, and compare it with other multi-objective optimization methods.

References

1. Agency for natural resources and energy. Japan's Energy Problems (Part 1) (2020). https://www.enecho.meti.go.jp/about/special/johoteikyo/energyissue2020_1.html
2. Gahm, C., et al.: Energy-efficient scheduling in manufacturing companies: a review and research framework. Eur. J. Oper. Res. **248**(3), 744–757 (2016)
3. Yabuuchi, M., Kaihara, T., Fujii, N., Kokuryo, D., Sakajo, S., Nishita, Y.: A basic study on scheduling method for electric power saving of production machine. In: Lalic, B., Majstorovic, V., Marjanovic, U., von Cieminski, G., Romero, D. (eds.) APMS 2020. IAICT, vol. 591, pp. 524–530. Springer, Cham (2020). https://doi.org/10.1007/978-3-030-57993-7_59
4. Nakayama, H., Sawaragi, Y.: Satisficing trade-off method for multiobjective programming and its applications. In: IFAC Proceedings vol. 17, pp. 1345–1350 (1984)
5. Tamura, H., Shibata, T., Hatono, I.: Multiobjective combinatorial optimization for performance evaluation by a meta-heuristic satisficing tradeoff method. In: Mertins, K., Krause, O., Schallock, B. (eds.) Global Production Management. ITIFIP, vol. 24, pp. 490–497. Springer, Boston, MA (1999). https://doi.org/10.1007/978-0-387-35569-6_60
6. Shirakawa, M., Arakawa, M.: Multi-objective optimization system for plant layout design (3rd report, Interactive multi-objective optimization technique for pipe routing design). J. Adv. Mech. Des. Syst. Manuf. **12**(2), JAMDSM0053 (2018)
7. Nakayama, H., et al.: Multi-Objective Optimization and Engineering Design-Supple Systems Engineering Approach-, Gendaitosho Co.,Ltd, Japa, Published in Japanese (2008)
8. ILOG CPLEX-IBM. https://www.ibm.com/jp-ja/products/ilog-cplex-optimization-studio

A New Representation and Adaptive Feature Selection for Evolving Compact Dispatching Rules for Dynamic Job Shop Scheduling with Genetic Programming

Salama Shady$^{(\boxtimes)}$, Toshiya Kaihara, Nobutada Fujii, and Daisuke Kokuryo

Graduate School of System Informatics, Kobe University, Kobe 6578501, Hyogo, Japan
shady.salama@kaede.cs.kobe-u.ac.jp

Abstract. Dispatching rules are extensively addressed in the dynamic job shop scheduling literature and are commonly adopted in many industrial practices. The manual design of dispatching rules is a tedious process that requires a great deal of time and experience. Due to the growth in computational power, the design process is automated using various machine learning and optimization techniques to evolve superior dispatching rules compared to human-made ones. Genetic Programming (GP) is one of the most promising approaches in the field of automated design of scheduling rules, especially under dynamic conditions. Considering a large set of terminals that reflects various job and machine attributes helps GP to obtain efficient rules, but in return extends the search space. Also, the impact of terminals can vary greatly among various scenarios, objective functions, and evolutionary stages. Therefore, an efficient feature selection mechanism can support the GP searching ability by eliminating irrelevant terminals and facilitating the process of high-quality rule search by focusing more on the promising regions in the search space. In this paper, we propose a new representation for the GP individuals that reflects the importance of each terminal in this rule. Also, an adaptive feature selection mechanism is developed that uses the information gained from the previous evolutionary step in restricting the search space at the current generation. Experimental results show that the proposed approaches assist the GP to obtain compact rules in a shorter computational time without sacrificing the performance compared with the standard GP algorithm and another representation from the literature.

Keywords: Genetic programming · Job shop scheduling · Feature selection

1 Introduction

Job Shop Scheduling Problem (JSSP) is a popular combinatorial optimization problem in which a variety of custom jobs are competing to be processed in a number of general-purpose workstations in a cost-effective manner [1]. JSSPs belong to a class of problems known as NP-hard problems which means that the time required to calculate an optimal

© IFIP International Federation for Information Processing 2021
Published by Springer Nature Switzerland AG 2021
A. Dolgui et al. (Eds.): APMS 2021, IFIP AICT 632, pp. 646–654, 2021.
https://doi.org/10.1007/978-3-030-85906-0_70

solution increases exponentially with the problem size. In Dynamic JSSP (DJSSP), jobs may arrive randomly over time with no operational information is available before their arrival. The main sources of dynamic behavior investigated in this paper are arrival time, operational sequence, processing time, and due dates. Dispatching Rules (DR) are frequently used to generate schedules in DJSSPs because of their simplicity, ease to understand, low computational complexity, and can respond instantly to dynamic events [2]. The manual design of sophisticated DRs is a trial-and-error-cycle which requires a great deal of time, code effort and domain knowledge [2]. Therefore, several scholars have suggested the use of machine learning methods to select or generate heuristics automatically for solving combinatorial problems called "hyper-heuristics" [3]. Due to the advances in computational power and optimization approaches, there is a growing number of articles in the field of automated heuristic design [2]. Recently, Genetic Programming (GP) has been successfully applied for the design of production scheduling heuristics. There are many representations presented in the literature depending on the requirements of DRs. The tree structure is the most common representation [4]. There are other representations, such as linear expression [5], grammar-based representation, and cartesian GP [3].

Recently, the authors in [6] proposed a new GP representation where rules are defined by two parts: the priority function presented in a tree structure, and an attribute vector. The attribute vector of a rule i is a binary array $vect_i = \{x_{i1}, x_{i2}, \ldots, x_{iA}\}$ with a length of A equals to the total number of terminals. If the attribute x_{ij} is 1, then this attribute is considered important (active), and the actual value of the attribute will be used, if included in the tree, in the evaluation of the priority function. In contrast, if x_{ij} is 0, the attribute is considered irrelevant (inactive), and its value will be set to 1 to exclude the effect of attribute x_j in estimating the priority value. The key limitation of this representation is that it ignores the situation where a certain attribute may not be present in the priority function. This makes the attribute vector not strictly linked to its corresponding priority function leading to the following limitations:

1. Attribute vectors do not provide sufficient, or even misleading, information regarding their priority functions. For example, all elements in an attribute vector may take the value 1 (active) even if the rule includes only one terminal.
2. Changing the activation state at a certain terminal will have no effect if that terminal is not present in this rule. However, it may have a future effect if this terminal emerges after the tree crossover or mutation, but that still is not certain.
3. The attribute vector mutation operator is applied in a uniform manner through all attributes (fixed mutation rate) without using any information gathered from previous generations and neglecting the relative importance of each terminal

One main challenge in using the GP algorithm is that there is a large selection of terminals in the dynamic job shop that can be provided to it. Although increasing the number of features in the terminal set can provide the GP reasoning mechanism with enough information to evolve competitive rules, it exponentially expands the search space which restricts GP's ability to identify promising search regions [7]. Therefore, feature selection is a critical GP issue that may speed-up the learning process and improve the performance of evolved heuristics by selecting only informative features and eliminating irrelevant ones. To the best of our knowledge, a limited number of articles have studied feature selection to improve the GP performance in DJSSP [8].

The aim of this paper is to develop an online feature selection method using a new computationally affordable representation and an adaptive selection mechanism to estimate the weight of each feature in the terminal set using the information gained from the past generation. The rest of this paper is organized as follows. The proposed approach is described in Sect. 2. Section 3 presents the experimental studies in different job shop settings. The results and analysis are provided in Sect. 4. Finally, Sect. 5 gives the conclusions and future research work.

2 Proposed Feature Selection Approach

The proposed framework extends the standard GP algorithm with two main points. First, a new representation of GP individuals is proposed by modifying the attribute vector representation in [6]. Second, a feature selection approach is developed which estimates the weight of each terminal as a probability to be activated in the next generation. As shown in Fig. 1, the algorithm starts by generating a population of dispatching rules using predefined sets of terminal and functions. Each rule is represented by two parts: the priority function in the standard tree structure and an attribute vector. The attribute vector proposed in this paper extends the binary representation in [6] where each terminal x_j can be active = "1" or inactive/absent = "0" to a ternary array where there are three states of each terminal. If a terminal exists in the dispatching rule, it may be active = "1", or inactive = "−1", otherwise it is absent = "0". This modification leads to two main advantages over the literature representation. First, it supports the attribute vector to be precisely bound to the structure of its corresponding rule. Therefore, the attribute vectors can be used to abstract the complex structure of dispatching rules which are used in the feature selection mechanism presented later. Second, this new representation ensures that any change (mutation) of the feature's state in the attribute vector will have a direct effect on the performance of the priority function. The performance of the initial rules is assessed using a Discrete Event Simulation (DES) Model. Then, a tournament method is used for selecting the fittest rules.

Regarding the feature selection approach, the attribute vectors of a subset s of the best select individuals are used to estimate the feature activation probability. Every generation, the activation probability of each terminal x_j is estimated using Eq. (1). The Activation Probability AP_j of a given terminal j is equal to the number of times it is active divided by the sum between the active and inactive times in all chosen rules. In the most optimistic case, if a certain feature is active in all the selected rules (very important) in the current generation, its activation probability for the next generation will be 1. On the other hand, if a certain terminal is inactive in all chosen rules (irrelevant), the activation probability in the next generation will equal to 0. The activation probability serves as on-the-fly feature selection mechanism that utilizes the past evolutionary information in estimating the importance of each terminal based on its impact in the best evolved rules. The estimated activation probabilities of all the terminals are derived to the GP algorithm. Then, generic operators are applied in two steps. First, the subtree crossover and mutation are applied on the rules' priority function to create new rules for the next generation. Second, the attribute vectors are passed from parents to offspring, then another mutation is applied to each terminal in the attribute vector. In the attribute vector mutation, the value for each attribute x_j is given using Eq. (2). For each rule i, in the absence of a certain terminal j, the value of x_{ij} in $vect_i$ will take 0. Conversely, if terminal j is presented, a uniform random number ($rand$) between 0 and 1 is generated, and two situations can occur. If $rand$ is less than or equal to its activation probability AP_j, then x_{ij} equals 1 (active), otherwise the terminal x_{ij} is inactivated and takes the value -1. Then, the new rules form the next generation. This evolutionary process is repeated until stopping criteria are met.

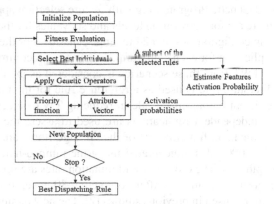

Fig. 1. The flowchart of the GP algorithm with the proposed feature selection approach.

$$AP_j = \frac{\sum_{i=1}^{|s|}\left(1, \textit{if } x_{ijk} = 1\right)}{\sum_{i=1}^{|s|}\left(1, \textit{if } x_{ijk} = 1\right) + \sum_{i=1}^{|s|}\left(1, \textit{if } x_{ijk} = -1\right)} \tag{1}$$

$$x_{ij} = \begin{cases} 0 & \textit{terminal j does not occur in rule i} \\ 1, & rand \leq AP_j \\ -1, & rand > AP_j \end{cases} \tag{2}$$

3   Experimental Design

A DES model is developed for the DJJ proposed in [9] to assess the performance of the proposed approach. Due to the importance of meeting job due dates, not only for on-time delivery jobs but also for customer satisfaction the Total Weighted Tardiness (TWT) is used as a performance measure. Also, computational time and the average length of evolved rules are considered. The job shop starts empty and jobs' arrival rate follows Poisson distribution based on the required utilization level. The total number of jobs is 2500 jobs. The statistics are collected from the 500th job (warm-up period) to the next completed 2500 jobs. The job shop settings are as follows.

- There are 10 machines in the shop floor.
- The jobs due date are assigned using the total work content [10].
- Jobs are given weights 1, 2, or 4 with probability 0.2, 0.6, and 0.2.
- The number of operations per job is uniformly distributed between 2 and 10.
- The operations processing time follows a uniform distribution between 1 and 49.

For comparison purposes, three experiments are developed to evaluate the performance of the proposed approach against the original representation in the literature [6] and the standard GP algorithm. The experiments are the Standard Genetic Programming approach (SGP), the Hybrid Genetic Programming using literature representation (HGP) [6], and the Proposed Genetic Programming with feature selection approach (PGP). As shown in Table 1, there are four utilization levels and six values for the tightness factors resulting in 6 training configurations and 24 testing scenarios. For the training phase, a single simulation replication for each configuration is used as recommended in [3]. The average normalized TWT from these scenarios is considered as the fitness for evolved rules. The WATC literature rule is used as a reference rule for the purpose of normalization as it is an efficient human-made rule in reducing TWT objective [7]. For each testing scenario, 20 independent replications are used to assess the generality of GP individuals. The terminal and function sets of the GP algorithms are given in Table 2. A population size of 1000 rules is generated using the ramped-half-and-half method with a maximum depth of 8. The crossover and mutation rates are set to 90% and 10%, respectively. The algorithm terminates after completing 80 generations. Most of these parameters are commonly used in previous studies [2]. The new parameters are the activation probability at the initial generation P_{int} and the number of selected individuals $|s|$ that are regulated to the proposed approach. Multiple pilot experiments are carried out to determine appropriate values for these parameters and evaluate their impact on the obtained results. Due to space limitations, the obtained findings are omitted and the P_{int} and $|s|$ used in the PGP experiment are 0.5 and 50, respectively. Regarding the HGP experiment, the attribute mutation probability is set to 0.5 for all defined terminals, as recommended in [6].

Table 1. The DES configurations for training and testing scenarios.

Parameter	Description
Utilization level	{0.8, 0.9} for training, and {0.8, 0.85, 0.9, 0.95} for testing
Tightness factors	{3, 6, 8} for training, and {3, 4, 5, 6, 7, 8} for testing

Table 2. Terminal and function sets.

Terminal	Description	Terminal	Description
JR	Ready time of the job	DD	Due date of the job
OR	Ready time of the operation	CT	The current time
RO	Number of operations remaining	SL	Slack of the job
WINQ	Work in the next queue	PT	Processing time
WT	Waiting time of the operation	WR	Work remaining
Npt	Next Processing time	JW	Weight of the job
Apr	Average processing time of queued jobs		
Functions	+, -, ×, /, min, max, abs, IF		

4   Results and Analysis

This section presents the obtained results for the three developed experiments. For the training phase, the three algorithms are examined using four performance indicators including computational time, total weighted tardiness, the average number of active terminals, and the average number of excluded terminals through generations. As shown in Fig. 2(a), although there is no clear difference in computational requirements between SGP and HGP, the PGP achieved the lowest computational time, especially after generation 35. The reason behind this is revealed by tracking the terminals' state across generations. The gap between the average number of active features in the case of PGP and SGP widens after the 35th generation. The same trend is revealed in the number

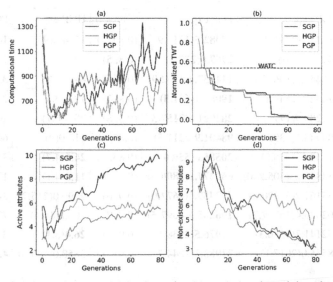

Fig. 2. The performance of the three algorithms during the training phase.

of non-existent features as depicted in Fig. 2(c, d). These findings demonstrate the superiority of the proposed approach in selecting critical terminals in the evolved rules resulting in shorter rules that accelerates the evolutionary process. To verify whether reducing computational time negatively affects the performance of evolved rules. The fitness value of the best rule at each generation is tracked, as illustrated in Fig. 2(b), PGP algorithm showed better convergence speed compared to the other methods with a slight difference from SGP in the last five generations, while the HGP method obtained the worst total weighted tardiness across the training scenarios. One reason may be that implementing a constant mutation probability ($P_a = 0.5$) for all terminals adversely affects the GP exploration ability. Finally, all three algorithms greatly outperform the WATC in minimizing the TWT objective.

To assess the impact of the feature selection approach on the generality of the generated rules in unseen scenarios. Table 3 shows the mean (standard deviation) of the test objective values of the HGP and PGP experiments in the 24 testing scenarios. Each scenario is denoted by a tuple (u, t) to represent a combination of job shop utilization (u) and tightness factor(t). SGP algorithm is not considered as the PGP algorithm reduced the training time by 21.8%, therefore it is not fair to compare SGP with PGP while the stopping criterion is the maximum number of generations. Also, the Wilcoxon signed-rank test with a significance level of 0.05 is conducted between the TWT obtained by the best rules of HGP and PGP in 10 GP runs as the two methods use relatively similar representations. The statistically significant better fitness values are marked in **bold**. As shown in Table 3, PGP significantly outperforms HGP in 19/24 test scenarios while HGP performed better in three scenarios. There was no significant difference between the testing performance in two scenarios.

Table 3. Mean and standard deviation of total weighted tardiness on the testing scenarios

Scenario	HGP exp	PGP exp	Scenario	HGP exp	PGP exp
(0.8, 3)	68172.2(2751.0)	**43382.5(1216.9)**	(0.85, 5)	1734.8(95.1)	**1471.8(215.7)**
(0.8, 4)	3412.4(73.0)	**2787.0(277.3)**	(0.8, 5)	192.8(12.9)	**115.9(28.4)**
(0.85, 3)	216447.2(10697.1)	**114657.4(1992.9)**	(0.8, 6)	44.4(7.8)	**32.8(5.8)**
(0.85, 4)	27432.1(1549.1)	**19087.1(631.5)**	(0.8, 7)	**19.9(3.6)**	28.7(6.1)
(0.9, 3)	571280.9(17721.8)	**282921.6(2157.3)**	(0.8, 8)	20.5(6.1)	20.9(2.7)
(0.9, 4)	189943.5(6390.6)	**98401.9(2211.5)**	(0.85, 6)	117.0(9)	**60.4(10.7)**
(0.9, 5)	31147.6(1538.5)	**20585.6(559.0)**	(0.85, 7)	**24.6(4.7)**	31.2(2.4)
(0.95, 3)	1348638.3(30529.0)	**662477.2(5800.0)**	(0.85, 8)	11.3(4.1)	17.8(5.7)
(0.95, 4)	833161.7(31990.6)	**397459.5(4677.0)**	(0.9, 6)	2699.0(215.7)	**2427.0(140.3)**
(0.95, 5)	402023.4(16257.7)	**196205.6(4597.5)**	(0.9, 7)	206.8(16.4)	**77.8(21.9)**
(0.95, 6)	152141.3(5686.3)	**81976.5(2588.6)**	(0.9, 8)	**26.4(5.1)**	35.8(2.8)
(0.95, 7)	38535.0(2017.1)	**21983.3(1044.7)**	(0.95, 8)	5858.0(335.6)	**4312.4(198.0)**

Moreover, the number of occurrences of each terminal in the best PGP rule is illustrated in Table 4. Two versions are shown, the "Original" version represents the tree structure without considering the attribute vector, and the "Modified" version utilizes the information given in the corresponding attribute vector to disable some terminals. The CT, PT, JW, WR, and SL terminals are the most common terminals which reflect the importance of these terminals in minimizing the TWT objective. An interesting observation is noticed, although DD terminal occurred three times in the original version, it is deactivated using the attribute vector indicating its negligible effect on the rule performance. This supports our claim that frequency analysis [7] commonly used in the literature is not an appropriate method for estimating the feature importance.

Table 4. The number of times each terminal occurred in the best PGP rule.

Version	IR	OR	RO	WR	PT	DD	CT	SL	WT	Npt	WINQ	Apr	JW
Original	1	1	0	2	3	3	4	2	0	1	1	1	3
Modified	1	1	0	2	3	0	4	2	0	1	0	1	3

5 Conclusions and Future Work

In this paper, we proposed a new GP representation and an adaptive feature selection algorithm to automatically evolve compact scheduling heuristics for the DJSSP. The new representation provides an abstract view of its corresponding priority function which is easier to understand and can efficiently control the complex underlying tree structure. Moreover, the feature selection approach uses an online learning technique by utilizing the information acquired from the best rules of the previous generation in estimating the weight of each terminal. The experimental results show that the proposed approach outperforms other literature methods in terms of computational time and rule length. In future work, more detailed comparisons will be performed between the proposed approach and other feature selection methods.

References

1. Ouelhadj, D., Petrovic, S.: A survey of dynamic scheduling in manufacturing systems. J. Sched. **12**, 417–431 (2009). https://doi.org/10.1007/s10951-008-0090-8
2. Branke, J., Nguyen, S., Pickardt, C.W., Zhang, M.: Automated design of production scheduling heuristics: a review. IEEE Trans. Evol. Comput. **20**, 110–124 (2016). https://doi.org/10.1109/TEVC.2015.2429314
3. Nguyen, S., Mei, Y., Zhang, M.: Genetic programming for production scheduling: a survey with a unified framework. Complex Intell. Syst. **3**(1), 41–66 (2017). https://doi.org/10.1007/s40747-017-0036-x
4. Shady, S., Kaihara, T., Fujii, N., Kokuryo, D.: A hyper-heuristic framework using GP for dynamic job shop scheduling problem. In: Proceedings of the 64th Annual Conference of the Institute of Systems, Control and Information Engineers (ISCIE), pp. 248–252 (2020)

5. Nie, L., Gao, L., Li, P., Zhang, L.: Application of gene expression programming on dynamic job shop scheduling problem. In: Proceedings of the 2011 15th International Conference on Computer Supported Cooperative Work in Design, CSCWD 2011, pp. 291–295 (2011). https://doi.org/10.1109/CSCWD.2011.5960088

6. Nguyen, S., Mei, Y., Xue, B., Zhang, M.: A hybrid genetic programming algorithm for automated design of dispatching rules. Evol. Comput. **27**, 467–596 (2018). https://doi.org/10.1162/evco_a_00230

7. Mei, Y., Nguyen, S., Xue, B., Zhang, M.: An efficient feature selection algorithm for evolving job shop scheduling rules with genetic programming. IEEE Trans. Emerg. Top. Comput. Intell. **1**, 339–353 (2017). https://doi.org/10.1109/tetci.2017.2743758

8. Zhang, F., Mei, Y., Zhang, M.: A two-stage genetic programming hyper-heuristic approach with feature selection for dynamic flexible job shop scheduling. In: Proceedings of the 2019 Genetic and Evolutionary Computation Conference, pp. 347–355. Association for Computing Machinery, USA (2019). https://doi.org/10.1145/3321707.3321790

9. Hunt, R., Richard, J., Zhang, M.: Evolving dispatching rules with greater understandability for dynamic job shop scheduling. School of Engineering and Computer Science, Victoria University of Wellington, 2016 (2016)

10. Shady, S., Kaihara, T., Fujii, N., Kokuryo, D.: Automatic design of dispatching rules with genetic programming for dynamic job shop scheduling. In: Lalic, B., Majstorovic, V., Marjanovic, U., von Cieminski, G., Romero, D. (eds.) APMS 2020. IAICT, vol. 591, pp. 399–407. Springer, Cham (2020). https://doi.org/10.1007/978-3-030-57993-7_45

A Study on Sharing Logistics Network Design Considering Demand Uncertainty

Asumi Ito$^{(\boxtimes)}$ ⓘ, Toshiya Kaihara ⓘ, Daisuke Kokuryo ⓘ, and Nobutada Fujii ⓘ

Kobe University, 1-1 Rokkodai, Nada, Kobe 657-8501, Japan
`asumi_ito@kind.ocn.ne.jp`

Abstract. The evolution of e-retailing is driving a rise in logistics costs and risk of late delivery. Collaborative logistics has become the key to help businesses eliminate inefficiencies, improve responsiveness to market changes, and reduce overall supply chain costs by adjusting transportation capacity efficiently. In this study, we propose a stochastic mixed integer linear programming model that incorporates shipper's transportation operations via truck sharing service. The model supports strategic network design decisions in uncertain market environments by optimizing the number of trucks under uncertain demand. Through several case studies on a small-scale truck sharing network, we show the influence of demand uncertainty on the network performance in terms of the on-time delivery ratio and the gross profit margin ratio. We also show the influence of the sharing platform features such as the transaction price and the number of available trucks, on shippers as well as a platformer in terms of the turnover of trucks.

Keywords: Supply chain logistics · Network design · Sharing logistics

1 Introduction

The growth of e-retailing market leads to the increase in freight and the shortage of trucks, and enterprises are facing a rise in logistics costs and risk of late delivery. Collaboration in logistics is even more critical to cope with uncertainty in their operation environment and to respond quickly to market changes. Vertical collaboration refers to the integration of organizations from different level of a supply chain. In contrast, horizontal collaboration refers to a collaboration between organizations from different supply chain at same level [1, 2]. As a part of horizontal collaborative logistics, truck sharing business has grown rapidly in some areas. Truck sharing enables users to react to demand by adjusting transportation capacity efficiently as well as to reduce the costs that come with ownership of trucks [3]. To address distribution network design that incorporates truck sharing, some contributions focus on the number of trucks for strategic planning and others consider routing and truck allocation for operational planning [4–7]. However, very few of them focuses on characteristics in sharing platform operations, such as pricing and geographical reach. Furthermore, several literatures apply stochastic programming to network design to capture demand uncertainty, but assume demand for only a single

© IFIP International Federation for Information Processing 2021
Published by Springer Nature Switzerland AG 2021
A. Dolgui et al. (Eds.): APMS 2021, IFIP AICT 632, pp. 655–662, 2021.
https://doi.org/10.1007/978-3-030-85906-0_71

item [8–11]. In other words, little literature exists that addresses logistics network design considering multiple independent uncertain demand.

In this paper, we propose an optimization model for the network design with truck sharing based on a stochastic programming. Through several numerical experiments, we evaluate the impact of truck sharing on the network performance in terms of cost and on-time delivery ratio. Also, we evaluate the effect of demand uncertainty on the optimal number of own trucks and on the expected profit of the platformer. Further, we show how the transaction price influences the number of shared trucks and promotes the truck sharing.

2 Problem Description

In this paper, we study transportation operations of multiple shippers who deliver items from their location to a warehouse by using trucks which they own or borrow through a sharing platform or lease from the outside of a platform. The objective is to minimize the fixed cost of own trucks and expected logistics cost by using a combination of these trucks depending on demand. On the platform a truck owner can lend its own trucks to others who need to satisfy demand when they are not in use. A percentage transaction fee is deducted from daily rental rate, and a lender keeps the remaining plus mileage charge. Thought the platformer also has a constant number of trucks, shippers may have to lease trucks from a leasing company due to a shortage of trucks available for rent. A borrower picks a truck up and returns it at the owner's location. Platformer-provided trucks are located at a dedicated parking spot. Leased trucks are located at the lessee's location.

3 Stochastic Collaborative Network Model

3.1 Notation

The notation introduced in the network design model is shown in Table 1.

Table 1. Sets, parameters and decision variables.

Sets	
S	Set of shippers
V	Set of truck owners
W	Set of scenarios
Parameters	
$D_{s\omega}$	Daily demand for shipper s's item in scenario ω
P_s	Gross profit of shipper s's item
Fix^C	Subscription charge for truck sharing

(continued)

Table 1. (*continued*)

Fix^V	Daily maintenance cost for truck
Fix^S	Daily rate to borrow truck on platform
Fix^R	Daily rate to lease truck from leasing company
Var^V	Freight cost per kilometer
Var^M	Mileage charge per kilometer
Var^F	Handling cost of one product
α	Percentage fee per transaction on platform
Cap^V	Loading capacity of truck
L_s^F	Distance from shipper s to warehouse
L_{sv}	Distance from shipper s to truck owner v
L_s^P	Distance from shipper s to dedicated parking spot
L^P	Distance from warehouse to dedicated parking spot
Q_p	Number of platformer-owned trucks
π_ω	Probability of scenario ω
m_s	Binary parameter to indicate if shipper s uses platform
Decision variables	
$x_{sv\omega}$	Percentage of demand for shipper s's item delivered to warehouse using v's own trucks in scenario ω
$x'_{s\omega}$	Percentage of demand for shipper s's item delivered to warehouse using leased trucks in scenario ω
$x''_{s\omega}$	Percentage of demand for shipper s's item delivered to warehouse using platformer-owned trucks in scenario ω
$z_{sv\omega}$	Number of v's own trucks used by shipper s in scenario ω
$z'_{s\omega}$	Number of leased trucks used by shipper s in scenario ω
$z''_{s\omega}$	Number of platformer-owned trucks used by shipper s in scenario ω
q_v	Number of v's own trucks

3.2 Model Formulation

Our objective is to minimize the total network cost of multiple shippers by making decisions on the number of owning and operating trucks. The first term of Eq. (1) represents the scenario-dependent cost of borrowing trucks on the platform, leasing trucks from the leasing company, delivering items to the warehouse, handling items at the warehouse, mileage charge and demand opportunity loss. The second and the third term represent the scenario-independent fixed cost of owning trucks and using the platform, respectively.

$$\text{Min} \sum_{\omega} \pi_{\omega} \left\{ Fix^S \left(\alpha \sum_s \sum_v z_{sv\omega} + \sum_s z''_{s\omega} \right) + Fix^R \sum_s z'_{s\omega} \right.$$

$$+ Var^V \sum_s \left(\sum_v \left(L_s^F + L_{sv} + L_v^F \right) z_{sv\omega} + 2L_s^F z'_{s\omega} + \left(L_s^F + L_s^P + L^P \right) z''_{s\omega} \right)$$

$$+ Var^F \sum_s \sum_v D_{s\omega} \left(x_{sv\omega} + x'_{s\omega} + x''_{s\omega} \right) + Var^M \sum_s \left(L_s^F + L_s^P + L^P \right) z''_{s\omega}$$

$$\left. + \sum_s P_s D_{s\omega} \left(1 - \sum_v x_{sv\omega} - x'_{s\omega} - x''_{s\omega} \right) \right\} + Fix^V \sum_v q_v + Fix^C \sum_s m_S \quad (1)$$

Subject to

$$\sum_v x_{sv\omega} + x'_{s\omega} + x''_{s\omega} \le 1, \quad \forall s, \forall \omega \quad (2)$$

$$\sum_s z_{sv\omega} \le q_v, \quad \forall v, \forall \omega \quad (3)$$

$$\sum_s z''_{s\omega} \le Q_p, \quad \forall \omega \quad (4)$$

$$1 + Cap^V (z_{sv\omega} - 1) \le D_{s\omega} x_{sv\omega} \le Cap^V z_{sv\omega}, \quad \forall s, \forall v, \forall \omega \quad (5)$$

$$1 + Cap^V (z'_{s\omega} - 1) \le D_{s\omega} x'_{sv\omega} \le Cap^V z'_{s\omega}, \quad \forall s, \forall \omega \quad (6)$$

$$1 + Cap^V (z''_{s\omega} - 1) \le D_{s\omega} x''_{sv\omega} \le Cap^V z''_{s\omega}, \quad \forall s, \forall \omega \quad (7)$$

$$m_s \le \sum_{\omega} \left(\sum_v z_{sv\omega} + \sum_{s'} z_{s's\omega} \right), \quad \forall s \ne v, s' \in S \backslash s \quad (8)$$

Constraints (2) ensure that the total number of items delivered from shipper s to warehouse does not exceed its demand. Constraints (3) ensure that the total number of v's own trucks used to deliver items does not exceed the number of that trucks q_v. Constraints (4) ensure that the total number of platformer-provided trucks used to deliver items does not exceed the number of that trucks Q_p. Constraints (5), (6) and (7) limit the number of trucks, considering the number of delivered items and the loading capacity of trucks. Constraints (8) ensure that a shipper lends or barrows a minimum of one truck in at least one scenario.

4 Numerical Experiment

This section elaborates on benefits of using sharing service under uncertain demand environment. Also, we show how the transaction price and the number of platformer-owned trucks have impact on the decision of owning and borrowing trucks and contribute to cost savings. Gurobi Optimizer V.9.1 was used to solve the stochastic problem.

4.1 Scenario Generation

The random numbers are generated following Pearson distribution characterized by average, standard deviation, and skewness, and partitioned into 7 small sets based on percentiles, as depicted in Fig. 1. We randomly select one set from all and define this combination with probabilities as a demand profile. The demand profiles of each item are combined into a demand scenario of a network. In following experiments, we consider the distribution network of 3 shippers whose items have the same demand profile.

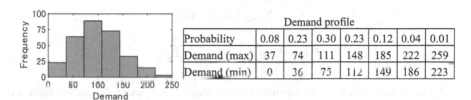

		Demand profile					
Probability	0.08	0.23	0.30	0.23	0.12	0.04	0.01
Demand (max)	37	74	111	148	185	222	259
Demand (min)	0	36	75	112	149	186	223

Fig. 1. Example of a demand profile

4.2 Results

The demand distribution is assumed to follow Pearson distribution with the average of 100 and the skewness of 0.5. It represents that low-demand scenarios occur with high probability. Figure 2 illustrates the cost distributions of the optimized network with and without truck sharing in different level of demand uncertainty. The figures in parentheses refer to 90th percentile cost. Those results indicate that shippers using truck sharing can deliver items at a lower cost compared to those who do so independently. While the 90th percentile cost difference at the low uncertainty level is 5.1%, that at the high uncertainty level is 9.7%. Truck sharing provides cost reduction more effectively in a high uncertainty environment.

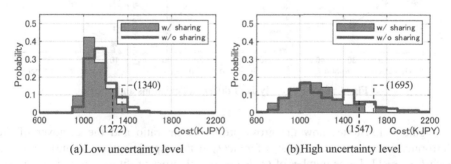

(a) Low uncertainty level   (b) High uncertainty level

Fig. 2. Cost distributions of a network with and without truck sharing

To evaluate the effect of the demand uncertainty and the transaction price, we introduce on-time delivery ratio γ and operation profit margin ratio δ as performance indicators. μ denotes the gross profit margin ratio of an item before subtracting logistics cost, and we set $\mu = 0.2$. The numerator represents the logistics cost, and the denominator represents the revenue in Eq. (10), where E and E^{Loss} denote the objective function value and the demand opportunity loss calculated with the optimal solution, respectively.

$$\gamma = \sum_{\omega} \pi_{\omega} \varphi_{\omega} \tag{9}$$

$$\delta = \mu - \frac{E - E^{Loss}}{\sum_s \frac{P_s}{\mu} \sum_{\omega} \pi_{\omega} D_{s\omega} \varphi_{s\omega}} \tag{10}$$

$$\varphi_{s\omega} = \sum_{\nu} x_{s\nu\omega} + x'_{s\omega} + x''_{s\omega} \tag{11}$$

$$E^{Loss} = \sum_s P_s \sum_{\omega} \pi_{\omega} D_{s\omega} (1 - \varphi_{s\omega}) \tag{12}$$

Figure 3 illustrates how the on-time delivery ratio, the gross profit margin ratio and the turnover of the platformer-owned trucks change across the deviation of demand at different transaction prices. In this experiment, we set the number of platformer-owned trucks $Q_p = 12$ and rate of leased trucks $Fix^R = 30$. The on-time delivery ratio is over 99% across the different deviations and prices. While the gross profit margin ratio reduces due to the increasing number of borrowed and leased trucks, the turnover of the platformer-owned trucks increases as the deviation increases. Although the increase in the transaction price leads to lower profit margin ratio, using truck sharing is consistently beneficial for shippers.

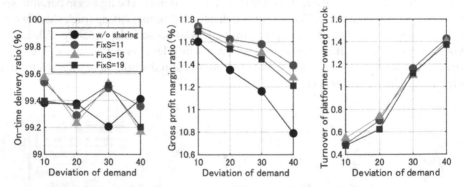

Fig. 3. Sensitive analysis of different deviations and prices

Figure 4 illustrates how the gross profit margin ratio and the turnover of the platformer-owned trucks change at different Q_p. In this experiment, we set the transaction price $Fix^S = 11$. Large number of Q_p leads to high gross profit margin ratio for larger deviation of demand due to a low cost of borrowing trucks. In contrast, the turnover is low for smaller deviation since there is a small change in the number of required trucks. Q_p and the transaction price together with other parameters such as fees and mileage charges, need to be adjusted to improve the robustness to demand fluctuations.

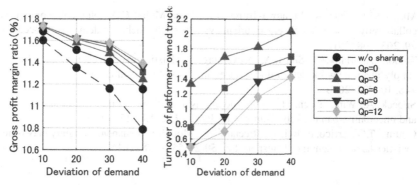

Fig. 4. Sensitive analysis of different number of platformer-owned trucks

5 Conclusion

In this paper, we proposed an optimization model for the network design with truck sharing based on a stochastic programming and perform analysis on several numerical experiments. Our results showed that the benefit of truck sharing increases irrespective of the transaction price and the number of platformer-owned trucks as the deviation of demand increases. However, several extensions for this model that consider, for instance, the area size and the number of shipper locations are suggested to better account for generalized sharing platform. Other sources of uncertainty, such as transportation lead time uncertainty, also need to be considered in terms of a platform management. Further, a heuristic method is required to solve the problem within practical time, since our stochastic approach may not address a large-scale network due to the increasing number of scenarios.

References

1. Bahinipati, B.K., Deshmukh, S.: Vertical collaboration in the semiconductor industry: a decision framework for supply chain relationships. Comput. Ind. Eng. **62**(2), 504–526 (2012)
2. Bahinipati, B.K., Kanda, A., Deshmukh, S.: Horizontal collaboration in semiconductor manufacturing industry supply chain: an evaluation of collaboration intensity index. Comput. Ind. Eng. **57**(3), 880–895 (2009)
3. Yu, K., Cadeaus, J., Song, H.: Flexibility and quality in logistics and relationships. Ind. Mark. Manage. **62**, 211–225 (2017)
4. Wang, Y., et al.: Two-echelon logistics delivery and pickup network optimization based on integrated cooperation and transportation fleet sharing. Expert Syst. Appl. **113**, 44–65 (2018)
5. Zhang, W., Chen, Z., Zhang, S., Wang, W., Yang, S., Cai, Y.: Composite multi-objective optimization on a new collaborative vehicle routing problem with carriers and depots. J. Clean. Prod. **274**, 1225593 (2020)
6. Cleophas, C., Cottrill, C., Ehmke, J.F., Tierney, K.: Collaborative urban transportation: recent advances in theory and practice. Eur. J. Oper. Res. **273**, 801–816 (2019)
7. Wang, Y., Zhang, J., Assoba, K., Liu, Y., Xu, M., Wang, Y.: Collaboration and transportation resource sharing in multiple centers vehicle routing optimization with delivery and pickup. Knowl.-Based Syst. **160**, 296–310 (2018)

8. Muroz-Villamizar, A., Montoya-Torres, J.R., Vega-Mejia, C.A.: Non-collaborative versus collaborative last-mile delivery in urban systems with stochastic demands. Procedia CIRP **30**, 263–268 (2015)
9. Tolooie, A., Maity, M., Sinha, A.: A two-stage stochastic mixed-integer program for reliable supply chain network design under uncertain disruptions and demand. Comput. Ind. Eng. **148**, 106722 (2020)
10. Snoeck, A., Winkenbach, M.: The value of physical distribution flexibility in serving dense and uncertain urban markets. Transp. Res. Part A **136**, 151–177 (2020)
11. Crainic, T.G., Errico, F., Rei, W., Ricciardi, N.: Modeling demand uncertainty in two-tier city logistics tactical planning. Transport. Sci. **50**(2), 559–578 (2016)

Reshaping the Supply Chain for Society 5.0

Rosanna Fornasiero[1]([✉]) [iD] and Andrea Zangiacomi[2] [iD]

[1] CNR-IEIIT, Via Gradenigo, 6, 35100 Padova, Italy
rosanna.fornasiero@ieiit.cnr.it
[2] CNR-STIIMA, Via Corti, 12, 20133 Milano, Italy
andrea.zangiacomi@stiima.cnr.it

Abstract. This work aims to study the evolution of Supply Chain (SC) towards Society 5.0 paradigm proposing a set of SCs to enhance the active role of involved stakeholders leveraging on digital technologies. Social macro-trends indeed strongly impact on companies' business creating the urgent need to significantly adapt the way their SCs are organized and interlinked. The work is based on a consultation with experts representing different kind of companies, industrial sectors, function, role in the SC and research fields. Results lead to the identification of possible SCs for the future, and among them, three solutions seems to particularly fit current challenges related to the evolution of society: Human-centric SC, SC for active citizens and SC in urban context. According to the identified SCs, specific issues are presented and possible solutions basing on new technologies have been mapped with the support of experts. The need to integrate strategies at industrial and societal level urge thus for a new holistic way where business eco-system capabilities merge with civil society needs for have people wellbeing as a major priority.

Keywords: Supply Chain · Digital technologies · Social trends · Industry 5.0 · Human centric approach

1 Introduction and Background

Nowadays, Supply Chains (SC) work in a global and complex environment, and in the future they will have to be more and more able to adapt and identify possible future evolutions to preserve their competitiveness and meet the challenges of this scenario [7, 8].

According to this view, digitalization and the adoption of Industry 4.0 (I4.0) paradigm represented an opportunity to be leveraged by the whole SC. SC processes are thus increasingly managed with a wide variety of innovative technologies and analytical methods to generate new forms of revenue and business value for all the involved actors, moving towards a "digital SC" [6].

However, despite I4.0 revolution is associated with various enabling technologies, such as artificial intelligence, Internet of Things, additive manufacturing, cyber-physical systems, cloud computing, automation and robotics in the manufacturing processes, until

© IFIP International Federation for Information Processing 2021
Published by Springer Nature Switzerland AG 2021
A. Dolgui et al. (Eds.): APMS 2021, IFIP AICT 632, pp. 663–670, 2021.
https://doi.org/10.1007/978-3-030-85906-0_72

now, it has primarily focused on digitalisation for increasing production efficiency and flexibility of companies and SCs and less on the original principles of social fairness and sustainability [14]. While the main concern in Industry 4.0 is about automation, the evolution towards Industry 5.0 will embrace a synergy between humans and autonomous machines, and the autonomous workforce will be perceptive and informed about human intention and desire [25, 26]. In the industrial context, indeed advances have still to be done for what concerns the human-centric approach. In order to ensure that both companies and workers benefit from the digital transition, rethinking and redesigning SC is necessary and workers should be involved in all step of the transition. The concept of Industry 5.0 provides thus a different focus, highlighting the importance of supporting industry in its long-term service to humanity and society. Most of contributions on Industry 5.0 address increased collaboration between humans and smart systems allowing to merge the high-speed accuracy of industrial automation with the cognitive, critical thinking skills of humans [1, 14]. The concept of Society 5.0 - or "super-smart society", presented and promoted by the Japanese government [9], is linked to Industry 5.0. It represents indeed the vision of a new human-centered society, where advanced technologies are applied in everyday life, and in different spheres of activity, to provide products and services satisfying various potential needs as well as reducing economic and social gaps, for the benefit and convenience of all citizens [14, 16].

Despite the advanced pace of technology adoption, humans will continue to play active roles even if these roles may change over time [28]. Human factors and ergonomics, knowledge, skills, and competencies will therefore be essential in guaranteeing and optimizing effortless and safe work processes [28, 29]. Moreover, social media and digitalization in manufacturing are creating a paradigm shift whereby end users are engaging in industrial processes. The main agents of the new society are indeed citizens that will play a leading role, for what concerns the transformation of cities, as innovators creating the desired urban environments [10].

In light of the envisaged scenario, the aim of this work is to reflect on the evolution of SC towards Society 5.0 paradigm proposing a set of SCs to enhance the active role of stakeholders such as workers, consumers, citizens and leveraging on digital technologies to enable manufacturing industry contribution to this essential change of pace. This concept till now has been partly applied in the factory context [11, 19] but a similar approach specifically addressing SC and its peculiar needs and potentials is still in its infancy and current research gaps call for novel contributions.

1.1 Societal Trends

Some important trends affecting the global scenario are related to the social dimension, in particular, changes in demographic, urban environment and customer habits. For what concerns demographic changes, the aging population has a prominent role: on one side by 2050 1 in 6 people in the world is expected to be over the age of 65, nearly doubling the quote of 2019 [30], on the other side a lack of awareness of new I4.0 technologies and related skilled workers is urging new actions [12, 22].

The growth of urban population and consequent emergence of megacities [30] will congest the urban environment due to larger transfer of people and goods and raise the need for the development of smart cities provided with sentient and intelligent infrastructure in order to improve people's quality of living, and sustainability levels [18]. Moreover, trends, such as the middle-class explosion and the rise of individualism and personalisation have increasingly orientated consumers towards extreme personalization requirements to satisfy their own personal needs [15] and will force companies to enrich customer relationship and ensure more flexibility in their SC [5]. Finally, rise of the "do it yourself" (DIY) paradigm in society, enabling customers to realize by themselves in small factories within the urban context, or directly at home, their preferred products [2, 24] also press companies to redefine their SC configuration to provide citizens with the accessibility to reliable means of production [2].

2 Methodology

In this paper, we report part of a study related to the definition of a set of SCs and research and innovation topics for digitalisation. More details on the results can be found in [1]. The work is based on a consultation with experts representing: companies (large, SMEs, start-ups), industrial sectors (i.e. automotive, steel, consumer goods, IT, fashion, transportation), function (CEO, Operation Mangers, SC manager, industrial and academic researcher), role in the SC (i.e. managers from focal company, suppliers, vendors, outsourcers) and academia (SC management and configuration, manufacturing, logistics, engineering, risk management, etc.). In particular, we report the results of two workshops organised in 2019 as face-to-face brainstorming sessions, each of them focusing on a particular topic, under the guidance of a moderator [17]: the first was dedicated to the validation of research and innovation in digital technologies, the second to the identification of possible SCs for the future. The interaction among participants was organized to be open-minded, with informal atmosphere to facilitate the generation of fast-result insights. Each workshop involved a sub-set of the whole group of experts according to the specific topics and aim of analysis to assure plurality of point of view and to cross-cut the results with double check. All in all, 40 experts were involved in the 2 rounds. The work has been conducted according to the following phases:

1. **Collection of Research and Innovation needs:** experts both from academia and from industry were directly involved through a workshop in order to collect ideas, opinions and proposals for the definition of the Research and Innovation needs to be addressed to face challenges impacting on SCs. Starting from a set of trends and related scenarios, experts discussed in small groups using brainstorming tools like posters, mind-maps, post-its.
2. **Clusterisation of ideas:** This phase supported the analysis of opinions collected during the workshops applying thematic analysis. This technique is a qualitative research method for identifying, analyzing, organizing, describing, and reporting themes found within the collected data [3]. This technique was used by the research team to summarize key features and produce a clear and organised output, to discover correspondences between the data collected and homogenously frame the results of the consultation [4, 27].

3. **Proposition of a set of SC strategies for the future:** in this stage, a dedicated workshop was held with a restricted number of experts in order to discuss how companies should adapt their networks to face evolutions identified according to the different trends impacting SCs and stay competitive. The research and innovation needs have been grouped and a set of strategies as the most promising to overcome SC challenges of the next decade were identified. In this insight, three of them are considered in relation to the specific societal trends.

3   Results

In the following the set of SC identified as prominent to face the societal challenges previously highlighted and to support the transition towards the Society 5.0 paradigm are presented.

3.1   Human Centric Supply Chain

The aim of the Human Centric supply chain (HSC) is enabling the valorisation of humans contributing to increase satisfaction and well-being of workers, consumers and citizens. SCs are expected to become increasingly inclusive, focusing on the involvement of all types of stakeholders, enabling the different actors to perform complex activities in an easy, safe and more secure way, supported by innovative digital technologies [31]. Therefore, the human centric technological change in the SC processes is aimed, not only at efficiency and flexibility but also in extended corporate responsibility by fostering socially and inclusive responsible practices [13]. Some issues emerging from the workshops with the experts regard:

- *Training programs for new SC skills*: given the gaps in specialised talent in SC workforce caused by digitalization, it is essential the context-aware identification of both hard and soft SC skills to manage networks in a sustainable way. Specialised skill programmes need to be designed according to human-centred organizational design principles basing on technologies such VR/AR. Also AI can be used to manage the skill gaps and propose appropriate training programmes to the workers.
- *Acceptance and awareness of new technologies*: when designing the future of work in SCs, it has to be taken into consideration the employee point of view to optimize technology-equipment user experience. In particular, cross-cultural acceptance of technological solutions needs to be successfully managed. When designing global SC processes, it is necessary to take into account the socio-cultural differences in the workforce spread in different premises around the world, as they affect the technology's perceived usefulness, user attitude and behaviour.
- *Safety and ergonomics in the work environment*: the potential of autonomous systems and collaborative robots is based on sharing work environment with humans, relieving them from risky and heavy tasks in SC operations. Advanced human-machine interfaces will facilitate the interaction and support ergonomic and safety. The use of exoskeletons will help workers (especially aged ones) in their activities, enhancing safety and productivity both in production and logistics.

- *Social Sustainability and ethical issues*: Health and Safety protocols and Corporate Social Responsibility protocols can be automatized and easily controlled sharing practices and real-time data in cloud based platforms accessible by all stakeholders. When developing decision systems based for example on machine and deep learning, natural language processing, ethical challenges have to be considered, to reduce the risk of unfair decisions and undesirable behaviours.

3.2 Supply Chain for Empowered Citizens

In recent years, citizens have been undergoing rapid changes in behaviour with an increasingly informed role, in a market with a choice of products wider than ever. Moreover, social media and enterprise mobility together enable new consumption patterns. Decisions along the SC thus need to be driven by customer's needs, expressing their own singularity in terms of products and services. The customer should also hold an active role in the SC as a co-creator [21] of her/his own product/service. Customer driven SC mainly rely on the agility concept, which aims for demand and production alignment, fast production and delivery of products in response to change in customer demand [23]. The following issues arise in this case:

- *Customer specificity*: each customer is different, and understanding customer demand is essential to assure inclusivity and that specificity of each societal groups are catched in SC value proposition thanks to technologies as Big Data and Analytics, social platforms and sensors. In this sense, the development of new models and tools for gathering and handling huge volumes of data from customers is needed. Moreover, also customer experience has to be enriched, for example with VR/AR technologies in the purchasing phase and sensors and AI to provide support in the post-sale.
- *SC Collaboration & Orchestration*: the development of new mechanisms based on digital platform and CPS to increase coordination and synchronization among all the actors of the chain is required to create agile/responsive SCs
- *Personalized shipping*: smart management of personalized goods grows the complexity shipping due to a set of factors (e.g. size, package, confidential information, lack of bundling opportunities). Localization and communication technologies are needed to properly handle multiple flows related also to the use of autonomous vehicles (e.g. drones)
- *SC traceability for customer trust:* in order to guarantee the quality, sustainability and originality of materials and processes for consumer trust it is necessary to implement technologies such as and track and trace systems, blockchain, sensor based real time monitoring (e.g. IoT).
- *IPR and privacy*: the increased involvement of customer and supplier concerned with the development of customization and personalization practices and the consequent data exchange requires properly handling IRP related issues. Data privacy should be taken into consideration too, especially when several actors are involved.

3.3 Supply Chain in Urban Context

The spread of new production technologies, such as additive and hybrid manufacturing, the increase in ecommerce and the rise of smart cities, characterised by high connectivity and new sustainable urban mobility [20] are changing the role of SC in relation to the urban context. The proximity of the end users largely influences the design of new processes for the SC. The focus will be on small scale manufacturing systems in urban areas, with the growing importance of fab-labs and local producers. The expansion of the urban environment involves a more complex development of the city logistics, impacting on the different flows (assets, people, vehicles etc.). The location of facilities in the city will also force companies and their logistics to be more environmental friendly and more resource efficient too. The following issues arise from the experts:

- *Coping with urban context*: it is essential to integrate manufacturing and distribution into the urban context and with smart cities infrastructures thanks to appropriate localization and communication technologies. SC should also optimize city logistics to efficiently implement last mile transportation and delivery thanks to Digital platforms.
- *Information and goods flows in urban areas:* issues such as traffic jam, overcapacity of some axis of circulation, local pollution etc., have to be overcome with advanced decision support systems based on AI (such as machine and deep learning) to optimize the flows of citizens and goods in a sustainable manner. At an even more radical level, automated driving will be ready for practical application.
- *Urban manufacturing*: due to automation and advancements in additive and hybrid manufacturing technologies, the development and implementation of modular facilities represent an enabler for the relocation of small manufacturing sites within urban areas and to exploit the DYI paradigm. Online platforms can support the shared management of both facilities and integrated purchasing of materials, enabling individual citizens to realize their own products.
- *New entrepreneurial generation:* the rise of DYI and personalization paradigm will impact the ambition of the new generation, which will exploit potential of digital technologies and social media to provide a service or a product to the society. This can be supported, for example, facilitating the creation of start-ups and fab-labs.

4 Conclusions

Global macro-trends such as the acceleration of technological developments, the demanding consumer needs and behaviors, the rise of aging population strongly impact on companies' business. This creates the urgent need to significantly adapt the way their SC are organized and interlinked. Companies are indeed forced, not only to identify new business model, but also to focus their strategy on redefining their value creation with upstream and downstream partners of their SCs.

This paper represents a first attempt to understand how SC can contribute to the rise of Society 5.0 accomplishing societal trends thanks to implementation of digital technologies. The work defines three possible type of SCs and define possible ways to answer in a proactive or reactive way to the societal changes. The need to integrate more than ever strategies at industrial and societal level urge for a new holistic way where business eco-systems merge with civil society.

Further research will be focused on deepening how the different enabling technologies can support the issues addressed in each of the three SC typology considered, with the aim to provide insights to the discussion on SC contribution to the development of a smarter and human centric society. Each SC typology need to be further designed along the most important dimensions like sourcing, purchasing, manufacturing and distribution to reshape the role of technologies and provide the opportunity for exploring new social paths.

Acknowledgment. This work has been partly conducted in the Next-Net project (n° 768884) (Next generation technologies for networked Europe), co-funded by the European Union under the Horizon 2020 programme. The authors wish to acknowledge the European Commission for their support. They also wish to acknowledge their gratitude and appreciation to all the project team for their contribution during the development of this research.

References

1. Atwell, C.: Yes, Industry 5.0 is Already on the Horizon (2017). https://www.machinedesign.com/industrial-automation/yes-industry-50-already-horizon
2. Bonvoisin, J., Galla, J., Prendeville, S.: Design principles for do-it-yourself production. In: Campana, G., Howlett, R.J., Setchi, R., Cimatti, B. (eds.) SDM 2017. SIST, vol. 68, pp. 77–86. Springer, Cham (2017). https://doi.org/10.1007/978-3-319-57078-5_8
3. Braun, V., Clarke, V.: Using thematic analysis in psychology. Qual. Res. Psychol. **3**(2), 77–101 (2006). https://doi.org/10.1191/1478088706qp063oa
4. Braun, V., Clarke, V., Hayfield, N., Terry, G.: Thematic analysis. In: Liamputtong, P. (ed.) Handbook of Research Methods in Health Social Sciences, pp. 843–860. Springer, Singapore (2019). https://doi.org/10.1007/978-981-10-5251-4_103
5. Brusset, X., Teller, C.: Supply chain capabilities, risks, and resilience. Int. J. Prod. Econ. **184**, 59–68 (2017). https://doi.org/10.1016/j.ijpe.2016.09.008
6. Büyüközkan, G., Göçer, F.: Digital supply chain: literature review and a proposed framework for future research. Comput. Ind. **97**, 157–177 (2018). https://doi.org/10.1016/j.compind.2018.02.010
7. Cannella, S., Dominguez, R., Framinan, J.M.: Turbulence in market demand on supply chain networks. Int. J. Simul. Model. **15**(3), 450–459 (2016)
8. Christopher, M., Holweg, M.: Supply chain 2.0: managing supply chains in the era of turbulence. Int. J. Phys. Distrib. Logist. Manag. **41**(1), 63–82 (2011). https://doi.org/10.1108/09600031111101439
9. Council of Science, Technology and Innovation: Fifth Science and Technology Basic Plan. Government of Japan, Tokyo (2016)
10. Deguchi, A., Sameshima, S.: Afterwords. In: Deguchi, A. (ed.) Society 5.0 - A People-Centric Super-Smart Society, Hitachi-UTokyo Laboratory (H-UTokyo Lab.), The University of Tokyo Bunkyo-ku, Tokyo, Japan. Springer open (2020)
11. Doyle-Kent, M., Kopacek, P.: Industry 5.0: is the manufacturing industry on the cusp of a new revolution? In: Durakbasa, N.M., Gençyılmaz, M.G. (eds.) ISPR -2019. LNME, pp. 432–441. Springer, Cham (2020). https://doi.org/10.1007/978-3-030-31343-2_38
12. European Commission: Europe's Digital Progress Report 2017, Integration of Digital Technology. https://ec.europa.eu/digital-single-market/en/news/europes-digital-progress-report-2017
13. European Commission: Unlocking the potential of industrial human–robot collaboration. A Vision on Industrial Collaborative Robots for Economy and Society (2019)

14. European Commission: Industry 5.0 - Towards a sustainable, human-centric and resilient European industry (2021)
15. Fornasiero, R., et al.: Paths to innovation in supply chains: the landscape of future research. In: Fornasiero, R., Sardesai, S., Barros, A.C., Matopoulos, A. (eds.) Next generation supply chains. LNMIE, pp. 169–233. Springer, Cham (2021). https://doi.org/10.1007/978-3-030-635 05-3_8
16. Fukuda, K.: Science, technology and innovation ecosystem transformation toward society 5.0. Int. J. Prod. Econ. **220**, 107460 (2020). https://doi.org/10.1016/j.ijpe.2019.07.033
17. Krueger, R.A., Casey, M.A.: Focus Groups: A Practical Guide for Applied Research, 5th edn. SAGE Publications, Thousand Oaks (2015)
18. Li, D., Ma, J., Cheng, T., van Genderen, J.L., Shao, Z.: Challenges and opportunities for the development of megacities. Int. J. Digit. Earth **12**(12), 1382–1395 (2018). https://doi.org/10. 1080/17538947.2018.1512662
19. Longo, F., Padovano, A., Umbrello, S.: Value-oriented and ethical technology engineering in Industry 5.0: a human-centric perspective for the design of the factory of the future. Appl. Sci. **10**(12), 4182 (2020). https://doi.org/10.3390/app10124182
20. Manville, C., et al.: Mapping smart cities in the EU (2014)
21. Martinelli, E.M., Tunisini, A.: Customer integration into supply chains: literature review and research propositions. J. Bus. Ind. Mark. **34**(1), 24–38 (2019). https://doi.org/10.1108/JBIM-07-2017-0162
22. Matt, D.T., Orzes, G., Rauch, E., Dallasega, P.: Urban production–a socially sustainable factory concept to overcome shortcomings of qualified workers in smart SMEs. Comput. Ind. Eng **139**, 105384 (2018). https://doi.org/10.1016/j.cie.2018.08.035
23. Medini, K., et al.: Highlights in customer-driven operations management research. Procedia CIRP **86**, 12–19 (2019). https://doi.org/10.1016/j.procir.2020.01.026
24. Mohajeri, B., Poesche, J., Kauranen, I., Nyberg, T.: Shift to social manufacturing: applications of additive manufacturing for consumer products. In: 2016 IEEE International Conference on IEEE Service Operations and Logistics, and Informatics (SOLI), pp. 1–6, July 2016
25. Nahavandi, S.: Industry 5.0—a human-centric solution. Sustainability **11**(16), 4371 (2019). https://doi.org/10.3390/su11164371
26. Nair, M.M., Tyagi, A.K., Sreenath, N.: The future with industry 4.0 at the core of society 5.0: open issues, future opportunities and challenges. In: 2021 International Conference on Computer Communication and Informatics (ICCCI), pp. 1–7. IEEE (2021) https://doi.org/ 10.1109/ICCCI50826.2021.9402498
27. Nowell, L.S., Norris, J.M., White, D.E., Moules, N.J.: Thematic analysis: striving to meet the trustworthiness criteria. Int. J. Qual. Methods **16**(1) (2017). https://doi.org/10.1177/160940 6917733847
28. Reiman, A., Kaivo-oja, J., Parviainen, E., Takala, E.P., Lauraeus, T.: Human factors and ergonomics in manufacturing in the industry 4.0 context–a scoping review. Technol. Soc. **65**, 101572 (2021). https://doi.org/10.1016/j.techsoc.2021.101572
29. Siemieniuch, C.E., Sinclair, M.A., Henshaw, M.D.: Global drivers, sustainable manufacturing and systems ergonomics. Appl. Ergon. **51**, 104–119 (2015). https://doi.org/10.1016/j.apergo. 2015.04.018
30. United Nations: World Urbanization Prospect 2019. https://population.un.org/wup/
31. World Manufacturing Forum (WMF): The 2019 World Manufacturing forum report-Skills for the future of manufacturing (2019). https://c00e521c-fc35-464f-8eef-9356e02fbfb5.filesusr. com/ugd/c56fe3_d617f7333fd347b0b2bb4a739ba72993.pdf

Supply Chain Risk Management Under Coronavirus

A Tabu Search Heuristic for the Robust Dynamic Bayesian Network Optimisation Problem Under the Supply Chain Ripple Effect

Ming Liu[1], Hao Tang[1], Feng Chu[2(✉)], Feifeng Zheng[3], and Chengbin Chu[4]

[1] School of Economics and Management, Tongji University,
Shanghai, People's Republic of China
[2] IBISC, Univ Évry, University of Paris-Saclay, Évry, France
feng.chu@univ-evry.fr
[3] Glorious Sun School of Business and Management, Donghua University, Shanghai,
People's Republic of China
[4] Laboratoire d'Informatique Gaspard-Monge (LIGM), UMR 8049,
Univ Gustave Eiffel, ESIEE Paris, 93162 Noisy-le-Grand Cedex, France

Abstract. Due to the impact of the global COVID-19, supply chain (SC) risk management under the ripple effect is becoming an increasingly hot topic in both practice and research. In our former research, a robust dynamic bayesian network (DBN) approach has been developed for disruption risk assessment, whereas there still exists a gap between the proposed simulated annealing (SA) algorithm and commercial solver in terms of solution quality. To improve the computational efficiency for solving the robust DBN optimisation model, a tabu search heuristic is proposed for the first time in this paper. We design a novel problem-specific neighborhood move to keep the search in feasible solution space. The computational experiments, conducted on randomly generated instances, indicate that the average gap between our approach and commercial solver is within 0.07%, which validates the performance of the proposed method.

Keywords: Ripple effect · Robust DBN · Tabu search

1 Introduction

In recent years, supply chain (SC) risk management has been a widely discussed topic in both industry and academia as a result of severe impact of the COVID-19 epidemic and some other natural or man-made disasters on SCs. Due to the growth structural complexity and increasing global scale of SC networks, the disruption of a supplier caused by these unpredictable disasters will probably propagate to the downstream manufacturers located in disaster-free areas. For example, the Japanese tsunami and earthquake in 2011 disrupted the production

© IFIP International Federation for Information Processing 2021
Published by Springer Nature Switzerland AG 2021
A. Dolgui et al. (Eds.): APMS 2021, IFIP AICT 632, pp. 673–680, 2021.
https://doi.org/10.1007/978-3-030-85906-0_73

of auto parts and image sensors suppliers, leading to the cease of production of auto companies and smart electronic devices manufacturers in other countries due to the shortage of necessary parts [7]. In another recent example, the sudden Texas winter storm strikes chip foundries, such as South Korea's Samsung Electronics Co., one of the world's biggest chip makers with about 28% of its overall production capacity in Austin facilities[1]. The impact of the disruption in the fragile chip industry, caused by the global COVID-19 epidemic and winter storm, propagates to auto automobile, mobile phone, game consoles and other downstream industries. These above facts embody the impact of a disruption or a series of disruptions along the SCs, i.e. the ripple effect. The ripple effect is introduced by Ivanov et al. [9], meaning the disruption risk of upstream partners in the SCs propagating to downstream partners. For a comprehensive review of this research area, interested readers may refer to surveys by Hosseini et al. [6] and Dolgui et al. [3].

To reduce adverse impact of the ripple effect and mitigate it at minimal costs, it is crucial to measure quantitatively the risk of disruptions propagating along SCs. Bearing this in mind, more and more researchers have proposed novel mathematical models and optimization methods to estimate adverse consequences of ripple effects [2]. Among these techniques, bayesian network (BN), capable of describing the ripple effect via a directed acyclic graph, is introduced for the disruption risk evaluation by Hosseini and Barker [5]. Due to the complexity of global SCs, it is worth noting that the disruptions of source suppliers have continuous effect, which can affect the SCs over several time periods [8]. To assess the disruption risk in a SC with two suppliers and one manufacturer over a time horizon with several periods, Hosseini et al. [7] further propose a simulation model based on a dynamic bayesian network (DBN). In their work, the inputs of DBN (i.e. the corresponding probability distributions) are assumed to be perfectly known. To overcome data scarcity in some real situations, Liu et al. [10] propose a new robust DBN optimisation model utilising the probability intervals to evaluate the worst-case disruption risk.

The new robust DBN approach opens a new perspective for disruption risk assessment, whereas the proposed algorithm in the former work can be improved in terms of both solution quality and computational time. Besides, as a result of the high level of complexity and uncertainty of global SC network, the state of SC may change at any time. Accurate and timely decisions will make a difference for mitigating the impact of disruptions. Motivated by the above two reasons, it is necessary to design efficient solution algorithm that can obtain risk assessment results within a reasonable amount of time.

As a main contribution of this paper, we propose a tabu search (TS) heuristic for solving the robust DBN optimisation model efficiently, which can provide

---

[1] Asa Fitch, 2021. Texas Winter Storm Strikes Chip Makers, Compounding Supply Woes. The Wall Street Journal. https://www.wsj.com/articles/texas-winter-storm-strikes-chip-makers-compounding-supply-woes-11613588617?mod=searchresults_pos3&page=1.

higher quality solutions within a shorter run time compared to that obtained by the simulated annealing (SA) algorithm developed in our former work.

The remainder of this paper is organized as follows. In Sect. 2, the robust DBN optimisation model is briefly presented for review. In Sect. 3, an efficient TS heuristic is designed for solving the problem, and computational experiments are conducted to evaluate its performance in Sect. 4.

2   Problem Formulation

In this section, we only restate the robust DBN optimisation formulation introduced in the paper [10] for simplicity. For a comprehensive description of the robust DBN approach, readers may refer to Liu et al. [10] and Hosseini et al. [7].

The notations and problem variables are defined the same as former research as follows:

Parameters

$\mathcal{I}$: the set of suppliers, $\mathcal{I} = \{1, \ldots, I\}$, indexed by i;

$I + 1$: the manufacturer;

$\mathcal{T}$: the set of periods, $\mathcal{T} = \{1, \ldots, T\}$, indexed by t;

$\mathcal{S}_i$: the set of states for the supplier or manufacturer i, $\mathcal{S}_i = \{s_{i1}, \ldots, s_{ij}, \ldots, s_{in_i}\}$, indexed by j, where n_i is the number of possible states of SC member $i \in \mathcal{I} \cup \{I + 1\}$;

s_{ij}: the jth state of the supplier or the manufacturer i, where $s_{ij} \in \mathcal{S}_i$, $i \in \mathcal{I} \cup \{I + 1\}$, $j \in \{1, \ldots, n_i\}$;

$\mathbf{M}_i$: Markov transition matrix of supplier i, where $i \in \mathcal{I}$;

$dom(c)$: the domain of the state-combination-index c, i.e. $dom(c) = \{1, 2, \ldots, n_1 \cdot n_2 \cdots n_I\}$;

$C(\bullet)$: unique bijection mapping $\mathcal{S}_1 \times \cdots \times \mathcal{S}_I \xrightarrow{C(\bullet)} dom(c)$ in the prior BN which maps a state combination to a state-combination-index;

$C^{-1}(\bullet)$: the inverse mapping of $C(\bullet)$, $dom(c) \xrightarrow{C^{-1}(\bullet)} \mathcal{S}_1 \times \cdots \times \mathcal{S}_I$, which maps a state-combination-index to a state combination;

$C^{-1}(c)(i)$: the corresponding state of supplier i, $i \in \mathcal{I}$, for a give state-combination-index c in the prior bayesian network (BN);

$dom(g)$: the domain of the state-combination-index g, i.e. $dom(g) = \{1, 2, \ldots, n_1 \cdot n_2 \cdots n_I \cdot n_{I+1}\}$;

$G(\bullet)$: unique bijection mapping $\mathcal{S}_1 \times \cdots \times \mathcal{S}_I \times \mathcal{S}_{I+1} \xrightarrow{G(\bullet)} dom(g)$ in each two-time bayesian network (2TBN) which maps a state combination to a state-combination-index;

$G^{-1}(\bullet)$: the inverse mapping of $C(\bullet)$, $dom(g) \xrightarrow{G^{-1}(\bullet)} \mathcal{S}_1 \times \cdots \times \mathcal{S}_I \times \mathcal{S}_{I+1}$, which maps a state-combination-index to a state combination;

$G^{-1}(g)(i)$: the corresponding state of supplier (or the manufacturer) i, $i \in \mathcal{I} \cup \{I + 1\}$, for a give state-combination-index g in each 2TBN;

$\underline{x}_{ij}^1$: the lower bound of the probability interval in the jth state for the supplier i in time period 1, where $i \in \mathcal{I}$, $j \in \{1, \ldots, n_i\}$;

$\bar{x}_{ij}^1$: the upper bound of the probability interval in the jth state for the supplier i in time period 1, where $i \in \mathcal{I}$, $j \in \{1, \ldots, n_i\}$;

$\underline{y}_{jc}$: the lower bound of the probability interval in the jth state for the manufacturer, conditional on the cth state combination in the prior BN, where $j \in \{1, \ldots, n_{I+1}\}$, $c \in dom(c)$;

$\bar{y}_{jc}$: the upper bound of the probability interval in the jth state for the manufacturer, conditional on the cth state combination in the prior BN, where $j \in \{1, \ldots, n_{I+1}\}$, $c \in dom(c)$;

$\underline{z}_{jg}$: the lower bound of the probability interval in the jth state for the manufacturer, conditional on the gth state combination in each 2TBN, where $j \in \{1, \ldots, n_{I+1}\}$, $g \in dom(g)$;

$\bar{z}_{jg}$: the upper bound of the probability interval in the jth state for the manufacturer, conditional on the gth state combination in each 2TBN, where $j \in \{1, \ldots, n_{I+1}\}$, $g \in dom(g)$;

Problem Variables

x_{ij}^t: the probability in the jth state for the supplier or manufacturer i in time period t, where $i \in \mathcal{I} \cup \{I+1\}$, $j \in \{1, \ldots, n_i\}$, $t \in \mathcal{T}$;

y_{jc}: the probability in the jth state for the manufacturer, conditional on the cth state combination in the prior BN, where $j \in \{1, \ldots, n_{I+1}\}$, $c \in dom(c)$;

z_{jg}: the probability interval in the jth state for the manufacturer, conditional on the gth state combination in each 2TBN, where $j \in \{1, \ldots, n_{I+1}\}$, $g \in dom(g)$;

The robust DBN optimisation model can be formulated as follows:

$$[\text{Robust DBN}] : \quad \max \left\{ \sum_{g \in dom(g)} z_{n_{I+1},g} \cdot \prod_{i \in \mathcal{I}} x_{i,G^{-1}(g)(i)}^T \cdot x_{I+1,G^{-1}(g)(I+1)}^{T-1} \right\} \quad (1)$$

Subject to:

$$\left(x_{i1}^t, \ldots, x_{in_i}^t\right) = \left(x_{i1}^1, \ldots, x_{in_i}^1\right) \cdot (\mathbf{M}_i)^{t-1}, \quad \forall i \in \{1, \ldots, I\}, t \in \mathcal{T}/\{1\} \quad (2)$$

$$x_{(I+1)j}^1 = \sum_{c \in dom(c)} y_{jc} \cdot \prod_{i=1}^{I} x_{i,C^{-1}(c)(i)}^1, \quad \forall j \in \{1, \ldots, n_{I+1}\} \quad (3)$$

$$x_{(I+1)j}^t = \sum_{g \in dom(g)} z_{jg} \cdot \prod_{i=1}^{I} x_{i,G^{-1}(g)(i)}^t \cdot x_{(I+1),G^{-1}(g)(I+1)}^{t-1}, \quad (4)$$
$$\forall j \in \{1, \ldots, n_{I+1}\}, t \in \mathcal{T}/\{1\}$$

$$\sum_{j \in \{1, \ldots, n_i\}} x_{ij}^1 = 1, \quad \forall i \in \mathcal{I} \quad (5)$$

$$\sum_{j \in \{1, \ldots, n_{I+1}\}} y_{jc} = 1, \quad \forall c \in dom(c) \quad (6)$$

$$\sum_{j \in \{1,\dots,n_{I+1}\}} z_{jg} = 1, \quad \forall g \in dom(g) \tag{7}$$

$$x_{ij}^1 \in \left[\underline{x}_{ij}^1, \bar{x}_{ij}^1\right], \quad \forall i \in \mathcal{I}, j \in \{1,\dots,n_i\} \tag{8}$$

$$0 \le x_{ij}^t \le 1, \quad \forall i \in \mathcal{I}, j \in \{1,\dots,n_i\}, t \in \mathcal{T}/\{1\} \tag{9}$$

$$0 \le x_{(I+1)j}^t \le 1, \quad \forall j \in \{1,\dots,n_{I+1}\}, t \in \mathcal{T} \tag{10}$$

$$y_{jc} \in [\underline{y}_{jc}, \bar{y}_{jc}], \quad \forall j \in \{1,\dots,n_{I+1}\}, c \in dom(c) \tag{11}$$

$$z_{jg} \in \left[\underline{z}_{jg}, \bar{z}_{jg}\right], \quad \forall j \in \{1,\dots,n_{I+1}\}, g \in dom(g) \tag{12}$$

The objective function (1) is to maximise the worst-case disruption risk, i.e. to estimate the robustness of the manufacturer in the final period T under disruptions. Constraint (2) represents the Markov transition equation for each supplier i. Constraints (3) describes the probability in each state for the manufacturer in the prior BN. Constraint (4) calculates the probability in each state for the manufacturer in each 2TBN. Constraints (5)–(7) guarantee the second Kolmogorov axiom of probability, i.e., the sum of probabilities in all states for a supplier or the manufacturer is equal to 1. Constraints (8)–(12) are the domains of probabilities in each state in all periods.

3 Solution Approach

Tabu search (TS) is an efficient iterative metaheuristic for finding optimal or near-optimal solution via memory structures and exploration strategies that can help escape from local optima [4]. Because of its outstanding performance, TS has become a popular tool for solving various difficult problems in many research fields. In the field of SC management and optimisation, researchers have applied TS for production and distribution planning problem [1] and multi-product, multi-echelon and multi-objective SC network design problem [11,12].

To solve the robust DBN optimisation model more efficiently, we devise a TS heuristic based on the characteristics of the model. In the following, the main components of the proposed TS heuristic are presented.

3.1 Solution Representation

From constraint (2), we know that the values of variables x_{ij}^t, where $t \in \mathcal{T}/\{1\}$, can be obtained once variables x_{ij}^1 have been determined. Thus, only variables x_{ij}^1, y_{jc}, and z_{jg} are encoded for representing the solution.

3.2 Initial Solution Generation

According to constraints (8), (11) and (12), the initial variables are randomly generated between their lower and upper bounds. Note that the solution may be infeasible due to violations of constraints (5)–(7) in the random generation process. Therefore, to guarantee feasibility of initial solution, the probability correction procedure proposed in paper [10] is applied after random generation.

3.3   Neighborhood and Move

As the number of suppliers gets larger, the number of variables increases exponentially due to the increase of the number of state-combinations in the prior BN and 2TBN. All neighborhoods of the incumbent solution, therefore, cannot be enumerated in bounded time. Besides, it has also been indicated that exploring complete neighborhoods may not be an efficient use of computing resources [13]. Thus, we merely generates partial neighboring solutions in each iteration.

Take the neighborhood move for variable x_{ij}^1 as an example. Two variables $x_{ij_1}^1$ and $x_{ij_2}^1$ for each supplier i are randomly selected and the values of them are changed as follows:

$$\begin{cases} x_{ij_1}^1 = x_{ij_1}^1 + \alpha \\ x_{ij_2}^1 = x_{ij_2}^1 - \alpha \end{cases} \tag{13}$$

where $\alpha = \min\left\{\beta \cdot x_{ij_1}^1, \bar{x}_{ij_1}^1 - x_{ij_1}^1, x_{ij_2}^1 - \underline{x}_{ij_2}^1\right\}$, and β is the adjustment rate, which is set to be 0.2 after initial experiments. The variation α will keep the neighborhood move within the feasible solution space. Likewise, for each state-combination c (g), the neighborhood move for variable y_{jc} (z_{jg}) is conducted by randomly selecting two variables $y_{j_1,c}$ and $y_{j_2,c}$ $(z_{j_1,g}$ and $z_{j_2,g})$, and changing their values in a similar way. Therefore, the number of neighboring solutions in each iteration is $I + n_1 \cdot n_2 \cdots n_I + n_1 \cdot n_2 \cdots n_I \cdot n_{I+1}$.

3.4   Tabu List Management and Aspiration Criterion

Based on initial experiments, the length of tabu list is set to be $|\mathcal{S}_{I+1}| \cdot I^2$, which is dependent on problem size. In the iterative procedure, tabu list is managed in a cyclical way using the first-in-first-out (FIFO) strategy. Besides, as a special case, whenever a move in tabu list yields a candidate solution better than the best solution so far, the new solution will be accepted and this move will be replaced at the end of the tabu list.

3.5   Stop Criterion

The search procedure stops when it reaches the maximum number of iterations or the maximum number of iterations without improving the best solution.

4   Computational Results

In this section, computational results on randomly generated instances are reported to demonstrate the performance of the solution method. The proposed TS heuristic is programmed in Python, and the commercial solver Yalmip (using Gurobi and Matlab built-in functions to compute lower bound and upper bound) is called in Matlab 2019a as a comparison. The computational experiments have been conducted on a personal computer with 2.4 GHz Core i5 and 16 GB Ram.

We generated 12 random instances with 1 manufacturer, 2–4 suppliers and 2–5 time periods, as the same way in our former research [10]. The numerical results are as follows:

Table 1. The Computational results.

		Yalmip		TS		
Number of suppliers	Number of periods	Objective	Time (sec.)	Objective	Time (sec.)	gap(%)
2	2	0.3512	3.60	0.3512	1.06	0.00
	3	0.2782	7.61	0.2782	1.76	0.00
	4	0.3710	13.96	0.3710	3.90	0.00
	5	0.2353	21.41	0.2353	3.97	0.00
3	2	0.3548	52.13	0.3548	16.49	0.00
	3	0.3327	176.68	0.3327	33.15	0.00
	4	0.3310	200.03	0.3310	45.21	0.00
	5	0.2932	278.40	0.2932	58.70	0.00
4	2	0.3511	414.14	0.3502	181.34	0.26
	3	0.3248	2038.50	0.3242	264.68	0.18
	4	0.0107	0066.10	0.3097	467.40	0.32
	5	–	3600.00	0.3445	439.84	–
Average		0.3213	596.60	0.3230	126.46	0.07*

'–': means Yalmip cannot output solutions within a time limit of 3600 s;
'*': the average gap is calculated except the '–' cases.

From Table 1, we can observe that the TS heuristic can provide almost the same solutions with an average gap of only 0.07% compared to the commercial solver Yalmip. In terms of computational time, our approach outperforms the commercial solver clearly. Especially when the solver cannot output optimal solution for the instance with 4 suppliers and 5 periods in 3600 s, the TS heuristic still can obtain good solution.

Compared with the SA proposed in former work [10], whose average gap with Yalmip on the same sized problems is 6.56%, the new solution approach proposed in this paper can provide better disruption risks assessment for SC managers to make better decisions to reduce adverse impact of the ripple effect.

Acknowledgement. This work was supported by the National Natural Science Foundation of China (NSFC) under Grants 72021002, 71972146, 71771048, 71432007, 71832001 and 72071144.

References

1. Armentano, V.A., Shiguemoto, A.L., Løkketangen, A.: Tabu search with path relinking for an integrated production-distribution problem. Comput. Oper. Res. **38**(8), 1199–1209 (2011)
2. Badurdeen, F., et al.: Quantitative modeling and analysis of supply chain risks using Bayesian theory. J. Manuf. Technol. Manag. **25**(5), 631–654 (2014)
3. Dolgui, A., Ivanov, D., Sokolov, B.: Ripple effect in the supply chain: an analysis and recent literature. Int. J. Prod. Res. **56**(1–2), 414–430 (2018)
4. Glover, F.: Tabu search: a tutorial. Interfaces **20**(4), 74–94 (1990)
5. Hosseini, S., Barker, K.: A Bayesian network model for resilience-based supplier selection. Int. J. Prod. Econ. **180**, 68–87 (2016)
6. Hosseini, S., Ivanov, D., Dolgui, A.: Review of quantitative methods for supply chain resilience analysis. Transp. Res. Part E Logist. Transp. Rev. **125**, 285–307 (2019)

7. Hosseini, S., Ivanov, D., Dolgui, A.: Ripple effect modelling of supplier disruption: integrated Markov chain and dynamic Bayesian network approach. Int. J. Prod. Res. **58**(11), 3284–3303 (2020)

8. Ivanov, D., Dolgui, A., Sokolov, B., Ivanova, M.: Literature review on disruption recovery in the supply chain. Int. J. Prod. Res. **55**(20), 6158–6174 (2017)

9. Ivanov, D., Sokolov, B., Dolgui, A.: The ripple effect in supply chains: trade-off 'efficiency-flexibility-resilience' in disruption management. Int. J. Prod. Res. **52**(7), 2154–2172 (2014)

10. Liu, M., Liu, Z., Chu, F., Zheng, F., Chu, C.: A new robust dynamic Bayesian network approach for disruption risk assessment under the supply chain ripple effect. Int. J. Prod. Res. **59**(1), 265–285 (2021)

11. Melo, M., Nickel, S., Saldanha-da Gama, F.: A Tabu search heuristic for redesigning a multi-echelon supply chain network over a planning horizon. Int. J. Prod. Econ. **136**(1), 218–230 (2012)

12. Mohammed, A.M., Duffuaa, S.O.: A Tabu search based algorithm for the optimal design of multi-objective multi-product supply chain networks. Expert Syst. Appl. **140**, 112808 (2020)

13. Reeves, C.R.: Improving the efficiency of Tabu search for machine sequencing problems. J. Oper. Res. Soc. **44**(4), 375–382 (1993)

A New Robust Dynamic Bayesian Network Model with Bounded Deviation Budget for Disruption Risk Evaluation

Ming Liu[1], Tao Lin[1], Feng Chu[2(✉)], Feifeng Zheng[3], and Chengbin Chu[4]

[1] School of Economics and Management, Tongji University,
Shanghai, People's Republic of China
[2] IBISC, Univ Évry, University of Paris-Saclay, Évry, France
feng.chu@univ-evry.fr
[3] Glorious Sun School of Business and Management, Donghua University,
Shanghai, People's Republic of China
[4] Laboratoire d'Informatique Gaspard-Monge (LIGM), UMR 8049,
Univ Gustave Eiffel, ESIEE Paris, 93162 Noisy-le-Grand Cedex, France

Abstract. Dynamic Bayesian network (DBN), combining with probability intervals, is a valid tool to estimate the risk of disruptions propagating along the supply chain (SC) under data scarcity. However, since the approach evaluate the risk from the worst-case perspective, the obtained result may be too conservative for some decision makers. To overcome this difficulty, a new robust DBN model, considering bounded deviation budget, is first time to be developed to analyse the disruption risk properly. We first formulate a new robust DBN optimization model with bounded deviation budget. Then a linearization technique is applied to linearize the nonlinear bounded deviation budget constraint. Finally, a case study is conducted to demonstrate the applicability of the proposed model and some managerial insights are drawn.

Keywords: Supply chain · Dynamic bayesian network · Bounded deviation budget

1 Introduction

The COVID-19 epidemic causes extreme disturbances for people's daily life. Supply chain (SC) is no exception. Especially, due to high structural complexity and increasing global scale, supply chain is fragile under disruptions, such as natural or man-made disasters. One example comes from the Japanese tsunami in 2011, which affected the production of auto parts' suppliers, leading to the reduce of production of auto companies [5]. Another example comes from the explosion and subsequent fires of BASF facility in Ludwigshafer, the disaster stops the production of raw materials, and its downstream manufacturer has a great difficulty to maintain production. According to [1], the propagation of the

© IFIP International Federation for Information Processing 2021
Published by Springer Nature Switzerland AG 2021
A. Dolgui et al. (Eds.): APMS 2021, IFIP AICT 632, pp. 681–688, 2021.
https://doi.org/10.1007/978-3-030-85906-0_74

disruption results in a revenue loss of 10–15% compared to the previous year. All these facts embody the impact of a disruption along the supply chain, i.e. the ripple effect. The ripple effect introduced by [9] means the disruption risk of upstream partners in the SC propagates to downstream partners. Due to the adverse consequences of ripple effects, the disruption risk propagation along the SC is the most notorious challenge that each enterprise must confront.

To mitigate the adverse results of ripple effects and maintain competitiveness for enterprises, disruption risk assessment has been given a high priority in SCM [7,10]. It is indispensable to adopt appropriate optimization methods to estimate the disruption risk quantitatively. Bayesian network (BN), first introduced by [3], is an outstanding representative. The BN describe the ripple effect via a directed acyclic graph. However, the temporal nature of the disruption propagation is not studied in his work. Considering the dynamics of the disruption risk propagation over a time horizon, [5] propose a dynamic Bayesian network (DBN). [11] indicate further that the probability distribution of each supplier's state and the disruption propagation in the SC can not be perfectly known under data scarcity. Thus they propose a new robust DBN approach, integrating the DBN and probability intervals, to evaluate the worst-case oriented disruption risk under data scarcity. However, [11]'s model focus on the worst-case situation in given probability intervals, which is too conservative for some decision makers. Therefore, in this work, we incorporate a bounded deviation budget constraint into [11]'s model.The bounded deviation budget constraint denotes the total sum of deviation (i.e., the part of decision variables deviates from the mean value of given intervals) no greater than the budget, which can reduce the robust properly. Moreover, the SC structure is built on partner relationships following [11]'s work. This study aims to aid decision makers to properly assess SC risk with bounded deviation budget. The main contributions of this paper include:

(1) To the best of our knowledge, we are first to combine DBN with bounded deviation budget, to evaluate the disruption risk propagation along th SC.
(2) A new robust DBN optimization formulation considering bounded deviation budget is developed.
(3) The linearization technique is applied to linearize the nonlinear constraint.

The rest of this paper is organized as follows. In Sect. 2, a brief literature review is given. Section 3 describes the addressed problem in detail and formulate a new robust DBN model for the worst-case oriented disruption risk estimation considering bounded deviation budget. In Sect. 4, the linearization technique is applied to linearize the nonlinear constraint. A case study is conducted in Sect. 5. Section 6 concludes this paper and outlines future research directions.

2   Literature Review

Since our study falls within the scope of SC disruption risk management problems, only most related works are reviewed.

The ripple effect is first introduced by [9]. [8] proposed an optimal control framework combined with a mathematical programming method to perform planning and execution control for SC resilience. Based on [8]'s work, [13] investigate the ripple effect in the SC from the structural perspective. [6] consider the structural and operational vulnerabilities of the SC under ripple effect simultaneously. [12] formulates a stochastic programming model and proposes multiple SC management strategy to mitigate the disruption risks under ripple effect.

Based on the dependence relationships between suppliers and manufactures, [2] propose a Bayesian network (BN) approach for measuring the resilience of SCs. Based on the BN approach, [4] propose a metric for quantifying the resilience of the SC. [5] joint consider the structural and temporal nature of the disruption propagation under ripple effect, and propose a dynamic BN (DBN) approach to analyze the disruption propagation in an SC. [11] develop a new robust DBN model for SC risk assessment under data scarcity.

Concluding, to the best of our knowledge, there is no result for evaluating SC disruption risks considering bounded deviation budget under data scarcity in the literature.

3   Problem Description and Formulation

For the addressed problem, we study an SC with multiple suppliers and one manufacturer, and the SC structure is based on partner relationships. When disruptions occur in suppliers, the disruptions propagate from the suppliers to the manufacturer. To emulate the disruption and recovery of each SC member, the Markov process is utilized to describe the temporal propagation of disruptions. We mathematically restate the DBN method proposed by [5] and adopt the same notation developed by [11]. We study an SC with a set $\mathcal{I} = \{1, \cdots, i, \cdots, I\}$ of suppliers and a manufacturer, denoted as $I+1$, over a time horizon $\mathcal{T} = \{1, \cdots, t, \cdots, T\}$. When an SC member suffers a disruption, its state can be represented by one in the set $\mathcal{S}_i = \{s_{i1}, \cdots, s_{ij}, \cdots, s_{in_i}\}$ of possible states, where $i \in \{1, \cdots, I, I+1\}, j \in \{1, \cdots, n_i\}$, and n_i is the number of possible states of SC member or partner i. The states in the set $\mathcal{S}_i$ are sorted in an increasing order of severity degree, i.e., s_{i1} signifies a fully operational state and s_{in_i} denotes a fully disrupted state. The states of the suppliers and the manufacturer in time period $t \in \mathcal{T}$ are denoted as $X_1^t, \cdots, X_I^t$ and X_{I+1}^t, respectively. For notation simplicity, the probability of random event $X_i^t = s_{ij}$ is denoted as x_{ij}^t (i.e., $x_{ij}^t = P\{X_i^t = s_{ij}\}$).

According to the DBN introduced by [5], the transition of the supplier i's state from s_{ij} in the previous time period $t-1$ into $s_{ij'}$ in the present time period t can be described by a probability $m_{s_{ij}s_{ij'}}$, where $t \in \{2, \cdots, T\}, j, j' \in \{1, \cdots, n_i\}$. All state transition relationships for the supplier i can be represented by a Markov transition matrix $\boldsymbol{M}_i$. In general, the probabilities in different states for the supplier i in time period t can be calculated as follows:

$$(x_{i1}^t, \cdots, x_{in_i}^t) = (x_{i1}^1, \cdots, x_{in_i}^1) \cdot (\boldsymbol{M}_i)^{t-1}, \quad \forall i \in \{1, \cdots, I\}, t \in \mathcal{T}/\{1\} \quad (1)$$

where $(x_{i1}^1, \cdots, x_{in_i}^1)$ and $(x_{i1}^t, \cdots, x_{in_i}^t)$ are the probability distribution of the supplier i in time period 1 and time period t, respectively.

Besides, the DBN structure consists of T sub-BNs, i.e., one prior BN and $(T-1)$ two-time temporal Bayesian networks (2TBNs). The state transition relationships for the manufacturer can be described by a conditional probability table (CPT). Especially, there are two types of CPTs, i.e., the $CPT_{priorBN}$ and CPT_{2TBNs}. Accordingly, the probability in jth state for the manufacturer $I+1$ in the prior BN and 2TBN can be described as formula (2) and (3), respectively.

$$x_{(I+1)j}^1 = \sum_{c\in dom(c)} y_{jc} \cdot \prod_{i=1}^{I} x_{i,C^{-1}(c)(i)}^1, \quad \forall j \in \{1, \cdots, n_{I+1}\} \tag{2}$$

$$x_{(I+1)j}^t = \sum_{g\in dom(g)} z_{jg} \cdot \prod_{i=1}^{I} x_{i,G^{-1}(g)(i)}^t \cdot x_{(I+1),G^{-1}(g)(I+1)}^{t-1}, \tag{3}$$

$$\forall j \in \{1, \cdots, n_{I+1}\}, t \in \mathcal{T}/\{1\}$$

The detailed notations and problem variables are defined as follows. Moreover, we formulate a novel robust DBN model with bounded deviation budget.

Input Parameters

$\mathcal{I}$: the set of suppliers, $\mathcal{I} = \{1, \cdots, I\}$, indexed by i;

$I+1$: the manufacturer;

$\mathcal{T}$: the set of periods, $\mathcal{T} = \{1, \cdots, T\}$, indexed by t;

M_i: Markov transition matrix of supplier i, where $i \in \mathcal{I}$;

$dom(c)$: the domain of the state-combination-index c, i.e. $dom(c) = \{1, 2, \cdots, n_1 \cdot n_2 \cdots n_I\}$;

$C(\bullet)$: unique bijection mapping $\mathcal{S}_1 \times \cdots \times \mathcal{S}_I \xrightarrow{C(\bullet)} dom(c)$ in the prior BN which maps a state combination to a state-combination-index;

$C^{-1}(\bullet)$: the inverse mapping of $C(\bullet)$;

$C^{-1}(c)(i)$: the corresponding state of supplier i for a given state-combination-index c (in the CPT) in the prior BN;

$dom(g)$: the domain of the state-combination-index g, i.e. $dom(g) = \{1, 2, \cdots, n_1 \cdot n_2 \cdots n_I \cdot n_{I+1}\}$;

$G(\bullet)$: unique bijection mapping $\mathcal{S}_1 \times \cdots \times \mathcal{S}_I \times \mathcal{S}_{I+1} \xrightarrow{G(\bullet)} dom(g)$ in each 2TBN which maps a state combination to a state-combination-index;

$G^{-1}(\bullet)$: the inverse mapping of $G(\bullet)$;

$G^{-1}(g)(i)$: the corresponding state of supplier (or manufacturer) $i, i \in \mathcal{I} \cup \{I+1\}$, for a given state-combination-index g (in the CPT) in each 2TBN;

$\underline{x}_{ij}^1, \bar{x}_{ij}^1$: the lower and upper bound of the probability interval in the jth state for the supplier i in time period 1, where $i \in \{1, \cdots, I\}, j \in \{1, \cdots, n_i\}$;

$\underline{y}_{jc}, \bar{y}_{jc}$: the lower and upper bound of the probability interval in the jth state for the manufacturer, conditional on the cth state combination in the prior BN, where $j \in \{1, \cdots, n_{I+1}\}, c \in dom(c)$;

$\underline{z}_{jg}, \bar{z}_{jg}$: the lower and upper bound of the probability interval in the jth state for the manufacturer, conditional on the gth state combination in each 2TBN, where $j \in \{1, \cdots, n_{I+1}\}, g \in dom(g)$;
  budget: the deviation budget.

Decision Variables

x_{ij}^t: the probability in the jth state for the supplier or manufacturer i in time period t, where $i \in \mathcal{I} \cup \{I+1\}, j \in \{1, \cdots, n_i\}, t \in \mathcal{T}$;

y_{jc}: the probability in the jth state for the manufacturer, conditional on the cth state combination (in the CPT) in the prior BN, where $j \in \{1, \cdots, n_{I+1}\}, c \in dom(c)$;

z_{jg}: the probability in the jth state for the manufacturer, conditional on the gth state combination (in the CPT) in each 2TBN, where $j \in \{1, \cdots, n_{I+1}\}, g \in dom(g)$.

$$max \quad x_{(I+1),n_{I+1}}^T \tag{4}$$

$$s.t. \quad (1) - (3)$$

$$\sum_{j=1}^{n_i} x_{ij}^1 = 1, \quad \forall i \in \mathcal{I} \tag{5}$$

$$\sum_{j=1}^{n_{I+1}} y_{jc} = 1, \quad \forall c \in dom(c) \tag{6}$$

$$\sum_{j=1}^{n_{I+1}} z_{jg} = 1, \quad \forall g \in dom(g) \tag{7}$$

$$\sum_{j=1}^{n_i}\sum_{i \in \mathcal{I}} \left| x_{ij}^1 - \frac{1}{2}(\underline{x}_{ij}^1 + \bar{x}_{ij}^1) \right| + \sum_{j=1}^{n_{I+1}} \sum_{c \in dom(c)} \left| y_{jc} - \frac{1}{2}(\underline{y}_{jc} + \bar{y}_{jc}) \right|$$
$$+ \sum_{j=1}^{n_{I+1}} \sum_{g \in dom(g)} \left| z_{jg} - \frac{1}{2}(\underline{z}_{jg} + \bar{z}_{jg}) \right| \le budget \tag{8}$$

$$x_{ij}^1 \in [\underline{x}_{ij}^1, \bar{x}_{ij}^1], \quad \forall i \in \mathcal{I}, j \in \{1, \cdots, n_i\} \tag{9}$$

$$0 \le x_{ij}^t \le 1, \quad \forall i \in \mathcal{I}, j \in \{1, \cdots, n_i\}, t \in \mathcal{T}/\{1\} \tag{10}$$

$$0 \le x_{(I+1)j}^t \le 1, \quad \forall j \in \{1, \cdots, n_{I+1}\}, t \in \mathcal{T} \tag{11}$$

$$y_{jc} \in [\underline{y}_{jc}, \bar{y}_{jc}], \quad \forall j \in \{1, \cdots, n_{I+1}\}, c \in dom(c) \tag{12}$$

$$z_{jg} \in [\underline{z}_{jg}, \bar{z}_{jg}], \quad \forall j \in \{1, \cdots, n_{I+1}\}, g \in dom(g) \tag{13}$$

The objective function (4) is to estimate the worst-case disruption risk, i.e., to evaluate the robustness of the manufacturer in the final time period T under disruptions. Constraint (1) denotes the Markov transition equation for each supplier

i. Constraint (2) and (3) calculate the probability in each state for the manufacturer in the prior BN and each 2TBN, respectively. Constraint (5)–(7) guarantee the second Kolmogorov axiom of probability, i.e., the sum of probabilities for a supplier or the manufacturer is equal to 1. Constraint (8) ensure the total sum of deviation no greater than the budget. Constraint (9)–(13) give the domains of probabilities in each state (in all time periods).

4 Solution Method

The above proposed model can not be solved by off-the-shelf solver, due to the Constraint (8). Therefore, we equivalently transform this constraint into a set of linear constraints which can be solved by GUROBI.

We first introduce a variable α_{ij}, where $\alpha_{ij} \geq 0, i \in \mathcal{I}, j \in \{1, \cdots, n_i\}$. Since we want to delete $|\bullet|$ notation, we let $\alpha_{ij} = |x_{ij}^1 - \frac{1}{2}(\underline{x}_{ij}^1 + \bar{x}_{ij}^1)|$, so we have

$$\alpha_{ij} \geq x_{ij}^1 - \frac{1}{2}(\underline{x}_{ij}^1 + \bar{x}_{ij}^1), \quad \forall i \in \mathcal{I}, j \in \{1, \cdots, n_i\} \tag{14}$$

$$\alpha_{ij} \geq -x_{ij}^1 + \frac{1}{2}(\underline{x}_{ij}^1 + \bar{x}_{ij}^1), \quad \forall i \in \mathcal{I}, j \in \{1, \cdots, n_i\} \tag{15}$$

Notably, as the objective value wants us to minimize the value of α_{ij}, $\alpha_{ij} = |x_{ij}^1 - \frac{1}{2}(\underline{x}_{ij}^1 + \bar{x}_{ij}^1)|$ can be guaranteed. Likely, given the auxiliary variables β_{jc} and γ_{jg}, where $\beta_{jc}, \gamma_{jg} \geq 0, j \in \{1, \cdots, n_{I+1}\}, c \in dom(c), g \in dom(g)$. We let $\beta_{jc} = |y_{jc} - \frac{1}{2}(\underline{y}_{jc} + \bar{y}_{jc})|$ and $\gamma_{jg} = |z_{jg} - \frac{1}{2}(\underline{z}_{jg} + \bar{z}_{jg})|$, and we can induce

$$\beta_{jc} \geq y_{jc} - \frac{1}{2}(\underline{y}_{jc} + \bar{y}_{jc}), \quad \forall j \in \{1, \cdots, n_{I+1}\}, c \in dom(c) \tag{16}$$

$$\beta_{jc} \geq -y_{jc} + \frac{1}{2}(\underline{y}_{jc} + \bar{y}_{jc}), \quad \forall j \in \{1, \cdots, n_{I+1}\}, c \in dom(c) \tag{17}$$

$$\gamma_{jg} \geq z_{jg} - \frac{1}{2}(\underline{z}_{jg} + \bar{z}_{jg}), \quad \forall j \in \{1, \cdots, n_{I+1}\}, g \in dom(g) \tag{18}$$

$$\gamma_{jg} \geq -z_{jg} + \frac{1}{2}(\underline{z}_{jg} + \bar{z}_{jg}), \quad \forall j \in \{1, \cdots, n_{I+1}\}, g \in dom(g) \tag{19}$$

A new model can be developed as follow.
New Decision Variables

α_{ij}: auxiliary variables, where $i \in \mathcal{I}, j \in \{1, \cdots, n_i\}$;
β_{jc}: auxiliary variables, where $j \in \{1, \cdots, n_{I+1}\}, c \in dom(c)$;
γ_{jg}: auxiliary variables, where $j \in \{1, \cdots, n_{I+1}\}, g \in dom(g)$;

$$max \quad x_{(I+1),n_{I+1}}^T \tag{20}$$

$$s.t. \quad (1)-(7),(9)-(19),$$

$$\sum_{j=1}^{n_i}\sum_{i\in\mathcal{I}}\alpha_{ij} + \sum_{j=1}^{n_{I+1}}\sum_{c\in dom(c)}\beta_{jc} + \sum_{j=1}^{n_{I+1}}\sum_{g\in dom(g)}\gamma_{jg} \leq budget \qquad (21)$$

$$\alpha_{ij} \geq 0, \quad \forall i \in \mathcal{I}, j \in \{1,\cdots,n_i\} \qquad (22)$$

$$\beta_{jc}, \gamma_{jg} \geq 0, \quad \forall j \in \{1,\cdots,n_{I+1}\}, c \in dom(c), g \in dom(g) \qquad (23)$$

Though the constructed model is still a nonlinear programming formulation, it can be solved by using the commercial solver GUROBI.

5   A Case Study

In this section, an illustrative example is presented to demonstrate the applicability of the proposed model. The model are coded in PYTHON 3.7 and combined with GUROBI 9.0 solver. Numerical experiments are conducted on a personal computer with Core I5 and 2.11 GHz processor and 16 GB RAM under windows 10 operating system.

Especially, we focus on the situation that the SC has three suppliers and one manufacturer, and the number of periods is set to be three. Each supplier and the manufacturer has two states, i.e., state 1 denotes a fully operational state and state 2 signifies a fully disrupted state. The Markov transition matrix of supplier i and the lower bound and upper bound of probability intervals are shown as follows.

$$\boldsymbol{M}_i = \begin{bmatrix} 0.549 & 0.715 \\ 0.451 & 0.285 \end{bmatrix}, \forall i \in \{1,2,3\} \quad \underline{x}_{ij}^1 = \begin{bmatrix} 0.209 & 0.360 \\ 0.000 & 0.151 \\ 0.073 & 0.046 \end{bmatrix} \quad \bar{x}_{ij}^1 = \begin{bmatrix} 0.718 & 0.513 \\ 0.775 & 0.718 \\ 0.710 & 0.665 \end{bmatrix}$$

$$\underline{y}_{jc} = \begin{bmatrix} 0.275 & 0.354 & 0.145 & 0.255 & 0.446 & 0.448 & 0.063 & 0.104 \\ 0.026 & 0.220 & 0.015 & 0.228 & 0.325 & 0.139 & 0.338 & 0.295 \end{bmatrix}$$

$$\bar{y}_{jc} = \begin{bmatrix} 0.984 & 0.774 & 0.986 & 0.857 & 0.849 & 0.608 & 0.988 & 0.503 \\ 0.626 & 0.717 & 0.890 & 0.599 & 0.931 & 0.992 & 0.582 & 0.799 \end{bmatrix}$$

Table 1. Different disruption risk probabilities obtained by different deviation budgets

budget	5	6	7	8	9	10
obj	0.239	0.252	0.261	0.267	0.268	0.268

The different disruption risk probabilities obtained by different deviation budgets are reported in Table 1. *budget* denotes the deviation budget and *obj* means the disruption risk probabilities. We can observe that with the increase of *budget*, *obj* increases first and remains unchanged later. It is natural that the worst-case risk estimations with large deviation budget are greater than those with small one. The experimental results are useful, since decision makers can adopt different deviation budget in line with their risk preferences to evaluate the disruption risk probability properly.

Acknowledgments. The authors are grateful for the valuable comments from the reviewers. This work was supported by the National Natural Science Foundation of China (NSFC) under Grants 72021002, 71972146, 71771048, 71432007, 71832001 and 72071144.

References

1. Dolgui, A., Ivanov, D., Sokolov, B.: Ripple effect in the supply chain: an analysis and recent literature. Int. J. Prod. Res. **56**(1–2), 414–430 (2018)
2. Hosseini, S., Al Khaled, A., Sarder, M.: A general framework for assessing system resilience using Bayesian networks: a case study of sulfuric acid manufacturer. J. Manuf. Syst. **41**, 211–227 (2016)
3. Hosseini, S., Barker, K.: A Bayesian network model for resilience-based supplier selection. Int. J. Prod. Econ. **180**, 68–87 (2016)
4. Hosseini, S., Ivanov, D.: A new resilience measure for supply networks with the ripple effect considerations: a Bayesian network approach. Ann. Oper. Res. 1–27 (2019). https://doi.org/10.1007/s10479-019-03350-8
5. Hosseini, S., Ivanov, D., Dolgui, A.: Ripple effect modelling of supplier disruption: integrated Markov chain and dynamic Bayesian network approach. Int. J. Prod. Res. **58**(11), 3284–3303 (2020)
6. Ivanov, D.: 'A blessing in disguise' or 'as if it wasn't hard enough already': reciprocal and aggravate vulnerabilities in the supply chain. Int. J. Prod. Res. **58**(11), 3252–3262 (2020)
7. Ivanov, D., Dolgui, A., Sokolov, B., Ivanova, M.: Literature review on disruption recovery in the supply chain. Int. J. Prod. Res. **55**(20), 6158–6174 (2017)
8. Ivanov, D., Hartl, R., Dolgui, A., Pavlov, A., Sokolov, B.: Integration of aggregate distribution and dynamic transportation planning in a supply chain with capacity disruptions and the ripple effect consideration. Int. J. Prod. Res. **53**(23), 6963–6979 (2015)
9. Ivanov, D., Sokolov, B., Dolgui, A.: The ripple effect in supply chains: trade-off 'efficiency-flexibility-resilience' in disruption management. Int. J. Prod. Res. **52**(7), 2154–2172 (2014)
10. Ivanov, D., Sokolov, B., Solovyeva, I., Dolgui, A., Jie, F.: Dynamic recovery policies for time-critical supply chains under conditions of ripple effect. Int. J. Prod. Res. **54**(23), 7245–7258 (2016)
11. Liu, M., Liu, Z., Chu, F., Zheng, F., Chu, C.: A new robust dynamic Bayesian network approach for disruption risk assessment under the supply chain ripple effect. Int. J. Prod. Res. **59**(1), 265–285 (2021)
12. Sawik, T.: On the risk-averse optimization of service level in a supply chain under disruption risks. Int. J. Prod. Res. **54**(1), 98–113 (2016)
13. Sokolov, B., Ivanov, D., Dolgui, A., Pavlov, A.: Structural quantification of the ripple effect in the supply chain. Int. J. Prod. Res. **54**(1), 152–169 (2016)

Stochastic Integrated Supplier Selection and Disruption Risk Assessment Under Ripple Effect

Ming Liu[1], Zhongzheng Liu[1], Feng Chu[2($\boxtimes$)], Feifeng Zheng[3], and Chengbin Chu[4]

[1] School of Economics and Management, Tongji University, Shanghai 200092, China
{mingliu,1830351}@tongji.edu.cn
[2] IBISC, Univ Évry, Université of Paris-Saclay, 91025 Évry, France
feng.chu@univ-evry.fr
[3] Glorious Sun School of Business and Management, Donghua University, Shanghai 200051, China
ffzheng@dhu.edu.cn
[4] ESIEE Paris, Université Paris-Est, 93162 Noisy-le-Grand, France

Abstract. The impact of the COVID-19 pandemic in the supply chain (SC) evokes the need for valid measures to cope with the SC disruption risk. Supplier selection and disruption risk assessment, as valid measures, have received increasing attentions from academia. However, most of existing works focus on supplier selection and disruption risk assessment separately. This work investigates an integrated supplier selection and disruption risk assessment problem under ripple effect. The objective is to minimize the weighted sum of the disrupted probability and the total cost for the manufacturer. For the problem, a new stochastic programming model combined with Bayesian network (BN) is formulated. Then, an illustrative example is conducted to demonstrate the proposed method.

Keywords: Supply chain disruption risk · Supplier selection · Disruption risk assessment · Stochastic programming model · Bayesian network

1 Introduction

The outbreak of the COVID-19 pandemic, viewed as a new type of disruption, has greatly impacted the supply chain (SC) (Ivanov and Dolgui [1]; Ivanov and Das [2]; Queiroz et al. [3]; Ivanov [4]). The COVID-19 pandemic has triggered the SC ripple effect (Ivanov [4]). Dolgui et al. [5] state that ripple effect describes the disruption risk propagating from the upstream to the downstream in a multi-tier SC. Therefore, the SC disruption risk should be properly managed by enterprises

Supported by the National Natural Science Foundation of China (NSFC) under Grants 72021002, 71771048, 71432007, 71832001 and 72071144.

under ripple effect (Ivanov et al. [6]; Ivanov et al. [7]; Ivanov and Dolgui [8]; Pavlov et al. [9]; Dolgui and Ivanov [10]).

To mitigate the impact of the SC disruption risk under ripple effect, supplier selection, i.e., selection of supply portfolio, can be applied (Tang [11]; Sawik [12]). Moreover, supplier selection plays a crucial role for reducing ordering cost (Sawik [13]). Disruption risk assessment is to quantify the SC disruption risk. A huge body of researches have been done on SC disruption risk assessment problems (Kinra et al. [14]). Bayesian network (BN), as an important tool, is introduced to assess the SC disruption risk under ripple effect (Hosseini et al. [15]).

However, existing works mainly focus on supplier selection and disruption risk assessment separately. In this work, we consider a two-tier SC, and investigate a new stochastic integrated SC disruption risk assessment and supplier selection problem under ripple effect.

The remainder of this paper is organized as follows. The relevant literature is reviewed in Sect. 2. In Sect. 3, we develop a new nonlinear stochastic mixed integer programming model. In Sect. 4, an illustrative example is conducted to illustrate the proposed method.

2   Literature Review

In this section, we review related studies from two aspects: SC disruption risk assessment under ripple effect, and supplier selection. The first aspect shows the significance of SC disruption risk assessment problem. The second aspect illustrates the supplier selection.

2.1   SC Disruption Risk Assessment Under Ripple Effect

There is a large number of studies about the disruption risk assessment under ripple effect. In this subsection, we only focus on related studies utilizing the BN approach, on which our model builds. Hosseini et al. [15] consider a SC resilience problem, and develop a BN approach. A case study is conducted to estimate the resilience of sulfuric acid manufacturer. Hosseini and Ivanov [16] consider a SC disruption risk assessment problem under ripple effect at disruption and recovery stages. The authors establish a new resilience measure based on a BN approach. Hosseini et al. [17] investigate a SC disruption risk assessment problem with different time periods. The authors propose a new model integrated a discrete-time Markov chain and a dynamic BN to estimate the SC disruption risk. Liu et al. [18] consider a SC disruption risk assessment problem in cases of data scarcity. The authors propose a new robust dynamic BN approach, and establish a nonlinear programming formulation.

2.2   Supplier Selection

Plenty of researches have been conducted on the supplier selection problems (e.g., Sawik [19]; Sawik [20]; Sawik [21]). Sawik [22] considers an integrated supplier selection and production and distribution scheduling in the context of the SC disruption risk. The author formulates a stochastic mixed integer programming model with the objective of optimizing the weighted-sum aggregation. Sawik [23] studies an integrated supplier selection and production scheduling of finished products problem. The author proposes a new efficient portfolio approach combining decisions made before, during and after the disruption. Sawik [24] considers a risk-averse supplier selection problem with resilient supply and demand portfolios in a geographically dispersed multi-tier SC network under disruption risks. The author establishes a multi-portfolio approach and a scenario-based stochastic mixed integer programming model.

To the best of our knowledge, no studies have been reported to investigate a stochastic integrated supplier selection and disruption risk assessment problem.

3   Problem Formulation

In this section, we first describe the studied problem. Especially, BN approach is applied to establish the propagation of SC disruption risk. Then, we introduce some notations and construct a new nonlinear stochastic programming model.

3.1   Problem Description

Consider a two-tier SC network with multiple suppliers and one manufacturer. Let $\mathcal{I} = \{1, \cdots, i, \cdots, I\}$ be the set of suppliers and $I + 1$ denotes one manufacturer. The states of SC participant i, $i \in \mathcal{I} \cup I + 1$, can be represented by $\mathcal{J}_i = \{J_{i1}, \cdots, J_{ij}, \cdots, J_{in_i}\}$. The states in the set $\mathcal{J}_i$ are sorted in an increasing order of severity degree. Denotes by π_i^j the probability of supplier i in state j. Let P^s be the probability that scenario s is realized, $s \in \mathcal{S}$, where $\mathcal{S}$ denotes the set of all disruption scenarios. There are a total of $\prod_{i \in \mathcal{I}} n_i$ potential scenarios. To formalize the one-to-one correspondence relationship between state combination of suppliers and disruption scenario, we define the following mapping. Let $G(\cdot)$ be a unique bijection mapping $\mathcal{J}_1 \times \cdots \times \mathcal{J}_I \xrightarrow{G(\cdot)} \{1, \cdots, n_1 \cdot n_2 \cdots n_I\}$. $G^{-1}(\cdot)$ represents the inverse mapping from a disruption risk scenario to a state combination (i.e., a set of states of suppliers), which is also unique, i.e., $\{1, \cdots, n_1 \cdot n_2 \cdots n_I\} \xrightarrow{G^{-1}(\cdot)} \mathcal{J}_1 \times \cdots \times \mathcal{J}_I$. Let $G^{-1}(s)(i)$ denote the state of supplier i in the sth potential scenario. For brevity, let $\mathcal{S}$ denote the domain of the scenario s, i.e., $\mathcal{S} = \{1, 2, \cdots, n_1 \cdot n_2 \cdots n_I\}$. Therefore, the probability of disruption scenario s realized is

$$P^s = \prod_{i=1}^{I} \pi_i^{G^{-1}(s)(i)}.$$

To portray the propagation of SC disruption risk, the BN approach is applied, which can be represented as a graph with a set of nodes (random variables) and a set of arcs. X_i denotes the state random variable of SC participant i,

$i \in \mathcal{I} \cup I + 1$. An arc from X_i to $X_{i'}$ denotes the dependence relationship. According to the studied two-tier SC structure, the joint probability distribution of the BN consisting of variables $X_1, \cdots, X_I, X_{I+1}$ can be expressed as

$$\mathbb{P}(X_1, \cdots, X_I, X_{I+1}) = \prod_{i=1}^{I} \mathbb{P}(X_i) \cdot \mathbb{P}(X_{I+1}|X_1, \cdot, X_I),$$

where $\mathbb{P}(X_1, \cdots, X_I, X_{I+1})$ represents the joint probability distribution over X_1, $\cdots, X_{I+1}$. $\mathbb{P}(X_{I+1}|X_1, \cdots, X_I)$ denotes the conditional probability distribution, which can be represented as a conditional probability table (CPT). In our work, the CPT for $\mathbb{P}(X_{I+1}|X_1, \cdots, X_I)$ is represented as follows:

$$\mathrm{CPT} = \begin{bmatrix} z_1^1 & \cdots & z_1^{|\mathcal{S}|} \\ \vdots & z_j^s & \vdots \\ z_{n_{I+1}}^1 & \cdots & z_{n_{I+1}}^{|\mathcal{S}|} \end{bmatrix},$$

where the number of rows corresponds to the number of possible states for the manufacturer $I + 1$; the number of columns represents the number of state combinations of all suppliers; z_j^s represents the jth state probability of the manufacturer in scenario s (Note that, z_j^s will be adjusted to $z_{r,j}^s$ later.).

Based on the above notations, the disrupted probability of the manufacturer (i.e., $\pi_{I+1}^{n_{I+1}}$) can be expressed as follow:

$$\pi_{I+1}^{n_{I+1}} = \sum_{s \in \mathcal{S}} \left(\prod_{i=1}^{I+1} \pi_i^{G^{-1}(s)(i)} \cdot z_{n_{I+1}}^s \right).$$

In our work, the supplier selection is considered, and the number of suppliers will be determined, which contributes to changing the BN structure accordingly. To adapt variable BN structure, the notation of CPT needs to be extended. The set of suppliers contains I suppliers, then the total combination number of selected suppliers is 2^I. Let r be the index of combinations of suppliers in the possible selection set (with 2^I elements). For clarity, we call r as the supplier-selection index. Let y_i be a binary variable, equal to 1 if supplier i is selected to supply material for the manufacturer. The supplier-selection index r can be calculated by $\left(\sum_{i=1}^{I} 2^{i-1} \cdot y_i + 1 \right)$ (That is, one-to-one correspondence between binary and decimal. For example, consider two suppliers. Supplier 1 is unselected, i.e., $y_1 = 0$, and supplier 2 is selected, i.e., $y_2 = 1$. Then, $r = 2 \cdot 1 + 1 \cdot 0 + 1 = 3$.). Therefore, an adjusted CPT, i.e., CPT^r, $r \in \{1, \cdots, 2^I\}$, which be represented as follow:

$$\mathrm{CPT}^r = \begin{bmatrix} z_{r,1}^1 & \cdots & z_{r,1}^{|\mathcal{S}|} \\ \vdots & z_{r,j}^s & \vdots \\ z_{r,n_{I+1}}^1 & \cdots & z_{r,n_{I+1}}^{|\mathcal{S}|} \end{bmatrix}, \quad \forall r \in \{1, \cdots, 2^I\}$$

where $z_{r,j}^s$ represents the jth state probability of the manufacturer given the supplier-selection index r in scenario s. Note that, when k suppliers, i.e.,

$i_1, \cdots, i_k$, are selected, the number of columns of actual CPT, i.e., $|\mathcal{J}_{i_1}| \cdot |\mathcal{J}_{i_2}| \cdots$ $|\mathcal{J}_{i_k}|$, is less than $|\mathcal{S}|$. Therefore, to encapsulate the actual CPT informations into CPT^r with fixed matrix size (i.e., $n_{I+1} \times |S|$), the elements of CPT^r matrix are reorganized by the following rule: $\mathbb{P}(X_{I+1}|X_{i_1}, \cdots, X_{i_k})$ is stored in $\mathbb{P}(X_{I+1}|X_{i_1}, \cdots, X_{i_k}, X_{i'_1} = J_{i'_1 1}, \cdots, X_{i'_{I-k}} = J_{i'_{I-k} 1})$. At the same time, the other elements in CPT^r are set to be 0, as they are no meanings.

3.2   Nonlinear Stochastic Programming Model

Problem parameters:

$\mathcal{I}$: the set of suppliers, indexed by i;

$\mathcal{J}_i$: the set of states of supplier i, indexed by j;

$\mathcal{S}$: the set of scenarios, indexed by s;

D: the total materiel demands of the manufacturer;

b: the unit penalty cost of unfulfilled demand of the manufacturer;

o_i: the fixed cost of ordering materials from supplier i;

u_i: the unit cost of ordering materials from supplier i;

W_i^s: the supply capacity of supplier i in scenario s;

π_i^j: the probability of SC participant i at state j;

$z_{r,j}^s$: the jth state conditional probability of the manufacturer given the supplier-selection index r in scenario s;

P^s: the probability of scenario s;

δ: the weight coefficient of the disrupted probability of the manufacturer;

λ: the weight coefficient of the cost.

Decision variables:

x_{ij}^{sel}: continuous variable, denoting the probability of the supplier i in state j after the selection (the supplier i can be selected or not);

y_i: binary variable, equal to 1 if supplier i is selected to supply material for the manufacturer;

w_i^s: non-negative continuous variable, denoting the supply volume of supplier i in scenario s;

ν_r: binary variable, equal to 1 if the supplier-selection index r is realised;

h^s: non-negative continuous variable, representing the volume of unfulfilled supply in scenario s.

Nonlinear stochastic programming formulation:

$$\min \delta \cdot \left[\sum_{s \in \mathcal{S}} \prod_{i=1}^{I} x_{i,G^{-1}(s)(i)}^{sel} \cdot \left(\sum_{r=1}^{2^I} z_{r, n_{I+1}}^s \cdot \nu_r \right) \right] + \lambda \cdot \left[\sum_{s \in \mathcal{S}} P^s (b \cdot h^s + \sum_{i=1}^{I} u_i \cdot w_i^s) + \sum_{i=1}^{I} o_i \cdot y_i \right] \quad (1)$$

$$w_i^s \leq M \cdot y_i, \quad i \in \mathcal{I}, s \in \mathcal{S} \quad (2)$$

$$0 \leq w_i^s \leq W_i^s, \quad i \in \mathcal{I}, s \in \mathcal{S} \quad (3)$$

$$D - \sum_{i=1}^{I} w_i^s \le h_s, \quad s \in \mathcal{S} \tag{4}$$

$$\sum_{r=1}^{2^I} r \cdot \nu_r = \sum_{i=1}^{I} 2^{i-1} \cdot y_i + 1 \tag{5}$$

$$\sum_{r=1}^{2^I} \nu_r = 1 \tag{6}$$

$$x_{ij}^{sel} \le \pi_i^j + M \cdot y_i, \quad \forall j \in \mathcal{J}_i \tag{7}$$

$$x_{ij}^{sel} \ge \pi_i^j - M \cdot y_i, \quad \forall j \in \mathcal{J}_i \tag{8}$$

$$x_{ij}^{sel} \le 1 + M \cdot (1 - y_i), \quad \forall j \in \mathcal{J}_i \tag{9}$$

$$x_{ij}^{sel} \ge 1 - M \cdot (1 - y_i), \quad \forall j \in \mathcal{J}_i \tag{10}$$

$$x_{ij}^{sel} \in [0,1], \quad \forall i \in \mathcal{I}, j \in \mathcal{J}_i \tag{11}$$

$$y_i \in \{0,1\}, \quad \forall i \in \mathcal{I} \tag{12}$$

$$\nu_r \in \{0,1\}, \quad r \in \{1, \cdots, 2^I\} \tag{13}$$

$$w_i^s \in \mathbb{R}^+, \quad i \in \mathcal{I}, s \in \mathcal{S} \tag{14}$$

$$h^s \in \mathbb{R}^+, \quad s \in \mathcal{S} \tag{15}$$

Formula (1) is the weighted objective function, i.e., minimizing the weighted sum of (i) disrupted probability of the manufacturer (i.e., n_{I+1}), and (ii) the total cost of the manufacturer. Constraint (2) guarantees that only the selected suppliers can supply materials for the manufacturer. Constraint (3) guarantees the supply capacity of supplier i in scenario s. Constraint (4) states that the unfulfilled material demand of the manufacturer. Constraints (5) and (6) guarantee that a specific CPT^r is utilized for the calculation of disrupted probability of the manufacturer. Constraints (7–10) ensure that the probability distributions of unselected suppliers are eliminated (i.e., the axioms of multiplication: for a specific number a, then $a \cdot 1 = a$). Constraints (11–15) are the ranges of variables.

4 An Illustrative Example

In this section, an illustrative example is conducted to illustrate the application of our method. Consider a SC with two suppliers and one manufacturer, of which have two states. Figure 1 shows the acquired probability informations in the BN based on our notations. In addition, D, b, W_i^s, o_i, u_i, δ, and λ are set to be 100, 2, 120, 100, 4, 100, 1, respectively. This example is solved by YALMIP. The solution is that the supplier 1 is selected, and the objective value is 300.

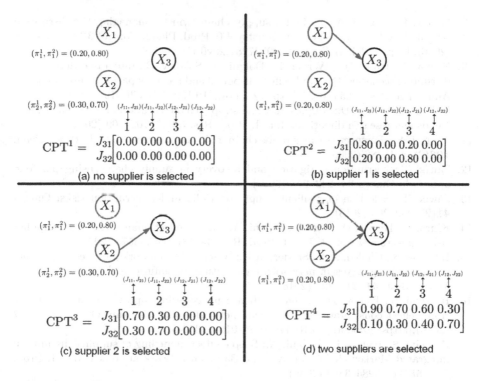

Fig. 1. The BN informations based on our notations of the illustrative example.

References

1. Ivanov, D., Dolgui, A.: OR-methods for coping with the ripple effect in supply chains during COVID-19 pandemic: managerial insights and research implications. Int. J. Prod. Econ. **232**, 107921 (2021)
2. Ivanov, D., Das, A.: Coronavirus (COVID-19/SARS-CoV-2) and supply chain resilience: a research note. Int. J. Integr. Supply Manage. **13**(1), 90–102 (2020)
3. Queiroz, M.M., Ivanov, D., Dolgui, A., Fosso Wamba, S.: Impacts of epidemic outbreaks on supply chains: mapping a research agenda amid the COVID-19 pandemic through a structured literature review. Ann. Oper. Res. **16**, 1–38 (2020). https://doi.org/10.1007/s10479-020-03685-7
4. Ivanov, D.: Predicting the impacts of epidemic outbreaks on global supply chains: a simulation-based analysis on the coronavirus outbreak (COVID-19/SARS-CoV-2) case. Transp. Res. Part E **136**, 101922 (2020)
5. Dolgui, A., Ivanov, D., Rozhkov, M.: Does the ripple effect influence the bullwhip effect? An integrated analysis of structural and operational dynamics in the supply chain. Int. J. Prod. Res. **58**(5), 1285–1301 (2020)
6. Ivanov, D., Dolgui, A., Sokolov, B. (eds.): Handbook of Ripple Effects in the Supply Chain. ISORMS, vol. 276. Springer, Cham (2019). https://doi.org/10.1007/978-3-030-14302-2
7. Ivanov, D., Dolgui, A., Sokolov, B., Ivanova, M.: Literature review on disruption recovery in the supply chain. Int. J. Prod. Res. **55**(20), 6158–6174 (2017)

8. Ivanov, D., Dolgui, A.: A digital supply chain twin for managing the disruption risks and resilience in the era of Industry 4.0. Prod. Plann. Control **32**(9), 775–778 (2020). https://doi.org/10.1080/09537287.2020.1768450

9. Pavlov, A., Ivanov, D., Werner, F., Dolgui, A., Sokolov, B.: Integrated detection of disruption scenarios, the ripple effect dispersal and recovery paths in supply chains. Ann. Oper. Res. 1–23 (2019). https://doi.org/10.1007/s10479-019-03454-1

10. Dolgui, A., Ivanov, D.: Ripple effect and supply chain disruption management: new trends and research directions. Int. J. Prod. Res. **59**(1), 102–109 (2021)

11. Tang, C.S.: Perspectives in supply chain risk management. Int. J. Prod. Econ. **103**(2), 451–488 (2006)

12. Sawik, T.: Disruption mitigation and recovery in supply chains using portfolio approach. Omega **84**, 232–248 (2019)

13. Sawik, T.: Selection of resilient supply portfolio under disruption risks. Omega **41**(2), 259–269 (2013)

14. Kinra, A., Ivanov, D., Das, A., Dolgui, A.: Ripple effect quantification by supplier risk exposure assessment. Int. J. Prod. Res. **58**(18), 5559–5578 (2020)

15. Hosseini, S., Khaled, A.A., Sarder, M.D.: A general framework for assessing system resilience using Bayesian networks: a case study of sulfuric acid manufacturer. J. Manuf. Syst. **41**, 211–227 (2016)

16. Hosseini, S., Ivanov, D.: A new resilience measure for supply networks with the ripple effect considerations: a Bayesian network approach. Ann. Oper. Res. 1–27 (2019). https://doi.org/10.1007/s10479-019-03350-8

17. Hosseini, S., Ivanov, D., Dolgui, A.: Ripple effect modelling of supplier disruption: integrated Markov chain and dynamic Bayesian network approach. Int. J. Prod. Res. **58**(11), 3284–3303 (2020)

18. Liu, M., Liu, Z., Chu, F., Zheng, F., Chu, C.: A new robust dynamic Bayesian network approach for disruption risk assessment under the supply chain ripple effect. Int. J. Prod. Res. **59**(1), 265–285 (2021)

19. Sawik, T.: A cyclic versus flexible approach to materials ordering in make-to-order assembly. Math. Comput. Model. **42**(3–4), 279–290 (2005)

20. Sawik, T.: Single vs. multiple objective supplier selection in a make to order environment. Omega **38**(3–4), 203–212 (2010)

21. Sawik, T.: Selection of supply portfolio under disruption risks. Omega **39**(2), 194–208 (2011)

22. Sawik, T.: Integrated supply chain scheduling under multi-level disruptions. IFAC-PapersOnLine **48**(3), 1515–1520 (2015)

23. Sawik, T.: A portfolio approach to supply chain disruption management. Int. J. Prod. Res. **55**(7), 1970–1991 (2017)

24. Sawik, T.: On the risk-averse selection of resilient multi-tier supply portfolio. Omega **101**, 102267 (2021)

Pharmaceutical Supply Chain Risk Assessment in the Time of COVID 19/Case Study

Jihene Jlassi[1]([✉]), Nesrin Halouani[1], and Abderrahman El Mhamedi[2]

[1] OLID Institut Supérieur de Gestion Industrielle de Sfax, Route de Tunis, Sakiet Ezzit, Tunisia
jihene.jlassi@isgis.usf.tn
[2] Laboratoire QUARTA/MGSI, IUT de Montreuil, 140 Rue de la Nouvelle,
93100 Montreuil, France
a.elmhamedi@iut.univ-paris8.fr

Abstract. As of March11, 2020 the world Health Organization (WHO) declared Corona virus disease 2019 (COVID-19) as a pandemic. The disastrous outbreak of Covid-19 is described as humanity's worst crisis since World War II. Effectively, not only has it caused severe disruptions around the world at different levels–social, economic, political-but it has also acutely disrupted supply chains worldwide. Pharmaceutical supply chain is a significant component of the health system as to supplying medicines. Today, pharmaceutical companies face a tremendous array of risks. The purpose of this research is to assess different risks in Tunisian pharmaceutical supply chain during this challenging period due to COVID-19 pandemic by providing quantified empirical results. Based on the review of literature, some major risks affecting the pharmaceutical supply chain are identified as regulatory risk, inventory risk, counterfeit risk and financial risk. The fuzzy AHP method is used, in this work, in order to identify the most important risk. It has to be noted that the top risk identified in pharmaceutical supply chain is that related to the Supply and suppliers.

Keywords: Supply chain risk assessment · Fuzzy AHP · COVID-19

1 Introduction

Supply chain has become an essential part of global business and economy in this rapidly changing world in terms of innovation and globalization (Kamalahmadi and Parrast 2016). In fact, supply chain is represented as a complex network. It includes procurement, internal operations, inventory, marketing etc. (Cooper 1997).

The risks in supply chains are mainly caused by operational fluctuations such as demand uncertainties, and price variability (Juttner 2005), natural events such as earthquakes, epidemics and manmade crises such as terrorist attacks and economic recessions (Kleindorfer and Saad 2005). Thereby, in the Supply Chain, risks can be found during a product delivery or service to a customer in terms of cost, timely delivery and impact on image.

© IFIP International Federation for Information Processing 2021
Published by Springer Nature Switzerland AG 2021
A. Dolgui et al. (Eds.): APMS 2021, IFIP AICT 632, pp. 697–704, 2021.
https://doi.org/10.1007/978-3-030-85906-0_76

Since 1950s, the number and impact of both human and natural catastrophes have been increasing (Boonmee 2017). Among the different types of disasters, epidemic disease outbreaks can pose tremendous treats for human beings (Büyüktahtakın et al. 2018), and it may, if ineffectively controlled, further become a pandemic and lead to a global crisis. Accordance to the World Health Organization (WHO), an epidemic outbreak is "the occurrence of disease cases in excess of normal expectancy", which is usually caused by an infectious disease through human-to-human transmission and animal-to-human transmission or by the exposure to radioactive and hazardous chemical sources (Yu et al. 2020).

The COVID-19 pandemic is impacting global health product supply chains, chiefly key materials and ingredients, finished health products, logistics and shipping. The Global Fund is constantly and closely working with suppliers and partners to assess the impact on core health product supplies and provide recommendations for implementing partners on how to manage the impact.

Furthermore, the pharmaceutical supply chain is a major component of the health system it includes all procedures, information, resources and players like suppliers, manufacturers, intermediaries, logistics activities, third-party service providers, merchandising and sales activities, finance and information technology (Jaberidoost et al. 2013).

The aim of this study was to analyze the overall impact of COVID-19 on pharmaceutical supply chain risks.

This paper is organized as follows: the Sect. 1 sheds light on supply chain risk management. The Sect. 2 represents risk definitions. The next two sections (Sects. 3 and 4) examine the pharmaceutical supply chain, focusing on coordination and decision making issues under business risks and also considering SCRM implementation issues for specific sectors as well as the application. Section 5 includes the closing remarks, identifies gaps in the research and proposes future research directions.

2   Supply Chain Risk Management

Supply chain, apart from being subject to different types of risks-organizational, operational, strategic, commercial or external, is also confronted with real threats relating to cost precariousness, materials scarcity, supplier financial problems and failures, and man-made or natural accidents.

The topic of risk is not novel in management, yet it is a newest area extending in the field of supply chain management. Supply chain risk management (SCRM) consists in taking necessary measures to determine measure and attenuate risks of the supply chain of an organization. The execution of risk management approaches can assist a firm to work more efficiently, decrease expenses and improve service customer.

SCRM can be considered as a significant part of Enterprise Risk Management (ERM) focusing on the execution of strategies operating with daily and occasional risks continuously across the supply chain, in order to decrease sensitivity and guaranty durability in risk event. Indeed, it decreases the vulnerability of the supply chain through a concerted and joint procedure, taking part in the supply chain all decision maker even subcontractors.

3 Pharmaceutical Supply Chain

Due to the difficulty and sensitivity of the pharmaceutical industry, the standard supply chain is very important and complex since this industry is exposed at the same time to rigorous control and good practices. Furthermore, the intricacy of pharmaceutical supply chain framework is aggravated with weighty supervising of controller, manufacturers, and consumers.

Numerous stressors are heightening, in most cases, the pharmaceutical supply chain with ever-changing regulatory requirements and client waiting due to the obvious development of the numerical economy. Theses supply chain obstacles can be surmounted by both analyzing tendencies in the pharmaceutical supply chain that are molding the future of this industry and considering their collective effect on several supply chain processes.

Therefore, the pharmaceutical supply chain is considered as an important element of the health scheme enclosing all the procedures, information, resources and actors such as suppliers, manufacturers, intermediaries, logistics activities, merchandising, finance and technologies information (Shah 2015).

Thus, the pharmaceutical supply chain delivers drugs in good quantity, in the best quality and to the right person, on the one hand. On the other hand delivery is at the same time, in the right locality and to the right purchasers, at the appropriate time and with weak charge under standard conditions (Jaberidoost et al. 2013). Thus, bad drug distributions affect reputations, profits of organizations and customer fulfillments in that they deliver patient recovery processes and generate negative impact on public fitness.

Actually, the pharmaceutical supply chain may be subject to risks yielding to wasted resources as well as menacing the lives of patients by restraining drugs access (Schneider 2010). Nowadays, these risks are rising proportionally.

The PSC was defined in previous studies as an "intricate suitable framework" and was employed as a pragmatic study purpose. From this point of view supply chains have a more general tendency to be exploited "like a system", and therefore to gain more interest they should be conceptualized, modeled and managed as such. Especially, the supply chain can be seen as a system including elements and connections of a socio-technical nature.

The vitality of pharmaceutical products as well as their availability and accessibility to companies and governments make the pharmaceutical supply chain very difficult. The PSC considered as a socio-technical system helps businesses not only in allowing the health status evolution due to drugs affording, but also in integrating additional and different process products and technologies.

Besides the various products types yielded from pharmaceutical supply chains, other specific problems exists like product variety, refund, prices quoted by ministries, sales models, 3PLs (Third Party Logistics), strict regulations, product life cycle rigor prediction, R&D products dispatching for health investigations. Pharmaceutical supply chain can be included in a new type named "life sciences" and "health supply chain (LSHC)", due to previous factors.

The pharmaceutical value chain is made up of many connected components that have been significantly decentralized and optimized to reduce production and distribution costs. The COVID-19 pandemic has further exposed the potential for disruption to the supply chain upon which this model is based.

4 Fuzzy AHP Method

4.1 Definition

The Analytic Hierarchy Process (AHP) is a method developed by Saaty (1980) to support the multi-criteria decisions. Ti is one multi-criteria decision making method, which has been extensively applied to a variety of decision-making situations.

AHP is probably the best-Known and the most widely used model in decision making. It is a powerful decision-making methodology in order to determine the priorities among different criteria.

To deal quantitatively with imprecision or uncertainty, fuzzy set theory is primarily concerned with imprecision and vagueness in human thoughts and perceptions (Beskese et al. 2004).

In this research, triangular fuzzy numbers, $\tilde{1}$ to $\tilde{9}$, are used to represent subjective pair wise comparisons of patient requirements in order to capture the vagueness. A fuzzy number is a special fuzzy set. F = $\{(x, \mu\ F(x), x \in R\}$, where x takes its values on the real line R, $-\infty \le x \le +\infty$ and $\mu\ F(x)$ is a continuous mapping from R to the closed interval [0 1]. A triangular fuzzy number is denoted as M = (a, b, c), where $a \le b \le c$, has the triangular-type membership given by Eq. 1.

$$\mu_{F(X)} = \begin{cases} 0 & x < a \\ \dfrac{x-a}{b-a} & a \le x \le b \\ \dfrac{c-x}{c-b} & b \le x \le c \\ 0 & x > 0 \end{cases} \tag{1}$$

One of the most important concepts of fuzzy sets is the concept of an α-cut.

For a fuzzy number M and any number [0, 1], the α-cut, M, is the crisp set (Klir and Yuan 1995) M = $\{x/\ M\ (x) \ge \alpha\}$. The α-cut of a fuzzy number M is the crisp set M α that contains all the elements of the universal set U whose membership grades in C are greater than or equal to the specified value of α. By defining the interval of confidence at level a, the triangular fuzzy number can be characterized (Cheng 1996, 1999; Cheng and Mon 1994; Juang and Lee 1991; Kaufmann and Gupta 1991).

4.2 Procedure of Fuzzy AHP

The procedure of fuzzy ahp is summarized as follows (Kwong and Bai 2002):

Step1: Comparing the performance score: triangular fuzzy numbers $\left(\tilde{1}, \tilde{3}, \tilde{5}, \tilde{7}, \tilde{9} \right)$ are used to indicate the relative strength of each pair of elements in the same hierarchy.

Step2: Constructing the fuzzy comparison matrix: by using triangular fuzzy numbers, via pair wise comparison, the fuzzy judgment matrix $\tilde{A}(a_{ij})$ is constructed as shown in Eq. 2:

$$\tilde{A} = \begin{bmatrix} 1 & \tilde{a}_{12} & ... & \tilde{a}_{1n} \\ .. & .. & .. & .. \\ .. & .. & .. & .. \\ \tilde{a}_{n1} & \tilde{a}_{n2} & .. & 1 \end{bmatrix} \tag{2}$$

Where $\tilde{a}_{ij} = \begin{cases} 1 & i = j \\ \tilde{1}, \tilde{3}, \tilde{5}, \tilde{7}, \tilde{9} \text{ or } \tilde{1}^{-1}, \tilde{3}^{-1}, \tilde{5}^{-1}, \tilde{7}^{-1}, \tilde{9}^{-1} & i \neq j \end{cases}$.

Step3: Solving fuzzy eigenvalues. A fuzzy set eigenvalue λ is defined by Eq. 3,

$$\tilde{A}\tilde{x} = \tilde{\lambda}\tilde{x} \tag{3}$$

where $\tilde{A}$ is a n*n fuzzy matrix containing fuzzy numbers $\tilde{a}_{ij}$ and $\tilde{x}_i$.

To perform fuzzy multiplications and additions using the interval arithmetic and α-cut, Eq. 1 is equivalent to Eq. 4.

$$\left[a_{i1l}^{\alpha}x_{1l}^{\alpha}, a_{i1u}^{\alpha}x_{1u}^{\alpha}\right] \oplus ... \left[a_{inl}^{\alpha}x_{nl}^{\alpha}\right] = \left[\lambda x_{il}^{\alpha}, \lambda x_{iu}^{\alpha}\right] \tag{4}$$

Where as in Eq. 5,

$$\tilde{A} = [\tilde{a}_{ij}], \ \tilde{x} = (\tilde{x}_1, ..., \tilde{x}_n), \ \tilde{a}_{ij}^{\alpha} = \left[\tilde{a}_{ijl}^{\alpha}, \tilde{a}_{iju}^{\alpha}\right], \ \tilde{x}^t = \left[x_{il}^{\alpha}, x_{iu}^{\alpha}\right], \ \tilde{\lambda}^{\alpha} = \left[\lambda_l^{\alpha}, \lambda_u^{\alpha}\right] \tag{5}$$

for $0 \leq \alpha \leq 1$ and all i, j, where i = 1,2,...,n, j = 1,2,...,n.

Degree of satisfaction for the judgment matrix $\tilde{A}$ is estimated by the index of optimism μ. The larger value of the index μ indicates the higher degree of optimism. The index μ is a linear convex combination (Lee 1999) defined as in Eq. 6:

$$\tilde{a}_{ij}^{\alpha} = \mu a_{iju}^{\alpha} + (1 - \mu)a_{ijl}^{\alpha} \forall \mu \in [0, 1] \tag{6}$$

Once α is fixed, the following matrix (Eq. 7) can be obtained after setting the index of optimism μ in order to estimate the degree of satisfaction.

$$\tilde{A} = \begin{bmatrix} 1 & \tilde{a}_{12}^{\alpha} & ... & \tilde{a}_{1n}^{\alpha} \\ \tilde{a}_{21}^{\alpha} & 1 & ... & \tilde{a}_{2n}^{\alpha} \\ ... & ... & ... & ... \\ \tilde{a}_{n1}^{\alpha} & \tilde{a}_{n2}^{\alpha} & ... & 1 \end{bmatrix} \tag{7}$$

The eigenvector is calculated by fixing the μ value and identifying the maximal eigenvalue.

5 An Illustrative Application

COVID-19 is the bad event that forced many companies, and industries, to transform their global supply chain model. As a matter of fact, corona-virus pandemic has affected almost all countries and has had a significant impact on the available healthcare facilities and treatment systems. In this way, all risks affecting the pharmaceutical companies could disturb the supply of medicines and affect the health system quality. The purpose of this research is to assess different risks in pharmaceutical supply chain by providing quantified empirical results. Based on the review of literature like in Table 1, some major risks affecting the pharmaceutical supply chain are identified as regulatory risk, inventory risk, counterfeit risk and financial risk. Accordingly, we opted for the application of analytical hierarchy process model.

Table1. Pharmaceutical Risks identified

Supply and suppliers risk (C1)	Delivery reliability (CR1)
	Environmental assessment (CR2)
	Technology level (CR3)
	Information systems (CR4)
	Technology development (CR5)
	Flexibility in delivering (CR6)
	Flexible quantities (CR7)
	Flexibility in product variety (CR8)
	Timely delivery (CR9)
	Quality management system (CR10)
Organization & strategies issues (C2)	Visibility on stock (CR11)
	Organization & process (CR12)
	Time to market (CR13)
	Production cost (CR14)
Financial (C3)	Tax payable change (CR15)
	Financial risks (CR16)
	Financial Tariff policies changes (CR17)
	Costs related to supply (CR18)
	Interest rate (CR19)
Logistic (C4)	Transportation (CR20)

An example of results is presented below in order to explain the procedures in this study as in Eq. 8:

$$c2 = FCM_2 = \begin{matrix} CR_{11} \\ CR_{612} \\ CR_{13} \\ CR_{14} \end{matrix} \begin{bmatrix} 1 & \tilde{1} & \tilde{3} & 1 \\ \tilde{1} & 1 & \tilde{5} & \tilde{1} \\ \tilde{3}^{-1} & \tilde{5}^{-1} & 1 & \tilde{1} \\ \tilde{1}^{-1} & \tilde{1}^{-1} & \tilde{1}^{-1} & 1 \end{bmatrix} \tag{8}$$

The lower limit and upper limit of the fuzzy numbers with respect to the α can be defined as follows, in Eqs. 9–13, by applying Eq. 4.

$$\tilde{1}_\alpha = [1, 3 - 2\alpha] \tag{9}$$

$$\tilde{3}_\alpha = [1 + 2\alpha, 5 - 2\alpha], \quad \tilde{3}_\alpha^{-1} = \left[\frac{1}{5 - 2\alpha}; \frac{1}{1 + 2\alpha} \right] \tag{10}$$

$$\tilde{5}_\alpha = [3 + 2\alpha, 7 - 2\alpha], \ \tilde{5}_\alpha^{-1} = \left[\frac{1}{7 - 2\alpha}, \frac{1}{3 + 2\alpha} \right] \tag{11}$$

$$\tilde{7}_\alpha = [5 + 2\alpha, 9 - 2\alpha], \ \tilde{7}_\alpha^{-1} = \left[\frac{1}{9 - 2\alpha}, \frac{1}{5 + 2\alpha} \right] \tag{12}$$

$$\tilde{9}_\alpha = [7 + 2\alpha, 11 - 2\alpha], \ \tilde{9}_\alpha^{-1} = \left[\frac{1}{11 - 2\alpha}, \frac{1}{7 + 2\alpha} \right] \tag{13}$$

For example, let $\alpha = 0.5$ and $\mu = 0.5$ all the α cuts fuzzy comparison matrices can be obtained as follows in Eq. 14.

$$c_2 = FCM2 = \begin{matrix} CR_{11} \\ CR_{12} \\ CR_{13} \\ CR_{14} \end{matrix} \begin{bmatrix} 1 & [1\ 2] & [2\ 4] & [1\ 2] \\ [\frac{1}{2}\ 1] & 1 & [4\ 6] & [1\ 2] \\ [\frac{1}{4}\ \frac{1}{2}] & [\frac{1}{6}\ \frac{1}{4}] & 1 & [1\ 2] \\ [\frac{1}{2}\ 1] & [\frac{1}{2}\ 1] & [\frac{1}{2}\ 1] & 1 \end{bmatrix} \tag{14}$$

Equation 3 and MATLAB are used to calculate eigen vectors for all comparison matrices.

$FCM_3^{0,5}$ can be obtained as shown below by Eq. 15 after applying Eq. 3.

$$C_3 = FCM3 = \begin{matrix} CR_{15} \\ CR_{16} \\ CR_{17} \\ CR_{18} \\ CR_{19} \end{matrix} \begin{bmatrix} 1 & 0,208 & 0,208 & 0,208 & 0,208 \\ 5 & 1 & 5 & 7 & 0,208 \\ 5 & 0,208 & 1 & 3 & 0,208 \\ 5 & 0,145 & 0,375 & 1 & 0,208 \\ 5 & 5 & 5 & 5 & 1 \end{bmatrix} \tag{15}$$

Let $FCM_3^{0,5} = A$, eigen values of the matrix A can be calculated as follows (Eq. 16) by solving the characteristic equation of A, $\det(A - \lambda I) = 0$, the largest value of λ_1 is $\lambda_1 = 6,0848$. The corresponding eigenvectors of A can be calculated as follows by substituting the λ_1 into the equation, $AX = \lambda X$

$$X_1 = (0,0672\ 0,4706\ 0,1959\ 0,1287\ 0,8480) \tag{16}$$

After normalization, the importance weights can be determined as shown below in Eq. 17.

$$C = [Wc_1\ Wc_4\ Wc_3\ Wc_2] = [0,360\ 0,310\ 0,220\ 0,110] \tag{17}$$

Following the similar calculation, the importance weights C1 to C4.

We notice that the pairwise comparison of the supply chain functions indicated that Supply and suppliers risk is the most important function to be managed with a priority of 0.360. Then we find Logistic (0.310), Financial (0.220), and Organization & strategies issues (0.110).

Nevertheless, before the lockdown caused by Covid-19 pandemic the financial risk has been ranked at the top of the list of risks.

6 Conclusion

Risks exist in all firms. Risk identification in pharmaceutical companies can increase business risk, and help health systems to meet goals of supply chain management. This paper has investigated risk assessment in pharmaceutical industry in Tunisia in the time of COVID-19 pandemic. Thus, the fuzzy AHP method is used. It has to be noted that the top risk identified in pharmaceutical supply chain is that related to the Supply and suppliers.

References

Beskese, A., Kahraman, C., Irani, Z.: Quantification of flexibility advanced manufacturing systems using fuzzy concept. Int. J. Prod. Econ. **89**, 45–56 (2004)

Boonmee, C., Arimura, M., Asada, T.: Facility location optimization model for emergency humanitarian logistics. Int. J. Disaster Risk Reduct. **24**, 485–498 (2017)

Büyüktahtakın, ˙I.E., des-Bordes, E., Kıbıs, E.Y.: A new epidemics–logistics model: insights into controlling the ebola virus disease in west Africa. Eur. J. Oper. Res. **265**, 1046–1063 (2018)

Cooper, M.C., Lambert, D.M., Pagh, J.D.: Supply chain management: more than a new name for logistics. Int. J. Logistics Manage. **8**(1), 1–14 (1997)

Yu, H., Sun, X., Solvang, W.D., Zhao, X.: Reverse logistics network design for effective management of medical waste in epidemic outbreaks: insights from the coronavirus disease 2019 (COVID-19) outbreak in Wuhan (China). Int. J. Environ. Res. Public Health. **17**, 1770 (2020)

Jaberidoost, M., Nikfar, S., Abdollahiasl, A., Dinarvand, R.: Pharmaceutical supply chain risks: a systematic review. DARU **21**(1), 69 (2013)

Juttner, U.: Supply chain risk management: understanding the business requirements from practitioners perspective. Int. J. Logistics Manage. **16**(1), 120–141 (2005)

Kleindorfer, P.R., Saad, G.H.: Managing disruption risks in supply chains. Prod. Oper. Manage. **14**(1), 53–68 (2005)

Klir, G.J., Yuan, B.: Fuzzy Sets and Fuzzy Logic Theory and Applications. Prentice Hall Inc., Upper Saddle River (1995)

Kwong, C.K., Bai, H.: A fuzzy AHP approach to the determination of importance weights of customer requirements in quality function deployment. J. Intell. Manuf. **13**, 367–377 (2002)

Kamalahmadi, M., Parast, M.M.: A review of the literature on the principles of enterprise and supply chain resilience: major findings and directions for future research. Int. J. Prod. Econ. **171**, 116–133 (2016)

Saaty, T.L.: The Analytic Hierarchy Process. McGraw-Hill, New York (1980)

Schneider, J.L., Wilson, A., Rosenbeck, J.M.: Pharmaceutical companies and sustainability: an analysis of corporate reporting. Benchmarking **17**, 421–434 (2010)

Author Index